Richard J. Aldrich was born in 1961 and was educated at Manchester, Aberdeen and Cambridge universities. He teaches international relations at the University of Nottingham and is the author of several books including most recently *The Hidden Hand: Britain, America and Cold War Secret Intelligence*, which won the Donner Book Prize 2002 and was shortlisted for the Westminster Medal.

By the same author

The Key to the South:
Britain, the United States and Thailand
during the Approach of the Pacific War, 1929–1942

Intelligence and the War against Japan:
Britain, America and the Politics of Secret Service

The Hidden Hand:
Britain, America and Cold War Secret Intelligence

WITNESS
TO WAR

DIARIES OF THE SECOND
WORLD WAR IN EUROPE
AND THE MIDDLE EAST

RICHARD J. ALDRICH

CORGI BOOKS

WITNESS TO WAR
A CORGI BOOK: 0 552 15108 4

Originally published in Great Britain by Doubleday,
a division of Transworld Publishers

PRINTING HISTORY
Doubleday edition published 2004
Corgi edition published 2005

1 3 5 7 9 10 8 6 4 2

Set in 9.75/12pt Palatino by
Falcon Oast Graphic Art Ltd.

Corgi Books are published by Transworld Publishers,
61–63 Uxbridge Road, London W5 5SA,
a division of The Random House Group Ltd,
in Australia by Random House Australia (Pty) Ltd,
20 Alfred Street, Milsons Point, Sydney, NSW 2061, Australia,
in New Zealand by Random House New Zealand Ltd,
18 Poland Road, Glenfield, Auckland 10, New Zealand
and in South Africa by Random House (Pty) Ltd,
Endulini, 5a Jubilee Road, Parktown 2193, South Africa.

The Random House Group Limited supports The Forest Stewardship
Council® (FSC®), the leading international forest-certification organisation.
Our books carrying the FSC label are printed on FSC®-certified paper.
FSC is the only forest-certification scheme supported by the leading
environmental organisations, including Greenpeace. Our
paper procurement policy can be found at
www.randomhouse.co.uk/environment

MIX
Paper from
responsible sources
FSC® C016897

Printed and bound in Great Britain by Clays Ltd, St Ives PLC

*For Libby
(in the white morning)*

CONTENTS

MAPS

Maps 1–6 are reproduced by permission of the *New York Times* Company.

ACKNOWLEDGEMENTS

Many have given generously of their time to assist me in understanding the secret life of diarists during the Second World War. Over two decades I have been privileged to speak to many who were tireless diary-keepers, and I should like to acknowledge my debt to them first and foremost. Their insights – sometimes breathtaking – have changed the way I think about not only the nature of the Second World War, but also the practice of 'making' history. Some of them have proved to be remarkably self-deprecating, being genuinely unaware of the value of their activity and of the material they have passed down to us. Sadly, not all of them have survived to see the completion of this project.

Several individuals have provided intellectual inspiration. Christopher Hill has edited the diary of the French soldier Gustave Folcher and, in passing, has offered one of the most powerful and persuasive commentaries on war diaries as the 'voice from below'. I have also been influenced by Alex Danchev, a dogged advocate of the importance of individuals, both high and low, in a field increasingly filled with depersonalized and abstracted interpretations of international affairs. Paul Fussell's reflections on 'wartime' and on his own experience of the Second World War remain one of the most striking accounts of the details of that conflict. These writers remind us that most human beings do not wage war: war is waged upon them, and usually with unintended consequences.

Many other individuals and institutions have offered kind support or advice about obscure locations where diaries might be found. I would particularly like to thank Matthew Aid, Antony Best, Robert Bothwell, Philip Davies, Anne Deighton, Saki Dockrill, Stephen Dorril, David Ellwood, Irving Finkel, M. R. D. Foot, Anthony Gorst, David and Joan Hamer, E. D. R. Harrison, Peter Hennessy, Rhodri Jeffreys-Jones, Matthew Jones, David Kahn, Saul Kelly, Sheila Kerr, Dianne Kirby, Paul Lashmar, W. Scott Lucas, Kate Morris, Philip Murphy, Robin

Neilands, David Painter, E. Bruce Reynolds, Annie Rigdeon, Aviel Roschwald, Anthony Short, Bradley F. Smith, Michael Smith, David Stafford, Wesley K. Wark, Donald Cameron Watt, Neville Wylie and John W. Young. Lee Smith offered a happy home in Washington DC for a visiting researcher and I would like to offer Lee, Al and Dela my thanks for all their kindness. Responsibility for interpretation and errors, however, remains with me.

Archivists, librarians and departmental record officers – tireless in their efforts – have extended their kindness to me; sadly, I cannot name them here. Stephen Walton, Roderick Suddaby and the staff at the Imperial War Museum, Patricia Methven and the staff at the Liddell Hart Centre for Military Archives in London, and Piers Brendon and the staff at the Churchill Archives Centre in Cambridge all deserve a special mention, as does John E. Taylor in Washington DC. Librarians at the University Library in Cambridge, the Lauinger Library at Georgetown University and the Hallwood Library at the University of Nottingham were unfailingly helpful and kind. Above all, it is the staff of the numerous archives and libraries, overworked yet unfailingly courteous – even when confronted with a slightly irascible researcher – who have facilitated the preparation of this book.

Many valuable papers and diaries have been lost down the years. Protecting what now survives is of crucial importance. Specialist archives are always welcoming to those who might help them expand their collections, and readers who might wish to consider depositing diaries and papers, or copies of them, can find details of how they might do this at the end of the book.

Permission to quote from books, manuscripts and private papers has been generously given by a great number of publishers, archives, libraries and individuals. The appropriate acknowledgements, along with full source information, are given in the references section at the end of the book. Every effort has been made to contact copyright holders. In the case of a few manuscripts and diaries held in museums this has not been possible. We would be grateful for any information that might help to trace those who are unknown.

Attempting to contact all these people has been an arduous task, and I would particularly like to thank the Churchill Archives Centre, the Liddell Hart Centre for Military Archives and the Imperial War Museum for their efforts on my behalf.

An army of postgraduate research assistants and helpers from many different universities have assisted in bringing this project together. Across the world 'secret diary investigators' have been delving into archives and libraries, often in countries that I could not visit personally, and have greatly extended the reach of this project. They have investigated, selected, noted, translated and typed with endless efficiency. I would like to offer my sincere thanks to Mahar Aziz, Corrie Burrow, Hannah Cameron, Carrie Deacon, Ingeborg Erikstad, Michael Goodman, Kathryn Hall, Chris Hawkins, Geoff Heyes, Naomi Hilliar, Sandanina Khan, David Layfield, Chiyako Matsumoto, Morjani Morisini, Aimee Olivo, Lisa Presgraves, Amanda Rowley, Danny Scatola, Asaf Siniver, Darren Solomon, Tom Steiner, Manuela Williams and Tom Wright.

There are a few individuals to whom I owe a particularly heavy debt of gratitude. Michèle Hutchison and Marianne Velmans at Transworld have been especially supportive and forbearing with a project that presented some unusual problems. Gillian Somerscales was tremendously effective in advising on and copy-editing the text. Andrew Lownie has not only offered continuous encouragement and inspiration, but also saved several rare diaries from continued obscurity. I owe an enormous debt to all my family for their encouragement over the years. My brother James cast his eagle eye over the finished text. As ever, my wife Libby has offered fantastic support, extraordinary knowledge and boundless love. My children, Nicholas and Harriet, deserve special thanks for their patience as they discovered increasing areas of the house rendered impassable by mountainous piles of diaries. All have tolerated this 'enemy occupation' with equanimity. Nevertheless, secretly they have longed for the day of liberation – which is now at hand.

INTRODUCTION

DIARISTS – THE FORGOTTEN
FOOT-SOLDIERS

FOR THE FIRST TIME in my life, this morning around five o'clock I heard bombs drop – and *recognised* them . . . Somehow, shaken out of my sleep I knew . . . I must record all this for my children to read someday. They must not forget. Today they were utterly unimpressed: bombing and invasion seemed just a lark to them – since we did not suffer. Of course they are only thirteen, ten and four . . .

ANNE SOMERHAUSEN wrote these sentences on the first page of her diary as war descended on the city of Brussels after long months of anxious apprehension.[1] By the spring of 1939, when many across Europe were already half-expecting it, city-dwellers in London, Paris, Berlin and Budapest were well informed about the nature of modern warfare. Radio and the cinema newsreels had allowed them to follow the course of the Japanese invasion of China and the Spanish Civil War, and so they anticipated destruction on an epic scale. Many predicted the complete levelling of the urban landscape in Europe by aerial bombardment. Accordingly, at the outset of the Second World War individuals from every walk of life, most of whom had never kept a diary before, began to chronicle their own private and personal responses to what they knew would be a unique moment in world history. Thousands of people who regarded their lives as

---

[1] Anne Somerhausen, *Written in Darkness: A Belgian Woman's Record of the Occupation 1940–1945* (New York: Knopf, 1946), p. 3. SEE PP. 462–3 AND 857–8.

unremarkable concluded that they had now become 'witnesses to war' – perhaps a war of biblical proportions, and one which might very well destroy their own society completely. Many believed that they would not live to see its end; and sadly, some of the voices captured in this collection were indeed silenced before it had run its course. When it had, most of those who had begun their journals at the outbreak of the conflict would stop as abruptly as they had begun.

Today, more than half a century after the end of the Second World War, these hidden treasures – the voices of the past – are still being unearthed. Each passing year brings to light fresh examples of the private journals of the war's participants and observers: some discovered by researchers in archives, others unearthed by relatives from attics and cupboards. The more famous diaries are readily available in print, but many others have received remarkably little attention. A considerable number were published in small print runs after the war and then forgotten. Anne Somerhausen's superb diary of her lonely struggle to care for her three children during the five years of German occupation in Belgium, *Written in Darkness*, was published in 1946, but is now almost unobtainable. Neil McCallum's delightfully sardonic account of the desert war, *Journey with a Pistol*, was published in 1959, but received almost no acclaim.[2] Other private accounts have languished unread for many years, either having been printed in small numbers for family and friends or, more often, untended and gathering dust in scholarly depositories around the world. The diaries selected here include many of both kinds, as well as secret service material in private hands or else recently cleared for release by MI5, and only just available for public inspection in the archives.

For two decades I have devoted myself to sustained research on the Second World War and its aftermath. Diaries have always

[2] N. McCallum, *Journey with a Pistol: A Chronicle of War (from Alamein to Sicily) from a Point of View other than that of Montgomery of Alamein's Memoirs* (London: Gollancz, 1959). Paul Fussell has commented on the extraordinary quality of Neil McCallum's writing, but otherwise he remains under-recognized. James Ambrose Brown is another superb 'desert diarist' of equal eloquence who shares his obscurity. See P. Fussell, 'The Real War', *Atlantic Monthly*, August 1989. SEE PP. 467–9, 528–9 AND 541–3.

been a special source of delight to me, and over time my work has allowed me to discover many obscure collections of papers and diaries and to develop contacts who have provided access to material in very diverse locations. Over 300 diaries, written by civilians and soldiers from both sides of the war and from all of the countries involved, have been chosen and extracted, and it is clear that they, more than any other medium, reflect the true human experience of war. They allow us to see through the eyes of those who were present at the time. They record first impressions, even those first impressions that in retrospect might appear odd. Oliver Harvey, private secretary to Anthony Eden, remarked that the whole value of the diary lies in its 'hotness', its ability to capture the spirit of the moment, without retouching or correction – the literary equivalent of the instant camera.[3]

The first volume of this anthology covers the Second World War in Europe and the Middle East; a second volume will address the war in the Pacific, against Japan. Any such division is bound to be artificial, for this was a war of global significance not easily divisible into separate sections. However, most diaries are concerned less with global strategy or high policy, and more with the private experience of war. The war against Japan had its own undeniable character, and devoting a separate volume to Asia and the Pacific allows us to capture the particular complexities of a conflict in which imperial power fought imperial power, anti-colonial agitator fought colonial oppressor and communist fought capitalist, all within the boundaries of a 'world war'.

A light narrative runs throughout each volume, summarizing the main events of each month and tracing the changing course of the war. One of the striking insights arising from this project is how little connection there is between the major contours of a global conflict and the everyday experiences of individuals as revealed through their diaries. Policy-makers and generals drew straight lines on maps and enjoyed a thoroughly ordered experience, whereas those below them in rank followed orders, with little notion of how the different phases of the conflict were

---

[3] J. Harvey (ed.), *The War Diaries of Oliver Harvey, 1941–1945* (London: Collins, 1978), p. 12. SEE PP. 438–9.

unfolding. The overwhelming sentiment was bewilderment – amplified by the absence of reliable information, a thick curtain of censorship and the superabundance of rumour. The course of the Second World War was determined by powerful men preoccupied with power, while others endured the consequences.

Much of the material in this collection was never meant to be read by anyone except its author, plus perhaps close family and friends. Joan Wyndham, a young diarist living a bohemian life as an eighteen-year-old art student, shrewdly observed that most diaries fall into one of two categories. The first are those written from the outset with the intention of publication, and crafted to present their authors in the best light. Second, there are those produced by people who 'write secretly and obsessively for themselves alone'. That was certainly how Joan Wyndham saw her diaries: she wrote them at night, 'scribbling away in the air-raid shelter by the light of a hurricane lamp', and hid them under her mattress 'in case my mother should read them and die of shock'. The majority of the diaries in this anthology are private diaries of this sort, rather than those written deliberately for publication.[4]

Godfrey Williams was one such very private diarist. He began his diary in January 1886 when he was ten years old, and his first tentative volume records the inner thoughts of a miserably unhappy schoolboy far from home and enduring the harsh regime imposed by Harrow College in the late nineteenth century. There, in an unforgiving world, any dissident action meant immediate punishment, and so the secrecy of his diary was one of his foremost concerns. Etched in thick black pencil around all four sides of the front cover are the words: 'Private, Private, Private, Private'. Opening the book, I found, on the first page, the words: 'Take NOTICE – all persons who look at this diary without my leave are Beastly Sneaks.' A fanatical diarist, Godfrey would maintain daily entries throughout his life, including every day of the First and Second World Wars, and onwards until his death in

[4] Joan Wyndham, Love Lessons: A Wartime Diary (London: Virago, 2001), p. 1. SEE PP. 203–4 AND 269–72.

1956.[5] Over his life he filled 76 volumes with his thoughts – a unique record of a life over three-quarters of a century.

Even peacetime diaries are often quintessentially private records. They set down thoughts and feelings that might cause hurt to others if revealed even to friends, family or close colleagues. In this very privacy lies their attraction to other readers. To be allowed to read another person's diary is intrinsically a privilege, akin to being allowed to walk around the secluded private garden behind someone's house. This sense of restricted access was heightened significantly during wartime, as privacy was overlaid with secrecy, and the hidden business of diary-keeping took on a new and more serious significance.

To those in particular peril – serving secretly behind enemy lines, imprisoned, or suffering maltreatment – keeping a diary provided a special kind of comfort. Perhaps the most remarkable example in this respect is the diary of Peter Moen, a Norwegian resistance worker. SEE PP. 661–3. Moen had been in charge of the underground newspapers in Norway and was arrested by the Germans in February 1944. He would eventually betray his friends under torture. His diary records his imprisonment and interrogation, interspersed with long periods of solitary confinement in which he describes the starkness of life in his cell. The most compelling sections of the diary are those that deal with his own mental self-torture over the betrayal of his comrades who were rounded up and eventually joined him in the same prison. It is clear that Moen suffered agonizing loneliness. He longed for comfort from his religious faith, but it never came; in his extreme isolation, his diary was his only solace. Remarkably, it was pricked out with a tack on lavatory paper and, each sheet carefully wrapped in another, unmarked sheet, dropped piece by piece through a grating in the floor of his cell. Moen's record is perhaps the ultimate secret war diary: painful, immediate and sincere, each recording dropped away into its hiding place with no possibility of revision or embellishment.

Moen's may be the extreme case, but wartime diaries were

[5] I am indebted to Irving Finkel, Curator of Mesopotamian Inscriptions at the British Museum, for allowing me to see this diary – and for sharing with me his thoughts on diaries.

often primarily a therapeutic response to acute loneliness and fear. Many people who were suddenly separated from their families or displaced from their homes found themselves with endless stretches of time in which to contemplate their psychological discomfort. War, after all, is legendarily ten minutes of action followed by ten days of waiting. Having witnessed extraordinary events, they needed someone to talk to: their diaries were conversations with themselves, serving as a psychological prop, providing consolation and opportunity for reflection when there was no other source of support. Most diaries are private and secret, not because they contain confidential material, but because they are a formalized conversation with the inner self. They are as intimate a picture of war as we are ever likely to find – evidence of the impact of war upon the soul of the individual.

Giovanni Guareschi offers us one of the best examples of this inner dialogue. SEE PP. 838–40. An Italian soldier who had decided to fight with the Allies against the Germans in 1943, he would later become famous as the author of *The Little World of Don Camillo*. By the end of 1943 Guareschi found himself a prisoner of war in Germany. For two years he collected 'everything I thought and saw' into three bulky notebooks that ran to over two thousand pages. He wrote in abbreviated form and when he returned home set about expanding his comments into a fuller account. As he did so, he reflected on what his diary was and what it meant. Guareschi realized that his journal captured the sense of an individual lost in the chaos of war. For long periods of his captivity he had no idea even of whether the Allies were winning or losing; there were no clear lines on the map, no obvious ideological choices – only confusion. Guareschi's own personal experience showed him that there were 'enemies who turned out to be allies, and allies that became enemies': in 1943 the Allies bombed his house in Italy, but in 1945 the same Allies liberated him from a German POW camp, looked after him and fed him. During these tumultuous years he realized that his diary was a sympathetic inner voice that offered calm and solace: 'I had no more influence than a nutshell tossed about on the ocean, and emerged without ribbons or medals on my chest. I emerged as a victor, however, because I came through the cataclysm without hatred in my soul and made the discovery of a precious friend, myself.'[6]

For Frances Partridge, member of the Bloomsbury set, translator and pacifist, keeping a diary was a means of 'relieving the various emotions aroused by the Second World War, ranging from boredom and horror to fear and disgust'. She described a rather agreeable time spent in rural Wiltshire at her large house Ham Spray, and noted that 'few passed a more sheltered war'. But although her own existence was relatively uneventful, she thought it vital to set down how the liberal and human values espoused by her family and their circle of friends stood up in the terrible times through which they were living. Above all, her diary is a testimony to the pacifist beliefs she had developed as a teenager in the First World War. Her observations being written down moment by moment, she wrote, 'I can vouch for their accuracy'.[7]

While private individuals kept their diaries hidden in order to conceal their inner thoughts, those in positions of authority were actually forbidden from keeping diaries at all. This was understandable. Those in possession of high-level secrets, such as future operational plans, or even information about the breaking of enemy codes, could not be allowed to risk this information becoming known beyond the inner circle: revelations of this sort might have severe consequences for many in the front line. Most countries made it a punishable offence for anyone in the military to maintain a diary – an offence even more serious if they were performing some kind of special or secret work. Fortunately for this collection, a remarkable number of individuals ignored this stricture. David Scholes DFC, a Royal Australian Air Force pilot from Melbourne who flew with the 5th Bomber Group famous for the Dam Buster and *Tirpitz* raids, noted in his diary on 17 September 1944: 'The Air Force allows no diaries and so, even with this lot, I could be hamstrung. I have mentioned little about tactics, secret instruments used by either side, weapons or to cut it short anything that would be really black, black.' David Scholes was flying Lancasters and was able to see all the early and very

---

[6] Giovanni Guareschi, *My Secret Diary, 1943–1945* (New York: Farrar Strauss & Cudahy, 1958), pp. xiv–xv.
[7] Frances Partridge, *A Pacifist's War* (London: Hogarth Press, 1978), p. 9. SEE PP. 176–7, 211–12, 348–50 AND 612–13.

secret aspects of the airborne 'wizard war', including electronic target location and radar jamming.[8]

Secret diary-keeping did not always sit comfortably with the regimented military mind and the consequent tension could have rather surreal results. Major J. W. Cockhill, who fought in France in 1940 and then in the Middle East in 1942, noted in his memoir that even though it was 'against orders to keep a diary' he had done so. Keen to make at least some gesture towards the regulation about 'no diaries', he concluded that the honourable thing to do was to censor it himself, and so he 'cancelled out' passages that he himself had written in his own diary, on grounds of security.[9]

Diaries were routinely captured and translated with real profit by the intelligence services of each side, revealing a wealth of detail about units, morale and the effectiveness of different types of weaponry. Shortly after enemy positions were over-run, the intelligence teams arrived and claimed abandoned diaries as treasure trove. Such was the volume of this sort of captured documentation that all sides set up special units in an attempt to translate them quickly for intelligence purposes. This anthology contains German and Italian examples of such material. The experience of being questioned as a prisoner by interrogators who have already perused your diary could be psychologically devastating.

Guy Liddell was a senior MI5 officer engaged in some of the most secret operations of the war, and aware of many other clandestine activities. He kept a remarkably detailed diary recording his daily dealings with German agents who had been skilfully turned against their masters and were now being 'played back' in order to deceive Berlin. He also rubbed shoulders with some of those who would later become famous – or infamous – as the heroes and villains of post-war British intelligence, including Kim Philby and Anthony Blunt. When the contents of a diary were this secret they were sometimes incorporated into the secure framework of the workplace: dictated to secretaries, and then confined to the safes and steel presses alongside classified

[8] David Scholes DFC, *Air War Diary: An Australian in Bomber Command* (Kenthurst, NSW: Kangaroo Press, 1997), p. 91. SEE PP. 586–8 AND 670–3.

[9] Major J. W. H. Cockhill, typescript memoir, 99/85/1, Imperial War Museum, p. 119.

documents. Guy Liddell's was such an in-house secret service diary, kept with official approval in the vaults at his MI5 office in Ryder Street. SEE PP. 794–5.

Not far from Liddell's office at MI5 were the offices of other wartime secret services. Malcolm Muggeridge, a journalist before the war, had joined the Secret Intelligence Service, often known as MI6. Muggeridge also kept a diary, but being a field officer he was constantly on the move in the uncertain terrain of neutral countries like Portugal or Mozambique. Muggeridge took the alternative path to secrecy, noting his exotic travel and private thoughts about the war, but recording almost nothing to do with his work, other than occasional evenings spent drinking with his fellow MI6 officer – coincidentally, Kim Philby. SEE PP. 406–8.

Joseph Goebbels, Germany's Minister for Public Enlightenment and Propaganda, served continuously from 1933 until his suicide in the bunker of the Reich Chancellery alongside Hitler in April 1945. A tiny but frenziedly energetic man, Goebbels was also a compulsive diarist, setting aside part of every busy day to maintain his voluminous personal record. He was assisted by chronic bouts of insomnia; but even so he could not keep pace with events, and under the pressure of his wartime duties he soon shifted from writing to dictating, barking out his long diary entries to stenographers who struggled to keep up with him. The result is one of the most detailed and revealing accounts left to us by any of Hitler's lieutenants. SEE PP. 818–20 AND 822.

Goebbels devoted attention to his diary almost as if it were a second self, the one true monument to his own lifetime's achievements. As the war drew to a climactic end, his own fate seemed obvious; but what was to become of his diary? Secrecy assured its preservation. The thousands of pages were copied meticulously onto photographic plates and buried in woodland outside Berlin. At the end of the war some of the originals were recovered from the chaos of the Reich Chancellery, and the photographic copies were unearthed from their hiding place in the countryside by the Red Army. Despite the recovery of two copies, significant sections of diary were claimed by its captors to be 'missing'. It is likely that these are portions which the Allies found to be too embarrassing to reproduce.[10]

[10] Foreword by John Keegan to F. Taylor (ed.), *The Goebbels Diaries 1939–41* (London: Hamish Hamilton, 1982), p. ix.

Prisoners and diaries go together, for captives found that time weighed particularly heavily on their hands. Some individuals captured at Dunkirk in 1940 had five years of free time to fill and many, when they could obtain notebooks, wrote remarkable journals. However, even after capture diary-keeping could be hazardous. For political prisoners, records which contained dissident thoughts might bring further punishment upon their owners. For those in enemy-occupied territory, or for anti-Nazis in Germany, diary-keeping could itself become an act of resistance and defiance; but the personal cost of discovery would be very high. For captured resistance workers even oblique notes about associates could result in their capture, or assist in the interrogation of others. Diaries kept by military prisoners might contain information from recent campaigns that could be useful to the enemy, if only for propaganda purposes; or information about illegal camp activities, including escape efforts. J. Ellison Platt was one of the longest-serving prisoners in Colditz Castle, a special German POW camp for Allied officers considered liable to escape. He made entries in his diary nearly every day over the five years of his captivity, compiling a record of life at Colditz that ran to nearly eight hundred pages by the end of the war.

Those incarcerated at Colditz were prisoners who refused to accept that their war was over. There was a constant game of cat and mouse between prisoners and guards. Ellison Platt realized that his bulky manuscript was almost certain to be discovered, given the routine of persistent security searches inside the castle, and he did not wish to give anything away; yet he wished to maintain his diary. So he adopted the clever approach of keeping an open diary of which the German authorities were fully aware. Every page carried the German censor's stamp, showing that it had been examined and approved. Indeed, it was read with an eagle eye by Captain Eggers, the German security officer. Much of the diary contains thoughtful social commentary on the psychological impact of prolonged captivity, on the prisoners' efforts to dispel boredom with lectures and plays, together with records of the main highlight of their existence – the arrival of Red Cross parcels.

Nevertheless, the high drama of the many Colditz escape attempts is also captured by Ellison in amazing detail. How was this achieved under the nose of the German censor? First, these entries in the diary were written up retrospectively, often after the Germans had uncovered an escape plan and knew all there was to know. Second, it appears that Ellison may have substituted more detailed accounts of some of the escapes after inspection of his diary, 'endorsing' them by forging the censor's stamp. Even with these precautions, some of his colleagues were unhappy about the diary. Rupert Barry, the British officer responsible for escape security in the camp, saw it as a potential source of trouble and wanted all diary-keeping to cease.[11]

While writing a diary was often a very private act, it could also signify a new connection with events in the wider world. It is not unusual for a diary from this period to begin in September 1939, or at a moment when the author began war-related work or moved from mundane military training to hazardous active service. Beginning a diary, for many, symbolized 'stepping into history': ceasing to be a spectator, and instead taking part in an extraordinary pageant. Very many individuals found that participation in the Second World War gave their lives and their activities greater meaning and purpose. This sentiment is understandable, but arguably it was misplaced, and nothing is more frustrating than seeing an excellent diarist put down the pen in August 1945 when the reader wishes to know what happened next. History had not stopped. But one has to concede that without this widespread conviction that the Second World War was a special event, we would be without the majority of diaries in this collection.

It is perhaps no accident that one of the most remarkable collective diary projects of modern times was created just as the shadow of war was creeping across Europe. In 1937 Tom Harrisson, a self-trained anthropologist and explorer, and Charles Madge, a poet and writer, set up a social investigation project which became the Mass-Observation Archive. By 1938 they were appealing for ordinary members of the public across Britain to become volunteer observers – to write down what they saw, heard and thought, and send in their diaries to the project. Certainly the advent of war brought many more volunteers: by

[11] M. Duggan (ed.), *Padre in Colditz: The Diary of J. Ellison Platt MBE* (London: Hodder & Stoughton, 1978), pp. 8–9. SEE PP. 457–9.

the end of the conflict Mass-Observation had 3,000 people on its mailing list, and some 300 of these kept full personal diaries, creating a unique body of material on the social history of Britain in the mid-twentieth century. Dorothy Sheridan, the keeper of this unique archive, now preserved at the University of Sussex, explains that for a while during the war this material was used by the Ministry of Information to gauge public morale. Charles Madge became disillusioned with the use of the diary project for what he called 'home front espionage'; Tom Harrisson, on the other hand, became an actual spy, joining the Special Operations Executive and undertaking missions in Japanese-occupied Borneo.[12]

While some had become 'diary volunteers', others were 'diary conscripts' on account of their military duties. Any historian of war soon discovers that it is not only people, but also units, that keep war diaries. Military formations in the mid-twentieth century forbade the keeping of personal diaries, but required the keeping of the regimental war diary, the squadron record book or the ship's log. In most cases these are dry affairs, but where we are fortunate the unit diarist or diarists abandons the tedious recording of stores and casualties and begins to write in the style of a personal journal. Such idiosyncratic accounts within official logs were especially common in irregular units and formations like the Commandos, the Long Range Desert Group and the Special Air Service, which attracted unconventional people. The eccentric individuals who joined these units were people who could not find satisfaction sublimating their personality within a regiment of the line.

Evelyn Waugh was one such eccentric and literary figure who found himself temporarily in khaki. His remarkable diaries reveal a character singularly ill suited to military life, but one for whom the war nevertheless provided boundless literary opportunities. The conflict not only offered up a remarkably rich cast of characters for his novels but also provided vast expanses of free time in which to write. Indeed, his diaries provide deep insight into his famous 'Sword of Honour' trilogy, which clearly drew heavily on his own war experiences. Waugh's minuscule military

[12] Dorothy Sheridan (ed.), *Wartime Women: An Anthology of Women's Wartime Writing for Mass-Observation 1937–1945* (London: Heinemann, 1990), pp. 4–5.

talents and cantankerous nature seemed purpose-designed to ensure that he was often under-employed and at a loose end. Perversely, his regimental postings seemed in inverse proportion to his martial abilities. By his own account he was perhaps one of the worst officers ever to have served in the British armed forces; nevertheless he managed to pass through the Commandos, then to the Special Operations Executive and then, in the final days of the war, to the Special Air Service. He socialized with some of the war's more famous heroes – including David Stirling, founder of the SAS. However, he was allowed to join these illustrious units only on condition that he spent his time writing and did not do anything so foolish as report for serious duties at headquarters.[13]

As Joan Wyndham noted, a small number of diaries were clearly intended for publication from the outset. Moreover, war diaries were immensely popular during the war itself. Indeed, some of the best diaries were written for immediate publication by journalists who were recording their experiences on a weekly basis and producing them as columns in newspapers. At the same time, however, these reporters were reserving additional diary material for retrospective publication in book form. For journalists this two-pronged approach was a weapon for use against their main enemy, the official censor. Equipped with a distinctive blue pencil, the censor rigidly restricted the publication of information that was current news – as potentially valuable to the enemy – but was often willing to pass the same information for publication in book form a year later. Even diaries of the Blitz, if published in newspapers, could be of use to the German forces, telling them if they were hitting their intended targets.

Charles Graves, the war correspondent of the *Daily Express*, is a good example of the journalist–diarist. He felt the effects of war personally: his own house was hit twice by incendiaries, although he survived the experience uninjured. Between 1939 and 1941 he spent time on Royal Navy destroyers, undertook two tours with the British Expeditionary Force in France and experienced two periods attached to the RAF at Bomber and Fighter Command stations in Britain. This gave him plenty to write about in his

[13] John St John, *To the War with Waugh* (London: Leo Cooper, 1974). SEE PP. 484–5, 692–4 AND 768–9.

newspaper; but security issues meant that much of what he saw could not appear in 'real time' in his *Express* column. The additional material, often on more intriguing subjects, was stored away in his diary. In 1942 he published his diary for the preceding two years, and this contained almost nothing that had already appeared in print; nevertheless, even then the full story could not be told and there remained a degree of both self- and official censorship. The published personal diary contained more expressions of Graves's own moods and emotions than had appeared in the press accounts, reflecting the changing taste of the readership. As the war progressed, published diaries were increasingly valued not only as a record of external events but also as a window upon the inner feelings of the individual, the 'war within'.[14] SEE PP. 312–13, 324–6 and 377.

Others, aware that their wartime work allowed them access to the 'inner circle' of power, were keeping diaries for publication far in the future, not necessarily even within the writer's lifetime. Some had been catapulted by the war into positions of particular power or significance; some worked at the right hand of significant figures. Two of the most spectacular diaries kept by those at the top are those of Hugh Dalton and Alan Brooke. Each kept a remarkably conscientious record of the war, expecting it to be made public at a later date. In his lifetime, Hugh Dalton merely used his voluminous diary as source material for a slim memoir. The vast bulk of his wartime literary endeavour would remain unpublished until after his death. SEE PP. 202–3. By contrast Alan Brooke, Chief of the Imperial General Staff, allowed the established historian Sir Arthur Bryant to draw heavily on his diary for a large two-volume biography published in 1957 and 1959, in which it was quoted extensively. As recently as 2001 the diaries themselves were published in unexpurgated form, and made the British bestseller lists. SEE PP. 472 AND 720. The post-war market for memoirs was buoyant, and the example set by Winston Churchill, who made millions from his six-volume semi-autobiographical history of the war, inspired many others, including Montgomery, into thinking about what they might write.

Winston Churchill was an early starter. Even in 1941 he had

[14] Charles Graves, *Off the Record* (London: Hutchinson, 1942), pp. v–vi.

already made it onto the American top ten bestseller list with *Blood, Sweat and Tears*, a collection of some of his more famous speeches from the darkest days of the war. But Churchill had been adamant that he would never write a diary. In late May 1943 Churchill and his senior generals joined General Marshall to visit General Eisenhower in Algiers for several days of rolling discussions about the future of Allied strategy. Eisenhower and Churchill were staying in adjacent houses at Eisenhower's HQ near Maison Blanche, and on the evening of Monday 31 May Eisenhower hosted a dinner for Churchill. Thirteen places were set at table – but the guests were anxious about the number thirteen, so Eisenhower's aide, Captain Harry C. Butcher, was drafted in as the fourteenth member of the party in deference to British superstition. Conversation at dinner turned to literary matters and Harry Butcher recorded in his own diary that at some point the question of diaries came up. Churchill asserted that 'it was foolish to keep a day-by-day diary because it would simply reflect the change of opinion or decision of the writer, which, when and if published, makes one appear indecisive and foolish'. Churchill added candidly that he would much prefer to wait until the war was over and then write impressions, so that, if necessary, 'he could correct or bury his mistakes'.[15] Churchill followed his own advice and instead of keeping a diary chose to write a personalized account of the war. Churchill's history, *The Second World War*, became one of the principal detailed accounts on which all other histories of the war depended, and it transformed his fortunes.

Still in 1941, two of the other top ten bestselling non-fiction books of the year in the United States *were* diaries of the Second World War. One of them was William Shirer's *Berlin Diary*, kept by the CBS correspondent who covered Hitler and his regime during 1940. SEE PP. *91–2* AND *174–6*. The other was the diary of a young Dutch boy, Dirk van der Heide, who recorded the experiences of his family under the first days and weeks of German occupation. Children's diaries of the Second World War are certainly among the most moving documents produced by that conflict. Dirk was described as a 'twelve-year-old blue-eyed

---

[15] Harry Butcher diary, 31 May 1943, Box 6, Butcher papers, Dwight D. Eisenhower Library, Abilene, Kansas. SEE PP. 469–70, 544–6, 561–3 AND 712–13.

Dutch boy with taffy coloured hair' who lived in Rotterdam with his mother, father and younger sister, Keetje. When the Germans invaded in 1940 he was encouraged by his mother to begin a diary to make a family record of their extraordinary experiences. Rotterdam was heavily bombed and as a result his mother was killed. His father had already departed to fight the invaders and so their Uncle Pieter arranged for the two children to make a dramatic escape to England. Arriving in London only to encounter a renewed German Blitz, they then embarked on a further adventure. They soon found themselves on a children's ship and had to go through a further hair-raising episode, braving the minefields and submarine attacks of the Northern Atlantic, before reaching eventual safety in America.

The diary not only has a wonderful sense of immediacy, it also captures the confusion of a child's mind, faced with traumatic events which seem to have no obvious explanation, as well as the intensity of family relations, the pathos of a family separated and children orphaned. Dirk van der Heide's diary is a fabulous evocation of small people caught up in the vastness of war. It is also a complete fake. Neither Dirk nor any member of his family ever existed. The account was created for the purposes of anti-Nazi propaganda and published in Britain with the connivance of the British publisher Faber & Faber. This fact was not revealed to its American publisher, Harcourt Brace, for the book was part of a vast campaign launched by the British secret services to secure American sympathy and assistance at a time when American isolationists were still attempting to keep Roosevelt's administration from involvement in the war.[16] Nevertheless, Dirk van der Heide's account of his family's struggles for survival under German oppression has simply been too good to sink into oblivion, and it continues to be read and commented upon as if it were real. Even in 1995 it was included in a widely read anthology of children's wartime diaries, without any attempt to distinguish it from the genuine material from which the other chapters were taken.[17] Tellingly, however, it is the only wartime

[16] Nigel West, *Counterfeit Spies* (London: St Ermin's, 1998), pp. 2–3; more generally, see N. Cull, *Selling War* (Oxford: Oxford University Press, 1997).

[17] L. Holliday, *Children in the Holocaust and World War II: Their Secret Diaries* (New York: Washington Square, 1995), pp. 33–54.

diary where the child adopts a pseudonym and no photographs of the family have ever surfaced.

Dirk van der Heide's diary confronts us with a serious question. How truthful are the real wartime diaries that have come down to us? The majority of diaries that have been forged or seriously tampered with have been identified. This is because few events take place under the gaze of a single human being, and so there is usually one brave individual ready to challenge dubious accounts. One such intrepid figure was a former German U-Boat telegraphist, Heinz F. K. Guske. During the war Guske found himself assigned to U-764 and was part of the crew for six missions until the vessel surrendered on 13 May 1945. He was then taken to Britain and remained a prisoner of war there for almost three years. As part of the U-boat's communications team, he was one of three who had been allowed to see the captain's diary. What he had seen there had shocked him to the core. He was astounded at the numerous false reports the captain had entered, but he was powerless to do anything about it, and after the war he forgot the matter entirely. Only in 1985 did he happen upon a copy of a magazine on German U-boat history, *Schaltung Küste*. From this he was dismayed to learn that his former captain had gone on to write a memoir based upon copies of his wartime diaries. Guske decided to come forward and reveal the deceptions in the diary and the memoir. His painstaking research and his first-hand knowledge of events finally enabled fact to be separated from fiction.[18]

Seriously falsified or forged diaries are not hard to identify. More problematic are those that have been lightly adjusted or enhanced. In the 1970s Donald M. McKale, a historian at Clemson University, set out to write the biography of Curt Prüfer, a German diplomat who specialized in Berlin's policy towards the Middle East. What McKale happened upon in the course of his exhaustive research was a great historical rarity: not one but two copies of Prüfer's diary. The first was the original; the second proved to be an adjusted version designed for public consumption after the war. Donald McKale has published the two versions alongside each other, providing us with an extraordinary visible record of Prüfer's attempt to rewrite history. Many of the

[18] H. Guske, *The War Diaries of U-764: Fact or Fiction?* (London: Thomas, 1996).

adjustments are subtle, often matters of emphasis or inflection, and without access to the earlier copy it is unlikely that the changes would have been identified.

The diaries of Curt Prüfer deal with the eventful year between October 1942 and September 1943 from the perspective of a pro-Nazi German diplomat in Berlin. They are all the more interesting because we have come to understand that pro-Nazi officials were not in the majority within the old institutions of the Wehrmacht and the German foreign office. (Indeed, one may search the innumerable post-war memoirs of those who served in the German armed forces without finding many dedicated Nazis.) Prüfer's accounts call this picture into question. The first version of the diary, which McKale has accepted as authentic and original, shows that Prüfer was supportive of many of Hitler's policies and of Hitler himself as a leader. The second version, produced by the author after 1945, contains many small additions, deletions and fabrications, including some direct criticisms of Hitler, and particularly of his war strategies.

McKale suggests that Prüfer modified his diary for various reasons. First, he wanted to distance the German people and himself from any direct responsibility for the Hitler regime's policies of aggressive war and the annihilation of the Jews. He also wished to suggest that the German population did not really require a tough post-war foreign occupation or extensive de-nazification. The revisions may also have been an exercise in self-deception. The most obvious fabrications involve the in-clusion of statements that implied sympathy for the German Jews, whereas the original, expressing Prüfer's true opinion of Jews, contains several derogatory passages. Above all it appears that Prüfer was motivated to revise his diaries as a result of the news coverage of the Nuremberg war crimes trials: he seems to have hoped to refute some of the evidence that was being brought against his former superiors. Some diaries believed to be genuinely contemporary with the events they described were employed as evidence by the Nuremberg tribunal, demon-strating the value of untarnished authenticity we generally attribute to them. Prüfer's was not among them.[19]

[19] D. M. McKale (ed.), *Rewriting History: The Original and Revised World War II Diaries of Curt Prüfer, Nazi Diplomat* (Kent, Ohio: Kent State University Press, 1988), pp. vii–xx. SEE PP. 493–4.

Prüfer's post-war attempts to revise history in a country under occupation and close Allied scrutiny are perhaps not as surprising as they first appear. However, they do provide a warning. What other diary material has disappeared or changed? All diaries must be approached with caution, for fear that they have been embellished. Moreover, there is also a grey line between memoirs and diaries written up some weeks or months after the event (sometimes because of a lack of access to writing materials at the time). Nevertheless, just like oral records, wartime diaries, if used with care, can shine a bright light into some dark corners of history. In particular, they often capture elusive subjects that governments might not wish to have illuminated at all.

Both Lord Halifax, the British Foreign Secretary at the beginning of the war, and his junior minister 'Rab' Butler had expressed admiration for Hitler and Nazi Germany in the interwar years. Henry 'Chips' Channon's diary records that in 1936 Halifax returned from a trip to Germany which he had visibly enjoyed. Channon took the opportunity to ask his friend Halifax for his detailed impressions. Halifax responded cheerily that he 'liked all the Nazi leaders, even Goebbels, and he was much impressed, interested and amused by the visit. He thinks the regime absolutely fantastic.' Halifax was especially taken with the regalia and liked the sight of Hitler in his 'khaki shirt, black breeches and patent leather evening shoes'.[20] Another diary, that of Alexander Cadogan, the most senior official at the Foreign Office throughout the war, records some of the many secret missives that went back and forth between London and Berlin in the period between 1939 and 1941 in search of some sort of peace deal. On the evening of 6 December 1941, less than thirty-six hours before the attack on Pearl Harbor, he wrote in his diary: 'I refused to see two of "C's" men about the peace offer, which is the same old stuff.' 'C' was the head of MI6. Hitler and Goebbels maintained an improbable belief that the British people would opt to avoid all-out war and instead choose a 'quisling' government under Lloyd George. Britain's First World War premier was personally obsessed with the danger of aerial bombing and anxious to avoid the destruction another war would wreak at

[20] Robert Rhodes James (ed.), *'Chips': The Diaries of Sir Henry Channon* (London: Weidenfeld & Nicolson, 1967), p. 499, entry for 5 December 1936. SEE ALSO P. 160.

almost any cost. Cadogan was no appeaser and had little time for such efforts, but others in the Cabinet were clearly more interested. When a published version of Alexander Cadogan's diary appeared in 1971, these matters were deemed still too sensitive to meet the public gaze and were edited out.[21]

Even matters simply too secret to be committed to official paper were captured occasionally when the right person was in the right place to record them in a diary. Although it has never been officially admitted, it is clear that by the latter stages of the war Britain's sabotage service, the Special Operations Executive, had begun to experiment with some nasty poisons and bacteriological weapons. The diary of Charles Sulzberger, an American journalist who frequented the circles of those on wartime secret service work in the Mediterranean, recorded his conversations with some of the wilder British operatives. His account includes details of the antics of Patrick 'Paddy' Leigh Fermor and Bill Moss on occupied Crete. The pair had already kidnapped a German general by wearing German uniforms, something which most undercover operatives were loth to do. Then, in September 1944, Sulzberger recorded that Bill Moss's most recent mission was to attack the headquarters of a division of Panzer grenadiers that was occupying Crete. 'He carried a bottle of germ fluid, which could give tertiary syphilis to five hundred men if mixed with their food, and kill them in forty-eight hours. He was dressed in Cretan costume and lay in a hole two hundred yards from the divisional headquarters.' Sulzberger does not record the outcome of the mission.[22]

Diaries can capture the very secret, but it is no less important that they can capture things that are regarded by contemporaries as being of little value – such as the history of prisoners of war (POWs) and of internees. Government record officers have regarded this as an especially unimportant area, and most of Britain's records regarding the management of German and

---

[21] Diary of Alexander Cadogan, Churchill Archives Centre, Churchill College, Cambridge, entry for 6 December 1941. The published version is D. Dilks (ed.), *The Diaries of Sir Alexander Cadogan, 1938–1945* (London: Cassell, 1971). SEE ALSO PP. 45–6, 247–8 AND 419–20.

[22] C. S. Sulzberger, *A Long Row of Candles: Memoirs and Diaries 1934–54* (London: Macdonald, 1969), p. 242.

Italian POWs have, in their circumlocutory language, 'not been selected for preservation'. Many other countries have gone down a similar road, making the history of prisoners and internees especially difficult to reconstruct. Nevertheless, a number of wartime diaries allow us to map the real treatment of prisoners of war in the field. Bill Moss of SOE had told Charles Sulzberger that 'the British in Crete turned over their prisoners to the local guerrillas who slaughtered them'. Within a few pages his diary records similar behaviour by both the Germans and the Russians. The juxtaposition is unlikely to be accidental. In June 1944 Sulzberger had visited Rome and heard that more than 300 Italian hostages had been slaughtered by the Germans in the local catacombs. He toured the location. It is the trivial details captured in his diary that carry conviction. Afterwards Sulzberger found it necessary to send his uniform to be dry cleaned and his other clothing to be laundered, but was unable to escape the stench because the putrefaction had seeped into the leather soles of his shoes. On the same page he records the activities of a Soviet officer in Yugoslavia who boasted that he had killed over 150 Germans. He was dismayed when the Allies offered safe 'surrender passes' to German soldiers to persuade them to give themselves up. Sulzberger's diary is just one of several private records that explicitly contrast the behaviour of the various Allied forces towards their prisoners.

Diaries offer a potential challenge to 'victor's history'. Traditional accounts by the victorious powers suggest that 'only' the Axis forces robbed or mistreated their prisoners and political internees. Diaries tell us a different story. In 1941 a Canadian diplomat serving in London, Charles Ritchie, recorded the fate of anti-Nazi refugees who had come to Britain in 1938 and 1939 and had been interned in May 1940. Finding itself over-burdened, he noted, Britain had asked Canada to accept some of these 'ferocious internees' who later turned out to be 'mostly entirely inoffensive anti-Nazi refugees'. This group, he added, who were for the most part middle-class anti-Nazi German intellectuals, had now been 'shovelled out to Canada at a moment's notice' and were likely to 'have a disagreeable time'.[23] Ritchie understated the

[23] Charles Ritchie, *The Siren Years: Undiplomatic Diaries, 1937–45* (Toronto: Macmillan, 1974), p. 61. SEE PP. 223–4 AND 707–8.

fate that awaited these 'good Germans'. From their initial internment on the Isle of Man through their eventual transportation
from Liverpool to their confinement in further internment camps
in Canada, they were routinely beaten and systematically robbed
by both British and Canadian soldiers. Conditions were appalling
and some of those subjected to this degrading treatment were
below military age or very elderly. Numerous diaries kept by the
individuals who endured this experience give eloquent testimony
to their suffering and were later used by the British Home
Office to try to bring some of the offenders to book. However, as
Ritchie records, these efforts were hindered by the fact that in
London the Home Office and the War Office were 'barely on
speaking terms'. This episode is perfect 'diary territory'. Accounts
by different internees allow for cross-checking and the construction of a narrative that is reliable and compelling.

Diaries do not provide us with a 'higher form' of historical source
material. They do, however, provide us with a more varied
historical diet. Ideally, in attempting to construct any historical
account we should draw on a great variety of sources, including
diaries, memoirs, oral history and press material as well as the
official records. In reality, however, the majority of Second World
War history has been written overwhelmingly from the official
record. In these records, as Christopher Hill has eloquently
reminded us, 'the people appear as objects not subjects'.[24]
Historians have used documents prepared by military officers or
civilian officials in the course of their duties, and then – perhaps
thirty years later – released into the public archives. Each year
historians eagerly await the arrival of the latest batch of material
in repositories around the world. The position of the historian in
this process is a somewhat passive one, and there can be no doubt
where authority lies. In 2000 historians of the First World War
were pathetically grateful when the British government decided
to allow them to see, for the first time, MI5 files generated during
that distant conflict. However, the material eventually released
represented no more than a slender sample of what had originally
been generated.

---

[24] C. Hill, '"Where Are We Going?", International Relations and the Voice from
Below', *Review of International Studies*, 25 (1999), pp. 107–22.

Inescapably, history written purely from the official record is effectively 'official history once removed'. This is not necessarily to impute improper motives to government. Understandably, officials at the time often failed to document matters that displeased their superiors; and, under pressure of war, issues that were interesting, but not pressing matters of the hour, went unrecorded. In subsequent years other officials perused the records that were made and 'weeded out' material that was thought unimportant. Still later, others would decide which elements of the remaining material should see the light of day and which should be withheld from the public gaze for longer periods. In short, official records are pre-processed and, used to the exclusion of all other material, can result in an impoverished version of history.

To enrich that account we can turn to an army of private diarists – the forgotten foot-soldiers of history. Many of them were themselves officials, diplomats and generals; but what they wrote in their journals was significantly different in texture from what they wrote in the files back at the office. At the same time, in thousands of quiet corners, normal people were also recording the unseen war in their own particular ways. How would the narrative of the Second World War sound if related by these private voices? *Witness to War* begins to give us some idea.

Inescapably, history written purely from the official record is effectively 'official history once removed'. This is not necessarily to impute improper motives to government. Understandably, officials at the time failed to document matters that displeased their superiors; and, under pressure of war, issues that were interesting, but not pressing matters of the hour, went unrecorded. In subsequent years other officials perused the records that were made and 'weeded out' material that was thought unimportant. Still later, others would decide which elements of the remaining material should see the light of day and which should be withheld from the public gaze for longer periods. In short, official records are pre-processed and, used to the exclusion of all other material, can result in an impoverished version of history.

To enrich that account we can turn to an army of private diarists – the forgotten foot-soldiers of history. Many of them were themselves officials, diplomats and generals, but what they wrote in their journals was significantly different in texture from what they wrote in the files back at the office. At the same time, in thousands of quiet corners, normal people were also recording the unseen war in their own particular ways. How would the narrative of the Second World War sound if related by these private voices? Witness to War begins to give us some idea.

1939

'I HAVE DECIDED TO begin this Notebook feeling that
this time we shall not escape. I should like to have
the perseverance, to be faithful enough to myself, not
to abandon it.

'I am afraid I shall not be able to submit to the sort of
discipline, of restraint, which keeping a diary demands
– or rather hope that I shall not; thinking that one is
seldom sincere in his supposedly intimate diary, and
that here more than elsewhere writing is artificial.
Thinking also that it is a proof of great vanity to note
one's own insignificant doings. But the war is here, it
will be here in a day, in an hour, and although I am still
at the Lys with G, in a peace disturbed only by the
wasps flying in swarms about the lindens, I know that
my turn is coming. And I go about repeating to myself
that the war ... the war ... the war ...'

Jean Malaquais' WAR DIARY, entry for 28 August 1939

JANUARY – AUGUST 1939

THE 1930S WERE NOT a peaceful decade. Although we date the beginning of the Second World War to September 1939, that spring saw the end of nearly three years of bloody conflict in Spain, where the Republicans had fought a desperate but unsuccessful campaign against General Franco's fascists; war had also been raging in China since 1937, between Japan and Chiang Kai-shek's Nationalist government, and throughout 1939 the Japanese army continued to make further cruel incursions into the vast Asian hinterland. Graphic images of the bombing of cities in both Spain and China found their way onto cinema newsreels across Europe, ensuring that by the beginning of 1939 few civilians were in doubt about what was coming. During the First World War, almost all the casualties had been military personnel; everyone knew the next European war would be very different.

In Germany, Hitler was possessed of his own limpidly clear vision of what lay ahead. By 1939 he had been promulgating his ambitions for *Lebensraum* – German expansion into new living space to accommodate population growth in the east – for more than a decade. Britain and France had come to a mutual understanding at an early stage that they would not resist German unification with Austria, and would press Czechoslovakia to come to an accommodation with Germany rather than embroil Europe in another large-scale war. The British Prime Minister, Neville Chamberlain, pursued a policy of appeasement which reached its climax at Munich in September 1938, in an agreement which allowed Germany to annex part of Czechoslovakia. Appeasement was founded upon two beliefs: first, that Britain was simply not ready for war in 1938; second, that Hitler was a traditional statesman who would keep his word – specifically, that this was the end of his territorial ambitions. Chamberlain was strongly encouraged in this policy by the US President, Franklin D. Roosevelt, and the American ambassador in London, Joseph P. Kennedy. Chamberlain was almost certainly right on the first count: in military terms Britain was lagging behind Germany and had little choice except to avoid war in 1938. But Hitler's own behaviour in Germany should have told him that he was dealing with someone who was neither reasonable nor responsible.

On 30 January 1939 Hitler gave a terrifying speech in the Reichstag which left little room for doubt about the nature of the Nazi state. He promised that if world war came he would ensure that it was accompanied by 'the annihilation of the Jewish race in Europe'. On 15 March he threw off all pretence of restraint and undertook the complete absorption of Czechoslovakia. The Munich agreement, and Chamberlain's reputation, now lay in ruins. German forces also began to encroach on Lithuania and Romania. Public opinion in Britain and France was outraged, although at this stage few demanded war. Paris and London responded by issuing guarantees to Greece and Poland against aggression by Germany or its ally Italy, with which it had recently signed the 'Pact of Steel'. Whitehall knew that war was not far away and introduced conscription.

In the summer of 1939 all eyes turned east towards Moscow, which would often be the fulcrum of the conflict which was to follow. At the time the Soviet Union was fighting an obscure limited war with Japan on its border with China at a place called Nomohan, but this passed almost unnoticed in Europe. Meanwhile the regime was being courted by two sets of European negotiators: an Anglo-French team who hoped to persuade it to restrain Germany, and a party headed by Joachim von Ribbentrop, Hitler's foreign minister, who sought an alliance. Ribbentrop believed that once he had secured agreement with Moscow, nothing could stand in the way of further German expansion. He was correct. On 23 August 1939 Stalin shocked the world by signing the Nazi–Soviet Pact, containing secret clauses that formed a prelude to a German and Russian division of Poland. By the end of August 1939 the British fleet was mobilizing and civilians had already begun to leave London.

Sunday 29 January – Sunday 19 March 1939

Miss H. P. L. Mott records her growing vexation with Chamberlain

Miss Mott was an elderly lady living with her sister in Teddington, just south-west of London. She was possessed of an excellent knowledge of world affairs and held strong political opinions. Her thirteen volumes of well-crafted diaries, written between 1939 and 1946, reveal the reaction of a politically aware middle-class woman to the failure of appeasement.

29 January

It seems *we* all wait to hear what Hitler tells us tomorrow. Why in heaven's name we (and by that I mean *every* nation, not Fascist or Nazi) can't tell *him* that, *no longer will we endure his threats* and if he moves one further step, the combined nations will swoop and *do* it. It should be *organised – all* stand together. One doesn't let the tiger taste blood and then say '*please* isn't that enough!'?

24 February

Chamberlain is to recognise Franco next Monday. A rotten and not understandable business – but on a par with the whole of his Czechoslovakia commitments and his Munich idiocy.

15 March

Hitler's troops march into *Prague* – The people hissed and booed and sang the Czech National Anthem. Czechoslovakia is referred to by Germany as *Czechei*!!! German troops entered *Slovakia* in response to an appeal from the Slovak Government. I wonder!!! So many lies are told and such atrocious deeds done that no reliance can be placed on any statement that comes out of Berlin. No words are fit for Hitler's war – maniac though he is – he is allowed to do anything without let or hindrance – to our everlasting shame . . .

Hitler left Berlin with a strong bodyguard for Prague . . . Chamberlain and Halifax by this juggling forfeit the right to be responsible Ministers – Are we gone supine? Have we lost every vestige of decency?

16 March

. . . 5,000 Czechs have been arrested by the Gestapo – Himmler is in Prague with Hitler (two fine specimens of cruel evil, ruthless brigands – I call them Castor and Pollux).

There is no intention so far of Chamberlain send[ing] protest to Germany – He is apparently in collusion. There seems no other interpretation to place on his silence.

19 March

Listened to the wild (animal) cheering in Berlin people seemed quite mad and disgusting – an orgy of frenzied shrieking. 'Hitler will show himself and then ask the people to go home' . . .

One cannot blame the German people for making fools of themselves in the eyes of the world. They are fed with Hitler's prowess like pap and allowed no other news and Goring and Goebbels tell them so many fairy tales and the perfidy of the other Powers – their brains being a bit weak and their powers of deduction nil – they believe just anything . . .

British public opinion was shifting fast in 1939 and Miss Mott's diary shows the importance of developments in Czechoslovakia for both Chamberlain and Hitler. Chamberlain had undertaken appeasement to buy time. With his background in the Treasury he was acutely aware of the poor state of Britain's defence capabilities as a result of the low levels of military spending that had been the rule in the mid-1930s. Britain was not ready for war in 1938; however, by 1939 the public had lost patience with the scale of broken agreements.

Miss Mott would survive the war and move to Greenwich, where she lived until her death in the early 1950s.

Friday 17 – Sunday 19 March 1939

Emil Dorian in Bucharest watches events in neighbouring Czechoslovakia

Emil Dorian was a Jewish writer and physician living in Bucharest, where he had been born in 1893. He kept a regular diary from the mid-1930s.

17 March

Although it was barely two months ago that Hitler hysterically roared to the world his sincere intentions – 'Wir brauchen keine Tschechen [We don't need any Czechs]' – he has just annexed Czechoslovakia to the Reich. And still Europe has not awakened. Within twenty-four hours, a country with its own culture and democratic institutions has disappeared from the map.

Sooner or later, Germany is likely to suffer the consequences of this action. The Sudetenland was as easy to devour as a soft piece of meat, but Czechoslovakia is a bone that will stick in the throat. For the people will no longer listen to the stale slogan: 'Our brethren are in chains, we must free them.' The repercussions in our country may be more serious than we think. Right now, however, Hungary's appetite cannot be satisfied. Germany cannot penetrate here without first preparing the climate of opinion. Might the knot be tied in Ruthenia? We are in the dark. Rumor has it that two battalions are stationed at our frontier with Hungary. Consultations, unrest, spreading panic.

19 March

The pressure of political events is growing from day to day and reaches unbearable proportions. So much terror in the world has disrupted life's simplest rhythms. People are again driven crazy by news, by threats, by uncertainty . . .

Dorian consoled himself by observing that he had lived through 'massive doses of history' in the last two decades and was too tired to be a victim of scaremongering. Nevertheless by the end of the month alarm was tangible. In Bucharest there had been break-ins at the savings banks and shoe shops; food prices were rising as people began to hoard supplies. Troops had been moved to the Hungarian and Bulgarian borders. SEE ALSO PP. 328–9.

Friday 28 – Saturday 29 April 1939

Count Ciano, the Italian foreign minister, compares developments in Berlin and Rome

Count Galeazzo Ciano was born in Livorno on 18 March 1903 into a prominent naval family. After toying with journalism, he eventually moved to Rome to pursue a political career. In 1930 he married Benito Mussolini's daughter Edda, and in June 1936 Mussolini appointed him foreign minister of Italy. His diary recorded his experience of the role in minute detail.

28 April

The Führer has delivered his speech [in Berlin]. It lasted exactly two hours and twenty minutes; it cannot be said that brevity is Hitler's most noticeable characteristic. Generally speaking, the speech is less bellicose than one might have supposed on the information coming to us from Berlin. The first reactions to the speech in the different capitals are also rather mild. Every word which leaves any hope of peaceful intentions is received by the whole humanity with immeasurable joy. No nation wants war today; the most that one can say is that they know war is inevitable ...

29 April

Council of Ministers [in Rome]. Some decisions are approved to increase the power of the armed forces. The

Duce is very much dissatisfied with them, with the exception of the Navy. He feels, and rightly so, that beyond appearances, which are more or less carefully kept up, there is little underneath. I think so too. I have no exact information as to the Army, but the many rumours which I hear are distinctly pessimistic. Also, some impressions which I formed on the occasion of the mobilization for the Albanian undertaking, which was after all a small mobilization, have increased my doubts. The military make great play with a lot of names. They multiply the number of divisions, but in reality these are so small that they scarcely have more than the strength of regiments. The ammunition depots are short of ammunition. Artillery is outmoded. Our anti-aircraft and anti-tank weapons are altogether lacking. There has been a good deal of bluffing in the military sphere, and even the Duce himself has been deceived – a tragic bluff. We will not talk about the question of the Air Force. Valle states that there are 3,006 first-line planes, while the Navy information service says that there are only 982. A gross exaggeration. I report the matter to the Duce. I believe that it is my duty to speak with absolute honesty about such a matter, even though it makes him bitter.

Early in 1939 Italy had attacked Albania. The campaign was accompanied by remarkable examples of military incompetence and disorganization, which partly reflected a culture of bluffing and self-deception within the Italian military. Italian behaviour in Albania was also accompanied by war crimes that were never investigated with any thoroughness after 1945 and which still remain almost unknown.

At the end of April 1939 Hitler made a crucial speech in which he demanded that Poland hand the city of Danzig over to Germany. In this month he also revoked the German Non-Aggression Pact with Poland and rejected US President Franklin D. Roosevelt's offer of mediation. Ciano feared that Italy was embarking on a war for which it was ill prepared. SEE ALSO PP. 46–7, 110–11, 335–7 AND 513.

Tuesday 2 – Tuesday 9 May 1939

Alexander Cadogan, the most senior Foreign Office official, works on replies to Hitler

Alexander Cadogan had made his name as a diplomat in China and had been Britain's ambassador in Beijing in 1935–6. He was then brought back to London and served as Permanent Under-Secretary of State at the Foreign Office from 1938 to 1946. His diaries are perhaps the most important personal record of the British government's inner circle during the war and describe conversations with some of the most senior figures in Whitehall, including Lord Halifax, at this point Foreign Secretary, and prominent advisers such as Sir Robert Vansittart.

Alexander Cadogan

2 *May*

Got Kirkpatrick's draft reply to Hitler before lunch and tinkered with it a bit . . . back at 2.30 to show reply to Hitler to H. [Lord Halifax – Foreign Secretary]. He made some suggestions, which I worked on and sent down to him at the H[ouse] of L[ords].

Saw H. at 7.20. P.M. [Chamberlain] wanted further alterations to reply to Hitler.

3 May

Putting finishing touches to telegram to Warsaw (which Van[sittart] says is 'admirable'!!!) About 4 o'clock got to work with H. on reply to Hitler. We got another draft into shape ... Went to see H.J.W. about a telephone intercept, which looks as if No.10 were talking 'appeasement' again. He puts up all sorts of denials, to which I don't pay much attention. But it's a good thing to show we have our eye on them.

9 May

Had a fairly quiet day and talk with H. about draft reply to Hitler, which P.M. wants, remodelled. Worked on this. And telegrams to Poland ...

Cadogan did his best to convey to Berlin the serious nature of Britain's promise that it would fight to defend Poland. However, neither Hitler nor the German people believed it. Neville Chamberlain did not help by attempting to water down the telegrams to Hitler. Cadogan was a vigorous opponent of appeasement and was keen to convey to No. 10 Downing Street that any backstairs diplomacy with the Germans would be picked up by British intelligence, controlled by the Foreign Office. SEE ALSO PP. 31–2, 247–8 AND 419–20.

Sunday 21 May 1939

Count Ciano visits Hitler in Berlin

I found Hitler very well, quite serene, less aggressive. A little older. His eyes are more deeply wrinkled. He sleeps very little. In fact less and less. And he spends a great part of the night surrounded by colleagues and friends. Frau Goebbels, who is a constant member of these gatherings and who feels very honoured by them, was describing them to me without being able to conceal a vague feeling of boredom on account of their monotony. It is always Hitler who talks! He can be Führer as much as he likes, but he always repeats himself and bores his guests. For the first time I hear hints, in the inner circles, of the Führer's affection for a beautiful girl. She is twenty years old with beautiful quiet eyes, regular features, and a magnificent body. Her name is Sigrid von Lappus. They see each other frequently and intimately.

The ceremony for the signature of the Pact was very solemn and the Führer was sincerely moved.

Goering, whose standing remains very high, but whose star is no longer in the ascendant, had tears in his eyes when he saw the collar of Annunziata around Ribbentrop's neck.

Von Mackensen told me that Goering had made a scene, complaining that the collar really belonged to him, since he was the true and only promoter of the Alliance. I promised Mackensen that I would try to get Goering a collar.

Ciano travelled to Rome on 21 May 1939, where he joined his opposite number, Joachim von Ribbentrop, in signing the 'Pact of Steel', which sealed the alliance between Berlin and Rome. Both Ribbentrop and Hitler repeatedly assured him that although they had some limited objectives, they wished to avoid a general war for at least three years. They were also keen to use the intervening time to bind Japan more closely to the German–Italian alliance. Having absorbed Czechoslovakia without provoking a violent reaction from London or Paris, they did not expect a foray into Poland to cause any more difficulty.

Ciano had a keen eye for the eccentricities of Hitler's entourage and repeatedly noted Hermann Goering's puerile obsession with medals and decorations. Later in the war, Ciano would arrange for Goering to receive 'The Gold Star of the Roman Eagle' and noted that 'he expressed his thanks so vociferously that his childish joy was obvious'. SEE ALSO PP. 43–4, 110–11, 335–7 AND 513.

Saturday 24 June 1939

Beatrice Webb on the widespread mania for worshipping leaders

Beatrice Webb and her husband Sidney were renowned campaigners for social reform and prominent members of the Fabian Society, widely revered for their commitment to improving the lives of working families by reporting on social conditions. Both were essentially nineteenth-century figures; Beatrice was in her eighties by the time the war began.

How amazingly personal the world has become: the mob idolizing particular individuals instead of claiming, as they did in the nineteenth century, the right of groups to govern themselves through mechanically ascertained majorities, without distinguishing one individual from another. And this idolization of persons on account of their assumed and exceptional goodness and infallible wisdom is not confined to the so-called totalitarian states. The British people, with their genius for compromise, have lit on the device for a robot King and his wife – who have no power but are treated with extreme deference and arouse in the mob worshipful emotion. The efficiency of the device has been shown by the enormous success of the British King and Queen not only in Great Britain but in Canada and the USA. They are ideal robots: the King kindly, sensible, without pretension and with considerable open-mindedness, and the Queen good-looking and gracious and beautifully attired, who blows kisses to admiring Yankees in New York but looks the perfect dignified aristocrat in London. Is this turn towards idolizing particular human beings characteristic of the last two decades, the reaction from a loss of faith in a supernatural god or gods? This mania for a *leader* seems a similar instinct to that shown by wolves – and even by dogs, when the dogs have lost contact with the idolized man. It is clearly a dangerous human instinct when manifested towards men who exercise personal power over multitudes of their fellow men, as do Hitler and Mussolini . . .

Beatrice Webb's diaries record the mindset of the inter-war socialist intelligentsia. They also reveal her fascination with the hypnotic power of modern leaders of all kinds and the way in which this was accentuated by the influence of radio and film. She was struck by the seemingly magical effect of the British royal family's visit to the United States and Canada in the summer of 1939. This was a masterstroke by Whitehall, for the King was a pleasingly apolitical figure and so did not attract criticism from American isolationists. The royal visit was hugely popular with the American press and public. SEE ALSO PP. 68–9 AND 200–1.

Friday 25 – Tuesday 29 August 1939

Geraldine Langhorne fears aerial bombardment like that she has seen on the newsreels

Geraldine Langhorne was aged forty-nine and divorced. She had been a newspaper reporter and was now working as a schoolmistress for the London County Council. She was keeping a diary for the Mass-Observation Archive, an innovative social survey project begun in 1937.

25 August
Nightmares and recurrent neurasthenia. Almost collapsed. LCC Doctor gives leave of absence till October, says I must go to Maudsley Hospital for treatment.

Hang on the end of radio for news. Keep making wild plans. Worried because my niece, a civil servant (aged 37 and very neurotic) looks like breaking down under the strain of being sent she doesn't know where for she doesn't know how long. My sister in an Essex village is nearly distraught at the thought of having evacuees thrust on her.

26 August
Felt guilty because my teacher colleagues are recalled and

working, but I feel bordering on lunacy, remembering news-reel pictures of bombardments. Cannot read or settle to anything. Notices about air-raid warnings garnish every blank wall and some shop windows.

29 August

I am going to see the new Lincoln film, or I shall go crazy waiting for news. Dreamed last night I was sorting rags in which maggots were crawling to make shrouds for school children. This morning I dreamed I heard a bell ringing with a beautiful deep note. I thought someone said 'Its Colonel Wrath come to billet the corpses on you. Don't keep him waiting he can be very unpleasant'. I thought he looked like Conrad Veidt (?) – when I wakened and found myself in my nightdress and dressing gown on the doorstep.

Geraldine Langhorne's diary is a classic example of 'the shadow of the bomber': the fear of aerial destruction that hung over the populations of western Europe even before war began. Conrad Veidt was a German actor who had become established in Britain in the 1930s. He specialized in horror, often playing zombie-like figures, so his films might not have been ideal viewing for someone in a nervous state.

Friday 25 – Monday 28 August 1939

Virginia Woolf's impressions of London on the brink of war

Virginia Woolf, a founder member of the Bloomsbury Group, was a lead-ing British novelist, feminist and literary critic. In her diary – as in her novels – she tended to make use of the 'stream of consciousness' technique, which involved the sporadic noting of spontaneous thoughts and associations. With her husband Leonard Woolf she had founded the Hogarth Press, beginning with a hand-press in their dining room in 1917. This became an important outlet for progressive thinkers and writers, and in August 1939 they were moving their London base to a new location at 37 Mecklenburgh Square.

25 *August*

Perhaps it is more interesting, to describe 'The Crisis' than R's love affairs. Yes we are in the very thick of it. Are we at war? At one I'm going to listen in. Its very different, emotionally, from last September. In London yesterday there was indifference almost. No crowd in the train – we went by train. No stir in the streets. One of the removers called up. Its fate, as the foreman said. What can you do against fate? Complete chaos at 37 [Mecklenburgh Square]. Ann met in graveyard [St George's Fields]. No war, of course not, she said. John said Well I don't know what to think. But as a dress rehearsal its complete. Museums shut. Search light on Rodmell Hill. Ch[amberlai]n says danger imminent. The Russian pact a disagreeable & unforeseen surprise. Rather like a herd of sheep we are. No enthusiasm. Patient bewilderment. I suspect some desire 'to get on with it'. Order double supplies & some coal. [Duncan Grant's] Aunt Violet in refuge at Charleston. Unreal. Whiffs of despair. Difficult to work. Offer of £200 from Chambrun for a story. Haze over the marsh. Aeroplanes. One touch on the switch & we shall be at war. Dantzig not yet taken. Clerk's cheerful. I add one little straw to another, waiting to go in, palsied with writing. There's no cause now to fight for, said Ann. Communists baffled. Railway strike off. Ld. Halifax broadcasts in his country gentleman's voice. Louie says will clothes be dear? Underneath of course wells of pessimism. Young men torn to bits: mothers like Nessa 2 years ago. But again, some swerve to the right may come at any moment. The common feeling covers the private, then recedes. Discomfort & distraction. And all mixed with the mess at 37.

28 *August*

I stay out here, after bowls, to say – what? On this possibly last night of peace. Will the 9 o'clock bulletin end it all? – our lives, oh yes, & everything for the next 50 years? Everyone's writing I suppose about this last day. I walked on the downs; lay under a cornstack & looked at the empty land & the pinkish clouds in a perfect blue summer afternoon sky. Not a sound. Workmen discussing war on the road – one for it, one against. So to bowls. I bowling am happy: I outside the

The German Invasion of Poland, 1939

garden what? Numb I think. Vita says she feels terror & horror early – revives then sinks. For us its like being on a small island. Neither of us has any physical fear. Why should we? But there's a vast calm cold gloom. And the strain. Like waiting a doctors verdict. And the young – young men smashed up. But the point is one is too numbed to think. London seemed cheery. Most people are numb & have a surface optimism. Hugh Slater yesterday, has an instinct that there wont be war. Old Clive sitting on the terrace says 'I don't want to live through it.' Explains that his life recedes. Has had the best. We privately are so content. Bliss day after day. So happy cooking dinner, reading, playing bowls. No feeling of patriotism. How to go on, through war? – that's the question.

The Nazi–Soviet Pact, signed on 23 August 1939, was an unpleasant surprise for all those with far left or communist sympathies, including many in Virginia Woolf's immediate circle. Communists had been in the forefront of the struggle against fascism in Britain through the 1930s – indeed, their anti-fascism had won them many converts – and few knew what to make of this turn of events.

Virginia reflected on these developments from her country home in Sussex, Rodmell. SEE ALSO PP. 221–2.

Sunday 27 August 1939

Joseph P. Kennedy collects an exhausted Lord Halifax from No. 10 Downing Street during the crisis over Poland

Joseph P. Kennedy, the US ambassador in London, came from an established Boston political family. His second son, John F. Kennedy, the future American president, was at Harvard University and his third, Bobby, was just about to go away to high school. Kennedy was a staunch supporter of appeasement and of the search for peace by Neville Chamberlain and his Foreign Secretary, Lord Halifax.

Stayed in bed, read the papers, went to 12:00 noon Mass, had lunch, went back to office. Had a call from Welles – anxiously awaiting news. I told him there was none until Cabinet met. At about 5 Cabinet broke up. I phoned and asked for Halifax. He came on the line and said, 'I'd like to see you.' He said, 'I'd like to see you but I'm terribly tired and I am going home to bed for a couple of hours.' And I said, 'Why don't I come down and drive you home.' He said that would be fine – come down in about 10 minutes . . .

Halifax came down and I told the detectives to get the crowd out of the way as I had to back the car up. Well, we both went out of the door [of 10 Downing Street] together. Halifax remarked jokingly as the crowd cheered, 'The 2 popular men in England.' I went alongside and got in on driving side and Halifax went other side. He is so tall he had great trouble getting into the seat alongside of me. He took off his hat and put his bags and umbrella on the back seat and I started off with the crowds cheering and the detectives waved me back when all of a sudden my bumper caught under the mudguard of a car at right angles to me and I was stuck. They waved me forward slowly and waved me back. I couldn't budge. The crowd laughed – they were very gay. Halifax and I both laughed heartily. Finally the police asked about 8 or 10 strong young Englishmen to come over and lift the car, which they did and so amidst the crowd's cheers they lifted the car up and put me on the road . . . While we were stuck, people stuck their head in the window – men and women – with 'God Bless you!' 'Please don't let us go to war.' 'You'll save us we know' 'I don't want to send my boy except to fight for Britain not Poland' etc . . . We drove home slowly and he gave me the story . . .

In late August 1939 Britain confronted new dangers as a result of the surprise agreement between two ideological enemies, Germany and the Soviet Union. This convinced Berlin and Moscow that they could act against Poland with impunity. Kennedy had met with his friend Neville Chamberlain a couple of days before and conceded that the Prime Minister looked 'like a broken man'. Chamberlain was extremely gloomy, predicting the deaths of 'millions of young men' and the destruction of Britain's economic and financial position. After the emergency Cabinet meeting that Sunday, the Foreign Secretary, Lord Halifax – nicknamed the 'Holy Fox' – told Kennedy that the British government would continue negotiating, but could not do anything that would mean abandoning Poland. German newspapers were full of wild stories about Polish atrocities against Germans in Danzig, and Kennedy could see that German public opinion was being whipped up. War now seemed inevitable. SEE ALSO PP. 64–5 AND 572–5.

Tuesday 29 August 1939

Sir Raymond Streat, a Manchester industrialist, encounters Nazi sympathies

Raymond Streat, a key figure in the Lancashire cotton industry, kept a diary from 1931 to 1958. He was Secretary of the Chamber of Commerce in Manchester and in 1940 would begin working in London as Chairman of the Cotton Board. His diary represents the outlook of the 'new' wartime civil servant, a middle-class provincial technocrat drawn into Whitehall by the mammoth expansion of government in 1939–40. Its perspective is one that originates in Manchester rather than London.

On Tuesday evening the dinner plan placed me next to a girl and next but one to her father. They sat silent whilst three or four Canadians opposite to them made no attempt to greet them. I therefore suggest I should introduce myself and them to the others at the table. The old gentleman responded at once, having evidently felt rather miserable until some-body spoke to him. It transpired he was a ship builder from Danzig. His town house adjoined his shipyards in which he was building two vessels for Poland and two for Germany. His state of mind had become fatalistic. He felt that what-ever happened must involve disaster for him. [He] was German born and bred but sprang from French-Huguenot stock and had gone to Danzig in 1920. He wanted Germany to make progress and recognised that the Hitler regime had achieved much for Germany. He thought the quarrel with England a fatal error and had tried several times in London and Berlin to see if he could not promote better understanding. Evidently he had influential connections.

The daughter was about twenty-four and had been 'finished' in London and Paris, speaking French and English with equal versatility. She was a devoted adherent of Hitler and said that all the young people in Danzig wanted it to be joined to Germany. She hated Poles and Jews with great fervour and admitted she never met or talked with either. She thought a vote would give a great majority in Danzig for joining the Reich and saw no reason why the ballot should not be conducted by the Nazi Gauleiter. Her father agreed that she represented the young people's views and to some extent his own. Much that I told her of the English attitude was obviously so strange and new to her as to be barely believable. She had had many English friends but had not been to England nor corresponded much for two years. In particular she did not realise at all that it was Hitler's broken promise when he took Prague which had made it impossible for England to trust him or his lieutenants, such as her esteemed 1939 Gauleiter in Danzig.

The Chamber of Commerce in Manchester afforded Streat a good vantage-point from which to follow world events. Many of the large cotton firms had representatives travelling in Europe, and their network ensured that Streat was closely informed about what was afoot. Most German businessmen did not want war with Britain and many had made strenuous efforts to improve relations. Equally, many felt that the Hitler regime had allowed Germany to secure some economic stability, perhaps preventing a takeover by the extreme left. Such views as those of the Danzig shipbuilder and his daughter were not untypical of those being offered up freely in Europe in the summer of 1939. SEE ALSO PP. 70–1 AND 853–4.

Wednesday 30 August 1939

Keith Vaughan watches preparations for war on Hampstead Heath

Keith Vaughan, born in Sussex in 1910, was a self-taught artist who developed his abilities through dedicated practice. He worked for the advertising agency Lintas *between 1931 and 1938. Loathing war, the military and the pomposity that military activities seemed to generate, he watched the transformation of London with horrified fascination.*

We wait still; war or peace. The governments have locked themselves in and continue exchanging letters; only we no longer know what they are saying. Tension has relaxed, simply because it was impossible to remain at that pitch of anxious fever for long. But the situation is the same. One hopes blindly for some miracle, but one dare not speak about it. People seem resigned, almost cheerful. 'I think we're going to have a slap at him this time.'

Sand everywhere. The weight of London must be increasing steadily by hundreds of tons an hour. The Heath is blighted by a plague of bull-dozers, their grinning steel faces burrowing into the sand like diabolical ostriches. Moist caverns yawn beneath the glare of paraffin arc-lamps as the frantic digging goes on all through the night. The familiar worn paths, the dry grass baked and trodden by countless feet, the hummocks and bushes which I have passed by since childhood, never questioning their permanence, are torn up and scarred by the steel caterpillars until the landscape is a nightmare filled with the shriek and clang of pulleys and chains and dim in a mist of dust and smoke. Groups of people hover in the shadows. Cyclists, workmen, young couples, gangs of excited youths, solitary old men, stand and watch and discuss the merits of different kinds of explosive and protection from direct hits as though they were already familiar with these things. The boys look proud and confident in their sleek blue uniforms posing gracefully on the backs of the new grey fire engines. They wave and are happy. They are part of something, vital and important; appointed to positions of conspicuous importance. And how absurdly easy. Just call at the office and sign your name and immediately you're somebody instead of nobody. The diabolical deception of war. How can they help but be disappointed now if it doesn't come. SEE ALSO PP. 272–3 AND 329–31.

Kevin Worth thinks about war and landscape

Kevin Worth was a fifteen-year-old boy living in Aldershot. Like Geraldine Langhorne, he had volunteered to keep a diary for the Mass-Observation Archive.

At breakfast, dad and I had an argument about the probable duration of a war if one should come. I maintained that it would last about 6 months, but Dad thought it would last at least 2 years. We didn't reach a satisfactory conclusion however.

After dinner, my mother and I went to Woking to visit my Grandfather and his wife. Apart from a speculation on how food rationing would affect us, there was no talk of war.

Grandfather and I went across the fields for a walk. Out there in the quiet, wars and talk of wars seemed impossible. I wonder if we got all the Heads of states out in the open air in a big green field with beautiful country stretching away all around them, and let them talk over their difficulties, would the surroundings would affect them [*sic*] so much that they would all negotiate these difficulties peacefully?

SEPTEMBER 1939

L IKE SO MANY twentieth-century conflicts, the German attack on Poland was not preceded by anything as gentlemanly as a 'declaration of war'. German forces began a Blitzkrieg campaign against their Polish opponents in the early hours of 1 September. Although German armour was relatively weak – certainly much weaker than it would be by May 1940 – the speed of the offensive and the use of Stuka dive-bombers against Polish forces, which had no anti-aircraft guns, was startlingly effective.

In Britain's House of Commons vicious attacks were made on Chamberlain and his failed appeasement policy. The Prime Minister, who appeared tired and ill, responded to his critics by sending Hitler an ultimatum on 2 September demanding German withdrawal from Poland. Hitler's reply was a deafening silence; accordingly, at 11.15 a.m. on 3 September 1939 Chamberlain made a dignified radio announcement to the nation declaring war on Germany. He spoke of Hitler and warned that 'there is no chance of expecting that this man will ever give up his practice of using force to gain his will. He can only be stopped by force.' As this speech was made on a Sunday, Chamberlain was listened to with rapt attention by almost the entire adult population of Britain. France, India, Australia, New Zealand and Canada quickly followed Britain in declaring war. There followed a frenzy of activity on the home front, notably the hurried evacuation of children from towns and cities considered vulnerable to bombing, and there was a curiously eager anticipation of the first air attacks.

By 10 September the first elements of the British Expeditionary Force were on their way to France, where they took up positions alongside their French allies. No significant action was taken to assist the Poles, who were still fighting but clearly doomed in the face of a combined onslaught by the German and Soviet armies. The only significant military action was at sea, where submarines quickly established themselves as a dominant element in the naval war. Within hours of Chamberlain's announcement a German U-boat accidentally sank a passenger liner, the SS *Athenia*. Then, in two separate 'friendly fire' incidents, three British submarines were mistaken for enemy vessels and attacked. In one incident, on 10 September, the British submarine HMS *Triton* fired two torpedoes at the British submarine HMS *Oxley* off the coast of Norway. Only three of *Oxley*'s crew of fifty-four escaped. Later in September, Royal Navy destroyers sank two U-boats in separate engagements, but on the 17th Germany's U-29 attacked and sank the British carrier HMS *Courageous* with three torpedo hits off the coast of Ireland.

By mid-September the Polish generals had begun to lose touch with unit commanders in the field, but Warsaw was still fiercely defended and German tank attacks were repulsed on its outskirts. On 25 September the Polish capital suffered very heavy bombing from 400 aircraft of the Luftwaffe and the resulting fires were uncontrollable. Two days later the Polish government surrendered. On 30 September a separate Polish government in exile was established in Paris, and the Polish resistance effort began.

Saturday 2 September 1939

Kay Phipps helps a German woman to the station on the day before war

Kay Phipps began the war working at a first aid post in Westminster and then became a probationer nurse at the Preliminary Training School for Nurses at University College Hospital, where she would train until May 1940.

Last night I went to the pictures, and when I came out I feared for the moment I had gone blind, for it was nearly pitch dark, not a street lamp as far as I could see and no lighted windows, except for one and there was a small crowd outside that and people saying 'you'll get us all killed' and a voice of Authority saying 'put out that light'.

The only bright thing was the tiny coloured crosses of the traffic lights. Cars had only side-lights and some had blue covers over their headlamps.

This morning I noticed that the police are decked out in steel helmets. The helmets have 'police' written on the front. Sauntering towards Victoria I met a woman carrying a suitcase, who asked me to direct her to the station, so I walked part of the way with her. To my surprise she told me she was a German who was trying to get home. She had worked in England for some years and had two sons in the German army. She became very upset when the ticket office could hold out no hope of getting her a boat. She thought she might get torn to pieces here if war broke out! I assured her that that would not be the case.

German citizens living in Britain, and British citizens in Germany, confronted the dilemma of what to do when war broke out. Some achieved repatriation, others decided to take their chances and stay on. For the next few months of the 'phoney war', Germans in Britain would for the most part be left to their own devices. SEE ALSO PP. 74–5.

Sunday 3 September 1939

ARP warden William Holl on the first air-raid warnings in London

William Holl, who lived in the Paddington area of London, was one of many who had volunteered to serve as an Air Raid Precautions warden in the summer of 1939 as British cities prepared for aerial bombardment. The authority enjoyed by these new figures on the streets was still uncertain.

Immediately following the unprovoked and sudden attack by Germany upon Poland, Britain declared war on Germany.

Our preparations in A.R.P. had been conducted upon the assumption that we would speedily be subjected to severe enemy air raids with consequential high casualties, so we were not surprised to hear the siren air raid warning sound at 11.34 hours on this Sunday morning. The Alert period did not last long, however, the 'All Clear' siren sounding at 11.55 hours, when street traffic, much of which had temporarily halted, resumed notional activity.

Perhaps the warning was due to an unidentified aeroplane buzzing around somewhere or it may have been a test warning; anyway, the sky was scanned for approaching aircraft by personnel of the various services who were either at their posts or were proceeding to report for duty, but nothing appeared. A small proportion of the public took to shelters or stood outside nearby; many windows were thrown open from which points of vantage, elderly women, with more curiosity than concern, searched their range of vision for the war to come – at one spot much to the indignation of a group of wardens on look out from the street outside their post who, equipped, and topped with steel helmets, felt they were not being treated with respect by these foolish people by such unorthodox behaviour. 'Where is this 'ere war?' asked one old chap with one eye cocked upwards, as he lit his pipe and passed on.

Dire forecasts of immediate and near-total destruction of cities by air raids had been a part of the approach of war. Accordingly, London was busy with the business of air-raid shelters and sandbagging even before war was declared. Home defence was given concerted thought by Whitehall, and as early as 1938 the Air Raid Precautions Department had appealed for one million volunteers. Extensive plans for the evacuation of children from London swung into action at the beginning of September, choking the railway stations. In practice, Britain had entered the period of the 'phoney war' and would remain in this state until the German advance westward in the spring of 1940.

Gladys Cox listens to Chamberlain declare war

Gladys Cox was a middle-aged housewife living in West Hampstead. Like the majority of the British population, she learned that war had been declared via the radio.

'Saturday'

Britain declared war on Germany at 11 o'clock this morning . . . On returning home, we turned on the wireless and heard there was to be 'an important announcement' by the Prime Minister at 11.15am. So, with bated breath – the whole world was on tip-toe of expectancy this morning – we settled ourselves in the sitting room and listened to Mr Chamberlain's broadcast.

He announced that, as there had been no reply by 11am to our ultimatum, we, as a nation, were at war with Germany.

I shall never forget the thrill of his closing words:- *'Now, may god bless you all. May He defend the right. It is evil things we shall be fighting against – brute force, bad faith, injustice, oppression and persecution. And against them, I am certain that the right will prevail.'*

Mr Chamberlain's speech was followed by the playing of 'God save the King' for which I rose and remained standing until it was finished.

Then, almost immediately, to our unspeakable astonishment, the air raid sirens sounded. Quickly turning off the gas at the main, catching Bob [pet cat] and shutting him in his basket, grabbing our gas masks, we struggled down several flights of stairs to the street, some yards along the pavement down the area steps, along dark winding passages, to our shelter. My knees were knocking together with weakness, while I stifled a strong desire to be sick. I was not exactly afraid, but nervous that I should be afraid; startled and bewildered, glimpsing dimly that all my known world was toppling about my ears.

It is possible that Gladys Cox may have rewritten or embellished her diary subsequently. One tell-tale sign is that 3 September is described in the diary as a Saturday, when in fact it was a Sunday. The phrase 'I shall never forget' also has the air of reminiscence rather than immediacy. However, it is often impossible to tell whether diaries were written hours, weeks or months after the event.

Although Gladys Cox would survive the war, she lost her house in the Blitz in October 1940.

Joseph P. Kennedy talks with his friend Neville
Chamberlain after war is declared

Joseph P. Kennedy

At the same time the broadcast announced that Chamberlain
would broadcast to the nation at 11:15. I cleaned up my desk,
sent for a small radio from the house in a hurry and had it
set up . . . I listened to the speech in my office with several of
the staff. It was terribly moving. And when he got to the part
of his 'efforts have failed', I almost cried. I had participated
very closely in this struggle and I saw my hopes crash too.
Immediately Chamberlain stopped speaking, I picked up the
receiver and asked for the P.M. I was astounded that he
should come right on the phone but he did at once. I judge it
was Horace Wilson who answered the phone because he
said 'hold the line for the Prime Minister.'

I said, 'This is Joe, Neville, and I have just listened to the
broadcast. It was terrifically moving.' He said, 'You heard
it?' And I said that it was great, really fine and it was terribly,
terribly moving. I said, 'Well Neville, I feel deeply our failure
to save a world war.' He said, 'We did the best we could have

done but it looks as though we had failed.' I said, 'It does indeed, Neville, but my best to you always.' He replied, 'Thanks, Joe, my best to you always and my deep gratitude for your constant help – Goodbye – Goodbye.'

I hung up. His voice still quivered, deeply moved after his broadcast and he spoke to me with real feeling.

Almost as I finished talking and was getting ready to go down to Parliament to take part in the proceedings, people rushed around saying the air raid warning was sounding. And sure enough it was. I urged every one to get out and they went to Molyneaux, the dressmaker across the street, who had a reasonably good basement . . .

And I noticed quite a few white faces amongst the men. Comments such as, 'He didn't wait long' – 'Isn't that like Hitler to hop in minutes after war was declared?' I went over to Molyneaux's to cheer people up and found most of them in pretty good shape.

Few felt the collapse of Chamberlain's appeasement policy more than Joseph Kennedy, who as US ambassador in London had supported him constantly. He predicted that the world would soon bear witness to the horrors from which Chamberlain had been trying to save it. More pragmatically, he argued that Chamberlain had been tactically astute in not going to war over Czechoslovakia a year earlier. The British public, he thought, would not then have been with the Prime Minister; some had even felt that Hitler's initial demands in relation to the Sudetenland – the German-speaking areas of Czechoslovakia – had been justified. The French were also less than resolute in their support of the Czechs. SEE ALSO PP. 53–4 AND 572–5.

The feminist and journalist Mollie Panter-Downes on the growth of women's volunteer organizations

Mollie Panter-Downes was born in London in 1906 and grew up in Sussex. At twenty-three she became the London reporter for the New Yorker *magazine and went on to describe British life for two generations of readers. Her writings provided one of the principal windows through which New Yorkers watched London and the home counties making the transition to war.*

All over the country, the declaration of war has brought a new lease of life to retired army officers, who suddenly find themselves the commanders of battalions of willing ladies who have emerged from the herbaceous borders to answer the call of duty. Morris 10s, their windshields plastered with notices that they are engaged on business of the ARP or WVS (both volunteer services), rock down quiet country lanes propelled by firm-lipped spinsters who yesterday could hardly have said 'Boo!' to an aster.

Although the summer holiday is still on, village schools have reopened as centres where the evacuated hordes from London can be rested, sorted out, medically examined, refreshed with tea and biscuits, and distributed to their new homes. The war has brought the great unwashed right into the bosoms of the great washed; while determined ladies in white VAD [Voluntary Aid Detachment] overalls search the mothers' heads with a knitting needle for unwelcome signs of life, the babies are dandled and patted on their often grimy diapers by other ladies, who have been told off to act as hostesses and keep the guests from pining for Shoreditch. Guest rooms have been cleared of Crown Derby knickknacks and the best guest towels, and the big houses and cottages alike are trying to overcome the traditional British dislike of strangers, who may, for all they know, be parked with them for a matter of years, not weeks.

The Home Secretary, Sir Samuel Hoare, had decided in 1938 that the ARP organization should be accompanied by a women's organization to assist with refugees and evacuation. As a result the Women's Voluntary Service for Air Raid Precautions (WVS) had been founded on 16 May that year. The WVS became the backbone of civil organization in Britain, with the Queen and Queen Mary, the Queen Mother, becoming joint patrons. By September 1939 it had 165,000 members, recruited from sections of society not otherwise involved in essential war work, including mothers and the elderly. One critical element of its role was to assist in the evacuation of over a million children from the major cities and towns to the presumed safety of villages in the countryside – where the new arrivals were not always warmly welcomed – and to supervise their hygiene, clothing, food and accommodation. SEE ALSO PP. 81–2, 106–7 AND 538–9.

Monday 4 September 1939

Miss D. M. Hoyles deals with the 'verminous heads' of evacuees on the south coast

Miss D. M. Hoyles was the headmistress of Albany Road junior school in London, which was evacuated to Dorset in September 1939. Her school became 'Evacuation Unit 418' and found new accommodation at the Central School, Cromwell Road, Weymouth. Like some other diarists of the period, she refers to herself in the third person.

Staff meeting at 9.30 a.m. Complaints about verminous heads was met by Miss Kerridge, Miss Bulloch and Miss Beedle offering to cleanse the children themselves as the clinic at Weymouth, consisting of three nurses only, was so busy with serious cases, that the only method used by them was to shave the head completely as the quickest means of care. Miss Hoyles went to the clinic to fetch soft soap and paraffin, and brought vinegar and a Derbac comb to cleanse the heads. On arrival at school the helpers found that the children were being treated by their foster mothers, but were able to give advice and materials for the cleansing. (These cases were few and not serious.) The rest of the staff were out interviewing foster parents. Every house was visited and the children rounded up to attend on the beach the next morning under the supervision of their teachers. Subjects discussed with the foster parents were:-

Clothes,

Cleanliness,

Early bed-time,

Postcards to parents,

Domestic questions,

Identity labels,

Arrangements for meeting . . . every day

Kemp threw toy of host's son into the sea and nearly lost his billet . . .

When the authorities began to evacuate children from London and other vulnerable cities and towns, some schools were evacuated en masse with their teachers, with classes kept together wherever possible. The Central School in Weymouth was destroyed during an air raid on the south coast in May 1942, prompting the return of the Albany Road pupils to London a month later.

Thursday 7 September 1939

Beatrice Webb, aged and eminent social reformer, experiences the first air-raid alert on the south coast

Our first air raid, which turned out to be a false alarm; the enemy aeroplanes never got beyond the east coast. A banging at the front door and grim voice calling 'Air raid'. I had just come from my bath and looked out of my window. There stood a man with a bicycle, his gas mask slung over his shoulder, who explained that a warning had been given from Portsmouth that German aeroplanes were in the neighbourhood. A few minutes later, I went into Sidney's room and saw him sitting up with his gas mask on! I suggested that he should take it off, which he promptly did. Mrs Grant had been in and was angry. '*You have no right* to tell Mr Webb to take his off,' she said in a menacing voice. 'Pardon me,' I laughed. 'I am his wife and the mistress of this house. Keep yours on if you like. It is damned nonsense putting on gas masks out in the countryside. The Germans won't waste their gas on us. Our only danger – if there is one – is an explosive bomb. Even a quarter of a mile off I am told it might bring our house down!' Annie and Jean were slightly excited and interested, but went on with their work. In two hours' time the all-clear was sounded. We who live round about the camps – there is a firing-range for tanks a quarter of a mile away – are fortunate in being in a *neutral* area – neither so dangerous for our own children to be evacuated nor sufficiently safe for strange children to come. We are free from lodgers and yet, for sensible folk, not subject to panic. So all is well . . .

In 1939 the Webbs joined 40 million others in preparing for gas attacks from the air. The whole population were issued with gas masks, including red 'Mickey Mouse' masks with bright eye-pieces that were intended to be attractive to children as well as specially adapted all-enclosed masks for babies into which mothers had to pump air with bellows. A variety of bags and boxes for carrying them became best-selling items in Woolworths in the autumn of 1939. Each side in the war built up substantial stocks of gas, and new and deadly agents such as nerve gas were invented. But the deterrent effect ensured that they were not used. The only victims of offensive gas in Europe would occur in 1943 in Bari in Italy, when American ships carrying mustard gas stocks were bombed, resulting in accidental release and over a thousand casualties. SEE ALSO PP. 48–9 AND 200–1.

Sunday 10 September 1939

Stanislaw Balinski finds bombs and counterfeit currency falling on Warsaw

Stanislaw Balinski, born in 1899, was a poet and journalist who witnessed the terrible bombing of Warsaw in 1939.

During numerous raids to-day the German airmen have dropped thousands of articles of various kinds, including packets of food and sweets. The population has been warned not to touch any of these things. During one of the afternoon raids the German bombers scattered Polish banknotes in large quantities; these were discovered to be forgeries of the Bank of Poland's banknotes. A large number of these forged notes were collected in Pulawska Street, in the centre of the city, and handed to bank experts. It is obvious that this scattering of notes is deliberate, and done with the intention of undermining the population's confidence in Polish currency.

The effects of yesterday's raids have proved to be worse than had been expected. Everywhere buildings are lying in ruins. The Hospital of the Transfiguration was set on fire; it was a ghastly sight, as it contained several hundred wounded. A soldier with both legs amputated was seen crawling out of the building on his elbows; other wounded men jumped out of the windows on to the pavement. Five doctors and several Red Cross nurses lost their lives. An emergency hospital is also in flames.

Although the populations of British cities were spared from bombing in 1939, others were not so fortunate. Polish cities were bombed extensively by the Luftwaffe and reports of these actions added to the incipient terror of air attack throughout Europe. Reports of air raids in Poland also increased the fear of special terror weapons. These included time-delay bombs that exploded long after they were dropped, rendering large areas impassable until they could be defused by bomb disposal teams. They also included booby-trapped personal items that maimed individuals who picked them up. Even more curious was the use of forged banknotes to undermine the stability of enemy economies. Germany had employed this technique against Britain during the First World War, and during the Second World War the practice of 'economic warfare' surfaced again.

Having experienced the aerial onslaught on Warsaw, Balinski escaped to London only to witness similar destruction there in the autumn of the following year. Uniquely, his diary sets the two events alongside each other.

Balinski would publish his diary under the pseudonym of Stephen Baley in 1941. He survived the war, dying in 1984.

Industrialist Sir Raymond Streat watches evacuees arriving in the leafy villages of Cheshire

As to life in Manchester and Wilmslow, the outstanding things have been the nightly black-outs, the evacuation of children and mothers and ARP. work. The black-out is astonishing. Stygian darkness on the roads from night-fall (about 8.15 p.m. now) until dawn. Motors are allowed a mere pin-prick of light covered with a shade to prevent it striking upwards. How people drive I do not know. There were five fatalities in Manchester during the hours of darkness on Friday. The great majority of people just stay in their houses. We have practically succeeded in making all our windows light-proof after a week's labour. It is curious to note the effect on one's mind – you feel as though you are shutting yourself up in a spiritual prison. I suppose we shall get used to it but it certainly brings home the realisation of being at war in a way that was never experienced in 1914.

The great evacuation is another astonishing thing. We are lucky with our enforced lodgers. They are nice people fundamentally and clean and decent. But many Wilmslow residents have found their evacuees, whether children or mothers or both, very hard to bear. Hundreds of mothers have returned with their children. The village of Wilmslow is crowded with a different class of person from the normal. I hear that it is almost the sole topic of conversation – hostesses exchanging stories of the worst cases amongst the evacuees and the evacuated mothers exchanging their woes. The husbands [of the evacuated mothers] appear at the weekend and hear it all over again. Our 'husband' came today for lunch at DSS's [Mrs Streat's] invitation, so I carved roast-beef for twelve – we five and Marjorie in the dining-room, four evacuees in the morning room and two maids in the kitchen. The wear and tear on the house if this is to last three years will be devastating.

ARP work is proceeding at a feverish pace. Cellars in Manchester are being commandeered as public shelters. Sandbags are being filled and piled against the lower windows in every street. Volunteers are being recruited for the Warden and Fire Services. Everybody in the streets has to carry his gas-mask, and a rare trade has sprung up in little satchels in which to sling them on the shoulder.

Plans for blackout and evacuation were in place well before war began. In Manchester, as in most cities, evacuation began on Friday 1 September, and Raymond Streat's evacuees arrived at his house in the affluent commuter village of Wilmslow, Cheshire, a day before war was declared. They consisted of 'a nice woman' and two little girls, and the house had plenty of space to accommodate them. However, for others in Wilmslow, and in the neighbouring well-to-do villages of Prestbury and Alderley Edge, space was often tight, and there was a mingling of classes and cultures that was as unexpected as it was unwelcome. Streat said that ARP or Air Raid Precautions was a dull phrase that did not describe the 'tremendous alteration in life and living considerations' that this meant for many people. SEE ALSO PP. 55–6 AND 853–4.

Monday 11 September 1939

Major Daniel Barlone, a French infantry officer, watches his men make themselves comfortable at the front

Major Daniel Barlone's war diary tells the story of a unit of the French 2nd North African Division, beginning with cheerful mobilization in 1939.

Holling. Arrived at Holling in driving rain, the night was as black as ink. Like all villages situated in front of the Maginot Line it has been evacuated by order; the inhabitants had had half an hour in which to prepare seventy pounds of luggage to take with them in the military lorries waiting for them. That was to be the sum total of their worldly goods.

In the course of the day I go for a walk in this charming Lorraine village, situated in the valley of the Nied which flows quite near by. The houses are large and opulent, the wide streets are bordered by the inevitable dung-heaps, dear to Lorraine. Countless herds of cows and pigs wander through the streets and fields. Our orders are to live on the produce of the country. Those of my men who are farm workers, and they are numerous, know what to do, only too pleased to resume something of their peace-time job. There are 800 to 900 men to be billeted in the homes of 250 inhabitants, as the Ambulance Section and the Artillery are quartered with us. Gangster methods are used to obtain the finest animals; soon my stable housed 30 superb pigs and 20 dairy cows, looked after by volunteer cowherds. That is our reserve; for immediate use we kill stray animals in the woods and in the fields. Everywhere friendly groups of men rig up their cook-houses; throughout the day the squeals of doomed pigs and poultry can be heard, whilst other men go off to thrash the walnut trees, shake down the mirabelles and the quetsches, unearth the 'spuds', uproot the salads. My men feed sumptuously, pastry-cooks make flans with the flour, found in abundance, and butter made in the dairy. This is the land of milk and honey.

The 'clearing up' goes on apace. I am taken, very secretly, to visit a still set up by the men. There they distil the contents of barrels of mirabelles and quetsches which the unlucky proprietors had put by. Within a few days we have in carboys more than a dozen gallons of wonderfully fragrant brandy. I intend keeping it for the days when things warm up.

Now the whirring of a threshing machine comes from a barn, and soon fifty sacks of good oats for our horses are lined up on our carts. No need to ask for volunteers, the NCOs and skilled army workers organize their teams and everything proceeds smoothly, no drunkenness, no quarrelling.

My headquarters are in the spacious café of the village. On the ground floor, in the large main room, the clerks play at Russian billiards when their work is done. The mess is behind. On the first floor is my bedroom, with marble wash-basin, handsome wardrobe, etc.

Holling was a small village of two hundred people situated on a tributary of the Moselle in the area of Lorraine. Located between the Maginot Line – a formidable series of French defensive emplacements – and the German border, it was at the western extreme of the frontier with Germany and not far from Luxembourg. Holling lay within an evacuated strip of France 10 miles deep which ran all along the northern border. Here civilians had been given only hours to pack a suitcase and depart, forcing them to leave behind everything the new inhabitants needed to make themselves at home. Living off the land had been the standard practice for French armies up to the First World War, when the invention of tinned food had enabled for the first time the centralized supplying and victualling of hundreds of thousands of men concentrated in small areas. SEE ALSO PP. 137–8.

Tuesday 19 September 1939

Student nurse Kay Phipps attends courses on gas and
treating gas casualties

Protective clothing has arrived in the Post, and gas lectures
started. I am fortunately exempt, owing to having taken it
last year. However we all had to practice decontaminating
the bathroom! The clothing consists of yellow oilskin
trousers, three quarter length coats ditto, wellington boots,
hood like head gear, gloves and masks. Ye gods what all this
must be costing the government. They told us at the
Aldershot Camp that one can't work more than half an hour
in this rig owing to the heat. We have been advised to buy
pots of bleach paste for personal use and to carry them
always in our gas cases. There is already a shortage.

Great arguments as to where wounded gas casualties are to
be treated, does one treat wounds first or gas? At what point
are they removed from contamination stretchers? Are con-
taminated dead to be decontaminated or kept separate from
the 'clean corpses'? If it wasn't so serious it would be
ludicrous . . .

Miss J. Twitters, Mrs S. D. Flaps and the outsiders who are
taking the courses snigger. I and a couple of others armed with
Chemical Warfare Certificates feel superior, remembering our
army instructor who made us all shout in chorus in answer to
his question 'what do you do first on receiving the warning
"Gas Attack"?'. 'ATTEND TO THE WANTS OF NATURE'.

All cinemas and theatres are closed throughout Britain, it
means we have nowhere to amuse ourselves in our off duty
[hours] . . . and one does want to get away, quite apart
from liking to see newsreels. Dreadful business about the
Athenia, they say hundreds of people drowned including
Americans. That should make the US sit up like the sinking
of the Lusitania in the last war. And our HMS Courageous
sunk in the British Channel [sic]. It seems dreadful . . . I
danced on her in Malta only last year . . . no not even
that, it was this year. I am very sad for that beautiful ship.

The SS Athenia, *torpedoed by the German submarine U-30, sank off Rockall Bank, some 250 miles north-west of Ireland, on 3 September 1939 – about twelve hours after the declaration of war. The loss was reminiscent to many of the sinking of the SS* Lusitania *early in the First World War. The* Athenia *had left Glasgow for Canada with 1,103 passengers trying to escape the war in Europe, over 300 of them Americans. Many survived thanks to the effective response of the crew. It was widely reported that the U-boat had shelled the lifeboats. In fact the German submarine had been forced to eject a faulty torpedo which had then detonated.*

Bleach paste, mentioned here as part of the nurses' kit, was the standard agent used to deal with unvaporized concentrations of residue after a gas bomb had exploded.

Kay Phipps would see a great number of Blitz casualties at the Emergency Medical Service Hospital in Ashridge, Hertfordshire (May 1940–October 1941), and then at the University College Hospital (October 1941–March 1942). After a period as a warden of a Women's Land Army Hostel near Baldock, Hertfordshire, during which she tried to recover from the psychological stresses of her work, she returned to nursing. She would spend the rest of the war at hospitals in Bradford and Yorkshire. SEE ALSO PP. 60–1.

Wednesday 20 – Thursday 21 September 1939

Wilhelm Prüller, an Austrian soldier, is captured by the Poles

Wilhelm Prüller was born in 1916; aged only twenty-two when Germany and Austria were united by the Anschluss, he lived out most of his conscious political life in Hitler's realm.

20 September

I look forward very much to the day when I can type these 'notes for a diary', and then keep them properly. The interesting thing about this diary is that it was written while we were in position, often under the heaviest enemy fire; for what I want, in case anything happens, is that you will be able through this diary, my dear Henny, to learn what I was doing up to the last minute . . .

13:00: I am looking at the countryside through my binoculars. Have the Poles surrendered?

13:30: Not a shot has been fired for two hours. And then – can you believe it! Polish soldiers are coming out of the woods, endless rows of 'em! Polish heavy guns are being carted off by our soldiers. Lorries are already moving to the woods to take the prisoners away.

21 September

I have been captured by the Poles! I don't know what will happen. I and my men and our guards are lying between German and Polish fire. A Pole has just been badly wounded.

Our troop was woken up early in the morning. Yesterday evening a Polish rider appeared and said that in some woods about ten kilometres away were some 400 or 500 soldiers who wanted to surrender. We had meanwhile withdrawn to a town called Lasczow. Our Oberleutnant gave Stuparits the order to send my troop to get the soldiers. A single-seater motor-cycle and one with a sidecar were assigned to us. At 5.00am we left.

The Polish rider went with us in the sidecar. At the place he described we dropped him off and waited for the Polish soldiers. A quarter of an hour or more went by. Our M/C combination went ahead to see what was happening. The fog was so thick that you couldn't see thirty metres ahead of you.

Suddenly the sidecar driver and the interpreter who was riding with him saw armed Poles advancing towards us. When he told us this, we mounted and withdrew a bit. A few minutes later some Poles actually showed up and gave themselves up. We took them along on our vehicle, and on the way back we kept losing time by having to pick up more Poles.

When we got to the crossroads, about four kilometres

from our troop, we heard an MG [machine-gun] firing right next to us. We had to stop. When we wanted to go on, the motor wouldn't start. It must have been hit. The MG was firing like mad. We went behind a hill and waited. The town lay to the left in front of us, to the right were huge swamps.

Then, from the side where we intended to take the prisoners, appeared Polish soldiers, all armed. Before we could take this in, Poles appeared from the town side as well. Did they want to surrender? Anyway I bring my MG into position, but find I can use it only in one direction. No point in shooting because the Poles are swarming in from all sides. In short we are surrounded . . . and disarmed.

We are made to follow them towards the right, into the swamp. The Poles are about company strength. Five soldiers are assigned to watch us. Then our MGs begin to shoot at the Poles from the direction of the town: the noise is stupendous, the bullets whistle past us and over our heads. We're sinking up to our chests in the swamp, and it takes a long time for us to advance several hundred metres. And all the while we're being shot at by our own side.

We come through some tall reeds. On the other side is a little wall, and there we take cover. The Poles cross over the wall and receive tremendous fire from that side, while our people are shooting at us from the other. Then the German mortars go into action. The shells land all round us, some of them 10 metres away. It's a terrible feeling to think you might get shot to pieces by your own troops.

The leader of the guards, a young chap, climbs on the wall. On the other side, soldiers are approaching. Enormous numbers. We can't see if they're German or Polish. In any case they shoot at us. The Pole who first climbed on the wall is hit by a whole round of MG fire, one shot through the penis, two in his legs. He's bleeding like a stuck pig and is in terrible agony. We bandage him. The other Poles hope that the advancing soldiers are ours. They want to be taken prisoner. But it's Polish cavalry that now appears.

*Poland had been invaded simultaneously by the Germans from the west
and their Soviet allies from the east at the start of September. When
Prüller's unit was captured not all of them were searched thoroughly,
although the Polish soldiers often kept whatever they found, including
money. Prüller was searched, but only in a cursory way, and so managed
to keep his diary, which he hid carefully 'next to his skin'. Being only
lightly supervised thereafter he was able to go on making entries, sometimes at night by candlelight. In common with many combat diaries,
Wilhelm Prüller's journal was originally recorded in a more abbreviated
note form and later typed up in full. It contains insights into the mind
not only of a long-serving soldier of the Wehrmacht but also of an
unrepentant Nazi. SEE ALSO PP. 79 AND 309–10.*

Friday 22 September 1939

Gunnar Hagglof, a Swedish diplomat, reflects on the stupidity of British foreign policy

*Gunnar Hagglof was born in Sweden in 1915. As a diplomat he was
critical of British policy towards Poland and the Soviet Union.*

There is something particularly sinister about the Russian
occupation of eastern Poland. I say sinister because that is
the word to describe the interplay between two deadly
enemies, Nazi Germany and the Soviet Union.

I must add that I understand Moscow's policy up to a
point. The unfortunate Conservative Government in Britain
has given the impression of wanting to come to an arrangement with Hitler, although they must have known that
Hitler would then attack Russia. It is certain that's how
Stalin interpreted Chamberlain and Munich. It was probably
then that he took the decision to make a *renversement des
alliances*.

Has British foreign policy ever been so mishandled?
Munich was a staggering mistake. Later, when the decision
was taken to change the policy, another major mistake was
made. Britain gave guarantees to Poland before trying to

come to an agreement with Moscow. Once the guarantee was given to Poland, Moscow could be sure that Britain would be at war with Germany before Hitler could attack Russia.

Gunnar Hagglof would go on to become Swedish ambassador in Paris and Moscow after 1945.

Monday 25 September 1939

Wilhelm Prüller is freed from Polish captivity by Soviet forces

Today is another day full of nerve-racking events, if I count the night as well. One is much like the other. We had to march with the Poles the whole night, despite pouring rain.

Wherever we look, German beacons, searchlights. Germans. We march and march . . .

We twenty-two prisoners make a break for it. It's our only hope. Are the Germans coming? Or Ukrainians? It's a foreign command anyhow! As I get out of the woods, I recognize them: *They are our Russian allies!*

I can't describe this moment. The emotions inside me can't be described. I felt no joy. I didn't laugh. Or cry. Or weep. I wasn't touched at all. Only someone who rises from the dead can know this feeling.

It was three Russians who took the Poles prisoners, one officer and two noncoms. They saw the Poles coming, hid in the bush, and when the Poles were in the woods, the Russians began to shoot. No one had thought of opposition. Whereupon the Polish officers took to their heels, and the men, one and all, came out of the woods. The Russian captain at once gave us arms. We're full-value soldiers again! The numerous wagons are emptied and the contents sorted. This keeps us busy till 14:00. Then we help the captain cart the things off. We're off for Tomaszow, a town already in our hands.

In the evening we get an excellent soup, with lots of game

and poultry in it. After the meal we push on. I haven't slept at all since yesterday morning. But perhaps I shall today?

Throughout Prüller's period of captivity German forces were never very far away, and sometimes German armour was as close as 7 kilometres. Within a day of their capture a Polish officer conceded that the Germans' imprisonment would only be temporary as Poland had already lost the war. He even refunded some of their confiscated money so they were able to buy food. They were moved about in a group of fifteen, no-one quite sure what to do with them. SEE ALSO PP. 75–8 AND 309–10.

OCTOBER 1939

THE LAST ELEMENTS OF Polish forces surrendered on 6 October and for the rest of the month most of the fighting took place at sea. Hitler announced that his desire to redress the injustices of the Versailles Treaty had been fulfilled and suggested a European peace conference. He blamed the state of conflict between London and Berlin on 'warmongers' like Winston Churchill, but his offer of peace negotiations was rejected by the British and the French immediately. The remainder of the British Expeditionary Force had now crossed the Channel and was positioned in France. To the dismay of his generals, Hitler decided that if a peace treaty were not secured quickly he would invade France and the Low Countries, and began military planning for operations the following spring.

On 13 October the German submarine U-47 made its way through the anti-submarine defences of the British naval anchorage at Scapa Flow in the Orkney Islands. At one o'clock the following morning Kapitänleutnant Prien sank the British battleship HMS *Royal Oak* with the loss of 883 hands. Despite being on the surface for much of the time, Prien was unopposed and escaped to the open sea. On his return to Germany he was personally decorated with the Knight's Cross by Hitler. However, by now naval operations were becoming more difficult for all sides with the extensive use of magnetic mines around the coasts of Britain and Germany. Mines were sinking more ships than U-boats.

For British civilians the big changes were on the home front. A massive programme to increase the distribution of gas masks ensured that they were available to everyone. There were differing opinions about when they should be worn and how they should be carried. The tops of post-boxes were treated with a special gas-detector paint and the public was given alarming leaflets about unpleasant poisons that might be dropped by the Luftwaffe. Civilians were also discovering that war preparations were expensive. In the last days of September 1939 the Chancellor of the Exchequer introduced a war budget and raised income tax from 5s 6d to 7s 6d in the pound.

The secret war was now under way. Although Germany had not yet begun its attack on France and the Low Countries, the Germans were reading French military codes, which allowed them to identify weaknesses in French defensive works such as the Maginot Line, and also some British naval codes. French and Polish codebreakers had begun to make headway against German communications; but before 1941 the German ability to read enemy codes was superior to that of the Allies.

Sunday 1 October 1939

Mollie Panter-Downes, *New Yorker* journalist, on the 'war of yawns'

Criticism is in the air these days, after pretty nearly a month of this curious twenty-five per-cent warfare. Everyone is slightly fed up with something or other: with the Ministry of Information, which doesn't inform; with the British Broadcasting Corporation, which is accused of being depressing and – worse – boring; with the deficiencies of the fish supply, which have made fishmongers hoard herrings for their regular customers as though they were nuggets; and even with the bombs which don't drop. The war of nerves has degenerated into a war of yawns for thousands of Air Raid Protection workers, who spend their nights playing cards, taking cat naps, and practically yearning for a short, sharp air raid. The fact that many of them are drawing an average of £2 10s a week for doing nothing much except waiting around has also caused a good deal of murmuring.

The Ministry of Information comes off worst with everybody. The man in the street feels, rather naturally, that he is paying plenty for this war, that he is entitled to know what is happening, and that he wants more to happen. He feels that something is rotten in a system which recently went through the most complicated acrobatics of releasing, suppressing, and releasing again even such a harmless piece of news as Her Majesty's return to London from a visit to the Princesses at Balmoral. The Englishman grumbles, but to be long on patience is one of the traditional strengths of the British.

During the phoney war, although there was no fighting on the Western Front, real change was taking place on the domestic scene. The British government was extending regulation to vast areas of society that had never before been touched by government officials. New departments had been created – such as the Ministry of Food and the Ministry of Information – and almost every form of production, whether industrial or agricultural, was now centrally controlled. SEE ALSO PP. 65–6, 106–7 AND 538–9.

Sunday 8 – Wednesday 25 October 1939

Janine Phillips (aged eleven) on passive resistance to German rule in Poland

Born in Poland in 1929, Janine Phillips kept a diary of the German occupation of Poland, based on what she saw around her. Her affluent family had fled Warsaw and were living in the countryside. Their access to an illegal radio set allowed her to listen to news broadcasts.

8 October

Everyone from our household, with the exclusion of Grandpa, Samson and Pempela had to report for potato harvesting in Jadwisin, the next village, on a farm which belonged to the Radziwil family. Now it seems to belong to the Gerries, like everything else. Not only our household, but most of the inhabitants of Borowa-Góra were summoned to work in the fields. There are an awful lot of soldiers and they need an awful lot of food. The confiscation of crops from our fields presents no problem to the Gerries. It comes to them as easily and as naturally as invading our country. At eight in the morning, Grandpa harnessed Samson to the cart and we scrambled onto it, wearing boots and working clothes and looking just right for the job. Though Papa, at first, appeared in his bowler, but Uncle Tadeusz lent him his bee-keeping hat. It sank over Papa's ears and I wondered if he would be able to see what he was doing. But Papa did not seem to worry unduly. Grandpa unloaded us at the potato field exactly at nine-thirty and, having warned us not to work too hard, he said he'd be back to fetch us for lunch. Presently, other people arrived for work, and a German soldier came as well to keep an eye on us, no doubt. No-one appeared to be down in the dumps, on the contrary, people were laughing and treating the enforced labour as a joke. A German mechanical digger, driven by another soldier, turned from the road into the field. Our task was to pick the potatoes and put them into big baskets. However, Uncle Tadeusz had a much better idea. He suggested, as quietly and as inconspicuously as it were possible under the circumstances, that some of the spuds should be put in a nearby ditch. Thus we laboured as fast as we could, tipping one basket onto a potato pile, and two baskets into the ditch. In spite of our legs, which were aching, and our backs, which were nearly breaking, we sang as we laboured along. But it was so good when, at last, our work was at an end and dear Samson came to fetch us back.

25 October

I asked Father Jakob yesterday if it were a sin to be nasty to the Gerries. Father Jakob scratched his head and said that under normal circumstances it would be a sin. But, taking into consideration the fact that we are at war, or be more precise, the Germans are occupying our country, God probably would be prepared to give us some sort of dispensation. Then I asked him, even if I were to kill a German, would I not end up in Hell? Father Jakob said that in self-defence killing is permissible, but not premeditated killing. He wanted to know whether I followed him and I said that I did, which is a lie, because I didn't. In actual fact, the more I think about the sin of killing the less I understand the whole business. To me, a killed man, for whatever reason, is a dead man, and to him surely it doesn't matter why he had died? His only worry is that he's dead and he can't do anything about it. Then I asked Papa if he would consider pinching spuds from the Gerries were a sin. Papa said it was most certainly not. He explained it to me like this: suppose a burglar stole my doll and I pinched it back. That wouldn't be stealing because the doll belonged to me in the first place. The same with the Germans. They have no right to be here. It is they who are the thieves. They are taking our crops from our fields and, on top of this, they are forcing us to work for them. Papa said it was a triple sin. I can always understand Papa and I hope God will remember to give the Gerries three bad marks.

In 1940 Janine would move back to Warsaw in order to continue her education. In 1944 she participated in the uprising against the Germans as a Girl Guide running a first aid station; she was captured and removed to Germany as a POW. After the war, at the age of sixteen, she moved to London and became a chemist. It was only when she returned to Poland in 1965 that an aunt produced her forgotten war diary.

Sunday 22 October 1939

George Beardmore looks into the window of Hamley's toy shop in Regent Street

George Beardmore, born in Staffordshire in 1908, had worked for an insurance company in north London in the 1930s. An aspiring writer, he held a long series of jobs, first at the BBC where his father-in-law also worked, and then for local authorities in London. He published his first novel in 1931. In 1939, working at BBC headquarters at the top of Regent Street, which were now heavily sandbagged and boarded up against bomb-blast, Beardmore was able to watch the transformative effect of war upon the landscape of London's West End.

Sovereigns, if any, are now worth 39/6d. Hamley's of Regent Street have their latest toy in the main window – 'Build Your Own Maginot Line'. On show is a cross-section of the tiered dug-outs and little men in them doing a variety of duties, a blimp hung up from a lorry outside, and an advance patrol crawling through the heavily camouflaged country, meeting with heavy fire. All right, it's only a toy, but a sudden realisation was brought home to me that, historically, purely defence-positions have never held out for long. Or hasn't the French General Staff read Plutarch?

Torches and gas-mask cases are for sale in Oxford Street. Here also a system of sand-bags and baffle-walls has been built round fire-alarms and police boxes. Rationing is to come in next month and even now the Government has put a top price on commodities like bacon, eggs, tea, and sugar . . .

An assistant at Milletts, from whom I bought a serviceable gas-mask container like a coffee-tin (the ones you are given soon fall to bits), told me that almost all the staff from his and other London branches had left their respective premises at 10 pm last night to report to a warehouse near Waterloo Station where they spent the night assembling gas-masks. They had given up at 5 am, gone home to snatch what sleep they could, and come back to serve in the shop at 10 am. 'Double time', the assistant said. 'All good money but I couldn't do *that* every day.'

For many, wartime offered welcome new opportunities, either for a return to employment or for additional part-time jobs. In 1938 the growing pace of rearmament had meant an effective end to the blight of inter-war un-employment and by 1939 there were labour shortages. Factory labour was increasingly scarce as 'soft' employment in war bureaucracies and wartime service industries became available. SEE ALSO PP. 89–90 AND 601–3.

Sunday 29 October 1939

Muriel Green describes the impact of refugees on a small east coast village

Muriel Green and her sister Jenny Green, aged eighteen and twenty-six respectively, were working in the family business, a village garage and sweet shop. Like Kevin Worth, they had both volunteered to keep diaries for the Mass-Observation Archive.

In the large houses the evacuees found the servants treated them badly. One said, 'the parlour maid giggles all the time, and the whole lot laughed when we asked how to light a fire with sticks'. [In] another house the servants would not let them have any water as they went home late, and told their mistress it was because they had come home drunk. Another woman said, 'I'm not saying anything against Miss, she is a lady, but them servants . . .' Three women said they were starving themselves in order to pay the fare home. Many evacuees returned to London because on the night of Sept 3rd and the morning of 6th there was an air raid warning. They said they thought they had been sent to safety areas but they decided they were no safer on the East Coast than in London especially as they have air raid shelters in their gardens and in the parks. There are none here. One woman said, 'In our own blocks of flats we have had ARP practices and know just what to do, but here there are no shelters and we seem to be in as much danger of passing raiders.' The first bomb in England fell in this village in the last war . . .

Other women said that they found such difficulty in the country shops. Food was much dearer at the village grocer's. Nothing can be bought ready cooked and they did not understand the coal cooking range of the country. They all grumbled at the inconveniences of travel, now only one bus each way was every two hours, and about 3 trains a day. They were not used to living three miles from a station and bus stop. Some said there was no cinema and one wanted to know where she could get her hair permed . . . They found the country very quiet and lacked amusement. One woman said, 'I'd rather be bombed on me own door step than stay here and die of depression.'

Difficulties for the hosts were the inconvenience of having other people in your house. Many grumbled at the dirtiness of the evacuees, and their bad language. I have never seen such dirty women with children. One woman who came to our shop smelt positively filthy and her clothes were disgusting. Most of the children had impetigo and red flea bites all over their bodies. One village woman rushed round to the organiser of the scheme and vowed she would not go home until he had fetched out the family he had taken into her nice home. I heard many instances of the evacuees not being 'house trained' and many carpets were ruined.

The village people objected to the evacuees chiefly because of dirtiness of their habits and clothes. Also because of their reputed drinking and bad language. It is exceptional to hear women swear in this village or for them to enter a public house. The villagers used to watch them come out of the pubs with horror . . .

Evacuation did not work out for everyone. Although some were received kindly, others were not; and the process of billeting, with evacuees sometimes being led from door to door and being turned away repeatedly, could be humiliating. Some chose to return to where they came from and take their chances in the cities. SEE ALSO PP. 109–10.

NOVEMBER 1939

NOVEMBER SAW THE first of many serious clashes between Hitler and his high command. Senior German generals were horrified by the thought of an attack on a major power like France. General Halder, the Chief of the General Staff, and his colleagues were in a mutinous mood and some officers even considered a *coup d'état*. Hitler, apparently sensing the strength of their opposition, backed down and postponed his plans for an offensive in the west.

Although British intelligence had a reputation for invincibility, largely derived from popular fiction, the real secret war initially involved disasters. Two officers from the Secret Intelligence Service (MI6), Captains Stevens and Best, were captured at Venlo on the border between Germany and Holland in a Gestapo 'sting' operation. One was carrying a list of British agents and this, together with skilful interrogation, resulted in the rounding up of many British agents in Europe.

At the end of November the Soviet Union attacked Finland and bombed Helsinki from the air. The tiny Finnish army began a magnificent defence against vastly superior Soviet forces. The British government decided to send British army 'volunteers' to assist the Finns, and a special fifth battalion of the Coldstream Guards was retrained in winter warfare. But neutral Sweden would not grant free passage for these forces across its territory to Finland.

Thursday 2 – Thursday 16 November 1939

George Beardmore, aspiring writer, tracks missing
ratepayers in Wembley

2 November

Have been working for Wembley Boro' Council this last
week, trying to find out where some of their missing ratepayers have disappeared to. Rates still have to be paid, war
or no war. Mostly they have gone, I find, to relations in
Yorkshire and Lancashire, and to hideouts made ready
months ago. Surely out of the seven jobs I have so far undertaken (this is the eighth) this is the only one that has allowed
me to come home in the afternoon for a nap – and please
myself whether or not I venture out again! I put in a moderate
number of calls on Monday and Tuesday, that is, arriving back
home about four in the afternoon, but was tipped off by the
other 'follow-upper' that I was doing too much and queering
the pitch. So I laid off. The technique is simple. You have to get
in touch with the missing household's milkman, who
apparently knows everything about everyone, including the
infidelities, and if he doesn't know, try the postman. Road-
sweepers and dustmen, too, are surprisingly knowledgeable.

The number of well-to-do people who have just upped
and gone is astonishing. At one house I found a back door
open, walked inside, and a *Marie-Celeste* situation presented
itself: breakfast-things unwashed, a half-smoked cigarette
dipped in tea to put it out, fruit going mouldy in a bowl, and
a mysterious note on the gas-stove that read: 'Grandma
Highgate Ponds 5.30'. Made me laugh. A neighbour told me
over the fence: 'You from the Council? I thought so. They've
gone to somewhere in Bedford.' But another house I tried
had so obviously been broken into that I dialled 999. The
police car when it arrived contained a fellow I had known
briefly at the Mortlake firm.

16 November

Came home for good at 11.30 am having done nothing more

important than have coffee with a fellow-collector. But what a worthwhile cup of coffee that was for he told me that the gas-meter men know even more than milkmen, particularly as to where the missing families can be found. 'They have to be told', was the explanation. So I have cleverly arranged to meet the gas-meter man every Saturday morning in the local Express Dairy when he will obligingly fill in the blanks on the list given to me by the Council's Treasurer's Department.

George Beardmore enjoyed the full benefit of the increasingly fluid labour market provided by the onset of war. Moving into jobs with ever higher rates of pay and ever lighter duties, by November 1939 he was working for Wembley Borough Council and enjoying himself enormously. Local authorities, working with the voluntary agencies, bore the brunt of the enormous upheavals caused by three waves of evacuation. The first, set in motion with the onset of war in September 1939, was largely reversed when no enemy bombers appeared and evacuees drifted back to the towns. The onset of city bombing in September 1940 would trigger a second wave of evacuation, and a third and final wave would follow the arrival of the V-1 'doodlebugs' in 1944. While struggling to cope with the increased demands posed by these movements of population, local authorities were beset by financial problems caused by the flight of ratepayers to the countryside. Those who had fled their town houses in Wembley were still liable for rates on their unoccupied dwellings, and Beardmore's job was to become an amateur sleuth, tracking them down and persuading them to pay. SEE ALSO PP. 85–6 AND 601–3.

Sunday 5 November 1939

William Shirer, American news correspondent in Berlin, on Hitler's breakfast

William Shirer was born in 1904 and grew up in Cedar Rapids, Iowa. The early death of his father, a lawyer, plunged the family into hard times, and William sold eggs and delivered newspapers to make ends meet. The latter task provided an entrée into journalism, and he was soon working on the local paper. In 1925 he was given the rare opportunity to go to Europe. Discovering a gift for languages, he rapidly acquired French, German, Italian and Spanish in order to become a permanent foreign correspondent based in Berlin. By 1937 Ed Murrow had persuaded Shirer to join the Columbia Broadcasting Service (CBS). From Berlin, Shirer offered a regular commentary on the rise of the Nazis in Germany. However, his reports from Germany were censored by Goebbels' propaganda ministry, and so he recorded what he could not print or broadcast in his diary.

CBS wants me to broadcast a picture of Hitler at work during war-time. I've been enquiring around among my spies. They say: he rises early, eats his first breakfast at seven a.m. This consists usually of either a glass of milk or fruit-juice and two or three rolls, on which he spreads marmalade liberally. Like most Germans, he eats a second breakfast, this one at nine a.m. It's like the first except he also eats a little fruit. He begins his working day by wading into state papers (a job he detests, since he hates detailed work) and discussing the day's programme with his adjutants, chiefly S.A. Leader Wilhelm Brückner, and especially with his deputy, Rudolph Hess, who was once his private secretary and is one of the few men he really trusts with his innermost thoughts. During the forenoon he usually receives the chiefs of the three armed services . . .

Hitler is a fiend for films, and on evenings when no important conferences are on or he is not overrunning a country, he spends a couple of hours seeing the latest movies in his private cinema room at the Chancellery. News-reels are a great favourite with him, and in the last weeks he has seen all those taken in the Polish war, including hundreds of thousands of feet which were filmed for the army archives and will never be seen by the public. He likes American films and many never publicly exhibited in Germany are shown to him. A few years ago he insisted on having *It Happened One Night* run several times. Though he is supposed to have a passion for Wagnerian Opera, he almost never attends the Opera here in Berlin. He likes the Metropol, which puts on tolerable musical comedies with

the emphasis on pretty dancing girls. Recently he had one
of the girls who struck his fancy to tea. But only to tea.

*Like Stalin and Churchill, Hitler was a film fanatic and also had a
private cinema constructed in his mountain retreat at Berchtesgaden in
the Alps. Hitler's tastes were wide-ranging and he liked all sorts of
Hollywood films, not least comedies and swashbuckling adventure films.
Curiously, Churchill and Hitler had the same favourite movie:* Lives of
a Bengal Lancer *with Gary Cooper. For Churchill it epitomized the
glories of the British Raj in India; for Hitler it showed how a small
number of Germans might rule effectively over many Slavs, and he
insisted that his SS entourage watch it repeatedly. SEE ALSO PP. 27 AND
174–6.*

Wednesday 22 – Saturday 25 November 1939

General von Bock on Hitler's unhappy relations with his senior army officers

*Fedor von Bock was born in 1880, the son of a Prussian general. He
loathed the Nazis but supported Hitler's military objectives. He participated in the German occupation of Austria and the invasions of Poland,
France and Russia. However, even in 1939 his dismay at Hitler's refusal
to accept the advice of his generals was already plain.*

22 November

Travelled to Berlin.

23 November

The *Führer* once again expressed to all the commanding
generals of the Armed Forces 'his unbending will' to see
the war through to total victory. Once again he justified the
compelling necessity to attack soon with the need for greater
security for the Ruhr Region, with the necessity for better air
and U-boat bases, and finally with the necessity to defeat the
enemy and thus assure a lengthy peace for Germany.

'One cannot achieve victory by waiting!'

'At last we are in the position we have longed for for sixty years, not to have to fight a war on two fronts,' he said, 'it would thus be a great mistake not to take advantage of this favourable moment, for no man can say how long it will last!'

The *Führer* took a firm position against any defeatism. He refused to accept the idea that our infantry was not as good as in 1914. The possibility of a revolution he rejected completely:

'There will be no revolution!'

A certain ill feeling toward the commander of the army was obvious in all his remarks. The Navy and Air Force were depicted as models of initiative. The reason is clear: the *Führer* knows that the bulk of the generals do not believe that attacking now will produce a decisive success. This is regrettable after the sacrifices and successes in Poland, for the army bore almost the entire burden of the campaign, because there was neither a Polish navy worthy of note nor a Polish Air Force to be taken seriously.

There had been a serious disagreement between the *Führer* and [General] Brauchitsch before the conference; the latter has nevertheless stayed on, and thus apparently intends to bear the responsibility for the planned operation!

25 November
Return trip to Godesberg.

As early as 5 November von Bock's colleague General Brauchitsch had participated in a stand-up row with Hitler over plans for a quick military drive to the west. The Chief of Staff, General Halder, was even exploring the possibility of a military coup as a preferable option, but had difficulty in getting support from younger officers.

Von Bock would become Commander-in-Chief of Army Group Centre during the Russian campaign of 1941, but was soon relieved of his command when he too complained of the strategic impracticality of Hitler's ideas. By this time Hitler had the psychological advantage, for the military had expressed deep anxieties about the campaigns in Poland and then in France; however, the ensuing victories had shown the military to be excessively timid. After 1941 Hitler would take even more operational control and displayed growing impatience with his commanders. Had von Bock not been killed in an air raid, he might well have been arrested or executed.

Late November – early December 1939

Anaïs Nin leaves some precious diaries in Paris as she flees to the United States

Anaïs Nin's father was the Spanish composer Joaquin Nin, her mother of mixed Cuban, French and Danish ancestry. She lived in Paris for the first eleven years of her life and then in 1914 moved to the United States, where she worked as a model and dancer, returning to Paris in 1923. Although she never completed her school education, she studied psychoanalysis with Otto Rank and was briefly a patient of Carl Jung. She was interested in the intersection between diaries, psychoanalytic therapy and eroticism, and believed that the writing of a detailed diary permitted self-knowledge and liberation. In 1935 she helped found Siana Editions in France which published erotica. In late 1939 she fled from Paris to New York and moved into Greenwich Village.

I left a Paris lit in a muted way like the inside of a cathedral, full of shadowy niches, black corners, twinkling oil lamps. In the half mist hanging over it, violet, blue, and green lights looked like stained-glass windows all wet and alive with candlelight. I could not have recognized the faces of those I was leaving. My bags were carried by a soldier whose shoes were too big for him. I suffered deeply from the wrench of separation. I felt every cell and cord which tied me to France snapping in me, the parting from a pattern of life I loved, from an atmosphere rich, creative and human, from intimacy with a people and a city. I was parting from a rhythm rooted very deeply in me, from mysterious, enveloped nights, from an obsession with war which gave a bitter and vivid taste to all our living, from the sound of anti-aircraft guns, of air-planes passing, of sirens lamenting like foghorns on stormy nights at sea.

I could not believe that there could be, anywhere in the world, space and air where the nightmare of war did not exist.

On the train to Irún. On the way to take the hydroplane from Portugal. It seems as if I will never tear myself away from France. Each mile of the journey, each landscape, each little station, each face, causes a painful separation. I carry with me only two briefcases filled with recent diaries. At the last moment, when I had taken all the volumes out of the vault in the Paris bank and packed them in two suitcases, I found that the cost of excess weight far exceeded the money I had. So the bulk of the diaries went back into the vault. And now, in the train, I feel despondent, ashamed to be saved from catastrophe, to abandon my friends to an unknown fate.

For the second time in my life, America looms as a refuge. My mind is journeying backwards in time. I think of the Maginot Line, which crossed near Louveciennes, in the Forest of Marly. We stumbled upon it one day on a hike. A young soldier took us through part of it. He was very proud. A cement labyrinth with apertures only for gun barrels. He showed us a vast empty pool, which he explained would be filled with acid to dissolve the bodies of the dead. I think of my concierge, who lost her husband in the First World War and might lose her son in the Second. I think of the Pierre Chareaus in danger because they are Jews, and those who escaped from Germany and are now once more afraid for their lives . . .

When we leave the Azores after refueling . . . I lie down and open my briefcases. I lie awake, rereading the last letters I received, and writing in the diary. The essence of all I have lived in the last ten years rests in these briefcases. I have run away with a part of my treasures, my memories, my obsession with preserving, portraying, recording. All of us may die, but in these pages we will continue to smile, talk, make love.

Anaïs Nin, whose lovers included Edmund Wilson, Gore Vidal and Otto Rank, published ten volumes of diaries in 1966. Although she was attacked as a supreme narcissist and fantasist, which she undoubtedly was, the feminist perspective of Nin's works, her psychological insight and her search for self-knowledge ensured her popularity in the 1960s and 1970s in American academic circles, where she was much in demand until her death in 1977. During this period she was bigamously married to two husbands, one in New York and one in Los Angeles, and commuted between them.

DECEMBER 1939

DECEMBER SAW THE first major naval action of the Second World War, the Battle of the River Plate in the South Atlantic. This saw the end of the German pocket battleship *Admiral Graf Spee*, which had been sinking British merchant ships in the Atlantic since the start of the war. With the appearance of a cruiser but the capabilities of a battleship, the *Graf Spee* and others like her had been designed by the Germans to evade the restrictions placed on their fleet by the Versailles Treaty. The British light cruisers HMS *Exeter* and HMS *Ajax* and the New Zealand cruiser HMNZS *Achilles* fought the *Graf Spee* in intense exchanges of gunnery. The *Exeter* suffered severe damage but the *Graf Spee* was also hit and eventually headed for the port of Montevideo in neutral Uruguay to make repairs. Efforts were made to convince the Germans that a large British naval force had assembled offshore to await the battleship's departure. The *Graf Spee*'s Captain Langsdorff consulted with his command in Germany. He was given various options but was not allowed to settle for internment in Uruguay. Believing his strategic position to be hopeless, he decided to save his crew and to scuttle his ship, sinking the *Graf Spee* in the Rio de la Plata estuary on 17 December. However, Hitler made known his extreme displeasure and shortly thereafter Captain Langsdorff committed suicide.

The 'Winter War' was now in progress in Finland, and was proving costly for the Soviet forces. Elsewhere there was little military activity. December was a time for reflection and reassessment. Throughout Europe there were active debates about

Hitler's personality and his real motives. Was he an opportunist and statesman in the vein of Bismarck? Or was he a madman bent on world domination? For the time being he had avoided total war and was proceeding by small shock campaigns that delivered dramatic victories after very little fighting.

Friday 1 December 1939

Anthony Weymouth talks to a captain in the mercantile marine

Anthony Weymouth was the pseudonym of the improbably named Ivo Geekie Cobb. He was born in 1887 and educated at Winchester before going on to medical school in London. During the First World War he had worked as a neurologist with the Army Medical Corps in France. A trained doctor and psychologist, he was also a wartime talks editor for the BBC.

This man has been through some ghastly times. He answered my questions quietly, but once he warmed to the subject, his descriptions were so vivid as to make me feel almost sick.

Here are two incidents he told me which I shan't easily forget.

On board the ship was a certain petty-officer – 'a grand chap.' He was marvellous at giving the ratings confidence, especially the young sailors. One day, news arrived that he had been awarded a decoration by the King. My companion took him to the Captain, who wanted to congratulate him.

An hour later he was walking along the deck when a young sailor came out of a cabin holding a revolver and playing with the trigger.

'You shouldn't do that, me lad,' the petty-officer said, 'it's dangerous. Never play with firearms.'

As he finished speaking the revolver went off and shot him in the abdomen.

They carried him into a cabin. As they were holding his

head, he told them not to punish the boy, 'as he didn't know any better.'

'You shouldn't 'a done that, laddie,' he gasped, and fell back dead.

The other story concerned the reaction young sailors show in their first experience of war.

He explained that most healthy young men are without fear, because they don't know what war is really like.

They are eager for a scrap and have no idea what ghastly sights they're going to see.

On one occasion, the ship was being shelled by a sub-marine, and the gun-crew were crouching inside the turret. One man had already been injured by a fragment of shell, and although he had been told not to, had crawled to the far side of the turret. A second shell exploded right on him and literally blew him to pieces, scattering fragments of his body over his comrades. Two were violently sick – and no wonder: the others turned bright green.

My Captain added that it is just these kind of experiences which young sailors find it difficult to face up to. On another and similar occasion when shells were bursting all round them, he saw a whole gun-crew jump over the side into the water. He added that the men literally didn't know what they were doing.

I came away shamefaced, feeling that I had no right to be living in comfort when men had to go through experiences like these – to feed me and others like me.

Lunch in the BBC canteen with Lord de la Warr and Mrs R S Hudson, wife of the secretary to the Department of Overseas Trade. We queued up for our trays, our knives and forks, and then chose our food.

It was a queer meal, for I could think of nothing else but the stories the sailor had just told me. I found myself looking at everything I ate, wondering whether it had been imported: and asking myself whether I had any right to eat food which perhaps had cost many men their lives.

I apologized for my dullness, explaining that I had just spent an hour with a merchant seaman. I gave some slight account of his story; but I discovered afterwards, what I didn't know at the time, that Lord de la Warr himself had served as a sailor during the Great War. So I probably was telling him the sort of thing he knew all about from personal experience.

At this stage of the war the threat to merchant ships came more from surface raiders and magnetic mines than from submarines. Only 40 U-boats were operating in 1939, compared to 400 by 1943. At the end of December 1939 Germany extended the threat of naval action to all those states selling or chartering ships to Britain. SEE ALSO *PP. 101–2, 139–40* AND *206–8.*

Monday 4 December 1939

Axel Heyst reflects on German attitudes to the 'phoney war'

Axel Heyst was a Swedish journalist living in London.

Yes, many people greeted the last war with a sigh of relief. Europe was bored with too long a period of peace. For many life had become too soft, too smooth. The legend of war, the myth of picturesque cavalry charges, sabres glistening in the sun, fascinated the imagination of the young. But soon this myth collapsed in the mud of the trenches, in the deadly suspense, and in the routine of life at the front . . .

This war offers a completely different picture. There were no sighs of relief in the West when it descended on us; and I am almost sure that, apart from the Nazi fanatics, there was no genuine enthusiasm and elation in Germany. I remember my impressions from a flying visit to Berlin in the first days of August this year. It was already clear that Germany had decided to strike at Poland; it was obvious that Germany was going to war, although she could have gained almost everything by sticking to her policy of blackmail and using combined political and economic pressure. The older generation in Germany was scared of war, and rather dubious about its 'advisability'. True, Germany was one armed camp, and her war potential was formidable; true, she could muster dozens of divisions, and her army was first-rate; true, she held mastery over the skies of Europe. But some people in Germany still doubted whether she could stand a prolonged war, and suspected that her staying power was over-rated by the Nazi leaders. I think that the majority of the German people, guilty of submitting all too readily to any doctrine of force and brutality, was in favour of a 'punitive expedition' against 'the insolent Poles', and a political conquest of Europe by means of pressure and a war of nerves. Even Germany, I am sure, is unprepared for a long and protracted war, for huge losses on the scale of the last war. True, the complex of Flanders, the complex of Verdun, which were the nightmares of Great Britain and France, was not matched by any similar fear in Germany; this was largely due to the great propaganda success of the 'stab-in-the-back' legend, and the myth of the 'invincibility of the German Army', and partly also to the more martial character of the German nation, which takes an enormous pride in all war-like things. While pacifism had been making rapid progress in the Western countries, militarism had been producing new myths in Germany. But, with all these reservations, Germany as a whole rather favours a short and victorious war – cheap, as far as biological losses are concerned – than a long and expensive adventure. Even in that misled and misguided nation, submissive to orders, fascinated by uniform, ready to goose-step even in their sleep – even in that barbarised Germany of today there were voices and feelings of apprehension, of doubt, and of fear. German towns at the outbreak of this war did not resemble German towns at the outbreak of the First World War. The fact that German propaganda was busy representing the war against Poland as a 'punitive expedition', to be over in a couple of weeks, seems to confirm the view that the German people were not too anxious for a real war. Hitler wanted to present his nation with an accomplished fact, and he did not believe that France and Great Britain would answer the war.

Heyst was particularly struck by the difference between the beginning of the First World War and the beginning of the Second World War. Since 1914 the world had been educated about the meaning of modern war, and by 1939 even Hitler had to be careful to offer the German people only short and successful wars.

Heyst is best known for his book After Hitler, *which was published in 1940. This presented Hitler in a less than critical light, arguing that he was a pan-Europeanist who wanted a better future for all. Thereafter he would be a marked man and had trouble finding a publisher. In common with some other diarists in this collection, Heyst complained that he had submitted the text of his diary numerous times to publishers but the wartime climate of censorship and indeed self-censorship had resulted in his manuscript being returned. In 1946 he was finally able to publish it.*

Tuesday 12 December 1939

Dr Anthony Weymouth offers a psychoanalytical view of Hitler

I have just read *Hitler Speaks*. It has confirmed the view I've held for some time that the German leader is suffering from schizophrenia. His split-personality must be very advanced, and I suspect will increase still more rapidly now that he has come up against the first serious reverses he has met with since his advent to power . . .

Psychiatrists will have no difficulty in recalling countless examples of schizophrenics who, within the limits prescribed by asylums, have behaved like Adolf Hitler has – and does.

Hitler's mental make-up is well known. He is a dreamer; a visionary; an ascetic. To-day, more often than not, his mind is occupied with his dreams, to the exclusion of the present.

It was this characteristic which, as an adolescent, led to his loneliness and to his failure to mix happily with others.

It is, of course, only the abnormal individual who finds it necessary to live the 'shut-in' life. This tendency is at once a symptom of mental instability, and a danger to what remains of sanity. A schizophrenic is always liable to pass over the borderline which divides eccentricity from insanity.

Now, so long as a human-being is associating with his fellow-creatures, some kind of social contacts are unavoidable. In asylums, schizophrenics avoid these by running away when anyone approaches. The same artifice can be used in a different way – the door of the mind can be bolted and barred against interference.

Adolf Hitler has used both methods. He has shut himself up in Berchtesgaden, and, gazing down on his Bavarian mountains, passed the hours in silent communion with himself . . .

Hitler was inspecting an institution when suddenly something upset him. Without any warning he began to bellow loudly. Then he flung himself on the floor, striking out wildly with his arms and legs and foaming at the mouth. Those present tried to pick him up, but he bit them on the hands.

After some time they were able to 'peg him down on a sofa' and cover him with a blanket. He bit the blanket and tore pieces out of it. Eventually he was quietened.

Hitler's psychological profile proved to be a matter of enduring fascination for publics and governments alike. Anthony Weymouth wrote popular psychology for public consumption. But behind closed doors the secret agencies of almost every power were busy preparing profiles of the German leader, drawing on his own writings and well-documented instances of his bizarre behaviour. Perhaps the most extensive was an analysis begun in spring 1943 by the American Office of Strategic Services, fore-runner to the Central Intelligence Agency. A team led by Walter C. Langer and including Professor Henry A. Murr of the Harvard Psychological Clinic, Dr Ernst Kris of the New School of Social Research and Dr Bertram D. Lawin of the New York Psychoanalytic Clinic laboured for months to produce their report. They concluded that Hitler's behavioural patterns were formed in childhood: 'He hated his father, distrusted his mother, and despised himself for his weakness.' They added that his 'distrust of both men and women is so deep that in all his history there is no record of a really intimate and lasting friendship'. SEE ALSO PP. 97–9, 139–40 AND 206–8.

Monday 18 – Thursday 21 December 1939

Paul Roubiczek reflects on honour, suicide and the scuttling of the *Graf Spee*

Paul Roubiczek was born in Prague in 1898. He spent much of the inter-war period in Berlin and later fled Hitler's regime by moving back to Prague and then to Britain, to take up a post at Cambridge University. Here he taught German and philosophy while struggling with the moral problems imposed by war. Temperamentally he was a pacifist, but he could not accept that the evils represented by Hitler could be dealt with by anything except force.

18 December

The German battleship *Graf Spee* has been scuttled. It is difficult to judge the situation which led to this decision and difficult too to judge the decision itself. Nevertheless I cannot help feeling that it reveals the Nibelung fondness for glorious destruction. Hitler himself is supposed to have ordered the scuttling. How many men have been sacrificed for an effect that is all too tempting for all too many Germans? Is this destruction for effect now being praised in exalted tones in Germany, and perhaps not only there, also really worth a single human life?

It would have seemed to me better policy to acknowledge defeat and save first and foremost the men, and then the ship as well, for the future. But the power addicted group dominant in Germany today is not, and never has been, capable of bearing defeat manfully. For a necessary part of doing that is to have a belief in life and the strength to fulfil life for its own sake without clinging to the prop of deceptive external aims. They distrust life – only that which receives the seal of death seems honourable. Is not here too again revealed that dreadful readiness, for destruction's sake, to sever oneself from the entire future?

19 December

Fortunately the crew have been saved. And the effect does not seem to have succeeded, at least not outside Germany. Germany's enemies are arguing convincingly that if the ship *had* to sink, it would have been more admirable, would it not, to seek destruction in open battle. The opposing British forces were not all that considerable, quite a lot of damage could have been done – to avoid battle by suicide was simply dishonourable and cowardly! To which the Nazi answer is that Uruguay is to blame! The ship could not be made ready for sea, she would not have been able to fight. That sounds less convincing. The Nazis are obviously merely looking for a scapegoat, as they always do, not having the courage to take each other to task.

A conflict of opinions all determined by the heroic ideal always has a seductive ring. The long dominance of an ideal always results in familiarity with that ideal down to the last detail, and everyone knows what to say in every situation. The British press is bound, after all, to present the matter in the manner most unfavourable to the Nazis. But I am not letting myself be carried away too quickly into passing judgement – will not the affair very likely sound just as plausible from the other side?

But it is wrong to let oneself be misled into passing judgement on this conflict of opinion! Heroism is the criterion employed on both sides – what matters is to have a new criterion!

21 December

The drama of the *Graf Spee* has today come to a moving end that sheds a shocking light upon the affair – the captain has committed suicide. By this act he confirms the British opinion – he too thought it dishonourable not to give battle and has made his protest against Hilter's will for self-destruction. Within the meaning of heroism all now seems clear. But this final point does, I think, point to other depths.

The Nibelung mania of Hitler, the Wagnerite, has meanwhile manifested itself in another way too. The *Columbus*, Germany's third-largest passenger liner has also been scuttled. Of course, with a vessel of that sort it is a different matter – she was not able to defend herself and would have been a prize for the enemy. But that she was the twenty-third ship to be dispatched on this death voyage by the Nazis does show how very much they stake on the last card – and also that they do not face up to the real situation. The *Bremen* has of course got back to Germany, but will she not be just as much sentenced to inactivity in her German port as other ships have been in neutral ones? It is merely a question of effect all the time, never of real sense, never of the living future!

But other depths are illuminated by the figure of the captain. In the British papers – and could such a thing be possible in the German? – he is depicted as chivalrous and noble, as concerned for his British prisoners as for his German crew, putting off suicide, which, by the code of conduct, would have been finer on the sinking ship, in order to see all his men to safety. Obviously he was the embodiment of old humane Germany. His telephone conversation with Hitler seems to have shaken him profoundly. But what was his response? Self destruction!

He did his duty – but what a terrible duty it was! Why did he obey a command he rejected as senseless, why not use his life to serve sense, instead of destroying his life after a senseless deed? . . .

The captain knew only two ideals – heroism and performance of duty – and when they came into conflict, he shot himself. But his very heroism provides a remarkable contradiction: concern of a high order for his crew whom in battle he would have sacrificed without a moment's hesitation! We assent to war and are powerless in the face of its real horrors but would still like somehow to help humanity into its own. The heroic ideal is no longer sufficient for men who have become human, and for that very reason it is subordinated to duty. But why does the knowledge of having fulfilled his duty still not save the captain?

Duty is one of the most dangerous of concepts. It is the form given to an activity – it says nothing at all concerning the nature of the activity; any activity can become the performance of duty. Duty, when its content is good, may be a very fine thing, and it may justify the worst of crimes – murder may be done as a duty too.

Roubiczek did not have all the facts of the Graf Spee *episode at his disposal; nevertheless, he had presciently identified 'duty' as a dangerous and ambiguous concept. SEE ALSO PP. 115–16.*

Wednesday 20 December 1939

Mollie Panter-Downes, journalist, on the movement of schools and colleges

The grade schools are not the only ones to be reshuffled by the march of events; public schools, too have done a sort of general post – Dulwich, for instance, has gone to double up with Tonbridge. There is even a story of two schools' simply swapping premises, with satisfaction to all concerned. Eton and Harrow are carrying on as usual, having built air-raid shelters expensive and expansive enough to satisfy the most fidgety mother. Harrow thinks that it won't be bombed anyway, since the Harrow church steeple was said to be a grand landmark to German aviators in the last war. Eton has made a stately concession to current happenings by partially abolishing top hats, which are tricky things to wear with gas masks.

At Oxford and Cambridge, the remaining undergraduates are either foreigners or under military age, but the population of both universities has been augmented by various transplanted government departments. Oxford, in addition, now houses the Royal Institute of International Affairs, which has roosted at Balliol. The nineteen-year-olds are taking an abridged course, which can be completed after the war if they feel like it. No one seems to know what has happened to the young men who voted a few years back that under no circumstances would they fight for King and Country.

*Elaborate school uniforms presented a tricky problem after the intro-
duction of rationing and clothing coupons. Some schools, such as Eton,
decided to lower their sartorial standards; others decided to carry on as
before. Christ's Hospital School continued to dress its 800 boys in an
elaborate and uncomfortable Tudor outfit consisting of an ankle-length
coat, knickerbockers and thick yellow socks. Almost all the boys' clothing
coupons were appropriated to ensure that they could acquire the blue-
coat uniform. SEE ALSO PP. 65–6, 81–2 AND 538–9.*

Thursday 21 December 1939

Jean-Paul Sartre hears of mass looting by French soldiers near the Maginot Line

*Jean-Paul Sartre was already in his thirties when he was drafted into
the French army at the outbreak of the Second World War. The phoney
war that ensued involved him in nine months of sitting about doing very
little. He was attached to a meteorological unit that monitored rainfall.
Sartre occupied himself by making a series of notes on his everyday
experience, with long digressions on philosophy, literature, politics,
history and autobiography. His diaries anticipate the themes of his later
philosophical works.*

This evening Klein, the colonel's driver, pays us a visit . . .
We offered him a slice of tart and he told stories. He's the
first fellow I've met who has really *seen* the state the evacuated villages are in. The other day they stopped in a
frontier-village, and while the colonel was going to the gun
emplacements, he asked a sergeant to open one of the houses
for him and show him the state of the furnishings. It was
edifying. Mirrors smashed on the wardrobes; pieces of
furniture split by bayonet-strokes; bed-linen looted – what
couldn't be carried away is torn. The tiles on the roofs are
smashed, the silverware has disappeared. In the cellars, the
lads drank what they could and then, when they could drink
no more, went off leaving the spigots of the barrels open; the

cellar is flooded with wine. A sewing-machine is split in two. By axe-blows? 'And yet it was cast-iron,' says Klein sadly.

Not long ago, some evacuees returned to this village and its neighbours on a 24-hour pass, to fetch bed-linen. When they left their houses, most of them were weeping in despair: they'd found nothing left. They complained to the commandant. But what could be done? The people responsible don't come from our division, nor in all probability even from the division which preceded us here. It goes back to the earliest days of the war. As Pieter rightly said, that was the time when everyone believed the war would be a cataclysm. The soldiers made haste to loot, thinking that the first artillery bombardment would wipe out all trace of looting, along with the very existence of the looted houses. And then, lo and behold, the war became a long tedium, a long wait, and the looted houses remain – shocking and indiscreet.

'It's not possible,' the sergeant was saying, 'it's not possible to give them back in that state; it'd cause trouble. They'll have to be told the Boches looted everything. But for that, the Boches would have to attack . . .' It seems that the officers set the example. At Herrlisheim, some wagons supposedly containing damaged ammunition were unsealed: they were stuffed full of underwear, sewing-machines, silverware. It's impossible to know whether the civilians who come to fetch warm clothes don't loot too. They have a free pass and that's all. Impossible to tell whether they really go to their own houses or into their rich neighbour's instead. Only the mayor could say, but the mayor isn't there, he's in the Limousin.

We talk about Strasbourg. He says the police there, by contrast, is well organized and strict. One old eccentric he used to know, an umbrella-merchant, wouldn't allow himself to be evacuated; he hid in his house and let the others go off, then lived alone, feeding himself from tins. In the end, he grew bolder and switched on the lamps of an evening. One night, as the constables were doing their rounds, they saw a light. They called and shouted, but the old man didn't reply. They called three times, but the old man still remained silent, terrified no doubt that he'd be evacuated forcibly. After the third time, they fired through the window and the first volley killed him stone dead.

By December 1939 the French army had made thorough and in some cases well-organized inroads into the property of French civilians who had been forcibly evicted from border areas at the start of the war. The military thinking had been wholly rational. The presumption was that matters would follow the same course as in 1914: fighting would break out shortly after the declaration of war, bringing first of all extensive German shelling, and then German looting. French divisional commanders thought to themselves that there was no point in the Germans acquiring all the loot from French areas and proceeded to help themselves. But three months after the outbreak of war, the Germans had still not arrived to cover up their handiwork, and French pilfering was increasingly plain for all to see. SEE ALSO PP. 125–6.

Wednesday 27 December 1939

Muriel Green, an eighteen-year-old garage attendant, sees a 'Nasty' from the kitchen window

We (Jenny and I) were cooking mince pies when we heard a very loud aeroplane and saw through the window a very peculiar looking plane. We both said at once, 'I am sure that's a Nasty.' But we both stood and watched making no attempt to take any precautions. About 5 mins later we heard more aeroplanes and Jenny rushed out and said she saw 3 Spitfires chasing over after the other aeroplane going very fast. A few minutes later the 1st plane went dashing back and the three others went over again, and Mother and Jenny rushed out in the garden and then rushed back declaring they could hear gunfire. The dog barked and jumped about and I was still eating my dinner and refused to get up and Mother announced that if there was anything to be seen she wasn't going to miss it. She said we might as well be killed while we were excited as anytime. Several times during the afternoon we heard the roar again of aeroplanes and Mother and Jenny dashed in the garden but saw nothing unusual. I felt so tired from the dance last night I could not be bothered to go and look. I remembered you should keep under cover but could not be bothered to go in the bathroom as arranged or get my gas mask from upstairs. I looked out of the window every time although I knew you should not. I did not feel in the least afraid but rather excited to think I had seen a Nasty.

The population of southern England was fascinated by the air activity that took place above them with increasing frequency while ordinary domestic scenes went on below. This diary entry may be mistakenly dated and may relate to December 1940, but it is not inconceivable that it is for 1939. The first Luftwaffe aircraft to be shot down over Britain was an He-111 bomber in November 1939. SEE ALSO PP. 86–7.

New Year's Eve, Sunday 31 December 1939

Count Ciano, Italian foreign minister, is gloomy about the future

Mussolini is once again suffering from a recurrent wave of pro-German sentiments. Now he would like to send Hitler some advice (which has so far failed to make an impression) and to inform him that Italy is continuing to arm. But what are we preparing for? We must not enter a war on the side of Germany, and we never will: it would be a crime and a folly. As for war against Germany, at the moment I cannot see any reason for it. In any case, if necessary I would accept fighting against Germany, never on her side. This is how I feel. Mussolini holds completely opposite views: he would never undertake war against Germany and, when we are ready, he would rather fight on Germany's side to defeat the democracies that, in my opinion, are the only countries with which we can deal seriously and honestly.

But for the moment, we should not talk about war, as we are totally unprepared for it. Today we are worse off than we were in September. Yesterday, General Favagrossa said that if he could get hold of all the material he had previously asked for – allowing our factories to work double shifts – we would be adequately prepared by October 1942. Generals Badoglio and Soddu agree that we could not enter a war in the near future.

This is the end of a year that has been so cruel in my personal life and so generous in my political life. The new year, I feel, will bring many surprises and perhaps we shall witness the rapid conclusion of a tragedy that humanity does not want or cannot understand. In the widespread inability to comprehend this absurd and inexplicable war, we may find the very key to its end.

Initially, Ciano had been in principle enthusiastic for an alliance with Germany; but he was less keen once he had got to know the leading figures in Berlin, and soon came to loathe Italy's Nazi allies. After a number of meetings with his partners, it was obvious that the Germans were determined to dominate and planned to pull Italy into war as quickly as possible. Prior to the German invasion of Poland, Ciano succeeded in restraining Mussolini, and the following day Italy declared its neutrality in that conflict. However, Ciano was dubious about how long he could hold Italy back from entry into war. SEE ALSO PP. 43–4, 46–7, 335–7 and 513.

1940

114 WITNESS TO WAR

'WE DROVE PAST many wrecked houses, the ruins of which were still smoking. Charred timber, twisted ironwork, piled up heaps of brick, all frozen over, lay around . . . Just at that moment the "All Clear" went, and almost immediately the silent and deserted streets began to be filled with people. They swarmed up like ants out of the shelters and holes of all sorts . . . We took another photograph near the Bank of Finland where four people were killed, next to the Scala cinema . . . I say "we," but I was busily writing up my diary as quickly as my shorthand would permit . . .'

Sir Walter Citrine, MY FINNISH DIARY, *entry for 2 February 1940*

JANUARY 1940

THE SOVIET WAR against Finland occupied newspaper headlines during January 1940. Although the Finns were under increasing pressure from the larger Soviet forces, they were inflicting severe casualties on their enemies. Few of the Soviet troops had proper winter equipment and some were found reading instruction manuals about how to use skis on the battlefield. Meanwhile Finland was supplied with additional aircraft from Sweden, Italy, Britain and the United States. Britain and France considered sending troops to assist Finland, but their main motive was a desire to leave some forces en route to garrison Norway against Germany.

On the home front in Britain, rationing began to make an impact. Meat rationing had begun the previous month and now bacon, butter and sugar were added to the list of restricted items. In France rationing was stricter, with only certain meats available on particular days of the week. January also saw a huge reverse flow of evacuees. Thousands of children who had been sent to the countryside in expectation of devastating air raids began to pour back into the capital. Some had already begun to trickle back within a month of the great exodus of September 1939, but by early 1940 this had become a flood. Of the London County Council's 900 schools, only 15 were operating in the second week of January, but soon many more were forced to reopen. The authorities reluctantly began a programme of school shelter building.

Over neutral Belgium, a German Messerschmitt passenger plane was forced down by fighters. On board were two German officers with plans for the German invasion of western Europe and they failed to destroy their documents. Because of this security disaster – and also because of bad weather – Hitler decided to cancel his attack until the spring. Accordingly, the phoney war dragged on until May 1940. However, the British and French failed in their efforts to use this incident to persuade the Belgians to abandon their neutrality. Freed from their task in the west, the German military high command began to plan the invasion of Norway.

Friday 5 – Tuesday 16 January 1940

Paul Roubiczek, an exiled Czech professor in Cambridge, reflects on the tension between anti-fascism and pacifism

5 *January*
Strange how empty the newspapers now are. Reports of the Finnish war are receiving maximum splash because there is apparently nothing else to report – or maybe too to mask the faint signs of peace efforts – the Papal Nuncio has been daily at the Wilhelmstrasse, Mussolini has still not been to the Pope. Apart from that there are tendentious reports of internal movements in Germany which to me seem neither reliable nor promising. One has the feeling that a very great deal is going on behind the scenes and that not much good can come of it . . .

16 *January*
And now at this point I may as well mention also something I ought to have mentioned long ago. A Czech National Committee has received recognition by the British Government, and consequently is able to call up Czechs living in Britain. I being over forty, this call-up will probably not affect me at once, but there is little doubt that it will get me sooner or later. The undeserved quiet I have been permitted to enjoy in the midst of war, will soon be over – I must make up my mind.

This brings me back to the question this diary opened with. Have I any right to keep out of the war – out of the armed struggle, when the fight is against the Nazis? It is over this concrete and decisive vital question where life is at stake, literally and figuratively, that must be shown whether my thoughts are of such moment and vitality as to be really capable of helping me, or whether they are merely formal and lead away from life and into the void.

What is certain is that the Nazis have to be fought. But that is because in them we are bound to recognize all that we fight in ourselves when struggling for a breakthrough of the human element – unbridled animal urges and destructive passions, presumption, contempt for others, the arrogance of allowing the validity only of our own opinions – not because they are right but to justify injustice to our own advantage – and a joy in destruction and self-annihilation. We have to recognize in them what we fight in ourselves, for only by so doing do we also recognize that we all are guilty of everything. And only in being destroyed by that sense of guilt do we experience the Absolute which can at the same time save us.

Stalin had hoped to cut Finland in two by attacking with two divisions at Salla, cutting across Finland and reaching the Swedish border at Tornio. The operation was a failure. The key battle was fought on the Raattee road near Salla in January 1940 – in temperatures of nearly 40 degrees Celsius below zero. Finland's armed forces encircled and destroyed the Red Army's 44th Division, which suffered 17,000 casualties in four days of fighting. But despite this intense combat Roubiczek suspected that elsewhere active measures were being taken to try to construct a peace settlement and bring the conflict to an end. It was partly for this reason that states such as Norway and Belgium opted to remain neutral, hoping that the war would now draw to a close. Peace efforts were indeed under way, but proved ineffective.

Paul Roubiczek's diary, in which he thought out his position on war, was effectively a dry run for his most important philosophical work, Thinking in Opposites, *which would be published in 1952. He remained in his adopted academic home of Cambridge until his death in 1969, before completing his last work,* The Necessity of Contradictions. *He was best known for his book on modern French philosophers,* Existentialism: For and Against. SEE ALSO PP. 103–6.

Thursday 18 – Saturday 20 January 1940

Jean Malaquais enjoys the cordial bureaucracy of the supply-man's war

Jean Malaquais, born Vladimir Malacki in Warsaw in 1908, had emigrated to France in 1926; a prominent writer and political activist, he had worked with many far-left groups. In 1939 he had been conscripted into the French army.

18 January

That's that, I have just been assigned to the supply service for automobile and truck parts. It's a vast shed built of old boards and divided into three compartments, and there are five or six fellows working there as storekeepers; most of them are metallurgical workers; they are jovial, optimistic, bursting with health, and display a simple and honest cordiality which enchants me. There is also a mascot, a little dog which is called Adolf, naturally, a good fire in the stove, numbered racks and bins, rubber stamps, chalk – in short, everything needed to win the war . . .

19 January

The incredible, the fantastic red tape in our supply service. For instance: each piece which we deliver, or which we order from the distributing service in Nancy, requires a voucher in six copies, all in different colors, each voucher bearing nine seals, also all different, which means fifty-four stamps for the smallest cotter pin as well as for a complete replacement motor. Same procedure for every article which is not as ordered, returned either to us or by us. And hundreds of replacement parts pass through our hands every day . . .

20 January

The variety of the names and appellations of the units which are supplied with automobile parts from our store is, soberly speaking, prodigious. Yet the sector which we serve is exceedingly limited. I can't convince myself that each of these units has a precisely defined role and function. My impression is that under the cover of military discipline and rigidity, a fantastic confusion is flourishing.

Sadly, Malaquais' appreciation of the state of disorganization, or over-organization, of the French military was accurate. Both the British and the French were still working up to war efficiency, whereas the Germans had been fighting for several months and were already there. SEE ALSO PP. 37 AND 126–8.

Saturday 27 January 1940

Sir Walter Citrine examines the Mannerheim Line in Finland

Walter McLennan Citrine was born in Wallasey in the Wirral in 1887. An electrician and union activist, he had risen through the union ranks to become General Secretary of the TUC. He was also President of the International Federation of Trade Unions. In 1940 he led a British labour delegation to see what was happening in Finland and visited Turku, a heavily bombed city.

We were now on the way to the famous Mannerheim Line, of which we had heard so much. On my remarking to one of the officers that it must have been a very costly job to build the concrete foundations of the line, he replied curtly: 'The Mannerheim Line is only a Russian legend. You will find nothing here like the Maginot Line in France.'

He then went on to explain that the Russians had deliber-ately circulated this story of an unassailable line of fortresses, to cover up their own inefficiency, and to give the world the impression that they had really as difficult a task to overcome the resistance of the Finns in this section, as the Germans would have to force the Maginot Line.

This officer carefully explained to me that the Mannerheim

Line, in fact, was little more than a natural defensive system which the country offered. What the Finns had done was to make the best use they could of lakes and forests, with which the Karelian Isthmus is crowded. They had certainly done everything they could to force the Russians on to the narrowest front possible, so that they could not make use of the large masses of men at their command. The Finns had constructed a good many small pill-boxes, and their tactics had made it difficult for the Russians to move anywhere but in the region of the roads between the forests, or across the ice.

The Russians could not take their tanks through the forests, of course, and hence their movements were restricted. I learned during the course of the day that the Mannerheim Line was very deep, and full of all sorts of ingenious obstacles which the Finns had devised to hamper and harass the Russians, a task in which they have been very successful with the small force at their disposal. I cannot give details as to the situation of the part of the line we visited for palpable reasons.

We passed down the narrow roads fringed by forests, being frequently challenged by soldiers with fixed bayonets who showed considerable alertness without too much heel-clicking. Time after time we came across evidence of the thoroughness with which the Finns were preparing their resistance. Tank traps and obstacles were frequent, and lines of granite blocks, many kilometres away from the front, showed how carefully things had been thought out.

In southern Finland, on the Karelian isthmus, the Soviet advance was held up by the defensive line named after Marshal Mannerheim, Commander-in-Chief of the Finnish army. Meanwhile, on Finland's eastern border, Soviet troops, who were obliged to use the roads, suffered ambushes and the attack halted.

Walter Citrine would be made Lord Citrine by the 1945 Labour government, and served on a number of public bodies, including the Central Electricity Authority, which he chaired from 1947 to 1957. SEE ALSO P. 113.

Late January 1940

Padre Alfred Leaney considers British army courts and justice

Alfred Leaney was born in 1909 and joined the 6th Battalion the Royal Sussex Regiment in October 1939 as a chaplain. He served in France in 1940.

I am writing at a busy moment very much without thinking twice – and what I want to say is on a subject of social importance.

One is struck by the completeness of the world of the army. Everything in the greater world is here in miniature: the army has its own everything, even its own Courts of Justice and its own Ministers of Religion. It is about justice that I want to write. I have seen several men in trouble. It has seemed often to me that the way a man will be dealt with depends enormously not on the application of real justice to his case but on the relative understanding or lack of it in those officers who happen to compose the tribunal . . .

Now, the officers who in fact compose the tribunal, being officers, are influenced by the very atmosphere towards taking a cynical view of what I will call abnormal behaviour (e.g. inexplicable insistence on overstaying leave, and throwing apparent fits – regarded as scrimshanking because not due to a physical cause). A great deal of this abnormal behaviour is of course as curable by punishment as a child's fears of the dark by flogging. I repeat that I am making no accusation of definite injustice. Methods of trial are most fair, the sentences not heavy, the rules stringently kept. I must place on record the acquittal on a technical legal point of a man who had in fact made a confession. All this, as in civil courts, is always impressive. My criticism is that so often the treatment given will not prevent a repetition of the error committed. To take the most extreme case, and the most ridiculous, to wet one's bed at night is automatically regarded as a criminal offence. It might be urged that [we create] . . . a system of justice in which qualified experts in the science of human character were widely employed. There are many ways in which the army would benefit itself besides becoming the institution by which men were re-made into useful citizens. It would have a greater proportion of reliable men, and be less embarrassed with recurrent hard cases and men temperamentally unfit to be soldiers, and the other rubbish which usually clogs the efficiency of a machine made of human cogs.

Leaney was alarmed by the attitude of soldiers to questions of religion, patriotism or social concern. He was not greatly surprised that the majority of soldiers had no wish to attend religious services, but he was surprised to find, during discussion groups which he chaired in 1940, that 80 per cent of the soldiers participating had no interest in the reasons for the war or its future course. He found the apathy of the average soldier 'colossal' and 'unnerving'. He also found his work frustrating as, aside from a brief period of fighting in May 1940, he would see little action between 1939 and 1944. In 1944 he was posted to the 4th Battalion the Dorset Regiment, which saw heavy fighting in the Nijmegen and Limburg areas of Holland. During August 1945 he was involved in the 'religious screening' of sixty-three German pastors who had belonged to the Wehrmacht or the Luftwaffe. In the 1960s Leaney was Professor of Theology at the University of Nottingham.

FEBRUARY 1940

BOTH JANUARY AND February were bad months for the Allies in the Atlantic, with 118 ships lost during the first two months of the year, mostly to a small number of German U-boats.

In the Soviet–Finnish 'Winter War' the Finns began to run out of ammunition and suddenly lost ground to the Soviet forces, who brought up large numbers of reinforcements. The Soviet

Union and Germany, although mere allies of convenience, deepened their co-operation, with Stalin supplying food and oil in return for German weapons. Germany was able to import supplies purchased from countries in the Far East using the Trans-Siberian Railway.

The British and French developed further amateurish plans to assist the Finns, but these were a transparent cover for their own efforts to gain control of Sweden and Norway and so prevent Germany gaining access to the vast reserves of iron ore that were available in Scandinavia. The British and French made ludicrous promises of support to Finland but did little to assist in real terms, and by the end of the month the Finns were prepared to capitulate to the Soviet Union.

Meanwhile in the west, the German army was known to be exercising and preparing for an attack on France, while the British and French continued to move more forces up to the German border. Military mobilization saw farms in England and Wales lose over 30,000 agricultural labourers to the armed forces by the end of February. Moreover, because war production began to provide more lucrative opportunities elsewhere, another 15,000 left the land to take up other types of employment. The resulting surplus of jobs offered agricultural labourers and others in poorly paid occupations a chance to escape the trap of low wages. One answer to the deficit of workers was to appeal to women to join the Women's Land Army (WLA), a volunteer force created during the First World War to address a similar shortfall. But the WLA could not fill all of the gaps, and the government had no choice but to tackle the problem with money. By June 1943 the minimum wage for an agricultural worker had almost doubled from its pre-war level to 65 shillings a week.

Within both Britain and France, strained nerves and security fears fed anxieties about the 'fifth column' – a popular term for groups within a country who were working on behalf of its enemies, often driven by ideology. In the 1930s most European countries, including Britain, contained elements sympathetic to fascism; but pacifist and socialist orientations could also attract suspicion of subversive motives.

Mid-February 1940

Anonymous diary of a volunteer in the British Auxiliary Fire Service

This diarist was determined to remain unknown, wishing his work to celebrate the bravery of his colleagues rather than his own actions. The writer worked in the scenery department of Ealing Studios and had joined the Auxiliary Fire Service (AFS) a few days after the declaration of war. He was based at a makeshift station in some sheds outside an infants' school in Aldgate. This was run by seven male and three female volunteers.

Two big fires since I last wrote were the Iceland Fur Company and a whisky warehouse. The Fur Company was a real big one; it kept burning for three weeks. I was on the job most of the time, with breaks of twenty-four hours every forty-eight for my leave. I got quite fond of that fire.

I had one very narrow escape. I and Marley were standing on a bridge between two warehouses. Suddenly we felt the bridge going under us. There were fires on both sides of the road, so that whichever way we went, we had to step off the bridge into a blazing building.

Marley went one way and I the other. Then abruptly the whole bridge went down. I was standing on the wall where the bridge joined the building and Marley was doing the same thing on the other side. But he was ok for the floor behind him was intact. When I looked round, however, there was nothing left for me to walk on except the burning joists.

The two floors below had already gone down, complete with joists and boards, so that as I made my way along the wall towards the stairs, there was nothing below me for forty feet. It was most unpleasant.

It was even more unpleasant though, when I got to the stairs and found they had gone too. Just as I was wondering where to go next, there was a hail from the part where the bridge had been and Adams appeared on top of the escape.

He was shouting at me to hurry up, because he didn't think the floor joists would last much longer. They didn't. I'd only just reached the escape and climbed on to it when down they went in a shower of sparks.

On the whisky job most of the men got tight from the fumes of the whisky. The vats burst and flooded into the fire! I myself got pretty funny about the head, and once I damn nearly fell from a window where I was holding a branch.

On another job a man was killed, and everybody seemed to think this quite all right because they said it was his own fault. I couldn't see that it made any difference whose fault it was. George argued, however, that if a man is bloody fool enough to climb off a ladder *on to* a window-ledge instead of *into* the window with one leg, no one but he is to blame if he falls and is killed. He was an AFS man, taken over by the LFB [London Fire Brigade] like myself.

I can quite imagine making the same mistake. The rule is that you must put one leg right over the sill into the room before you take the other foot off the ladder. It's a good rule. Poor chap, he took three days to die after he'd fallen about sixty feet into the street. He must have been pretty tough.

That's the first death of a fireman on any fire I've attended. But he wasn't from our Station.

The Auxiliary Fire Service had been set up under the Air Raid Precautions Act in 1939. This made each local authority responsible for taking extra steps to prepare for air attack as part of its provision for civil defence. The fire in the fur company described here was a routine event and was not caused by enemy air action, but such incidents offered the newly formed AFS valuable experience. When the Luftwaffe attacks on south-east England began in earnest in the summer of 1940 the London Fire Brigade would suffer serious casualties, and their depleted ranks were often filled by AFS volunteers. SEE ALSO PP. 131–2.

Saturday 17 February 1940

French philosopher Jean-Paul Sartre watches farewells on
the platform at the Gare de l'Est

I want to recount my journey. The day before yesterday, 15
February at around eight-thirty I donned anew my military
uniform, all tidied up by a civilian tailor. I had new puttees,
ski shoes (those I'd worn till then belonged to the Beaver
[Simone de Beauvoir]), and was neater than I'd ever been
since the war began. At nine o'clock I arrived on the
platform at the Gare de l'Est, where I found a corner-seat
without any trouble. There were many women seeing off
soldiers, very few men. The women were clinging to their
arms and looking at them with a kind of ferocity. But most of
the soldiers, washed and shaved and likewise neater than
they'd ever been before, weren't looking at them: they'd
already left and were gazing into space or else looking at the
other soldiers.

I'm not making hasty generalizations. I walked the whole
length of the platform and everywhere I was struck by those
odd little groups . . .

Strange social event, in dirty grey and smudged khaki:
that utterly primitive separation of the men, who were all
being taken away, from the women – ill made-up, disfigured
by the sleepless night, hastily clad – who were going to stay
there.

There were two trains opposite each other and mine was
leaving second. At 9.30, when the other one left, I saw a
parade of women. The couples whose males were taking my
train had retreated a little, and watched the parade in
silence. The women clasping their men's arms were doubtless thinking that, a quarter of an hour later, they'd be like
that. It was a slow, silent parade with a kind of hesitant
grace. With two or three exceptions, all the women were
weeping, it was almost comical: old women and young
ones, tall ones and dumpy ones, blondes and brunettes
intermingled, with the same red, dark-ringed eyes. One or

two of them caught my attention – one in particular, a tall elegant blonde with a fur coat and face past its prime, who wasn't weeping but walking with long strides, her head turned to one side and gazing at our train with a look of kindly distraction: that one struck me as being groggier than the rest. Another one too: a little girl with just the same bearing and expression as women returning to their seats after communion. At the sight of her vague inward smile and lowered eyes, it seemed to me she could feel her memories within her like a consecrated wafer.

The Gare de l'Est in Paris, close to the Place de la République, is a place saturated in collective emotion. In 1940 it was the major point of departure for those heading for the front and those going on or returning from leave. The sentiments of the crowd were probably intensified by strong memories of the thousands of young men who had passed through the same station on their way to the Western Front only two decades earlier. Many of the mothers there in 1940 would remember the lines of First World War soldiers, with their distinctive leggings, leather belts and clanging mess-cans, who left but did not return. Later on during the Second World War, the Gare de l'Est would also become the main point of departure for the 20,000 Parisian Jews sent to the concentration camps. The camp at Auschwitz was already being constructed in the spring of 1940. SEE ALSO PP. 107–9.

Saturday 24 February 1940

Writer and socialist Jean Malaquais is kept under close observation in a French military hospital

24 February
Nine a.m. I just got into a pretty mess. About an hour ago I got up to drag myself to the lavatory. Coming back into the ward, I saw the envelope containing my medical chart lying on the nurses' table. Out of sheer curiosity, although I knew that it was forbidden, I took the chart out of the envelope and looked at it. And at the bottom of the same, written in

large letters framed in green ink, I suddenly see: *'Patient to be watched closely. Makes syndicalist-communist speeches.'* I turn the paper around in my fingers, read the inscription again, twice, four times: I think it must be a hallucination due to the fever. I remember having exchanged some remarks with other patients, notably on the relations between officers and men, and between the fighting men themselves (some of the wounded come from the Sarre front); but nothing incendiary, certainly nothing which could prompt this incredible 'notice.' There I stand, shivering, turning the paper over and over in my hands, and, like a fit of coughing, a towering rage takes hold of me little by little, clouding my sight. I bound into the corridor like someone stricken with madness, and open door after door, looking for the lieutenant doctor whom I suspect of having penned this extraordinary composition. Finally I come upon him as he sits tranquilly reading his paper, and in a voice over which I have absolutely no control I throw in his face that he is acting singularly in excess of his prerogatives as a physician when he assumed those of a stool pigeon. Suffocated by the vehemence of my attack, he is dumbfounded at first, but, recovering himself quickly enough, he retorts that I had no right to examine my medical chart, and that he was going to have me brought up before a court-martial. He was shouting and I was shouting, forgetting that I was dealing with an officer, too exasperated to be prudent. I said that I was very glad that I had been curious, that he was free to have me brought before anyone he pleased, but that in the meantime I demanded that he efface what he had written, failing which I myself would go to the colonel in command of the hospital – and we would see whether it was compatible with the honor of an officer and a physician to play the role of an informer. My man turned green, then pale, then green again, ordered me to stand at attention (which I did, bellowing the while), bumbled a couplet on the country in danger and the Fifth Column: 'I am told that you have uttered seditious remarks. Is that true?' I flatly refuse to answer; that is none of his business, his task being to concern himself with the condition of my bronchial tubes and not with tittle-tattle about the things I have said. (It's fantastic, how fever inflates you with courage . . .) Thereupon he, the lieutenant, turns his back on me all of a sudden, and says, 'All right, that will do. Dismissed!'

On 20 February, Jean Malaquais had been struck with a fever and taken to hospital. The remarks on his notes derived from the fact that he had been ordered to write a play for the entertainment of visiting staff officers, who, when they saw it performed, judged it to be 'terribly subversive'. He was then identified for close scrutiny by his commanding officers. On 2 March Malaquais would be moved to a better-quality hospital in a school at the centre of the town of Nevers. Finding himself in a clean bed in a pleasant town far from the front, he observed: 'What a joy to be sick.' Like so many intellectuals and thinkers pressed into wartime service, he found these moments of enforced inactivity great opportunities for writing and reflection. Not only was he able to reread and think about the nature and purpose of his diary, he was also able to gain surreptitious access to the hospital typewriter.

Later in 1940 he was taken prisoner, but by 1942 he had managed to escape the Germans and make his way to Venezuela. By 1943 he had moved to Mexico, and eventually he settled in the United States, where he lectured on European literature in universities and colleges. A renowned political activist, after the student protests of 1968 he moved in radical circles with Norman Mailer and Herbert Marcuse. He died in Geneva in 1998. SEE ALSO PP. 37 AND 117–18.

MARCH 1940

THE FINNS BEGAN to negotiate for peace on 7 March 1940 and on 12 March signed the Moscow Peace Treaty. Announcements by Chamberlain and Daladier that Britain and France would assist the Finns merely made their own governments look incompetent. Chamberlain's Cabinet appeared increasingly shaky. Daladier was forced to resign on 20 March and was replaced by Paul Reynaud. Britain and France began detailed military talks about Norway, but the meandering thoughts of their staff officers were soon to be overtaken by German action. Norway's refusal of the British and French offer to station troops in the country was a serious blunder.

Although the prospect of British troops fighting with the Finns against Soviet forces was now over, London worried about the Baku oilfields inside the Soviet Union. Secret overflights of the area arranged by British intelligence from airfields in Baghdad were busy photographing these top priority strategic targets.

Meanwhile Hitler took the opportunity to meet up with Mussolini at the Brenner Pass. Although there were areas of rivalry and disagreement between the two Axis leaders, especially over central Europe, they nevertheless agreed on a timetable for attacks on France and the Low Countries. Mussolini's foreign minister, Ciano, was again dismayed by Mussolini's subservience to Hitler.

Tuesday 12 March 1940

General Edmund Ironside despairs of Chamberlain's War Cabinet

Tall and powerfully built, 'Tiny' Ironside began his military career in the Boer War. In the First World War he had fought at Vimy Ridge in 1916 and at Passchendaele in 1917. A year later he was in northern Russia with a British force sent to assist the Whites in the Russian civil war. A tough-minded individual, he was made Chief of the Imperial General Staff at the War Office in September 1939 and would remain in that position until after the fall of France.

Chamberlain has made his speech in the House, more or less at the request of the French, saying that we are prepared with 'all our resources'. And yet we cannot even say that we have a sporting chance of getting to Finland. We gave a guarantee to the Poles which couldn't be implemented . . .

We had a dreadful Cabinet. Everybody had a different idea upon how much force we would have to use at Narvik.

In the end, the Prime Minister was persuaded to see the Admiral [Sir Edward Evans] and the General [Mackesy] – and he said he could see them tomorrow afternoon. When I explained to him that the men were commencing embarkation [for Norway], they all seemed surprised. A more unmilitary show I have never seen. The Prime Minister began peering at a chart of Narvik and when he had finished he asked me what scale it was on. He asked what effect an 8-inch shell would have on a transport and finished up by saying that he was prepared to risk a 4-inch shell, but not an 8-inch shell. He then asked what the weight of the shells were. Chatfield, an Admiral of the Fleet, first said that we should not risk firing at the Norwegians, and then said that he thought we ought not to be bluffed by a mere Lieutenant in charge of a shore battery. The Cabinet presented the picture of a bewildered flock of sheep faced by a problem they have consistently refused to consider. Their favourite formula is that the case is hypothetical and then they shy off a decision.

I came away disgusted with them all.

Ironside had protested for a long time that Britain was behind in the rearmament race with Germany. He regarded Britain's promises of assistance to the Finns as ludicrous and despaired of the Cabinet's plans for military action to reinforce them by moving through Norway. In any case, Oslo had not given its approval and no-one was sure whether Norway would offer military resistance to these efforts to protect it against Germany. SEE ALSO PP. 158–9.

Thursday 14 March 1940

Nella Last on the changing place of women

Nella Last was a housewife married to a joiner and lived in Barrow-in-Furness, a port which would be subjected to heavy bombing raids. She had begun a diary in September 1939 as a volunteer for the Mass-Observation Archive.

I reflected tonight on the changes the war had brought. I always used to worry and flutter round when I saw my husband working up for a mood; but now I just say calmly, 'Really dear, you *should* try and act as if you were a grown man and not a child of ten, and if you want to be awkward, I shall go out – ALONE!' I told him he had better take his lunch on Thursday, and several times I've not had tea quite ready when he has come in, on a Tuesday or Thursday, and I've felt quite unconcerned. He told me rather wistfully I was 'not so sweet' since I've been down at the Centre [probably the WVS], and I said, 'Well! Who wants a woman of fifty to be sweet, anyway? And besides, I suit *me* a *lot* better!'

Nella Last's diary is interesting not only because of the picture that it offers of a small town under the pressure of war, but also because of her reflections on the changing role of women. Many women found the pressing need for their services as volunteer workers outside the home liberating, even though their husbands did not always welcome it. It was soon clear that this change in attitude and practice would endure, with many women quickly resolving not to return to the restrictions of life as they had known it in the 1930s. SEE ALSO PP. 235, 537–8 AND 593–4.

Mid-March 1940

Our anonymous diarist in the AFS watches auxiliary firemen practise sheet-jumping and ladder exercises in north London

During our exercises last week we had sheet jumping. This was the first time I'd done it. That went for Ikey and Art. Of course George Stiles had his laugh, because he had been through it many times before.

We went down on the tender to a training centre some- where in the north of London, and there in the middle of a yard was a tower some fifty feet high. We had to climb up the tower one after another and jump first from ten feet and then twenty feet into the sheet.

The slogan is: 'If you don't want to do it again, don't look down . . .' In other words the correct way of doing the jump is to walk off the tower looking straight in front of you. You have to rely on the men below to catch you in the sheet (or mat as it is sometimes called).

I don't really mind heights very much, and I've done quite a bit of high-diving in swimming baths, but Ikey hates height in any form, and he had to jump three times before he did it without looking down. Of course the officer in charge has no real power to make them jump, but the moral persuasion is pretty strong. None of the men who were new to it actually funked jumping.

It is a very strange sensation and when you land in the sheet it doesn't hurt a bit. As soon as it is over you feel wonderfully excited, and almost as if you'd had a number of quick, strong drinks.

As I was sailing earthwards (or 'sheetwards', so I hoped) I remembered childish nightmares in which I'd been falling, and I can honestly say that the nightmares were far more frightening than the real thing.

Training was essential for the volunteers of the AFS. Even so, although these programmes were carried out, when the main force of the Blitz hit London in August 1940 some AFS men had never attended a serious fire. SEE ALSO PP. 123–4.

Hector Bolitho at the Air Ministry receives ideas on ways to win the war

Hector Bolitho was born in New Zealand in 1897 and came to Britain in 1922. He became a famous author, mostly of non-fiction, and was well known by this time as a sympathetic writer on the history of the British royal family, notably for his biography of Prince Albert called Albert the Good. *At the outbreak of war he joined the RAF and was initially put to work in the Air Ministry in Whitehall.*

Some cranks, and a few wise men, send in suggestions for winning the war. One correspondent has gone so far as to propose that we drop bombs 'down the throat of Vesuvius' and thus 'explode Southern Italy'. The same idea has come from educated people, in South Africa, Australia and America. The thought is painful to those of us who dream of returning some day to the enchanting coast that runs south from Naples.

Pilots who find their tasks monotonous might like the plan of another correspondent who asks for a 'fleet of fighter planes, thirty strong' which would pretend to 'run away from the enemy'. While pretending, they would 'squirt out from the rear of each aircraft a fine spray of chloroform or the strongest narcotic possible'. The trusting German pilots 'would fly into this strata and so lose control of their machines'.

There is another plan, to drop 'enormous quantities of sticky stuff, like treacle, in front of advancing German troops'. If this failed to stop them, 'coils of barbed wire could then be dropped, to trip and entangle them'. Another patriot suggests that 'you can buy a kind of open-work dishcloth with a wide mesh for washing greasy dishes'. These could be 'scattered among the enemy formations to entangle their airscrews'. A less gentleman-like suggestion is that 'long projecting knives of razor-sharpness' should be fitted to the undercarriages of obsolete and unemployed planes: thus equipped, 'they could chase the enemy airman who baled out and fly over him in such a way that the knives would cut the parachute cord, thus causing the Hun to drop to the earth with a bump'.

A correspondent from Durban proposes that 'millions of snakes' should be shipped from South Africa and released from our aircraft 'on dark nights only', over German towns. He also suggests that 'millions of cabbage leaves' should be steeped 'in a deadly poison' and dropped among the livestock in the German and Italian fields. The same man from Durban wrote, 'The war will finish 2.30 p.m. 4th May, 1945, with Britain on top.'

During the First World War the cartoonist Heath Robinson had drawn several volumes of extremely popular cartoons featuring unlikely secret weapons that might win the war. However, during both the First World War and the Second World War they faced stiff competition from members of the public who flooded the Air Ministry, the Admiralty and the War Office with 'helpful' suggestions that were at least as bizarre. It was Hector Bolitho's task to respond with polite letters of thanks. As it happened, his correspondent from Durban was adrift by only a few hours: the German high command signed an instrument of surrender at Montgomery's tactical headquarters on Lüneburg Heath at 1820 hours on 4 May 1945. SEE ALSO PP. 279–80.

Thursday 21 March 1940

Sven Hedin meets Heinrich Himmler to discuss Tibet

Sven Hedin was a Swedish geographer and explorer who had led four major expeditions to Central Asia between 1899 and 1939. He was also ardently pro-Nazi and conducted private diplomacy to enhance relations between Germany and neutral Sweden. Hedin was seventy-five years old when he met Himmler in 1940, but still appeared youthful and vigorous; on the Swede's same visit to Berlin Hitler, a hypochondriac, asked him for the secret of his remarkable good health. Hedin explained that it was yoghurt.

On the afternoon of 21st March I made my way to the Gestapo Headquarters, where guards gave the military salute at the entrance and on the stairs. Heinrich Himmler, Reichsführer SS and supreme chief of the Secret Police, received me politely and pleasantly and invited me to sit down at a small table. He had none of the look of a cruel and ruthless despot and might just as well have been an elementary school teacher from some provincial town. One felt a lack of character and pregnancy in this face, of the strongly moulded lines that tell of will and energy. It bore not a trace of the classical beauty of Greece and Rome, not a suspicion of race or culture. His face was everyday, common-place and uninteresting, and the pince-nez did nothing to remedy the absence of intelligence, warmth, cruelty, hard-ness or any of the other qualities that usually betray their presence in a pair of human eyes. His expression could only be called indifferent and colourless, his eyes lacked life and fire. Himmler, in a word, left the visitor completely unmoved . . .

But Himmler's outwardly insignificant appearance may possibly have been only a mask which he used to hide the fact that he strove to become as powerful as, or even more powerful than, Hitler. Our German friends expressed very varying opinions of him. We met ladies who declared that he was a charmer whom no one could help but love and admire. Cautious men said nothing, while others hinted that the Chief of the Secret Police was after all the most hated and feared man in all Germany.

Just as simple and unassuming, almost bare indeed, was Himmler's office and reception room, in which his desk by the window, a sofa, some chairs and a table by the inner wall constituted the only furniture. The elegance which characterised the offices of all the other Ministers was completely lacking here. It struck one altogether as old-fashioned and make-shift.

Himmler opened the conversation by telling me about the able and successful expedition into southern Tibet, led by the young Dr Ernst Schäfer, who had recently returned. Schäfer had already made one or two trips to Tibet, chiefly for zoological and botanical research, and I had read his accounts of them. He was consequently no stranger to me. I had not known, on the other hand, that his expedition had been under Himmler's patronage and still less that the Reichsführer SS took such a keen and enlightened interest in the snow-lands north of the Himalayas. He told me now that Schäfer and his companions had spent forty days in Lhasa and had brought back from their travels, among other things, a successful film. Himmler was eager that I should see this film and give my opinion on it.

Anthropology and ethnography were of central importance to a Nazi ideology obsessed with race. Nineteenth-century German scholars had speculated that a light-skinned group of warriors in Tibet might have been the original source of the Aryan 'race'. Although appearing some-what banal in conversation, Himmler was in fact an obsessive mystic and fascinated by the Tibetan link. In 1935 he had set up the Ahnenerbe or Ancestral Heritage Organization, a research institute to study Aryan origins. Some of this research was undertaken by Dr Ernst Schäfer, a young German anthropologist and captain in the SS, who studied the mathematics of racial difference. As early as 1937 Schäfer had expressed enthusiasm for the ideals of the SS, and in 1938 Himmler had despatched him on an expedition to Tibet looking for relics of the lost Aryan precursors. This mission was the inspiration for Steven Spielberg's film Raiders of the Lost Ark, *starring Harrison Ford. However, in reality Schäfer was also engaged in secret efforts to use Abwehr (counter-intelligence) agents to encourage tribal revolt on the North-West Frontier of British India.*

Sven Hedin's diary claims that at his meeting with Himmler in 1940 he complained about the treatment of Jews in Poland. Sven Hedin was partly Jewish himself, and although his sympathy for Nazism was driven mostly by anti-Soviet feeling, nevertheless this section of his diary seems to be of dubious authenticity. His diary would be published in 1949 by Euphorion books in Dublin, which had been set up by Oswald Mosley to publish far-right material that British publishers would not touch after the war. At the time of his death in 1952 Hedin remained unapologetic about his contact with the Nazis.

Monday 25 – Tuesday 26 March 1940

Major Daniel Barlone admires the British and French forces waiting in France

25 March

Yesterday was Easter Day. Fine football matches between British and French military teams at the stadium of Valenciennes. Crowds present. The bands of the Welsh and Scottish regiments have a well-deserved success with their precise and rhythmic movements. They give an impression of calm, of finish, of will-power which reflect the qualities of Britain. The Highlanders, with their green bag-pipes, short kilts, dark jackets and bonnets, present a picture of beautifully blended colours. Our team of dragoons beats the Welsh by one goal to nil. The 11th Zouaves have a drawn game with the Scots. To-day the team selected from the division has beaten that of the Valenciennes Athletic Club by one goal to nil . . .

26 March

. . . A night manoeuvre by the 11th Zouaves in which I participate with a part of the company. At the starting-point, where all the regiment has to march past at a given time, I meet General Dame and his Staff. The soldiers, relieved of their packs, which are carried on the transport wagons, march by briskly and alertly in files, one on each side of the road. Each battalion takes 12 to 14 minutes to pass accompanied by their lovely police-dogs leashed in pairs and so intelligent looking. The dogs have daily training in message carrying from point to point. After the infantry come a group of the 40th Artillery, half French, half Algerian. They also have their liaison dogs, which they carry in travelling cages.

Behind these come the Anti-Tank Defence Battalion, with their very modern-looking guns, low mounted on rubber tyres. The battalion commander, Captain Marcel, has just returned from the camp at Mailly, where the gun-layers have shown themselves to be first-class with 96 per cent of the shells on the mark; five out of six reached 100 per cent on moving targets. This is thanks to the daily training which they undergo in all weathers and over all types of ground. If all commanding officers are like him, what splendid results we will get! The new guns at 1200 yards range will penetrate three normal plates of German tank armour spaced an inch or so apart. If the army had these guns in sufficient numbers, Marcel told me, not a single tank could reach our lines.

Not everyone shared the optimism of Daniel Barlone. German armour, used in combination with air power, would soon create havoc in the French lines. General Charles de Gaulle, in command of most of his country's army, was beginning to discover that despite having mobilized 5 million

men France was woefully short of both aircraft and tanks. Meanwhile the
determination to fight was growing on all sides, and on 28 March Britain
and France agreed that neither would make a separate peace with
Germany.

After the armistice of June 1940 Barlone would escape to Dunkirk.
Curiously, he then opted to return to France briefly via Cherbourg, before
escaping again, to north Africa, and eventually joining de Gaulle and the
Free French. SEE ALSO PP. 72–3.

APRIL 1940

ON 9 APRIL Germany invaded Denmark and Norway. This widening of the conflict signalled the end of the phoney war, or what some had come to refer to as the 'Great Bore War'. Although the Germans suffered losses, including the sinking of the heavy cruiser *Blücher* as she made her way up the Oslo Fjord, they secured control of the vital air bases. As so often, the German offensive had been well planned: these air bases proved critical as the campaign developed. The German navy fared badly, with nine destroyers sunk at close quarters in the port of Narvik as the result of dramatic action by British destroyers. However, by the end of the month British and French forces in Norway were in retreat, despite the fact that they outnumbered the Germans. On the last day of April, King Haakon of Norway and his government were evacuated by a British cruiser, together with all the Norwegian gold reserves.

War in the air was still the aspect of the conflict that caused most anxiety among civilians. Before September 1940 there were only limited air attacks on British cities, and air-raid shelters were not well organized. Shelter policy was a matter of fierce public debate. In March 1940 the government had begun a programme of building larger shelters in cities, each designed to protect around fifty people living in the same street. Constructed from brick and concrete they provided a higher level of protection than the domestic 'Anderson' shelters in people's back gardens, made out of steel sheets and first introduced in February 1939. However, there was a severe shortage of building materials, and this slowed down the building of the larger shelters. By now, worries about gas attack had abated and few people carried their gas masks as a matter of routine.

April 1940 was the last full month of the Chamberlain government. Neville Chamberlain appointed the press baron Lord Beaverbrook as Minister of Aircraft Production. This move underlined the drift towards a total war that would eventually be won by industrial capacity. Rationing continued to intensify, and restrictions on petrol for civilians saw the use of private cars dwindle virtually to nothing.

Tuesday 9 April 1940

Anthony Weymouth, in the Talks Department of the BBC, responds to news that the Germans have invaded Denmark and Norway

At seven minutes past eight, when I was still in bed, the telephone rang, and I was asked by an official of the BBC whether I had listened to the eight o'clock news. I hadn't.

'Well,' said the voice, 'Germany has invaded Denmark; and Norway and Germany are at war.'

I said I would dress and get in a taxi: which, after a hasty cup of coffee, I did.

A conference on what to do in the matter of talks and discussions. The first conclusion we arrived at was to the effect that the existing discussion must be shelved, and in its place we must have one on Denmark and Norway.

The international situation of the past year or two has made it imperative for the BBC to know where they can lay their hands at once on authoritative speakers on almost every subject to do with geography, history, economics, politics, and so on. The man for this discussion was obviously Bjarne Brattoy, a Norwegian journalist, born in America and now correspondent of a Swedish newspaper – a man who has an intimate knowledge of these countries.

I telephoned to him, and he told me that as soon as he had finished the article on which he was engaged he would come to Broadcasting House.

At twelve o'clock precisely we sat down, with a map of Scandinavia on the wall and a typist at the table. We dictated our discussion straight on to the typewriter. At two o'clock we took the script to a rehearsal studio, and at 2.30 we went on the air. I am quite sure that these discussions are the easiest way to learn geography, and I do not mean only for myself (though this is quite true), but for the listener; for the questions are designed to be those which the average man with only an average knowledge of the subject is asking himself as he reads the news.

The afternoon programme, 'In England Now,' had to be altered at the last minute, for no listener overseas would, in view of this important news, have wanted to hear the programme we had planned. So in the morning we had telephoned to a journalist and asked him to walk round London and pick up the reactions to the German invasion of Denmark and Norway. He produced a most interesting account of the Londoner trying to understand the swift move of events. Most of the people he spoke to were of the same mind – that it was a good thing the deadlock had come to an end, and that this time Hitler had bitten off more than he could chew.

The BBC had been set up in 1927 as a broadcasting monopoly, run by a board of governors and a director-general. Then as now, it was a public service broadcasting organization funded by a licence fee at a rate set by Parliament. Although it was experimenting with television in the late 1930s, this project was put into mothballs at the start of the war while the BBC focused on provision of a wartime radio Home Service, which replaced the peacetime national and regional programming. The BBC was still a very formal organization in which all announcers wore dinner jackets while on air, and the new service was initially filled with organ recitals and serious public announcements. By April 1940, however, the Corporation had launched its more popular 'Forces' programme for the troops in France, and the informal style of these broadcasts would be the model for the future. SEE ALSO PP. 97–9, 101–2 AND 206–8.

Saturday 13 – Tuesday 30 April 1940

Arthur Turner on HMS *Hero* takes part in the Second Battle of Narvik

Arthur Turner was born in Coventry in 1909 and had joined the Royal Navy as a 'boy 2nd class' at the age of fifteen. By 1940 he was serving as a rating on the destroyer HMS Hero *during fearless attacks on the German navy during the Second Battle of Narvik. Like many of the ratings on the destroyers that fought at Narvik, he had not seen serious action before and was amazed by the resulting destruction.*

13 April

'Hero' became 'Guide of the Fleet' and with [the destroyers] 'Icarus', 'Foxhound' and 'Forester' swept the channel for mines starting at 0530. All hands closed up about 0515. Weather was very cold, slight mist and snowing at intervals. The entrance to the Fiord was very narrow with snow covered mountains on either side.

It looked very beautiful and it was difficult to realise that hell would let loose within a few hours.

10.50 Battle Ensigns were hoisted and we entered the Fiord.

11.00 Submarine reported by 'Eskimo'. Depth charges were dropped to keep her down while we passed. The hills were scanned for land batteries but the only sign of life was a group of Norwegians waving their caps and cheering.

12.25 Enemy in sight. One destroyer coming towards us out of the mist.

12.30 'Forester' and 'Foxhound' opened fire and enemy destroyers withdrew. A minute later the mist lifted and more enemy destroyers were sighted and engaged. Land batteries opened up and 'Warspite' engaged with 15" [gun]. She destroyed two with three salvos. By now the mist had lifted altogether and Narvik was in sight.

12.55 Torpedo fired at us and missed.

13.35 'Hero' stopped to get in provisions and immediately came under heavy fire from the enemy who must have thought we were damaged. We were continually straddled; the extreme range probably saved us from a direct hit. During this period 'Foxhound' was slightly damaged.

One German destroyer suddenly burst into flames. Another with smoke coming from her engine room was aground. Her aft gun kept firing so 'Warspite' blew her out of existence with the first salvo.

14.22 The enemy retired up Rombako Fiord under cover of a smoke screen.

The next destroyer which we were engaging was seen to receive several direct hits. She stopped and the crew abandoned ship. Attention was then turned to the remaining shore batteries.

14.23 'Eskimo', 'Forester' and 'Hero' followed the enemy into Rombako Fiord. The entrance was barely 50 yards wide, so we could enter only one at time. 'Eskimo' entered first and reported two destroyers which she engaged. 'Forester' followed and opened fire as soon as she was clear of the hillside. We could only get our bows into the fiord, as it was only 3000 yards long and 300 wide. Only one enemy was in sight, the other having retired round the corner at the end of the Fiord.

14.52 The enemy destroyer fired six torpedoes, then beached herself and the crew abandoned ship. Forester was able to dodge, but 'Eskimo' was unable to swing for lack of room. A sheet of flame shot up from 'Eskimo', and her bows disappeared. B gun's crew, with the bow shot away beneath them, continued to fire. They deserved the cheer we gave them.

15.00 We entered the Fiord and allowed 'Eskimo' to retire.

15.10 Aircraft from 'Warspite' reported three more German destroyers round the corner. 'Hero' took the lead to investigate, being cheered by 'Eskimo' and 'Forester' as we passed them.

One destroyer was sighted which we immediately engaged. No reply came from the enemy so we went right round the bend, 'Icarus' and 'Kimberley' coming up astern in support. After a few rounds the ships were observed to be sinking and their crews abandoned ship and commenced to climb the hills.

Shortly afterwards two of the three destroyers sank. The third remained afloat with fire raging beneath the depth charges.

16.15. 'Hero' sent a boarding party to the remaining destroyer. She was the 'Hans Ludeman'. Many articles of German kit were brought back. One of the boarding party entered the Wireless Office and saw the two operators sitting by their desks with their heads blown off. He decided not to investigate the office further. One wounded man was brought back to 'Hero' but he died later and was buried at sea.

17.20 Fired a torpedo into 'Hans Ludeman' and commenced to retire out of Narvik.

17.45 to 19.30 Four enemy aircraft alarms no bombs dropped. The following seven large German destroyers were sunk during the action:- 'Drether von Roker', 'Hans Ludeman', 'Wolfgang Zenker', 'Bernard von Arnia', 'Erich Koellmer', 'Hermann Kunne', 'Erich Giese'.

14 April
Re-entered Narvik and bombarded shore positions and took on board survivors from 'Hardy'. We then carried out patrols until we left for Scapa a fortnight later.

28 April
Arrived Scapa. Snowing and Blowing like blazes.

29 April
Left Scapa for Greenock.

30 April

Arrived Greenock. During the afternoon a terrific explosion was heard and it was found that the French destroyer 'Maille Breze' was on fire. A torpedo had left her tubes and exploded under her bridge. The fire trapped many of the crew who were sleeping on the mess deck. Boats from all ships went out to the rescue but nothing could be done as the portholes were too small to get through.

Through each porthole a man's head was showing. Their cries and screams were terrible as they slowly burned to death, and all we could do was watch.

(The Admiralty has since ordered all destroyers to be fitted with escape ports forward and aft).

Arthur Turner

When Germany invaded, Denmark capitulated at once, but Norway fought on against landings at many of its major ports. In the First Battle of Narvik on 10 April a flotilla of British destroyers sank two German destroyers and damaged another five, also sinking six supply ships. Although the British had lost two destroyers in this engagement they returned with a stronger force on 13 April using the battleship HMS Warspite *and several destroyers, including* Hero. *Pushing up the fjord and risking air attack, they engaged seven German destroyers at short range to great effect. However, Germany was consolidating on land elsewhere in Norway and the strengthening German air power eventually forced the British and French to withdraw their troops.*

The French ship Maillé Brézé, berthed at Greenock, was a large destroyer, almost a cruiser, and a relatively new vessel, commissioned in 1933. On 30 April the safety mechanism failed on her torpedo tubes and a torpedo slithered along the main deck, hitting part of the bridge structure. The explosion wrecked the whole forepart of the ship, and set fire to the fuel oil and everything combustible, including, eventually, the forward magazine. She eventually sank. The incident left thirty-eight dead and forty-eight wounded.

We have no record of whether Arthur Turner survived the war.

Saturday 20 April 1940

Howard Clegg prepares for action in Norway, but then is stood down

Howard Clegg was a young married apple-farmer living at Ganges harbour near Vancouver on the west coast of Canada. His apple business produced 4 million apples per year, about half of which were sent to Europe, and he resented Hitler's activities on economic as well as political grounds. In 1939 many of his young friends had joined up even before war was declared and he felt 'left at the post'. By the end of September 1939 he had joined Princess Patricia's Canadian Light Infantry – a regiment formed in 1914, shortly after Canada's entry into the First World War. Its founder, Lt-Col. Francis Farquhar, DSO, sought and gained the permission of the Governor-General, the Duke of Connaught, to name the regiment after the Duke's daughter, Princess Patricia of Connaught, who was highly regarded in Canada because of her appreciation of the country's landscape and people. After training at Work Point Barracks, Esquimalt, he set sail for Europe on 22 December 1939 and the following spring found himself in Scotland awaiting deployment to fight in Norway.

We drew more and more equipment this morning – rubber
boots, ankle high; wool gauntlet mittens with a thumb and
first finger separately provided for.

An hour before lunch we paraded in our landing equipment, with ammunition and arms.

The Colonel inspected each man. He found that I for one
was carrying too many rounds, that I had the special cotton
bandoliers slung over my webbing instead of under (I had
forgotten till after I was dressed about this additional
trapping – containing fifty rounds of emergency ammunition), and told me to demonstrate how I proposed to
relieve myself of all my equipment in one motion if my landing barge or boat or whatever should be sunk under me. I
said, 'It couldn't be done, sir.' Whereupon he told me to
remove the bandolier, undo the belt and straps of my
webbing, and let my equipment hang loose, as I would have
it on the barge. This I did. 'Now let me see you get out of it
in one motion,' he said. I did.

Now he knows that I can do it, and that should mean that
everyone can. But he did suggest to the O.C. that we were
carrying too much ammunition – 'unless you have mighty
strong men.' The O.C. ordered a reduction. As a matter of
fact, I think the N.C.O.'s gave us each a hundred rounds
more than the O.C. intended. But it was all a very happy
ending, for I for one was worried about the fatigue of storming a sloping shore with so much weight aboard. We do, of
course, have to consider the possibility of our party being
cut off and having to hold out for a considerable time. Too
many rounds may be a lesser worry than too few.

We are taking iron rations for forty-eight hours against
this possibility. Nothing but rations in our haversacks –
rations and socks – not even a razor or a toothbrush.

We have a very strange look. Quite the appearance of
warriors in that ancient period when warriors wore flat helmets like our little battle bowlers and chain-mail head
protection like our Balaclava caps – coats of mail down to the
thighs like our leather jerkins. This outfit – helmet, balaclava,
jerkin over battle dress, webbing (including four large pouches
of ammunition), a water-bottle, haversack on back, rifle,
bayonet, and service knife – is our order for landing. Were it

not for the great weight of our ammunition we should, for the first time, feel like 'Light Infantry.'

The weighty back pack, sleeping-bag, etc., are in the second and third echelon, coming ashore later.

Howard Clegg was excited to be in the company allocated the task of being first ashore, having excelled on manoeuvres. But after their infinitely detailed preparations – including making their own 'Death's Head' flag to carry ashore when storming the beach – they were stood down as the Norwegian campaign faltered under the pressure of poor Allied organization and massive Axis air power. SEE ALSO PP. 194–5.

Tuesday 23 April 1940

John Davies gets ready to pay the real cost of war

In 1940 John Davies, originally from Dolwyddelan in north Wales, was a lecturer teaching at the Technical School in Liverpool. His diary covers the period from September 1939 to December 1940, and consists mostly of brief summaries of national and international news for each day. But it also contains some personal observations about lighting restrictions, gas masks, rationing and tax.

Today the Budget is introduced. A new tax, introduced by Sir John Simon [the Chancellor], is the new Purchase tax, whereby everybody in the country will be forced to pay his share of the costs of the war. By means of this tax everything we buy will be taxed 2½%, i.e., everything, except those articles already heavily taxed, and food, drink and services like gas and electricity.

The letter post goes up from 1½d. to 2½d. and Post Cards from 1d. to 1½d. Telephone charges are increased, and beer, tobacco and cigarettes. 8½d. each for a packet of 10 cigarettes instead of the prewar 6d. is pretty stiff, and 3d. on an ounce of tobacco.

It is essentially a 'pay to victory' budget, and people

accept it as National duty. At least it is an attempt to pay our way, thus obviating the necessity of resorting to borrowing, the folly of which was seen after the last war.

Sir John Simon has estimated the war will cost some £2,000,000,000 by the end of next March.

'Fear of falling' was a major factor underpinning the British government's search for appeasement in 1938 and 1939. Many in the British Cabinet were anxious to avoid not only a repeat of the terrible human casualties of the First World War, but also the economic damage it caused. Some believed it would be the end of the British Empire, and all believed that Britain would emerge from a war owing the United States colossal sums. In some respects they were right. By 1945, the UK national debt would stand at £21 billion.

MAY 1940

MAY 1940 WAS one of the most eventful months of the war. The Norwegian campaign, although successful in parts, was clearly being directed in an amateur way. On 10 May Winston Churchill replaced the exhausted and widely discredited Chamberlain as Prime Minister and formed a coalition government. Lord Halifax, the Foreign Secretary, might have been the preferred choice of leader for many, but it was felt that the Prime Minister must sit in the Commons. On the same day German forces began their attack in the west against neutral Belgium and Holland. On 14 May Rotterdam was very heavily bombed by 900 aircraft even before a German surrender deadline had expired.

Within a few days French forces collapsed under the onslaught of the German panzers. By 15 May the French Prime Minister, Paul Reynaud, had all but accepted defeat. Privately, the British Cabinet had begun to give up on France and decided to send no more precious fighter aircraft across the Channel. By 18 May the British commander in France, General Gort, realized that he had no choice but to order a headlong retreat to the French coast and to attempt evacuation by sea from the beaches of Dunkirk. On 22 May Churchill was in Paris attempting to persuade the French to counter-attack, but it was clear that they had few reserves left and more importantly, no will to resist.

On 26 May orders were given to begin Operation Dynamo, the evacuation from Dunkirk. On 31 May alone 68,000 troops were evacuated. During the last days of May and the first days of June some 225,000 British and some 160,000 French troops escaped capture in this way. General Alan Brooke, commander of II Corps, was one of those to escape. General Ironside wrote in his diary, 'I still cannot understand how it is that the [Germans] have allowed us to get [our troops] off in this way. It is almost fantastic that we have been able to do it in the face of all the bombing and gunning.' In fact, it is likely that Hitler ordered a halt to his tanks some way off Dunkirk because of anxieties about the flat boggy land. Some believe he was still hoping to reach an accommodation with the British before beginning his attack on Russia.

On the home front, Britain began to form the Local Defence Volunteers or 'Parashots' – soon to be rechristened the Home Guard. On Tuesday 14 May Anthony Eden appealed on the six o'clock news for men between the ages of seventeen and sixty-five to form anti-paratroop units to guard local key points of strategic importance. The response was amazing. By the beginning of June 400,000 men had joined and by late July the force numbered no fewer than 1,300,000. The government had originally expected about a quarter of a million to come forward. The numbers would peak at 1,793,000 in 1943. It is rarely realized that their main role was anti-aircraft duties, or that there was a women's section – the Home Guard Auxiliaries – that numbered around 30,000. Meanwhile the WVS was preoccupied with 20,000 refugees from France and the Low Countries.

'Fifth columnists' or enemy sympathizers were thought to be widespread and draconian emergency regulations were passed to allow their detention. Churchill issued his famous 'Collar the Lot' order and most German nationals, regardless of their political persuasion, were rounded up and interned; among them were many fervent anti-Nazis and German Jews who had fled Hitler. Using Defence Regulations 18B, the arrest and internment of fascists in Britain was also stepped up. Sir Oswald Mosley, the leader of the

British fascists in the 1930s, was detained. Nevertheless, numerous members of the establishment who were known to be sympathetic to Germany were left at large.

Sunday 12 May 1940

Harry Seidler, an anti-Nazi refugee from Germany, finds himself interned

Harry Seidler was born in Vienna in 1923, the younger of two sons in a middle-class family. In March 1938 the arrival of Hitler's troops in Austria had prompted his flight at the age of fifteen. His family had arranged for him to be looked after by Edith, Lady MacAlister in Cambridge, where he had completed a building course at the Technical College.

Harry Seidler

Today was the most dreadful day that I ever experienced in England. The whole thing began in the afternoon. I got home at lunchtime and Lady MacAlister told me that a policeman had been there and wanted to see me. As I wasn't there, he said that I should come to the police station immediately. At first I thought it was something to do with my post.

Straight after lunch I went to the police with no idea of what awaited me there! I noticed that there were several other refugees as well as me. They told us that we would be taken to the Guildhall – why, they didn't say. So, five of us were put in a police car and off we went to the Town Hall. There were two plain-clothes policemen in the car with us.

At the Town Hall there was already quite a crowd of Germans, almost all of whom I knew, at least by sight. Only now did I begin to understand what it meant – WE WERE ALL TO BE INTERNED. I was greatly upset by this and then also noticed that we were under guard. All the exits were guarded by policemen. There were about 100–150 people in the hall and every couple of minutes new people were brought in. It was now about 2.30. I started to think over the whole situation. INTERNED. I was immediately convinced that the new government must have done this. That meant that they thought we refugees were spies, or believed that there were spies among us. Us – spies! Isn't that ridiculous? We, exiled from Germany, are suspected of being spies for our deadly enemies! Nevertheless the situation seemed quite serious. We were being watched and were considered dangerous. If you tried to talk to the policemen, you got no information – they knew nothing.

Some people began to work out all the things that they wanted to have with them. They even began to send us home one by one, under guard, so that we could pack some necessary things. I worked out what I wanted, too, and then I had to wait. At last, at 5, my name was called. A plain-clothes policeman came with me; another refugee who lived near me came in the same car.

I asked the policeman to wait in the hall while I packed my bag, but he said that he had to go everywhere with me, that he could not let me out of his sight. Isn't that something to make you laugh? Or should it make you cry? He had to guard me as if I were a criminal, so I wouldn't escape. The situation embarrassed me. Here was Lady MacAlister and everyone else in the house and my every move was being followed by a policeman! I packed all my things and said good-bye to Lady MacAlister; then we drove back to the Town Hall. There were far fewer people there now: all the others had already been taken away. I had to wait again.

We left about 7. We were now only about 50 people and we were loaded into a double-decker bus. None of us knew where we were going. We chatted, told each other jokes and forgot that we were prisoners. At 8.30 we arrived at Bury St Edmunds. Here we parked in a street and saw two other buses in front of us in which were all the other refugees who had arrived earlier. The streets were full of inquisitive spectators and now we had a military guard. A soldier stood in the doorway of each of the three buses with a fixed bayonet. If you wanted to get off the bus for a few minutes, you had to do so under military guard. This amused the spectators on the streets. And we waited . . .

About 10 we became impatient – we all wanted to go to bed – but that would not be possible for some time. It was dark and hours went by and they seemed to have forgotten about us. In this situation you get terribly tired. This morning we would never have believed that in the evening we would no longer be free and would be prisoners of the English. Time passed dreadfully slowly. We were hungry and tired. It was 11, 12 . . .

Harry Seidler and his brother were interned as part of the 'fifth column' panic in May 1940 when it was expected that Germany would attempt to invade Britain. Not quite everyone was caught in the net – anti-Nazi Germans with good society connections escaped internment – but some who had been in Britain for over thirty years and could not even speak German found themselves behind the wire. After being moved to a camp at Huyton in Liverpool, Seidler was interned on the Isle of Man. Germans had been interned here during the First World War, and the same procedure was followed in 1940. Existing property, mostly requisitioned bed-and-breakfast houses or hotels, were cordoned off and used as a series of 'camps'. Different camps catered for different nationalities – women and children were housed around Port Erin and Port St Mary in the south, to which access from the rest of the island was controlled; British fascists and Italians were interned at Peel; and a section of central Douglas promenade was cordoned off for use as a series of male camps. SEE ALSO PP. 190–2 AND 342–4.

Tuesday 14 May 1940

Sir John Colville, private secretary to Winston Churchill,
surveys the Prime Minister's night-working arrangements

*Jock Colville served as one of Winston Churchill's private secretaries
during the war and came to know him extremely well.*

After dinner I went to Admiralty House, where Winston
proposes to work at night. He has fitted up the ground floor
for this purpose: the dining room in which the private
secretary and one of Winston's specially trained night-
women-typists sit; the lovely drawing room with its curious
ugly dolphin furniture, which is used as a kind of
promenade; and an inner room in which the Great Man himself sits. At the side of his desk stands a table laden with
bottles of whisky, etc. On the desk itself are all manner of
things: toothpicks, gold medals (which he uses as paper-
weights), special cuffs to save his coatsleeves from becoming
dirty, and innumerable pills and powders.

*Churchill's night-time working habits exhausted his colleagues and
became notorious. Colville would obtain Churchill's permission to join
the RAF in 1944, but after only a few weeks as a fighter pilot he was
recalled to duty in the Prime Minister's office. SEE ALSO P. 829.*

A British intelligence officer watches the German advance at Sedan

*The author of this excellent diary was an army officer appointed to serve
in air intelligence liaison under the GHQ Military Adviser, Col. J.
Woodhall, on the staff of Air Marshal Sir A. S. Barratt, who was
Commander-in-Chief of the British air forces in France during 1939–40.
He chose to publish his journal almost immediately and it appeared in*

1941, quickly going through six impressions. However, as he continued to serve in the army and diary-keeping was an offence, publication was anonymous; his identity remains a mystery.

1415 hours. The French counter-attack at SEDAN was delayed 30 minutes. A fatal pause. The Germans have meanwhile delivered a further stroke and have widened the gap on either side by 3 miles each way and have penetrated forward 3 miles into open country. The French have lost the whole of their artillery.

Not so very long ago I went right through the fortifications on this front and estimated that a well-organised and determined resistance would cost the Germans half a million casualties if they were to break through. And what has happened? The Germans have walked through 5 miles of fortifications in depth with a loss of probably 500 men. It appears that as the SEDAN sector was considered so strong the most inferior of the French divisions were posted there to hold it. They were mostly Parisians and their morale of the very lowest order. When the dive-bombers came down on them they stood the noise – there were hardly any casualties – for only 2 hours, and then they bolted out with their hands over their ears like a lot of frightened old ladies. One cannot be surprised at the tears of the General Staff.

The French army was dogged by out-of-date operational doctrine and an absurdly complex decision-making process with far too many levels of command. There was also an overlapping of responsibilities and a lack of centralized intelligence. Tragically, the French had ample armour to repulse the Germans in this sector but simply could not organize themselves. The German breakthrough at Sedan was psychologically critical, and thereafter high-ranking officers shifted from the absurd self-confidence of the phoney war to abject defeatism.

Thursday 16 May 1940

General Sir Otto Marling Lund travels with Churchill to
see the French

*Otto Lund was born in 1891 and joined the Royal Artillery in 1911.
Having fought in the First World War he then went on to take part in
the British Expeditionary Force deployment to Russia in 1919. By
September 1939 he had become Deputy Director of Military Operations
at the War Office, one of the key staff appointments. In May 1940 he
accompanied Churchill on a visit to meet Paul Reynaud, the French
Prime Minister, Edouard Daladier, now the Minister of War, and
General Gamelin, the senior French commander.*

We took a Flamingo, our escorts were three Spitfires, and as
the usual route had not yet been closed, we went by
Shoreham, Treport and Paris.

Winston's flying technique is very interesting and it never
varies. On this occasion, as on all others, he first put on his
overcoat, then he got in the plane. Then he wrapped a rug
round his legs, took something black out of his pocket,
removed his hat and sat down. The black thing turned out to
be a woollen band which he put on top of his head, as you
would wear a crown, and then he had a good look round.
The first time I saw the thing perched on his head, I could
not for the life of me think what it was, and knowing his
passion for odd hats, I thought it was a special flying con-
trivance. Not at all. The moment we were up in the air, he
pulled it down over his eyes, and went fast asleep, at once.
He has that great blessing – he can sleep at any time, anywhere; so many great men have had this in common . . . The
moment we touched ground, he woke up and Sir Ronald
Campbell, who met us, drove us to the British Embassy,
where Lady Campbell offered us tea. Winston looked aghast
at the suggestion; Sir Ronald ordered whisky and soda, and
then we went straight off to the Quai d'Orsay [the French
Foreign Office] . . .
We were shewn into Reynaud's study and with him were

Daladier and Gamelin, both of whom looked saturated with gloom and depression. Gamelin was Dejection personified. Reynaud not so.

The room was arranged in a rather surprising way; in the middle was a large easel with a big map of France on it. By the side of it stood the interpreter, in front, four very superior gold chairs. Behind the chairs was Reynaud's desk and out of the windows to the right I could always see the little man running to and fro, madly burning the archives. In the first chair Gamelin sat himself, then Daladier, Winston, and on the outside Reynaud, all facing the map and the interpreter, like a lot of schoolboys. Ismay [War Cabinet Secretary] and I stood behind, but finally got tired and sat ourselves on the edge of Reynaud's desk. The procedure at these meetings with the French was always the same. We would start off very correctly with an interpreter and by keeping minutes. Winston would stick this for just about a quarter of an hour, and then his impatience would break through – he would start to declaim in the most astounding and surprising French, waving his hands and repeating time after time, a particularly pleasing phrase that he would get hold of, so literal a translation of the English was it that even I could understand it. The accent had to be heard to be believed. I found it most enjoyable. After Winston's break through the whole thing would become entirely unorthodox.

On this occasion Winston ran true to form; in no time the interpreter, a very good one, was discarded. The Prime Minister must have sensed immediately the defeatist attitude of Daladier and Gamelin, and his irritation was slowly mounting. Among his many attributes, first place must surely be given to his mental attitude towards disaster. It is the bravest I know. The worse things go, the more pugnacious and aggressive he becomes. On this occasion his theory, quite rightly was that of ATTACK! 'Attack! attack! attack! That's what we must do. Attack! What did it matter if the French had had a slight (! tactful) reverse on the Meuse? Fill up the gap with Reserves. What did a slight reverse matter? Attack all the time. We could do the same in Belgium. Attack! They must pull up their socks!' And then he got hold of an expression which so fascinated him that he repeated it over and over again. 'Our Air Force will nettoye le ciel' and he waved his hands with a broad sweeping gesture. 'Nettoye le ciel, comprennez vous, nettoye le ciel, and the French must, in co-operation with us, attack and attack again and again. That was the thing. Nettoye le ciel and attack and fill up the gap with Reserves.'

When this tirade was over, Reynaud said he quite agreed. He still seemed to have a lot of drive left in him, and struck me as being the best of the three Frenchmen. Gamelin then made his only contribution to the meeting, historic, in my opinion. 'We have no reserves. There is nothing between Paris and the leading elements of the German Armoured Divisions.' No more and no less, and no mean contribution from one on whose shoulders rested a major part of the responsibility. Already in his mind he was defeated . . .

. . . I looked at Winston; his face had that bull dog look on it and he growled, a habit he has when things of a startling nature are handed out to him . . .

. . . To hear that the French had no reserves was a shock, to say the least of it. I had always suspected it to be so, but how could I have really known? Certainly not through the way Ironside had behaved. We had been fed on the glorious might of the French Army; there were supposed to be millions of soldiers to hold the enemy. To be told that there were no reserves was indeed a setback of the first magnitude.

As I said, Winston took it quite calmly, growled, and began to ask some pertinent questions about the 9th Army under General Corap. Where was it? In what state was it? Incredible as it may sound, it seemed that it had disappeared; no one knew where it was! So then we discussed the best thing to do.

Churchill met with the French again on 22 May, by which time it was clear that the situation was completely hopeless. Although he had failed to inspire the French to greater military efforts, these visits did permit the Prime Minister to gain a very personal and graphic appreciation of the real situation, allowing him to plan accordingly. After the war

Lund would use his specialism in artillery, becoming Director Royal Artillery, War Office, 1944–6 and General Officer Commanding-in-Chief, Anti-Aircraft Command, 1946–8. He died in August 1956.

Monday 20 May 1940

General Edmund Ironside realizes that the French generals are now mentally beaten

We arranged to get the 50th Division and 5th Division down towards Arras. Also the 44th Division on our extreme left to be relieved by the Belgians. This would make a beginning towards facing the gap in the south. I then went down the Béthune to find General Billotte, the C-in-C of the Armies in the North. The road's an indescribable mass of refugees, both Belgian and French, moving down in every kind of conveyance. Poor women pushing perambulators, horsed wagons with all the family and its goods in it. Belgian units all going along aimlessly. Poor devils. It was a horrible sight and it blocked the roads, which was the main difficulty. I then found Billotte and Blanchard at Lens (1st Army), all in a state of complete depression. No plan, no thought of a plan. Ready to be slaughtered. Defeated at the head without casualties. *Très fatigués* and nothing doing.

I lost my temper and shook Billotte by the button of his tunic. The man is completely beaten. I got him to agree [to a plan] and Blanchard [Commander of the French 1st Army] accepted to take Cambrai. There is absolutely nothing in front of them. They remain quivering behind the water-line north of Cambrai while the fate of France is in the balance. Gort told me when I got back to his Headquarters that they would never attack.

On 20 May General Heinz Guderian's XIX Corps took Amiens and then Abbéville. Meanwhile, last-minute changes of command at the top of the French forces exacerbated growing tensions in the lower echelons of the army. At the same time the 7th Panzer Division was advancing under General Erwin Rommel. Rommel, born in 1891, was a professional soldier who had served in the First World War and remained in the army after 1918. During the inter-war years he taught in a military academy and the publication of his lectures on strategy brought him to Hitler's attention, ensuring his promotion in the late 1930s. Although his advance on Arras was halted by a British tank attack on 21 May, the success was not exploited and the Allied retreat continued.

Ironside would retire in late 1940. SEE ALSO PP. 129–30.

Sergeant L. D. Pexton of the British Expeditionary Force in France is taken prisoner

Refugees still coming through from somewhere. Saw two men running down the road. Refugees said they were parachutists. Captain Martin and myself called on them to halt but they didn't. Not immediately. Dropped them. Both dead when we got to them. 10 a.m. Fun began. Germans came from nowhere. Properly surprised us. Got down to it in the open and fought for all we knew how. Getting wiped out this time all right. Got back out of the farm buildings, and he's sending everything he has at us. 11 a.m. Still holding out and there's a bit of a lull. Kid on my right will keep sticking his head up above the clover. He's sure to get his soon, I'm thinking. Can't really remember much about the next hour. Remember the order 'cease fire' and that the time was 12 o'clock. Stood up and put my hands up. My God, how few of us stood up. German officer came and spoke in English. Told us to pick up the wounded and carry them to the road. There aren't many that need carrying. We have to leave our dead. Took us off the road into another field. I expected my last moments had come and lit a fag. Everyone expected to be shot there and then. Patched up our wounded as best we could and were taken back about two miles. Stayed the night in a Roman Catholic church. Learned this village is called Ficheaux. Note: out of appr. 1,400 men only 425 spent the night in this church.

Pexton's unit had been fighting in the areas around Cambrai and Arras, familiar battlegrounds of the First World War, as part of a British effort that halted Rommel's division for some time. Eventually they succumbed to superior German numbers and air support and took heavy casualties. Pexton, aged 24, would become prisoner 8806 in Stalag XXA (17). Like many prisoners, both British and French, he eventually found himself employed as a farm labourer in Germany. Although this was technically illegal under the Geneva Convention it probably offered the POWs better conditions than they would otherwise have had.

Thursday 23 – Friday 24 May 1940

Henry 'Chips' Channon MP buries his diary near his home at Kelvedon in Essex

Henry 'Chips' Channon was a wealthy American-born British politician and socialite. A junior minister at the Foreign Office, he was also a superb diarist, and his writings offer a fabulous inside view of the political circles around Chamberlain and Halifax. With the prospect of German invasion looming closer, the question was, what to do with these potentially revealing diaries?

23 May

Honor and I have decided to bury my diaries in the church-yard; Mortimer has promised to dig a hole tomorrow evening after the other gardeners have gone home: perhaps some future generations will dig them up.

The news on the radio was grave. Winston announced to the House that Abbeville had fallen and that Boulogne was the scene of a great battle . . . It is maddening not to be in the House in these momentous days . . .

The roar of planes immediately overhead woke me; and I counted 21 fighters rushing towards the coast: they were barely over the tree-tops. The war is at our door.

24 May

This evening we buried two tin boxes three feet below the

earth's surface in the little churchyard under a tree near the brick wall – the West wall, which divides the churchyard from Honor's private garden. The larger, lower, box contains my diaries, the smaller box my best bibelots, watches, Fabergé objects, etc. Mortimer, who dug the hole, is discreet, and he waited until all the gardeners had gone home; we watched the earth cover them over; may they sleep in peace. Mother earth must hold many other such secrets in her bosom.

Channon was an unrepentant appeaser and did not expect Churchill to save Britain. He knew that the 'miracle' of Dunkirk was a defeat presented as a victory and acknowledged that 'we are in an appalling position'. Indeed, he wrote, 'is this really the end of England?' This was not a question asked publicly, but privately it was in everyone's minds in May and June 1940. SEE ALSO PP. 31–2.

Wednesday 29 May 1940

Leslie Barter is wounded and taken prisoner in France

Leslie Barter, a despatch rider with the Royal Army Service Corps, had been sent to France in October 1939 and served in Belgium and around the Maginot Line in France. He was helping to transport wounded in a truck near St-Valéry when he too was wounded . . .

About four thirty p.m. three or four of us got down beside a wagon and started to get a much needed drink of tea and a bite to eat. The activity was particularly heavy at this time, the Gerry infantry were only a matter of a quarter of a mile to half a mile away. I had just stood up to get my mug filled when 'whoof' over I went on the side of the road, thereby saving my life because a couple more bullets came against the wheel of the truck.

I tried to rise but unfortunately was unsuccessful. My trousers were loosened and shirt pulled out to find out where they hit me. Imagine my thought when I found a nasty looking jagged tear in my abdomen. Gosh what a mess

I was in. I thought my inside was hanging out, but the best part was I was still alive, I vaguely remember lying back on a stretcher and away I went a passenger in my own ambulance. The next thing I remember was lying in a cow shed on some straw, with a couple of lads who were also hit. They told me I had been unconscious for nearly two days, and we were in a village occupied by the Germans.

Crikey that was good news to wake up to!

A little later a German came in with some thin soup stuff and put it down beside us at the same time as motioning us to eat. For the life of me I couldn't have eaten the best meal going let alone that stuff he brought in. By this time I was smelling horrible, my trousers and shirt were simply filthy due to my wound, and all I wanted was water and more water which never came . . .

The next morning there was great excitement in the village, followed by firing and shouting. The next instant motor bikes were going by the barn and we could just see through the door that the Germans were leaving the village. Our thoughts were would they take us or leave us. What actually did happen was the most murderous action I think was ever possible for a man to make. Towards the last of the party's moving out a German came running through the doorway. We thought he was coming in to take us. He practically did, only it was to send my two fellow sufferers to hell, and me very nearly there.

The man must have been mad, he came in, stood for a moment and then flung a hand grenade against the barn side. Luckily for me I was in the last stall at the end. As it exploded I was partly protected by the side of the stalls. Nevertheless, I was hit twice; once in the abdomen again and once alongside my right temple. The whole roof collapsed on the other two chaps. Whether they died through the shrapnel or through the roof I never knew.

I had passed out. What happened I cannot say but I do faintly remember a long time later it seemed having a sip of tea from a lovely red X nurse. I found out that I was near Ypres. I remained there until Gerry captured the whole . . . twelve hundred wounded men on the morning of the first of June.

Once captured, Leslie Barter spent the majority of the war as a prisoner, but life was not uneventful. In February 1942 he would be court-martialled for striking a German officer and sent to work in the salt mines in Poland; 1944 saw him employed as a street-sweeper in Danzig; and by the end of the war he would be in the Stalag IVB prison camp at Mühlberg on the Elbe. The camp was bombed by the Americans at the end of the war before being liberated by the Russians in April 1945. Barter would be finally repatriated by American forces at the end of May 1945.

JUNE 1940

MANY OF BRITAIN'S difficulties in the 1930s had stemmed from trying to contain and restrain not only Germany but also its allies, Italy and Japan. During 1938 and 1939 British diplomacy had sought to pull Italy away from the growing Axis alliance. At that juncture Mussolini's Italy had not been ready for war and had watched events in Europe with hesitation. But in June 1940, with the French in retreat, Mussolini was no longer able to resist the temptation of easy spoils. He declared war on Britain and France on 10 June, seizing soft areas of southern France after Germany had done all the fighting in the north. However, the Italian war effort was immediately beset by disasters. In one of the first Marshal Balbo, the Italian Governor and Commander-in-Chief in north Africa, was killed by anti-aircraft fire from Italian guns while flying over Tobruk.

The French government fled Paris ahead of the Germans, who finally entered the French capital on 14 June. Churchill made a perilous visit to France between 11 and 13 June to appeal to the French to hold on and also to ask them to transfer their resources to Britain. This met with an ambiguous response. On 16 June, Marshal Pétain became the new premier of France and quickly sought an armistice with Germany. It was signed on 22 June. On 28 June General de Gaulle was recognized as leader of the Free

French, of whom over 100,000 had made their way to Britain.

On the home front Churchill remained defiant, and on 4 June he delivered his most famous wartime speech, insisting, 'We shall fight them on the beaches . . .' Churchill was buoyed up by an excessively optimistic view of when the United States would enter the war. Although this was still a long way off, the United States was already acting as the 'arsenal of democracy' by helping to replace the heavy equipment that had been lost at Dunkirk. Meanwhile the British police continued their investigation of fifth columnists. Subversion was a widely offered explanation for why France and the Low Countries had fallen so quickly to the German onslaught. The rounding up of enemy aliens and German sympathizers in Britain gathered pace in preparation for an invasion that many thought was not far away.

Thursday 6 June 1940

Cecil King, newspaper editor, talks to Lloyd George

Cecil King was born in 1901 and was related to the great newspaper barons of the early twentieth century, Lord Northcliffe and Lord Rothermere. King joined the Daily Mirror in 1929 and rose to be chairman, gradually moving the paper in a radical anti-establishment direction and becoming a vocal critic of appeasement and the upper classes. He was part of a vibrant journalistic team, including Hugh Cudlipp, Guy Bartholomew and William Connor, which revitalized much of the British newspaper industry and began the modern 'tabloid'-style newspaper in Britain.

Lloyd George also mentioned meeting Hitler and spoke of him as the greatest figure in Europe since Napoleon, and possibly greater than him. He said that we had not had to deal with an austere ascetic like Hitler since the days of Attila and his Huns, who curiously enough attained the success he did by mounting his whole army on horses and bewildering his enemies by the speed of his movements. I gathered that Lloyd George's opinion of Hitler was based not so much upon the impression he received when talking to Hitler face to face, as on his achievements, though Lloyd George evidently judges people a lot by their faces. In this connection he was very severe about Gamelin [Commander-in-Chief of Allied Forces] – said the lower half of his face was weak.

In June 1940 much of the establishment, including Lloyd George, advocated reaching some accommodation with the Germans. The former Prime Minister feared that Britain's cities would be completely destroyed by German aerial bombardment. Some argued that this course should be followed because Europe's common enemy was the Soviet Union and Bolshevism. Others, like Britain's leading strategist Basil Liddell Hart, argued for peace with Germany simply because he believed Britain's military position was now virtually hopeless.

Cecil King would later become a director of Reuters. He died in 1987.

Friday 7 June 1940

Alexander Werth observes Anglo-French relations from a beleaguered Paris

Alexander Werth was born in Russia in 1901 but had come to Britain with his family in 1917 to escape the Revolution. He became a foreign correspondent for British newspapers and had been based in Paris throughout the 1930s. From the French capital he covered the increasingly frantic diplomacy between London and Paris, which involved personal visits by Churchill.

As regards the personal relations between the BEF and the French Army, the latter – not unnaturally – felt some envy for the British soldiers, who were paid 2 shillings a day as against the French private's 1½d. It is true that the French private had free cigarettes and cheap railway fares, and his family lived rent-free; but the attempt made by M Frossard, the Minister of Information, to explain in a broadcast in April that the Tommy was really no better off than the *poilu* was unconvincing; and, knowing M Frossard, and his friendship for M Laval [a pro-German media magnate], one wonders whether he meant it to be convincing. It is true that French soldiers in the 'battle zone' were paid, from December, 10 francs a day (about 1s 2d); but they were only a minority. Further, in some of the towns where numerous British troops were stationed, the local inhabitants complained of the 'overbearing' manner of the British troops, and of their 'noisiness,' especially at night. In such towns, the presence of the British troops also tended to send up the cost of living.

The Germans exploited this relative unpopularity of the 'rich' British soldiers and officers, for instance by dropping 'transparent' postcards from their planes. The postcards showed French soldiers attacking barbed-wire defences. On top, above a large blank space was written: 'Where are the Tommies?' and when you held the blank space up to the light, you saw a picture of British officers, looking like conquerors, making bold advances to French girls and women.

Werth was at this time war correspondent of the Manchester Evening News, *and his diary, although claiming to be 'personal', was clearly written for publication. It would first appear in September 1940 and was reprinted eight times in the period up to Christmas of that year. His diary was of a particular type – that written by a knowledgeable correspondent for subsequent publication, helping to satisfy an almost insatiable public appetite for detail on international affairs. However, the value of his particular diary was, as he himself suggested, that it was not about high politics, but instead about the ordinary Parisians and how they reacted to defeat. For Werth himself, the diary provided a way of 'letting off steam'. The French government press censors took a very restrictive approach to the information that could go back to his paper in England, and so what they would not pass he put in his diary. Keeping such a journal and publishing its contents some months after the event was an increasingly common tactic by journalists in the face of press censorship. SEE ALSO PP. 422–3.*

Wednesday 12 June 1940

An Italian pilot at Assab in Eritrea watches a night attack
on his base by a single RAF aircraft

*This diary belonged to an Italian pilot who fought in Eritrea, east Africa,
in 1940 and 1941. He arrived at Assab, the main port of Eritrea, on
5 June and his regiment was soon established at the main air base outside the town. The pilots mostly flew Fiat CR-42 Falcos, obsolete biplane
fighters which the Italians would continue to manufacture until 1943. A
week later the area was reconnoitred by British aircraft, and the Italians
were bombed for the first time during lunch on 12 June. As with many
diaries captured and translated by British military intelligence, the
names of the author and the translator have not been recorded. It is
nevertheless a poignant personal record.*

That evening, I return to the airport, tired and exhausted
from the tension and the heat of the day. I stay a while under
the shower and, after dinner, I take another shower and get
on the bed still wet and under the fan, hoping to drop off to
sleep. I hear the faint hum of a motor which gets louder and
louder. I listen, almost bursting from holding my breath, as I
instinctively know that this can be nothing less than a plane.
I jump out of the hut and look up at the sky. There was a faint
semblance of light in the sky, although there was no moon,
and between the many stars, I make out a small white light
moving slowly. Then in the dark after a fraction of time I see
from the direction of the airport the red lights which mark
the boundaries of the airfield for night landings. I take it that
it must be one of our planes, which, without warning, had
had to land here.

Then I hear the distinct sound of a plane whistling in a
dive. A second later a bomb explodes. I understand. Again
a dash across the sand and I am in the first funk-hole. Once
there I find myself with VANNONI, RONDELLI, CARINI
and a few others. In the meantime, the plane is still overhead. It makes a wide turn and dives in our direction. It is so

low, about 300 ft., that I can make out its shape, black, slow, with large wings. So, in its subsequent attacks, I can easily follow the direction of the dive and in this way can guess the destination of the bombs which are dropped as it begins to come out of the dive.

After the third attack, the matter began to get troublesome, in fact it worried us, as, often as not, bombs were dropping only a few yards away and each one was a hundred pounder.

To end it, the plane made six attacks, diving and dropping six bombs in all and, all the time with its light on, went calmly off over the sea in the usual direction.

All this at 8 o'clock in the evening. After an hour and a half that damn thing returns again with its deadly load. This time he doesn't find the airfield so easily. In fact, no light in the buildings is seen as before, but with this difference. The moment the plane was heard Col. FEDELI gave the order to turn off the lights from the main and the man in charge, in his agitation, instead of turning off the lights, illuminated the landing ground. The plane only waited for this, for him, fortunate incident, to start the fun fair. The damn plane, as we called it [translator's note: he uses the word 'Avioneta' which is repeated several times and which I shall use], again makes two attacks, dropping bombs as before, and flares, some of which remain in the air, others which are incandescent, light up the airport, deserted and silent. And off he goes.

From the brilliant light of the flares, it was evident from our expressions that there were signs of uncertainty and hate against these unexpected night operations.

But we had not foreseen what was to come, the rest of the night. How could we rest? Already shaken as we were it was difficult to reason things out or to decide what to do. Most of them by now had run off into the scrub or to the sea-shore. At last we made up our minds.

After a few minutes the Avioneta could be heard again, damnation. This was the height of cheek. This time, with better results, and with the aid of flares still burning (!) on the ground the plane dropped several incendiaries and some H.E. [High Explosive] One hangar is on fire and in a short time some of the askaris' [native African soldiers'] houses.

Besides the fire, incendiaries dropped on a lorry loaded with 12.7 cartridges, arrived only this evening, and for use of the M.Gs of our CR 42s.

The Airport had a sinister and desolated appearance. Firemen gone, our officers gone, the fire which was burning more fiercely and the explosion of the cartridges which got worse and worse. But the greatest torture of all was to see us running out from the airport with mattresses over our heads. I, and a few others taken by surprise, completely nude, sweating from the exertion of running and the weight of the mattresses, walking and running across the scrub, thorns, tree stumps and behind us the glare of the fire and the explosions one by one of 3,000 cartridges destroyed in a little less than an hour. Midnight was past when, with mattresses and sheets on the ground in that hot night full of eruptions, we tried to find a little peace and sleep after a day of bombardment, chasing them in our fighters, of heat and thirst. And tomorrow it will start all over again.

The author of this diary avenged the night-time attack the next day by catching and shooting up an RAF Blenheim over the Red Sea – his 'first encounter' – returning to base to treat his comrades to a few victory rolls before landing.

East Africa was one of the few places where the Allies were winning in 1940. Despite the fact that the Italians outnumbered the British and Commonwealth forces in the region by some five to one, Italian military organization was appalling and, as this diary revealed, morale quickly plummeted. We shall return to this journal in May 1941. SEE ALSO PP. 293–6.

Sergeant Harold Watt narrowly fails to escape at St-Valéry and becomes a POW

Harold Watt had joined the Royal Engineers in the third week of September 1932 and served in Palestine and Iraq. By 1938 he had been promoted to colour sergeant. He went to France with the British Expeditionary Force but did not keep a diary while actually on campaign; it was written up later.

Given orders by O.C. [officer commanding] on roadside to cut across fields on our left and told that St. Valery was to our left. Started to cross field when fired on by light automatic using tracer bullets!! Safely across field, we halted and found myself with C/Sgts Bright and Collins and approx. 30 men mostly of No. 1 Section. We decided to carry on and we eventually reached main road. I decided road was too dangerous and we carried on until we came to top of cliffs about 1 kilo to the right of St. Valery . . . Reached top of cliffs about 1.30 a.m. Had a talk with two officers who said it was impossible to get into St. Valery owing to Ger[man] machine gun nests covering all entrance so started to search for way down cliff. Came to the only real way down. A fissure which still left 150 to 200 feet to the beach. The place was simply packed with French and a few English tommies gave a hand to make an improvised ladder but it was far too short. Eventually by taking all ropes off covers of lorries a rope long enough had been secured and a start was made to lower men to the beach . . . The tide was in and a boat standing by . . . there was no time to hesitate but slung the rope over my shoulder, walked backwards, and gave the signal to lower away. I risked one look then shut my eyes quickly. It was very unnerving descent as I kept twirling one way, stop, then twirl the other way. But I reached the beach safely undid the rope and gave the signal to haul back . . .

We threw our ammunition belts and rifles as far as we could out to sea, stripped off, I kept only my trousers on, and started to wade out to the boat. She was lying about 300 yards. We had to swim the last 100 yds or so as we found it hard going as the current was strong. There was a crowd all clambering round a rope ladder hanging over the port side so we made for another knotted rope hanging near the bows . . . A shell landed right amidships apparently in the engine room for there was a terrible noise of escaping steam. Two quick firing guns on deck were still firing madly away, I had climbed the rope just to the left of the port gun and my head was aching horribly from the concussion. Everyone that could find the space lay flat on the deck and we could feel the shock as several shells hit the ship mostly about the waterline. Found out later that the Germans had gained the cliff tops and we were a grand stationary target. They opened with anti-tank guns and I should say anti-tank rifles because holes started to appear in the sides above our heads. Men all around were hit, very few escaping injury, some were killed at once and many dying after only a few minutes. When the ship was first hit, those who were on deck had dived overboard and made for the shore, many had run the gauntlet of shell and machine gun fire ... we eventually made our way onto the deck, we had been below in the forecastle [*sic*] and we found the bridge and stern of the ship blazing fiercely and every few seconds violent explosions could be heard and felt from the inside of the ship ...

Just as dusk was falling a German officer came onto the beach and shouted across to us that if we did not come ashore at once we would be killed ... We replied that immediate attention was necessary for the injured. His reply was that nothing could be done about them until the morning and repeated his order that all able bodied men come ashore at once or we would be killed.

There was nothing for it but to obey so we started to climb overboard and swim shorewards ... We were met on shore by the German officer and soldiers and were given a drink of spirits which was very welcome as it was now very cold and of course we were wet. The injured we had managed to bring ashore were examined and taken away immediately to a field dressing station, including Bright ... the rest of us were taken to an artillery camp on top of the cliffs, provided with towels to dry ourselves, discarded our remnants of wet clothing and were given Ger[man] overcoats and a blanket and shown a bivouac, complete with straw to sleep in. A Ger[man] soldier slipped me a packet of French cigarettes. The inevitable reaction now set in and after smoking a very welcome fag we were soon asleep.

The remains of the 52nd Highland Division were trapped on the beaches at St-Valéry-en-Caux after Dunkirk had fallen. The Royal Navy rescue operation tried to pull them off the beach but couldn't get anywhere near the coast on the night of 11 June because of heavy fog which appeared off shore. By 12 June 8,000 Highlanders and their supporting units had been captured. Sergeant Watt used the time in captivity to compile his diary account.

Thursday 13 June 1940

George Bilaikin discusses the fall of France with an angry Joseph Kennedy

In 1940 George Bilaikin was the diplomatic correspondent for Allied Newspapers in London. Now aged thirty-seven, he had been in the job for many years and had excellent contacts within London's many embassies.

Turning again to France, Kennedy said: 'I always told your people you were not ready last September. I said it was no good, you'll remember my words, putting out the tongue when you must be able to hit the other man in the jaw. You'll remember, too, I told you the British people would yet put up a memorial of gratitude to Chamberlain, for Munich. Now supposing he had led the country into war in 1938, what would have happened? Through Munich you gained a year in which to prepare – and yet, nine months after that, you are in the position of having only two or three divisions fighting in France.'

I suggested here that we ought to be preparing for events towards the end of this year, when American supplies might come in time to refresh and ultimately save the democracies.

'For Heaven's sake, George, come down to practical politics,' he thundered angrily. 'This is not a question of months, and you know it. It's a question of days.'

Back at his table now Kennedy said, 'It's no use, as a friend of the democracies, for me to have gone on saying the things people wanted to hear. From the start I told them they could expect zero help. We had none to offer and I know we could not give it, and, in the way of any material, we could not spare it. I could have easily said the usual blah and poppycock, but, what's the bloody good of being so foolish as that? An ambassador's duty is to be frank, not to mislead. I considered that my duty and I discharged it. What the hell are you worth if you just mislead them?'

Churchill, according to Kennedy, has much more drive than Chamberlain, but time is running away. I said: 'It may be your fault: it may be ours; it is probably the fault of both. But the fact remains that, if France is compelled to give up, and if we are conquered, you will be invaded, after Russia, in six months.'

Kennedy answered: 'Yes, that's possible. Nobody here seemed to take any notice when I kept on telling them about the strength of the Germans, and, of course, nobody dreamed that they would achieve so much in a month's warfare. Don't forget, the war has only been on since May 9th or 10th.'

Joseph Kennedy had based his support for Chamberlain's policy of appeasement on his belief that Britain and France were not ready to fight Germany in 1938–9, and he now felt vindicated. Kennedy's views were of increasing importance, for President Roosevelt was in two minds about whether to send significant supplies to Britain. Was it worth sending armaments across the Atlantic that might quickly fall into the hands of the Germans? However, Kennedy's caution was countered by William J. Donovan, who was sent by Roosevelt to Britain on special assignment to investigate the situation, and whose upbeat views would eventually outweigh those of Kennedy.

At the end of the war George Bilaikin would be sent on an investigation of conditions in newly occupied Europe, and reported from Paris, Berlin, Prague and Belgrade for the Daily Mail.

Saturday 22 June 1940

William Shirer, American correspondent in Europe,
watches the French surrender

William Shirer (centre)

On the exact spot in the little clearing in the Forest of
Compiegne where at 5 a.m. on November 11, 1918 the
armistice which ended the World War was signed, Adolf
Hitler to-day handed *his* armistice terms to France. To make
German revenge complete, the meeting of the German and
the French plenipotentiaries took place in Marshal Foch's
private car, in which Foch laid down the armistice terms
twenty-two years ago. Even the same table in the rickety old
wagon-lit car was used. And through the windows we saw
Hitler occupying the very seat on which Foch had sat at that
table when he dictated the other armistice ...

The time is now three-eighteen p.m. Hitler's personal flag
is run up on a small standard in the centre of the opening.

Also in the centre is a great granite block which stands
some three feet above the ground. Hitler, followed by the
others, walks slowly over to it, steps up, and reads the
inscription engraved in great high letters on that block. It

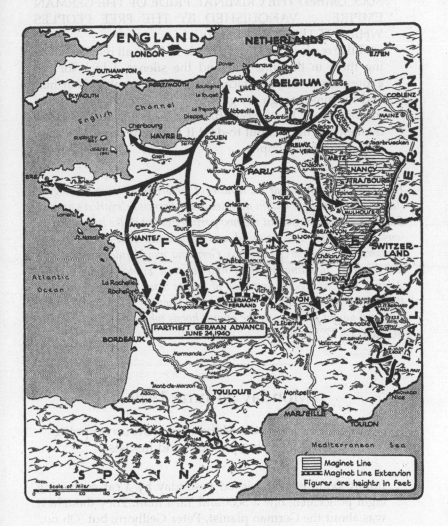

The Battle for France, 1940

says: 'HERE ON THE ELEVENTH OF NOVEMBER 1919 SUCCUMBED THE CRIMINAL PRIDE OF THE GERMAN EMPIRE ... VANQUISHED BY THE FREE PEOPLES WHICH IT TRIED TO ENSLAVE.'

Hitler reads it and Goring reads it. They all read it, standing there in the June sun and the silence. I look for the expression on Hitler's face. I am but fifty yards from him and see him through my glasses as though he were directly in front of me. I have seen that face many times at the great moments of his life. But to-day! It is afire with scorn, anger, hate, revenge, triumph.

Hitler did not wait to hear the reading of the armistice terms, but signed the document and left within minutes of the French delegation's arrival. Salutes were exchanged but the two parties did not shake hands. France was now divided into occupied and unoccupied zones, with a rigid demarcation line between the two. Germany would rule three-fifths of the country, including northern and western France and the entire Atlantic seaboard. What remained of France would be administered by the French government at the little spa town of Vichy, where each ministry fought for space in the quaint hotels where they were billeted.
SEE ALSO PP. 27 AND 90–2.

Monday 24 June 1940

Frances Partridge of the Bloomsbury Group on police raids targeting pacifists and fascists

Jimmy Bomford was visited yesterday by a car containing eight policemen, one a Scotland Yard man. They thought it was about the German pianist, Peter Gellhorn, but 'Oh no,' they said, 'we've come about *you.*' They then went over the house from top to bottom, searched all the men bodily, and took away all Jimmy's papers and farm accounts. They would not say what were the grounds of suspicion, but they came to the conclusion it was village gossip, their having foreign friends, and Jimmy wearing a beard. When I tried to ring them up I was told the line was 'out of service'. I then tried to get onto the Wests and got the same answer. Surely *they* can't be searched too? But they had been, and came to tell us so. The police were there for about six hours and took away all their foreign books, maps and guides, and even some toy soldiers belonging to Anthony! They took him to Marlborough police station, where the Chief of Police was hectoring and disagreeable: 'And by the way that's a pretty nasty shirt you're wearing.' One of the things the police had against him was that he knew the Bomfords and Brenans! So I shan't be at all surprised if it's our turn to be searched next. I actually wandered round looking for things the police would be silly enough to carry off if they came here. Hugo's *German*, perhaps? Or Clive's pacifist tract? Or this diary, I suppose.

By June 1940 a 'spy scare' in both Britain and America resulted in a tightening of measures against all fringe political groups, including fascists, communists and pacifists. A substantial number of those who had befriended Oswald Mosley, the British fascist leader, were well-to-do and one official remarked that Defence Regulation 18B, if implemented properly, would mean locking up half of the House of Lords. MI5 and the Special Branch investigated pacifists and members of the Peace Pledge Union, suspecting them of spreading disaffection in the armed forces.

Frances Partridge was born in 1900 into a literary family. She worked as an editor and translator and became a central member of the Bloomsbury Group; her wartime diaries capture her life in the Wiltshire countryside with her husband, Ralph, and son, Burgo. Their literary friends included Jim Bomford, Rebecca West and Gerald Brenan, as well as Arthur Conan Doyle and Henry James. Both she and Ralph were dedicated pacifists, and in the summer of 1940 they found themselves the subject of growing attention from the police. In September 1940 Gerald Brenan would come close to internment because his name had been found among the charred remains of Oswald Mosley's private papers and he was therefore thought to be a secret associate of the Blackshirt leader. In fact his name had been in the papers because he had once written an open letter to the Daily Telegraph *urging that Mosley be arrested.* SEE ALSO PP. *19, 211–12, 348–50 AND 612–13.*

Flora Stark and Herbert Young are interned as enemy aliens at Asolo in Italy

Flora Stark was an artist and textile designer who lived among a community of British artists and writers that had existed in northern Italy since the nineteenth century. Separated from her husband, the painter Robert Stark, she had lived in Italy since the turn of the century with her two daughters, Freya and Vera. Herbert Young, a long-standing friend and godfather to Freya, lived not far away. Vera Stark eventually married Count Mario di Roascio. All had been involved in a family arts and crafts business which absorbed most of Flora Stark's time. After Italy's declaration of war on Britain in June 1940 Italian behaviour towards enemy aliens varied greatly, and some individuals were simply ignored by the authorities; but Flora Stark and Herbert Young (who was eighty-five years old in 1940) were two of the many British citizens initially interned. It was thought that this behaviour was a reprisal for anti-Italian propaganda by Flora's daughter, Freya Stark, who had begun working for the British authorities in the Yemen at the start of the war.

Two quiet, well-dressed men, accompanied by the local Brigadier of Carabineers, called at 2 o'clock to tell us that our presence was required at Treviso to give some information. They had a car waiting outside and told us we might be detained late and to take money and things for the night. Fortunately H Y took a note of L1,000 with him and off we drove with the two detectives and the Carabineer. I did find a moment in which to whisper to our maid, Emma, to telephone to M[ario] that we had been carried off to Treviso.

We arrived there in pouring rain about 4.00pm. Called at the Questura, where our passports were given up, and then drove straight to the prison, a fact we did not at first realise.

We were shewn into a little room where an official made us give up all our 'connotati' and a much-surprised and agitated Governor was called and told he must put us up. He looked at us in despair. He had evidently been disturbed in his afternoon siesta and had on his pyjama jacket.

We were called into the little room again and told to give

up all money and valuables, and the Governor disappeared to return in full dress uniform. He consigned H Y to the care of a guard, sending him off to the left, while a small young woman, much alarmed, had to take charge of me. She conducted me to the women's side, where I found a narrow stone corridor with many women standing about, some in ordinary dress and some in convict garb with shaven crowns.

The Governor, or 'Capo' as they called him, followed us presently and ordered one of the cells to be cleared out. Two of the convicts set to work. I saw pails of creosote doused on the floor of an inner cell, palliasses made of sacking and straw being taken out and others being taken in, and heard much discussion, remonstrances and grumblings, while I sat on the only chair and looked on, stared at by curious and pitying eyes. Finally my cell was announced ready and I was invited in.

A cell, with three small windows high up, heavily barred, one small shelf against the wall at one end and four truckle beds, in a space of three metres by five. My little gaoler followed me in and, apologising, proceeded to feel me all over for secret papers, money or knives. A gentle, nice little woman.

I asked her whether a cell to myself were not possible, but she said the women's quarters were terribly restricted and that this was the best they could do for me; that the most decent women had been picked out to share my cell. This, of course, had failed to please the others who had formed friendships when in my cell; others were jealous of a supposed preference.

The Governor harangued them, exhorting them to good behaviour and kindness, and then left.

Presently a bell rang and all had to turn into their respective cells. Three cells – fifteen women, so I was fortunate in having only three more in mine.

The food for the day had been distributed at midday, and there was nothing for me. But the little Signorina, as the gaoler is called, went out and procured some milk and bread, and presently I sat on my 'branda' (truckle bed with straw sack) eating out of a tin bowl with a rough, large wooden spoon (no metal ones allowed because of possible aggressions) while the others sat at theirs and devoured large chunks of bread and cold soup left from midday.

Under each 'branda' was a tin chamber and a small basin filled with water.

By dint of some gymnastic activity one woman had succeeded in attaching a piece of string, secreted somehow, and to which Signorina shut a charitable eye, and clothes were hung on this. I, as a great favour, was allowed to keep my small bag and was able to cram all my clothes into it, after removing my nightdress, etc. The daylight waned, a feeble electric light shone between the bars of one window and we proceeded to undress. The women were polite and truly considerate. They examined my bed and piled their spare blankets on to the straw sacking and one extra blanket was folded into a pillow instead of the straw roll given out. Then I sat with my back to them while they made their arrangements for the night. One went to bed in all her clothes, the others in their day chemises, and each thought it polite to ask my leave before passing water.

When they were all asleep at 8.30 I undressed and washed (they had all taken up a position with their backs to me) and then to bed, where I lay and stared at the bars and the ironbound door and wondered where Freya was. Fervently did I pray for her, and that God would grant wisdom to our leaders, both civil and military.

That first night was terrible. In spite of creosote and soap, black beetles ran gaily across the floor in every direction, and once I saw one crawl on the wall over the head of 'Maria'. I called to her and told her and she simply took up her shoe and squashed it and went to sleep again, but I now perceived the use of the voluminous white dusters they all tied around their heads on going to bed. Then I saw a large spider over the head of another woman, Maria del Son. Again I called out and she killed it.

Then I passed hours thinking on what I had better do. This impossible place! Poor H Y perhaps in the same case, though I was told at once by the Capo that the men's quarters were much better and he was probably by himself or with one 'persona scelta'. Had I better remonstrate bitterly and make things difficult (I could see that that was what they feared) or had I better make the best of it and make friends all round. It was obvious that, from the Governor down, they were all sorry, and I decided on the latter course and finally went to sleep.

I woke up to find two large forms bending over me in the half light and plucking at my sheet. 'Cerchiamo le cimici' ('We are looking for the bugs') and there they were! My first meeting with them. The two kind women plucked, evincing all the pleasure of the chase, and I lay still and said 'Thank you,' and presently we all went to sleep again.

Asolo, a village in the foothills of the Dolomites and close to Venice, was Flora Stark's family home, and she had lived there much of her life. Her internment was brief and she was soon freed and allowed to return home. Her daughter Freya Stark continued to work for British propaganda organizations in Yemen, Beirut and later in Baghdad, where she befriended the MI6 officer Nigel Clive. In Beirut she undertook information work, making use of her excellent Arabic, Spanish, German and Italian. Immediately after the war she edited and published her mother's diary.

JULY 1940

On 2 July 1940 Hitler ordered preparations to be made for the invasion of England. Early German planning projected an attack force of between twenty-five and forty divisions. The German high command sent out an order entitled 'The War against England', which initially emphasized increased air attack and intensified sea blockade. Accordingly, the first stage of the invasion called for an air war over the English Channel, with much of the Luftwaffe activity directed at coastal shipping. This would become known as the 'Battle of Britain'.

As the threat of invasion loomed, some British families began to send their children overseas to America, South Africa and

Australia, but this process was itself hazardous. The summer and autumn of 1940 were the heyday of the German U-boats. Later in the war U-boat crews would look back on this period and refer to it as 'the happy time'. Between July and October 1940 German submarines, often acting independently, attacked Allied shipping almost unmolested. German U-boats sank an average of eight ships on each patrol and their commanders became the 'stars' of the German navy.

One of the casualties of the tightening blockade was the British transport ship the *Arandora Star*, which was sunk close to the coast of Ireland. It was carrying 1,200 enemy aliens who were being sent to Canada; of the total number of 1,673 on board, 805 were lost. Most of the passengers were anti-Nazis and some were German Jewish refugees who had fled Germany for Britain in 1938 and 1939. Britain had persuaded Canada to take many of its German internees because of the overcrowding of internment camps in locations such as the outskirts of Liverpool and the Isle of Man. The 'fifth column' panic was producing more internees than the system could handle, and the conditions which they endured were often unpleasant.

Suspicion of undercover enemy activity had become little short of a mania in Britain by July 1940. Wild stories circulated about German parachutists disguised as nuns, and secret agents arriving from overseas hidden in coffins or crates of bananas. Everyone was on the look-out. By night the Home Guard were out patrolling the streets looking for saboteurs and detaining unlikely suspects.

On 1 July the decision was taken, during a very secret meeting held in Anthony Eden's office, to create the wartime sabotage organization called the Special Operations Executive. The SOE incorporated a range of existing small secret outfits, including a sabotage unit from the secret service called Section D, a similar unit from military intelligence in the War Office called MI(R) and a black propaganda unit called Electra House. On 16 July Churchill asked Hugh Dalton, the Minister of Economic Warfare, to take charge of the new body; the War Cabinet confirmed this decision and Dalton was given the new and secret title of Minister of Special Operations. Although this sounded very exciting, it was some months before the SOE began substantial activities.

Even now, debate continues as to whether Hitler ever

seriously intended to invade Britain in 1940 or 1941. On 19 July, in a speech in the Reichstag, he issued a public appeal for 'common sense', offering Britain a peace deal. This was rejected equally publicly by London three days later. Meanwhile the German high command had already begun to plan for the campaign that was closer to Hitler's heart: the 'total' war in the east against Russia.

Tuesday 2 July 1940

Diana Falla (aged twelve) hears that Guernsey has been occupied by Germany

Diana Falla and the rest of her class at school had been evacuated from Guernsey without their parents at midnight on 20 June 1940. Embarked on the Dutch steamer Batavier, they arrived in Rochdale on 22 June. Diana was sent to a reception centre called Roylelands in the Manchester Road. She was able to receive only a little news about her parents in Guernsey through the Red Cross.

Black Tuesday

Once a week we stay and do the housework at Roylelands and our turn was today. We had cornflakes for breakfast. At dinner time the bomb-shell came. Guernsey had been occupied on Sunday June 30ᵗʰ by the Germans. I was very glad I had not been to school as I heard there had been some very sad scenes. I was so dazed I did not cry. To take our minds off the news the staff arranged sports in the afternoon at the park with chocolate for prizes. I came second in the ball and spoon race. [In the] morning I received a lovely box of bars of chocolate from Mrs Payne. We had stew for dinner. Everyone was very kind to us. We had our tea and then went to bed in a very miserable state.

In mid-June 1940 there had been a mass evacuation from the Channel Islands, particularly Guernsey, ahead of an expected German invasion. Approximately 30,000 people decided to leave. Many of them had since arrived at reception centres in the north-west of England or in

Scotland, from where they were gradually dispersed around the country.
After the war Diana Falla would study art at Reading University and
later went on to be a sculptor.

Wednesday 3 – Monday 15 July 1940

German internees are robbed while in transit from Britain to Canada

This anonymous diary of a German anti-Nazi internee was obtained by
Home Office censors through postal interception. The Home Office hoped
to employ this diary to try to identify those who had systematically
robbed and brutalized German internees on their way to camps in
Canada.

3 July

... What we suspected the other day and what I hinted at in
my last letter ... has now happened with extraordinary
suddenness ... there was a week's guessing with the odds on
Canada since we had read in papers about the proposal of the
Canadian Government to accept interned refugees. The day
before yesterday it transpired that we would leave the following day. We were still without money, which had not been paid
out (our money that was impounded at Bury St. Edmunds
seems to be completely lost), without the documents that had
been impounded, many without shoes, lots of people for various reasons very unwilling to go ...

Yesterday after lunch 360 of us left the old camp [at
Douglas on the Isle of Man] ... we got to Liverpool this
morning. After hours we were led on the ship in single file.
We had made plans for trying to get a nice outside cabin in
a good part of the ship, on a high deck etc. Our hopes sank
when we were taken right down in to the bowels of the ship.

She is a troop-carrier with large rooms (mess-decks) with
low ceilings. 1000 internees were crammed together in three
such rooms on top of each other. At first the conditions were
indescribable. People waited all day in these rooms in a

frightful atmosphere. There were ventilators but the portholes had to remain closed. There were twice as many
people as the rooms should hold. The officers (so we were
told) had also come to Liverpool the same morning; they
were completely helpless and refused to see us . . . The worst
thing was that we had not been given anything to eat for
almost 28 hours . . . We left Liverpool about 8 p.m.

4 July

Yesterday was taken up by caring for the sea-sick. There was
not much of a sea, but by 4 p.m. practically everyone was
sick who had not managed to get up on deck. People's bad
nerves and lack of food the previous day probably
accounted for the disproportionate amount of sickness. At 4
p.m. everyone except myself and two other people lay in
their hammocks either violently sick or at least unable to
move. I spend hours carrying buckets or broom or shovel, or
helping people with water. It was hopeless to do much in the
terribly congested room and the foul air. In the evening more
than 100 on my deck were still sick and our evening meal
was a rather improvised affair on a table as far away from
the worst cases as possible . . .

5 July

. . . while most of the others were on the top deck in the fresh
air we went at our place with brooms, brushes and dis-
infectant. Working from 10 a.m. till 2 p.m. we got the place
clean and more or less tidy. There was still a large number of
victims although the sea was pretty calm. One grand
Viennese spent an hour playing the accordion and singing
while himself all the time fighting against sea-sickness. After
an hour's sleep I went up on deck for the first time. We are
now allowed to go up there in double shifts of two hours
each. One lies about reading or playing cards and enjoying
the fresh air . . . In the evening I took part in the worst scenes
that happen here – washing up on the next deck above. A
frightful scramble of 30–40 people around a table with huge
bowls of hot water, trying to steal each other's cutlery and
plates (most tables haven't got enough), all of it in semi-
darkness and in state of indescribable filth and din. I went to

bed rather early, feeling tired and unwilling to do any more organising. With difficulty I managed to find a place for my hammock in the opposite corner of the deck. Two of my blankets were stolen. I kept only one and felt very cold through the night.

6 July
I have now at last caught up with the chronology and can devote myself to a little reflection and description . . .

Our group has, in the main, been selected from among the unmarried between 20 and 30. These young people had mostly come to England only a few months or years ago and are losing little. They take their fate stoically and with as much humour as they can muster. There are some older people who are leaving their wives and children, their property and position in England. They are pretty miserable and a few have broken down and can hardly be comforted. I continue my tactics of keeping myself too busy to think too much.

7 July
Another day on the ship . . . a rather unpleasant interlude with the military. In the morning, when one shift of 300 odd people was taken on deck and they were kept in one corner of the deck to wait until the previous shift had gone downstairs, a sergeant, whilst trying to push people back, suddenly pulled out a long hard rubber truncheon and started beating 10, 15 people right on the head as hard as he could. He simply lost his head and temper. It was a disgusting performance in front of the eyes of the (German) prisoners of war (there were 450 of them on board, kept apart from the internees) who stood on the other side of the partition and no doubt enjoyed this re-enactment of concentration camp scenes. The sergeant even tried to grab a rifle with a bayonet from one of the sentries but the sentry decently refused (he was later charged by the sergeant for disobedience) . . .

8 July
In the afternoon again discussions with the other deck chiefs on the food question. Further endless difficulties with

shouting groups clamouring for more food. Thank God, it is only another four or five days . . .

9 July

. . . a longish meeting with the captain-interpreter in charge of us. We tried to drive home for the nth time since our internment that we are refugees from Nazi oppression – not Nazis; and we insist on our status as 'temporarily interned refugees' . . .

10 July

This morning I heard in a fairly authentic form a rumour of which I heard the first trace some days ago, namely that a previous ship with internees and prisoners of war which left England Thursday before last ('Arandora Star') was torpedoed off the coast of Ireland and sunk with the loss of 3000 men – only 700 odd being saved. It is an appalling thought. There may have been many among the internees who had been in earlier camps with us . . .

11 July

On our right, far away, we saw the first piece of America, the south coast of Newfoundland . . .

12 July

To-day it is two months since our internment . . .

13 July

Before breakfast we reached the St. Lawrence River and went upstream . . . By 10 a.m. everyone had been taken up on to the front top deck with all their luggage. The view was heavenly. We were going slowly upstream – on both sides the banks of the river – some 500 yards apart – hilly with villages, houses, woods and fields. The weather was wonderful, and we enjoyed one of the most beautiful sceneries I have ever seen. At first, people were so wrapped in the view that they hardly noticed how the time passed as they were crowded together on the front deck, unable to get down again and waiting for our arrival. Soon it became necessary for some to go to the lavatory. I spent the next three hours, at first trying to get permission for them which was terribly difficult and then letting groups of five tortured people go down at intervals after hours of waiting ... We docked at 1.30 p.m. By then people had waited for three hours and a half on the deck in the sun. The Colonel who was in command of the transport was getting more and more nervous, being unable to cope with the disembarkation proceedings; he raged about, shouting at everyone. One of our internees, a little Jewish boy, was kicked by him and beaten with his stick, accompanied by the words: 'Get back you lousy lot'. Later he ordered the sentries to use their bayonets against us (which they did not do). Colonel Freesen will stay in our memories for a long while yet!

After docking at the quay nothing happened for hours. The prisoners were disembarked first. In the meantime we waited and waited for hours, getting hungrier and some getting desperate, as they were again not allowed to go to the lavatory. At about 3 p.m. we managed to get the officers to have some buckets put up one deck below, and I spent three ghastly hours organizing the traffic to these buckets ... At 7.30 p.m. at last we were taken off the ship. Our heavy luggage had previously been collected and taken off the ship by porters. We marched down the gangway in single file and made very consciously our first step on American soil. We were taken to buses in groups of 20 and after every piece of luggage down to the last bread carrier and violin had been torn out of people's hands and added to the luggage we were taken in buses through Quebec.

By about 8 p.m. we once again reached barbed wire. We drove into the compound and we unloaded in the sight of a large number of well-constructed and nicely spaced-out wooden huts ... we had to undress ... and one by one every item of our belongings taken away from us by sergeants and privates. Most of the things were put into green bags with our names on them and lists were made with the articles. But we soon found that soldiers were taking cigarettes and later also watches, fountain pens, money etc. without putting them down. We were all terribly weary (the last group was not searched until 5 a.m.) and did not offer any resistance ...

14 *July*

We soon found out that in our hut there happened to be a group of some 30 people (out of a hundred) who were Nazis or at least on the side of Germany ... before the meal, therefore I was elected hutfather over the pro-Nazi vote (the latter supported by most of a group of Roman Catholic priests) ... in the afternoon, we had a meeting with Captain Milne ... and a Canadian Lieutenant. In the discussion we were soon surprised by the way in which both officers assumed as a matter of course that we would be interned for the duration.

15 *July*

... In the course of the morning began the procedure of returning to us our luggage and confiscated goods which was to occupy everyone in the camp for the next two days. When the green bags were opened in front of the officers to be examined for impoundable articles it was soon found that the sergeants and privates had used the unrivalled opportunity of the night to steal on a colossal scale. Money, watches, pens, cigarettes, lighters, everything of value has been appropriated by them. By the evening it was discovered that money and articles to the value of altogether £1200 were missing, not counting some 20,000 cigarettes. At the same time our luggage was put up in a long row in the street outside the barbed wire for examination and collection. Here the robbery started again. The soldiers stole several typewriters in front of the eyes of their owners; later they 'confiscated' all sorts of useful objects from suitcases. Most of them disappeared and have not been seen again ... The whole search had been illegal. It should have been carried out by officers, not N.C.Os. and privates ... Later a military court of enquiry was set up ...

History is often written by the victor, and the conventional view is that the Axis monopolized the dispensation of degrading treatment. The diary of this internee suggests otherwise. It is remarkable for the light it casts on the deplorable British treatment of German civilians who were expressly anti-Nazi. Of equal significance is the manner in which it captures orchestrated crime by a military unit, something which military historians know is common in every conflict but which is rarely glimpsed, still less documented in detail. (Similarly, oral history suggests, for example, that systematic looting by firemen and policemen during the Blitz of 1940 was rife; but it remains almost impossible to document.)

This particular incident did not go uninvestigated. The internees were personally powerless, but not without significant friends. Some were academics with international connections, and the Society for the Protection of Science and Learning would soon be pressing their case with the Department of Internment Operations in Ottawa.

The keeper of this diary is still unknown. The authenticity of its content was confirmed by the subsequent investigation. More diary material and letters by other individuals were sent by this group of internees in sections through the post to relatives. En route to the recipients, they were secretly intercepted and would eventually end up in the hands of B.3 Division of the Home Office, which was investigating the incident. The material was collated and it all told the same story, complaining of valuables stolen, 'inhuman treatment', and transport on a 'slave ship' which was designed to carry 2,000 but had set sail from Liverpool with over 3,400 passengers. The Canadian government informed the Home Office that courts martial were under way against young Canadian soldiers who had participated in the theft of valuables. However, they also asserted that most of the stolen goods were in the hands of the British escort, adding that 'on no less than three occasions successful attempts were made to steal the cash and effects of the internees who passed through England'.

Sunday 14 July 1940

Harry Seidler, anti-Nazi internee, arrives in Canada and is robbed by troops

We hadn't eaten anything for 17 hours! Soon many loaves of bread were brought to the kitchen next door – our mouths watered but they didn't give us any. At 2 am we were led off in small groups under guard to another hut. Here there were many tables to which we were taken one by one. What then followed is typical of how we are treated.

I went up to a table at which a soldier told me to put my name on a form and my signature on a blank piece of paper. I did so – then the search began. I had to undress and all my clothes were searched minutely. The contents of my pockets were put out on the table – my watch was there, too. Then the soldier began to write the names of the objects on the piece of paper I had already signed. Since my signature was already on it, all he had to do was to record what he wished. For example, if he wanted to keep my watch for himself he could simply leave it off the list and pocket it. No one would ever know that I signed the paper beforehand without understanding what for! EVERYTHING was taken from me – even my handkerchief. The most incredible thefts were perpetrated during this dead-of-night search. The things taken from us were put in paper bags if not in the soldiers' pockets. I was disgusted: they let us starve for 17 hours during which they stood us in the sun, they make us wait and then at 3 o'clock in the morning they rob us! And so 'welcomed' we were taken into another barrack-hut where we finally got something to eat.

Groups of 100 then went into huts with bunks on top of each other. I went straight to sleep as I was – we didn't have any nightwear. We had to get up at 7. There was a wash-house but we couldn't make good use of it as we didn't have soap or toothbrushes. We got little breakfast. The weather was beautiful. We lay out in the sun on a little hill behind our hut. It got terribly hot around midday – over and over again we would go to the washhouse and shower to cool ourselves.

We had already elected a hut representative who went to the meeting with the commandant. He told us that we had been sent here from England as 'dangerous people' – so here they believe we're simply 'fifth column' (and that's how we've been treated). Telegraph to England is not allowed – they hope we'll be allowed to write soon.

Now it is official – the transport before ours was sunk. I can imagine what a state *Mutti* in England will be in when she hears about that!

This afternoon a crowd of German prisoners of war arrived in our part of the camp – they occupied one of the huts. They walked about the camp freely in their uniform and were allowed to mix with us. So we've sunk this low: mixing with NAZIS. It was bad enough on the ship, where we were only occasionally together – but now we have direct contact! I was enraged and stayed well away from those uniformed figures. Do these Canadians or Englishmen know what they're doing to us when they keep putting us with Nazis? No – surely not – they think we're one and the same – all GERMANS. This evening the Nazis marched, singing, out of the camp – hopefully for ever! Tonight we had to go to bed unwashed again and sleep in our clothes – we haven't seen our bags since we arrived.

In May 1940 Harry Seidler and his brother had been interned as enemy aliens on the Isle of Man by the British authorities. Two months later they were sent to Canada.

Few forms of historical evidence are more compelling than diary entries compiled independently by different individuals which tell the same story. Harry Seidler's diary confirms the violent and dishonest treatment that anti-Nazi refugees – many of them fleeing from the German persecution of the Jews – received in Britain. The irony was not lost upon the diarist. As Seidler was marched along a Liverpool street by soldiers and prodded with a rifle, the locals shouted 'down with fifth column'. He could see little difference between this and the sort of treatment he had seen the SA and SS handing out in Germany in the 1930s – though treatment of political suspects in Germany and Britain was, of course, vastly different. The greatest difficulty for the British authorities was having no records on the internees, and therefore no reliable paperwork that allowed them to sift dangerous individuals from the harmless majority. The inability to discriminate had some tragic results. One internee, Ernst Scheinberg, had already suffered badly in a Nazi concentration camp before fleeing to Britain. He found the experience of a second confinement in Britain and then a third in Canada too much to bear, and after arriving in Canada became mentally unstable and was placed in isolation. On the night of 16–17 July 1940 he was shot while trying to escape. SEE ALSO PP. 150–2 AND 342–4.

Sunday 14 – Tuesday 16 July 1940

Sir Cuthbert Headlam watches Whitehall's preparations for a German invasion of Britain

Sir Cuthbert Headlam, born in 1876, was a long-serving Conservative MP and a big wheel in the party organization in the north-east of England. He sat in the House of Commons on and off between 1924 and 1951. Prior to that he had worked as a clerk in the House of Lords before leaving to serve in the Bedfordshire Yeomanry during the First World War.

14 July

Winston spoke on the wireless tonight – a fine effort – less bombastic than usual and full of vim. The recent successes of the RAF have clearly cheered him up a lot. He assured us that we now have a million and a half men under arms in this country, and, in addition, another million in the Local Defence force which he preferred to call the Home Guard. (To do him justice he did not try and make us believe that this latter force was yet armed!) It is clear, I think, now that we are in a position to resist an invasion should the Germans risk one . . .

16 July

London is rapidly become like a besieged town – or, rather, is being converted into a defended zone. Whether all the barbed wire defences and machine-gun posts in the Whitehall area are erected to cover the last stand of Winston and the rest of us against the invading Germans, or whether to prevent the government offices being raided by 'Fifth Columnists' and parachutists, one does not know. They are certainly formidable obstructions to most of us especially in the hours of darkness when one is confronted by barriers in the most unexpected places. I am told that Winston is mainly responsible for them and takes the deepest interest in them. He appears to spend a lot of time inspecting our defences all over the country. It is certainly his hour – and the confidence in him is growing on all sides.

Headlam was an astute politician and had weighed up the qualities of Churchill as a wartime PM quite precisely. He thought of him as an erratic but indispensable genius who found it hard to delegate and who would be hard to work with.

On another level, Headlam's diaries are fascinating on the subject of party organization in his constituency, where bickering over money and personalities was constant. They are full of references to hopes and promises for advancement, and disappointments. SEE ALSO PP. 825–6.

Tuesday 23 July 1940

Howard Clegg, a Canadian infantryman, encounters the Home Guard on his way back from the pub

'Time gentlemen! Time!' cries the landlord.

Out comes the Jeep, and we head out to collect the boys that we left to admire the hedgerows.

There's a barricade.

'Halt! . . . Advance and be recognized.'

The sergeant gets out and advances. Two bayonets flash in the dark. There's the poor serg. With steel skewers jammed up against his uneasy ribs on each side. A third guard comes up and starts asking questions. To satisfy him that we aren't phoney the serg. reaches for his pay-book. That has almost done it. The bayonet thrusters take a firmer hold on their rifles. You can hear a light exclamation from the serg. As one of those blokes takes the first pressure on his trigger.

'Don't get windy, mate,' says the serg., who is experiencing the feeling of being extremely windy himself. These windy blighters are young L.D.V.'s. They really are determined to protect England and their own precious hides against whatever they have taken us to be. At last the sergeant is released. A civie car drives up from a cross-road.

The command to halt is promptly, too promptly, obeyed. The L.D.V. boys say, 'Drive up a bit closer.' But the motorist has met guys like these before.

'You come here' says he.

'Nothing doing,' say the L.D.V.'s, 'bring that car up here.'

The motorist is adamant as he looks along the barrels of two pointed rifles.

'Well, you can stay there all night,' threaten the L.D.V.'s. Perhaps he did.

We pushed off wondering which side would first get up the courage to approach the other. Farther along the way we came to another guard, soldiers this time. They had their bayonets fixed as per regulation; but their weapons were slung on their shoulders. They took a peek at us. We passed a few abusive remarks to show that there was no ill-feeling, and that was that.

The Local Defence Volunteers or 'Home Guard' had been formed in May 1940, but it was a few months before they were fully supplied with uniforms and weapons. An appeal was issued for the public to donate their shotguns and pistols, and eventually over 20,000 private weapons were distributed among them. An already diverse armoury was supplemented with home-made weapons including clubs, coshes, spears and dummy rifles. Much of the initial training was in techniques of sabotage against invaders using home-made explosives and petrol bombs. By the autumn of 1940, however, they would be receiving proper uniforms and organized training. Later in the war, after the threat of invasion melted away, the Home Guard would be occupied in capturing German airmen whose planes had been shot down over Britain. As well as guarding ammunition dumps, factories and aerodromes, they organized road-blocks and checked people's identity cards.

Clegg survived the war to return to his Canadian apple farm. SEE ALSO PP. 145–7.

AUGUST 1940

O N 1 AUGUST 1940 Hitler issued Directive 17, which dealt in more detail with the planned invasion of Britain. This was a troublesome document and caused heated argument in Berlin among the service chiefs, who disagreed on how the operation should be organized. The directive called for an all-out Luftwaffe offensive to secure air superiority over the English Channel, followed by an amphibious attack. German commanders hoped to land 160,000 German soldiers along a 40-mile coastal stretch of south-east England. In the summer of 1940 the Germans assembled a large armada of vessels, including 2,000 barges moored in German, Belgian and French harbours. The German army and navy argued bitterly about this operation throughout August, and Hitler had to intervene to resolve matters on more than one occasion.

In the air, the Battle of Britain was now reaching its height. Hermann Goering's Luftwaffe had 2,800 aircraft stationed in France, Belgium, Holland and Norway, and this force out-numbered the RAF four to one. However, endurance and range were critical factors, and the British had the advantage of being closer to their airfields. German fighters could stay over England for only about half an hour before flying back to their home bases. The RAF also had the benefits of an effective radar early-warning system. The RAF was shorter of pilots than of aircraft; fortunately, in many cases pilots were able to bail out over friendly territory and were recovered. The heaviest fighting occurred on 8 August when the Germans lost thirty-one aircraft to the RAF's twenty. Numbers of aircraft lost were announced on the radio and although these figures were eagerly followed by the domestic population as a barometer of success, in fact they were less im-portant than the RAF's refusal to cede air superiority.

In mid-August the Luftwaffe began a concerted offensive against the RAF and its airfields, focusing on the south-east coast from Kent to Hampshire. They also attacked the vital radar sites, which were enabling the RAF to deploy its resources with maximum efficiency. Inexplicably, Goering soon ordered the Luftwaffe to cease attacks on radar stations. However, the raids on RAF airfields were taking their toll and on 24 August the fighter airfield at RAF Manston was so badly damaged that it was put out of action.

Italy continued its opportunist activity in the hope of fulfilling Mussolini's dreams of an African empire that recalled the glories of imperial Rome. On 3 August 1940 it invaded British Somaliland. Italian forces vastly outnumbered British units in the area but were badly organized. The RAF began bombing industrial targets in Turin and Milan.

Wednesday 7 August 1940

Colonel-General Franz Halder attends a conference of the German General Staff to plan the invasion of Britain

General Franz Halder had served in the First World War and in 1938 had replaced Ludwig Beck as Chief of Staff of the German army. He had supported Hitler in his invasion of Poland but, being cautious, counselled against the invasion of France in 1940. He was heavily involved in the planning for Operation Sealion – the abortive invasion of Britain – and later for Operation Barbarossa, the invasion of Russia.

Conference results merely in confirming the existence of irreconcilable differences between us. Navy maintains that landing is possible only on the narrowest frontage, between Folkestone and Beachy Head, and feels confident of being able to assure a continuous shuttle service to the lodgement. However, this front would be too narrow for us, all the more so as it leads into a terrain that offers backbreaking obstacles to any swift advance. A landing between Folkestone and Ramsgate is held practicable by Navy only after coastal defences have been rolled up from the landside. Navy opposes any westward extension of the assault front out of fear of Portsmouth and the British High Seas Fleet. There could be no adequate air defence against these threats.

In view of the limited transport resources, completion of the cross-Channel operation on a broader frontage would take 42 days, which is utterly prohibitive for us. The issue must therefore be settled on higher level.

The German General Staff had no experience of amphibious operations. Invasion barges were amassed at the Channel ports, but were heavily bombed by the RAF. Hitler hoped that London would do a deal with Berlin. Military planners were eventually spared these anxieties when Hitler's eye began to shift to Russia, which it did even during 1940. SEE ALSO PP. 307–8 AND 360–1.

Saturday 10 August 1940

Giuseppe Bottai attends a meeting of the Council of Ministers in Rome

Giuseppe Bottai, the son of a Tuscany wine trader, was born in Rome in 1895. Like many of Mussolini's followers he was a disillusioned soldier who had suffered in the First World War. He was also regarded by many as the 'most fascist of the Fascists', being more interested in racial laws than many other Italian party members. A controversial personality who held in succession the posts of Governor of Rome, Minister of National Education and then Minister for Industry, he was also an avid diarist.

Usual improvisation and lack of planning. Mussolini opens the meeting with an update on the invasion of British Somaliland. The papers have already received news of our advance; we have provided a conservative estimate, as our troops have already started climbing the mountains near Berbera. 'We need to remember,' the Duce observes, 'that percentages are the basis for any peace settlement, and by this I mean that those who have conquered more will be able to carve a bigger slice. The occupation of new territories will reduce our obligation to make final concessions that might be requested by both our enemies and friends.' He then moves on to Cyrenaica: 'It's time to push into the country. Our armed forces are powerful: men, tanks and planes. It's true, there is a desert to cross, but we cannot stop there, we must march through it. We cannot keep wavering, we must take action.' He turns his attention again to military preparations: 'There is still a lot to do to teach the Italians precision and attention for details. There is always something missing. For example, we send tanks and then we realise that the compasses don't work as they are mounted on iron bars'. He fidgets on the armchair and gesticulates to show his disgust: '*Pressapochismo* [inaccuracy] is a widespread disease. All this proves that we must take the Revolution further. We can't keep swaying from public to private.' And here is the enemy: the bourgeoisie. He becomes even more agitated: 'The upper class is the most unruly. I have formulated a definition of bourgeoisie, which I find truly satisfactory and accurate: a bourgeois is someone who is neither a farmer nor a worker; this description is based on economic characteristics. However, if we want to give a psychological portrayal, we shall say that a bourgeois is someone who is only concerned with his own interest.' He returns to military preparations: 'Our air force is excellent; our land forces are heavily armed. By 1941 we will be able to manufacture 30–35 tanks and 30–35 cannons per month. The morale of our troops is very high, despite some disagreements among the officers. Even here we can find the bourgeoisie at work.' . . .

After the meeting, I go with Galeazzo [Ciano] to the Lido. He sounds tired and pessimistic: Britain will fight hard and America is preparing to enter the war. If the conflict lasts beyond the current year, everything will become more difficult. He disagrees with the optimistic assessment made by the Duce on the state of our armed forces: even assuming that we will be in the position to produce 30 tanks every month, this still amounts to 400 tanks per year, which is very little. He has spoken to Graziani who does not wish to attack Cyrenaica. As to Badoglio, Ciano thinks he has started bluffing: he does what everyone else is doing at the moment.

Giuseppe Bottai, like many Italians, had a realistic assessment from the outset of the state of Italian preparations for war and also the desire of the average Italian soldier to fight. By contrast, Mussolini was obsessed with a fear that Italy would be left behind in a vast land-grab that would take place across the Mediterranean and north Africa, and which he expected would involve claims by Franco's Spain as well as Germany. Bottai shared Ciano's distaste for their German allies. Remarkably, in 1943 he would reject Mussolini and change his name to André Bataille and, despite his advancing years, fight the Germans as a corporal in the French Foreign Legion.

Wednesday 14 August 1940

Social reformer Beatrice Webb experiences the all-out attack on airfields in the south of England

Yesterday morning, as I was enjoying my hot bath, there opened a roar of aeroplanes overhead, then machine guns and rapid explosions, shaking the walls and the roof. 'I must not be found naked,' I thought, and hurriedly put on my underclothing. Mrs Grant, white and trembling, was downstairs and stationed herself in the back kitchen with white face and her hands folded: whilst Annie went about her business preparing our breakfast. Apparently there was a battle in the air between seventy German aeroplanes and the Longmoor and Bordon air defences. The roar overhead raged for half an hour and then slowly died away. At one o'clock the BBC mentioned the Hampshire camps as one of the targets for the four hundred German invading aeroplanes. The usual disproportionate German losses were announced during the day ... The best we can hope for is that we shall not be conquered, that Germany will become more hopelessly paralysed by the battles in the air than we shall be ... Anyway there is a growing anger against Germany – not only within the armed forces but among ordinary men and women carrying on the civil life of the nation. Disillusioned but determined to best the invader sums up my impression of the national consciousness. Those who desire to make peace with Hitler before we have beaten his dream of conquest decisively are a tiny minority of the governing class and they judge it better to be silent.

Beatrice and Sidney Webb lived in the Hampshire countryside, near to large RAF airfields and the barracks at Bordon near Alton, and Longmoor near Petersfield. During August the Luftwaffe were still attacking these military targets and doing severe damage to the RAF's defensive capacity.

Beatrice Webb would die of old age in 1943; her husband Sidney survived to see the end of the war but died in 1947. SEE ALSO PP. 48–9 AND 68.

Thursday 15 August 1940

Suburban commuters going home to Surrey watch aerial warfare near London

This diary of a trader on the London Metal Exchange was published anonymously during the war; we know nothing of the author beyond what emerges from his depiction of the impact of the changing nature of aerial warfare upon London and also the growing importance of war controls for the economy. In the City of London, the copper, lead and spelter markets were closed during August 1940 because these commodities had come under the direction of the Ministry of Supply.

Paid a visit to town and was on my way home by train when a flight of planes roared overhead. Then came a series of explosions followed by a continuous rattle like pebbles falling on galvanized steel sheeting. The train pulled into a suburban station, the porters shouting 'Air Raid – Take Cover'. This was the real thing. Passengers poured out calmly into the subway; I took doubtful cover in the booking-hall. After a couple of minutes, the porters yelled 'The train's going on. Take your seats if you want to'. Going out on to the platform I joined a small group gazing into the sky. A diamond-shaped cluster of enemy bombers and fighters was sliding away almost overhead towards the south-east. The sky was blue and almost cloudless. There were the puffs of bursting shells, the rattle of machine guns and the tiny shapes of our own interceptor fighters darting into the swarm. The battle moved out of sight swiftly and simultaneously some local humorist started the alarm sirens working. But amusement turned to dismay when one looked towards the west. Three vast columns of smoke were rising over there to a terrific height. Something had been hit just behind the hill and must have caught fire. It was queer to see these signs of cruel warfare so close to thousands of pleasant little suburban houses whose windows seemed to smile down pleasantly upon the railway in the valley. I felt a strange exhilaration nevertheless.

In August 1940 the population of London still regarded air attack with a degree of equanimity – as a source of dismay rather than horror – for the heavy bombing of London had not yet begun. By January 1941 everything would have changed, and the same diary later recorded that the landscape around St Paul's near the Metal Exchange looked 'a bit like Ypres in 1918' or like pre-war photos of Barcelona during the Spanish Civil War. The diarist's personal view was that this was the end result of Germany's huge inter-war effort to increase its metal production – aluminium for aircraft and magnesium for fire-bombs. For years he had watched the output statistics for German metal production rise; now it was 'flowering in the orgy of destruction'.

Wednesday 21 August 1940

Hugh Dalton, Minister of Economic Warfare in London, discusses bribery

Hugh Dalton was the minister responsible for propaganda and sabotage; Vansittart was one of his advisers. Dalton enjoyed control of the new Special Operations Executive organization (SOE), which had been set up the previous month with the objective of, as Churchill memorably put it, 'setting Europe ablaze' with its resistance efforts.

In the afternoon go with Vansittart to see Halifax [Foreign Secretary], and *his* Man Friday. The purpose of the talk is to discuss how rude we can be to the men of Vichy. The answer is 'as rude as you like'. Halifax says, wonderingly and with a faint smile, 'I have often wondered whether it would not have been possible to bribe Mussolini, but I do not think we could ever have offered him enough to tempt him, and Lorraine always disliked the idea of offering anything to Ciano. He never felt able to hand him £50,000 on the golf links.'

Although the SOE is best known for its work in supporting the French resistance, some of its most successful operations involved money rather than guns. Franco's regime was kept neutral by the dispersal of large amounts of cash, and the SOE undertook similar activities throughout the Middle East, where Arab leaders were kept friendly, or at least neutral, by the payment of secret subventions. Percy Lorraine was the British ambassador in Rome. SEE ALSO P. 26.

Friday 30 August 1940

Joan Wyndham discusses the price of contraception with her boyfriend Rupert

Joan Wyndham was a well-to-do Catholic girl living in south-west London. She attended Chelsea Art College and studied under Henry Moore in 1940. Living with her family but permitted to rent a studio to herself for daytime activities, her half-hearted efforts to remain a virgin were never likely to be effective. Her subsequent experiences were chronicled by night in the family air-raid shelter, where she wrote obsessively about the extraordinary times she was living through.

Didn't see Rupert for a few days, as I was busy at the post – kept thinking about Squirrel and hating her.

Tonight when I went round to the studio just for a check-up, I was surprised to hear the doorbell ring. It was Rupert, who seemed to have something on his mind. After some casual conversation he suddenly said, 'Oh by the way, I was looking through my pockets for some money this morning and I found half a crown in my dressing-gown, so determined to prove my manly powers, I leapt on to my bicycle and went to the chemists down the road and bought *three* contraceptive apparatuses! "Three French letters! The cheapest you've got and be quick before I change my mind!" I cried. "You'll feel more through the three and sixpenny kind, sir" said the chemist. "I don't care about the feeling this is a job of work," I replied sternly.' There was a pause. 'So what do you think about that, eh Joanie?'

I thought it was very funny and rolled on the floor laughing. 'Oh dear, dear,' I thought to myself. 'What a funny life.'

He went on to tell me that when he was at Marlborough all the boys had catalogues of French letters and the cheapest was sixpence. It would last a year if carefully washed, rubbed with French chalk and put away in the box after use. This 'low priced sheath' was known as the Workman's Friend. At least Rupert had spent 2/6.

Joan Wyndham's diaries offer remarkable insight into the world of young people in wartime Britain. They record the attitudes of a teenage girl from an affluent background, discovering love and sex for the first time in one of the more bohemian areas of London. They also capture the deep ignorance of teenagers about these subjects, and the views of her male companions. Joan's boyfriend Rupert was unashamedly lavishing his attentions on two women simultaneously, and Joan was obsessed with her rival 'Squirrel'. Joan's affections had previously been bestowed on a German anti-Nazi refugee called Gerhart, but in May 1940 he had been interned. A month later he had been sent to Canada on the ship Arandora Star, *which had been torpedoed off Ireland. Although there were 868 survivors, Gerhart was not one of them.* SEE ALSO PP. 16 AND 269–72.

SEPTEMBER 1940

T HE TURNING POINT IN the Battle of Britain had occurred in a major aerial engagement at the end of August 1940. Unusually, the British had suffered the more serious reverses, losing fifty aircraft compared to Germany's forty-one. Even more damaging than the straightforward ratio of aircraft losses was the severe pounding that was being delivered to the RAF's infrastructure, including aircraft factories and airfields. The RAF appeared to be losing the air war over Britain.

Fortunately, Hitler chose this moment to make one of his dramatic personal interventions. He ordered a change in tactics and insisted that the Luftwaffe switch its attack from airfields, factories and ports to the terror bombing of civilian targets, and especially London. This was unfortunate for Londoners, who hitherto had not suffered greatly, but it was also a calamitous strategic error on the part of the Germans. Hitler's decision was partly driven by a desire to carry out reprisals for a British bombing attack on Berlin that had been ordered by Charles Portal, the new head of Bomber Command. It also reflected an agreed strategy by Hitler and Goering, who believed that an attack on London would force the RAF to commit all their fighter reserves. The first major attack on London came on 9 September: it consisted of a day raid followed by a night raid, involved over 1,000 German aircraft and resulted in widespread damage.

On 15 September the Luftwaffe made another major effort against London, sending two waves of bombers. But after more than a month of air activity, the Luftwaffe was short of fighter escorts and they lost sixty bombers in this attack, with many others damaged. Most importantly, it was now abundantly clear that the RAF was not close to defeat (as some in Berlin had suggested). At one stage the German bombers were engaged by 300 RAF fighters, and German aircrews were dismayed to see that the British could still field a defence on this sort of scale. Air superiority had not been achieved by the Germans and on 17 September, with winter weather coming on, Hitler postponed

Operation Sealion – the invasion of Britain – until further notice. London, however, continued to suffer heavy bombing raids, and large numbers of civilians had taken to sleeping in underground stations.

Throughout the war and afterwards there were vigorous debates about the extent to which a nation could be defeated by a strategy of intense aerial bombardment designed to deplete industrial capacity and to break morale. The evidence remains ambiguous; in the British case, rocket attacks by German V-1s and V-2s towards the end of the war may have had more impact upon the British population than the Blitz of 1940.

September also marked the beginning of the desert war, in which opposing forces chased each other backwards and forwards across the coastal areas of north Africa. On 13 September the Italians began to push forward slowly from Libya into Egypt. Their commander, Marshal Graziani, had thirteen divisions with which to pressurize Britain's Western Desert Force of two divisions under General O'Connor.

Saturday 7 – Thursday 12 September 1940

Anthony Weymouth, psychologist and BBC talks editor, experiences the first heavy air raids on London

7 September

Mark this day in your memory. For it has seen the opening of the first serious air attack on London. The morning was quiet; it was yet another of those marvellous still, sunny days which have made this summer so exceptionally beautiful . . .

Well, about tea-time came the now familiar wailing note. We moved into the hall. Hoddy [Weymouth's son] was out. He had bicycled to Hendon to see a Messerschmitt which is on view. I passed some anxious moments until he arrived, somewhat breathless. He explained that there was nothing going on overhead, so he had decided to make a dash for it.

We waited for an hour or so, some of us sitting on the mattresses which are now a permanent part of our hall furniture, some squatting on the floor. Audrey put on her tin hat and went round her sector to see if she was needed. She returned to tell us that a big fire was raging in the City. Soon after, the All Clear sounded and we climbed the stairs to the roof. Up five flights – the lifts are not working during an alarm and for sometime afterwards – and along our roof to its most easterly part.

There stood St Paul's with a semicircular background of red. The flames looked perilously near the dome: while to the left the pall of smoke was black – a dark pillar which drifted uneasily upward . . .

8 September

We are alive, but we have passed a night such as I never wish to spend again. We have been lying in the dark on our mattresses for eight hours listening to the characteristic drone of the German aircraft. They seemed to be flying round and round our flat. How close are they? Have they passed? Yes. No – for the exhaust, which was becoming less loud, is now increasing again. And then – the first bomb fell. I could hear the swish and then the explosion, which shook even this apparently sturdy building. I switched on a torch, as I heard Audrey say, 'Steady, peoples.' It seemed a matter of seconds only before a new sound reached us. The clanging of bells, as one after another, the fire-engines raced along the Marylebone Road. The sounds grew in intensity, then became less and less. They were going in the direction of the City.

I switched out the torch and lay down. I could hear Hod turning over on his mattress. Quite suddenly I heard the drone of an aeroplane, and, almost immediately, the shattering noise of a bomb exploding. How near was it? We had no experience by which to judge. All I knew was that the building shook, and my heart raced. Subconsciously, I was waiting to hear the crash of falling masonry. But silence followed the shattering crash. Once more I lay down, my heart thumping against my ribs. Would this nightmare never end? It was only just after two o'clock. The Huns could – and doubtless would – keep it up till daylight.

And they did. A constant drone and bomb after bomb.

We heard the All Clear about 4.30 and promptly went to sleep on our mattresses.

11 September

... I looked at my watch by the light of the torch. It was only three o'clock. Another two hours before dawn would force the bandits of the air to race for safety.

I lay as patiently as I could, thinking about the future. One decision I came to in that long period of excruciating anxiety – Audrey and the children should leave London once this ghastly night had come to an end ...

12 September

... Then on to Beaconsfield. We are welcomed by a kind of family, with whom I leave my children. This country village is full of refugees. I don't wonder. You would scarcely credit that within a score of miles all hell has been let loose. For here all is quiet. I am assured that one bomb was dropped about six miles away – but no one seems to know where.

Many evacuees almost had 'commuter' status. A vast number of children had been evacuated to the countryside in the first days of the war, but most had drifted back after weeks and months without any aerial activity. The beginning of the serious bombing of London in September 1940 prompted a return to the countryside as parents sought to deposit their children with friends and distant relatives. In 1941, when things quietened down, they would begin to drift back once more.

In 1942 Weymouth would publish a popular diary of the period between September 1939 and March 1941 which offered psychological insights into world affairs and also chronicled some of his meetings with famous figures such as the Fabian and playwright George Bernard Shaw and Jan Masaryk, foreign minister in the Czech government-in-exile.

Anthony Weymouth would retire from the BBC after the war; he died in 1953. SEE ALSO PP. 97–9, 101–2 AND 139–40.

Thursday 12 – Friday 13 September 1940

Veronica Goddard, living in west London, survives a bad night in the Blitz

Veronica Goddard was a teenager living with her family at 45 Warwick Road, Earls Court; she kept a diary of her family's experiences of bombing and rationing.

Veronica Goddard

A terrific night. First and foremost we had a new anti-aircraft barrage which continued almost unceasingly through the night. Crack after Crack, bang after bang – it went through one. And bombs – they fell like hailstones. High explosive, incendiaries and time bombs. There was no scarcity of any of them. Down they whistled, crash and then 'Where was that?' Always that question. We never knew, but we had a good guess; more often than not we were streets out in our surmisings. But no-one cared. A 1,000 lb. time bomb was

dropped in Trebovir Road; – Coleherne Road and Courtfield
Gardens had them too. Incendiaries fell in Penywenn Road
doing considerable damage to a number of houses; the
Princess Beatrice's Nursing Home suffered also – so did
Finborough Road and no end of other spots in the
neighbourhood. But worst of all was Warwick Road – not
only because it was very near to us, but it really was a dreadful sight. A large four-storeyed Victorian house lay right
across the road – one mass of rubble. The result of one of
Jerry's finest H.E.'s. As we sat in our shelter we heard it coming. It whistled down. It sounded a long way off at first, then
nearer and nearer it came. Our hearts stopped beating and
then with one final shriek it dived straight down, crashing
on a private hotel two hundred yards away. Then all was
confusion. For one second everything seemed to be crashing
and breaking round us. Luckily the hotel was empty. So the
debris only consisted of brick, wood and mortar – one consolation anyway. But all the houses opposite were ruined;
not a door or window was left intact; railings were smashed
and bent; brick-dust and rubble lay everywhere. Even our
house was in a mess. A thick coating of dust covered everything and anything and glass from the broken windows was
scattered all over the place. Dad lost the two big windows in
his room; the windows in the Dining Room also went and
the fan-light. So we were very lucky. As we stood on the
front doorstep at 5.45 A.M. we looked in the direction of
High Street Kensington. A nasty red glow greeted us from
the sky. Yes. Our Lady of Victories it was. Our beautiful
parish church was blazing furiously, as the result of one of
Jerry's oil canister bombs to say nothing of several
dozen incendiaries which disappeared down at the same
time . . .

*The incendiaries dropped on London in 1940 were of many types. Some
were large oil canister bombs, in which a flammable liquid was used
with an explosive charge. The intention was to cause some blast
damage with the explosive, but mainly to spray the burning oil over a
large area and cause widespread fires that were difficult to isolate and
deal with. Already, oil canister bombs were being overtaken by smaller*

and more fiercely burning bombs made of magnesium. These weighed only a couple of pounds, so could be dropped in their thousands, and often came down by parachute. Some of these were coupled with a small explosive charge, which went off when the magnesium was well alight in order to spread the fire over a wider area.

Veronica Goddard would stop writing her diary in 1943 when it seemed the air raids had ceased, but felt obliged to begin a new notebook with the appearance of the V-1 rocket bombs in the summer of 1944. In April 1945 she became a clerk at the Admiralty.

Saturday 14 September 1940

Frances Partridge, Bloomsbury Group pacifist, on the
selection of evacuees

Mrs Hill on the telephone again! 'I've just heard that twenty refugees are arriving in half an hour. Could you have some more?' R., Burgo and I drove down to the village and waited. Then the bus came lumbering in, and children ran to gape and stare. One very small child thudded along screeching out 'VACU-EES! VACU-EES!' As soon as they got out it was clear they were neither children nor docksiders, but respectable-looking middle-aged women and a few children, who stood like sheep beside the bus looking infinitely pathetic. 'Who'll take these?' 'How many are you?' 'Oh well, I can have these two but no more,' and the piteous cry, 'But we're *together*.' It was terrible. I felt we were like sharp-nosed housewives haggling over fillets of fish. In the end we swept off two women about my age and a girl of ten, and then fetched the other two members of their party and installed them with Coombs the cowman. Their faces at once began to relax. Far from being terrified Londoners, they had been evacuated against their will from Bexhill, for fear of invasion, leaving snug little houses and 'hubbies'.

During 1940 large numbers of people were evacuated from London and the south-east. Although the authorities had the power to billet them on local house-owners, some simply refused to comply and would not take strangers in. Most of those who were willing were 'picky' about their new house-guests. Whereas the first waves of evacuees had come from London and consisted mostly of children, sent away in anticipation of large-scale city bombing, later groups included entire families that had lost their homes in the Blitz of 1940. After Dunkirk in May 1940 there had been growing fears of a full-scale invasion of Britain from the continent, beginning in the south-east, and this prompted an additional exodus from coastal towns that were thought to be vulnerable. SEE ALSO PP. 19, 176–7, 348–50 AND 612–13.

Sunday 15 September 1940

General Raymond E. Lee, American military attaché in London, predicts British victory

Raymond Lee was the United States military attaché and also de facto the head of American intelligence activities in London. He was immensely pro-British and did not like his ambassador, Joseph Kennedy, or his views. Lee, being a mere military attaché, was under-estimated by British intelligence, but proved to be an important influence on his superiors in Washington, who read his reports avidly, not least because they offered the inside track on the London political and social scene.

This is the date after which I believe Hitler's chances will rapidly dwindle. The weather holds good in a miraculous manner but there are faint premonitory puffs of wind from the southwest and a chill in the air. Reports show that he has gathered great numbers of steamers and barges across the Channel, but it's growing a little late for such a campaign . . .

If there was ever a time when one should wear life like a loose garment, this is it. I particularly admire the little tarts who wander about the streets of Mayfair every afternoon and evening in their finery. When everyone else is hurrying for the air raid shelters, they are quite indifferent and continue to stroll unperturbed.

After finishing in the office in the middle of the afternoon, I went for a walk. There are now four big craters in Green Park. Guardsmen are digging rifle pits around Buckingham Palace, I suppose against parachute attacks. In the one air raid of today, which was quite a lively one, with brisk fighting overhead, a number of German machines were brought down. One landed at the entrance to Victoria station, a complete wreck; another on the roof of a house a couple of blocks further on and firemen were trying to get it down . . .

I can't for the life of me puzzle out what the Germans are up to. They have great airpower and yet are dissipating it in fruitless and aimless attacks all over England. They must have an exaggerated idea of the damage they are doing and the effect of their raids on public morale. At the end of this month of blitzkrieg, the British are stronger and in a better position than they were at the beginning.

8.15 p.m. Just as I finish writing this, the heavy guns commence giving tongue – wha-a-am! whaaam! whaaaam! – and the little Irish maid comes in to turn down the bed. She went over to Victoria to see the plane which crashed there and is very pleased because she saw the dead German crew extracted from the wreckage.

It has been a rather good thing that Buckingham Palace was bombed. The people feel that the King is in the same boat with them all and is being as unperturbed and dogged as a British King should be.

Many in the United States were anxious about sending supplies to Britain for fear that the country would soon collapse: Raymond Lee had to work hard to correct this erroneous impression, arguing that Britain would hold out. Lee was competing for the ear of Washington with the American ambassador in London, Joseph Kennedy, and his colleague the naval attaché, who were both loudly predicting imminent British defeat. SEE ALSO PP. 231–2.

Monday 16 September 1940

Walter Musto watches the Blitz from his kitchen garden

Walter Musto, a civil servant approaching retirement, lived in a 1930s semi-detached house in East Molesey, Surrey with his beloved wife Alice Mary and their ageing dog Nell. He had begun his diary on 1 January 1939 at the first signs of impending war. He was a keen gardener and a naturist, and loved being outdoors; nothing gave him more pleasure than pottering in his greenhouse, or sunbathing in the nude among his flowers, interrupted only by the wailing of an air-raid siren or plain bad weather. Walter was too old to fight, but he organized his ARP firewatch unit and, spurred on by the cry of 'Dig for Victory!', grew mountains of vegetables for the war effort.

While harvesting my main crop of potatoes yesterday and tending the kitchen garden, I dreamed as I watched the flights of Spitfires and Hurricanes passing overhead that a titanic struggle was going on in our south-eastern skies between the rival air forces. That Germany is making a terrific bid for the mastery of London is certain; that we are more than holding our own in the air is equally certain. True, Buckingham Palace was again bombed, wrecking the Queen's private apartments, as well as many other buildings, but this morning's announcement of the destruction by our grand RAF boys yesterday of no less than 185 planes out of some 400 launched against us, with a loss of no more than twenty-five, is the best evidence of the price Hitler is paying for his reckless disregard of our decencies. And on this Sabbath day at St Paul's cathedral an unexploded bomb weighing one ton, which had buried itself 27 feet below road level in stiff subsoil and was menacing the fabric of the old church as well as much property around, was lifted out, loaded on to a lorry and removed to Hackney Marshes, there to explode in safety. I cannot imagine any other act calling for such a rich degree of courage as the cool removal in the face of sudden death of this infernal machine. With the fourth raid of the day still in progress we have already spent five of our working hours in the office shelter. But I see no sign of any move by the authorities to turn this time to account or to devise some plan whereby the intentions of Hitler to paralyse production can be circumvented. The same difficulties in going home will confront London's workers tonight, as the nightmare of Friday. Then most of the terminus railway stations were closed, the buses were full to capacity, with queues at every stop patiently waiting in the drizzle. The majority of drivers of private cars appeared indifferent to the appeals of the anxious folk who hailed them. At Eccleston Bridge Green Line bus stop, where I waited over an hour, a riot occurred when a stampeding queue tried to board a bus that pulled up a couple of lengths in advance of its stand. The entrance became so jammed with struggling humanity that passengers could neither alight nor enter and the transport officials seemed powerless to help matters. On the other side of the road an objectionable bus conductor received a crack on the head which necessitated first-aid treatment.

Between 13 and 16 September London received a terrible battering as the Luftwaffe launched another of its strategic raids with two waves of bombers. In fact the raids of 15–16 September marked a significant point in Hitler's fortunes in the west, with 187 German aircraft brought down for the cost of only 25 British planes and the loss of 12 pilots. Both sides tended to exaggerate their victories, but it was clear that the German decision to shift raids from British airfields to the bombing of towns had given the RAF a vital respite. SEE ALSO PP. 242–3 AND 726–8.

Tuesday 17 September 1940

A. J. Sylvester encounters Lloyd George's paranoia over air raids

Albert J. Sylvester was a long-standing denizen of Whitehall and Westminster, having been Lloyd George's personal secretary for more than two decades. He had recorded the former Prime Minister's reactions to appeasement, and then to the outbreak of war.

We motored off to Churt. On arrival LG [Lloyd George] and I enjoyed an Irish whiskey and water and Megan had sherry. LG at once wanted to know whether there had been any air activity and, leaving his drink, he insisted that I should accompany him to the air-raid shelter to decide where we should sleep. He led the way to a most luxurious under-ground apartment which, when I last saw it, was merely being dug out of the ground. There were a number of beds. There was a reading-lamp by the side of each, an electric fire, with furniture made of non-flammable material. The cup-board contained everything that one might require: drinks, eatables, fruit, cigars. I saw, I listened, I wondered, I wondered exceedingly whether he would in this state ever take office again, how he would function. I felt unhappy.

As we left, he suddenly stopped, and holding up his finger, to emphasise the point he was about to make, he said: 'Do you know the Prime Minister and his family sleep in an air-raid shelter at 10 Downing Street every night? Winston told me that himself.'

Megan told me that Dame Margaret had had a terrible time with LG in Wales. That he thought of nothing but air raids, that he had got them completely on his mind, and that they were afraid he would make himself really ill.

Lloyd George, the former Liberal Prime Minister, had been a formidable critic of Chamberlain both before and after the outbreak of war. However, without a party machine behind him he was now no more than an orator and increasingly bewildered by old age and the gathering pace of inter-national events. Air raids in particular proved more than he could cope with. Sylvester's honest diary underlines how many people within the British establishment were still toying with the idea of appeasement, and these attitudes probably persisted until Hitler attacked Russia in June 1941.

Sylvester continued to serve Lloyd George through the war; after the latter's death and the end of the conflict in 1945, he retired and became a leading light in the Imperial Society of Teachers of Dancing. In 1977, aged seventy-eight, he was thought to be the oldest competitive ballroom dancer in the world.

OCTOBER 1940

DURING OCTOBER 1940 the main focus of attention shifted to the Battle of the Atlantic, where Allied shipping losses were horrendous. U-boats accounted for more than three-quarters of the 443,000 tons of shipping sunk during this month. They tended to attack on the surface at night, making them invulnerable to echo-location techniques such as ASDIC, an early form of sonar. They were also faster than many of the surface vessels and tended to get clean away, even after staging daring close-range attacks.

The Battle of Britain continued, but the Germans were now bombing at night-time only. Although some attacks would continue into November, the Air Ministry regarded the last days of October, with the developing bad weather, as the effective end of the campaign – one in which the Luftwaffe had been decisively repelled. Officially, Hitler had merely 'deferred' the invasion of Britain until the spring of 1941; but in reality he was already preoccupied with planning the invasion of Russia.

Meanwhile, both Italy and Germany were becoming interested in the Balkans. On 6 October 1940 German troops were 'invited' into Romania by pro-fascist forces and Germany secured access to vital Romanian oil. Mussolini secretly planned to invade Greece but, typically, did not inform his allies in Berlin or Tokyo. The Italians presented the Greeks with an ultimatum on 28 October, but this was a mere pretext for war and – in the spirit of the age – Italian troops began to move into Greece even before the deadline had expired.

Wednesday 2 October 1940

Colin Perry, aged eighteen, travels from Tooting to
Mitcham to see a Heinkel 111

*Colin Perry was a London teenager who enjoyed the vicarious thrill of
the Blitz. Although it was disturbing, it was also far and away the most
exciting thing he had ever seen. Born in Camberwell in 1922, at the start
of the war he had been working as a junior clerk with the California
Standard Oil Company, subsequently moving to the Royal Bank of
Canada in the heart of London.*

Tonight we all drove out to Mitcham. We had heard so many
tales about land-mines that we determined to see for ourselves. My God, it was no exaggeration. The church just
behind the Clock Tower was completely removed; behind, a
street had literally been destroyed. House after house lay in
piles of dust. It was utter, complete annihilation. The famous
Cricketers also lay crumpled, razed to the ground. In fact
Mitcham had more than caught a packet. On the green, a
crowd of small boys romped gleefully over a light, or
medium Heinkel 111. I surveyed this smashed, dark green
vulture. Outwardly a beauty of a machine, just like a Comet.
(7.50 p.m. There go the nightly sirens: we stay put by a cheerful fire.) Pitcairn Road, Tooting, also all round the Junction
Station, H.E.'s have wreaked their trail of death and
destruction. They are closing in. Each side of us there are
time bombs. However, there is now cheering news of a new
weapon; a sort of rainbow, apparently – seen over France
and here – A ray? Trust the British people to invent something. But I do not intend putting any more news of bombed
areas in this journal unless I or my people have actually seen
the areas.

*By the end of 1940 almost every boy in London had a collection of
shrapnel, usually small jagged pieces of iron, kept carefully in a box. This
material was admired, discussed and swapped at school. Particularly*

prized items included fuses, nose-cones and anything with German writing on it. Civilians developed an alarming habit of collecting un-exploded ordnance, especially incendiary bombs, which were small and sometimes failed to detonate. Most highly valued of all were souvenirs from German aircraft, which would often be stripped clean of anything detachable within hours of being shot down. SEE ALSO PP. 220–1.

Monday 7 October 1940

Emily Riddell tries to buy an air-raid shelter in Barnehurst, Kent

Mrs Emily Jane Riddell was forty-nine years old and lived with her husband John in a new house on an estate at 133 May Place Road East in Barnehurst, Kent. Her husband had joined the Royal Army Service Corps in 1939. They had three sons and a daughter. Her youngest son was evacuated to Wales.

Black day for me. Dad wrote to say we were not entitled to a free [Anderson] Shelter, so after washing went to Town Hall to see if I could buy one. Nothing doing. Don't know where to turn for help. Cannot see the likelihood of getting one under £40. Dad said order one, but it isn't so easy, he did not say where the £40 was to come from. I have about £8 we have had about 12 bombs dropped today just around us. I feel thoroughly depressed having no shelter. What a life. Pipes are leaking in the bathroom again . . .

Anderson shelters were made from curved steel sheets fixed together at the top, with steel endplates, and could just about hold six people each. They were supposed to be buried in the ground, with a thick layer of soil on top. The entrance was protected by a steel shield and an earthen blast wall. Anderson shelters were free to the poor and supposedly cost £7 if bought by anyone else. (The suggestion here that they cost £40 is puzzling.) By early 1940 more than 2 million people had them built in their gardens. Over time they were eclipsed by Morrison shelters, iron cages that provided a place of refuge inside the house.

Emily Riddell's eldest son joined the RAF and would be killed while training in the United States in May 1945.

Sunday 13 – Monday 14 October 1940

London teenager Colin Perry witnesses the 'Hell' beneath the Balham High Road

Sunday night, the 13th, saw one of the heaviest raids of the war upon South London. Balham, the suburb of ordinary people, was again bombed. One bomb has fallen in the centre of the High Road (obviously aimed for the railway close by) and I do not know whether the bus which I saw sunk in the crater this morning drove into it or was blown there. Whatever, only a few inches of the double-decker is peeping above the roadway.

This bomb I think penetrated the steel-encased Tube below the ground, and I hear too that something, by a million to one chance, went down the ventilator shaft of the underground station. The water main was burst and the flood rolled down the tunnels, right up and down the line, and the thousands of refugees were plunged into darkness, water. They stood, trapped, struggling, panicking in the rising black invisible waters. They had gone to the Tubes for safety, instead they found worse than bombs, they found the unknown, terror. Women and children, small babes in arms, locked beneath the ground. I can only visualize their feelings, I can only write how it has been told to me, but it must have been Hell. On top of this there came a cloud of gas. People not killed outright were suffocated, the rest drowned, drowned like rats in a cage.

On 14 October 1940 a bomb exploded directly above Balham tube station. Partly because of large ventilator shafts, the bomb blast went through the road above and penetrated into the tunnel causing terrible damage, severing major water mains and sewage pipes, with the result that the tunnels below ground were quickly flooded. Sixty-seven people were killed and many more were injured. Twenty people had already been killed the previous month after a direct hit on Marble Arch tube station.

Colin Perry would stop writing his diary in November 1940 when the bombing of London diminished and he joined the merchant navy. SEE ALSO PP. 218–19.

Sunday 20 October 1940

Virginia Woolf salvages books from her bombed flat at 37 Mecklenburgh Square

The most – what? – impressive, no, that's not it – sight in London on Friday was the queue, mostly children with suitcases, outside Warren St tube. This was about 11.30. We thought they were evacuees, waiting for a bus. But there they were, in a much longer line, with women, men, more bags & blankets, sitting still at 3. Lining up for the shelter in the nights raid – which came of course. Thus, if they left the tube at 6 (a bad raid on Thursday) they were back again at 11. So to Tavistock Sq. With a sigh of relief saw a heap of ruins. Three houses, I shd say gone. Basement all rubble. Only relics an old basket chair (bought in Fitzroy Sqre days) & Penmans board To Let. Otherwise bricks & wood splinters. One glass door in the next door house hanging. I cd just see a piece of my studio wall standing: otherwise rubble where I wrote so many books. Open air where we sat so many nights, gave so many parties. The hotel not touched. So to Meck[lenburgh Square]. All again litter, glass, black soft dust, plaster powder. Miss Talbot & Miss Edwards in trousers, overalls, & turbans, sweeping. I noted the flutter of Miss T's hands: the same as Miss Perkins. Of course friendly & hospitable in the extreme. Jaunty jerky talk. Repetitions. So sorry we hadnt had her card . . . to save you the shock. Its awful . . . Upstairs she propped a leaning bookcase for us. Books all over dining room floor. In my sitting room glass all over Mrs Hunter's cabinet – & so on. Only the drawing room with windows almost

whole. A wind blowing through. I began to hunt our
diaries . . .

Virginia Woolf

*In October 1940 Tavistock Square, where Virginia Woolf had lived
previously, and her garden flat at 37 Mecklenburgh Square both suffered
bomb damage. In one sense she was faintly relieved, for she now hoped
to escape London and its wartime pressures to a house in Lewes. The
diaries that she was 'hunting out' were almost certainly the twenty-six
handwritten volumes of her own journal, which she called 'a great mass
for my memoirs'. But she never wrote them. On 28 March 1941 at
Rodmell in Sussex, after writing to her husband, Leonard, and to her
sister, Vanessa, she walked into the River Ouse, put a large stone in her
pocket, and drowned herself. Her body was found by children a fortnight
later. SEE ALSO PP. 50–3.*

Saturday 26 October 1940

Charles Ritchie, a Canadian diplomat in London, joins a
bomb rescue squad at World's End

*Born in Halifax, Nova Scotia, Charles Ritchie had studied at Oxford,
Harvard and L'Ecole des Sciences Politiques in Paris before joining the
small Canadian diplomatic corps in 1934.*

Margery, Frank and I went after dinner at this club off the
King's Road to their house in Blantyre Street; they are still
living in this dangerous outpost near Lots Road Power
Station. It is the only street in World's End which has not yet
been bombed. Their house, like the others, is a little square
box of bricks of the type that falls down when a bomb comes
anywhere near it. On this occasion the bomb fell in the
next street. We all rushed out and I found myself helping to
remove the people from the remains of three bombed
houses. There was a large crater where one house had been,
and in the centre of the crater were Margery and a doctor,
trying by the aid of a torch to see who was
injured and how badly. People were being pulled and
pushed up the sides of the crater, to be taken off to the nearest pub to wait for the ambulance to come. These were the
'shock' cases – an old man who let them make an injection in
his tattooed arm without question or even tension of the
muscles – an old distraught mother gasping for breath and
trying to collect what had happened to her – a tall, scraggy
daughter, her cheeks blackened with smoke powder and her
hair wisping wildly about her head. Margery called in
imperious tones from her crater, 'Hot water.' I rushed panting through the dark and empty streets to the nearest police
station then to the nearest public house in search of water. By
now the sky was an ugly 'fire pink' glow from a row of
houses burning noisily in a street nearby. Bombs were
steadily falling and the members of the Air Raid Precautions
and Rescue Squad whom I encountered in the streets

cowered in carefully restrained attitudes against walls as the bombs came down. In the end when I came back with the hot water it was only to find that full supplies had been brought up already. It was the same with everything I tried to do. I helped shock cases to walk to the First Aid station when it was plain that they needed no help. Frank and some men in tin helmets emerged from the crater carrying a wounded woman stretched out on one of the doors of her house. We carried the stretcher Frank calling, 'Go easy there,' 'Gently now.' When we put the woman down on the pavement a man came out of the mobile ambulance, felt her pulse and heart and said, 'She is dead.' Frank contradicted in a pettish tone, 'The other doctor found a pulse.' 'No she is dead.' 'Do not cover her face up,' said Frank as we walked away. We all went to a pub where a fat landlady, her hair in papers, was offering cups of strong sweet tea, while her husband with a conspiratorial air offered to break the law and give us beer or 'take-away ports' although it was two a.m.

We all went back to Blantyre Street and slept on the floor in the basement passage.

The Canadian diplomatic service had been founded in 1909 with an annual budget of $13,550, two clerks and premises over a barber shop on Bank Street, Ottawa. By the 1930s, Canada had diplomatic missions in London, Paris, Washington, Geneva and Tokyo. Canada had joined the war against the Axis one day after Britain. The 24-hour delay was meant to underline that there was a real process of deliberation, signifying a growing sense of independent statehood. SEE ALSO PP. 33–4 AND 707–8.

Sunday 27 October 1940

Mrs Cecilie Eustace on Cub Scouting and the Blitz

Cecilie Eustace and her husband Don assisted in the evenings at the local ARP post at Chiswick in west London. Cecilie also ran the local Cub Scout pack. Hers is one of the many civilian diaries now preserved at the Imperial War Museum.

A whole book might be written about A.R.P shelters, but no words could do justice to their smell. Don and I go on duty two nights a week to make hot drinks, but we kip up in the church – we'd sooner be bombed than poisoned.

Houses were destroyed in our road at the beginning of the raids, and three people were killed . . .

Bombing is so wholesale and regular that Cubs barely discuss it, even when their homes are quite badly affected. Even quite large explosions during pack meetings merely draw forth a laconic 'Time bomb!' Little John Abbess was five minutes late for Pack last week and came in full of apologies. 'Sorry Akela, but our house was bombed last night and when we went back this morning we couldn't find my uniform' and no further mention was made of the subject.

SEE ALSO PP. 238–9.

Late October 1940

Naomi Royde Smith follows developments on the home front in Winchester

Naomi Royde Smith was born in the 1880s and had become an established novelist and playwright. Before the First World War she had been the literary editor of the Westminster Gazette *and her social circle included writers and poets such as Rupert Brooke. For a long time she lived with Walter de la Mare as his lover. During the Second World War she continued to write novels and reviewed books on an almost weekly basis for the* Times Literary Supplement.

Griselda came in at tea-time and told me about a local farmer who had refused to comply with instructions from the Ministry of Agriculture and was shot dead by a policeman. 'Of course', she said, 'the farmer had shot seven policemen himself first, because he wasn't going to plough up any of his pasture as the Ministry of Agriculture wanted him to, so it was justifiable homicide.' She had driven the ambulance which conveyed one of the surviving victims to the Inquest, and had remained with him in court till it was over.

When she had gone I tried to listen to the Symphony Concert at eight o'clock. In the middle of *L'après-midi d'un faune* the voice of Haw-Haw filled the air from Milan to Beromünster. There was no getting any other noise. It declared the Portal family had conspired with the Rothschilds to put Mr. Churchill into power in order that the Insurance Companies might wring 100% profits out of the compulsory insurance against air-raids now being forced on the oppressed victims of Democratic Capitalism. Is the sneering contempt in this being's delivery of his lunacies directed against people like myself who are idiotic enough to listen to such poisonous nonsense? I managed to hear part of the Moussorgsky-Ravel *Pictures from an Exhibition* on the short wavelength, but even that faded out after the first bars of *The Hut of Baba-Yaga*. At 9.30 no British, French or German station could be disentangled from the general cacophony – only Soittens broadcasting a very competent performance of a piano concerto I did not recognise was, as usual, perfectly clear. I left it on for the *Bulletin d'Information* which announced that le marechal Petain had emerged from a month's official silence during which he had arranged for the repatriation of 3,000,000 Frenchmen and the reorganisation of transport in occupied France, and then went on to give a far more pro-British resume of the day's debates at Westminster than it had been doing in September.

In September 1940 Naomi Royde Smith had decided to begin a diary using some old notebooks. She was struck by the marked difference between official persons, who seemed to know what was going on, and ordinary mortals, who were often told very little. Her diary therefore had a particular purpose, which was to show 'what people will believe when they may not hear the truth and also how buoyant rumour, as distinct from propaganda, generally is' during wartime. Like the majority of British people during the war, she searched the airwaves for news and listened to many radio stations, Allied, Axis or neutral. Much of her most reliable information came by letter from friends in London who were 'in the know'. Naomi Royde Smith died in 1964.

NOVEMBER 1940

ALTHOUGH THE BATTLE of Britain was by now effectively over, the air war continued. The RAF now began to step up raids against German cities including Berlin, Essen, Munich, Hamburg and Cologne. Although these RAF raids were light compared to what was to come, 1,300 tons of bombs were dropped on Germany in November 1940.

Over Britain, the Luftwaffe turned its attention to provincial cities, most notoriously to Coventry. On the night of 14 November 450 German aircraft attacked the midlands city, reportedly in retaliation for a raid on Munich the previous week. Munich was where the Nazi party had been founded and Hitler demanded revenge for this insult. The ensuing assault, codenamed Operation Moonlight Sonata, was an indicator of the increasingly scientific nature of war. The attack was led by bombers of Kampfgeschwader 100 – a 'pathfinder' squadron which was equipped with crude on-board 'computers'. These used what was known as the X-Gerät or X-beam system to guide them to their target. The aircraft listened in to a continuous radio beam which changed its note if the aircraft strayed from its line. When they approached the target a second and a third beam cut across the first, telling them to begin their bombing sequence. Later, a young British scientific intelligence officer named R. V. Jones identified the X-beam and arranged for it to be jammed.

The Italians had continued to try to push into Greece, now supported by German air power. However, by 10 November the Italians were already getting into difficulties, and the Greeks took 5,000 Italian prisoners near Mount Pindus. By the end of the month, the Italians had virtually been driven out of Greece. The Italians also suffered reverses at sea. On 11 November the British Mediterranean fleet carried out a brilliant attack with torpedo aircraft against the Italian harbour at Taranto. This was the first concrete indication of how important naval air power would be in this war and prefigured events at Pearl Harbor.

In Warsaw the Germans turned a large segment of the city into a vast Jewish ghetto, into which they herded the local Jewish population. Here the occupants were worked mercilessly as slave labour and endured terrible conditions. Other ghettos were constructed across Europe, but Warsaw was by far the largest.

Friday 1 – Monday 11 November 1940

WAAF Edith Heap finds and loses a fiancé in the air war

Edith Heap was serving in the WAAF at Debden, a little to the south-east of Saffron Walden. This was a sector station for fighters of No. 11 Group. On the night of 1 November she became engaged to Denis Wissler, an RAF fighter pilot flying Hurricanes with No. 17 Squadron who was at the same base.

1 November

Denis and I managed to fix a 24hr pass in due course ... I could only have one night off camp. We went to Cambridge, but we couldn't get in at the Garden House. Denis came out saying 'There's only one double room, so I said no, that was right wasn't it?' 'Yes' I said, and wondered later if he would have asked me to marry him if I had said 'No'. Eventually we got into the Red Lion at Trumpington. Oh place of sublime happiness, had dinner and lots of chat. It was getting late and Denis came with me to my room, sat on the end and asked me to marry him. 'Yes' of course, and he went to order a bottle of champagne, which the manager brought up himself and wished us well. I was surprised that he didn't say anything about Denis being in my room, definitely not done ... He needn't have worried however, after all the bubbly we went to our respective beds.

11 November

17 [Squadron] were scrambled in a hurry and soon in the thick of it and having had a field day with the Stukas a day before, they ploughed in regardless again. Just before we came off at 1200 hrs there was a cry of 'Blue 4 going down

into the drink!'. I was paralysed, and luckily, not frantically
busy, we were down on the floor for the first and only time,
plotting on the black board with more time to listen. The
battle was over suddenly, as usual, and the aircraft returned
to base. One landed very shot up, the pilot died, at Manston,
and I KNEW who had gone into the drink, though I could
hardly believe it and allowed myself to hope. They were still
not all down when we left ops. I didn't bother with lunch but
went up to M.T. [motor transport] to talk to old friends.
When I got back to Saffron, Bill was waiting for me. They
hadn't been able to find me, and hadn't tried the min camp.
Yes it was true. Denis was missing, no parachute.

*Edith and Denis had met at a party at RAF Debden on 7 October 1940.
The connection was immediate and they were engaged in less than a
month. Denis Wissler was heir to the Marmite fortune. He had already
been wounded on 24 September, when he had been shot down by a
Messerchmitt 109 and crash-landed. On 11 November he was shot
down again while attacking a JU-87 Stuka over the Thames Estuary and
did not manage to bail out.*

Later Edith became engaged again and ended the war as Mrs Kup.

Tuesday 5 November 1940

Chaim A. Kaplan watches the children of the Warsaw Ghetto

*Chaim A. Kaplan was born in 1880. He founded a pioneering Hebrew
school in Warsaw, and also spent a lot of time writing for Hebrew and
Yiddish periodicals. His diary of the Warsaw Ghetto, originally recorded
in careful Hebrew script, offers a meticulous report of the Nazi occupation of Warsaw and an extraordinary record of the destruction of the
Jewish communities of Poland. He had begun his journal with
the German invasion in September 1939.*

They have begun sending children of various ages to peddle
in the streets. I saw a boy of six selling 'badges of shame',

conducting his business with eagerness and industry. Little vendors like these are hard to catch, because they are fleet-footed and quick to slip away – and when they are caught their liability is not great. So boy vendors fill the Jewish section with their deafening cries. They are either hawking their wares at the top of their lungs or else running from the pursuing police. Either they laugh raucously or they whine and plead for their lives before the captors who lead them, and their merchandise, to the police station.

The sidewalks are crowded beyond belief. Most of all, mothers take up positions on the sidewalks with their children's cradles, and they lean against the sides of build-ings all along the street. The conquerors have closed the city parks to us. Anywhere that a tree has been planted, or a bench has been placed, Jewish children are forbidden to derive enjoyment. It pains the heart to see the sorrow of our little children. Children who have never known what it is to sin are forced by order of the cruel conquerors to stay out-side while children their age are romping in a half-empty park. But there is nothing which does not become second nature through use. The Jewish mothers have already gotten used to their bad fortune, and in order not to deprive their babies of the sunlight, they take their stand with their cradles wherever there is a square or a vacant lot, or a sidewalk covered with sunlight.

A second phenomenon – characters out of Mendele. The inescapable beggars and paupers have gathered in Warsaw from all parts of the country. And they are types the like of which you have never seen before. By the thousands they beg for food and sustenance in the streets of the Jewish quarter. They surround you and tug at your sleeve wherever you turn. This is not ordinary panhandling, it is artistry. Every business likes to try new things in order to succeed, and those who work at this one are adept at it, as is proven by their inventiveness and originality in appealing to the hearts of passers-by. Thus at one intersection you encounter a group of children of poverty ranging in age from four to ten, the emissaries of mothers and fathers who supervise them from the side-lines. They sing, and their voices are pleasant and their songs permeated with Jewish sorrow and grief. The music touches your heartstrings. Little groups of idlers and strollers stand near the childish quartet, their eyes filled with tears; they find it hard to leave. At infrequent intervals someone turns up who drops a miserable penny into the hands of the little singers. May the philanthropist be blessed!

Three weeks after the Germans attacked Poland in 1939 they had decided that Jews would be restricted to particular areas in cities and towns. These 'ghettos' were effectively large concentration camps, hemmed in with barbed wire and guarded. Jews in the countryside were dispossessed and moved to ghettos in towns and cities. Two major ghettos were constructed in Warsaw and Lodz. The ghetto in Warsaw was the largest and constituted a significant section of the city, with no fewer than twenty-two guarded entrances. A Jewish Council (Jüdenrat) of twenty-four elders ran a police force which was used to keep order in the ghetto and to round up people for labour duties. Later in the war large numbers of the ghetto's occupants would be moved to extermination camps. SEE ALSO PP. 433–4.

Thursday 7 November 1940

General Raymond E. Lee, American military attaché in London, reflects on German espionage capabilities

[Brigadier Arthur] Harker, the [Deputy] head of MI-5, came to see me at Claridge's at half past five to discuss the possibility of American observers coming over to study the fine arts of counterespionage, countersabotage and censorship. He is very anxious that the people who come should not be either politicians or temporary appointees. He told me that at the trial of Tyler Kent and Anna Wolkoff, which closed today, sentences were for Kent seven years and for Wolkoff ten years of penal servitude. Tyler Kent was a code clerk in our Embassy who gave away the whole cipher system and all the despatches to the Gestapo. He was the son of an American consul general. She, Wolkoff, was the daughter of a Russian admiral. When they were captured they were living together. I could not help but remember that Tyler Kent was the subject of a conversation with an acquaintance whom I happened to meet in Bermuda on the way over here and who had been with Kent in the Embassy in Moscow.

Harker confided in me that to their great surprise his organisation had apparently rounded up practically all of the active German operatives in the first swoop at the beginning of the war. He went on to say that they had been watching for a recrudescence of activity but, professionally, he said, 'I am greatly disappointed in what the Germans have managed to do. They are not in the same class as they were in the last war.'

The recruitment of Tyler Kent was one of the better German spy operations of the Second World War, providing them with significant insights into Roosevelt's policy towards Europe. By contrast, German efforts to send additional agents to Britain after the outbreak of war were amateurish in the extreme, and MI5 could hardly believe that they had successfully rounded up the majority of these pathetic creatures. They would eventually be offered the prospect of being executed in the Tower of London or being played back as deception agents. Most chose the latter option, thus providing the foundation of the famous Doublecross operation that would deceive Germany about the location of the D-Day landings in 1944. SEE ALSO PP. 212–13.

Friday 15 – Tuesday 19 November 1940

Clara Milburn watches a devastating air raid on Coventry

Clara Milburn was born in 1883. By 1940 she was living in the countryside with her husband about six miles from Coventry. Although her village was not bombed, the war touched her personally: her son spent most of it as a POW. Her diary gives a clear picture of the impact of war upon a middle-class household and also documents the bombing of Coventry.

15 November

We had a terrible night – not so much for ourselves personally as for the people of Coventry. Jack and I stayed in the
house till 11.15, then he said: 'Well, of all air raids, this is the
one when we ought to be in the shelter.' So he went down
and later came back for me, as Florence and Kate elected to
stay in the house. When we went out the searchlights were
probing the clear sky, the stars looked very near, the air was
so clear and the moonlight was brilliant. I have never seen
such a glorious night. Wave after wave of aircraft came over
and heavy gunfire followed. Scarcely once was there a lull
the whole night. I should have said they came over sometimes at one per minute.

Once or twice we came up the dugout steps and looked
out at the lovely moon and sky, saw the flash of the shells as
they burst high over the oak tree and the sudden glare as the
big gun held forth away to the east. Always there was the
sound of enemy aircraft, and as the near guns fired down we
went and closed the lids above us. We read at first, then tried
to sleep, but I had the only chair down there and Jack sat on
the bench, which was very uncomfortable. He went up once
and came back with a cushion for my head, which improved
matters for me.

The planes ceased going over for a few minutes now and
then towards 4 am and at 4.20 we came up tired out, finding
that Florence had gone to bed and Kate was still sitting in a
chair in the kitchen with her toes tucked up nice and warm.
I then lay down on the living-room sofa, still clad in my fur
coat, for it was very cold and the frost was white on the grass
and the roofs as we came in. We slept a bit and about 5.30,
after ten hours, the sound of planes ceased and the guns fell
silent, so at 5.45 we stumbled upstairs and tumbled into bed.

Poor, poor Coventry! The attack is described on the wireless 'as a vicious attack against an open town comparable to
one of the worst raids on London, and the damage very considerable'. The casualties are in the neighbourhood of a
thousand, and the beautiful fourteenth-century cathedral is
destroyed. I feel numb with the pain of it all. We hear from
here and there of this and that place demolished, damaged
or burnt. The Curtises say their Works is burnt down and we

hear of fires spreading because of the lack of water, as the water main is damaged. One cannot judge the reports as there is no telephone communication with Leamington, Coventry and several places round. Often reports are grossly exaggerated and one dare not accept them.

19 November

Presently my party [of refugees] came along – a woman and two children, and then two more boys, all eating sandwiches! – and we set off to Bickenhill, a few miles distant. I had instructions to take them to the First Aid Point, but the baker of whom I asked the way said it had a time bomb there, dropped last night. I went on and soon a policeman stopped me, told me to get away at once and directed me to the other side of the village – scarcely a village, a mere hamlet. There was a lovely old church and farm close together, and beyond them the vicarage, which was the First Aid Point which harboured the time bomb.

I met the billeting officer along the road, picked her up and drove to the farm, where a kindly soul clad in a tin hat received us. They were a little upset there because everything was all arranged for their visitors – the stage set, so to speak – and then it could not be used. However she soon took them off and we all waved goodbye to each other, myself having enjoyed the warmheartedness of the lady in the unbecoming tin lid! And so back to the schools to find no more transport was needed. But oh the filth, which the energetic teachers were clearing up! They were all wonderful and getting on with the job in an amazing fashion.

The raid on Coventry of 14 November began at 7.20 p.m. with the dropping of phosphorus incendiaries to mark the target. Ten minutes later the main bomber force arrived and dropped 500 tons of bombs, creating a firestorm. Over 4,000 homes were destroyed and three-quarters of the city's factories were damaged. Many of the basic services including gas, electricity and water were heavily disrupted, and many schools destroyed or badly damaged. The tram system was reduced to chaos and half the city's buses were lost. Large numbers of people would be evacuated to surrounding towns and villages.

Friday 22 November 1940

Nella Last, a housewife in Barrow-in-Furness, on the freedom brought by war work for women

My husband said, 'You look lovely tonight,' and I got up and had a good look in the mirror. My crisp set waves certainly *were* lovely, but my face was no different, and I said, 'Would you always like me to look like a doll with a wig on?' He said, '*Yes*, if you mean looking like you do tonight, and I would like you to never have to work, or worry over *anything*, to see you in the glowing silks and velvets I know you always admire in the shops, and fur, jewellery, perfume, lace – everything I've ever known you admire.' I said, 'I suppose you would only think I was putting a brave face on if I told you I'd sooner *die* than step into the frame you make for me. Do you know, my dear, that I've never known the content – at times, real happiness – that I've known since the war started? Because you always thought like that and were so afraid of "doing things", you have at times been very *cruel*. Now my restless spirit is free, and I feel strength and endurance comes stronger with every effort. I'm *not*, as you always fear, wearing myself out – and even so, it's better to wear out than rust out.' Gosh, but I hope he never comes into money. It would be really terrible to be made to 'sit on a cushion and sew a fine seam'!

See also pp. 130–1, 537–8 and 593–4.

Wednesday 27 November 1940

Hannah Senesh debates the fate of refugees trying to reach Palestine

Born in Budapest in 1921, Hannah was the daughter of playwright Bela Senesh and displayed a similar literary talent, winning a scholarship at an early age and writing plays while still at school. She had begun her diary when she was thirteen years old. Anti-semitism was responsible for her being removed from her elected post as president of her school's literary society, and helped to turn her interest towards Zionism. At the age of seventeen she began to learn Hebrew and immediately after leaving school in 1939 she left Hungary for Palestine. By then her father had died; her mother remained in Budapest. In 1940 she was studying at the Nahalal Agricultural School.

A ship filled with illegal immigrants reached the coast. The British would not allow them to disembark, for 'strategic reasons', and for fear there might be spies among them. The ship sank. Part of the passengers drowned, part were saved and taken to Atlit. I brood over this and ask, What is right? From a humane point of view there is no question, no doubt. One must cry out, Let them land! Haven't they endured enough, suffered enough? Do you want to send them far away until the end of the war? They came home; they want to rest; who has the right to prevent them from doing so? But from the point of view of the country . . . really, who knows? They come from German-occupied countries. Perhaps there are elements among them likely to endanger the peace of the Land, particularly at a time when the front is drawing closer.

We argued about these matters among ourselves today. I tried to take the side of the British, but didn't believe in my own argument.

At this time Jewish refugees were arriving in Palestine having fled persecution in Europe, but controversially the British authorities, who since 1920 had run Palestine under a mandate from the League of

Nations, were turning them away, citing security hazards and the difficult ethnic relations within the territory. Many ships filled with refugees were sent on elsewhere, some as far as New Zealand.

The writings of Hannah Senesh, a popular Joan of Arc figure in the history of Israel, offer a remarkable insight into Jewish life in Budapest during the German domination of Europe and also into the activities of the early Zionists in British-controlled Palestine. SEE ALSO PP. 516–17 AND 526–8.

DECEMBER 1940

ALTHOUGH THE WINTER weather provided some respite from air attacks, the Luftwaffe kept up its damaging night raids on British cities. During December 1940 almost 4,000 people were killed by these raids, which hit not only London but also Sheffield and Liverpool. Attacks on London at the very end of the year were particularly heavy.

General Sir Archibald Wavell, Commander-in-Chief of British forces in the Middle East, was given additional resources to launch an offensive against the Italians in the western desert. Although the Italian forces were more numerous, they fought poorly and were quickly broken up into isolated pockets and then defeated.

In London, Anthony Eden replaced Lord Halifax as Foreign Secretary and so joined Churchill's War Cabinet.

The Italians continued to be hard pressed in the Balkans, with Greek forces advancing and prompting the resignation of the Italian commander General Badoglio. The Germans decided to move a great deal of their air power into the Mediterranean, particularly to southern Italy and Sicily, and this was to prove decisive in the coming months.

On 17 December, President Roosevelt announced Lend-Lease, a scheme by which Britain would be supplied with war materials without immediate payment.

Sunday 8 December 1940

Cecilie Eustace feels a shadow fall over the Cub Pack at Chiswick

Since last I wrote a real war-time tragedy has cast its shadow over the Pack and Troop. A bomb made a direct hit on Malcolm's home when he, his mother and Mr. and Mrs. Rooke were all preparing to go to the school shelter, as early as 7 o'clock in the evening. Of all the family, only Malcolm's arm was found, and at least we can be thankful that death must have been instantaneous. And they suffered nothing. For Tony it was different – at one fell swoop to lose all that his schoolboy life had loved. Parents, home and, since he must now live with relatives at Gidea Park, school friends, and Scouts.

We have done our best to help, linking him up with a new Troop at Gidea Park, and our boys are going to buy him a new uniform and stave as a Christmas gift – the last I heard from his uncle was that he was settling down quite well.

Malcolm was the only son of a widowed mother, with most engaging manners and a great friendliness for all the world. It was this very friendliness that led me to suspect a very real loneliness of spirit. Long before he was Cub age he used to long to join us when the Pack played games in Gunnersbury Park, and always had to be driven off home when we left. Although only about five years old, he would always hold his own with the rest of the Pack, but I never expected him to join us when he was older, because of the long journey from his home to H.Q. However, on his eighth birthday along he came, and he was most popular with the rest of the Cubs, largely because he was very much ahead of them in his ways and education, besides being full of ideas and conversation. I found myself when planning my programmes, thinking, 'what will Malcolm get out of this', and his passion for stories led me to buy at least two new books. I shall never read another yarn to the pack without feeling a small shape pressing against my left side (always my left side) absorbing every word with the most passionate interest. I could always feel his concentration; and at the end I shall always hear a quite subdued voice 'Ah – just one more story, Akela, please'. We were reading a story when they told me of his death, and I still don't really believe it. He was so very, very vital and alive, so happy and full of promise that I am selfish enough to grieve at his passing, even while I know that . . . he has passed to a higher service. I must get hold of photo, though . . .

Cubs and Scouts remained active throughout the war. Boys aged eleven moved up from Cubs to Scouts, and more than sixty thousand were awarded a National Service Badge for their efforts on the home front. They fulfilled a myriad of roles, including first aid, signals and telephony; they worked as ARP messengers and stretcher-bearers, Coast Watch, Home Guard instructors and rest centre assistants; they also helped with evacuation of children and with harvesting. By 1945 some eighty Scouts would have won Scouting gallantry medals. SEE ALSO *PP. 224–5.*

Christmas Day, Wednesday 25 December 1940

Laird Archer, an American aid worker, recounts German action against Corfu

Laird Archer was Chief of Mission for the Near East Foundation in Athens. Founded in 1915, this was an American humanitarian organization that focused on rural development, health and education.

Children of Corfu were bombed today in the public square as they were opening their Christmas packages dropped shortly before by British fliers. Four hundred are dead, scores wounded. We have sent bandages and first-aid equipment in the government plane flying nurses and doctors to the scene.

That defenseless town of Corfu has suffered terribly in the past two months. Under an international agreement, it has been unfortified, hence easy game for the Black Shirt bombers. More than a thousand homes have been crushed, nearly all public buildings, including hospitals and orphanages. For sixty days, more than twenty thousand have practically lived in the subterranean shelters of the ancient Venetian and British fortresses which grace with their mossy walls the picturesque cliffs of that charming old town. Twenty-eight days out of the sixty have been a holocaust of bombing and strafing. After each, the people have emerged from their ancient shelters to bury the dead, care for their wounded, and clear away the debris. Early in the war many took shelter in the famous seventh-century Byzantine church where the body of St Stephan is buried, prayerfully hoping that the church would be spared. Now that likewise is gone.

The Allies were hopelessly outnumbered in the skies over Greece. In terms of modern aircraft there were only a handful of Hurricanes to oppose growing Axis air power. Some Commonwealth pilots serving with 80 Squadron operating from Yanina were flying Gloster Gladiator biplanes. Their main target was the Italian tri-motor bomber known as the S-79. SEE ALSO PP. 274–5 AND 284–5.

Christmas 1940

Vera Reid watches Christmas arrive for the underground dwellers in London

Vera Reid was a WVS worker in London between August 1939 and May 1941. She was mostly concerned with the evacuation of pregnant women and schoolchildren and the distribution of gas masks, but also helped with the outfitting of a volunteer military group for Finland and assisted Belgian and Dutch refugees. She had watched the devastation in Oxford Street during a particularly bad raid on 28 September 1940.

Christmas trees for those who shelter in the tubes. And a special train to bring Christmas dinner. How quickly it has all become an organised part of life this living in shelters. At first confusion was bad. People rushed out when the all clear sounded and then went back again at once so that they spent all day and all night below ground. Then came the time when no one was allowed to stake a claim for the night before 6 o'clock. I used to watch them on my way to the club waiting on the platform with large bundles of luggage until the time came when they could get settled down. After that tickets were issued and bunks put up. The bunks were a great improvement. Before that people used to sleep two deep against the walls of the stations while others lay in rows with their feet pointing towards the rails. In consequence there was only just room to walk along the edge of the platform. Not a nice feeling when the train was moving.

The night life differs in every tube station. At St. James Park all is very decorous and quiet. Everyone is asleep or at least lying down when I pass there at night. At Piccadilly there is much more life and variety. People play games, have parties and meet together. At Leicester Square they eat sausages and play toss half penny. Baker Street . . . dull. No cards or games and sleeping people.

Although this diary entry is ascribed to Christmas 1939, the degree of organization described in the tube shelters suggests that it is much more likely to be Christmas 1940.

Vera Reid would lose members of her own family as the result of a major raid on London on 13 May 1941.

Saturday 28 December 1940

Evelin Jackson, housewife, on the perils of travelling and rationing

It was Christmas Eve and I had taken the precaution of securing an Emergency Ration Card before I left home, and came to spend Christmas in Gloucester. I went into the first shop to get my meat ration. I waited my turn very patiently, but it was useless. No meat to be had. A tall man in the rear, very dirty, was hailed with joy by the butcher who had refused me, 'What can I do for you Sir? A nice leg of mutton?' He answered grandly, 'Yes, that will do.' One more effort I thought. 'Couldn't I have a few pork chops?' There they were, most temptingly, on the counter in front of me. 'Well', he said grudgingly, 'I could give you one.' I had visions of returning to the family with but one large pork chop and wondered how far it would go among the three of us. I begged for two thin ones and came away in triumph.

Most people supplemented their diet with additional material derived from 'special sources', whether private connections, local shopkeepers of long acquaintance or the black market. This was true all over Europe; in Germany, civilians prized what they called their Quellen or private sources of supply. However, anyone travelling or undergoing evacuation suddenly found themselves detached from this local network and then the basic ration appeared very meagre indeed.

New Year's Eve, Tuesday 31 December 1940

Civil servant Walter Musto, living in East Molesey, on bomb damage in London

Said a neighbour's wife to him, in her flat, toneless drawl, in reference to the bombed-out area in York Road, Wandsworth, which we passed in his car on our way up to town together, 'I once thought it was nice to have houses all in a row, to save trailing about collecting rents, but when so many can be destroyed by one bomb, it isn't so good.' I was shocked by her outlook, and a further shock awaited me later when she remarked that it were better that the National Gallery had been bombed instead of Hampton Showrooms, as the destruction of all their beautiful furniture almost made her cry. And again, what did the wrecking of London's Guildhall matter? After all, it was an old building. Her chief regret at the end of the day's town shopping was the neglect, through her own indecision, of a bargain offer of a large lampshade, going cheap from a partly wrecked store, 'Oh, it was marvellous!'

Said her husband, 'You already have a good one in use at home, why want another?'

The loss of possessions and physical comforts was not unimportant. For many people who had struggled through the hard years of the 1930s to purchase domestic essentials such as furniture, the level of destruction of household items was genuinely galling. In July the government had published an information booklet entitled After the Raid is Over, *on compensation for injury, insurance, rent and repairs. It went through six editions in two months. In September the government had agreed to pay compensation of up to £2,000 for each house destroyed in the Blitz. SEE ALSO PP. 214–15 AND 726–8.*

Joseph H. Wellings, assistant US naval attaché, sees in the New Year at Scapa Flow on HMS *Hood*

Joseph H. Wellings was born on 23 April 1903 in Boston. The third of four sons, all of whom became rear-admirals in the United States navy, he was commissioned in 1925. In 1938 he had been working in the office of the Chief of Naval Operations in Washington and was already a rising star. In 1940 the British and American navies had substantially accelerated their co-operation and Wellings was one of a team of officers sent to Britain to assist. His speciality was fleet operations, and accordingly he was attached to the cruiser HMS Hood *to observe British tactics.*

Last day of 1940 – up at usual time 0745 – breakfast, a good 1½ mile walk on quarterdeck, more snow last night – Hills are really very pretty – wish I were home. On bridge watching ship shift berths – Not a very good job – cut mooring buoy. Watched the crew get their ration of rum – quite a ritual. Called on the Warrant Officers – had a gin(s) (2).

Lunch, read, nap – First Lieut. in for a cup of coffee at 1730. Dressed for dinner – at 1830 called on the midshipmen in the gunroom and the Warrant Officers before dinner. Had a very fine turkey dinner.

After dinner remained in wardroom – talked with Warrand, the navigator, and Owens. Just before midnight the officers returned from the C.P.O. party. Browne (Lt. Paymaster) rigged up ships bell in Anteroom of wardroom. At 2400 bell was struck 16 times, an old custom. Captain, Admiral, his staff, exec. and practically all officers returned to Wardroom. We all drank a toast to 1941 – Peace and Victory. One of the midshipmen from the gunroom came in with a bagpipe and played Scotch tunes. Everyone started to dance the various Scotch dances from the Admiral down to the lowest midshipman. The Wardroom tables were cleared away and a regular party was in full swing. It was a very unusual sight to see the Admiral, Captain, staff, Wardroom, gunroom, and Warrant officers dancing. Included in the party but not dancing was the Chief master-at-arms and Sergeant Major of the marines. Such a comradeship one would never suspect from the English who are supposed to be so conservative. I was impressed very much. Such spirit is one of the British best assets. This spirit will go far to bring about victory in the end. At 0145 I left the party in full swing and turned in but not before thanking God for his many blessings in 1940 and saying goodnight to my two sweethearts.

– Farewell 1940 – all in all not a bad year although I regret to say I will remember this year as the year my mother died and the year in which I was separated from my sweetheart, for five months. With God's will may 1941 bring peace to the world and happiness to us all – Ring in 1941.

Joseph Wellings soon returned to the United States to report on his experiences aboard HMS Hood *and later went on to have a long and successful naval career. The* Hood *would be sunk on 24 May 1941 when she engaged the German battleship the* Bismarck.

1941

'I STILL FEEL THE shock from the Gestapo adventure,
but so far nothing has happened, and as I am going
to take the diaries to my friends, the Hamkes, I feel
better when I think of a search being made of my
cabin. One night I woke up with a terrible scare. I
dreamt the police had found the books in the potato
box, where I had hidden them, and of course it was
silly to put them there . . . That very night I got up and
fetched the bundle by the light of a torch. But where
could I hide it?'

*Grete Paquin, near Göttingen, entry for 13 May, after being
interviewed by the Gestapo*

JANUARY 1941

JANUARY 1941 WAS A quiet month from the point of view of military operations, these being mostly dependent on reasonable weather. Only in the desert were operational conditions at their peak. Here Allied forces, bolstered by the arrival of the 6th Australian Division, did well against the Italians. Around 30,000 Italian prisoners were taken in Bardia on 3 January 1941. The Italians fell towards Tobruk. Under the command of General Wavell, the Allies advanced rapidly on through Libya against the Italians and took Tobruk on 22 January.

By the middle of the month it was clear to Hitler that his Italian allies had become something of a liability. The proud Mussolini remained reluctant to accept German assistance, yet it was now evident that the Italian forces needed serious support to avoid being crushed completely; Germany would have to intervene in north Africa if the Axis were not to be evicted from that theatre. From this conclusion sprang the decision to establish the Afrika Korps. Italian forces were also on the run in Greece, Albania and Eritrea. Air power had become the critical factor in the Mediterranean war. The Luftwaffe's powerful 10th Air Korps had been established on Sicily, from where it fought a protracted duel with the RAF on the beleaguered fortress island of Malta.

In London, officials struggled to organize facilities for Allied representatives who had become permanent guests for the duration of the war. These included the free governments-in-exile of over a dozen European countries, including France, Czechoslovakia and Norway, which had set up station across London, most of them in the second-class hotels of Kensington and Bayswater. Much of their activity was concerned with resistance intelligence, deception and sabotage and could be troublesome. A range of buildings in south-west London became home to the substantial secret services of the French and the Poles – shadowy organizations which tended to act as if they were a law unto themselves, sometimes even kidnapping people off the streets whom they considered a danger to their own interests.

Wednesday 1 – Thursday 9 January 1941

Alexander Cadogan, the top official at the Foreign Office,
on Admiral Muselier of the Free French forces

1 January

Got further evidence against Muselier ... Talked to A.
[Anthony Eden] about Muselier. P.M. of course wants to
hang him at once. I pointed out possible effects on de G.
[Charles de Gaulle] movement and suggested we must
consult de G. first. A. agreed. Home about 7.

H. H[opkinson] rang up to say Morton [Churchill's
intelligence adviser] instructed by P.M. to proceed at once
against Muselier and Co. I said P.M. ought to talk with A.
first. A. rang up later. P.M. still insists. I said all right
provided he realises what is at stake. Awful lot of work ...

2 January

12.30 A. and I saw de G. and broke to him the news about
Muselier and Co ... de G. affects to be sceptical about
Muselier.

3 January

de G. came to see me and A. at 10.45. He made an im-
passioned but quite undocumented, defence of M.[uselier].
Of course he doesn't want a scandal! We promised an im-
partial investigation ... I tried to get the Muselier story
straight. There isn't a case – yet ... It was that baby dictator
Winston who ordered immediate (and premature) action ...

9 January

X has now confessed that the Muselier documents are
forged! So we are releasing everyone and P.M. apologised to
de G. at 5 this afternoon! I gather he did it fairly well, though
he said to A.[nthony Eden] before 'When I'm in the wrong'
(I didn't know he ever admitted he *was*) 'I'm always very
angry'!

In early 1941 the British Secret Intelligence Service (often referred to as MI6) acquired documents from Vichy French sources that seemed to implicate Admiral Muselier of the London-based Free French organization in treachery. He was accused of betraying a military expedition against Dakar to the Axis via spies based in the neutral Brazilian embassy in London. He was also suspected of conspiring to hand over the Free French submarine Surcouf to the Vichy French. Cadogan found Churchill's impulsive approach to foreign affairs testing, for the Prime Minister would not wait to get the facts straight before acting, and most of Whitehall was frightened of him. The incriminating documents soon proved to have been forged by two British security officers on loan to the Free French who had a grudge against Muselier. The authorities immediately had Muselier released from Brixton prison, where he had been held. The Muselier episode was one of many vexations caused by Britain's hosting most of the Free European governments-in-exile, together with their secret services, which were also based in London and were superintended by MI6. SEE ALSO PP. 31–2, 45–6 AND 419–20.

Saturday 11 – Sunday 12 January 1941

Brigadier Vivian Dykes tours the Bardia battlefield with US General William Donovan

Brigadier Vivian Dykes was born in 1889 in Kent and had served in the Royal Engineers during the First World War. In the troubled winter of 1940–1, with the United States still reluctant to enter the war, Dykes was chosen for a vital and sensitive mission: to guide the legendary Colonel 'Wild Bill' Donovan on an investigative tour of the Mediterranean requested by Roosevelt. By January 1941 they had reached north Africa, where the British had just defeated the Italians at Bardia.

11 January
We got off from Heliopolis at 9.30 a.m. with Longmore and Whiteley in a Lockheed, arriving at Sollum at 12.00. General ['Jumbo'] Wilson [General Officer Commanding-in-Chief,

Egypt] met us. Air Commodore Collishaw showed us his Air
Operations Room located in the old Egyptian barracks, or
rather what was left of them after the bombardment. From
there we went on by car to Advanced Headquarters, British
Troops Egypt, at Capuzzo, where they are very uncomfortably lodged in a tent. After lunch General Wilson took us for
a conducted tour of the Bardia battlefield. We started on the
west side, at the point where the Australian Division
breached the perimeter with an infantry assault one hour
before dawn. Their sappers had blown a gap in the wire with
Bangalore torpedoes and they had then made a small bridgehead to cover the filling-up of the anti-tank ditch. The 'I'
[infantry] tanks had then gone through and moved down
along the perimeter systematically knocking out all the
Italian guns. The Italian dispositions were very unskilfully
made, consisting of a very widely-extended outer perimeter
which was completely unsupported from the inner defences.
Neither line of defences had any depth at all. Nevertheless, the
assault had been carried out with great skill, as it is perfect
machine-gun country. The point of assault was very cleverly
chosen so as to give the maximum observation for our own
troops, with some defilade fire [positions] on both flanks and
for the forming up position. I suspect that Jumbo Wilson with
his extraordinary eye for country had had a good deal to do
with the choice.

The Italian strong-point at the point of assault was very
solidly constructed with covered trenches, but all their
weapons were poorly protected. The natural result had been
that the garrison had been more keen to stay in their underground protection than to come out into the open and man
their weapons. The 'I' tanks had apparently stood up to
field-gun fire extraordinarily well.

We next went over the eastern side of the perimeter and
looked at some of the Italian battery positions in a wadi
which had held out for a long time. There were some pretty
ancient weapons there, including six-inch guns without any
buffers. The gunners' bivouacs were very bad considering
the time they had been there. They had been living in low
sangars [look-out posts] about three feet six inches high,
with groundsheets rigged up to give some cover. All over the

place were masses of equipment and troops' letters. I read several of these and was interested to see that among a couple of dozen there was no sign of the 'dynamic spirit of Fascism' – they were all rather pathetic ones which seemed to show that the heart of the Italian people was not in this war at all.

12 January

The dust-storm was too bad to look at any of the other Australian units or headquarters, so we left at 11.15 with visibility down to a few yards. On arriving at Sollum at 2.10 we found that it would not be possible to take off until later, when it was hoped that the dust would have decreased a little. To fill in time we went down to have a look at Sollum Harbour with Wilson and Longmore ... All over the place there were swarms and swarms of Italian prisoners. Like a litter of pigs, the healthy ones got to the outside where the food and air was; I think some of the ones in the middle of the jam must have been having a rather uncomfortable time. These crowds of prisoners are a great feature all through the Western Desert. You see a column of 2,000 or 3,000 marching along from one camp to the next, most of them with their little handbags packed, and one British soldier at the head and one at the tail of the column. 'Join the Italian army and see the British Empire' is the motto.

Vivian Dykes had worked in the military intelligence section of the War Office that dealt with Italy during the mid-1930s, and had excellent Italian, so the possibility of inspecting the Italians at first hand was more than fascinating for him. By 1942 he would be the first British Secretary of the Combined Chiefs of Staff Committee in Washington, and lived at the centre of Allied co-operation, becoming a key figure in the construction of the wartime Anglo-American 'special relationship'. Dykes was one of the most talented and respected staff officers of the Second World War; sadly, he would be killed in an aircraft accident while returning from Washington in January 1943.

Tuesday 14 January 1941

On queueing and the 'backlog' of death at the cemetery in the Lodz Ghetto

The Lodz Ghetto in Poland maintained its own remarkable collective diary or 'chronicle' which, although written by many, has a strikingly personal quality. Its main architect was Julian Cukier, the son of a prominent Lodz industrialist and a successful journalist who began working on the diary as soon as the Ghetto archives were created in November 1940. He was assisted by six other 'diarists' of widely varying ages and past occupations who all worked together, producing material in different styles. Although Cukier would die of lung disease in April 1943, a team of chroniclers continued the remarkable work. The journal was written partly in Polish and partly in German; the continuous production of six copies would ensure its survival.

'You can't die either these days,' complained a woman who had come to arrange formalities in the mortuary office in connection with the death of her mother. There is nothing exaggerated about such complaints if one considers that, with the current increase in the death rate, a minimum of three days' wait to bury the dead, sometimes even ten days, has become an everyday occurrence. The causes of this abnormal state of affairs are worth noting. There are scarcely three horses left in the ghetto to draw the hearses, a totally inadequate number in view of the current increase in the death rate. Several times, there was such a 'backlog' in the transporting of bodies to the cemetery that, out of necessity, a side-less hauling wagon had to be pressed into service and loaded with several dozen bodies at the same time. Before the arrival of the current frosts, when the death rate in the ghetto did not exceed 25 to 30 cases per day (before the war the average death rate among the Jewish population of the city amounted to six per day), there were 12 gravediggers employed at the cemetery. Today there are around 200. In spite of such a horrendously large number of gravediggers, no more than 50 graves can be dug per day. The reason: a lack of skilled labor, as well as problems connected with the ground being frozen. And this causes the macabre 'line' to grow longer.

Lodz, a city in central Poland, housed the second largest Jewish community in Europe, numbered at close to a quarter of a million, and smaller only than Warsaw. From September 1939 there had been daily round-ups of Jews for forced labour as well as random beatings and killings on the streets. The Germans quickly forced Jews to wear an armband on their right arm, a forerunner to the yellow star that would be introduced more universally at the end of that year. The Lodz Ghetto was created in the northern sector of the city on 8 February 1940. Order was maintained by rationing food, which was always in pitifully short supply. Malnutrition and cold resulted in an appalling death rate. SEE ALSO PP. 320 AND 667–8.

Sunday 26 January 1941

General John Kennedy at the War Office reflects on diaries and Winston Churchill

John Kennedy had been an artillery officer at the 1916 Battle of the Somme, and had subsequently served in the expeditionary force against Bolshevik Russia in 1919–20. During much of the Second World War he served as Director of Military Operations and worked very closely with the Chief of the Imperial General Staff – for most of the war, General Alan Brooke.

It is very difficult to keep any sort of personal record that will be worth having. My day is so full that it is both difficult to give any adequate account of one's activities and almost impossible to find the time and energy to do so. As a rule I have not a moment of leisure till 11p.m. or later except for meal times which I like to keep free by way of respite. There is also the problem of secrecy, one may become a casualty too and it is awkward to avoid compromising papers.

Another difficulty is that it is very hard to be fair in giving an account of what happens. It would be easy by a cunning or biased selection of evidence to give the impression for instance that the P.M's strategic policy was nearly always at fault and that it was only by terrific efforts that he is kept on the right lines – and it would be easy to do likewise with all the Chiefs of Staff individually or collectively. The historian who has to deal with the voluminous records of this war will have a frightful task. I suppose no war has ever been so well documented. Yet the records do not often reveal individual views. It is essentially a government of committees. Opinions are nearly always collective or anonymous.

Winston is of course the dominating personality and he has in his entourage and among his immediate advisers no really strong personality. Yet Winston's views do not often prevail if they are contrary to the general trend of opinion among the service staffs. Minutes flutter continually from Winston's typewriter on every conceivable subject. His strategic imagination is inexhaustible and many of his ideas are wild and unsound and impracticable. Days and hours are spent discussing his projects and it seems impossible to kill them quickly – but in the end they are killed if they are not acceptable – either by persistent, if not very pronounced, opposition on the part of the Chiefs of Staff or by the impact of realities when they see the light of day and are referred to Commanders on the spot or to the foreign states upon whom execution may in the end depend.

The maintenance of elaborate diaries by some of the senior figures involved in the running of the war is a truly extraordinary achievement. The volume of their work was at times crippling, and the ability of men like Hugh Dalton or Alexander Cadogan to write a detailed personal account at the end of a punishing day is amazing. Some were clearly fired by an early decision to write personal accounts and memoirs after the war – as, indeed, John Kennedy did, drawing on his journal. However, his memoirs, published as The Business of War *in 1957, would be much more cautious and restrained than his diary entries. Kennedy was well positioned to observe the interface between Churchill and Britain's military strategy. He rightly noted that although*

Churchill could be a bully, he was not a dictator. When the Chiefs of Staff put their foot down he did not get his way, although the process of battling with him – often late into the night – could be exhausting. SEE ALSO PP. 367–8.

FEBRUARY 1941

ALTHOUGH THE NUMBERS of operational German U-boats were quite low they continued to take their toll: in February they sank thirty-nine vessels, almost 200,000 tons of shipping. Matters were made worse by a foray into the Atlantic by the German cruisers *Scharnhorst* and *Gneisenau*, which slipped out of the Baltic to sink a further twenty-two ships during this month. Frustratingly, the German cruisers then returned unmolested to the safety of the French port of Brest.

Large-scale Italian surrenders continued in the western desert at Beda Fromm and Benghazi. Two divisions of British, Australian and Indian troops destroyed ten Italian divisions and took 13,000 prisoners, while suffering only 2,000 killed and injured. However, the British forces were now exhausted. Troops that might have been used to reinforce them were being diverted to assist the Greeks against Italian incursions from the Balkans. On 12 February General Rommel arrived in Tripoli, together with the first units of what would become known as the Afrika Korps. German and British forces clashed in the desert for the first time on 20 February.

In Somaliland, a force under General Cunningham broke through the Italian front line at the Juba River and took Mogadishu on 25 February; in Ethiopia, the British brought back Emperor Haile Selassie, who since 1936 had been in exile in England, to help organize local tribal resistance to the Italians. Captain Orde Wingate, a champion of irregular warfare and already a somewhat mystical figure, worked with guerrilla bands known as the 'Patriots' to harass the Italians.

In the United States, Roosevelt was sounding more bellicose.

The previous month he had emphasized his idea of the American defence of 'Four Freedoms' – freedom of speech and worship, and freedom from want and fear – in his State of the Union address. As yet, Roosevelt continued to promise American families that their children would not be sent to fight in foreign wars, but he also insisted that the price of this was that America would have to serve as the 'arsenal of democracy'. He then brought forward the critical Lend-Lease bill, which extended greater material assistance to Britain with the additional provision that the recipients would not have to pay for the materials until after the war was over. American isolationists resisted this measure fiercely and the debate, which lasted for much of February, was intense. Prominent opposition spokesmen were the former ambassador to London Joseph Kennedy and the famous First World War aviator Charles Lindbergh. They would have been appalled to know that British and American staff officers were already meeting secretly to co-ordinate plans in the event of a war with both Germany and Japan.

Tuesday 4 February 1941

Mihail Sebastian compares the Holocaust with other pogroms in history

Mihail Sebastian, a Romanian Jewish writer, had been born in 1907 at Braila on the Danube. By the 1930s he was living in Bucharest and was a rising novelist, playwright, poet and journalist, moving in a circle of intellectuals and social sophisticates in one of the main centres of east European culture.

I cannot (and would not wish to) forget the horrors through which I have lived. For the last few days, all I have read are the chapters in Dubnow's *History of the Jews* about the great pogroms of the late Middle Ages. Whether the official figure is correct (three hundred Jews killed) or the much higher one that people mention in whispers (six hundred to one thousand), the fact is that we have experienced one of the worst pogroms in history. It is true that there have been moments in the past when the butchery was greater (during the First Crusade, eight hundred were killed in Speyer, eleven hundred in Mainz – and again very many in 1348, at the height of the Black Death), but the average for a single pogrom was usually much smaller – fifty, eighty, or a hundred dead is the kind of figure that appears in Jewish martyrology, and Dubnow sometimes writes at length about smaller losses that have nevertheless remained in memory.

The stunning thing about the Bucharest bloodbath is the quite bestial ferocity of it, apparent even in the dry official statement that ninety-three persons ('person' being the latest euphemism for Jew) were killed on the night of Tuesday the 21st in Jilava forest. But what people say is much more devastating. It is now considered absolutely certain that the Jews butchered at Straulesti abattoir were hanged by the neck on hooks normally used for beef carcasses. A sheet of paper was stuck to each corpse: 'Kosher Meat.' As for those killed in Jilava forest, they were first undressed (it would have been a pity for clothes to remain there), then shot and thrown on top of one another. I haven't found anything more terrible in Dubnow.

Mihail Sebastian's diary catalogues the infatuation of many Romanian intellectuals with the pseudo-science of fascist philosophy during the 1930s. He also described the appalling repression of Jews, gypsies and communists in Romania. He was interested to examine these issues in cultural and historical terms, comparing them with pogroms of the past, but found no parallel for this new level of savagery. Even in Romania his diary would remain unpublished until 1996, and when it appeared it caused an uproar. Here the blame for the Holocaust had been laid at the door of Germany alone, but Sebastian's diary made it plain that a large part of the Romanian population was implicated. SEE ALSO PP. 303–4 AND 321–2.

Thursday 13 February 1941

David Lawrence, journalist, reflects on America and the swelling tide of war

David Lawrence was a leading American journalist and publisher. Born in Philadelphia in 1888, he had attended Princeton University and began working for Associated Press as a reporter while still a student. In 1926 he founded the United States Daily, *which reported on the activities of federal government, and as early as 1931 made an unsuccessful bid to buy the* Washington Post.

The whole question of American policy is at the moment more military than anything else. The experts who study the hypothetical in warfare must assume that Hitler might attack us through the air as well as the sea if he conquers England, and from bases in Latin America as well as Africa. Confronted with that military contingency, the experts want an armament set-up far beyond anybody's dream of two or three years ago. Likewise, the experts feel that plans for defense only are no longer effective and that a sound defense plan means taking into account ways and means of striking offensive blows.

Thus, in planning bombers for our own use, it is essential that long-range craft be built. The fact that nobody in Europe has built them yet is one reason why American experts want them built.

By and large the debate in Congress centers on some really undebatable points because nobody can assure America against attack and nobody can say that mere defensive weapons will be enough in case of attack. With war on in Europe, the disinterested expert will recommend that any and all weapons be made at once. As for Britain, the theory that it is better to help her fight off the nazis rather than to take a chance on having to do the job ourselves alone two or three years hence is accepted one hundred per cent by the Administration and unquestionably is taking hold with

258 WITNESS TO WAR

the American people, judging by comments received here.

The division of opinion in America, while substantial, is by no means as great as it was in 1915 and 1916 when open sympathy for the Central Powers was expressed and publicly defended. Today the isolationist or non-interventionist bloc insists it is anti-Axis, but is opposed only to war involvement for ourselves.

In 1942 David Lawrence would publish his diary, asserting its value as a kind of anti-history of current times. He insisted that he disliked historians because their books were always coloured by self-satisfied comments and criticisms made after the fact. They enjoyed the unfair advantage of knowing 'the way the plot actually worked out'. Lawrence claimed that his diary was an alternative kind of history writing – devoid of hindsight and drawn up when the writer could not possibly have known what the future held in store. Some of his diary was published as a newspaper column at the time, but a lot more of it was generated in the form of a circular letter sent only to a few friends and relatives. This extract reveals the extent to which many Americans in February 1941, although still anxious to stay out of war, also had a growing sense of the American continent as a beleaguered fortress in a troubled world. The arms industry in America was now running at a fantastic pace. Few could see this boom coming to an end soon, for Germany looked unlikely to be defeated, whereas the defeat of Britain, in Lawrence's view, would only prompt America to rearm more vigorously.

Saturday 15 February 1941

Private Steve Lonsdale, en route to the British 8th Army via South Africa

Private Steve Lonsdale served in the British Army Dental Corps 131st Mobile Dental Unit, part of the 8th Army in the Middle East, and later with the Long Range Desert Group that carried out raids deep behind enemy lines. His diary was kept primarily for his wife Una.

During our stay in Durban we changed ships on to the Orbita, a positive hell ship. A terrible ship, stinking and rotten, one had to sleep and eat on the mess tables, crowded and herded like cattle. The first two nights we had to sleep where we could. I got curled up on deck, it wasn't too bad seeing we had Durban to sweeten it. Then on Saturday 15th February, the day to leave Durban came. We had our first dinner on board, IT WAS CRAWLING WITH MAGGOTS, my God, what a start. Mutterings were heard from all tables. The Officers came, complaints were made, talks of leaving the ship were heard. Then, headed by the Dental Corps, all the chaps trooped on deck to leave the ship. An Officer blocked the gangway, it looked like being good, one man did get off. It all quietened down and the ship put off in a hurry out of the dock.

We were promised better food but it was terrible, dysentery broke out, hundreds a day going down with it. I had a touch of it and believe me it is no joke being on the run all day and night. The tea wasn't bad, the meat you dare not touch, so I lived on a bread and butter tea. Potatoes all went rotten, more than two hundred sacks were thrown over-board and tons of black slime that had once been spuds scraped up and slung. The whole ship was in a filthy state, the decks all filth and flies. We were told that the Air Force had got it in that state. Before we left it was looking like a ship. I still carried on with my batman job. Had to clean the things in the officers cabins, no room anywhere else.

Moving round the Red Sea, the heat was terrific, I did not think it possible to sweat as much. On board we had wash-ing parades. Had to wash our clothes on deck owing to the water shortage. When one thought of the number of good ships that had been sunk and a ghastly wreck like this had missed it all – well it made one wonder if there was any justice. However, good things and bad things must end, and on 8th March, we arrived at Port Tufay at the entrance to the Suez Canal and on the 9th March we disembarked. The dis-embarking and the getting on the train was the quickest move I have ever made in the Army. We got straight on the train and were away within the hour. At the station we were given tea and a cake, it was very welcome. Then we started on our journey into the unknown.

The transport described here was part of the rapid build-up of forces in the Middle East that prefaced further action in the desert, in Syria and in Greece. It has often been pointed out that conditions in the desert were tough, but the journey made by Lonsdale and his fellows from Liverpool to Durban, then on to Cairo (the direct route via the Mediterranean was impassable to Allied ships) was also a real test of endurance. Troop transports varied enormously: some were purpose-designed vessels, but ships of all sorts pressed into service.

Later in the war Private Lonsdale served at the 64th Field Hospital in Alexandria and, during 1945, with 5 Field Dental Lab. Steve Lonsdale would return home safely to Wickersley near Rotherham in July 1945.

Monday 24 February 1941

Able Seaman Charles Hutchinson enjoys some shore leave in Alexandria

Able Seaman Charles Hutchinson served on the anti-aircraft cruiser HMS Carlisle *off the coast of Norway in 1940 and then in the eastern Mediterranean during 1941. His diary records life ashore during periods of leave as well as naval action.*

I heard there was a spot of bother at the 'Maltese Club'. Only Petty Officers were invited, but some merchant seamen had gate crashed and after a few drinks, some bother had taken place, and everyone was fighting. One stoker P.O. was knocked down and then kicked on the ground by ten merchant seamen and was carried out in a bad way, smothered in blood. After it had subsided a little up comes Jack, and thinking the P.O.'s were having a rough house they all piled in and set about them. They were turned out and the doors locked, but they all mustered together again, and came flying in through windows and doors, and it was like all hell let loose. The patrol was called in and when all was at peace in marched the Egyptian police with rifles and bayonets. When it came for the time to leave the Chief of Police asked for naval protection, he said he was afraid of the sailors outside

... A lot of the sailors here have had a hard life on these small boats mine sweeping and take no notice of anyone ashore.

Alexandria was a major port and a recreational area both for soldiers fighting in the desert and for sailors on leave. It was the base of the Royal Navy's Mediterranean Fleet. Public order was always a problem. Egypt was no longer a colony, having gained its independence in 1935; however, much of the infrastructure was still run by the British. The police force was bolstered by a dozen senior officers, called the 'Indispensables', who had stayed on, but no amount of bolstering could contain the widespread troublemaking of sailors on shore leave. Many of them had been cooped up in small ships and had endured weeks of dangerous work minesweeping the Suez Canal; they did not much care what happened to them once they got on shore. It was not unusual for the Fleet Club to be closed because of disorder, or for orders to be given to cease serving beer at the various bars for a period. SEE ALSO PP. 282–3.

Wednesday 26 – Thursday 27 February 1941

William Hares battles incendiaries during a raid on east Bristol

William Hares lived with his wife and children at 9 Merchant Street, Bristol. The first serious raids on Bristol had begun in the autumn of 1940 and were terrifying to a population that had not experienced this sort of bombing before. William Hares was an ARP warden operating from a post near his own street, in a district with a number of warehouses which were major targets.

Planes over. Heavy gunfire. Am relating a few past experiences to the new voluntary watchers, when a plane comes in very low and lets go several bombs. We all fall flat and expect a lot more, but nothing happens.

There's a huge glow in the sky from Eastville way and one

of the watchers tells of a huge momentary flash. Incendiaries are falling away to the east of us mixed with a few H.E.s.

Fire-watchers are discussing the whereabouts of the fires when all at once the familiar hiss of a shower of incendiaries sends us all scuttling for cover. I am standing in the doorway with F.K. The other two men are in the boiler house having supper. As I dive through the door I notice some fire bombs in the Friars, one in Evans' and the street littered with them – a pretty sight! Looks as if the whole neighbourhood is on fire.

Top floor is ablaze. My pals tear up over the stairs with me. What a sight meets our gaze! There is a fire dripping through from the office into the carton room, and all the boxes are blazing. Up the stairs again there is molten magnesium flowing from the top floor setting the lift shaft alight. The incendiary in the office is certainly going some, and I can see in S.'s room there is another making a hell of a mess. It's a fire-fighter's bad dream – you don't know which to start on first.

My three mates are on the top floor giving another the works. So I tackle the one in the office. No time for 'finessing' with stirrup pump or other fancy tackle. Two buckets of water straight on the damn thing, and up she goes. Then some sand on top. I rush down to the boxroom on the next floor. Another couple of buckets of water dampens down the blazing cartons, and J. throws some more over the now burning woodwork.

Up into the form room where another incendiary is lodged in the rafters. We throw water, but cannot reach it. We throw sand over the burning papers, drench the bench with water. Leave that and dash back to the office where the first one is getting a hold on the tables and stock. C. goes up to the bomb, thinking it is a blazing gaspipe, as it is lodged on the wall horizontally. Approaches the bomb with a bucket of water, and attempts to pour the water on to the fire. The bomb blazes more furiously; C. jumps! And throws the bucket as well. It makes me laugh.

Things are getting pretty sticky with fires going in five different places, so J. puts a call through for the Fire Brigade. We keep pegging away at the fires, first one then the other, and gradually get all of them under control. It's the hottest thirty minutes I have ever experienced, and by the time the Brigade arrived they were only needed to extinguish a fire in the Mail Coach.

I then look out, and think that I shall see the whole neighbourhood on fire. But all the fires are well under control now, and have been 'outed' successfully. It was some damn good practice for all of us, and I feel proud the way my crew dealt with the situation. There is no doubt that if any one of us had funked it the whole building would have gone up, as we had no assistance from outside.

Planes were still over, but it seemed that the raid had fizzled out and an early All Clear gave us a chance of looking back on a job well done.

ARP wardens and firemen had to gain experience of dealing with different types of bombs and particularly with incendiaries. Sand was the ideal medium for extinguishing oil- or magnesium-based incendiaries, while water often made the situation worse. Some wardens displayed incredible nerve and put out incendiaries by stamping on them with their boots or picking them up with a shovel.

MARCH 1941

THE AMERICAN LEND-LEASE Act was passed on 11 March and extra supplies began to flow across the Atlantic. The additional food provided was vital, for British stocks were dwindling. The government had been forced to bring in unpopular legislation that forbade the feeding of pets with material that was fit for human consumption. Dog-lovers and cat-lovers protested.

Although the Lend-Lease programme allowed Britain to defer payment for supplies, in order to help the passage of the bill through Congress Britain had to demonstrate that it had lost all of its assets, and in order to do this a number of British companies, such as Courtaulds, were instructed by the government to sell their American subsidiaries at knock-down prices. This expedient dealt a significant blow to the fortunes of many companies and would have repercussions after the war.

An isolationist motion in Congress forbidding US warships to offer convoy protection in the Atlantic was defeated. Germany responded by increasing U-boat operations in what became the Battle of the Atlantic. Nevertheless, three of the more experienced U-boats were lost during the sea battles of March 1941.

As the weather improved the war in the air began to gather momentum again, and London suffered three major raids during March. Liverpool, Glasgow, Bristol and Plymouth were also subjected to heavy attacks. British bombing increased in volume with the arrival of the four-engined Halifax bomber with its longer range and greater capacity. Kiel, Hamburg, Bremen and Brest were all bombed during this month.

In east Africa the British continued to have success against the Italians, but in the western desert the more experienced troops were withdrawn for service elsewhere and the remaining troops had few tanks with which to resist Rommel. This pointed to future trouble.

Saturday 8 March 1941

Eric Baume, New Zealander and journalist, is caught
in a raid

Midnight. There has been a hell of a raid. The Café de Paris got some direct hits. The bombs came through the Picture Show on top, and Ken 'Snakehips' Johnson and others of the band were killed, as well as many of the dancers, including several Canadians. A Canadian Service girl, whose name I don't know, did some good work in rescuing the injured. Just heard that Edgar Percival, the designer of the Percival Gull, and the pilot who used to work for us on the old *Guardian* in Sydney years ago, has been badly injured.

There were plenty of bombs in the Savoy area, and we had

several shakes. I was playing chess with Larry Rue down in Tich's Bar. Bottles and the chessmen were strewn all over the place. As always happens on these occasions, Ed Beattie, of the American United Press, wandered in to say good-day. He and Ben Robertson, of PM, are always on the job when bombs are falling thickest. So is EW McAlpine, one of the Australian editors.

Of course, the censor won't let us mention the Café de Paris . . .

Ken 'Snakehips' Johnson had been Britain's first black swing band leader. He was inspired by the sounds of the orchestras he heard when he had worked in Hollywood in the 1930s, and came to London where he formed the West Indian Orchestra, the first regular black band of any size in Britain. They became London's leading swing band in the late 1930s and 1940s and were the toast of London's café society. Johnson was only twenty-six when he perished, together with the majority of his band, in the worst raid on London since early January 1941. Although it was not on the scale of the raids conducted during the Blitz of October 1940, 156 people were killed; the worst single incident occurred at the Café de Paris, where 34 dead and 80 wounded were initially reported. Press censorship forbade the reporting of the bombing of specific locations for fear of giving the enemy free intelligence on the accuracy of their attacks.

Eric Baume was a larger-than-life figure who by dint of some technical knowledge had become editor of the New Zealand newspaper the Sunday Sun *by 1935. In 1939 he was in London on business when the war broke out and resolved to stay on as a war correspondent. He took a job as London bureau chief of the Sydney-based* Daily Mirror, *set up his offices in two adjoining rooms in the Savoy Hotel, and used his newspaper expense account in the bar and restaurant to entertain widely and pick up good stories. He was the bane of the British censors. SEE ALSO PP. 296–7.*

Sunday 9 March 1941

Arthur Street on pigs and policemen in Hyde Park

A. G. Street was a farmer, broadcaster and writer whose essays appeared regularly in Farmer's Weekly; *he also wrote numerous books about farming and country life in England. A farmer in Wiltshire, he had been disturbed by the changes he had seen in the countryside in the decade after the First World War, and in 1932 he had published* Farmer's Glory, *which documented the transformation he had observed since the turn of the century. As food and farming became major wartime issues he emerged as a champion of the farmer's cause amid a jungle of red tape and bureaucracy, one of the most influential voices of the countryside in the 1930s and 1940s.*

My last broadcasting job was fun all the time. On this occasion it was farming in London, in Hyde Park of all places. The other morning I walked across that park for the first time in my life. I was trying to follow rather vague directions, when a policeman informed me that I could not proceed down a certain path. 'But I've been sent to see the police pigs,' I said. Whereupon he waved me on. Apparently pigs are now a potent password to any member of the Hyde Park Division.

Pigs are pigs all the world over, but these were something special. Granted, they had been born in rural surroundings, but now they were the property of the Hyde Park Police Pig Club, which was started last September. The policemen bought some materials from bombed houses, and with these in their off-duty hours built a pig-sty. I could tell at a glance that policemen had built that sty. Whatever else might happen to its inmates none would ever escape, for it was built solid, like a gaol. Perhaps this was wise, for the other day an odd bomb fell just behind that sty, and it only shuddered a trifle, while none of the pigs was even put off its feed.

Since the forming of this pig-club the pigs have been

bought by policemen, fed by policemen, and most of their food collected from police barracks by policemen. The allure of these pigs is so great that all this work is eagerly done by policemen during their off-duty hours, the club made a handsome profit from its pig-keeping; and the Sunday morning Hyde Park Parade is now composed mainly of policemen's wives and families visiting their pigs. Moreover, when you catch, as I did, a London policeman, out of uniform and wearing an apron of bagging while he mixes up the pigs' food, well, he doesn't look like a London policeman at all. Instead, he looks just what he once was, an English Countryman, and this particular bobby talked to his pigs in broad Devon.

But unfortunately for reasons of policy the best story of this pig-club was banned from the air. One day while off duty one of the smartest sergeants in the division, dressed in old civvies and wearing a disreputable cap well down over one eyebrow and a muffler round his neck, attempted to push a barrow-load of pig-swill that he had just collected across Hyde Park Corner towards his beloved swine. He was sternly admonished by the latest-joined constable to the effect that he was pushing his barrow to the danger of the public. Whereupon he lifted his cap a trifle, and said, 'You ignorant something something. Can't you see whom you're talking to?' Whereupon the culprit stopped all the traffic at Hyde Park Corner from every avenue, and the swill proceeded to its destination in triumph.

Street was dismayed to see the passing of the 'spacious days' of English agriculture and recalled the time when tenant farmers had been relatively well-to-do and played golf or tennis. Farming, he complained, was becoming a 'business', but at the same time the farmer was being economically squeezed. Farmer's Glory *became a bestseller and was widely read in schools.*

Friday 14 March 1941

Captain John Mansel on the importance of personal space in a POW camp

Captain John Mansel was born in London in 1909. He served in the Queen's (West Surrey) Regiment and had been captured during the fall of France in 1940. A qualified architect with skills in technical drawing, he soon became his prison camp's resident forger and developed a reputation for work of extraordinary quality. These secret activities were only hinted at in his diary, which is, for the most part, a superb record of the social life of a prison camp.

Everyone has his particular habits which in normal circumstances one would never think of taking offence at. I will illustrate a few in our room, without any mention of names. The fellow who always hums to himself very quietly when he is reading or you are talking to him. The man who persistently is stroking the long ends of his moustache with his tongue. The man who quietly spits out stray ends of tobacco from his cigarette; who eats abnormally slowly and endlessly chews a bit of nothing which I myself have swallowed in one. The man who dresses slowly and meticulously, looking no better for it, if anything rather a twirp. The man who you can rely on to produce an argument and who will always disagree with anything which is said. The man who is never present when he should be, who, being a bookworm, will pick up any book that comes into his line of vision, open it at the middle and page hop. The man who visits our room for this special purpose, who spends the whole day playing double pack Patience – and thereby taking up more than his fair share of room. And above all the man who *must* be first with the news or acknowledge with 'oh yes' news started by someone else, showing that he knew it already, and who likes to show that he is the origin of all communal benefits or news by the incessant use of the first personal singular. That will do for today.

Many ordinarily trivial matters assumed enormous significance within the confines of a prison camp. No issue became more important for those who were 'waiting on winning' for their release than news. Some of the more organized camps addressed this thirst for information by making use of secret radios and then circulating the information via underground newspapers. Great ingenuity was required, but in fact the guards were sometimes helpful. They too were eager for accurate news, as opposed to propaganda, and would impart information which they had heard from contacts, or from listening to the radio broadcasts of neutral countries such as Sweden late at night.

Although he aided many others in their escape attempts, John Mansel would remain a POW for more than five years. In 1952 he married the daughter of a fellow POW; the couple had two daughters. He died in 1974.

Monday 24 – Thursday 27 March 1941

Joan Wyndham, a Chelsea art student, gets ready to join the WAAFs

24 March

Letter from the WAAFs at last. They order me to report immediately to Victory House for my medical and end, 'Yours sincerely, Commandant in charge of WAAF recruiting. PS. Do not come when your period is in progress.'

Went to Knightsbridge and saw old Bolitho [Doctor], but the cap hadn't come yet.

25 March

Ten a.m. Victory House

Was interviewed by glamorous officer called Pearson, the first WAAF to be decorated for gallantry. She was charming to me, asked how long I'd been an arts student and whether I'd enjoyed it and so on. Then she put me down for special duties which are very hush-hush – map plotting and so on – and sent me in for my medical to see whether my eyes were good enough. After sitting in a vast room full of girls all shaking with nerves, one or two with suitcases and in tears, I was sent by a corporal into an inner room and made to sign a paper saying I had never suffered from fits, bed-wetting, suppurations of the ears, St Vitus's dance, or venereal disease. I wrote 'no, no, no' till my hand was exhausted but noticed my neighbour, earnest and sweating, giving each item her full consideration, with pen poised doubtfully over sleeping sickness.

I finished the list and was pushed into another room, weighed, measured – "at orf, coat orf, be'ind that screen' – and wrapped in a dirty towel while my hair was searched for nits.

The next stop was a canvas booth with partitions, where a bored and weary woman murmured without opening her eyes, 'Please pass water for me, dearie,' and handed me a bottle. I managed to oblige her after strenuous effort, poured the result into a UD milk bottle and marched back through the crowded room carrying it in front of me with some embarrassment. Horrified mutterings from the girls who were waiting. 'Cor! Look wot they make you do!'

'Looks orlright to me!' said the lady who'd first seen me, holding it up to the light, then, turning on me again, 'Dress orf, undies orf, be'ind *that* screen!' There I was confronted by a lesbian-looking doctor, completely hung around with stethoscopes. 'Undress!' she said in a deep bass voice.

'Completely?' I asked nervously.

'Completely!'

She then punched and pummelled me, listened to my heart, hit my reflexes with so much force that my foot shot up and nearly knocked her out and then finally said, 'Well, you seem pretty fit,' and then, with biting scorn, 'And what brought you in then? Mr Bevin?'

'Not at all,' I said huffily, 'I just got sick of my job. I was at the first-aid post and there didn't seem enough to do.' Finally, after someone had stuck tubes down my ears and blown down them, I had the dreaded eye test. Of course I couldn't see a thing on the chart without my glasses, but I fooled them because I had learnt lots of it off by heart while I waited my turn.

So I was passed, registered as fit for special duties, and

told to be ready for call-up in five to six weeks' time.

Bought some Maltesers and went to the Forum to see Peter Lorre in *Island of Doomed Men*. Wish I could write about important things instead of the nonsense that I do. Sometimes I feel the significance of what is going on in the world, but even then I can't put it into words. This war is probably the biggest thing that's happened in history, one half of the world trying to destroy the other. Nothing will ever be the same again – we are gradually reaching starvation point as rationing becomes stricter. Civilians, for the first time, are living under fire. We are expecting the invasion in the spring, poor Rupert's going to sea and may be killed, bombs fall every night and so on, but I don't feel any different to what I did in peacetime, except that I'm a bit happier.

In Zwemmer's window today I saw a huge print of Picasso's *Guernica*. It made me feel something of the awful chaos in which we live. I was considerably moved, but normally I just don't think about it.

27 March

Great day. Had my cap fitted and found I could get it out quite easily this time. It's a sort of twist and a wriggle; you soon get the knack of it, like getting winkles out with a pin. In fact I got it out right first try, much to Bolitho's admiration.

He was very sweet and kind and said it should be almost impossible for me to get pregnant wearing that cap, but I should use Volpar Gel as well. Also be careful in the WAAF and hide it when they have kit inspection – if necessary put it where its meant to go until the danger's past!

Then he told me it would be a guinea, wished me the best of luck and off I went with it in a little box.

The Women's Auxiliary Air Force (WAAF) had been formed in July 1939. Women were not permitted to undertake front-line service; initially they were used to increase the size of the Royal Observer Corps who spotted enemy raids, and maintained and flew barrage balloons. Aerial warfare was increasingly a battle of technology. Many WAAFs were involved in 'special duties' connected with radar, radio direction-finding or photo-intelligence interpretation. The radar control system was vital during the Battle of Britain and later in the war for guiding night fighters towards the Luftwaffe bomber formations attacking British cities under cover of darkness. By 1945 WAAFs would number more than 153,000.

Contraceptive preparations such as those made by Joan through a private doctor were available only to those with money. SEE ALSO PP. 16, 25 AND 203–4.

Late March 1941

Keith Vaughan, artist and conscientious objector, enjoys the intellectual life of the Non-Combatant Corps

Most of the people here are younger than I and better read. University students, school masters, young dons from Oxford and Cambridge. The daily routine of coolie labour keeps our bodies occupied but not our minds. Talk is mostly on the Big Subjects, art and life, literature, truth and philosophy. The only ones with whom there is no contact are the religious groups, Plymouth Brethren, Four Square Gospellers, Jehovah Witnesses. They form an entirely separate group to themselves, and spend much of their free time in prayer. Kneeling by their bedsides in long new woolly pants they look like new-born elephants. It is very much a society of individuals and eccentrics. Consequently I feel more at home than I have ever done before. I am accepted with no difficulty as an 'artist'. A year ago at Guildford such a thing would have seemed impossible. There is no need any longer to use this journal as a refuge and escape. The war is something remotely distant. Private life and its problems seem of no importance. There are days when I feel more alive, vigorous and happy than I can ever remember. If only one had more time and leisure and the work were not so physically exhausting.

The Non-Combatant Corps (NCC) had been founded during the First World War and had grown to 16,000 men by 1918. About 60,000 men and 1,000 women were conscientious objectors during the Second World War; all those of military service age and fitness were required to sign up for some kind of approved work, and about a quarter, of whom Keith Vaughan was one, served in the NCC. Conditions for and attitudes to COs had improved markedly since 1914–18, and some were publicly praised for acts of heroism performed while undertaking civilian rescue activity. Keith Vaughan found the company exhilarating because the NCC was a home for all kinds of fascinating intellectual and artistic misfits. SEE ALSO PP. 57–8 AND 329–31.

APRIL 1941

APRIL 1941 WAS a month of German successes. Rommel began to advance in the desert against weak and disorganized Allied forces under Wavell, the British Commander-in-Chief in the Middle East, and the Italians recaptured Benghazi. On 6 April two British generals, Neame and O'Connor, were captured by a German patrol and on the same day German forces attacked Yugoslavia and Greece. The crucial factor in the Greek campaign was air power. The German forces enjoyed support from 1,000 aircraft, whereas General 'Jumbo' Wilson, commanding the British effort in Greece, had only 80 at his disposal. It was rumoured that Wilson had always regarded Greece as untenable and would have preferred to see Allied forces deployed against Rommel in the western desert. On 19 April General Wavell arrived in Athens to hold a conference with General Wilson and the commander of the Australian forces, General Blamey. They agreed that within a week or two they would probably be forced to evacuate from Greece, but also accepted that they had to be seen to support their allies. Accordingly, they decided to hold on for as long as the Greeks were able to offer organized resistance.

In east Africa, British, Indian and South African units continued to have success against the Italians, but as the Italians weakened all spare units were diverted north to reinforce Egypt, which was coming under pressure from Rommel.

The widening war stretched all participants during April. Events in Greece and particularly in Yugoslavia had taken Hitler by surprise, for Mussolini had told the Germans little about his Balkan ambitions. The necessity for the German armed forces to support their Italian allies in the Balkans would delay preparations for Operation Barbarossa, the attack on Russia, until June. Some eminent historians have speculated that, had this latter attack been launched two months earlier, the Germans might have captured Moscow before the onset of the bitter Russian winter – and indeed, that the eventual outcome on the Eastern Front might have been defeat for the Russians.

Monday 7 April 1941

Laird Archer, an American aid worker, watches the bombing of Piraeus harbour

Wakened at 4 am with a blast of ungodly sound and weird blue light. Our casement windows blew open and we were literally shaken from our beds.

The whole southern sky flamed over Piraeus, an unearthly brilliance that silhouetted the calm Parthenon in stark ghostly beauty. The continuing explosion left Peggy and me with wits shaken, speechless and a sense of the world's end. From neighboring houses came sounds of maids screaming, and the wild cries of a macaw. Nothing in all the sound effects of catastrophe in Hollywood films could match the crashing thunder, the crackling individual blasts under the greater roar, the howl of the dogs and human shrieks.

Later we learned that the eleven o'clock raid last night had struck a tanker which flamed, setting fire in time to a ship loaded with TNT. A British destroyer then had entered the harbor and had tried to tow the munitions ship out to sea. The tow line broke three times. But the destroyer got the freighter outside the breakwater before it exploded – taking those brave British boys and their ship to destruction with it.

Harbor installations, buildings and homes in a rim around the sea were flattened but the city in general was spared. The Greeks will never forget the sacrifice of those British seamen.

During a spectacular night attack on Piraeus harbour, Stuka pilot Heinz Schmetz achieved a direct hit on the British ammunition ship SS Clan Fraser. *The ammunition train alongside her also exploded. Although the Royal Navy pulled the ship some distance from the dockside, the resulting explosions were still devastating, sinking three other ships and flattening much of the port. The Australian ship HMAS* Perth, *moored 200 yards away, survived but was lifted clean out of the water by the explosions and her mooring lines snapped. In late 1943 the same ace pilot would secure a similar success, hitting the British battleship* Warspite *and sinking the Italian battleship* Roma *which by then had joined the Allies.* SEE ALSO PP. 239–40 AND 284–5.

Easter Sunday, 13 April 1941

Kenneth Slessor, Australian Official War Correspondent, Greece

Kenneth Slessor was born in 1901 at Organe in New South Wales and had worked as a professional journalist in the inter-war years. He was also a poet and had several volumes of verse published during the 1930s. From 1940 Slessor was Official War Correspondent with the Australian Imperial Force (AIF), serving with the rank of captain in the United Kingdom, Greece, Palestine, Syria, Libya, Egypt and New Guinea.

At 7.00, Parer and Silk returned from a trip up the line to get pictures. They said that the news was that the anti-tank regiment had suffered severely in the withdrawal, through lack of infantry support – found themselves surrounded by Germans, could not make effective use of their anti-tank guns against them, lost 120 men missing out of 130 or so, and twelve guns out of twenty-four – sounds tall and is unconfirmed. News also that General Mackay has not been located yet. Also stories of other heavy Australian losses, all of which I won't accept until a better source gives it. Parer said that it was reported that British complained that Australians had attacked against orders, also that Australians refused to take prisoners, and Germans accordingly did the same. Germans said to be using all kinds of guile – one tank stopped in front of Australians, and an officer with an English accent in the tank shouted 'Cease fire!' The Australians ceased fire, thinking it was a British tank, and an English officer with them approached tank, saying 'What regiments are you?', where upon he was shot by a pistol from the tank – and the Australians emptied a whole Bren magazine into the German officer. Long, Hetherington and I decided to go up the line early tomorrow morning, to try and get a coherent story for despatch in the afternoon.

Kenneth Slessor

Kenneth Slessor's diaries capture the chaotic nature of the fighting during the fall of Greece and the ubiquitous tensions between British and Australian troops. Greece was invaded on 7 April and surrendered before the month was out. The Allied evacuation was relatively smooth, and although several destroyers and transports were lost to enemy air action, 50,000 troops were rescued, the last of them taken off the beaches on the night of 28–29 April. This achievement would stand in contrast to the shambolic evacuation from Crete a month later. SEE ALSO PP. 352–3.

The German Invasion of the Balkans, 1941

Easter Monday, 14 April 1941

Robert Menzies, Australian Prime Minister, observes and evaluates Churchill

Robert Gordon Menzies served as Australia's Prime Minister for seventeen years. Born in 1894, he was one of five children of the keeper of a grocery store in the town of Jeparit in Victoria. He graduated from Melbourne University with a first-class law degree in 1916 and slowly moved from law into politics. He had become Prime Minister in April 1939.

The position in Libya becomes worse, and Egypt is threatened. In Balkans, the Jugo-Slavs are going to collapse, and as the Greeks have not withdrawn their Albanian divisions, the Aliakhmon line [the main Greek defensive position] will probably be turned and our Greek position rendered untenable.

At War Cabinet, WC [Winston Churchill] speaks at length as the Master-Strategist – 'Tobruk *must* be held as a bridgehead or rally post, from which to hit the enemy'. 'With what?' says I, and so the discussion goes on. Wavell and the Admiralty have failed us. The Cabinet is deplorable – dumb men most of whom disagree with Winston but none of whom dare to say so. This state of affairs is most dangerous. The Chiefs of Staff are without exception Yes Men, and a politician runs the services. Winston is a dictator; he cannot be overruled, and his colleagues fear him. The people have set him up as something little less than God, and his power is therefore terrific.

Today I decide to remain for a couple of weeks, for grave decisions will have to be taken about ME [Middle East], chiefly Australian forces, and I am not content to have them solved by 'unilateral rhetoric'.

With Rommel advancing in the western desert and a German attack on Yugoslavia and Greece under way, Menzies came on an urgent tour of

Britain and the Middle East to assess Churchill and his running of the war effort. A high proportion of the troops in the Middle East were Australian and he wanted to know that they were being deployed sensibly. He was also pressing for the redeployment of more Australian troops for home defence. Menzies was not happy about what he found in London and would have liked to see Churchill replaced. SEE ALSO P. 281.

Thursday 17 April 1941

New Zealander Hector Bolitho experiences the bombing of the Savoy Hotel in London

We have been through London's most terrible night. It is not easy to write down anything about it because I still feel as if I have been hit on the head with a mallet . . . I was dining in the River Room of the Savoy: it was all pretty and gay, and there was music.

We took the sirens for granted when they sounded, about nine o'clock. About ten o'clock there was a nervous movement beyond the restaurant door. I went out and found a few people going down to the shelter. With calm curiosity, of which I would have been incapable a year ago, I walked on to the Embankment . . . a bomb fell, near enough to deaden the world for a moment. Then came the noise of hurrying people; little crouching ghosts, moving against the crimson glow of the river. Flare fell in the east and the gunfire grew into wilder thudding than ever before.

I went back. People were coming down from the heights of the hotel in their pyjamas and dressing-gowns. About half past ten the bombs began to fall like loosened hell. I recall the clatter of the chess players in the bar and an old woman on a sofa, opening and shutting her bag – a nervous occupation for her crinkled hands. There was a jovial Army officer who tried to make a joke of it all, and a little man who simply curled himself up near the door of the ladies' lavatory and went to sleep.

It must have been about midnight when I went into the

street again. The doorman, George Chamberlain, was standing there, erect and correct as ever. Soon the night became scarlet . . .

Three more hours passed before the most terrible bomb of all fell, within a few yards of the hotel . . . The building staggered. I imagined that the vast stone structure was cracking, like biscuits, and that I was living in the last second before death. Glass was flung at us, like hail through an open door. Then I smelled falling masonry. I do not remember a cry or a movement from anybody. We stood still, in the hall, waiting. The silence yielded nothing for a moment. Then I realized that the hotel was still above us. We walked over rubble and glass; then there seemed to be nurses, and people bleeding, and George Chamberlain being carried in. There was complete orderliness: injured people in a line, their faces cut, their hands cut – one with her face slashed, carrying a bottle of brandy in one hand and powder-puff in the other. 'We were blown out of bed in our flat,' she said. There was only one noisy person; a warden who had been wounded, while he was on duty beside the river. They carried him in. He cried out: 'I must go back to my post! I must go back to my post!'

Seven months before this attack, the Savoy had been the site of protest by East Enders. The scale of air attack on London before September 1940 had been fairly light, and accordingly air-raid shelter provision was limited. In the East End it was particularly poor, and after repeated bombing in the autumn of 1940 the residents had had enough. On the night of 15 September over 100 people from the East End burst into the Savoy Hotel, demanding shelter. The size of the building convinced people of its relative safety. With the air-raid warning sounding, the influx from the streets had to be accommodated. The police were called but before any action was taken the 'all clear' sounded, and the populace retreated.

After the war Hector Bolitho would resume his career as a prolific writer of non-fiction. He died in September 1974. SEE ALSO PP. 132–4.

Friday 25 April 1941

Robert Menzies visits tube shelters in London on Anzac Day

Anzac Day. Lay a wreath on Cenotaph, and walk up Whitehall . . .

At dusk, visit Air Raid Shelters in the *Tubes* at King's Cross and Old Street. Indescribably pathetic. Malodorous, or rather stuffy. Bunks of wire arranged in tiers of 2 or 3 along the platforms and in the recesses. Canteen arranged. Little children staggering in beneath bundles of bed-clothes. Old women & men, going down to their nightly burial, for this happens every night, and not just when the alert blows. These people are 'deep shelter conscious'. They are drab, dreary, and look infinitely sad – standing in the queues for their places, for which they have tickets. Squatting on the metal treads of narrow stairs, there to hunch up asleep all night. Stretched out in a bunk, with electric trains swishing and roaring past every few minutes.

To Supper with Noel Coward and Clemence Dane . . .

During the early phases of the war, and despite elaborate air-raid preparations, Herbert Morrison, the Minister for Home Security, opposed the idea of using the London Underground stations as public air-raid shelters. However, shelter provision in the East End of London was worse than elsewhere and the use of the tube for shelter proved popular with those who had no other refuge. Travellers on the Underground in wartime London became quite used to passing through stations crowded with hundreds of sleeping men, women and children together with their bundles of possessions. It is estimated that by 1941 there were 140,000 Londoners using the Underground for that purpose.

Menzies spent five months in Britain and his prolonged absence from Australia would allow intrigue against him within his own party to develop, leading eventually to his own political demise. He would resign in August 1941, after two years in office, but return to power in 1949 at the head of the new Liberal Party, remaining Prime Minister thereafter until his retirement in 1966. SEE ALSO PP. 278–9.

Saturday 26 – Sunday 27 April 1941

Able Seaman Charles Hutchinson evacuates soldiers from
the Greek beaches to the island of Crete

26 April

We cruised around off Souda Bay [Suda bay in Crete] all
night and our orders are to join up with the Admiral of Light
Forces at 1 p.m. . . . our group consists of Salween (2500), the
two destroyers are to have 300 each and we are to take 500
troops.

We went into action this morning, but ceased firing as the
aircraft dropped recognition lights, and were Blenheims, 3 of
them, they were a bit late in signalling, but we soon
reminded them. Just before dinner we were attacked by 12
Junkers 87's [Stukas] . . .

Tomorrow we are on emergency rations, corned beef for
dinner and bread and salmon for breakfast for the next two
days we are told we are on that, but we don't mind as the
Galley is to be used to cook hot meals for the troops. We shall
be packed like herrings. I won't be sorry when we get the job
over – I reckon it will be red hot tomorrow. All the lads are
cheerful cracking jokes etc. I hear Churchill speaks tomorrow, I hope he doesn't count his chickens before they are
hatched, we've two day trips ahead of us.

5 p.m. just steamed through a long patch of thick oil and
all around were dozens of small life saving rafts and two
open boats, all empty, and a lot of wood and wreckage. I've
heard it was a ship that was sunk earlier in the day.

27 April

We made our destination last night at 7.30 and started getting troops on board immediately. We all had our boats
running as we could not get close in, and we left at 4 a.m.
instead of 3 a.m. as we had to take more troops, as there were
about two thousand more than were estimated. Instead of
our five hundred we have twelve hundred on board, and all
the ships are packed . . .

One thing I didn't mention, and that was when we took the troops on board, and on checking them up it was found that we had two Greek girls on board dressed up in battle dress and tin hats. They did weep as they thought they were going to be put ashore again but they were kept on board and put in a cabin, and put ashore here [on Crete]. They wanted to stay on board, and when they [finally] went ashore they were dressed in their normal clothes. I think they would be about 18, and they were very good looking. I think they were homeless and did not like to stay behind and face the Germans. Also we had a small boy with the troops – he would be about 10 years, and he had been with the troops for a while. He was found wandering around on his own as his home and his parents had been destroyed and killed, and he had been following his brother at the front and he had also been killed, so this section adopted him, and he was kitted up in battle dress. He did look pitiful, the uniform was miles too big for him, and you could hardly see him under his tin helmet but he was quite cheerful, and I hope he is looked after. I think he will be . . .

Charles Hutchinson was serving on the light anti-aircraft cruiser HMS Carlisle. Although the evacuation from the beaches in Greece was conducted under cover of darkness, there was then a long and nerve-racking daylight journey back to Crete under constant threat of air bombardment. The Germans had no ships in the Mediterranean but they controlled the air. In the light of this the Royal Navy did well not to be obliterated in the eastern Mediterranean during the operations of April and May 1941. On 27 April two destroyers were lost off Greece while trying to evacuate soldiers from a burning troop transport that had already been bombed. On 22 May 1941 the Carlisle would be damaged by air bombardment during the Battle for Crete, and she endured further aerial attack on convoy runs to Malta during 1942. On 9 October 1943 her luck ran out when she was attacked and badly damaged by Stuka dive-bombers off the island of Kos (the accompanying destroyer HMS Panther was sunk). Carlisle was never fully repaired after this. Charles Hutchinson, however, survived this attack – and the war. SEE ALSO PP. 260–1.

Monday 28 April 1941

Laird Archer observes the German use of 'occupation
marks' in Athens

Wholesale and retail shops are being systematically cleared
out.

This is done by the polite method of 'purchase' with
freshly printed Occupation Marks, of no value outside of
Greece. Early this morning, all troops in Athens not on detail
were issued one hundred of such marks each, the equivalent
of five thousand drachmas (about thirty-five dollars) in
purchasing power. They were sent into the shops to buy anything from women's stockings to electrical equipment. They
took their 'purchases' to the parcel post office or to the railway express and promptly shipped them home to the Reich.
This organized looting will serve a triple purpose: it will
please the Nazi troops, it will make their people at home feel
they're getting something out of the endless fighting, and it
will help to enfeeble Greece. Everywhere, I hear of shopkeepers trying to hide things from their shelves only to meet
with abuse or arrest. A truckload of silk goods being
delivered to the smart Etam Shop was seized, truck and all.
Prices have gone up alarmingly in the effort to discourage
the loot-buying but without effect except on the people of
Athens. I saw a squad of soldiers, who had cleaned out a
small leathergoods shop, carry their new suitcases to
a clothing store to be filled. The Eastman Kodak store has
been emptied of cameras.

*Laird Archer, being an American citizen, and therefore neutral –
although the degree of American neutrality was increasingly in question
– was able to remain in Athens. Here he witnessed a phenomenon
common to almost all occupied countries, namely the legalized robbery
of every shop by means of 'occupation currency' which was given to
garrison troops in large quantities and which had no value outside the
occupation area. Shop-owners were required to accept this currency and*

were punished for attempting to hide their better stock. As the war progressed, one of the activities undertaken by the Allied secret services was the forging of vast amounts of such occupation currency in the hope of undermining or subverting the Axis war economies.

After the war Laird Archer would continue his career with humanitarian relief organizations. SEE ALSO PP. 239–40 AND 274–5.

Wednesday 30 April – Friday 2 May 1941

Maurice Hankey, with Robert Menzies, attempts to 'bell the cat' at No. 10

Maurice Hankey was born in 1877 and had begun his career in the Royal Marines before moving into intelligence work. Proving to be an able staff officer, he had been Secretary of the Committee of Imperial Defence during the First World War and became Cabinet Secretary for most of the inter-war years. By 1941 he was Chancellor of the Duchy of Lancaster and then Paymaster General, although he was strongly associated with the preceding Chamberlain government. In common with Robert Menzies and the Australian Minister of Defence Paul Shedden, and many of the senior military figures in Whitehall, he was dismayed by the way in which Churchill was running the war.

30 April

Shedden lunched with me today. He was at the Defence Committee last night with Menzies. His account tallied with my own experience at the War Cabinet on Monday – a monologue by one man – Churchill. Menzies had gone there to find out about intentions if things went wrong in Libya, where the largest forces are from Australia and N.Z. Apparently Churchill burst out into one of his fervid orations about how nothing would induce him to make plans or order preparations for such a contingency. If it leaked out, our army would be demoralised. They had to contest every inch and fight to the last and sacrifice their lives if necessary to defend Egypt and Palestine and so forth. No one else spoke a single word and Shedden gathered from

Menzies that this was what happened every time he attended the War Cabinet. Menzies at first had fallen for Churchill, but gradually he had changed. He admitted now that it was dangerous to go to Chequers and spend an evening, because Churchill was so persuasive. Shedden with his incisive mind had seen through the humbug of the present regime and is absolutely shocked . . .

I am puzzled what to do . . . It is hopeless to approach Churchill direct because he does not like me; would not take my advice even if he did; and has deliberately smashed up the [Cabinet] system to increase his own power . . .

1 May

Walking to the office this morning I was caught on the Horse Guards Parade by General Kennedy D.M.O., one of the best of the younger generals. He at once tackled me about the Supreme Control of the War; said he was very anxious about it; believed that we should lose the war if it was not put right; Pug Ismay [War Cabinet Secretary] was completely bemused by Churchill . . .

After lunch I bade Menzies farewell. He leaves tomorrow . . . I walked away down Park Lane. We heard someone running and, lo and behold, it was Menzies himself. He burst out at once about Churchill and his dictatorship and his War Cabinet of 'Yes-men'. 'There is only one thing to be done and that is summon an Imperial war cabinet and keep one of them behind, like Smuts in the last war, not as a guest but as a full member.' . . .

At 4.45, therefore, I went to see John Simon [recently retired Chancellor of the Exchequer], at the House of Lords, and under seal of personal secrecy told him the whole story. He was very concerned. We talked for nearly an hour. His final advice was as follows:- 'the best plan is to get Menzies to "bell the cat" before he leaves: he has become a great Imperial figure. He has a big stake in the war; and is entitled to speak his mind: if he will not play, there is nothing for it but for you Hankey to see Winston yourself: you cannot ignore all this knowledge which has come to you . . .'

So I went back to the office, and after long delays managed to get Menzies on the telephone and asked him to tackle

Churchill when he went to say good-bye. He said he had already decided to do so. I begged him to urge Churchill to drop his dictatorial methods.

2 May

Shedden came to say good-by about tea-time. Menzies it seems got no change out of Churchill. In effect his answer (elicited from Shedden confidentially) was, 'you see the people by whom I am surrounded, they have no ideas.' . . . It leaves me in a difficult position. Check-mate in fact!

Hankey's diary, perhaps more than any other private journal, captures the widespread anxiety about the way in which Churchill had come to dominate the machinery of government and the manner in which this had eroded any meaningful Cabinet committee system. It does not reveal everything, for Menzies was wondering about actually replacing Churchill with a Commonwealth figure as head of a revived Imperial War Cabinet. However, there was also something in Churchill's rejoinder. In fact it was the energetic figures that he himself appointed – including Alan Brooke and Montgomery – who would eventually prove to be his equals and resist his more eccentric ideas. It has become more fashionable to criticize Churchill's leadership in recent decades; however, his belief that the United States was the key source of strategic salvation for Britain was wholly correct.

Hankey survived the war and died in 1963.

MAY 1941

IN THE EARLY PART of the month the Blitz on London reached new heights. On 10 May the Germans carried out their largest raid of the entire war, killing over 3,000 people and destroying part of the House of Commons. Nevertheless, the shift away from the earlier strategy of bombing airfields continued to offer the RAF breathing space, and so the Luftwaffe was still denied air superiority over Britain.

In the middle of May 1941 one particular Luftwaffe aircraft made a remarkable flight to Scotland. It contained Rudolf Hess, Hitler's deputy, who landed by parachute near Glasgow. Many believed that this was a personal peace initiative, or even a scheme for *rapprochement* sponsored by Hitler as a prelude to his attack on Russia. The true purpose of his visit was a cause of endless speculation at the time, and it continues to be so more than half a century later, remaining one of the most mysterious episodes of the Second World War.

In early May the Middle East was preoccupied with large numbers of evacuees arriving from Greece, while German troops attempted to lay siege to Tobruk. The Middle Eastern theatre was also, for no apparent reason, the birthplace of a remarkable range of special force units or 'funnies' that were either exalted or hated by senior commanders. They had their origin in brilliant but eccentric individuals who could see the potential of small raiding forces working behind enemy lines. These new units included the Special Air Service and some of the first sophisticated units created for perpetrating deception.

Intelligence had a critical role to play in the battle for Crete. Although the reading of German communications had yielded precise details of the German plans, the British commander on Crete, General Bernard Freyberg, had been given strict instructions to be cautious in using the information, for fear of giving away what they knew. The German airborne attack began on 20 May 1941 using the 7th Paratroop Division. The fighting on Crete was bloody and chaotic. Eventually the Germans gained control of Maleme airfield and were able to fly in reinforcements. Although the German paratroopers were victorious, they suffered horrendous casualties, and because of this experience never attempted another airborne attack for the entire duration of the war.

In east Africa Axis forces suffered defeat. The Italian commander, the Duke of Aosta, surrendered on 20 May and Churchill announced a victorious end to an offensive that had lasted only four months. A key factor had been support from the local indigenous tribes or 'Patriots', advised and assisted by Colonel Orde Wingate. While the British treated surrendered Italian personnel well, the local tribes were extremely bloodthirsty and rarely accepted surrender.

ABOVE: Hitler's troops entered Austria in 1938 and received a jubilant response from the local population.

BELOW: German and Russian soldiers meet in Poland: in September 1939 some German soldiers were captured by the Poles but then released by the Russians as Hitler and Stalin divided Poland between them.

RIGHT AND BELOW: Miss D. M. Hoyles, the head teacher at Albany Road junior school in North London, found that her entire school was evacuated to Weymouth in September 1939. See p. 67. The children from Albany Road (pictured) enjoyed the seaside but Weymouth offered only relative safety as it also was to suffer bombing.

OPPOSITE: ARP wardens like William Holl (p. 61) found that London residents awaited the arrival of the German bombers with a mixture of fear and fascination.

BELOW: German internees en route to the Isle of Man in May 1940. The diaries of people like Harry Seidler (p. 150) reveal that many were treated badly in Britain and later in Canada.

ABOVE: The Home Guard improvised all manner of dangerous weapons. Here they attack a dummy 'German tank' with Molotov cocktails in 1940.

BELOW: The Local Defence Volunteers or LDVs were renamed 'the Home Guard' soon after the war began, and started searching for saboteurs and parachutists.

ABOVE: WAAFs like Joan Wyndham (p. 269) played an important part in the Battle of Britain and their number rose to over 153,000 by the end of the war. Their achievements refuted the RAF's initial claim that WAAFs were not strong enough to handle barrage balloons.

BELOW: The desert war in Libya: the first stop for the wounded was the Regimental Aid Post, a grim sorting centre for separating the treatable wounded from the dying.

When Rudolf Hess's aircraft crashed in Scotland in May 1941 journalists such as Eric Baume (p. 296) could get no information from a bemused Whitehall.

LEFT: In 1941 British women were conscripted for the services and for the factories. Women like Kathleen Church-Bliss and Elsie Whiteman (p. 507) chose to work on lathes at light engineering factories.

BELOW: A bombed house in suburban London with its Anderson shelter. This form of shelter was a cheap, safe and accessible refuge for thousands of Londoners. Families on low incomes were provided with free shelters.

ABOVE: James Ambrose Brown (p. 439) and Neil McCallum (p. 467) noted how allied soldiers greeted the desert Arabs with fascination, but treated the urban population of Cairo with disdain.

BELOW: In the dust and confusion of the desert war, a surprising number of senior British officers were taken prisoner. Some escaped, but the rest were flown to Italy.

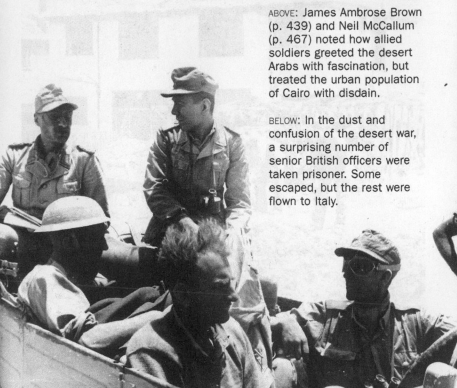

The last days of the month also saw a major sea battle. On 24 May the German battleship *Bismarck* and her escort the *Prinz Eugen* sank the elderly British battleship HMS *Hood* and damaged the more modern HMS *Prince of Wales* in the North Sea. After an extended pursuit, the *Bismarck* was sunk by combined air and surface action off the coast of Brest two days later. In the Atlantic, the Allies lost almost sixty ships to U-boats, partly because Germany had shifted operations to waters that were less well protected off the coast of Africa. However, in the British code-breaking centre at Bletchley Park Luftwaffe codes were already being read, and progress was being made against the operational codes used by the German navy.

Monday 5 May 1941

The Countess of Ranfurly calls on Peter Fleming and Bill Stirling in Cairo

At the outset of the war Dan Ranfurly had been sent out to fight in the Middle East with his Nottinghamshire-based regiment, the Sherwood Rangers. His young wife, Hermione, decided to follow him to Cairo, despite the fact that this was not allowed by regulations. Hermione Ranfurly was not the sort of person who took no for an answer. Born in 1913, she remarked that life began as a disappointment because she 'was not born a boy', and continued to be a disappointment because she later discovered that she 'was ugly'. She had kept a diary since she was five years old and used it to capture her experiences and adventures.

Peter Fleming, just returned from Greece, came to see me. The boat he was escaping on was bombed. One of his men was killed and he was wounded.

On my way home from work I called on Peter and Bill Stirling whose flat is close by our Embassy. I wanted to give them my news of Dan. Mo, their Sudanese Sofragi, opened their door furiously brandishing a dustpan. Apparently the Stirlings went to a party last night, lost all their money at cards and rode home on a 'borrowed' donkey which they inveigled up to their third-floor flat. Mo found it in their drawing room when he arrived in the early morning. Since then it had refused to go downstairs and had thoroughly manured the carpet. Mo, erupting in rage, said to me, 'I give notice many time to Mr Stirling but he only laugh. First they scramble eggs in my tarboosh [the Egyptian variant of a Fez]; next they hire one damn bad cook who chase me with chopper; and now they catchit one donkey who sheet everywhere. It's too heavy to carry downstairs . . . Last week they sit in drawing room and practise their revolvers at wall and bullets come through wall into dining room where I lay table and I have to leave in hurry on stomach . . .' I suggested he find a safer job, which made him more angry: 'you know they give me awful times but you forget they are my very best friends and I never, ever, work for nobody else.' I patted his shoulder and he began to laugh: 'No ever any dull times,' he said and wandered off to the kitchen.

Hermione Ranfurly's journey to the Middle East was full of adventure. Once there, she would soon find work in the local headquarters of the SOE, whose low profile suited her own illegal presence in Cairo. She became familiar with a host of famous figures including Peter Fleming, a deception officer and peacetime adventurer (and also brother of Ian Fleming, the naval intelligence officer who would later create James Bond). She spent time in the company of Bill and David Stirling, who were then attempting to set up the Special Air Service (SAS). People of this kind were an asset on the battlefield, but were also sufficient to try anyone's patience when allowed to enjoy themselves in Cairo.

Hermione was initially hunted by the military police; eventually, however, General Wavell, the Middle East commander, relented, deciding that she was best used to keep an eye on the SOE, over which he had no control. Hermione was soon working for SOE Cairo during the day, but then informing on its activities to Wavell during the night. Documents were smuggled out of the SOE headquarters, copied and returned in the early morning. SOE Cairo was especially troublesome and was the subject of a secret investigation in 1942. Such 'friendly spying' was not an unusual state of affairs within wartime secret services, which expanded quickly and caused immense problems with command jurisdictions and personal rivalries. SEE ALSO PP. 447–8 AND 721–2.

Wednesday 7 – Thursday 8 May 1941

R. Peat helps with first aid during an air raid in central Hull

Just before the outbreak of war, Peat had been a member of the St Mary's and St Peter's Boy Scout troop in central Hull, and in 1939 he was asked to volunteer to assist with air-raid precautions. Initially this just involved filling sandbags and then assisting at a warden's post. In 1940 he became a member of the Cyclist Messenger Corps and by 1941 he was working at a first aid post (FAP) in North Road with his brother.

The sirens sounded and although I went straight to the FAP the sky was red with fires before I arrived. My name was put on the blackboard to go out with the first ambulance. We could see we were in for a terrible night. The first call came for us to go near the side of the Riverside Quay. On leaving the Post I was told there would be no fire engines available. I set off at great speed and was joined by my Div[isional] Officer. As we neared the docks we could hear a bomb getting nearer and nearer but neither of us wanted to be the first to lay down but the decision was made for us by the bomb. The dock was blazing from end to end and we found a public shelter had been hit. Police Constable No. 902 hung his oil lamp on a tree and took our names. We were told to wear our goggles. The full length of the street was blazing. The ambulances became blocked in the street so it was decided to remove casualties to another public shelter nearby. On one journey the street was covered in fire bombs and I flung myself in the shelter doorway and others doing so lay on top of me. Looking up I saw for the first time some children on bunks round the side of the walls although they must have known the people we laid on the floor of the shelter they hadn't made a sound . . .

We were so jammed in the entrance to the shelter the policeman blew his whistle for others to help us. I was then given a message to take to control asking for more rescue parties. When the road was cleared we took the dead, each with a printed form attached to them, saying where they were found, to Alber Ave Mortuary. The injured, who had been given morphine, and the letter 'M' marked on their foreheads to say so, we took to the Western General Hospital on Anlaby Road, and laid them on the floor on their stretchers. They would be seen by a doctor if a bed became available, would be washed, but most were eventually transported by buses fitted out with beds to Driffield or Beverley Base Hospitals . . .

We were sent out straight away to the corner of Regent Street on Anlaby Road where firemen were reported dead and injured. I set off down Hessle Street to go through to Anlaby Road when I was surrounded by shrapnel. In the distance I saw a woman running and thought she must know where to take cover so I went after her. She turned into a terrace and jumped into a shelter and I did the same. She publicly thanked me in front of everyone for looking after her. I didn't tell her why I had run after her and of course had to continue my journey. She was on her way to Baume Chapel to open it up for people bombed out of their homes.

I then came across a house that was covered in fire – obviously an oil bomb had dropped on it. A policeman was stood in the doorway said people were in the house but there was nothing we could do.

The firemen were laid on the road and asked me if I had any cigarettes. We also found a dead firewatcher. I was told to go from this incident to investigate a report of a body laying in Ferensway. I found an ARP man laid on the road that was dead. A policeman, who said he was looking for missing policemen, said he was seeing to the casualties. I could see Hammonds had a small fire burning on the top and a ladder was resting on the building when suddenly fire spread right across the roof as though an oil bomb had hit it.

On returning to the FAP I came across huge bomb damage at Stirling Street and saw some of our First Aiders. I was asked to check under beds in damaged houses to see if anyone was hurt.

Arriving back at the FAP we were given toast and cocoa

and sat in a semi-circle dead quiet. Some of the men were crying. We received instructions not to talk to civilians about the fires to try and stop panic. We went home and went to work.

It is frequently asserted that the city of Coventry was the most intensively bombed city outside London, but the facts reveal otherwise. Coventry certainly suffered one of the most sustained and destructive aerial attacks of the entire war, but thereafter it suffered only one further substantial attack by the Luftwaffe. Hull was the seventh most heavily bombed city after London. In terms of tonnage of bombs dropped, after London, the order was: Liverpool/Birkenhead, Birmingham, Glasgow/Clydeside, Plymouth/Devonport, and Bristol/Avonmouth, followed by Portsmouth, Hull, Belfast, Sheffield, Newcastle/Tyneside and Nottingham. Hull was bombed very heavily between 7 and 9 May by Luftwaffe units diverted from their primary targets of Liverpool and Sheffield. There would be further heavy attacks on Hull during July and August.

Thursday 8 – Thursday 22 May 1941

An Italian pilot is captured by the British at Asmara in Eritrea

The diary of this unknown Italian pilot was captured with its owner towards the end of the east African campaign in May 1941 and trans-lated immediately for intelligence purposes. The Italians' air base had been overrun and they joined a convoy of hundreds of motor vehicles fleeing from Addis Ababa towards Amba Alagi and Asmara. Halting by night, they sheltered under canvas but by now had run out of food. In the rain they drank the last of their rum and listened to a gramophone record of Chopin's Opus 42. They knew capture was not far away and noted 'there is so much sadness in us'.

8 May
By now we realise that we are surrounded, and at dusk we withdraw to the road where there are some vehicles ready to take us further up ALAGI hill.

At midnight a D.R. [despatch rider] arrives with the order that the men belonging to S. & T. should go up together with our own men. These men number about 200 and 30 of us. We arrive at the bake-house and then make our way to an arch under the road, waiting for daylight. We are awakened by the sound of rifle fire from the rebels [local tribesmen supporting the British] and we can see them advancing hidden from sight of those on the crest of the road. We have barely time to jump into a car and dash to the bake-house to report to the officers who are sheltering underground. Two M.Gs [machine-guns] are placed in position under a curve in the road which dominates the whole valley beneath. Then rifle fire is opened up by our soldiers, all belonging to different units, who are without control and without orders. The officers, as usual, are all sheltering in the grottos, unaware of their responsibility at the present time . . .

10 May

The dawn of a new day, a grey dawn which finds us near our M.G., pale and weary after a sleepless night, although quiet. The first sounds of the enemy fire don't wait long to make themselves heard; ever stronger, ever more insistent. About 0800 hrs rebel patrols of 15–20 men advance and take some of our positions. Our fire is slowed up because the rebels are mixed up with our own soldiers who have been taken prisoner and who are waving white flags. From where I am I can see soldiers piling into lorries at the supply depot, waving white flags and going down the road to surrender. By now the position is lost. Some officers give the example, raising their hands above their heads. Some rebels have climbed up the road and start firing on them. Beneath me I see some ruffians working up to my position to take it. I put the M.G. out of action and with the few remaining soldiers I make my way to the road and have just time enough to snatch a few underclothes from my suitcase and get aboard a passing lorry and get further up the hill towards TOSELLI Pass. Here I find Capt. BAROZZI already snugly settled in a cave. All the other men of our unit have been taken prisoner.

I climb up a height where I find FENZI with two A.A. guns emplaced. He kindly invites me to his cave where he is working on making it even deeper. But the rebels think otherwise and tomorrow we can expect another attack with its consequent retreat. One lone Gloucester [*sic*: an RAF Gloster biplane fighter] all day long attacks our A.A. gun emplacement flying low and machine-gunning. Arty [artillery] is firing continually and from the hospital a stream of ambulances goes loaded with wounded to MAI CEU, now in the hands of the British. This means that we have no medical stores to care for the sick and wounded who completely fill the hospital. The soldiers are aware of this and perhaps that is why they fight with such little spirit. In fact, they don't fight . . .

14 May

After two days of subterranean life, I come out in the evening like a bat, with my limbs cramped and rheumatic pains. I am placed under orders of Capt. BAROZZI, who is in command of certain gun posts on the Southern slope of AMBA mountain. Once again I have to seek hospitality from my friend POZZI, who offers me a corner in his narrow and low cave. I believe that my pilgrimage has now come to an end, as in the position in which I find myself, I can retreat no further, and I shall be taken prisoner when the whole of AMBA ALAGI falls.

22 May

At about 1600 hrs we arrive at ASMARA at BALDISSERA Fort. We are taken within the usual barbed wire fences. That evening we get nothing to eat. We sleep on the floor of a large room all bunched together, breathing foul air of about a hundred tired and dirty men. The rotten soup which is handed out to us at noon and in the evening has no nourishment in it and doesn't sustain me. My inside protests strongly. Ah! if only I could have a piece of bread. I have never been vengeful towards anyone, but the day that the British are our prisoners, I promise that I shall make them suffer what I have suffered and am suffering now.

By 24 May this pilot was one of 7,000 Italians commanded by the Duke of Aosta who had surrendered at Amba Alagi, marking the end of Italy's east African campaign. He received food – mostly rolls of local black bread – and smoked English cigarettes. Suffering from rheumatic fever and running a temperature of 102 degrees, he was also receiving medical attention. Later on he recognized that the quality of his care was good and noted thankfully, 'I get into a bed which is soft and I have a pillow at long last.' Nevertheless, the sheer numbers of Italians taken prisoner at the end of this campaign stretched the British authorities and they had difficulty making adequate provision for all of them. SEE ALSO PP. 167–9.

Monday 12 – Wednesday 14 May 1941

Journalist and New Zealander Eric Baume locks horns with the censors in his attempt to report the flight of Rudolf Hess to Scotland

12 May

Midnight. We're all going crazy now. Rudolf Hess has landed up in Scotland, and the raid – even though the streets are still bloodstained and littered, has been forgotten. The censor is very strong about the whole affair and forbids us absolutely to say that Hess had a letter for the Duke of Hamilton (who was the Marquis of Clydesdale, the boxing peer). We can't mention where Hess landed; we can only say Scotland. And we can't give any of the 'human interest' details about how he was found by a farmer.

The German Propaganda Bureau has been working overtime; their reports said that:

a) Hess had disobeyed the Fuehrer's orders, being ill, had gone up in a plane and been killed.
b) He jumped out of a plane.
c) He was insane.

All the official statements from Downing Street say that Ivone Kirkpatrick, a Foreign Office official, has definitely verified that the man is Hess.

I was able to get one good sidelight from Oliver Hoare,

who knew Hess and Goering well. Hoare says one of two things has happened – either Hess is bringing peace proposals, or else he is leading a party which wants to get Hitler out . . .

13 May

Still Hess. Had a long argument with the censorship about mentioning the name of the Duke of Hamilton . . .

14 May

They have released the news that Hess was going to visit the Duke of Hamilton. People are getting very annoyed, because they now learn that Hess 'enjoys a light diet of chicken, fish and eggs.' . . . It seems, however, that the Hess affair goes far beyond the limits of ordinary news. Meanwhile Churchill's attitude is to keep whatever information Hess may or may not have given him as the property of the War cabinet. No one else knows what Hess has said.

Rudolf Hess was the deputy leader of the Nazi party and also second in line to replace Hitler, after Goering. He had fled to Scotland hoping to contact the Duke of Hamilton, whom he had met and come to know tolerably well at the 1936 Olympics in Berlin. Oliver Hoare's estimation of Hess's motives represented the kind of intelligent speculation indulged in by many. Both London and Berlin were taken off guard by this remarkable development and handled their propaganda badly, the Germans making a number of contradictory statements and the British being exceedingly coy, which drove the press men wild. Martin Bormann took over Hess's position in Berlin on 13 May.

Back in Australia after the war Eric Baume would become a famous television personality and radio commentator. SEE ALSO PP. *264–5.*

Wednesday 14 May 1941

Anthony Eden, Foreign Secretary, battles with Churchill on the Hess issue

Anthony Eden was born in 1897 at Windlestone Hall, Bishop Auckland. He had fought in some of the major engagements of the First World War, including the Somme, and was lucky to survive (his younger brother was killed). After 1918 he went into politics and was soon identified as a rising star, being appointed Parliamentary Private Secretary to Austen Chamberlain at the Foreign Office. Eden became Foreign Secretary himself in 1935 but resigned over appeasement in 1938. When Churchill replaced Neville Chamberlain as Prime Minister in 1940, Eden became Foreign Secretary for a second time. His diaries are fragmentary and were never published but are preserved at the University of Birmingham.

Winston rang me up late with the text of a statement he wants to make in House tomorrow about Hess, quoting trend of his statements. I protested, urging Germany must be kept in the dark as to what Hess had said. Winston then demanded alternative draft and I struggled out of bed and produced it and telephoned it. A few minutes later Winston telephoned he did not like it and Duff [Cooper] was much upset. On the other hand Max [Beaverbrook] agreed with me. Which was it to be, his original statement or no statement? I replied 'no statement'. 'All right, no statement' (crossly), and the telephone was crashed down. Time 1.30 a.m.

No-one knew what to do with Hess. He remained in custody for the rest of the war, being moved around the country and interrogated by a number of individuals, including the former MI6 Head of Station in Berlin. Churchill approached this issue using his infuriating predilection for small-hours consultation. SEE ALSO PP. 420–1 AND 607–8.

Tuesday 20 May 1941

Martin Pöppel, a German paratrooper, joins the costly airborne attack on Crete

Martin Pöppel's remarkable diary traces his life from his early days in the Hitler Youth, describing his training and his feelings as a young soldier eager for battle, to his maturity as a war-weary veteran who just wanted to bring his men home safely. He records his feelings at the loss of valued comrades during many battles, first in Holland and then in Crete, Russia, France and Italy.

When we see a mountain range in the distance, we know that we are near Crete. We check our gear one more time, particularly the fastener on the end of the jump line. The aircraft achieves the correct height for the drop and soon we're over the coast. 'Prepare to jump' – signal – and out. My God, we've been lucky. Our jumpmaster has located the dropping zone perfectly and at 15.40 hours we drift to earth, about 12km east of the town of Rethymnon and 1.5km north of Episkopi. Miki and I end up in an olive tree, but one somersault and we're on the ground. During the drop there's been nothing more threatening than a few shots. After a short time the Company has assembled, and it appears that just one aircraft complement has been put down in the wrong place and is missing. Even now, as we fetch the weapons containers, we're getting damnably hot – the heat is almost 50 degrees and we're all breathing heavily already. First of all we just have to get acclimatised to it. Clearly our leaders were well aware of the heat, but we've been sent into battle in full uniform and with para jumping overalls as well. Absolutely bloody crazy! We're scarcely likely to be pleased with our rations of salty ham either. It's not long before some men, myself included, have taken off their jackets and hidden them in the undergrowth . . .

In the grey light of morning we storm the vineyards on the hills at the edge of the airfield. Now our objective is before

us. But they've spotted us and give us hell – and real hell at
that. I see one badly injured Oberjäger holding his torn
abdominal wall closed with both hands. When we stop to
help him he just says: 'Get down there first, then fetch me!'
Unbelievable. Oberjäger Rudi Freisch has the most enormous
stroke of luck. He gets a bullet through the nose, but it goes
in one side and clean out of the other. (After a few days he
could even blow his nose again.)

It's no good. People are getting hit all around us, and the
air is full of their groans and cries of pain. We're forced to
withdraw from this hill of blood and so fail to achieve our
objective. Firing continues on both sides. We manage to find
some cover on the rear slope, then move quickly to a white
house where we can care for our wounded. The medical
orderlies really have their hands full now. Then to a shallow
ditch, and leap over the road into a little hollow. How many
of us there now, thirty men, forty? A heated debate follows.
An Oberleutnant Hintz or Hintze from another unit wants to
give the order to surrender. A Feldwebel replies curtly:
'Quite out of the question'.

*Crete was the location of the largest, and perhaps the most disastrous,
German airborne operation of the war. Of the 15,000 airborne troops
despatched, nearly 4,000 were lost – killed and missing – in the assault.
Crete was a vital target for the Germans because the British airfields
there could be used to bomb the vital Ploesti oilfields in Romania. Oil
was one of the weaker components of Hitler's war economy. Despite their
air superiority, the Germans did not have enough transport aircraft to
take all their forces across at once, so instead they went in two waves,
one in the morning and another in the afternoon. The Germans had
expected only light resistance. The turning point was probably a tactical
mistake by the Allies when they withdrew from positions that
dominated the airfield at Maleme. Pöppel's diary confirms a frequently
made observation about German troops, that they would rarely
surrender unless they received permission from an officer or NCO.*

Tuesday 27 – Wednesday 28 May 1941

Grete Paquin, a German smallholder and anti-Nazi, hears
of the loss of the *Hood* and the *Bismarck*

In 1938, after her four children had left home, Grete Paquin opened an
advisory bureau for students in the German town of Göttingen.
Although she lived in an apartment in the town she spent a great deal
of time on a smallholding that she had acquired in the nearby country-
side. She was a committed anti-Nazi and her diary gradually became an
outlet for dangerous political opinions; she had come to the attention of
the local Gestapo because of her anti-war sentiments and also through
writing to relatives overseas. She chose to hide her diaries with friends
and spent almost all her time on her smallholding, with its cabin, which
offered some insulation from the war.

27 May

Last year we marched into Holland. Another year has gone
now, and we are in Crete.

People told me about the battle of Iceland. The *Hood* has
gone down with 1,500 men, and the German *Bismarck* is
fighting against the British Navy. I remembered the night
when I came back from England on the *Europa*, a wonderful,
calm summer night, the boat bright with lights, and we met
the *Bremen* on her voyage to America. Light greeted light,
friend greeted friend.

28 May

The *Bismarck* is gone! The young housemaid at the Ruprechts
has lost her fiancé who was a sailor on it. He is one among
thousands, and on the other side it is the same.

I sat in my office all the long hours during the battle, as
one sits at the bedside of a beloved sick friend, and could
only pray that God might have mercy. In the evening we
sang Psalm 98 'Let the sea roar, and all that fills it . . .' But
this sea in the Psalm is a different one, the music is full of
peace; just waves going up and own in harmony. David did

not know battleships, torpedoes, explosives, burning iron, and burning sea. Those are the gifts of our time.

Early in the morning of 24 May the British cruiser HMS Hood and the German battleship the Bismarck identified each other in the North Sea. Hood fired first, launching her first salvo at 5.52 a.m., and the Bismarck returned fire, beginning the Battle of the Denmark Strait. Eight minutes later, a massive explosion ripped the Hood into two and the ship disappeared. Only three men survived out of a crew of 1,400. Hood's armour was not of battleship strength and a shell had penetrated an ammunition store. Hood's sister ship, the HMS Prince of Wales, hit the Bismarck twice, inflicting damage which slowed her down. As a result, Bismarck was sunk off the French coast on 26 May, after taking some four hundred further hits on her massive armour during a long pursuit. Grete Paquin's horror at the loss of both ships was typical of her humanitarianism. SEE ALSO PP. 245, 383–5 AND 515–16.

JUNE 1941

THE WORLD WAS taken aback when Hitler launched Operation Barbarossa – the German invasion of Russia – on 22 June 1941. This massively expanded the scope of the Second World War. Remarkably, Soviet intelligence had received no fewer than eighty-eight separate warnings of the impending German attack. German reconnaissance planes equipped with large mapping cameras had even crashed deep inside Russia while photographing likely routes for the advancing panzer forces. However, these clear indicators of imminent invasion were dismissed as German bluffing – Stalin thought that Hitler would soon present Moscow with an ultimatum demanding more territory in eastern Europe. Stalin was not the only leader who found the suggestion of a German attack in the east hard to believe; the idea that Hitler would deliberately open up another front to the war took everyone by surprise. Even though intelligence from Bletchley Park had pointed to this for some months, it was only in late May that senior figures in London and Washington had begun to accept that Hitler really did mean business; and when London did eventually send Stalin warnings, he thought this might be some British ruse to drag Russia into the war.

In the western desert General Wavell launched Operation Battleaxe, which was designed to relieve the siege of Tobruk. Poor-quality British tanks were soon stopped by Rommel's defences and by 17 June it was clear that the offensive had failed. Churchill was furious at this inability to defeat a numerically smaller German and Italian force.

Most British cities were enjoying a welcome respite from aerial bombing because of the movement of German aircraft to the east to support the beginning of Operation Barbarossa. Only Manchester suffered heavy air attacks during June. British air operations concentrated on the Channel ports where there were U-boat pens, such as Brest, which was repeatedly bombed. Losses of shipping in the Atlantic continued to be heavy, but the tide was turning slowly in the Allies' favour. Escort carriers designed for convoy protection duties had begun to make their appearance and a new radar that would detect submarine periscopes was also coming into service.

Sunday 1 June 1941

Mihail Sebastian, a Romanian Jewish journalist, learns
that a German attack on Russia is certain

And Russia? Could there be a war between Russia and Germany? For three days everyone has thought one imminent. Since yesterday we have had a climate of mobilization in Bucharest. On Friday there was a blackout; yesterday an order was issued that air-raid shelters must be built in every yard in a maximum of two weeks. Today a number of trains have been cancelled, probably because of troop movements. There is a wave of call-ups and requisitioning. At the height of the working season on the farms, horses and cattle are being taken away from people. Those who have been to Moldavia (eg G M Cantacuzion) say that there is a clear war zone in the region of the Prut. On the streetcars, in the streets and restaurants, people talk of war, war, war. From a political point of view, it seems unlikely to happen. But the actual state of things cannot be denied. Is it again a big bluff? But such a *mise en scène* would be too costly and, in the end, without any point. The same comedy could be acted with less ostentation and equally good results. In the space of a year and a half I have seen the most absurd happenings, the most incredible turnarounds. I should stop trying to judge, to understand, to predict. The facts carry more weight than anything else.

Mihail Sebastian moved in well-connected circles in Bucharest, but he was not privy to any inside government or military knowledge. Rather, his conclusions were typical of millions who observed the vast preparations for Operation Barbarossa that could not be disguised from anyone living within 100 miles of the Russian border. SEE ALSO PP. 255–6 AND 321–2.

Staff Sergeant Raymond Ryan, Australian Army Pay Corps, is captured on Crete

Ray Ryan was one of two brothers who had joined the Australian Imperial Force in 1939. Ray Ryan joined the Pay Corps and his younger brother Laurie joined the 2/11th Infantry. Both sailed from Fremantle Harbour on the troopship Nevassa *on 20 April 1940.*

Capture

The next morning the 1st June 1941, a Sunday. I woke to find white flags fluttering everywhere. I didn't take much notice of that as it didn't mean much to me. Then I saw a group of chaps talking quietly with gloomy faces. On enquiring as to what was up, I was sent right back to be told that HQ had gone during the night, leaving orders to surrender and that the Germans would arrive in a few hours. I could hardly believe this and went up to the HQ at the cave and found only the familiar litter of scattered documents which by now always indicated a hurried retreat. We were at a loss as to what to do next. We learnt that General Freyburg had gone off by seaplane and with him the big nobs. A battalion had been ready to go into the line at 4am when it was told that all had finished. Everyone felt rather savage at just being left high and dry without warning, mingled with speculation as to what our fate would be in the near future. The general opinion was that the Aussies and Kiwis would receive short shrift, being volunteers and also blamed for the Greek mutilations. Another opinion reckoned that all the NCOs would receive harsh treatment. With these ideas in their minds, many Australians took care to remove all AIF insignia and posed as Tommies until they realised their error some days later. Some NCOs both Tommies and Aussies took down their stripes. One Aussie sergeant yelled out 'I'm not staying here to be murdered' and forthwith blew his brains out. On the other hand there were many optimists. It was rumoured that the Aussies had just captured 20,000 Germans in the desert and we would soon be exchanged. Others hoped the island would be recaptured in a few days by our forces, or that we would never reach Greece as the navy would intercept the prison ships and rescue us. I didn't agree with any of these yarns, but anticipated we would have a tough time due to lack of food and comfort, without any physical ill treatment. About 9 o'clock the Germans arrived and rounded us up into a group of several thousand. Shortly after, their planes came over and not knowing we were brand new prisoners, attacked with MG and bombs.

The half dozen Germans who had taken us over waved a swastika flag until they themselves had to dive for cover. Several of our chaps were killed and many wounded as we were such a large body of men and made a perfect target. As I lay there, the bullets thudded into the ground all round us without hitting any of our party.

The shock of the first few hours of being a POW was lessened slightly by the keen interest with which I observed the first German soldiers I had ever seen. They were in high spirits at their success and addressed us through an interpreter.

'For you the war is over. How do you like our Stukas? All quiet now. There will be no more bombing'.

Retreating Allied forces on Crete were led towards the embarkation point of Sphakia Bay by Cretan guides. When they reached the headland they were marshalled by military police for evacuation. They handed some of their ammunition to local Cretans who were going into the mountains to continue the war on a guerrilla basis. There was a great deal of bitterness about the process of evacuation. Senior officers were rescued from Crete in the closing days of the campaign while some junior officers made sure they were first in line for evacuation on the beach. Throughout the bitter campaigns in Greece, and then in Crete, the main problem had been overwhelming German air superiority. Matters were not helped by the time of year, with a full moon in a clear sky and very short nights, offering only short periods of semi-darkness for cover.

Many were not evacuated from Sphakia, and by Sunday 1 June large white sheets had been spread over the hills to indicate surrender in order to try to prevent further bombing. The response of the rank and file to the news of surrender varied. Many reacted with shock; some found that they were stricken with incontinence and there followed a rush into the bay to clean their kit. Sadly, there was more than one suicide, particularly among those who had been POWs in the First World War and who felt they could not face another prolonged period of captivity. Those who took this drastic option removed a boot and sock and used a toe to discharge their rifle into the roof of their mouth.

Laurie Ryan was also taken prisoner on Crete and accompanied his brother to captivity in Germany. SEE ALSO PP. 379–81.

Saturday 21 June 1941

Georgi Dimitrov in the Moscow Comintern hears rumours of attack everywhere

Born in 1882 in Kovachevtsi in Bulgaria, Georgi Dimitrov was first a printer and an active trade unionist. Later, as a socialist MP, he campaigned against the country's involvement in the First World War.

This led to his being imprisoned for subversion. In 1929 he became head of the Central European section of the Comintern – the international organization dedicated to fomenting national communist revolutions – and so moved to Berlin. When the Reichstag caught fire on 27 February 1933 he was arrested by the Nazis on trumped-up charges and imprisoned. On his release in February 1934 Dimitrov moved to the Soviet Union, where he was promoted to Secretary-General of the Comintern.

A telegram from Zhou Enlai in Chongqing to Yan'an (to Mao Zedong) contains among other things an indication that Chiang Kai-shek is declaring insistently that Germany will attack the USSR, and is *even giving a date*: 21 June 1941!

Rumors of an impending attack are multiplying on all sides.

Have to be on guard . . .

Although the Comintern was not strictly an intelligence organization, in practice Dimitrov's job ensured that he rubbed shoulders with senior intelligence officers and received a continual stream of valuable information. Like many, he was aware of the countless warnings of what was about to take place. SEE ALSO P. 543.

Sunday 22 June 1941

Colonel-General Halder of the German army on the invasion of Russia

The morning reports indicate that all Armies (except Eleventh) have started the offensive according to plan. Tactical surprise of the enemy has apparently been achieved along the entire line. All bridges across, the River Bug, as on the entire river front, were undefended and are in our hands intact. That the enemy was taken by surprise is evident from the fact that the troops were in their quarters, that planes on the airfield were covered up, and that enemy groups faced with the unexpected development at the front inquired at their Hqs in the rear what they should do . . .

[General von] Paulus communicates to me at 1100. State Secretary von Weizsaecker's appraisal of the situation: Britain will first feel relieved by the news of our attack on Russia and will rejoice at the 'dispersal of our forces'. But a rapid advance of German troops will soon bring disillusionment, for the defeat of Russia cannot but lead to a marked strengthening of our position in Europe.

As to Britain's readiness for an accord with us he has this to say: The propertied classes will strive for a settlement leaving us a free hand in the East, but it would involve the renunciation of our claims to Holland and Belgium. If these tendencies are to prevail, Churchill has to be overthrown, as he relies on the support of the Labour Party, which is not interested in a peace concluded by the propertied classes. Such a peace would bring the propertied classes back into power, whereas the Labour Party wants power for itself. The Labour Party will therefore continue the war until the propertied class is entirely eliminated. Under what conditions it would eventually be willing to come to some terms with Germany, cannot be predicted. Probably vehement opposition to National Socialism, by reason of strong Jewish influence and Communist connections. For the time being, in any case, the Labour Party will not be disposed to put an end to the war.

Stalin was so shocked by the attack that he retreated to his dacha in the country for a week and issued no orders. In the summer of 1941 Nazi officials in Berlin were still hoping for an accommodation with London, but were gradually realizing that this was unlikely. They attributed this partly to presumed Jewish and Communist influence within the British Labour Party. Meanwhile, Weizsäcker, Ribbentrop's state secretary at the Foreign Ministry, was right to presume that there remained some sympathy for Hitler's anti-Bolshevism among the English elite and even among some British army officers. SEE ALSO PP. 197–8 AND 360–1.

Monday 30 June 1941

Lieutenant Wilhelm Prüller of the German army enters Ukraine

Wilhelm Prüller had been briefly captured by Polish troops and then freed by his Russian allies during the invasion of Poland in 1939. Now the Russians were his enemies; but inside the Soviet Union he found other, unexpected allies.

At 5.45 were up again. Our major is to report to Regiment Headquarters. The road is the worst imaginable: deep sand and then huge craters right across the whole road, and this mile after mile. I write the orders on the road.

My eyes ache from looking at so many vehicles, one after the other as far as you can see. We arrive about 15.00, after travelling along these impossible roads, in Busk, where there's still fighting going on. The western entrance of the town is jammed full of our vehicles, and all you can see there is dust, but the Russian guns are still barking away at the eastern end. On the other side of the bridge an armoured scout car is burning; the bang of its ammunition covers the noise of our armoured columns.

They are hauling some Russians out of the houses – disgusting creatures. Our colonel sits at a table, completely calm, and gives his orders. Among a batch of Russians who are in the process of surrendering we catch sight of a wounded, uniformed Russian woman. She's the first skirt in uniform we've seen in Russia so far. Neither Red Cross nurses, nor anything else, but actually soldiers!

This region has quite a lot of Ukrainians. In every village we're showered with bouquets of flowers, even more beautiful ones than we got when we entered Vienna. Really it's true! In front of some villages they have erected triumphal arches. Some have the following inscription in Russian and German: 'The Ukrainian peoples and their liberators, the brave German army. Heil Adolf Hitler!'

The people here are overjoyed, and it's a special piece of luck for us to be here too. For we're fighting this battle not only against the world's poisoners, but in the case of the Ukraine we are liberating a people from an almost unbearable yoke. We are so proud, so happy!

As Wilhelm Prüller advanced into Russia he took particular pleasure in seeing the Germans separate out the Jews from the rest of the local population, remarking, 'That's the way it should be in the whole world!' Other groups in the Soviet Union greeted the Germans with pleasure, and in Ukraine the Germans managed to raise an entire division of Waffen-SS troops to fight on their behalf. This became known as the Galician Division. In 1945 this Ukrainian SS division would be brought back from Italy to the UK almost intact for reasons that remain unclear even now, but were probably related to the emerging Cold War.

By the end of the war Prüller would have fought in four campaigns – in Poland, in France, in the Balkans and then on the Eastern Front – and reached the rank of Oberleutnant. He never lost his commitment to the Third Reich and when, in 1959, he sought to have his diaries published, he was still wearing a heavy gold ring embossed with the runic sign of the SS. SEE ALSO PP. 75–8 AND 79.

JULY 1941

DURING THE FIRST few hours of the German attack many Soviet troops had been under strict orders not to fire on the invaders, and so they simply took to their heels and ran. There followed several weeks of headlong retreat. At the start of July 1941 the Germans captured the city of Minsk, and by 11 July they had taken a third of a million prisoners. However, Hitler was increasingly disinclined to leave operational matters to the generals and instead began to interfere in the detailed running of the war. This would become a growing trend. He ordered a reluctant General Guderian south towards Kiev, and consequently slowed the advance towards what Guderian regarded as the vital objective – the city of Moscow.

In the conquered territories, Germany had already begun to implement Hitler's 'new order'. National minorities who had been oppressed by the Soviet Communist Party, such as the Ukrainians and the Volga Germans, welcomed their new conquerors with open arms, while Jews and others deemed undesirable were sifted from the local population. In the Baltic states, eastern Poland and Ukraine, local volunteers assisted with the elimination of many local Jewish populations, often with great enthusiasm. However, the scale of the task of 'racial cleansing' that lay before them was seen as a problem by the German army.

In the Middle East, the failure of Operation Battleaxe prompted Churchill to replace General Wavell with Claude Auchinleck. Churchill accepted that Wavell had been weighed down with political duties and so created the post of Minister of State, resident in the Middle East, to handle these regional administrative affairs. This new post was taken by Oliver Lyttelton and later by Lord Moyne. July 1941 also saw the launch of Churchill's 'V for Victory' campaign. Some thought this to be a silly idea but it proved to be a very popular symbol, and in occupied countries everywhere the V sign was chalked up on walls and doors as a symbol of resistance.

By now it was clear to leaders in both Tokyo and Washington that they could not stand on the sidelines indefinitely. It was increasingly a matter of when, rather than if, they would join the struggle. In the summer of 1941 Roosevelt realized that staying out of the conflict and allowing the Axis to grow stronger was now positively dangerous. Although using coded language, he said as much in his Independence Day speech on 4 July. This was underlined a week later when Roosevelt appointed William J. Donovan as his 'Co-ordinator of Information'. This post would eventually develop into the Office of Strategic Services, America's main wartime agent-based secret service.

Saturday 5 – Sunday 20 July 1941

Charles Graves prepares for the German invasion of London

Charles Graves, born in 1899, was a reporter for the Daily Mail *and the* Sunday Express, *a novelist and a busy socialite. When not on assignment, he spent his time patrolling the London clubs and hotels in search of senior officers for news about the war. In 1941 he was enjoying the success of his recently published fictional account of life in the RAF,* The Thin Blue Line, *and trying to interest the leading actor Leslie Howard in the film rights to his forthcoming book on the naval war,* Life Line. *Graves joined the Home Guard and when in London enjoyed the regular exercises, although they sometimes had a slight element of farce.*

5 July

Home to lunch. It was blazing hot. Went on a Home Guard parade, where we were photographed, and then took part in a new scheme for defending Regent's Park from parachutists. Was informed that I am now second-in-command of the new headquarters platoon, and that we will have flame-throwers, Molotovs, hand-grenades, tommy-guns, anti-tank rifles and sticky bombs. In fact, we have them already. The men were delighted at the new order whereby they can now take their rifles home with them. This is to save time in the event of being called out for an invasion. After the parade heard that Castlerosse had been quoting someone as saying that Russia would be out of the war in a week. Duff Cooper said yesterday that the Russian situation was much better than the pessimists thought. Dined with Jesse Heinter and went on to the Liaison Club, where we found Nat Thorpe, now Chief Superintendent at Scotland Yard. He says that Thurston [criminal being sought by the police] is a rat and depends on women to hide him, that the gang warfare in Soho is very genuine. He also said that two sailors who were arrested for breaking into a house and banging someone on the head with a sandbag claimed that they had been waiting for — [name withheld], with whom they had a rendezvous. There is a murmuring campaign against the Prime Minister over Wavell and his alleged insistence on complete control of all three fighting Services. It is a fact that Wavell wanted to go to Tripoli and not to Greece, but was overruled . . .

20 July

Took a slow train back to London, arriving late for lunch. Changed into uniform and hurried off to Hampstead Heath, where a demonstration by the Royal Tank Corps was being provided. An officer with a loud-speaker described to everyone present – hundreds of civilians, perhaps Quislings among them, in addition to the 3,000 Home Guards – all the best ways of destroying our latest Valentine tank. Actually it seems that it takes a tank to kill a tank, but still . . . Today is the great V day [V for Victory]. You see Vs on walls and posters, even chalked inside restaurants.

By 1941 the Home Guard was better organized than it had been in its early days, and central training schools were being established to provide courses on heavier weapons; however, the threat of invasion was already fading. Pessimists had predicted that the Soviet Union would be knocked out of the war in a few weeks, but by the last week of July 1941 resistance was stiffening and the scale of the task that Hitler had taken on was becoming clear. SEE ALSO PP. 25–6, 324–6 AND 377.

Monday 7 July 1941

Jean Offenberg, a Belgian RAF pilot, blacks out over the English Channel

Jean Offenberg was born at Laeken in Belgium in 1916. In the spring of 1940, when he began his diary, he was serving in a Belgian fighter squadron at a small airfield near Nivelles. The aircraft used was the Fiat CR-42, an Italian-made biplane that fired its gun by interrupting the propeller in true First World War style. After the fall of Belgium,

Offenberg refused to give up and travelled to France, north Africa and then Gibraltar, where he joined a motley group of Poles, Belgians and French all sailing for Britain in search of a chance to continue the fight. Offenberg then became a fighter pilot with 145 Squadron at Tangmere; by 1941 he was based at Biggin Hill and flying Spitfire Mark Vs with 609 Squadron.

We escorted four Stirlings to Albert, near Amiens. The raid was carried out without incident and we did not meet the least opposition. It was almost kid glove warfare. But I was certain that it would not continue like this and that sooner or later a cloud would disclose a swarm of Messerschmitts. For a good hour we had been frolicking with impunity above their territory and nothing had happened.

I was Blue 1, and all went well until we got over Le Touquet, when I noticed an Me 109 attacking my No. 4.

'Blue 4, break immediately. Break, break . . .'

He broke off and I banked to port without getting excited. Yesterday in the same manoeuvre I had only managed to go down in a spin. Gently . . .

The Bosche dived below me. I did a roll on the way down. I followed suit and we both dived almost vertically.

I must get him . . . I must get him . . .

He had seen me and continued in his breath-taking dive.

The water rushed up towards me and I was suddenly afraid. I no longer dared to look at my air speed indicator.

I was following him at 400 yards exactly on a line with him.

We should both break our necks if we went on at that speed. The water drew dangerously close and I was afraid of a black-out. I pulled on the stick, flattened out and then for a second I saw nothing. I really had blacked out . . . It was the end. I have no idea how long I was in this state.

As soon as I could see again I noticed an enormous splash in the centre of a fleet of a dozen fishing boats some miles from the French coast.

The Me[sserschmitt], in his crazy dive, had not been able to pull out and had crashed at 500 m.p.h. into the sea.

I had not fired a single bullet, but Sergeant Evans, my No. 4, was missing. I did not think that the Messerschmitt was in a good firing position when I first spotted him.

At about 15.00 hours the Prime Minister, Winston Churchill, paid a visit to the squadron. The group captain introduced me and almost made me blush when in front of me, he described this morning's combat.

By July 1941 the pressure on RAF fighter squadrons was easing off a little. Large numbers of German bombers and fighters were drawn off to fight on the Eastern Front. Although the bombing raids against major British towns continued, they were less frequent, and Fighter Command was at liberty to extend its operations over the Channel. Spitfires lacked the range to escort bombers over Germany but, operating at the very limit of their endurance, they were able to escort medium bombers on their attacks against France. They were also sent on 'rhubarbs' – single-aircraft fighter sweeps over coastal areas of France looking for targets of opportunity, such as goods trains or the German fast attack vessels known as E-boats. Increasingly they also fought over the sea. SEE ALSO PP. 322–4.

Saturday 12 July 1941

Diary of Blutordenstrager Felix Landau

Felix Landau was an SS officer from Vienna assigned to Galicia in eastern Poland, where he kept a remarkably graphic diary of his activities.

At 6.00 in the morning I was suddenly awoken from a deep sleep. Report for an execution. Fine, so I'll just play executioner and then gravedigger, why not? Isn't it strange, you love battle and then have to shoot defenceless people. Twenty-three had to be shot, amongst them the two above-mentioned women. They are unbelievable. They even refused to accept a glass of water from us. I was detailed as marksman and had to shoot any runaways. We drove one kilometre along the road out of town and then turned right into a wood. There were only six of us at that point and we had to find a suitable spot to shoot and bury them. After a few minutes we found a place. The death candidates assembled with shovels to dig their own graves. Two of them were weeping. The others certainly have incredible courage. What on earth is running through their minds during those moments? I think that each of them harbours a small hope that somehow he won't be shot. The death candidates are organized into three shifts as there are not many shovels. Strange, *I am completely unmoved. No pity nothing.* That's the way it is and then it's all over . . .

And here I am today, a survivor standing in front of others in order to shoot them. Slowly the hole gets bigger and bigger; two of them are crying continuously. I keep them digging longer and longer; they don't think so much when they're digging. While they're working they are in fact calmer. Valuables, watches and money, are put into a pile. When all of them have been brought to stand next to one another on a stretch of open ground, the two women are lined up at one end of the grave ready to be shot first . . .

As the women walked to the grave they were completely composed. They turned round. Six of us had to shoot them. The job was assigned thus: three at the heart, three at the head. I took the heart. The shots were fired and brains whizzed through the air. Two in the head is too much. They almost tear it off. Almost all of them fell to the ground without a sound.

Felix Landau was not an especially important Gestapo officer. However, he would come to public notice in 2001 when artists discovered the murals painted by Bruno Schulz, a Jewish art teacher, on Landau's orders in a tiny pantry of the Villa Landau, a three-storey house that had once belonged to Landau in his role as the chief Gestapo officer in the town of Drohobych in Galicia. This area of eastern Poland was inhabited by Jews, Germans, Russians and Ukrainians, and would be transferred to Ukraine in 1945. Schulz even provided illustrations of the Grimms' fairy tales in the nursery of Landau's young son. These included a princess, a king in high heels, a clown, a jester and a coach driver. Bruno Schulz was later shot and killed by another SS officer. Landau offers us the prospect of a Gestapo officer who was both a connoisseur of art and a callous mass murderer.

Sunday 27 July 1941

Catherine Harrison of the Citizens' Advice Bureau in Catford, south-east London, writing in her sister's diary

Helena Harrison lived in Beckenham in Kent with her sister Catherine and their 85-year-old mother. Their house was fairly close to the airfield at Biggin Hill and was provided with 'a good cellar' for use during air raids. They also had two maids who were German Jewish refugees, but in May 1940 one of them had been interned on the Isle of Man. Helena had written a memoir of her time serving with the British Red Cross Voluntary Aid Detachment in Kent during the First World War. She also kept an excellent diary from 1939 to 1944, with interesting descriptions of air raids and local ARP arrangements. It also depicts her voluntary work for the Women's Voluntary Service and Citizens' Advice Bureau in Beckenham and Lewisham. Added to the diary were further entries by her 42-year-old sister Catherine, made while working in Catford Citizens' Advice Bureau, one of which is reproduced here.

Life is mostly 'Citizens' Advice Bureaux' . . . Last week I was asked to resolve the following situations:- Unknown to anyone a shell cap lodged in the gutter of next-door (semi-detached) house. It had set up a short circuit in the electricity and when meter was next taken it was seen to have been racing in an absurd way. Shell cap only discovered some time after this. Electricity company claim the full bill must be paid. Householder claims she is not liable. She came to us. We think it is a war damage claim. But Assistance Board have already turned this down! Want to send her to the Legal Bureau – but she is over the scale – suggest her writing for advice to the War Damage Dep[artmen]t – and let us know developments.

Personally I should let such a thing come before the magistrates from sheer curiosity!!

Case of XXX [name withheld] is half-funny – Soldier called to know what he should do. Wife deserted him for

another man taking all her daughter (15)'s clothes! Helped
him to transfer Army allowances to daughter and advanced
girl money till transfer was arranged – As soon as it was
arranged the wife returned home, begging to be taken back
– he gladly agreed and once more we helped him do the
transfer. A short time after the soldier calls again – wife has
gone off again and again taken the girl's clothes (most of
which we had provided!) once more we arrange the transfer
– as soon as it is done the wretched woman once more goes
off and we transfer the money to the girl! The mother does it
again but we make man keep it in daughter's name – and I
believe daughter remarks she never wants to see mother
again (she goes to live with aunt) ... I wish I had kept a
diary last year – the Blitz period would be so interesting to
me now – will only remember fragments of my feelings in
another year ...

*The first Citizens' Advice Bureaux (CABs) had been set up in September
1939. They provided an important service, for it rapidly became obvious
that many people would need considerable help in the face of the dislocation and hardship inflicted by the war. Quite often staff working in
CABs were confronted with very grim personal situations. During the
worst of the Blitz, mobile CAB units were provided near devastated
areas to help relocate people who had lost their homes. Many found it
hard to cope with the mass of regulations that came with the system of
food and clothes rationing, and many lost their vital paperwork
when their houses were bombed. Conscription often meant disruption
of employment or a lowered income, and advice over matters
of debt were much in demand. The CABs' war-related work would
continue beyond 1945 as they sought to track down missing relatives.*

AUGUST 1941

G ERMAN U-BOAT successes continued to decline and total Allied shipping losses this month were low at only 130,000 tons. RAF Bomber Command stepped up its operations against Germany, but fighter cover forced them to continue to carry out night-time raids, which were increasingly revealed to be inaccurately targeted. Berlin was bombed by both British and Soviet planes.

Between 9 and 12 August Churchill and Roosevelt met at Placentia Bay in Newfoundland. This famous meeting was most memorable for the signing of the Atlantic Charter, which asserted the right of all countries to hold free and fair elections. However, controversially, Churchill would later maintain that he thought it applied only to European countries, and not to areas of the British Empire that were still under imperial rule, such as India, where demonstrations in favour of independence were gathering strength.

In north Africa the Allied situation was deteriorating. The Australian government was increasingly concerned about its troops, who had been besieged in Tobruk in conditions similar to the trench warfare of 1914–18. The Australian forces defended Tobruk with remarkable tenacity, living for months like troglodytes in caves and bunkers while enduring terrible heat and bombardment.

On the Eastern Front the Germans continued to make rapid gains, cutting the railway line between Moscow and Leningrad. However, Hitler's generals resented the emphasis on the push south beyond Kiev; they would have preferred to move against Moscow, in the hope of knocking the Soviet Union out of the war by forcing a surrender. Right across Hitler's new eastern domain the process of racial cleansing gathered pace. Experiments were now being conducted at the Auschwitz concentration camp to examine methods for killing large numbers of people, including the use of Cyclon-B gas.

Friday 1 August 1941

A youthful smuggler escapes the authorities in the Lodz
Ghetto, recorded in the ghetto's collective diary

The Smuggler Zawadzki who recently escaped from
Hospital No 1, where he had been under guard by the Order
Service, was apprehended in the city and placed under
arrest. When interrogated, he stated that he had executed his
escape with the aid of a Jew and had paid a policeman 500
marks for his help. The Order Service man who had been on
duty in the hospital was summoned to Kripo (German
criminal police), and in spite of his passionate assurances
that he was innocent, was only released two days later. He is
now receiving medical attention. Zawadzki, a fourteen-year-
old boy, was the major smuggler both into and out of the
ghetto. He supplied saccharine, vaccines, medicines, etc, and
earned colossal sums of money. His escape was executed in
a highly ingenious manner: Zawadzki stated that he wanted
to go to the bathroom, where the stalls were set up so that the
user's feet were visible. When, after a rather long time,
the patient had not come out and did not respond to
knocks, the door was forced open. To their astonishment it
was discovered that Zawadzki had left his shoes to deceive
the guard while he escaped through a window.

*Probably the majority of the food eaten in the ghettos of Lodz and
Warsaw was smuggled. There was a smuggling hierarchy: at the top
were the organized crime networks, involving Germans, Poles and Jews,
who worked together to form an upper layer of large-scale activity; at
the bottom were armies of children who scaled walls and undertook
extraordinary trickery to smuggle food into the ghetto. Hunger was so
extreme that they engaged in this activity despite proclamations ordering the death penalty both for Jews who left the ghetto and for those who
helped them. Children were frequently shot while engaged in smuggling.
   At the end of 1941 the Germans would begin to deport large numbers
of Jews from Lodz to the death camps. SEE ALSO PP. 251–2 AND 667–8.*

Saturday 2 – Monday 4 August 1941

Mihail Sebastian, Romanian Jewish journalist, on the
rounding up of Jews in Bucharest

2 *August*

All Jews aged twenty to thirty-six must report to police
headquarters this evening or tomorrow morning, with three
days' food and a change of clothes. That means both Benu
and me. For a moment I felt dumb-founded, petrified, desperate. Then came my old sense of futility, of submission in
the face of adversity, of open-eyed acceptance of catastrophe.
And now, this evening, after a few hours of fretting, I
promise myself that I will sleep and try to forget. We'll see
tomorrow.

4 *August*

Early this morning the sergeants and policemen went from
house to house in various parts of town – and woke people
to inform them that not only Jews aged twenty to thirty-six,
but also those aged thirty-six to fifty, must report to police
headquarters. The alarm I felt at first is returning. Are we
again facing a mass roundup of Jews? Internment camps?
Extermination? When I went out at ten, the city had a
strange air: a strange kind of nervous animation. Agitated
groups of people hurrying around. Pale faces lost in thought.
Looks that wordlessly question one another, with the mute
despair that has become a kind of Jewish greeting. I quickly
did some shopping to prepare our rucksacks for this afternoon, for when we had decided to present ourselves. Shops
were taken over by Jews buying all kinds of things for their
departure. After a couple of hours there were no more rucksacks on sale anywhere. The shops selling canned goods had
only a few odds and ends (it was impossible to buy a tin of
sardines, for example). The price of the simplest things
suddenly shot up. I went to Calea Vacaresti to buy a couple
of canvas hats.

In 1941 General Ion Antonescu, a right-wing militarist who was obsessed with 'law and order', established a military dictatorship in Romania with German support. Events in the summer of 1941 resulted in Romania entering the war, and also accelerated action against the Jews. The Romanians did much of this on their own initiative and massacres took place at Iaşi before the main German concentration camps were established. The Romanians constructed a sinister experimental 'death train' which killed hundreds of Jews by asphyxiation in sealed compartments on a journey heading nowhere. Large numbers of Jews in Germany had seen what was coming and had decided to flee before 1940; by contrast, many Jews in eastern Europe, including those in Bucharest, had been less prescient, or more optimistic, and now found themselves trapped.

Bizarrely, Mihail Sebastian would survive both the war and the Holocaust, only to die in a car accident in early 1945. When his brother emigrated from Romania to Israel in 1961 he arranged for Mihail's diary to be taken out of the country in the safe pouch of the Israeli embassy's diplomatic mail for fear that it might be lost or damaged. SEE ALSO PP. 255–6 AND 303–4.

Thursday 7 August 1941

Jean Offenberg provides fighter cover for Air–Sea Rescue in the English Channel

Jean Offenberg sometimes refers to himself in his diary in the third person, either as 'Offenberg' or by his nickname 'Pyker'.

It was not quite seven o'clock when Pyker took off from Gravesend with twelve aircraft from 609. Mission – to escort a Lysander of Air Sea Rescue over the Channel along the English coast. They flew in very open formation over Dover on course 100°. All eyes scanned the sea looking for a sign, the yellow patch of a rescue launch, a man hanging in his rubber dinghy, being buffeted by the waves. They saw nothing. The sea was a vast expanse and the water looked very cold in the grey morning light. The cliffs of Dover struck by the sun's rays seemed whiter than usual. The white cliffs of Dover . . .

This was the first time that Offenberg had had time to admire them. Beyond stretched the green meadows of England, the vast English countryside which had grown so familiar. This land which he had defended so unswervingly, was now in part his country – a second country where he did not feel in the least foreign. He checked his weapons, glanced at the gonio[meter] and saw the luminous circle. All was well. He was leading his section, his No. 2 close to his wings, a little above him. He could see the pilot's head when he turned round.

Suddenly Gilroy called on the intercom. 'Beauty leader – four bandits at three o'clock.'

Four Messerschmitts were flying in from the east out of the sun. They were slightly lower – 2,000 feet perhaps – and still some distance off.

Blue Section climbed to the south.

Offenberg turned, gave full gas, climbed with his section on the course received, banking slightly to keep an eye on the enemy formation. Me 109s making straight for them . . . They were trying to shoot down the Lysander which was close to the water. A Messerschmitt broke away and dived on the reconnaissance plane, whose machine-gunner opened fire. Tracers flew . . . Red 1, Gilroy, attacked another 109 from very close quarters but missed it. His No. 2, Choron, who had remained behind the squadron commander, opened fire in turn on the tail of the German fighter. He almost rammed it. Pieces of the enemy aircraft broke off. It dived almost vertically and Offenberg saw it crash into the sea. A great patch of oil appeared at the place where it had hit.

Choron was French and Pyker could not help congratulating him: 'Bravo, la France.'

Pyker, at 5,000 feet in position with the sun behind, dived into the fray. He chose a Messerschmitt, approached at a terrific speed and took careful aim. 500 yards . . . 300 . . . He fired. His machine-gun spat a long burst but his cannon jammed. The machine-gun bullets seemed to rake the Me 109 without having hit it in its vitals. He broke away to port and returned. From some distance he fired a very long burst with all his ammunition. He could no longer fire, although he still had 120 shells in his wings. Nevertheless he continued to fight, dived on one of the Messerschmitts, which broke and fled to France.

Pyker pursued him for fun. The German pilot was fleeing for his life before an unarmed Spitfire. Had he known for a moment that the man behind him was quite harmless even if he came within fifty yards of his tail, he would have shot him down. But the Luftwaffe pilot knew nothing and thought he was saving his own skin. Off Calais Offenberg gave up the chase, set his course for the Thames estuary and reached Gravesend.

Offenberg's diary captures the constraints on fighter pilots flying even advanced machines such as the Spitfire Mark V. Despite being continually improved, their range remained short and it was not uncommon for pilots to have to ditch their aircraft in the English Channel through lack of fuel. Ammunition was also limited, and the combination of machine-guns and 20mm cannons could be fired for only a few seconds before all the ammunition was spent.

Offenberg was an excellent pilot who survived the deadly battles of 1940 and 1941. Sadly, he would die on 22 January 1942 as the result of an air accident when two Spitfires collided over RAF Digby in Lincolnshire. The tail of his plane was cut off and at an altitude of only 1,000 feet it was impossible to bail out. SEE ALSO PP. 313–15.

Friday 8 – Friday 15 August 1941

Charles Graves of the Home Guard patrols Hyde Park with an umbrella

8 August

Went to the Home Guard School in Surrey with Harry Foster. By great good luck we were able to fire tommy-guns, light automatics, heavy machine-guns, and Northover projectors. The latter are wonderful weapons. It rained all day, but that didn't damp our enthusiasm for two kinds of flame-thrower, land mines, Very lights, smoke-bombs, and all the other tricks of the trade. Altogether great fun. Unfortunately we had to parade for a further demonstration in Regent's Park. Once again our Headquarters Section had to adopt the role of parachute troops. For three hours we waved umbrellas. At least it was good exercise for the arms. Didn't get home until 10p.m., and was too tired to go out. Still no news of Churchill's return . . .

10 August

Another Home Guard parade. This time it was arms drill and bomb-throwing.

Still no sign of Churchill, although the Germans have been broadcasting his absence for over a week.

After lunch went to the Admiralty to see R. and acquired some more information for the book [on naval warfare].

A wet night, so we stayed home. One unexpected bit of luck was getting a packet of ten Players in the pub next to Company Headquarters. It's extraordinary how life alters. With the exception of the Coq d'Or and the Moulin d'Or we eat infinitely better at home than anywhere else in London; cigarettes are very hard to acquire; bottled beer is equally scarce except in public-houses.

The Queen and Quentin Reynolds both broadcast tonight . . .

15 August

Returned to London in time for the dress rehearsal of a street-fighting exercise of the Home Guard. Once again I lead the troops dressed up as Germans. It seems to be my fate. Went to the Savoy later for supper, and thereafter listened to the midnight news. Russia seems to be having a bad time.

Although efforts were made to offer centralized training for the Home Guard, the standard of weapons handling was generally poor. This problem, combined with their local enthusiasm for constructing and testing a great variety of improbable home-made weapons, resulted in many accidents. Although the Home Guard had only limited contact with the enemy, other than manning AA batteries and rounding up the odd parachutist, it nevertheless suffered no fewer than 1,206 deaths (killed on duty or died of wounds) and 557 injuries during the war. Others were killed by V-1s when on air-raid duties. An alarmingly high proportion of these deaths resulted from training with live ammunition. Six died and fourteen were injured in one incident when a grenade exploded during a lecture.

Charles Graves also noted Churchill's mysterious absence during the middle of August 1941, when the Prime Minister had travelled to Newfoundland for important meetings with Roosevelt on HMS Prince of Wales *and* USS Augusta. SEE ALSO PP. 25–6, 312–13 AND 377.

Saturday 9 August – Monday 1 September 1941

Log of Police Battalion 322 at Bialowieza Prison Assembly Camp in Poland

9 August

0.00 – Start of evacuation action against Jews in Bialowi(e)za. All male Jews aged 16 to 45 were arrested and brought to the assembly camp. All remaining Jews of both sexes were evacuated by lorry to Kobryn. The Jews had to leave behind everything in their homes apart from some hand-luggage. Confiscated articles of value were collected in Bialowieza Hunting Lodge and handed over to the Ortskommandantur. The homes of the evacuated Jews were locked or boarded up.

10 August

7.00 – Liquidation of Jews housed in the Bialowieza prison assembly camp. 77 male Jews aged 16 to 45 shot.

5 Jewish tailors, 4 Jewish cobblers and 1 Jewish watchmaker were not shot since their labour was urgently required by the company.

11 August
In Olschowka SS base a Jewish prisoner and 2 young White Russian peasants shot for looting.

12 August
Morning exercise training. Afternoon overhaul of weapons and cycles.

14 August
4.00 – Jewish action in Narewka-Mala. 259 women and 162 children transferred by lorry to Kobryn.
282 Jews were shot.
During the action one Pole was shot for looting.
18.00 – Hauptmann d Sch Podlesch arrived in Bialowieza and informed the company that it would soon be relieved by Battalion 323.

31 August
15.00 – Jewish action in the city of Minsk ghetto.
9th Coy manned the outer cordon while 7th Coy, NSKK Coy and the SD carried out search. All Jews aged between 15 and 60 were apprehended. In addition all Jewesses who were not wearing the prescribed yellow star on their clothing. A total of 916 (?) Jews of both sexes were apprehended and taken to the police prison.

1 September
5.30 – Execution of Jews apprehended yesterday some 10 km east of Minsk, north of the Minsk–Smolensk–Moscow highway. Three Execution Kommandos were deployed. The Kommando from 9th Coy shot a total of 330 Jews (of whom 40 were Jewesses).

The dense, dark forest at Bialowieza held many secrets during the Second World War. It was the site of extensive testing and development of the V-2 ballistic rocket, which the Germans would fire with devastating effect against Britain and Holland in the closing stages of the war. This site, like other missile testing and production sites, used slave labour. Bialowieza was also the location of a former tsarist prison, where

328 WITNESS TO WAR

100,000 Poles were imprisoned and executed between 1939 and 1945. In December 1942, 300 Poles would be executed here for partisan activity.

Monday 11 August 1941

Emil Dorian, a physician in Romania, watches the mounting tide of local 'Jew-hatred'

Anti-Jewish measures, unexpectedly harsh, have spread throughout the country. Jew-hatred has become hysterical. All the versions and explanations of the execution in Iaşi, and all we know through official channels, fall short of what really happened. After the Iaşi executions, Jews were rounded up in villages throughout Moldavia and evacuated in sealed cars, where many died a horrible death of thirst and asphyxiation. The tragic details are endless. The most sadistic imagination could not equal what happened at those train stations where the sealed cars with their load of doomed people stopped. Hundreds of women, children, men, herded into freight cars, licked the sweat off one another, drank their own urine to quench their thirst, screaming in agony until they perished. Crazy stories: a man paid twenty thousand lei for a glass of water; others offered priceless jewellery for a sip. A Romanian officer, crazed by the unearthly screams of the dying, jumped onto the platform carrying a bucket of water. When a sergeant stopped him with the butt of his rifle, he cried: 'I am a major in the Romanian army! Shoot me, but first let me give them some water!' For those who survived, the road ended in a concentration camp.

Emil Dorian survived the increasing numbers of attacks on Jews in Romania because of his medical training, which made him invaluable to the authorities. Anti-semitism had been strong in Romania even before 1939, but became worse after Russia annexed a sizeable area of Romania in the summer of 1940. Hungary and Bulgaria seized other areas of Romanian territory, and what remained became an ally of Germany on

23 November 1940. Thereafter it was rumoured that all Jews were traitors, communists, saboteurs or spies. Dorian would write later in 1941 that he 'could write a diary of rumours: a notebook would fill up in no time'.

By the time he died in 1956 Dorian's diaries filled twenty-two notebooks. They survived in the hands of a family friend and were later taken to his son in Berlin, who arranged for their publication. SEE ALSO
PP. 42–3.

Thursday 28 August 1941

Keith Vaughan, artist and conscientious objector, enjoys a walk in the moonlight at Melksham

Talk is now all on the question of transferring; giving up our protected status and joining a combatant unit or volunteering for bomb disposal. Everywhere there is a restlessness and exasperation with the boring and trivial routine of daily life. Bill has been offered an attractive job in the RE [Royal Engineers], Cosmo could get a job in intelligence which would take him to a training depot in Oxford where he would be among old friends. People are being worn down by the daily humiliation of going about with NCC flashes on their shoulders. There have been one or two unpleasant episodes with combatant units in the YMCA, though curiously not with the Guards regiments. I resist this with every argument that I can muster. Partly because I think it is a definite policy of the authorities to try to break up the Non-Combatant Corps, but mostly because I cannot bear the thought of losing this society and these people and being thrown back once again on myself.

About nine o'clock C. [name withheld] and I walked across to the cookhouse to see if we could find something to eat. It was full moon and the wind was pulling at the guy-ropes and the marquees were swaying like galleons. Inside, Bill was sitting in his shirt sleeves at the table writing. The lantern in front of him lit his face and arms and a strip of his shoulder with a deep bronze radiance. Other figures sat around in the shadows. The air was warm after the clear windy night and everywhere was the hum of conversation. We made tea and ate sausage rolls out of a box on the floor. The box was quite invisible and everyone tripped over it as they passed, but it never seemed to occur to anyone to pick it up. Presently Bill got up and stood away from the table by the fire and out of the light of the lantern. I stood near him drinking my tea which C. had brewed. C. moved about quietly collecting bread and bits of jam from various tins while the others sat around the table talking. I did not listen to what they were saying but looked at Bill once or twice and he smiled – the smile one gives when one has nothing particular to say but wants to acknowledge the other person's presence. When the conversation began to get animated I walked towards the door so as not to be drawn into it. I was aware of that sense of magic, of something unique and un-repeatable that such moments can sometimes hold. Bill followed me and we walked out into the sudden lustrous moonlight and fresh warm wind. The tents were like geometric impressions of mushrooms, hardly distinguish-able from the colour of the dull grass. Clouds were mounted over the horizon, the rest of the sky was clear and star-lit. I put my arm around his shoulders, and he put his arm round my waist and we walked across the muddy grass back to the tent.

Although Keith Vaughan found the intellectual life in the Non-Combatant Corps stimulating, the hard manual labour in which they were engaged by day did not suit everyone. In July and August 1941 his unit found themselves quartered in tents at Melksham where they were engaged in quarrying gravel. Life largely consisted of swinging a pick, eating and resting. He found relief from the tedium of 'navvying' in speculation about the possibility of transferring to non-combatant work that was less physical, and in his affection for 'Bill G'. In other units homosexuality might have presented more problems, but in his own unit attitudes were more liberal.

Though Vaughan hated war, paradoxically these years were the making of him as an artist, giving him time to paint – albeit at night, after hard physical work during the day – and ample subjects. After the war he would teach painting at Camberwell and in the late 1950s at the Slade. By the time of his death in 1977 he was regarded as an important British artist. SEE ALSO PP. 57–8 AND 272–3.

SEPTEMBER 1941

IN 1941 THE AXIS continued to perform better at codebreaking than the Allies. The German codebreaking service – B-Dienst – was reading a great deal of Allied naval communications traffic in the Atlantic. Moreover, in September Italian agents from the Servizio Informazione Militare (Italian military intelligence) acquired the cipher used by the American military attaché in Cairo, Colonel Bonner Fellers, who was sending detailed reports of Allied dispositions back to Washington. This would provide Rommel with priceless operational intelligence on the desert war all the way through to the summer of 1942.

An American destroyer, the USS *Greer*, was attacked by a German U-boat on 4 September after being mistaken for a British ship. Roosevelt presented this as an example of German aggression and ordered the US navy to shoot at German military vessels on sight. In reality this was merely justification for something that was already happening. During the second half of September the US navy took over responsibility for escorting many of the convoys from Canada to the UK, and also ships going to Iceland.

On 19 September the major Soviet city of Kiev fell to the Germans. Soviet losses in this one battle were almost half a million men. But German losses were also high, amounting to 100,000 well-trained and well-equipped troops. Germany, accustomed to short 'Blitzkrieg' campaigns, had not yet experienced casualties of this kind and scale, and the lost formations would not be easy to replace. Moreover, the Russian winter was now not far away.

Further south, British and Soviet troops jointly occupied Iran, allowing Allied access to critical oil supplies and providing a southern route for US supplies to the Soviet Union. On 29

September the first convoy carrying such supplies – PQ-1 –
paused at Iceland and then set out for Archangel. Throughout the
rest of 1941 this regular supply traffic proceeded without hindrance from the Axis.

Monday 1 September 1941

Sergeant James Gray is thrilled to see bombing in Newcastle

*James Gray's well-written and sometimes outspoken diary records the
life of a man from Hove in Sussex who had enlisted in the Territorial
Army in November 1938 in response to the Munich agreement. He
served as an NCO in searchlight and anti-aircraft units in Hastings and
Dover before converting to coastal artillery in late 1940. From March
1941 he was serving with the 348th Coast Battery, 508th Coast
Regiment RA, at Tyne Coastal Defences, South Shields.*

James Gray

This evening paid my, by now, weekly Monday visit to Newcastle for the dance at the Oxford galleries. I had my usual good evening there and as I was walking down Granger Street the syrens [*sic*] sounded. Almost at once planes were overhead and the A.A. guns and searchlights went into action.

I stood outside the station watching the S/L's [searchlights] and gun bursts and then as I went inside the station one plane zoomed very loudly overhead and down came three bombs with almost ominous wail!! They all dropped fairly close to the station and before long the glare of flames in the sky showed that some building nearby was on fire. The guns still roared and further bombs were dropped. My train which was due to leave at 10.45 p.m. for South Shields was delayed and we didn't leave until after 11 p.m. We crossed the bridge over the Tyne and then as we rounded the curve in the line leading into Gateshead station we came upon an awe-inspiring sight. On the Newcastle river-bank, quite close to the station a large building, which appeared to be a store of a warehouse, was blazing furiously and quite literally was alight from one end to another.

Bombs were still falling and more damage was apparent at Pelaw and Fellin. Everyone seemed tremendously excited about this raid, which although slight when compared with the London blitz seemed to be considered of some magnitude in this district. I learned next day that 20 people had been killed and that it was Newcastle's heaviest raid of the war, to date.

All coastal cities were vulnerable to bombing, not only because they were often ports, but also because they were easier for bombers to locate. Fortunately, although parts of Newcastle were badly damaged in this raid, including the Forth Goods Station near Newcastle's Central Station and some parts of nearby Jesmond, the city was shielded from some of the worst effects of the German bombing by deception and camouflage methods. The Civil Defence had decided to light tar barrels along each side of the Tyne whenever major air raids were predicted to make a large smokescreen which hid the river and some of the main buildings.

In common with many who began the war as NCOs, by 1945 Gray would have been promoted to captain.

Early September 1941

Friedrich Reck-Malleczewen comments on 'how we live in Germany today'

Friedrich Reck-Malleczewen's diary is one of the most fascinating journals of the Third Reich. An anti-Nazi Prussian aristocrat and monarchist living on his estate in Bavaria, he describes the horrors of the 1940s through the eyes of the upper classes. Unable to disguise his true feelings, he described the Nazis as beast-like 'half-men'.

Recently, when Herr Gauleiter Wagner honoured our little town with his presence, practically every chicken in the area was slaughtered to meet the needs of his entourage of drunkards and felons. Herr Hitler has his own private vegetable farm in Solln, near Munich, where SS guards patrol an electrically charged fence enclosing the hothouses of our vegetarian Tamerlane.

In the meantime the plebes are feeling the full fury of a German food industry gone chemical-crazy. Sugar is now made out of fir-wood pulp, sausage out of beechwood pulp, and the beer is a stinking brew made of whey. Yeast is made out of a chemical, and marmalade is coloured to fool people into thinking it is the real thing. The same for butter, except that the colouring matter here also contains a vile and in-digestible substance poisonous to the liver and doubtless responsible for the biliousness so common today. Everyone's eyes are yellow, and if I am to believe friends of mine who are doctors, the incidence of cancer has doubled in the last four years.

A true Prussian, an old hand at 'improvising' his life out of garbage cans, is in his glory when he can sweep away the natural abundance of Germany, which is more than enough to satisfy demand, and put in its place the substitute, the ersatz. Canned vegetables are also artificially colored. The wine, except for what is guzzled by young officers, or black-marketed by Army paymasters, is unholy snake poison. The soap stinks as badly as 'New German' corruption, and the soles of the ski shoes I bought last winter after a series of battles over the ration coupon, turned into a sodden mess of cardboard after a half hour's walking.

   ... The consequences of all this are already beginning to be apparent. As a result of the fermentation and gas result-ing from pulpy, clayey bread, the air in the cafes is pestilential. No one even bothers anymore to hold back his wind. As a result of this systematic poisoning of the blood, people go about with boils and abscesses and their body liquids are fouled. The daily hunt for immediate necessities and envy of one's darling neighbours have combined to pro-duce a nastiness, and a slackness in behaviour, such as would have been impossible even a short time ago.

In the latter months of 1941 Friedrich Reck-Malleczewen began to note the impact of 'total war' upon the German people. Previously they had reaped the benefits of plundering neighbouring countries conquered at low cost, but after June this year the German people found that their industry and agriculture were increasingly feeling the strains of all-out war. The German economy would nevertheless enjoy some protection until late 1942. Reck-Malleczewen also expresses the bitterness of an old and privileged elite displaced by the Nazi party, whose upper echelons were untouched by these privations. SEE ALSO PP. 485–7.

Monday 22 September 1941

Count Ciano, Italian foreign minister, records the death of Mussolini's son Bruno

I have come back to the Ministry after a prolonged absence due to a throat infection, which forced me to undergo surgery. Almost two months without any contact with the Duce apart from the very sad day of Bruno's death. I have found the Chief in good physical and mental shape; he has recovered from the blow. As usual, the dominant note in his speech is the progress of the war. He claims that the anxiety of the Italian people is due to the fact that they are not taking part in the broad military campaign on the Russian front. I do not agree with him. The Italian people are not particularly interested in the Russian war; their uneasiness is due to lack of bread, fat, eggs, etc. However, this does not seem to overly concern the Duce. But it does worry [Adelchi] Serena who is now responsible – or at least is regarded as such – for food supply. The Party made a great mistake when it decided to assume responsibility for a problem that is likely to generate even more discontent, because if now the situation is alarming it is not difficult to foresee that this crisis will become more acute as lack of fodder and scarce fertilizers will cause crops and production to drop to lower levels.

Many of the world's leading statesmen found that their children were in uniform by 1941, Roosevelt, Stalin, Churchill and Mussolini among them. Bruno Mussolini had served in the Italian air force in Abyssinia in 1937 and had been much criticized for his outspoken comments about the pleasure of machine-gunning 'natives' from the air. He later undertook more hazardous service in the Spanish Civil War. However, Bruno died not in action but away from the front line at the large aircraft factory at Pontedera. Previously a specialist air-engine factory, it now produced a range of fighters, transport planes and bombers. One of these, the Piaggio 108, an experimental four-engine bomber, crashed in the countryside outside Pisa on its first test flight on 7 August 1941. Everyone on board died except for the co-pilot. The chief pilot was Bruno Mussolini. Benito Mussolini was very close to his children and suffered shock and deep grief when he learned of the death of his son.

Ciano had married Mussolini's daughter but did not share his father-in-law's views. Mussolini wanted Italian troops to join Bulgarian and Romanian units that were already fighting on the Eastern Front alongside their German allies, in an effort to show Axis solidarity. There was even a volunteer unit of Spanish fascists – the 'Blue Division' – fighting there. In contrast, Ciano knew that Italy had already bitten off more

than it could chew with its own battles in the Mediterranean. SEE ALSO
PP. 43–4, 46–7, 110–11 AND 513.

Thursday 25 – Saturday 27 September 1941

Commander George Blundell struggles with torpedo damage en route to Malta

George Blundell

*George Blundell had spent much of his naval career on large battleships.
In the 1920s he had served as a midshipman on HMS* Hood, *and by
1941 he was second-in-command of HMS* Nelson. *He wrote one of the
great personal records of the naval war.*

25 September
The operation we are in is entitled 'Halberd': it is nothing
more than getting another convoy through to Malta ...

Group 1 is Nelson, Ark Royal, Hermione, Cosack, Zulu, Forsyte, Forrester, Laforey and Lightning, and our group goes straight up the middle of the Mediterranean well ahead of Group 2 as if we were the normal Force H out on a club run. Group 2 consists of P[rince] of W[ales], Rodney, the convoy, Sheffield, Kenya, Edinburgh, Euryalus and the rest of the destroyers.

26 September
... At dawn we were between Majorca and Algiers. Group 1 was on its own all day: we saw no shipping and only one snooper which Ark's fighters failed to sight. It's noticeable how difficult the fighters find it to see a snooper, although they carry an observer gunner.

27 September
At Dawn we joined up with Group 2 who were to the north of us ...

The convoy consists of 8 ships, Clan MacDonald, Clan Ferguson, Ajax, City of Lincoln, City of Calcutta, Imperial Star, Dunedin Star, and Rowallan Castle, also the AMC Breconshire. All destroyers are spread out in a vast screen 5,000 yards ahead and the 'umbrella' so formed sheltering the convoy and a large area in which the Ark Royal can operate. Ark is keeping eight fighters in the air all day.

Well! The day has been exciting, but tragic for us in Nellie. The forenoon was peaceable enough, but at 12.01 a big attack by Torpedo Bomber aircraft developed. They were Italian S.79's and B.R.20's, the big 3 engined machine. At first they were all over the port wing side and we could see Rodney, P of W, cruisers and destroyers that side opening up on them.

They dropped torpedoes ahead of the screen but some machines seemed to get between the battleships and the convoy. Nobody was hit and one or two planes were brought down. One of the machines, gradually losing height, glided right down along the line of destroyers, looking as if it was going to pancake right on top of them, but it fell into the water just ahead of it, sending up a huge sheet of flame and a puff of white smoke as it struck. It must have been an awe inspiring sight from the destroyer!

Then we had a big attack our side. They came right over our screen which seemed to have no deterrent effect on them. One machine dropped its torpedo away from us but a 2nd came on and the ship turned towards it. When it was about 20 degrees on our starboard bow and 800 yards off it dropped its torpedo, but we couldn't see any track as it seemed to have run deep. But to our horror the track suddenly appeared, not more than 200 yards ahead, coming straight for us on an absolutely opposite course. There was simply nothing we could do. Had we turned, and there wasn't time, we should get it on our side. The only thing that could of saved us was to walk the ship sideways and that was obviously impossible. I was on the Bridge and the track came straight to our stern, perhaps just to port, and I felt by some miracle it might miss or turn or run deep. And then I thought it must have gone under us or down our side, because although the track had reached us, and to my eyes had disappeared under the overhang of the bow, there was no explosion. Then, just as I was breathing again, there was that horrid underwater thud, the whole bow rose and quivered, and the ship shook like a mighty animal. But the splash was amazingly small, only as if a small sea had slopped over the side with a momentary vibrant haze. This happened at 13.31.

Another plane dropped a torpedo on our starboard bow and we turned towards this but it harmlessly ran down our starboard side and the plane came so close that one felt one could knock it down with ones fist. We hit this machine and it came down. I myself, saw no more, although there were more attacks after this, because I rushed down to ginger up the repair parties . . .

[I] went down to the Communications mess deck. Here water was gushing through a gash in the deck under the hammock netting port after side just forard of 60 bulk head and there was about 2 feet of water. The whole deck seemed to be heaving and through the jagged edges of the hole I could see the blue glistening sea. I organised a party to remove the hammocks and lockers, mess stools and tables in the vicinity to give some space to work in. Then, with not much success, we banged at the torn edges of the plate to try

and even them down, stuffing the hole which seemed about
4 feet square, with hammocks, over which we put tarpaulins
– backed with sawn planks and shored the whole thing
down to form a big pudding . . . the pressing need was for
wood for shoring.

Eventually electric light got supplied everywhere, parties
brought up enough wood and the engineers rigged up their
75 ton portable pumps putting the suction down into the
Communications mess deck. The H.O.'s and torpedomen's
mess decks came to look like forests with the amounts of
vertical shoring erected!

The bow has gone down about 6 feet and, looking along
the Upper Deck, the ship looks most peculiar as if she were
plunging down hill. If one stands at the stern it feels as if one
could just step straight off into the sea.

*Damage control was a critical skill for the officers of the Royal Navy
serving on convoys running through the western Mediterranean to
Malta. Plagued by bombing and aerial torpedo attacks launched from
Sicily, the ability skilfully to limit the flood or fire damage from an
explosion could often save a ship. Their twin enemies were first, panic on
the part of ratings who feared both drowning and asphyxiation when
hatches were closed, and second, poor design on ships that had in many
cases been laid down during the First World War. Ships built after 1935
enjoyed much better compartmentalization and hence had better chances
of survival. When the HMS Nelson was torpedoed much of the flooding was attributable to a worried stoker leaving a single hatch open. On
the return journey to Gibraltar the accompanying aircraft carrier, HMS
Ark Royal, was torpedoed and eventually sank after a fourteen-hour
battle to keep her afloat, although only one rating was lost. SEE ALSO PP.
452–5.*

OCTOBER 1941

D URING SEPTEMBER AND October a further series of relief operations was mounted to assist the besieged port of Tobruk. By
night fast transports and destroyers brought in about 13,000 fresh
troops, mostly Poles, and evacuated 14,000 Australians, who had
fought doggedly for months and were now exhausted.

Tobruk was not the only city under siege. The Germans had
already surrounded Leningrad and on 2 October they launched
Operation Typhoon, their bid to capture Moscow. By 16 October
the city was in panic, with foreign diplomats and government
officials preparing to flee to the reserve capital of Kuibyshev.
Those who could made an undignified exit by train, car and lorry.
However, heavy rain was now falling and this turned the battleground into a sea of mud, slowing the German advance to a
crawl. At the end of October the ground froze permanently. In the
south, German forces reached the Sea of Azov to the east of the
Crimea and cut off 600,000 Soviet troops. Odessa had to be
evacuated by sea.

With so much of the Luftwaffe engaged in Russia, the RAF
decided to undertake bolder incursions into Europe. Even with a
proportion of German air strength diverted to the Eastern Front,
however, RAF bomber losses over German industrial cities continued to be heavy, and so alternative strategies were tried in an
effort to stretch German air defences. During September and
October the RAF mounted numerous fighter sweeps over France,
attacking opportunistically. Many of the pilots were Belgians,
Frenchmen, Czechs and Poles who had escaped capture in 1940
and who in some cases were now attacking targets in their own
countries. In France, the resistance was gathering pace. On 20
October the German commander in Nantes was shot by the
underground movement. Fifty French hostages were shot as a
reprisal. Another assassination took place in Bordeaux a few days
later and also resulted in vicious retribution. These punishment
measures were widely publicized by the Gestapo in an attempt to
deter further attacks.

Saturday 4 October 1941

Harry Seidler, an anti-Nazi German, is released from
internment in Canada after seventeen months of captivity

This is the greatest day of my life. The day of my RELEASE.
It ends a very sad period of my life – INTERNMENT.

I did not sleep much at night. Thinking, thinking, I try to
count but it helps little. All I get is about two or three hours'
sleep. I am up early and try to make myself look civilised.
Wearing a tie certainly is very unusual and uncomfortable.
At 9 we are all at the gate and are led out to the officers. The
six being released are asked in one by one. The interview
with the immigration officer takes about half an hour. He is
an ordinary looking chap and rather friendly at times. He
cross-examines me about every period of my life. What I did
in Vienna, what my father did – when I left Vienna for
England. In between he makes a remark which makes me
realise my position better than anything else. He says, 'It is
understood that you are not to talk to anyone about the conditions in this or any other camp nor about experiences you
have had during your internment. We have ways and means
of finding out if you do and you know what happens.'
Meaning, of course, that the way back to camp is always
open to me in case I don't behave outside. I get a conditional
permit for six months which can be prolonged if I behave
during that time.

After the immigration officer has dealt with us we are
interviewed by a police officer who provides us with
registration cards. We then bring our luggage to the outer
compound where everything is searched. I am rather
nervous because there are some things in my trunk which
they might take away. I have, for instance, got a prisoner's
shirt with the red back, my diary etc. But, as usual, I am
lucky. The censor, a very nice chap, is looking at my things
and is not too particular about it. He just opens the trunk,
looks at the top layer of things and – okay. So I can keep my
souvenirs – diary and shirt.

Meanwhile, the thirty people going back to England have also come outside. People in the camp stand behind the wire wishing luck and giving addresses (I have about 30 people to write to for friends inside). I speak to Marcell [his brother] – poor chap – the fact that I must leave him behind certainly mars the joy of my release. But I am confident that I'll be able to do something for him. We can take our separation well. After all it is nothing sad – on the contrary, a step towards freedom for both of us.

Internment has brought us both very much nearer to each other. Going through all those difficulties side by side binds two people more than anything. He has become a real pal of mine.

Our train leaves at 3.30. Tickets are bought for the other five and mine is brought up from Sherbrooke by the Canadian Pacific Railways agent. We get our money from the commander (I get $100) and off we go. A truck takes us down to the station. At 3 pm we cross the wire – I do hope for good. What a feeling! FREE!!! I somehow can't believe it – it must be a dream. Maybe I'll wake up in a camp again. We pass houses – cars – PEOPLE!!! At the station we register our luggage (my large trunk right through to Winnipeg) – then the train pulls in – one car occupied by our people going back to England – heavily guarded – we get on the train and sit down. I get my pals to punch me in the arm. Yes, it does hurt – so I must be awake.

People are very French. Girls are frightfully painted and everyone dresses in conspicuous colours – some of us go to the dining car to have coffee. White table cloths – china plates – and the food! It is all like a miracle. Just behind us is the car full of Pioneer Corps men. They don't eat in luxury like we do. Why? Because they go back to fight for England, guarded. But we can be completely free in a peaceful country just because we happen to be under 21 and have someone who pays for us. The world is standing on its head!

We sit in our armchairs – look at the landscape – yes, we are really free.

At about 6.30 we get into Montreal. Three of us have our sponsors waiting and, for the remaining three, Mr Goldner

and Mr Raphael have come down. They shove us in their car
(a beauty) and drive us round a bit. Goldner is very glad to
have us out. After all, it is one of the first successful schemes
to get refugees out. We do some calls and drive around the
city. It's a beautiful place. Terrific buildings, parks, posh cars,
lights – for us like a dream. Goldner then treats us to a
dinner at a very modern restaurant. We eat REAL soup,
chicken, pudding – all things I have not tasted for 1½ years.
Then he dumps us at the Ford Hotel (also a pretty posh
place) and leaves us. He was certainly very decent and kind
to us – the three of us walked down town – St Catherine's
Street is our objective. With plenty of plans in mind we go
off. Little comes of it. We walk up and down, look at the busy
life – the shop windows, and then end up in a soda fountain.
This hour of strolling in the busiest street of town has done
the job with me – I am no more frightened. I am quite used
to civilised life again. After all THIS is normal and not
my immediate past! For the first time I sleep in a real bed
with WHITE SHEETS over it. The loveliest thing in the
world.

*Some Germans had escaped internment by volunteering for the Pioneer
Corps, an unarmed unit concerned with construction and road-building.
Harry Seidler, aged eighteen at the time of his release after seventeen
months of internment, was soon studying at the University of Manitoba.
There it was compulsory to join the university Officer Training Corps
and so, ironically, he would find himself almost immediately in Allied
uniform. Seidler had endured an unpleasant period of incarceration but
now had a bright future ahead. After a period working as an architect
in the United States he emigrated to Australia in 1948, becoming one of
the country's leading architects of the modern movement and the first in
Australia fully to express the principles of the Bauhaus. His major
works include the Australian embassy in Paris. SEE ALSO PP. 150–2 AND
190–2.*

Monday 6 – Monday 13 October 1941

Surgeon Ralph Marnham arrives at No. 62 General Hospital, Tobruk

Ralph Marnham was a surgeon in the Royal Army Medical Corps and was having a quiet war in Jerusalem when he found his unit was to be moved by sea to the besieged town of Tobruk, where it was attached to No. 62 General Hospital.

In September we heard rumours that we were leaving Jerusalem and that No. 6 Australian General Hospital was to replace us. Basra, Turkey and Cyprus were all suggested as our possible destination. On the 26th September we heard we were moving in two weeks time without equipment and on the 30th the advance party of the No. 6 Australian General Hospital arrived. On the 6th I was informed that I was to command the Advance Party, 10 Officers and 50 Other Ranks (Official), there were in fact 51, how and why I never discovered. The Officers were told camp beds were not required, that we could take what we liked but what we took we would have to carry ourselves. I settled for a standard pack and a valise and for home comforts I put in a thermos of tea and two bottles of whisky. On the 8th at 16.30 hours we assembled at the Hospital and I sent off the baggage party with Lt. Ramage, Corporal Dodsworth and four Other Ranks. Major Gowans protested about being parted from his baggage and it was only when I said this was an order not a basis for discussion that he complied. I happened to know he had lost his on two occasions between England and the Middle East. At 18.30 hours we entrained at Jerusalem and were on our way . . .

The all night journey from Lydda to Kantara East was not uneventful. Our party was accommodated in one third class coach and two box trucks and were frequently disturbed by drunken Australians running from coach to coach and offering liquid refreshment to all and sundry. The train stopped thirty miles short of Kantara East to water the engine and two of the worst offenders were disembarked and told to finish the journey on foot. The end of a noisy nuisance. Feeling I should at least look respectable I shaved with the help of hot tea from my thermos. We had breakfast at Kantara East crossed the canal and finally left Kantara West at 16.00 hours but this time in peace and comfort in 1st and 2nd class coaches . . . [and then on to Tobruk by sea]

Some impressions of No. 4 A.G. Hospital, charming officers commanded by Colonel Spears . . . No discipline which resulted in more dirt and disorder than any of us had ever seen in any hospital or Unit.

Colonel Spears and I were walking from the Main Gate of the Hospital towards the Officers' Mess, a distance of some 50 yards when shells began dropping in and around the Compound. The Colonel proceeded at an unhurried pace and I, having no alternative, with him. At the same time there was a scurry of orderlies from the Administrative Block making for adjacent slit trenches. I can still see one of the junior clerks, a tall thin man with a high stepping gait, leading the rush and still clutching the ledger in which he had been entering the admissions. 'Get back to your work' shouted the Colonel, 'look at me, I am not hurrying'. A voice from the trenches rang out 'Neither would we if we were your age, you silly old b—. What have you got to live for anyway'. No action was taken, all the Colonel said as we pursued our leisurely way was 'High spirited lads aren't they!!' That night when I joined the Colonel for a drink after dinner I found his sergeant clerk already there, both in their shirt sleeves. 'Don't worry' said the Colonel 'he is my stock broker when we are at home.'

The sea journey to Tobruk could be undertaken only during hours of darkness, for air superiority in the Mediterranean had long since been lost to German fighters and bombers operating from Sicily. Casualties were gradually being evacuated out of Tobruk on the decks of destroyers for movement to better hospitals in Cairo. On arrival in Tobruk, one of the first people Marnham met was Colonel Spears, the commander of a remarkably casual Australian hospital unit which they were replacing and which would be taking their place in Jerusalem. Marnham soon found himself operating in the thick of the fighting where casualties could be accessed more quickly. SEE ALSO PP. 358–60.

Tuesday 21 October 1941

René Mouchotte, a Free French pilot flying with the RAF, on preparations for escape and evasion

René Mouchotte was a Parisian, born in 1914, who became a sergeant in the French air force. When France had surrendered in 1940 he seized an aircraft and fled from Oran in north Africa, landing at Gibraltar where he volunteered his services. His outstanding aptitude as a pilot and a leader was soon noted and so he had become leader of the famous 'Squadron Churchill', a unit of French pilots that would attack German targets along the coast of northern France during 1942.

We take some elementary precautions before flying over enemy-occupied country. Above all, I never fly without my English uniform, which will give me a few hours' respite if I am taken prisoner before being recognized as French . . .

Handicapped as I am with an unshakeable French accent, I doubt whether I shall be taken for an Oxonian. I have anticipated this difficulty by wearing the word 'Canada' on my shoulders. So now I am a citizen of Toronto, as long as I roll my 'r' as they do in Périgord. Without any papers whatever, my pockets absolutely empty. I go off with a light heart, in the conviction that my lucky star and my guardian angel will turn aside the bullets meant for me. These precautions are unnecessary, really: we fly like swallows scenting the storm and there is no likelihood, whatever of our being taken prisoner and every likelihood that we shall test the temperature of the Channel deeps or the resistance of the English plane when it crashes at 400 kilometres an hour in some kitchen garden in one of the New Order countries! But regardless of these lofty considerations, the English amuse themselves by encumbering us with a quantity of small objects of undeniable usefulness 'if' fate should make us the quarry in some absorbing manhunt. More than once, I admit, I have thought about this kind of sport. It must be extraordinarily exciting, and once the first agonizing minutes were over being French would make my task easier. We go with our pockets stuffed with odd paraphernalia: compasses hidden almost everywhere in the form of trouser buttons, propelling pencils and collarstuds; miniature hack-saw sewn into the belt; maps, on silk, of Holland, Belgium and France hidden in shoulder pads. We carry nutritive chocolate, pills to stop us going to sleep, an ampoule of morphine with a needle to inject it, tablets to purify water and a great deal of French and Belgian money. With all that, we are ready to face the terrors of a grand pursuit . . .

Pilots were more valuable than aircraft. Accordingly, by 1941 the RAF had applied extraordinary ingenuity to the matter of escape kits for pilots who were shot down over France. There were tunics with silk maps sewn into secret hiding places; there were oilskin-covered packets of French francs; and, inevitably, there were compasses and revolvers. Some pilots even carried specially made civilian clothes to assist their evasions if they were shot down. There were those who found these materials genuinely useful, and quite a number made their way back to Britain via Spain. But others looked on such preparations with amusement or disdain, thinking them signs of a defeatist mentality, and took to the air without them. SEE ALSO PP. 415–16.

Thursday 23 October 1941

Frances Partridge of the Bloomsbury Group on the horrors of wartime executions

This morning Burgo hurried in with the news that the rats had eaten a hole in the passage carpet 'big enough to put your waist through'. True enough. They had gnawed two very large holes in the floorboards and dragged the carpet through them, presumably to make nests with.

The Germans have shot fifty Frenchmen in cold blood as a

reprisal for the shooting of two of their own officers. They say they will shoot fifty more unless the man who killed the officers gives himself up. I was surprized when R.[alph] said in a voice of great emotion: 'There's one thing too horrible to talk about – the shooting of the fifty French hostages.' In the conversation that followed I understood that, apart from everything else, he was entering into the state of mind of the German soldiers who had to shoot these fifty innocent and irrelevant individuals, and that this action performed completely in cold blood has a horror for the person made to do it which distinguishes it sharply even from the action of a man who picks off a sniper with his rifle in the heat of battle. R. has told me everything that happened to him in the First War, with the greatest detail and vividness; but there is one he cannot describe without his voice breaking; when he was the captain ordered to take a squad of men to shoot one of our deserters, and had to give the signal to fire. It's for this reason that the last act of *Tosca* is almost unbearable to him. And by infection to me also.

Frances Partridge (left)

Frances Partridge's comments on her husband's sensibilities regarding execution show very clearly the long shadow cast by the First World War over an entire generation. Ralph had been head boy at Westminster

*School and won a classical scholarship to Christ Church, Oxford in
1913. By 1918 he was a 23-year-old major who had been awarded the
Military Cross and bar and the Croce de Guerra. He had been wounded
twice and had narrowly escaped death when he was buried alive as the
result of shellfire. The experience of presiding over the execution of a
deserter was especially troubling for him, given that he himself was
moving towards an intellectual position wherein he regarded all war as
'murder'. Over 300 British soldiers were executed for desertion,
cowardice or similar offences during the First World War. This included
two men who were shot for 'sleeping on post' in 1917. The war affected
Ralph Partridge deeply and he had become disillusioned with violence.
During the Second World War, like Frances, he was a conscientious
objector and spent his time distributing food to refugees in Wiltshire. SEE
ALSO PP. 19, 176–7, 211–12 AND 612–13.*

Saturday 25 – Wednesday 29 October 1941

Mrs Trowbridge, a housewife in Bradford, on eggs and wartime crime

25 October
'Eggless' week again! Yet shopkeepers are selling eggs 'off
the ration' at 1d each. Woolton must have discovered a huge
consignment hidden away – eggs which should have been
offered to the public before they went bad. No thank you!
I'm not buying his rotten eggs.

29 October
At last we are beginning to find out where the eggs have
gone. 150,000 in one Black Market prosecution alone, and
there's probably 150,000 other cases that ought to be brought
to light. The news yesterday that the transport of food is to
be curtailed and kept 'regional' isn't very pleasant reading
to us in this part of the world. We produce nothing eatable –
what are we going to do?

*By 1941 most foods were rationed. In a week an adult ration book pro-
vided for: 3 pints milk, 1lb meat, 3–4oz cheese, 4oz bacon and ham, 2oz*

tea, 8oz sugar, 2oz butter and 2oz cooking fat. Eggs were rare, and an adult was allowed one egg or a packet of dried egg every two months. Stories about 150,000 black-market eggs created intense public anger, and the authorities took stern action against those who broke regulations, even in a minor fashion. This included using undercover inspectors to identify shopkeepers who were not demanding coupons for everything that was sold. Food crime was sometimes carried out on a grand scale. A food control officer in Brighton discovered that 80,000 ration books had been stolen from the Brighton Food Office. An under-cover policeman was eventually offered the missing books on the black market. When the gang was arrested, it was discovered the ring-leader was actually the woman enforcement officer at the Brighton office who had reported the theft; she was sent to prison for three years.

Mrs Trowbridge was a Mass-Observation diarist who was active in the WVS and the University Women's Federation, looking after billeted soldiers and refugees.

NOVEMBER 1941

B Y NOVEMBER 1941 Churchill was increasingly desperate for victory in the desert war. Recognizing that the British now enjoyed numerical superiority over their opponents and that Rommel was facing severe supply problems, he urged his commanders to push forward in the hope of relieving the siege of Tobruk. This attempt took the form of a new British offensive, Operation Crusader, which was launched on 18 November across the border from Egypt into Libya. Rommel's attention had been focused on a final attack on Tobruk and because of this, together with deception measures by the British, he reacted slowly.

Special operations of various kinds were a growing part of the desert war. In early November, just prior to this major British offensive, Rommel was fortunate to evade a secret attempt to eliminate him and his headquarters with a Commando raid. Although the Commandos reached their objective, Rommel was not there: he had flown to Rome for consultations with the

Italians. He had found them in less than buoyant mood, for in east Africa their forces were close to total defeat.

Allied losses in the Battle of the Atlantic in November were the lowest for many months, partly due to the growing pace of the desert war, which was prompting Germany to send many of its U-boats into the Mediterranean. As a result of this transfer of German submarines Allied shipping in the Mediterranean was at greater risk, and the British carrier HMS *Ark Royal* was torpedoed and sunk close to Gibraltar on 14 November as she returned from operations to resupply Malta with fighter aircraft.

On the Eastern Front, fighting had now slowed to a crawl. The invaders' grip on Leningrad intensified with the severing of the rail route into the city. However, the German army realized that it was neither properly trained for winter fighting, nor, more importantly, adequately equipped with the appropriate clothing and supplies to deal with the severity of the Russian winter, which proved to be the coldest on record. Wisely, the Soviet commanders now chose to bide their time and prepare for a counter-offensive once the weather had taken its toll of their enemy.

Monday 3 November 1941

Kenneth Slessor, Australian war correspondent, watches Nazi films in Cairo

At 12.30, to Diana Theatre, where the [captured] German films screened before the British Ambassador (Miles Lampson), Commander-in-chief Auchinleck, all the Hats of GHQ, war correspondents and the hush-hush parachute unit. The films terrible and terrifying – designedly so, of course, since they are propaganda to cow and scare the smaller neutrals. Some extraordinary shots from the air of cannon-projectiles in flight, and hitting vehicles on the ground – also of German parachutists descending on the Corinth Canal. Several Australians photographed amongst the British prisoners shown (with hands up 'kamerad' style – not the Australians) – some close up, and could easily be recognised by their friends. The films are remarkably well-photographed, obviously in the thick of the fighting, and well presented, but leave out all the other side of the picture (Germany's own losses). Shots of dozens of corpses being dragged out of bombed buildings in Russia and dumped in holes. Films now re-edited with British commentary, thus reversing the propaganda.

Randolph Churchill, Winston Churchill's son, served in Cairo and was helping to make a documentary film about a new Allied parachute unit. Like many in the upper social circles, he had drifted into the world of special forces and secret service 'funnies'. While involved in filming he invited the local war correspondents, including Kenneth Slessor, to view two captured German propaganda films dealing with German parachutists in Crete and also the German war against Russia.

At the end of the war Kenneth Slessor would return to the Sydney Sun *as a leader writer and literary editor until 1957, after which he wrote for the* Daily Telegraph *and* Sunday Telegraph. *He died in 1971.* SEE ALSO PP. 275–6.

Monday 10 – Wednesday 19 November 1941

Lieutenant-Colonel Robert Laycock leads a night-time Commando attack on Rommel's HQ

Robert Laycock was born in 1908 and educated at Eton and Sandhurst before joining the Horse Guards in 1927. Between February and August 1941 he had commanded a special service brigade called 'Layforce', which was later depicted in Evelyn Waugh's semi-autobiographical 'Sword of Honour' trilogy, with Laycock thinly disguised as Tommy Blackhouse. Waugh would later comment that Laycock was one of the very few true military heroes he had ever met. In August 1941 Laycock had become commander of the Commandos in the Middle East.

Lt-Col. Geoffrey Keyes

[The submarines] TORBAY and TALISMAN slipped [anchor] and proceeded from Alexandria on the evening of 10 Nov. 1941 and the 4 day passage westwards was made in fair weather without incident though the wind freshened gradually throughout. Conditions in the submarines were naturally somewhat cramped and surfacing after dark each evening was a relief. All ranks were greatly interested in what was to us a novel way of approaching our objective . . .

A successful periscope recce was carried out by both submarines during daylight on 14 Nov, and that night TORBAY closed the beach shortly after 1830 hrs . . .

The nights were extremely cold . . .

[On the evening of 18 Nov.] No.1 Detachment was guided to within a few hundred yards of the house by friendly Arabs and lay up awaiting zero hour (2359hrs.)

They were here apprehended by another party of uniformed Arabs, presumably carribineri [*sic*], whose suspicions were however allayed by Capt. Campbell explaining to them in German that our forces were part of a German unit . . .

All parties were in position just before midnight and a recce was made of the house. Unable to find a way in through the back premises or windows, Col. Keyes' party walked up to the front door and beat upon it, Capt. Campbell demanding access in German.

The door was eventually opened by a sentry who was set upon but who could not be overpowered silently and was therefore shot by Capt. Campbell which aroused the H.Q. and the vicinity.

Two men tried to come downstairs from the first floor but thought better of it on being met by a burst of fire from Sgt. Terry's Tommy gun. No one attempted to leave the rooms on the ground floor but the lights in them were turned out.

No enemy emerged from the guard tent or the Hotel but two Germans carrying lights appeared running towards the house where they were shot by our sentries.

Keyes and Campbell started to make a search of the ground floor but the occupants of the second room they entered were waiting for them and Lt. Col. Keyes, who had opened the door, was met by a burst of fire and fell back in the passage mortally wounded.

Sgt. Terry emptied 2 magazines of his Tommy Gun into the darkened room and Capt. Campbell silenced the party by throwing in a grenade and slamming the door. Together they carried Lt. Col. Keyes outside where he died almost immediately. While he was attending to him, Capt. Campbell was hit by a stray bullet which broke his lower leg.

On the whole, the enemy seems to have been taken completely by surprise and put up little resistance. Two German Staff officers are known to have been killed and others wounded, whilst several soldiers were killed and wounded. It is however, particularly unfortunate that General Rommell [sic] himself was absent attending a birthday party in Rome. Later information received from Arabs confirmed those 3 German Lt. Cols. were killed. A few shots were heard at some distance from the house but as they did not come from the direction in which our own troops were posted, it is hoped that the enemy were shooting at each other.

Captain Campbell, who was now lying wounded outside the house, ordered Sgt. Terry to concentrate the detachment and tell them to throw all remaining grenades through any available windows before returning to their operational R.V. [rendezvous] preparatory to withdrawal to the beach.

Capt. Campbell, realising that a super-human effort would be required to carry him back over 18 miles of precipitous country entailing a descent of some 2000ft., ordered himself to be abandoned . . .

During the night of 17/18 Nov. I again revisited the beach but weather conditions were still hopeless and no sign could be seen of TALISMAN.

In late 1941 a plan was conceived to raid four strategic locations that were all close to Sidi Rafa on the coast of Cyrenaica, 200 miles behind enemy lines. The raid was timed to coincide with the 8th Army's advance and was designed to cause maximum disruption. The most audacious target was a building at Sidi Rafa itself which Field Marshal Erwin Rommel was reported to use when visiting his logistics chief. Other detachments were to attack the main Italian HQ, an Italian intelligence centre and a communications centre. On 10 November four detachments of Commandos consisting of nine officers and fifty-six other ranks boarded two submarines. The weather was rough, and on arrival there were problems disembarking all the Commandos to move ashore. A diminished force of only six officers and twenty-seven other ranks attacked their objectives, but the main party of nineteen Commandos led by Lieutenant-Colonel Keyes failed to locate the sought-after prize of Rommel and suffered casualties, including the death of Keyes himself.

After the attack the raiders' problems began in earnest. All the detachments retreated to the beach, but found it impossible to return to the submarines because of the rough weather and the loss of boats. Located by the enemy, the Commandos scattered in small parties in the hope of making it across the desert to their own lines. Some were killed; most were taken prisoner. Laycock and Sergeant Terry were among the small number of the original party who made it back to British lines at Cyrene some forty-one days after landing from the submarines. They sat down to dinner at 8th Army headquarters on Christmas Day.

Robert Laycock's account was actually written out in longhand for him by Hermione, Countess of Ranfurly, who was working in the headquarters of SOE Cairo at the time and visited him in hospital. (She incorporated some of the story into her own diary.) Laycock would survive the war and receive a copy of each of Waugh's novels with fulsome dedications in the front. Laycock enjoyed a lifelong association with special forces and was Colonel Commandant of the SAS in the 1960s.

Thursday 20 November – Friday 5 December 1941

German army Field Pastor Sebacher feels the onset of the Russian winter

20 November

I slept a few hours on something that goes by the name of bed. The houses all look as if they had witnessed some fierce fighting and that the Germans got the worst of it. Helmets, machine-gun equipment, blood-stained clothes and the like were scattered anyhow in the straw. How much more pleasant the war was in summer-time than now!

29 November

Already in the summer the thought had occurred to me once that really this country was made for winter, for snow and icy cold. Everything round about is clad in white and all the time you are haunted by the thought that a snowstorm may bury every trace of a road. It is this that makes the Russian winter so horrible. Oh Russia, what have you still in store for us, what cruelties will you still inflict upon us?

5 December

I did some fighting on my own account this morning and casualties were not few, either: I shook a couple of hundred lice and nits out of my shirt and jacket. I felt dispirited when I realized I would not be able to get rid of these pests altogether. That was too much for me. I wonder if this is the last sacrifice that Russia will exact.

By the second half of November the German attack on Moscow was paralysed by temperatures of –20°F. Many German soldiers were deliberately wounding themselves to avoid further service, and incidents of cowardice were common. Sebacher's diary would be captured by Soviet forces at the end of 1941, but little is known of him or his ultimate fate.

Friday 21 November – Wednesday 10 December 1941

Surgeon Ralph Marnham operates during heavy fighting at Tobruk

In the first 7 days we were dealing almost exclusively with garrison troops attempting a link up with 13th Corps, 606 were operated on and these were arriving on an average within six hours of being wounded.

In the second period of thirteen days the casualties were mostly from 13th Corps and had passed through Casualty Clearing Stations, 561 were operated on, the average time since wounding 30 hours. Forward Surgical Units were sited at Sidi Mahmoud and dealt with the most serious cases before passing them on to the Town Hospital. The less serious were sent there direct and they also had some additional admissions. The following is an account of how three surgeons, two specialist surgeons, two neuro surgeons, and six general duty officers did 1167 operations in 20 days, or one every 24 minutes. I was at Sidi Mahmoud for seven days, 21.11.41–27.11.41, there were two surgical teams (A) Griffiths, Wallis and Johnstone as one and (B) Myself, Douglas and Johnson as the other. Major Wallis, the Ophthalmic Specialist, in addition to dealing with all eye cases, did duty as an anaesthetist.

On 21st we started operating at 14.00 hours and with half an hour off for breakfast, other meals were taken in theatre, continued for 25 hours, when (A) team went off for three hours returning at 18.00 hours on the 22nd, and after 28 hours in the theatre (B) team went off for a similar period returning at 21.00 hours . . .

For my rest periods I always left the caves, which were hot and smelly, and went to a small derelict shed, rather like a garden shed, where I slept soundly in spite of the sound of battle and occasional bombing raids on adjacent targets, about 10 blankets beneath me and as many as I wanted on top. At the end of my second spell of operating I noticed that my legs were twice their normal size. A colleague suggested putting a knife into one to see what came out. As a conservative surgeon I did not accept his offer and a few hours on my back put matters right . . .

It was noted by the Colonel that when German wounded were brought into the theatre the Polish surgeon would have nothing to do with them so he was sent for and the following conversation took place. Colonel 'Captain . . . you must deal with the wounded as they are brought in irrespective of race,' Captain 'Is that an order Colonel.' Colonel 'Yes, captain it is.' Captain 'Very good Colonel I will obey but you must understand that with regard to the Germans my mortality rate will be 100%'. The point was not pressed and other members of the team dealt with them.

How I was nearly court martialled. We were all flat out in the Theatre, all three teams at work. An orderly appeared and said could I send someone to his ward to certify death as he had two dead patients and wanted their bodies removed. I told him to go to the Pathologist's room and ask him to deal with the matter. A few minutes later he returned and said the Pathologist said it was not his job. In a flaming temper I left the theatre, went to his room switched on the light, he was apparently asleep. I went across and to wake him took a flying kick at his bed, I had forgotten that it was of the camp variety with a canvas bottom, the result was dramatic, he was up and on his way in no time at all. He reported me to the Colonel for assaulting a junior officer. I refused to apologise. The Colonel pointed out this was a Court Martial offence but that if I would leave the matter with him he would do his best. That I did, and heard no more about it.

Ralph Marnham's first duties at Tobruk were as part of a forward surgical unit set up in four caves at Sidi Mahmoud, close to the front line, ready for the major battle to relieve Tobruk which began on 21 November. By February 1942 the surgeons at Tobruk would have treated 5,497 battle casualties with only 90 deaths – a mortality rate of only 1.6 per cent. Marnham would survive the war, reaching the rank of brigadier, and died in 1984. SEE ALSO PP. 345–7.

Sunday 30 November 1941

Colonel-General Halder on Hitler's style of command in the Russian campaign

First Panzer Army, against which the enemy has launched an enveloping attack in such overwhelming strength that army reserve (14th Armored Division) had to be committed on the very day that it reached its new position in the withdrawal. Even so, First Panzer Army could not prevent local penetrations; now it has to fall back once more.

The Fuehrer is in a state of extreme agitation over the situation. He forbids withdrawal of the army to the line Taganrog–Mius–mouth of the Bakhmut River, and demands that the retrograde move be halted farther east. Alongside this, there is even talk of an attack by Seventeenth Army on Voroshilovgrad. These people have no conception of the condition of our troops, and keep grinding out ideas in a vacuum.

ObdH was ordered to the Fuehrer at 1300. The interview appears to have been more than disagreeable, with the Fuehrer doing all the talking, pouring out reproaches and abuse, and shouting orders as fast as they came into his head. Regrettably, ObdH yielded to the Fuehrer's insistence and has issued the order not to fall back to the aforementioned line in one move. Field Marshal von Rundstedt's reply was that he could not comply with the order and asked that either the order be changed or he be relieved of his post. Inasmuch as the Fuehrer had reserved the decision for himself, the request was passed on to the Fuehrer in its exact wording. In tight situations such as these, only the commander on the spot can have a complete picture, and his decision must be trusted. Such confidence would certainly be in order in the case of von Rundstedt. The people at army group have done everything in their power. Let them have a free hand, and they will handle their end of the job.

By November 1941 the German offensive in Russia was slowing badly, and the drive for Moscow faltered only 50 miles short of its objective. German forces, who had begun the invasion too late in the year, found themselves at the end of hopelessly over-extended supply lines and without proper winter clothing. Soviet forces were determined to exploit the weather and used the frozen Lake Ladoga around Moscow to move in supplies to assist the defenders. Hitler involved himself in the minute detail of the campaign, and his rantings are barely captured in Halder's understated diaries. Hitler's reaction to reverses was extremely volatile: he would often scream and shout when confronted with the obstinate realities of war. He gave impulsive orders regarding small operational units and over-ruled commanders on the ground. His insistence had delivered stunning success in Poland and France during 1939–40 against the pessimism of the German General Staff, and so few now had the courage to contradict him. The situation was different in Britain, where the Chiefs of Staff – especially Alan Brooke – did an effective job of containing some of Churchill's wilder notions, although they found the task exhausting.

Halder was by now Commander-in-Chief of the German army; however, he would be replaced in September 1942 by Kurt Zeitler after a disagreement with Hitler over the direction of the war in Russia. In 1944 he would be arrested by the Gestapo and accused of being connected with the bomb plot which came close to assassinating Hitler in July of that year. He was taken to Dachau concentration camp but survived. Ironically, his sojourn in Dachau probably saved his life, for when he gave evidence at the Nuremberg war trials in 1945 he was perceived as an enemy of the regime. In fact his arguments with Hitler had been military rather than political. SEE ALSO PP. 197–8 AND 307–8.

Fear and confusion during Reginald Crimp's first desert night patrol near Sidi Omar

Reginald Lewis Crimp was a City of London clerk turned rifleman. His experience of war was made doubly uncomfortable by joining a formation – the 8th Army – that was made up mostly of regular soldiers who had been serving since before the war. His diary captures many of the more elusive yet omnipresent aspects of ordinary soldiers' experience, including dirt, confusion, flies and fear.

Mr R, primed with full instructions and a stiff whisky from the Company Commander, announces that our platoon has been chosen for the job. 'Gym shoes will be worn, for the sake of quietness. Tin hats will not be taken – they might fall off and make a noise. Every man to be sure he's got fifty rounds. Cpl Gardner's section in front, the other behind in diamond formation. Start off in ten minutes'. So that's that – one of those moments you always knew would come, and here it is . . .

By now the half-moon is well up in the eastern sky. Everything's quiet, only our footfalls can be heard. For half a mile we pad along over the desert, beginning to hope for a picnic after all. Then suddenly somewhere in front, there's a series of explosions, and we fling ourselves to the ground. Lying absolutely still, peer up from the corner of my eye: strings of luminous yellow slots speed overhead, like beads on a rod, hissing. My heart beats heavy hammerblows. This is deadly! The missiles soon cease, however, and after several minutes' silence we get up and move forward, very warily. But we've only covered forty yards when: bang, bang, bang! And again we have to lie flat while a further instalment of vivid gashes pursues unerring flight over us a few feet above the ground. Thank God for these small scrub bushes! – mere bumps of sand with a few twigs sprouting, but it's surprising how much happier you feel with one in front of your nose . . .

For a long time we stay motionless, pressing our noses into the sand. A night breeze blows cold. Then Mr R signals the next move, and a stealthy mass-wriggling across to the left begins, everyone painfully and determinedly propelling himself horizontally over the ground by fin-movements of hands and feet, with any amount of rustling and scraping, hoping thus to remove ourselves from the direct line of fire. When at last the advance is resumed on foot, the platoon appears scattered and depleted. Pedlar is still with Mr R in front. The sergeant has decided to cover the rear, 'to whip up stragglers.' Ernie and Sam, out on the flank, look like two of the Seven Dwarfs, crouching double and lifting their knees in exaggeratedly high strides as though they're playing musical chairs . . .

Meanwhile Mr R is getting very impatient. He keeps looking at his watch and peering strenuously ahead for signs of the enemy dispositions. He even crawls forward and disappears for ten minutes on a solo recce. On his return he says he thinks he knows where the enemy are and starts making plans for an attack. Pedlar, however, points out that the bulk of the platoon has melted away, and suggests it may be rash to try an assault with the few chaps that remain, against an enemy whose strength is still uncertain. All that are left of us, in fact, are Pedlar, Bob Harris, Ernie and Sam, five chaps from other sections, Arthur and myself. Mr R, fortunately, has enough sense to see the snags, but he's very disappointed at the way things have turned out. Obviously he doesn't at all relish having to report back to the Company Commander the failure of his first important mission. So we wait a bit longer, to give the stragglers a chance to catch up.

The situation is quiet again. We lie inert, alongside one another under cover of the sand-rampart. Arthur is next to me, and although the night strikes very cold, blissful snores soon reveal he's asleep. I even feel like that myself, the peace and quiet are so relaxing after our recent spell of tension. I rouse myself after a while, however, and glancing across his motionless back, can't discern any of the others. Arthur, unwillingly returning to consciousness, is as surprised as I am and can't account for their disappearance. No doubt his neighbour signalised an impending move-off by a prod in the ribs (to avoid the noise of speech) and Arthur, of course, was oblivious. So we creep forward together, very

cautiously, in the hope of regaining contact. But not a trace
do we find in the darkness . . .

Half an hour's steady marching brings us back to the foot
of the cud. It looks quite empty in the sour light, but we're
challenged by a section of 12 Platoon who're dug in at the
bottom of the path. From them we learn that Mr R and his
remnants arrived back two hours ago, having jagged in the
twitch because of inadequate numbers. Some of the other
chaps have been back since soon after midnight, and
nobody's missing.

*Sidi Omar was on the border between Egypt and Libya. This attack was
part of a general drive forward from British positions on the border in
an effort to relieve the siege of Tobruk. In front of the minefields the
British faced Italian and German units which had adopted fortified
positions stretching from Bardia to Sidi Omar and onwards to the
Halfaya Pass. Crimp's diary dwells not on strategic or operational
issues, but instead upon the 'worm's-eye view' of war. Here he offers a
perceptive evocation of the fear, confusion and backsliding involved in
the mounting of an 'aggressive' night patrol. Most platoon leaders soon
came to realize that every group of men consisted of a few natural
leaders, a large number of 'sheep' who followed along behind, and a few
shirkers who always drifted to the back. Crimp's superb diary also
captures the growing sense of desert-weariness that many men felt by
the end of 1941. The most obvious signs were extreme mental 'sluggish-
ness', pronounced physical apathy and a strong aversion to exertion in
every form. Mundane activities such as cleaning a rifle or making a cup
of tea required a tremendous effort to perform. SEE ALSO PP. 474–5.*

DECEMBER 1941

POLITICIANS AND GENERALS alike, preoccupied with events in the
Middle East and Europe, had almost deliberately ignored
Japan. However, by the end of 1941 Japan was under strong

pressure from the United States to withdraw from its gains in China and felt that it would be compelled to enter the wider war sooner or later. Roosevelt had also concluded that the United States would soon be forced into the war, but by putting economic pressure on Japan through sanctions he had 'passed the buck' to the leaders in Tokyo. Decision-making in the Japanese capital was increasingly erratic. Eventually a consensus view emerged that, with the passing of time, Japan would only get weaker; accordingly, it chose to attack Pearl Harbor on Sunday 8 December, simultaneously moving on the Philippines and British Malaya. The entry of Japan into the war ensured American military support for Britain and – in the long term – Allied victory. In the short term, however, it meant even greater losses for British troops and shipping and new threats to vital supplies of food and oil. Hitler declared war on the United States on 12 December; however, the Soviet Union and Japan chose not to fight each other and respected their non-aggression treaty signed the previous year.

In December 1941 many British people began to believe that they would eventually win the war. The real turning point had been June 1941, when Hitler's invasion of Russia had embroiled the Nazi state in an exhausting conflict that was quite different in character from anything it had yet experienced. At the time, many had seen this as only a temporary respite, believing that Soviet forces would collapse in a few weeks; however, as the year drew to a close it was clear that the German armies were suffering in the snows of the Russian winter.

By 2 December German forces reached the outer suburbs of Moscow; but winter blizzards had arrived and commanders, as well as front-line troops, were incapacitated by weather and illness. On 6 December Soviet forces began a series of successful counter-attacks. During the course of the month Hitler replaced most of the senior generals involved in this campaign, including Rundstedt, Bock and Brauchitsch. Hitler himself took over Brauchitsch's role of Commander-in-Chief and ordered the German army to stand fast.

In the desert, Rommel initially succeeded in holding off the Allied advance, but his forces were tired. Unlike the Allies, he was not receiving regular supplies of fresh equipment or new formations. By 11 December Rommel had given up on the siege of

Tobruk and the city was relieved. He then began a long retreat through the Libyan desert towards more easily defended positions. The retreat was well organized and his periodic counter-attacks inflicted a lot of damage on the British. Hitler decided to send much of his air power south to assist Rommel in the desert, and Germany's forces were now over-stretched.

In Britain, life was also getting tougher on the home front, with further cuts in rations. On 4 December the House of Commons passed a National Service Bill that allowed for the compulsory conscription of unmarried women between the ages of twenty and thirty.

Monday 1 – Friday 5 December 1941

Gertrude Bathurst counts her rations in Streatham

Mrs Gertrude Elizabeth Bathurst (née Ransom) was born on 4 July 1881 and had married James Thomas Bathurst in 1915. She lived at 99 Penwortham Road, Mitcham Lane, Streatham, London SW16 throughout the war. She kept a diary of key developments in the Blitz and also relating to rationing.

1 December
We have not been able to buy any tinned food for the past month, but today starts the rationing of them, we are allowed 16 points per month. Tinned salmon, sardines and American meats 16 points per lb. but beans in sauce 8 points per lb. We shall be glad to get sardines for a change for breakfast as eggs are terribly short, only one each in October and November, also fish is scarce. We had a 2 lb. pot of marmalade this week, the first for three months.

5 December
It is surprising how easily things adjust themselves, shopkeepers are not allowed to use paper for wrapping up so everyone has to take a bag or paper themselves. The butcher asked Jim this week to please bring a cloth. We have a sack

to collect all paper, tins cartons and bones in, and we take it to a particular house once a week for the man to fetch it. The Personal Service League have asked for volunteers to buy 10 lbs. of oiled wool, 2/- per lb. to make into stockings and helmets for Russian soldiers by Dec. 31. I wonder what a banana would taste like. Oranges arrive in different parts of the country sometimes and are sold to folk who hold childrens food cards. A letter has arrived from Mrs. Gardiner of Toronto to ask me for news of London and how we are faring. She wants to send some baby clothes, made by herself and friends to Ramsden Road Church for bombed out people's children.

In November 1941 rationing had been extended to cover milk, and in the following month the Ministry of Food not only extended it to cover new items but also introduced the points scheme for items hitherto not rationed, such as canned meat, fish and vegetables. This too was continually extended and eventually covered foodstuffs such as rice, canned fruit, condensed milk, breakfast cereals, biscuits and cornflakes. Everyone was given sixteen points a month, later raised to twenty, to spend as they wished at any shop that had the items they wanted. Although no-one liked having these additional items on ration, for some time past they had barely been available at all, so in practice the change was minimal. Although she would survive the war, nothing is known of Gertrude Bathurst after 1945.

Friday 5 December 1941

General John Kennedy, Director of Military Operations, discusses the Middle East with Churchill

Winston sent for me at 1 o'clock and I went to No. 10.

Maisky [the Soviet ambassador] was with him but went just after Davidson [Director of Military Intelligence] and I had arrived.

Winston was sitting alone at the long Cabinet table with his back to the fire, in air force blue rompers, with an extinct cigar with ½ inch of ash and looking pale pink and rather unwholesome. But he was in fairly good heart, having apparently got over his fit of depression.

He asked what I thought of the situation in Libya. I said it was a setback. On the information we had it looked like bad leadership on the whole. But this was a phase the British Army always had to go through. I thought that if the hard bitten and experienced Rommel had led the attack it would have succeeded. But our forces probably had another kick in them. This might be sufficient to tip the balance and then the whole thing would slide quickly. If not we should have to stage another offensive which might take some weeks. He signified assent except to the last statement and thought delay seemed to be unnecessary. He asked for information about the tank situation in Egypt, the contents of recent convoys and especially the amount of transport. I having said that the size of the force was limited by [vehicle] maintenance. He said he could not understand why, with a force of 750,000 men, more could not be deployed . . .

Speaking of Japan Winston said the Japs were fools if they came in. Hong Kong will be a gone coon I suppose he added mournfully. I said that on balance we stood to gain if America came into the war. He agreed . . .

Last Thursday 4th Dec. WSC [Winston Churchill] held a meeting of the Chiefs of Staff at 10 p.m. at which certain plans for raiding Italy etc. were turned down because of naval pre-occupation with Japan – At midnight Winston banged his papers on the table and walked out saying the COS [Chiefs of Staff] frustrated him in all his offensive projects. Brooke gave us a most amusing account of it next morning.

In early December 1941 Churchill was obsessed with British reverses in the Middle East. He could not understand why success was not forthcoming with so many British and Commonwealth troops deployed there, and was increasingly minded to sack generals. Partly for this reason, he was determined to ignore the growing threat from Japan, while insisting on diverting all resources to the desert war for a new offensive. The British Chiefs of Staff resisted, being increasingly anxious about the situation in the Far East. SEE ALSO PP. 253–4.

Sunday 7 – Thursday 11 December 1941

Breckinridge Long in the State Department hears of the attack on Pearl Harbor

Breckinridge Long was born in 1881 in St Louis and had attended Princeton University and then Washington University Law School. Involved with the Democratic party for many years, he was eventually made an assistant secretary of state in 1917. Having failed to enter the Senate, he was appointed ambassador to Italy by Roosevelt in 1933. He left government service in 1936, but returned to the State Department in 1940. One area he supervised was immigrant visas, in which capacity he was notoriously unsympathetic to those fleeing Nazi persecution, and so earned the enmity of Eleanor Roosevelt.

7 December

The Japanese problem is practically at a crisis. They have answered in an equivocal way the question put by the President. They have not replied to the basic questions raised by Hull in the paper he handed to them. In the meantime they are reinforcing their troops in southern Indo-China and forwarding trucks, artillery, supplies of all kinds – bicycles, sawed-off shotguns, etc. Their transports in flocks of twenty and thirty land at Saigon and some move west around the southern corner toward Bangkok. They plead that their moves are simply defensive against China – but they are moving away from China toward Siam. They claim Vichy authorizes their activity – but Vichy has weakly tried in spite of German pressure to relieve itself of the consequences of its earlier consent to collaboration in Indo-China.

Here Nomura and Kurusu kill time. Many of the Japanese officials here – including some of the Embassy staff – are on the way out, some to South America, some to Japan . . .

The President sent a communication to the Emperor of Japan – to keep the record straight and ask his help in preserving peace. But the chances of peace are slim . . .

Momentous things happen these days – and, because there are so many of them and our stake so great – we handle them without excitement, in ordinary course, and with dispatch, though any one of them a few years ago would have thrown the Foreign offices of the world into excitement and confusion.

8 December

Sick at heart. I am so damned mad at the Navy for being asleep at the switch at Honolulu. It is the worst day in American history. They spent their lives in preparation for a supreme moment – and then were asleep when it came. At the Defense Communications Board this morning I learned of the extent of our losses – and it is staggering.

All day we have been in hectic steps of transition from a peace basis to a war basis. There are so many things to arrange for.

11 December

A very busy day. Germany and Italy declared war on us and we on them. With the Secretary and Berle and Hackworth drafted resolutions of war – one for Germany – one for Italy – and the President's address to the Congress – and got it to the White House late . . .

And a hundred other things I can't remember and am too tired to record. It has been a hectic day.

Breckinridge Long's diary captures the exasperation of many officials in Washington who were surprised by the attack on Pearl Harbor, despite the warnings they had received. As his diary makes clear, everyone knew that war with Japan was just weeks, perhaps even days away; and yet American bases, not only in Hawaii but also in the Philippines, would suffer devastating surprise attacks. Historians continue to argue as to why this was.

Long would leave the State Department in 1944 and died in 1958.

Tuesday 9 December 1941

Vere Hodgson in Notting Hill Gate hears of the attack on
Pearl Harbor

*Vere Hodgson read history at Birmingham University in the 1920s and
then taught at schools in Tuscany and Folkestone. Thereafter she worked
for a charity in Notting Hill Gate caring for victims of bombing. She kept
a meticulous diary recording the reactions of Londoners to the Blitz and
the news of each phase of the war.*

We are now at war with Japan – and the Whole World is in
it. Air-raid warnings in San Francisco, and though I do not
wish anyone to be bombed, a little wholesome shaking-up is
good for people who contemplate the sufferings of others
with equanimity. Like we did the Czechs – and only woke
up when we came within the orbit of the enemy ourselves.

Listened to the Midnight News on Sunday, after they told
us at 9 p.m. that American bases in the Pacific had been
bombed. Studied the map of the area, found Hawaii, and it
looked so far from Japan – but we had forgotten Aircraft
Carriers.

Poor dear people in those islands of bliss, sunshine and
fruit drinks. They must have had an unpleasant Sunday
afternoon. Lots dead, they say. Honolulu had a few bombs.
The Americans seem to have leaped to their feet like one
man. I should think Colonel Lindberg has retired to a room
with dark blinds – not to be heard of for many a long day.

Listened to Roosevelt at 6.30 p.m. and heard all the applause.
They sounded happy as sand-boys. Then Churchill at 9 p.m.
Apparently he looked very serious in the House with a
heavy scowl. He just told us we must work, and work and
work. Well, if I must go, I must. The Calling-Up Date gets
nearer to me; but it will not be until after Christmas. I shall
let things take their course . . . I wish I had a private income
– then it would hold no qualms for me . . .

Vere Hodgson's diary reveals a city whose ears were glued to the radio at times of crisis. Although visual image was not yet important, oratory was, for speeches were increasingly broadcast live and sound quality was improving markedly. Her diary also makes interesting comparisons between the policies of two appeasers, Roosevelt and Chamberlain. Both had viewed the Axis as a problem for others but had found that it had eventually come to pay them a personal visit. In fairness to Roosevelt, the US President had probably realized that American entry into the war was inescapable in the summer of 1941.

Vere Hodgson's last sentence is a small but telling reference to the mobilization of women. Being drafted into war work could be a problem for those already in employment if it resulted in a drop in pay. Some found they could no longer pay the rent on their existing accommodation with their changed income. SEE ALSO PP. 744–6.

Wednesday 10 December 1941

Graham Greene sets sail with a convoy en route to Freetown in west Africa

During the war, Graham Greene was employed by MI6 doing what he called rather coyly 'government work of an ill-defined nature'. He was a close friend of Kim Philby, who belonged to the same organization. Greene was also a volunteer fireman in the London Blitz until he was sent to become a wartime intelligence officer in west Africa in 1941.

We leave after breakfast. Passengers are to man three four-hour watches during the day: two men on machine-guns above the boat deck for aircraft, and two below the bridge for submarines. The Glasgow man is head of my watch. One climbs a short vertical steel ladder into a kind of conning tower containing each a gun with steel shield. A sailor shows us how to tilt the gun and fire: he is one of the few who were in this ship last trip. Two ships were torpedoed the first night out from the Mersey, but the passengers' watches had only continued two days. The submarine watchers had watched from the bridge, but they had got so drunk the captain had refused to allow them there again. Little fear of that this time – we are a very sober, sedate company. The siren keeps on blowing – rather disturbing as one must count the blasts – seven short and a long for boat stations.

A cold grey day: the sea getting up: soldiers in Balaclavas by the Bofors: a black steward making water in the bilge.

Two hours watch, and a half an hour as well relieving the previous watch for lunch. Then an hour on submarine watch – bitter cold especially to port. Even a bird can look like a periscope. At dinner the Chief told us that in weather like this it was easy for a submarine to follow a ship unobserved during the day above water and submerge at night for the attack. Two ships in which he had served had been torpedoed after he had left them. One hopes his luck will hold. Never more than five days' leave between voyages.

An hour with the machine-gun – a little less cold up there. The steel shields like the wings of black angels. Past the Isle of Man, and a plane in the sky, presumably one of ours. News on the wireless of the sinking by the Japs of the *Prince of Wales* and the *Repulse*.

It's odd how on submarine duty one thinks only of that danger and on machine-gun duty only of the air. Perched up above the deck one hears the wind in the wires like choral singing from inside a church.

Felt sea sick at tea and lay down till dinner. In the bitter cold of the bows recited Hail Marys to distract myself.

During his voyage from Liverpool to Freetown Graham Greene kept a journal, although he had no book in mind at the time. Axis submarine activity was a threat all the way to his destination, and numerous Allied ships were being sunk in the South Atlantic. When not taking turns on watch he read a detective novel by Michael Innes which had eventually 'set his mind' towards the possibility of writing on security issues, and he began to think about a short story – which he later called 'The Ministry of Fear'. He did not continue his diary once he arrived in Africa and would come to regret this five years later when he began his novel The Heart of the Matter *in which he drew on his wartime African experiences. After the war Greene would be an unsuccessful publisher – he found this role boring – and then a fabulously successful novelist and writer of screenplays. Many of Greene's novels reflect his wartime experiences in Africa and the world of espionage.*

Thomas Meredith helps to swipe the Spanish ambassador's briefcase in Cardiff

In 1938 Thomas Meredith was twenty-two years old and had been finding occasional work on the Isle of Wight as a relief bus conductor during the summer season. The following year he joined the RAF to escape unemployment in south Wales. He was stationed at No. 14 [Barrage] Balloon Centre in the Ely district of Cardiff. In April 1941 he was approached by a local MI5 officer called Frank River, who was based in Cardiff and who was undertaking work against fifth columnists in the dock area. Thomas was asked if he wanted to join River's 'Group'. He continued to serve in the RAF by day, but would turn out by night for MI5 operations and receive additional pay.

Christmas dinner dance at the Park Hotel. Frank found out that the Spanish Ambassador was staying there, and was carrying information that could be useful. The Spanish being pro-Nazi this was quite possible, so Frank decided we should try and get hold of his briefcase. We bought four tickets and during one of the dances, Frank slipped upstairs to the Ambassador's room. Charlie went with him to watch out in the corridor. Irene was dancing with the Ambassador's bodyguard, and I was in the foyer, a taxi waiting for me outside. Charlie came down with the briefcase, gave it to me, and I was away to Frank's house in Ely to put the briefcase in his safe. I arrived back at the hotel within 35 minutes. There was a bit of fuss going on, and the briefcase had obviously been missed, but no one suspected us, and we enjoyed the rest of the evening.

Thomas Meredith enjoyed his part-time work for MI5, but it was not without danger. The previous year one of the 'Group' had been acting as a courier with a briefcase chained to his hand. He was found dead by the side of a railway line, missing both the briefcase and his hand. Wartime operations against enemy sympathizers in Britain remain unknown territory; Meredith's diary, which chronicled this hidden war, remains unpublished. His work for MI5 came to an end in February 1942 when he was posted to Egypt.

1942

'TIMING THE PUBLICATION of a War Diary is a very tricky business. If you wait too long it becomes stale. If you bring it out too soon it is certain to be heavily censored. I prefer the deep blue sea of blue pencilling [by the censors] to the devil of staleness.'

Charles Graves, preface to OFF THE RECORD, *his war diaries for 1940–1, published in 1942*

JANUARY 1942

IN THE MEDITERRANEAN a desperate air duel between the islands of Malta and Sicily continued. German aircraft made strong attacks on the Malta garrison, and the Italian navy put to sea in strength to try to protect convoys resupplying Rommel in north Africa. In the desert the British took the Halfaya Pass on the border between Libya and Egypt, and captured 5,500 Axis troops; but on 21 January Rommel began a series of effective counter-attacks. Some experienced Australian troops were withdrawn from the desert theatre so that they could be sent east to oppose the Japanese, who were advancing into south-east Asia. As a result the Germans found a number of soft spots in the British defence and pressed forward. On 29 January German forces re-took the key town of Benghazi in Libya and began to push quickly along the coast.

With the help of a bitter Russian winter, the Red Army threw the Germans back in the area immediately in front of Moscow; meanwhile, partisan activities in the German rear were taking their toll on long and troubled supply lines. The Russian commander, General Zhukov, was suffering interference from Stalin, who insisted on a counter-attack across a broad front, spreading Russian resources thinly. This was the same sort of political interference that the German generals had to tolerate from Hitler. Extraordinarily low temperatures continued on the Eastern Front and there were appeals across Germany for people to donate extra winter clothing, skis and snow-shoes for the troops at the front. The civilian population in Germany began to realize that the Eastern Front would not offer an opportunity for another of Hitler's quick victories.

On 20 January 1942 the Nazi leadership gathered at a conference at Wannsee near Berlin. Here Reinhard Heydrich, in euphemistic language, presented plans for the 'Final Solution', which involved the transportation of all of Europe's Jews to extermination camps. Adolf Eichmann was put in charge of the element of the SS responsible for implementing this plan.

Churchill and Eden returned from their own conference with the Americans. Codenamed Arcadia, this addressed major questions about the future direction of the war. Within weeks of the American declaration of war on Germany the first permanent bases for US troops had been constructed in Britain.

Thursday 1 January 1942

Staff Sergeant Ray Ryan, an Australian soldier captured with his brother in Crete, experiences a hungry New Year in Stalag VIIIB

The New Year was heralded by several days' continuous snow and I didn't like the look of it at all each morning, as I looked out the window at it falling silently and ceaselessly hour after hour. The typhus scare was now over and the Germans felt that they could once more enter the barracks without fear of infection. As a result parades were resumed and we had to turn out each morning at 7am in the cold and dark.

The racketeers were also able to resume operations. The rackets were the predominant feature of life at VIIIB, and were so notorious that when we went to a new camp later, an appeal was made to keep out the 'Lamsdorf rackets'. Hundreds of POWs were getting extra spuds and bread which adversely affected the issue to the rest. Some days we only got one sixth of a loaf, owing to the shortages caused by thefts. On bread and soup days, fifty loaves were supposed to go in to the soup, but only twenty five went in. The resulting watery soup can be imagined. Everyone engaged on any sort of a barrack duty at all got double rations but as the German Quartermaster only rationed one ration a man, we footed the bill again. There were also coal rackets.

There was no hot water available even in the depths of winter and it was a terrific ordeal to bathe under a cold tap on a stone floor once a fortnight with the snow and ice outside. I was only able to wash a single article a day, immediately after soup, when I felt slightly warmer. After ten minutes in the water, my hand would turn blue and the pain so intense that I had to stop and swing before continuing. How eagerly we looked forward to the summer, which seemed so long in coming that we wondered if we would ever see a fine day again.

Anticipations for the year were fervent and hopeful. Most people thought or hoped that it would be a three year war and would finish at the end of 1942. The burning question was 'When will the invasion and Second Front start?'. We reckoned six months from then would see us released. There certainly was not much to justify any optimism during the first half year. Every morning we heard Haw-Haw, via the loud speakers telling us of fresh set-backs. The Russians were falling back, the Japs were pushing on, and every week the 'Camp' published more sinkings by subs and fresh air raids. The Germans used to laugh and point at the Aussies, saying 'Japan haben Australian'.

We soon had something else to think about. The grim days of living on issue rations alone had gone with the advent of Red Cross parcels. Or so we thought. Life in the stalag which had been bearable suddenly changed for the worse, when the supply of Red Cross parcels stopped. Once more we went back to living on one issue soup, one fifth of a loaf and three or four spuds. The next few months were the worst spent in Germany.

The long and cold days passed very slowly. There were very few books or cigarettes and it was impossible to think of anything else but the next food issues and at night it was very cold and I used to go to bed nearly fully dressed. Even then I used to dream I was walking into Carter's and other shops at home and ordering loads of bread and meat. On Saturdays, two days' bread was issued at once. This was invariably eaten the same day and left none for Sunday. As a result, I came to hate Sunday and called it in my own mind 'Black Sunday'.

Staff Sergeant Ray Ryan and his brother Laurie had been captured at Sphakia Bay in Crete in June 1941 and transported via Greece and Serbia to Stalag VIIIB at Lamsdorf in Germany. Supplies of food and cigarettes were thin and the Red Cross parcels, sometimes arriving weekly, provided much-needed supplements to the diet. Racketeering was rife and to acquire food on the black market one needed money. During the period following their capture some soldiers sold everything they had – not just valuables, but also shirts, pens, tunics and boots. One soldier even sold his trousers and walked about in his issue pyjamas.

A few weeks after arriving at Stalag VIIIB both Ray and Laurie would secretly 'swap identities' with two RAF prisoners in an adjacent camp, and so secured a move to Stalag Luft III at Sagan. Ray found the life of the flyers much more chivalrous. Their own NCOs were polite rather than domineering, and the German camp commandant saluted the parade each morning and offered them a cheery 'Guten Morgen'; best of all, there were few rackets at Sagan. In the four years in which they were prisoners, Ray continued his diary, while Laurie wrote verse. They would be liberated on 7 May 1945 and flown to Brussels and then England, before beginning a long voyage home to arrive in Sydney harbour in July 1945. SEE ALSO PP. 224–6.

Sunday 4 January 1942

Victor Klemperer, slave labourer, tries to piece together the state of play on the Eastern Front

Perhaps the most highly regarded account of life inside the Third Reich is the diary of Victor Klemperer. In 1933, when Hitler had come to power, Klemperer had been a distinguished professor at the University of Dresden; in the First World War he had served in the front line as a German soldier. He survived the initial pogroms because of his marriage to a German Aryan, but was forced into slave labour in a factory in appalling conditions. His will to survive came in part from a deep desire to make a chronicle of the extraordinary times through which he had lived.

382 WITNESS TO WAR

Situation obscure. The Neumanns did not know either, where the Eastern Front stands. – The lies outdo and contradict one another. First the word was: Into winter quarters, we are shortening our line, let the Russians claim that as a success, we are masters of the situation ('we have the initiative'). Then Ribbentrop explained: The Russians are attacking our rear. Now Hitler has issued two New Year messages. One to the nation: Should it become necessary, we too shall make the greatest sacrifices. One to the soldiers ('*My* soldiers') which talks frankly about the Russian offensive, which 'must and will' fail.

The Neumanns in Kötzschenbroda: The Russians attack on horsedrawn sledges and with cavalry, tanks frozen up. Retreating Germans are losing immense quantities of equipment. – Hitler has not only dismissed Brauchitsch, but something like thirty generals altogether or 'Brauchitsch and something like thirty others have left of their own volition' or 'have been shot'. Reason: Brauchitsch had already considered winter quarters necessary in the autumn but when Smolensk was reached, Hitler ordered the advance to continue. – German tank divisions are massed on the Spanish frontier. Against Gibraltar? To protect the Portuguese coast? Will Spain remain neutral? Which side will it join? Where does the German Eastern Front stand? Nothing but questions without answers . . .

Klemperer's diary captures the unique horror of life for Jews during the Third Reich. It also captures elements of the common predicament of ordinary people trapped by war everywhere, including a lack of access to reliable information that was not tainted by propaganda. Klemperer particularly wanted to know about the progress of the fighting on the Eastern Front because it was already recognized that events in Russia were likely to determine the course of the war. Like ordinary citizens everywhere, he depended on news from 'contacts' who had other 'contacts' on the inside as much as on newspapers and radio. The fact that General Brauchitsch and other military leaders had been dismissed by Hitler suggested to him that all might not be well on the Eastern Front – and he was right. SEE ALSO PP. 643 AND 649–51.

Tuesday 6 January 1942

Nan le Ruez enjoys a leaflet raid on Jersey

Nan le Ruez was the daughter of a dairy farmer and in her mid-twenties during the war. She kept a rather personal diary of everyday life during the full five years of occupation.

RAF dropped leaflets early this morning. Laurence found one and Joyce found one in our garden near the bee-hive! They were all written in French. They were not addressed specially to Channel Islanders. German officers were searching the countryside for them but our eyes are sharper than theirs! It is nice to think that our British friends were close to us today. We are not forgotten after all!

Propaganda leaflet drops were a prominent feature of the Second World War. During 1939 most of the RAF's activities over Germany had involved leaflet drops; as the war progressed these became more sophisticated, sometimes dropping forged currency in order to undermine the economy of the country in question, or safe-surrender passes intended for use by enemy troops. By 1944 even some V-1 pilotless aircraft would be carrying German leaflets that were dropped before impact.

Tuesday 6 – Tuesday 13 January 1942

Grete Paquin, a dissident German tending her smallholding, is forced to give up her skis for use on the hard-pressed Russian Front

6 January
Some more students have come back from Russia. They get used to civilian life very slowly, to a bed, to regular meals, to sleep and work. They tell me about conditions out there, the

wounded have to be packed on sledges and brought back, sometimes for over sixty miles. They have no warm things and there are more casualties by frost than by the enemy. I looked through my own things and found an old pullover, mended it, and sent it away.

13 January

We are ordered to give away our skis. I hate Goebbels for this trick, and I waited until the last day even then trying to keep them. Lots of people do. But then I thought better of it. It really will help those poor boys who are out in Russia and I will remember them later on when I see – and certainly it will happen – that the Party members have kept their skis or get new ones.

I did love my skis. I got them when I was sixteen and only pleasant memories are connected with them. Woods deep in snow. I loved the hissing noise they made, I loved to walk for hours among the trees without any path, alone or with friends in snow, ice, and the fresh coolness of a winter day.

I took them to the old schoolhouse [where the skis were being collected] and left them there in the dust and smell, good old things!

The early arrival of unseasonably cold weather in the winter of 1941–2 was not entirely disadvantageous to the German advance. It ended the period of heavy autumnal rains which had transformed the roads of central and northern Russia into rivers of mud. From the beginning of November these roads had been frozen and so trucks and tanks were able to move again. Even heavy snow was not always a disaster. It protected some surrounded German units from being completely eliminated, since neither side could conduct operations in such conditions. However, at the end of December General Heinz Guderian, who was in charge of the 2nd Panzer Army, had berated Hitler about the lack of winter clothing in forward areas. He had already lost twice as many men to frostbite as he had lost to enemy fire. The Nazi party then began an emergency Christmas campaign among German civilians to collect winter clothes and skis, but this amateurish effort came much too late. German troops had to strip extra clothing from dead corpses in an effort to keep themselves alive, and by the end of the winter a quarter of a million Germans would have fallen victim to frostbite of varying degrees. SEE ALSO PP. 245, 301–2 AND 515–16.

Thursday 8 January 1942

Second Lieutenant John Guest goes .303 target shooting with his artillery troop in Ayr

John Guest was born in 1911 in Warrington, Cheshire, and had been educated at Pembroke College, Cambridge. His first job was as a proof-reader and he later became a junior editor for Collins. During the war he would serve in England, Africa and then Italy; by 1942 he was a junior artillery officer.

To-day I had a minor triumph. Our troop was billed to go down to the range to fire .303 at miniature targets. In preparation for this I gave an hour's talk on the sighting and firing of the rifle, and I'm afraid I allowed a slight attitude of over-confidence in the subject to creep into the talk – passing reference to Bisley days, competing in the Gale & Polden and all that, you know. At any rate, directly or indirectly I let them know that I considered myself to be a bit of a shot – very unwise. This afternoon on the range I spent a lot of time correcting positions, advising on breathing, urging them to rest if they got wobbly, and so on. Each man had five rounds only to fire, and then, at the end, came the shock: 'There are five rounds over, Sir: we drew them for *you*.' They all but raised their hands and laughed behind them. I was certainly caught and I only hope that my 'Ah, good!' didn't sound too hollow. A silent semi-circle (David Langdon faces) formed behind me, and I knelt on the butts as for execution. If I didn't shoot well I was going to look damned silly – and they knew it. I tried the trigger pressure, came up to the aim, got wobbly, eyes bleary, and came down for a rest (I had been urging them to do this, and they doubtless thought I was rubbing it home). I came up again and fired. The spotter reported a bull. My palpitations increased. Every shot I got so dithery I had to come down and aim again. The second shot, however, cut the first, enlarging the hole. The third shot cut the second and the first, enlarging the hole again. The fourth shot cut all three, blowing a half-inch hole out of the centre of the bull. The silence behind me changed its mood and it was now desperately important that I should get a good last round. After a lot of trying to steady my hands, clear my eyes (all cloudy and full of barrage balloon liver spots), and quieten my heart, the worst thing happened: I had already taken first pressure when suddenly the rifle went off before I was ready. I hadn't the faintest idea where the round had gone. And where do you think it went? A half inch from the hole in the bull, making a one-inch group in all!

It was only then that I realised what a fool I was: the obvious thing to have done would have been to fire deliberately wide of the target so that they would have assumed that the last round went clean through the hole! But at any rate I was saved. I know it reads like a school story, but I cannot tell you how exciting it was. One thing is certain: I must never *never* shoot again with the troop, who now regard me as an absolutely dead-eyed Dick!

I was so pleased with the target that I cut the bull out and shall send it home. Both my mother and father fancy themselves with a .22. They rush about the garden shooting at roses and twigs and dandelions, and bickering at whose turn it is to have the rifle. My mother, I think, always visualises the probability of having to defend the house from the spare-room window against paratroops!

Military training in which the officer was required to participate alongside his men was always the young subaltern's nightmare, whether it was shooting, map-reading or some other martial activity. At least the surroundings in which Guest was training were pleasant, for in December 1941 the artillery regiment had been moved to new quarters at Ayr racecourse. The gun battery HQ was in the Tote, the officers' mess in the clubhouse and the men in the horses' boxes. He added that 'it was not as bad as it sounds', for each loose-box provided a comfortable room for two soldiers with its own little stove. SEE ALSO PP. 397–9.

FEBRUARY 1942

A T THE BEGINNING OF February the Germans began to use a new cipher system called Triton for communicating with their U-boats. This involved using a new and more complex Enigma cipher machine with four wheels rather than three. Four wheels offered a greater number of possible cipher combinations, making the already fiendishly difficult task of reading the Enigma code yet more complex. This was a setback for Allied codebreakers, and it would take them until the end of 1942 to penetrate this new system.

However, the anti-submarine war was being fought on many fronts, and the arrival of escort carriers and of more aircraft with greater range was no less important, making the life of the U-boat crews progressively more perilous. An aerial reconnaissance 'gap' in the mid-Atlantic was gradually being closed. Nevertheless, in February 1942 Axis submarines sank eighty-five ships. During the spring of 1942 the Germans would also launch their first submarine support ships, which allowed refuelling at sea and effectively doubled their range. U-boats then became more adventurous and spent more time in the western Atlantic, where they sank no fewer than twenty oil-tankers in this area during February and March 1942.

In the Mediterranean, the loss of some airfields in Libya as a result of Rommel's rapid advance along the coast was making the air war more difficult for the Allies. This in turn was both making it harder to interrupt Rommel's supply lines across the Mediterranean from Italy and resulting in greater pressure on the fortress island of Malta.

In the Far East, British and Commonwealth forces, mostly from India and Australia, faced disaster. On 15 February 1942 General Percival, the British commander in Malaya, decided to seek surrender terms from his opposite number, General Yamashita. Over a period of two months, an Allied force of 138,000 had been defeated by a Japanese force half that size. Japanese forces had triumphed because they were battle-hardened troops facing new and inexperienced units. Japan also had air superiority. This was the largest British military defeat in history and reverberated in every theatre of war. The large numbers of troops captured, especially Australians, and the immediate threat to Australia from Japanese forces pushing into Indonesia, called Churchill's war leadership directly into question and his political future looked uncertain. Many believed he would soon be replaced and some were even searching for a likely successor.

Friday 6 – Saturday 7 February 1942

John D. Phillip, an American merchant seaman, finds his oil-tanker attacked by U-boats in mid-Atlantic

6 February

13th day at sea – U-boat attack

This night at 2200 we were attacked by submarines, and a minute later the general alarm went off as the first depth charge was released.

As we gathered on the 4'50 gun platform where our gun was ready for firing, we noticed the destroyers and corvettes all moving to the port side at the head of the convoy. Apparently they had picked up the sub, and were now making the move to pounce upon it. The stern remained open.

Three minutes later the troop transport was hit, we heard the explosion and saw two red flares released into the sky.

Training our gun in that direction, we remained silent as we watched.

Within a minute the tanker, second ship back of us, was hit. By the time the destroyers had assembled in their former position, they released depth charge after depth charge. Also releasing white flares which lit the water up and by this means it was possible to tell whether the subs had been hit, by the wreckage and floating oil that might be on the surface.

Another explosion and the tanker on the starboard stern received hers. The Lieutenant had remained on the stern gun to personally take charge in the event the sub might appear. Among the faces of the crew were some puzzling looks as we all watched with eagerness to fight if we had to.

Five minutes later all was quiet, until another ship which happened to be a liberty was hit as the flares pierced the sky once more. We began to wonder if any of the survivors had been picked up. The way the escort ships were releasing depth charges, not a soul could stand the concussion in the water, in the event they were able to escape from the sinking afloat.

Up to 2300 all but four ships remained afloat. Finally the Lieutenant, sensing the sub's approach, dismissed half the crew for coffee, which came in handy at this time.

Drinking our coffee in the mess hall, we sensed the danger closing in on us, and being allowed five minutes to ourselves, we took advantage of it, then the alarm sounded once more. Rushing up to our guns we noticed the destroyer on the starboard side maneuvering with considerable force in the water as the depth charges went off. The ships had spread out and it seemed as if every ship was on its own.

The first ship back of us was hit on the starboard side; we noticed the flares piercing the sky once more. Knowing that she was close, the Lieutenant posted each man around the gun turret, with the indication that if a torpedo was launched, we would be able to spot the wake and with quick action stop the deadly missile before it proved destructive to our ship.

Once the destroyers released white flares, as they scanned the surface once more for sub wreckage. We believed at this time the sub could send up her periscope, and with no trouble take bearing on a ship, as it would be light enough for them to see.

Another explosion and a tanker received a tin fish [torpedo] in her belly. About 400 yds away, we noticed a life boat. Apparently the survivors had managed to escape, but it would be some time before a destroyer could go to their assistance.

A half hour later the destroyer on the bow patrol cut through the convoy for survivors – at the same time two more flares pierced the sky as the explosion sounded once more.

It was 0100 by this time and somehow the crew began to get restless as we remained at our stations. With depth charges going off every now and then, we wondered how long the attack would last.

Off the starboard stern we noticed two ships getting close and as they turned into the same direction, seconds later they rammed. The concussion was terrific as they pulled away and once more came back at each other. Some time later we learned that one ship was stricken so badly, that one destroyer had to sink her with continuous shell firing . . .

7 February
14th day at sea – U-boats resuming the attack.

During the night the attack by U-boats commenced. Off the starboard stern a ship was hit, and the flares pierced the sky once more, as the escorts went about pounding depth charges into the bulky subs wherever they might be.

Having trained our 4'50 in that direction once more we eagerly watched as the destroyers maneuvered in the water trying to find some possible way of trapping the under sea raiders.

By this time the second ship off port side received a tin fish in her belly as blue flame flushed the sky. That meant a tanker had been hit – and no sooner had that happened than the liberty off our starboard side got hers. Anyway she sure sounded loud, and that meant she wasn't very far from us.

Although this night wasn't as lit up as the night before, the U-boats worked with rapid marksmanship, and after a half hour, the action died down – apparently the U-boats were put to rout.

Duty on board oil-tankers was considered particularly unattractive by merchant seamen. Plying the Atlantic, they had little chance on board such a vessel if hit by a torpedo because the ships burned rapidly with distinctive blue flames. Any who survived impact and jumped overboard were unlikely to last more than a few minutes in the freezing waters of the Atlantic. Larger quantities of oil were being moved across the Atlantic in 1942 in support of expanding air operations and also in preparation for Operation Torch, the Allied landing in north Africa in November 1942. In late 1942 refuelling at sea would be introduced for the convoy escorts, which meant even more oil-tankers crossing the Atlantic. Quite a few Allied merchant seamen were captured by the Germans, mostly by surface raiders, but some by submarines. As civilians these sailors were supposed to be repatriated, but instead they were taken to Germany and initially imprisoned in the Sandbostel Concentration Camp; then they were forced to build their own camp, which they would christen Milag Nord.

The US Maritime Commission constructed ships for the British merchant fleet, using a British design for a basic 11-knot, 10,800-ton dry cargo ship that was fitted with oil-fuelled steam engines. The design allowed for mass-produced welded construction. The result was the famous 'liberty ship'. Although fitting turbine engines would have improved their speed, turbines were in short supply and so used only for fighting ships. The Commission had ordered 260 'liberties' in early 1941 and the first had come into service on 11 September 1941.

Sunday 15 – Wednesday 18 February 1942

James Chuter Ede MP on the problem of replacing Churchill

James Chuter Ede was born in Epsom in 1882 and had been a schoolmaster until 1914, when he became a teaching union representative. This position served as a springboard into politics, and he became Labour MP for South Shields in 1923. His diary is a remarkable record of wartime politics and social change from the perspective of a junior minister. As Parliamentary Secretary of the Board of Education he observed much of the revolutionary thinking on education that would lead to R. A. Butler's 1944 Education Act.

15 February
After a very early lunch I caught the 1.17 train and went from Waterloo to Euston, where Miss Horsbrugh had already reserved two seats . . . She told me that Hore-Belisha, Granville and Morris-Jones, who left the National Liberal

Party last week, were lining up behind Cripps in a determination to make him Prime Minister. Granville had said Cripps brought Russia into the war and was very angry when she said that Hitler brought Russia in. We listened to the Prime Minister's sombre broadcast at 9 pm in which he announced the fall of Singapore. He went on to make an advance attack on those who would try to upset the Government because of this. We discussed the situation at some length. I said it did not seem possible that the 1922 Committee would support Cripps. We ran through the whole list of critics of the Government and they did not make an alternative team or one that would coalesce easily . . .

18 February

This third volume [of the handwritten diary] comes to an end when our arms have encountered severe and humiliating reverses. Our counsels are divided. Parliament is given over to intrigue. Yesterday I saw Bevan, Horabin and Cunningham-Reid in close consultation. The PM's position is very difficult but he is still too strong for direct attack. Faith is sorely tried but if the rank and file can be jolted out of complacency our trials, costly as they are in life and suffering, may be worthwhile. There is no doubt that we go forward into a very dark and devastating storm.

In February 1942 Chuter Ede was summoned to see Churchill, who offered him promotion to the Ministry of War Transport. Passionately interested in education and a rebellious sort, he refused to move. Churchill was taken aback. While talking, Churchill outlined his plans to open up the great public schools – Haileybury, Eton, Harrow – to the urban working class after the war.

As dissatisfaction with Churchill grew, the far left favoured Stafford Cripps, Britain's ambassador to Moscow, while in the Empire and Commonwealth there were moves to find a leader for the Commonwealth war effort who might not be drawn from Britain at all. Churchill would survive this plotting because there was no consensus candidate who could bring together the many different groups who disliked him. SEE ALSO PP. 510–11.

Thursday 19 February 1942

Adam Czerniakow notes cases of cannibalism in the Warsaw Ghetto

Adam Czerniakow was born in Warsaw in 1880. He taught engineering in the Jewish community's vocational school in Warsaw and had been elected to the Polish Senate in 1931. Shortly after the city's surrender to the Germans in September 1939, Czerniakow was made head of the 24-member Jewish Council responsible for implementing German orders in the Jewish community. This was a cruelly invidious position: Council members tried to mitigate the impact of German orders but felt the ignominy of being indirect instruments of German rule – and for Czerniakow the burden was a heavy one.

On February 19th, on order of the *Kommissar*, 59 persons (prisoners) were taken from the Jewish detention facility and transported to the Western Station under an escort of the German police; one might guess they were directed to Treblinka. Each prisoner was given a pound of bread for the trip. The *Kommissar* needed some construction workers.

At this very moment (11:33) Colonel Szerynski, the chief of the Order Service, has reported a case of cannibalism in the Jewish Quarter. Mother-child. Here is the report:

D Szwizgold, *patrol leader 1845. The report refers to a case of cannibalism.* At the request of the supervisor of IV sector of the ZOS [Jewish Social Welfare], Nirenberg, I proceeded to No 18 Krochmalna street, apt 20, where I found, lying on a bunk, the 30-year-old Urman, Rywka, who stated in the presence of the witnesses, Mrs Zajdman, Niuta, the secretary of the House Committee, and Murawa, Jankiel, that she was guilty of cannibalism, involving her own 12-year-old son, Berk Urman, who had died the previous day, by cutting out a piece of his buttock.

Signed D Szwizgold, patrol leader 1845
Patrolman M Grossman 393

J Murawa, Chairman
February 19, 1942

In the morning the *Kommissar* came to the Community with a senior SS officer and some Swiss national (a doctor?) who was asking questions about the ghetto and the typhus. Before he arrived, Auerswald forbade me to make any mention of the mortality rates. In January the mortality was 5,123 persons.

Even in February 1942 conditions in the Warsaw Ghetto were appalling. Many were starving to death, while others were deported to Treblinka, which was already recognized as a death camp. Worse was to come: in July 1942 the authorities would begin preparing for mass deportations from the Warsaw Ghetto to Treblinka at a rate of 6,000 a day, and the Jewish Council was ordered to provide lists of deportees and their addresses. All Jews in Warsaw would be moved east except for those working in German factories, Jewish hospital staff, members of the Jewish Council, members of the Jewish police force and their families. Czerniakow would seek additional exemptions for sanitation workers, husbands of women working in factories and some students, but despite all his pleading he was unable to obtain an exemption for orphans. Having failed to secure this he returned to his office and took some cyanide that he had been keeping for such an eventuality. In a suicide note he explained that he could no longer bear the burden and felt that this course was the honourable one to follow. He died in the Warsaw Ghetto on 23 July 1942.

MARCH 1942

MARCH 1942 MARKED a turning point in the air war. New British equipment started to come into service, including the Lancaster bomber, a large and reliable four-engined aircraft with significant range that would become the mainstay of RAF Bomber Command by 1943. There were also changes in policy.

'Bomber' Harris, who the previous month had replaced Air Marshal Sir Richard E. S. Pierse as head of Bomber Command, believed that the war could be won by attacks from the air that broke enemy morale, and so he chose targets that would burn well. This decision partly reflected continuing problems with navigation and aiming which made precision bombing difficult, especially at night.

In Britain there were other significant command changes. The rather somnolent Admiral Dudley Pound was replaced as Chairman of the Chiefs of Staff by the more sprightly General Alan Brooke, who had a broader perspective on the war and did not hesitate to stand up to Churchill. Brooke also maintained one of the most compelling diaries of 'war at the top' as seen from the War Office, Whitehall and Westminster.

On the Eastern Front, the Red Army pushed forward in the Crimea and the Germans admitted they had lost more than one and a half million men in less than a year of fighting inside the Soviet Union. Elsewhere the spring thaw resulted in torrents of mud and roads became impassable. The only significant military activity in February was being carried out by the growing numbers of partisans behind the German lines. The Germans responded ruthlessly to any such resistance.

On 28 March British Commandos carried out a raid on the docks at St Nazaire, specifically attacking the gates of the dock because it was the only one on the Atlantic coast of France that could accommodate the powerful German battleship the *Tirpitz*. British casualties were considerable, prefiguring the even costlier raid on Dieppe later in the year. Meanwhile the *Tirpitz* prepared to launch operations against Arctic convoys from bases in Norway.

At Auschwitz on 20 March mass exterminations using gas chambers began.

Early March 1942

Cecil Beaton, official war photographer, in the desert to the west of Cairo

Cecil Beaton was born in 1904. He was an amateur photographer who had received no formal training, yet he soon became well known as one of the top fashion photographers for magazines such as Vanity Fair *and* Vogue. *He quickly became a society figure himself, moving in the worlds of film and theatre. From 1939 he became an official war photographer working for the Ministry of Information and produced images of striking clarity.*

The bedouins, in the wadis near the shore, watching the battle wage backwards and forwards along the tableland, consider the protagonists mad. They see first one army then another retiring in haste, leaving behind a wonderful amount of loot. The Bedouins steal forward and sell their spoils to the conquering army. A few months later the victors are vanquished; again the Arabs find great booty. They are the only people, so far, to win on this hazardous chess-board, where invariably the winner loses with his long lines of communication. Only the Arabs understand how to live here in the desert. They have learnt little else. After the battle, in which tanks are set on fire, and their occupants fried alive, the fluid field of battle moves on, and the Arabs arrive to pick up, among the useless relics and impediments of destruction, the gold rings, wrist-watches, cameras and souvenirs from the stiffened bodies lying in the sun. They will sell the silver strap of a wrist-watch that is worth fifteen guineas for a few pounds of sugar. Occasionally they are punished with the loss of an eye, hand or arm; for the Germans sometimes leave behind them fountain-pens and Thermoses which, when opened, ignite the secret fuse – then bang!

Beaton deliberately abandoned his exotic inter-war photographic style and sought to represent his wartime subject-matter in a very direct and striking way. His work covered the home front as well as the front line in the Middle Eastern, Indian and China theatres, and his remarkable photographs captured an extraordinary range of wartime activity. His greatest interest lay with those standing on the sidelines of war and as he travelled around the world he was perhaps unique among official observers in taking an interest in the impact of war on indigenous peoples.

Wednesday 4 March 1942

John Guest, an artillery subaltern training in Scotland, changes trains in Glasgow and London – with all his kit

Travelling in trains is always bad for crises: it is partly the insistent rhythm, the temporary isolation, the panorama of scenery that is wound past, the hours when one is prevented from doing anything but think. Coming on top of everything else, the journey north nearly finished me off. On arrival at home, the first thing I was shown was a telegram recalling me immediately to Ayr. This was awful. The following morning I set out again, thinking, thinking, all the time in the train. I missed the connection at Carlisle, and arrived late at night at Ayr, worn out. There I was told that I was to come on this [training] course, that I was to leave early the following morning – so again the next day I set out for London.

Only one particular incident marked the journey. At Glasgow I had to change not only trains but stations. This, with an enormous valise and a suitcase, and with only twenty minutes to get from one station to the other, was nerve-racking. After some mild panicking when I couldn't find a taxi, I was approached by a villainous-looking old man with a hand-cart who offered to wheel my stuff to the other station for two shillings. I agreed, and we set off down the slope at a smart pace which I found hard to sustain, weighed down as I was with webbing, haversack rations, water-bottle, pistol, pouches of ammunition, gas-mask and tin hat. At its mildest, the traffic in Glasgow is murderous: in the morning rush-hour it is like a battle-front. The old man with his hand-cart plunged into the thick of it and simply disappeared in a blur of lorries, trams, taxis and bicycles. Incredible as it may sound, he vanished before my eyes. We were at a cross-roads and he was certainly on none of the main streets. I couldn't even remember whether I had told him I was going to London. Being in an already nervous state, this seemed to be the last straw and I began to lose my head. I felt immediately that he must have made off to a 'fence' with all I possessed. I started running along the street, barging into people and peering up alleyways and passages. In the end, sweaty, exhausted and unhappy, I arrived at the station to find him sitting patiently on my valise at the right barrier. He immediately seemed a most kindly and rather pathetic old man and I gave him an inordinately handsome tip. By the time I got to London it was, of course, far too late to come on here, so I stayed the night.

Next morning I arrived at Waterloo three-quarters of an hour too early for the train. The crisis was still at full pitch. Outside it was pouring with rain, and the station was crammed with soldiers, tired, over-laden and miserable. Over the loud-speakers, which usually announce departure times, they were relaying the most wonderful music – Delius, I believe. I wandered up and down in a daze: everywhere were faces, faces and music. I was in a ridiculous state – on the verge of tears! I didn't know what to do. I went into the buffet for a cup of coffee. Hardly had I sat down than I noticed a girl of perhaps twenty in a loose-fitting Harris tweed coat with a bright silk handkerchief round her neck. She had fair hair done in a bun and an open-air complexion. She was slightly made-up, and very pretty. To my delight she came and sat at my table with her coffee, so I offered her a cigarette and for the next half-hour we talked. She was open and unreserved without being naïve; pleasing without a trace of subtlety. Her mother was Hungarian, her father English. Her effect on me was extraordinary. As she talked everything seemed to fall into perspective again – at any rate, I took a turn for the better, and from that moment until now I have thoroughly enjoyed myself down here.

For everyone in the services, travelling between postings was a legendarily troublesome process. The pitfalls were trying to manage efficient travel to and from destinations for leave that was all too infrequent – and then being recalled for no apparent reason. The whole world seemed to be on the move, while the bombing of communications links disrupted transport continually. However, the supreme challenge presented by wartime movement was how to pack all one's kit into a rucksack, a suitcase and a duffel bag.

After the war Guest would become a literary adviser to the publishing firm Longmans with the task of revitalizing their general trade list, at which he was very successful. He later moved to Penguin after a merger, remaining there until his retirement. He was a Fellow of the Royal Literary Society and edited the first anthology of the work of his friend, the poet Sir John Betjeman. He died in August 1997. SEE ALSO PP. 385–6.

Monday 9 – Saturday 14 March 1942

Friedrich Schmidt of the Secret Field Police executes young Russian partisans

Friedrich Schmidt was reported to have served as secretary of the Secret Field Police, attached to the German 626th Group, 1st Tank Army, stationed near Rostov during the spring of 1942. Little more is known of him.

9 March

The sun is out in all his glory, flooding the snow with a dazzling light. But even old Sol can evoke no joy in my heart. I have had a distressing day. I woke up at 3 o'clock, startled by a terrible dream. I had been thinking about the thirty youngest that I had to kill to-day. After all, the war on the Eastern front is a horrible thing. At 10 am they again brought me two girls and six boys who had crossed over from Yeisk. I had to give them a merciless beating. Many arrests are being made. Yesterday there were six and today thirty-three.

I'm simply suffocating here and losing my appetite. It won't go well with me if I am caught here. I no longer feel safe in Budennovka. Everybody must be hating me. If my people at home only knew what a distressing time I have had today. The ditch is almost full of corpses. And how heroically these young Bolsheviks go to their death! What is it, anyhow, that makes them so? Love of country? Or Communism that has entered their blood and suffused the whole system? It really must be so if some of them, particularly the girls, do not shed a tear when they are beaten and do not flinch when they are led to execution. There is valour for you! One young fellow even demanded that they shoot him right in the heart. If they get me here I am done for . . .

14 March

Very cold weather once more. I'm not feeling well again. My stomach is out of order and I have pains round the heart. I ordered the doctor to be called. He diagnosed the case as indigestion and a nervous condition of the heart. He ordered me to stay in bed but I could not follow his directions. Today the remaining two parachutists with all their equipment will be brought to me. Now I have two Russian automatics, a great number of cartridges and an ample supply of Russian hand grenades. I issued an order today that Ludmila Chukanova, a girl 17 years old, be shot this evening. I was almost entirely indifferent when I gave this order. I have to decide on the death of such youngsters. Such is my lot! That must be the reason for the nervous condition of my heart. During the night Bolsheviks again crossed the ice and attacked Natalyevka.

There is no question that the war against partisans conducted by specialist German units was characterized by extreme brutality. There is also no doubt that a security police officer called Friedrich Schmidt existed and had been involved in the execution of Jews in Poland in 1941. However, the text exists only as a collection of 'captured' German war diaries published from Soviet sources during the war. It is likely to be genuine, but it may also be embellished and is illustrative of the problems presented when not much is known about the provenance of a diary.

Thursday 12 – Saturday 21 March 1942

Odd Nansen describes life in a concentration camp at Grini in Norway

Odd Nansen came from a Norwegian family with a proud record of humanitarian commitment and in 1937 had founded the Nansen Help organization to supplement the work of his famous father Fridtjof, who had been an Arctic explorer and had then turned his hand to famine relief and work in the repatriation of war prisoners. His father won the 1922 Nobel Peace Prize and in 1931 the League of Nations honoured him by creating the Nansen International Office for Refugees. An active anti-Nazi and protester on humanitarian issues, by 1942 Odd was in a concentration camp in Norway.

12 March

Tonight we've had a farewell party for Oftedal, who is leaving tomorrow . . . Oftedal has a lot to tell about the origins of Grini, both jest and earnest. And yet the whole thing gets to be sinister in a peculiar way, even though we can say with our hands on our hearts that we have had a pleasant evening.

At one moment we got talking of the worst things that have happened here at Grini, at the Terrace and at No 19. Incredibly frightful things have happened and are still going on. People have been beaten up and tortured and tormented beyond all bounds. Some held, others cracked. No one dare sit in judgement. One man cracked and had the death of others on his conscience: well, he's been shot too. But first he lived through a ghastly time. A little poem on the wall of his cell in No 19 gave expression to his mental agony. I don't remember how it went, but he does not value or esteem himself as a rotten herring.

Sigurd Johansen, Thorsvik and Lea used to be room-mates here at Grini. None of these three were expecting the worst. All hoped, or were almost sure of a light sentence. Then they were all three shot. They had only to run away. Sigurd

Johansen and Thorsvik had been in Oslo any number of times *without* a guard, and come back here like sheep to the stall. Meekly they let themselves be led to the shambles. It makes the whole outrage twice as scurvy. First there is a raking in of confidence and upright dealing by every means, and then it is rewarded by a volley of musketry.

What is now lying black and heavy on people's minds is the news that Fraser and Svae have been condemned to death! Now I suppose they are at Akershus, waiting for the time of grace to run out. They can't have much chance to speak of. And poor Birkevold, their leader, who is lying here in hospital, has been told. He took it splendidly, we heard from one of the male nurses today. He said he was glad to have been told; it was better than lying there knowing nothing. And so he is a hundred per cent certain to be shot on his discharge from hospital, unless something should have happened by then.

21 March

The teachers are streaming in. Yesterday and today two hundred and fifty have arrived, and it looks like continuing. One can't deny that there is something melodramatic about this national migration to Grini, but at the same time it is sinister. The treatment they are getting here is still frightful. It was not just a demonstration of welcome. All the Germans yell in copybook style when they come across teachers either singly or in a squad, and then they kick and cuff a little for safety's sake, to indicate more precisely what they mean.

This afternoon I had the pleasure of setting a hundred and thirty-five teachers to work shovelling snow and clearing the hut sites on the 'upper plateau'. It went nicely; everyone got hold of some object or other to indicate work, a pick, a spade, a shovel or something else with which they could either poke at the stumps or 'move the snow'. Properly they should all have had spades, but we are short of spades, and so we have to eke out with other implements. All went well, and it rapidly developed into a grand-style penal comedy out on the clearing, where the whole gang stood round in the snow and poked. They began to get back their spirits, which perhaps had drooped a little at their reception in the *Vermittlung* and afterwards when they were 'shown round' inside the hotel. Then the guards came along and began yelling: 'Faster, man! Can't you work? Faster, I said; get on, get on! Don't you understand, blockhead? Damned Norwegian! And you call yourself a teacher. That's impossible! You'll have to learn something yourself first, blockhead! Get on!' and so on. But it didn't proceed to blows this afternoon as far as I know. Only bellowing. And one soon gets familiar with the yelling. It is really worst for themselves. In the long run it must be a strain upon the throat and the vocal cords.

Nansen's diary is one of the more detailed records of Nazi oppression in Norway, one aspect of which was the rounding up of large numbers of schoolteachers who were regarded as non-compliant. He spent a long time in concentration camps in Norway and later in Germany and, as a meticulous observer, recorded all that he saw there. SEE ALSO P. 776.

APRIL 1942

IN APRIL 1942 Sir Charles Hambro, a former City banker, was appointed as the executive head of the Special Operations Executive. This reflected the idea that sabotage would concentrate on economic warfare. However, the new organization provoked many bureaucratic quarrels: Churchill had exhorted the subversives to 'set Europe ablaze', but after a year of activity it was Whitehall that they seemed to have set on fire. Hambro would be later replaced by his deputy, Major-General Colin Gubbins, who had previously been in military intelligence. Gubbins stamped his identity on the organization, giving it a more military aspect and turning it into a 'secret army'. He would remain as head of the SOE until it was disbanded on 15 January 1946.

Despite the squabbling in Whitehall, the various national resistance movements in Europe were growing in strength and confidence. On Wednesday 15 April the French resistance attacked the German HQ at Arras with hand grenades. At the end of the month the Belgian resistance destroyed Tenderloo chemical works, killing more than 250. There were, inevitably, reprisals, with executions by the Germans reported to be running at twenty-five to thirty a month in Belgium.

On the last day of April, Hitler and Mussolini met at Berchtesgaden to discuss future Axis strategy in north Africa and the Mediterranean, where Rommel's Afrika Korps was on the offensive. Their main objectives were the reduction of the fortress island of Malta and the seizure of the Suez Canal.

During the spring of 1942 there was a renewed effort to improve domestic food production in Britain, as German U-boat attacks in the Atlantic bit deeper into supply traffic from North America. Areas of uncultivated land, even in the major public parks in London, were being turned over to vegetable production. By 1942 large numbers of women were working in the Women's Land Army and a major programme of training had begun, with 'tractor schools' springing up in every region.

Thursday 16 April 1942

Naomi Mitchison in Scotland listens to an English officer talk about invasion

Naomi Mitchison was a British writer known as an outspoken feminist and free-thinker. The daughter of the physiologist John Scott Haldane and the suffragist Kathleen (Trotter) Haldane, she had begun to study science at Oxford University but left in 1915 before completing her degree to become a VAD nurse. In 1937 Naomi Mitchison moved to a large house at Carradale on the Mull of Kintyre, where she would remain throughout the war.

In the evening to Campbeltown with Davie Oman to this lecture on When Invasion Comes. It was given by the officer in command of this military sub-area, an English gentleman, and all that, who was in command of the Highland Area. He began by some preliminaries about the Boche and the Hun who has had world conquest in his veins since the beginning of history, said invasion was inevitable, the Germans would want the aerodromes on the west coast, there were some fine ones on islands. I imagined them landing on Tiree! Then blood-curdling invasion details, how all Germans were treacherous, had no idea of 'fair play', the paratroops on Crete were all doped and so turned bright green when dead ... After this I decided this lecture was hardly for my intelligence group. But I waited for practical things; he explained that he wanted to keep the civilian population occupied as otherwise it would be so boring for them to stay put during an invasion and they might panic. He suggested they might observe things and send in reports, become stretcher bearers, clear debris from roads, help ARP etc. None of it seemed to apply. There were to be Invasion Committees (each to include one lady, jolly good idea . . .), one in Campbeltown. They could have copies of his lecture notes.

At the end he didn't even ask for questions; I rather furiously got up and said I represented the Carradale Farmers and we wanted to know what we should do about crops, stores, etc. Should we burn them? Oh no, he said, I wouldn't do that if I were you. After all, we'll get these fellows out in ten days and it doesn't matter what they do in the mean time. I said what about cattle, did we or didn't we want to inconvenience the invader? He said we shouldn't do anything. Should the Village Hall burn 40 gallons of petrol? Oh no, it wasn't worth while. Should the Head Forester burn the saw-mill? On no, he shouldn't do that, should he? So much for scorched earth. I don't think anyone else thought much of it. Commander Moir smiled sweetly and said it was a little bit old-fashioned. Donald Jackson and Hugh (I didn't know they were coming) agreed it was complete balls. Davie Oman was utterly unimpressed, and felt this was the kind of thing the English did. I tried feebly to say that all soldiers weren't quite as bad. But I wonder if they realise what an effect bastards like this produce.

Naomi Mitchison maintained a generous pattern of hospitality at her house in Carradale, entertaining a continuous stream of left-wing intellectuals, writers and politicians, as well as a curious collection of friends and acquaintances from around the world. In her later years she would become a travel writer. Although she produced three volumes of memoirs, her diaries best capture the irreverence and creative chaos of her wartime years. The officer who met with her disapproval may have been Major James Campbell, who commanded the Southern Highland area. Pompous British officers being sent to take charge of the Highlands was just the sort of thing that was likely to provoke her fierce critical intelligence. In any case, by April 1942 public fears of a cross-Channel invasion were evaporating, for it was clear to everyone that Hitler was in deep trouble in Russia. In fact, unbeknown to the British public, Operation Sealion, the planned invasion of Britain, had been formally cancelled by the German high command on 13 February 1942.

Naomi Mitchison would write more than seventy novels, biographies and books of poetry. She died on 11 January 1999 at the age of 101.

Thursday 16 – Sunday 26 April 1942

Malcolm Muggeridge discusses fighting to live 'as we were accustomed to'

Malcolm Muggeridge began his intellectual life as a dedicated Fabian socialist, spending time in Russia, but later became a public advocate for Roman Catholicism. He worked mostly as a journalist, but spent the Second World War in the Secret Intelligence Service (MI6). In April 1942 he was in Portugal.

16 April

Lunched with Rita Windsor and others from the Embassy, including Press Attaché, at English Club, piece of land forever England, leather chairs, subdued light, florid men reading newspapers, etc, etc. Inevitably discussed war. Rita said we were fighting for a chance to go on living as we were accustomed to, though as a matter of fact there was no possibility of our doing so in any case. It was, I said, like fighting a duel over a woman who was in fact dead and buried. But suppose, a little man called Bush said, you won and had to sleep with the corpse. I agreed that that was the most appalling prospect of all. Bush took me afterwards to see the procession in connection with installation of the President for his third term of office. Troops, cavalry, naval contingent, etc, etc, and President Carmona driving by in open carriage with coachman of English type (in 17th and 18th centuries, France copied; in 19th England; eg in uniform peaked caps, now Germany is beginning to be copied), with the Prime Minister, Salazar, beside him. Dense, but not particularly enthusiastic crowds.

24–26 April

Unquiet, apprehensions coming in crowds, sense of the war, its unreality, unreality of my situation here and of the journey soon to be undertaken, empty words sounding in my ears, echoing emptiness in my heart. What is to happen? What can happen? How can any happening be of significance? Why? No interest in 'Why?'; no real interest. Drifting onwards, drifting onwards. Life's a poor *pension* ... Confused, unhappy, futile thoughts passing through my mind, and always the clear, permanent thought – it will always be the same. Go here, go there; be this, be that, it will always be the same.

Spoke with Mrs K about the war and why it should seem so dreamlike – because we had been so fed on lies. I looked back with disgust on the teeming lies of recent years – lies about wealth, lies about poverty, lies about strength, lies about weakness, hopeful lies and despairing lies, all lying, in spoken as well as in written words, in thoughts even, as many and as varied lies as there were slimy things with legs crawling about the Ancient Mariner's slimy sea. And now there is no longer the possibility of lying because there is no truth left, no means of detecting or estimating lies. When currency inflation goes beyond a certain point there ceases to be any currency; only soaring figures. So with lying. Perhaps the war has never taken place, perhaps it will never end; its beginning was announced without it being begun; its end may be announced without it being ended. There is no possibility of knowing anything about it; begotten and conducted on lies, it will end in lies.

Lisbon, the capital of neutral Portugal, was one of the espionage capitals of the world and hosted a large British intelligence station. MI6 officers who spent time there included Graham Greene and his boss Kim Philby as well as Malcolm Muggeridge. Although Muggeridge left MI6 at the end of the war, he continued to be employed by the 'office' on occasional tasks. He was somewhat critical of both the British establishment and the senior officers in his own organization. His diary captures the tension between patriotism and an intense sense of dissatisfaction with the staleness of what many took to represent Britain and British society. Like many other intelligence officers who kept diaries – including Graham Greene – he wrote very little about his work. After the war he would work on the Telegraph *and then became editor of the humorous magazine* Punch. SEE ALSO P. 21.*

Sunday 19 April 1942

Flight Lieutenant Harold J. Dothie of the RAF reflects on diaries and correspondence

Harold Dothie was a Canadian serving in the RAF and was trained on multi-engined aircraft, reflecting the growing focus on the bombing of Germany.

Today I read in the papers that a man has been fined £10 for keeping a diary on board ship, and had made notes on sinkings in convoys etc. He had hidden this diary in a funnel, and it was discovered by a Customs Official. So I must be careful what I put in these pages, but it seems that most of it these days is concerned with personal matters.

I am now definitely and 'officially' engaged to Joyce, having told this fact to my mother and to various relations, although I have not yet given her a ring. I am in fact saving up for one, but so far have not succeeded in saving a single bean. I always seem to spend all my money. Until last Christmas I was writing to Joyce approximately once every two months, and she complained bitterly in her letters about the scarcity of mail from me. But since the New Year I have been writing to her a lot more often. I have now sent her 10 letters, (against her 35 to me!) besides several cables and quite a number of airgraphs. She was always very depressed when there were big gaps between my letters and when she received one her joy knew no bounds. Now she writes in a much more satisfied tone. She is very good to me, writing regularly once per week constantly. Its quite clear that she is deeply in love with me, and is building her whole life around me. Yet I cannot escape the dread that she does not know me really well enough, has put me on a pedestal, and is weaving all kinds of dreams about me. It has been my experience that girls who have felt that way toward me on previous occasions have quite suddenly, and usually after a period of about two months, found the pedestal completely collapse.

Harold Dothie's diary reveals the hazards of keeping diaries and the anxiety that the practice could induce among serving personnel. It also reveals the stresses placed on relationships by long periods of service and short periods of leave. Many servicemen were married after only short courtships, or returned from long periods overseas to realize that the war had changed them considerably. Dothie's own absence from Canada was prolonged. In May 1943 he would be posted to 51 Squadron RAF after converting to Halifax bombers and the following month was shot down over Krefeld in northern Germany. Having bailed out successfully he would spend the rest of the war as a POW and after his release in 1945 joined BOAC as a pilot.

Tuesday 21 April – Sunday 17 May 1942

The SOE and MI6 discuss plans to assassinate Mussolini and Farinacci

At various points in the war the British secret services developed plans to assassinate both Hitler and Mussolini. The plan to assassinate Hitler – Operation Foxley – revealed in 1995, is now well known. Less well

known are the plans to assassinate Mussolini, which were recorded in a
Special Operations Executive unit war diary in 1942. Unit war diaries
were sometimes rather impersonal records, but where they were the
responsibility of one individual they could take on the character of a per-
sonal journal, capturing fleeting conversations or private impressions.
The writer, however, is unidentified.

Mussolini and Farinacci: London asked Cairo to read a
telegram from C. [the Chief of MI6, Sir Stewart Menzies]
(apparently dealing with a project to assassinate Mussolini)
and to discuss it with C's representative [in Cairo]. Cairo
were to telegraph whether they considered the scheme
feasible. Cairo replied that they intended to proceed with the
scheme unless further study disclosed major difficulties.
London told Cairo that in the view of the Italian Section the
target should be Farinacci and not Mussolini, as he was
Mussolini's spur in Italy: his removal would be popular with
all classes. To remove Mussolini before Italy had suffered
further defeat and while Farinacci was still powerful might
easily result in the rallying of the fascist party and an
increase in German control.

[Major Pearson of SOE argued that although] Mussolini
was now discredited in the eyes of a proportion of the
population he was still idolised by large sections and his
removal would make him a martyr. Farinacci, more than any
other, was the sponsor of collaboration with Germany and
the mainstay behind Mussolini. He was moreover more
easily accessible: he was frequently to be found taking an
aperitif at public bars. Mussolini on the other hand was not.
Whatever means were used they would have to be taken in
by the agent as they could not be supplied by local purchase
or by our own people in country. We would not consider
endangering any of our local contacts by assisting this
operator and he would therefore have to make his own
arrangements.

[Mr Roseberry told Brigadier Gubbins, a senior SOE offi-
cer] that it was a rather scatterbrained project but if Cairo
were satisfied that the man had possibilities of perfecting
such a job we ought to allow him to pursue it . . .

Cairo cabled on 16th [May] that the individual was now

undergoing a facial operation and would be ready for action
in the middle of June . . .

---

*The Allied secret services did not shrink from contemplating the
assassination of enemy leaders during the war. However, the prospect
presented awkward questions. What if the Fascist successor to Mussolini
proved to be more effective and more popular than the person who had
been removed? There can be little doubt that Hitler's bizarre behaviour
served Britain well more than once, and his decision to invade Russia,
informed by a belief that the Slavs were 'a weak race' and would be
easily defeated, proved to be one of the decisive turning points of the war.
Both Mussolini and his Fascist ideologue Farinacci were incompetent
and potentially beneficial to the Allied cause. Perhaps for this reason, the
operation was never launched. Farinacci was secretary of the Italian
Fascist party and after 1943 would be Mussolini's delegate to the
German command in Italy. Like Mussolini, he was captured and shot by
partisans in 1945.*

Wednesday 29 April 1942

Marion Kelsey excels at tractor school in East Sussex

*Marion Kelsey was a young Canadian woman serving in the Women's
Land Army in East Sussex. A relative offered her the price of the boat
ticket so that she could travel across the Atlantic to be near her husband,
who was serving in the Canadian army in Britain. She would spend
four years planting crops, milking cows – and driving a tractor.*

Tractor School Cralle Place
I have been here twenty-four hours. We live in converted
brooder houses, eleven other girls and myself. Instead of a
foster-mother, warming fifty little chicks, in each room there
is one Land girl, one bed (one thin mattress on three-ply
wood, no spring), one small ply-wood wardrobe, and one
chair.

But I have learned to forage, like Caesar's men and the
Canadians. I found that a few planks, scrounged from

underneath the chicken-coop and arranged on a couple of saw-horses, also scrounged, make an excellent dressing table and desk combined. My books on the table, my sepia print of Tintern Abbey on the wall, and a big bowl of primroses in the honey-pot which Mrs Moss gave me, make me feel very much at home.

I was off to a flying start this morning. Mr Winters, our instructor, told me to hitch on to the roller and stood watching carefully while I did so. While he held up the draw bar I backed straight in, leaned back and dropped the pin in the hole. Mr Winters looked at me with awe.

'By gum,' was all he said, and I was forced to confess that I had driven a tractor before. I swapped the roll for harrows, and as we have had no rain for weeks, I was enveloped in clouds of dust all day.

I called Nunningham at noon and asked if Fatty Cornford, the local carter, could bring over my working kit, which I had left at the farm. I expected him to come when he had a trip in this direction, but he made a special one and arrived just as I came in from work. He is a great friend of Walter's and we sat on the step and had a real old gossip. Fatty was glad to see his 'little ol' de-ar,' as he and old Dan call me, and I was delighted to talk to an old friend.

When he had gone I disrobed piecemeal on the doorstep, and whacked the dust out of my clothes on the outside wall. I gave my hair a good brushing and then washed, 'up as far as possible, and down as far as possible. Poor possible,' as the Welsh girls I met in Sutton used to say. As yet we have no bathroom facilities and may bathe, only on sufferance and advance notice, at the big house.

Two years ago tomorrow I sailed from New York to a British Port.

The girls change and rush off to the Pig and Whistle every night. I have not yet grown accustomed to unescorted pubbing, but I can see that I soon shall or else be dubbed a snob.

Last night, George, who is farm manager, asked me if the girls had gone off and left me alone. When I explained that I had not wished to go, that I had been busy unpacking, he said that if I were through and if I felt lonely, his wife would be glad to have me spend the evening with her. I walked up this evening to thank her. She is a plump, cheerful person, about my age and they have a practical, modern cottage.

Tomorrow night is pay night and George says that Mr Winters tries to make it Land Girl night at the Pig and Whistle. He and Mrs George go, and all the girls. I may as well give in gracefully and brush up on my dart game.

Some women joined the Land Army in preference to the armed services, thinking that it might be less demanding. In fact the life was very tough; not everyone was up to the job, and there was quite a high rate of departure. Marion Kelsey had been in the WLA in Britain since 1940. The nature of the women's work depended very much on the farms to which they were sent. In some cases Land Girls quickly found rewarding and responsible work; elsewhere they might be used for low-grade tasks, performing odd jobs around the farm and domestic tasks in the farmhouse. Most girls worked for individual farmers, but a proportion stayed in hostels and were deployed on areas run by the Forestry Commission or in teams under the control of the County War Agriculture Executive Committee. SEE ALSO PP. 416–18.

MAY 1942

ON 8 MAY A new German offensive began on the Eastern Front, with attacks by the 11th Army in the Crimea. The Germans had prepared well and by the end of the month they were driving Soviet forces back in the area of the Donnets river (a tributary of the River Don), taking a quarter of a million prisoners.

The fortress island of Malta was successfully resupplied with aircraft in a joint Anglo-American operation which involved sailing aircraft carriers within flying distance of the island. Malta itself was effectively used as a large aircraft carrier from which planes could harry German supply routes in the Mediterranean. When Malta was almost out of serviceable aircraft and fuel, the

May 1942 operation delivered sixty-four much-needed Spitfires.

On 26 May Rommel began a major new offensive in the western desert, sending his armour in a wide, sweeping manoeuvre to the south; however, the Italian elements in his force became confused and lost their way. Axis armour was outnumbered and the British were assisted by the arrival of new American types of tank that were replacing the inferior British vehicles. Rommel's offensive continued until 28 May, when some of his tanks began to run out of fuel. Two days later he was forced to pull his forces back into a defensive position in the so-called 'Cauldron' – an artificial redoubt consisting of barbed wire and large minefields.

Resistance activity was becoming ever more ambitious. At the end of May 1942 Czech underground fighters, armed and trained by the SOE, launched Operation Anthropoid, which would result in the assassination of the leading Nazi official SS Obergruppenführer Reinhard Heydrich in Prague. Operatives from Czechoslovakia who had been trained by the SOE were parachuted back into their own homeland, where they mounted their attack on 27 May; their quarry died of his wounds a week later. The mechanics of Operation Anthropoid were strikingly different from those of the plan to assassinate Mussolini and Farinacci, or indeed the plan that would later develop for the assassination of Hitler. They involved patience, professionalism and support from the local population. Heydrich has often been described as 'the perfect Nazi' and only four months earlier had convened the Wannsee Conference, where the 'Final Solution' was agreed.

On the night of 30–31 May RAF Bomber Command mounted a famous raid on Cologne, using 1,000 bombers. This operation stretched the RAF to its limit and every available aircraft was deployed, some of them with barely trained crews. There were risks involved, but the casualties were remarkably light, with only 40 aircraft lost. The impact on Cologne was immense: 1,455 tons of explosive were dropped, destroying 600 acres of built-up area, killing 486 civilians and making 59,000 people homeless. This attack also underlined the increasing pressure that would fall on Germany from now on as the tide of air war was reversed.

Friday 1 May 1942

René Mouchotte, a pilot leading a Free French unit of the
RAF, survives a desperate dogfight over the English
Channel

*In November 1941 most French pilots in Britain had been sent to
Turnhouse in Scotland to form a dedicated Free French unit. René
Mouchotte had been appointed commander of the new squadron on 15
March 1942. It battled with the fighter escorts of German bomber raids
and specialized in cross-Channel operations.*

This morning I had the most memorable combat of my life.
Ten minutes' dog-fight with a Boche who, unlike his fellows,
would not let go. And no one to help me! The bandit
attacked from above and I could do no more than turn at the
opportune moment, trying to give him a few bursts in passing. He must have been a tough one, one of those veterans
who hang on to their prey. Each time he made for me I
clenched my teeth and everything else, wondering if this
was it. I was alone over the Channel with this bellicose
brother, showing me his white belly, his fine black crosses and
the dangerous red lines of tracer. He let me go in the end, in
disgust, but I admit that more than once I should have liked
to say, as in my childhood days, when I realized I was losing
a game, 'Pax! Pax! The game's over. I won't fire at you any
more but do let me go!'

I thank Heaven for having given me such good sight and
such a long neck. Unfortunately I have a very sensitive
stomach which makes its presence strangely felt before each
sweep, but once I have my backside on the pilot's seat and
my 1,200 horses are crackling, I couldn't feel better! The
mind works fast in the air but if I meet the enemy I know
perfectly well that I do not *think* what I am doing. My nerves
respond like clockwork. I no longer have time to think, to
feel, to consider. There is no trace of fear but an enormous
excitement, an intense mental effort. The proof that one does

not think during these moments of combat is that on landing it is very hard to remember all that has happened. A few images or impressions are photographed, but the more one ponders them the more they change. A striking incident may remain before the eyes, but the most difficult thing is to remember what one has done in a particular situation. After a good night's sleep it is rare for any details of a combat on the day before to be remembered . . .

A major task for Free French air units would be providing operational air cover for the raid on Dieppe on 19 August 1942. By then BBC radio broadcasts to France praising him as an example of Free France continuing the fight against the Nazis had made Mouchotte quite famous. He was awarded the Distinguished Flying Cross in the autumn of this year and by December his unit would be training for duty on aircraft carriers. Based at Biggin Hill from March 1943, Mouchotte would continue to fly on almost every mission that his squadron undertook and was close to exhaustion. He was shot down by an FW-190 on 27 August 1943. SEE ALSO PP. 347–8.

Saturday 2 May 1942

Marion Kelsey, a Canadian from the Women's Land Army working in Sussex, makes a find at the local store

Tractor School

At present we must eat in the house, in a tiny room allotted us by Mrs Batten, and we are considered an unavoidable and not even necessary evil. A Land Girl is a person who feels forced to intrude in the house, and who comes in muddy boots and with greasy finger-nails to eat, bathe, or telephone.

The weekend began well. Saturday morning was one of brilliant sunshine and my tractor behaved beautifully. My ploughing is improving too. It is so glorious out there on the hill, little pink-breasted chaffinches, with blue caps and barred wings, diving, sweeping swallows, and tail-tipping magpies, all following the plough, picking up grubs on the newly turned earth. I found and gathered an enormous bouquet of foxglove on my way back at lunch time.

And I had a very satisfactory afternoon. I walked along the road to the little cottage which is the Post Office and general store.

'Have you any cigarette papers?' A routine question.

'Well, I can let you have one package.'

'I suppose it is useless to ask for cigarette tobacco?'

'Well, you may have one ounce.'

This was really deep in clover, so we talked a little and I explained how hungry we girls were at night. I said that we were able to have a bit of bread but that there was no jam or cheese to spare. By then a pot of honey had appeared on the counter and two little triangles of processed cheese, and finally some chocolate. I left feeling like an antique dealer who has made a genuine find.

I have been here about two weeks now, and with the addition of two or three embryonic tractor drivers, I am no longer the newcomer. I have little to offer to make me one of the group, but as we all have a meeting-point in our work, we get along well together.

We are all in different stages of proficiency. The newer girls cruise around on tractors to get used to driving. The next step is rolling, which initiates one into driving with an implement, gauging the turning space, and learning to drive straight and to measure out a field. Several stages follow, until one proud morning one hitches on a plough and proceeds to realize that the three levers which one must master each produce a multitude of results.

Last week I came in for a job I did not relish. Like each of the other girls, I had a two-furrow Cockshutt and was really beginning to get the knack of it, when one of the newer girls graduated into the ploughing contingent. We were one plough short, and much to my disgust, I was given a three-furrow International. I was not sure enough of myself with a two-furrow to carry on easily with a three, and in addition to my lack of skill, the plough proved to have something wrong with it.

We began at the front and adjusted the hitch differently but there was no improvement. We changed the set of the coulters, adjusted the tension of the axle on the furrow wheel, then on the land wheel. After four days of adjustment and experimentation we discovered that the trouble was in the set of the rear wheel. A morning's work, removing the wheel, trying on one from a new plough, taking both to the blacksmith, and finally resetting the repaired wheel, resulted in three identical furrows turning smoothly over the moldboards.

They say that it takes twenty years to make a plough man and I can well believe it. However I can now cut out well, set my plough with some method, plough comparatively straight and evenly, but I still make a dreadful mess of closing up. The tractors themselves are all 1942 Fordsons and run beautifully. These girls must experience ploughing, which requires full concentration, while at the same time they are nursing along an old worn-out tractor which is always most cussed at the critical moment. I had just such a problem on Brian Moss's old 1932 tractor, and I breathe deeply on these perfect WAEC machines. Certainly we have much to learn.

By July 1942 the friends that Marion Kelsey had made at tractor school began to disperse to their new assignments. Marion was allocated by the East Sussex War Agricultural Executive Committee to a farm at Broomlye, near Newick, to assist with the harvest. She would be directed in her work by a Mr Botting, who took her to the fields that she was to plough and left her to it. When she had finished a field he made 'no complaint' but also made no remarks.

Marion would stop farming in 1944 when her husband was badly wounded at Falaise. They eventually returned to Canada. Marion Kelsey now lives at Hunts Point, Nova Scotia. SEE ALSO PP. 411–13.

Sunday 3 – Tuesday 5 May 1942

Alexander Cadogan, the top Foreign Office official,
worries about appeasing the Russians over their demands
in eastern Europe

3 May

Maisky [the Soviet ambassador in London] has given [the]
Soviet reply to our draft Treaties. Pretty bad: they cut out all
we had put in to save the Polish case and American
susceptibilities. It's curious that A.[nthony Eden], of all
people, should have hopes of 'appeasement'!! Much better
say to the Russians 'We can't discuss post-war frontiers: we
want to work with you, now and later: let's have a mutual
guarantee. Frontiers can easily be agreed on later. If you like,
we will try to get U.S. collaboration – so far as their
Constitution allows them to go. If not, we offer you all *we*
have. But don't ask us *now*, at the cost of all our principles,
to agree to a situation which *we* can't influence!' I believe,
still, it would be better not to crawl to the Russians over the
dead bodies of *all* our principles.

4 May

4.30 meeting with A. and others about Soviet. Glad to find he
realises we can at least go no further, and no use haggling.
5.30 Cabinet. Not much news ... Short discussion after
about Russia. All members of Cabinet sound (except perhaps
Cripps, [previously British ambassador in Moscow] who
didn't know what he was talking about, as he hadn't seen
the drafts of the Treaties).

5 May

[Invasion of] Madagascar was launched this morning, but
don't know how it is going. Roosevelt has played up well ...
Meeting in A.'s [Eden's] room at 10 p.m. on Russia. Glad to
find he is determined at least not to throw the Poles down
the drain and faces the possibility of a failure of the
negotiation. I urged again that we should try to switch

the discussion on to some alternative form of Treaty – mutual guarantee, or something. No use haggling – as all through the summer of 1939 – on the present drafts. Agreed Department should try to draft something.

Alexander Cadogan found the problem of negotiating a treaty of alliance with the Soviet Union to be one of the biggest diplomatic headaches of 1942. Stalin wanted the treaty to include British approval of Soviet control over many of the territories that Soviet forces had gained in 1939, when they were in alliance with Hitler. This would have meant Britain abandoning its principles, and also betraying the Polish government-in-exile in London. For Cadogan, who had vociferously opposed appeasement in 1938–9, this was distasteful in the extreme. Eventually a formula was found that did not address sensitive issues of territory and the Soviet Union was persuaded to sign it. Cadogan noted in his diary 'Winston relieved and delighted', and recorded that 'bouquets were heaped' upon his master, Anthony Eden.

Immediately after the war Cadogan was appointed Britain's first ambassador to the UN. Between 1952 and 1957 he was Chairman of the BBC. SEE ALSO PP. 31–2, 45–6 AND 247–8.

Tuesday 12 May 1942

Anthony Eden discusses with Churchill what to do with the boisterous Max Beaverbrook

Winston asked me to come round and talk to him in morning. I found him struggling with his bath towel, like a Roman Emperor with his toga. We spoke of Max [Beaverbrook]. Winston doesn't like him loose and wants him to replace Edward [Lord Halifax, Britain's ambassador to the United States] at W'ton [Washington]. He maintains that Max has entrée to the President which is all that matters, that he would do as told or be recalled, that he would get us what we wanted as no other could etc. I cited obvious objections. Eventually we agreed that Winston should send a private telegram to Harry H [Hopkins] to sound him out. When I saw Winston later he showed me a draft which amounted to asking for an 'agrément' [formal acceptance of a proposed ambassador]. I persuaded him to add 'This is not official, please tell me frankly what you think'.

Anthony Eden

This entry from Eden's episodic diary captures his relationship with Churchill perfectly. Churchill intervened impulsively in both diplomatic and military affairs, often to the complete exasperation of his colleagues. They in turn attempted to steer him towards sensible action and proper protocols, combining public firmness with private fury, which they vented in their diaries. Max Beaverbrook, the former press baron and wartime aircraft production minister, was certainly close to Roosevelt and admired by him, but he was also a maverick and so a risky choice for a post that required tact and delicacy.

Harry Hopkins was one of Roosevelt's closest confidants and served as his special assistant between 1942 and 1945. SEE ALSO PP. 298 AND 607–8.

Whit Monday, 25 May 1942

War correspondent Alexander Werth sails with convoy
PQ-16 to Archangel

I don't know when exactly the little bastard joined us, but he's been circling round and round the convoy all day. He is keeping well outside the range of the guns on the destroyers, and sometimes he disappears, but before long he, or his relay, turns up again. He's a Fokke-Wulf, and the crew, who are irritated by his presence, refer to him as 'George.' At 5 this morning the first alarm went, and I dressed in under three minutes, but nothing happened. Then, at dinner-time, the alarm bell rang again, and the destroyer fired several rounds at our German 'escort,' but he was out of range, and for the rest of the afternoon he gave us no more trouble, except by being *there*. The crew looked longingly at the catapult Hurricane on the *Empire Lawrence*, but apparently it was decided not to waste the Hurricane on chasing George, especially as there was much cloud, and he would probably have escaped had the Hurricane been sent after him. At 6.30 the alarm went again – and this time it was the real stuff.

They appeared in the distance, on the starboard side, low above the water: three – four – five, then three more, then four or five after that, further to the right. We were all on deck – the R.A.F. boys, with their tin hats, and the deck-hands, the cabin boys – and we counted and watched. Eleven, twelve, thirteen . . . Something was already happening ahead of us. The gunners had rushed up to the gun-turrets. The two cruisers which had suddenly joined us earlier in the day, and the destroyers on the edge of the convoy, were firing like mad. It was a beautiful bright day, the sea calm and blue like the Mediterranean, and the sky was now dotted with specks of smoke from the flak shells. They went in a half-circle round the front of the convoy, then, after a few seconds of suspense, they came right out of the sun. They swooped over us, two or three in succession, and from their yellow bellies the yellow eggs dropped, slowly, obscenely. They were after the cruisers, in the middle of the convoy. The tracer-bullets from our Oerlikons were rushing at the yellow belly of the Junker 88 as he swooped over us. A loud squeal, growing louder and louder, and then the explosion, as a stick of bombs landed between us and the destroyer, on the port side. Three pillars of water went high up in the air, and the ship shook. As he dived, almost to the water level, our tracer-bullets followed him, but he got out of their way, and on the bridge Captain Dykes, wearing a wide navy-blue beret, was waving and shouting frantically: 'Don't fire so low! You're hitting the next ship!' Then after a few minutes they came again, out of the sun – three of them. This time they seemed to make a dead set at the cruisers. On the upper deck, on the fo'c'sle, the Flight-Lieutenant was looking on, his long hair waving in the wind. He had his life-jacket on, with a drawing of naked 'Loulou.' The R.A.F. boys and I and ginger-haired Harry with the blackheads, stood amidships, watching the battle. Suddenly something happened. The cruiser, which had put up a very impressive barrage, had got one. He began to reel and swoop down, on our port side, then he staggered over us. It was like a football match. Harry and the R.A.F. boys were shouting: 'He's on fire! He's on fire! That's it! He's *down!*' Harry jumped about with joy, frantically. He *was* down. Something brown and large and soft detached itself from the plane, and the plane itself slid into the water, without much of a splash. The barrage was still going full blast, but a destroyer sailed up to the brown parachute or whatever it was, and proceeded to pick them up. Meantime the catapult Hurricane on the *Empire Lawrence* had leaped swiftly into the air, in pursuit of the dive-bombers. Swiftly it went in a wide circle round the convoy, ready to pounce on one of them; but here something unfortunate happened; one of the American cargoes, no doubt mistaking the Hurricane for a German plane, fired what gun or machine-gun it had at him, and the next thing we saw was the pilot baling out by parachute, with nothing to show for his exploit, and with the Hurricane nothing to show for its £5,000. Again the destroyer, which had just picked up the Huns, came to the rescue, and picked him up wet, swearing, but uninjured – so we were later told.

After about three-quarters of an hour the attack ceased, and in groups of twos or threes, the Germans gradually disappeared. They had lost one plane for certain, and another was said to have been seen staggering away, its engine on fire. Bombs had burst and pillars of water had gone up all over the place, but after their first dead set at the cruisers, they seemed to have been unnerved by the terrific barrage the convoy put up, the two cruisers and the destroyers and the corvettes and most of the convoy ships firing like mad, with everything they had, and they did not come near the cruisers – and, therefore, near us – again.

I am trying to remember how I reacted to the whole thing. My first feeling when the deafening barrage went up from the whole convoy, dominated by the great bangs of the naval guns, and the planes swooped over us, and the blue sky was dotted with hundreds of little circular black and white clouds – my first feeling was one of surprise – the surprise of being right in the midst of a naval battle. After that, the dominating feeling was not fear, but excitement; it was the same football match excitement that had sent little ginger-haired Harry into his dancing antic, when the German plane plunged into the water. It was sensationally *new* . . .

When the Wehrmacht had smashed into Russia in June 1941, the Soviet Union and Britain had found themselves in alliance against Germany. As a result Britain agreed to supply the Soviet Union with materials and goods via convoys through the Arctic seas (although the greatest material support still came from the United States). Convoys taking supplies to Russia sailed from Scotland or Iceland, heading for the northern ports of Murmansk and Archangel. The main hazard they faced was travelling close to the German-occupied Norwegian coastline, which left them vulnerable to air attack. These convoys were known as PQ convoys and those returning were called QPs. The series of shipments had begun in the summer of 1941 and up to early 1942 losses had been slight. However, when PQ-8 sailed in January 1942 a U-boat had sunk the escorting British destroyer HMS Matabele north-east of the Kola peninsula with the loss of almost all hands. This pointed to future trouble. In the week following 24 May the Luftwaffe made nearly 250 bomber and torpedo attacks on PQ-16, with which Alexander Werth was sailing, sinking five of its 30 ships. This was the most serious *attack on any convoy in the Arctic so far, but worse was to come.*

In the immediate aftermath of the war Werth became the Sunday Times *Moscow correspondent. During the 1950s and 1960s he produced a stream of serious books and articles about Soviet politics and foreign policy. SEE ALSO PP. 165–6.*

JUNE 1942

R EINHARD HEYDRICH WAS head of the RSHA, the central SS department with authority over all police and security organs throughout the Third Reich, and the Reichsprotektor of Czechoslovakia. On 4 June 1942 he died of wounds he had suffered when attacked by the resistance the previous month. Hitler swore revenge and demanded the killing of thousands of Czechs. The Karl Borromaeus Church, where the operatives and more than one hundred members of the Czech resistance had been hiding, was besieged. The operatives committed suicide; everyone else in the church was killed by the SS. At the village of Lezaky, to the east of Prague, where an SOE radio transmitter was discovered, every adult was killed. The children were forcibly removed to Germany; only two of them would survive the war. At dawn on 10 June all the men of Lidice, a village ten miles outside Prague, were killed.

On 3 June more Allied spitfires were ferried to Malta by the aircraft carrier HMS *Eagle,* and a further consignment arrived on 9 June. Malta was close to Sicily, where the Germans had based very considerable air power, and so it was pounded continually. Efforts to resupply the island by convoy had limited success, with only about half of all shipping getting through. The fighting both in the air and at sea was fierce, but the balance of the supply war in the Mediterranean was gradually shifting in favour of the Allies.

In early June General Ritchie, commander of the 8th Army, attempted to mount attacks on Rommel's defensive positions in the 'Cauldron'. Unfortunately, the British units either blundered into minefields or lost contact with each other. On 11 June Rommel's forces broke out of the Cauldron and threatened Tobruk. The next day the Guards' defensive position at the 'Knightsbridge Box', an area of strong-points defended with wire and mines, came under heavy pressure and the British lost many of their tanks. Knightsbridge was finally abandoned and South African and British infantry began to pull out of their defensive lines at Gazala, fleeing back into Egypt in considerable disorder. On 16 June British forces also abandoned the town of El Adem, and there was clearly no chance of defending Tobruk.

Rommel seized his advantage. Although his forces were exhausted and very short of supplies, they began an attack on Tobruk on 20 June. Within two days the garrison had fallen, with 30,000 prisoners taken. The victors also captured extraordinary quantities of stores, including half a million gallons of petrol. Replenished with this remarkable bonanza, Rommel was given permission to drive on into Egypt. German forces crossed the border on 23 June, causing panic in Cairo and Alexandria. On 24 June General Claude Auchinleck sacked General Ritchie and took control of the battle himself. Auchinleck decided to make a stand at El Alamein.

Tuesday 9 – Wednesday 10 June 1942

Brigadier Claude Vallentin suffers a surprise in the desert south of Tobruk

On 31 May Rommel had launched an attack against the main British defensive position on the Gazala Line to the south of Tobruk. On 5 June General Auchinleck, the British commander in the Middle East, ordered a counter-attack, but British armour was poorly handled and the operation went badly wrong. Some units became trapped in minefields; others attacked the wrong positions. Many British tanks were lost, and by 5 June Auchinleck had decided to halt and await Rommel's next move, which was not long in coming. One of the more experienced formations fighting on the Allied side was the 5th Indian Division, commanded by General Frank Messervy. On 9 June he had directed his forces to set up defensive positions at Trigh Hacheim. Brigadier Claude

Vallentin, aged forty-six, was an experienced officer in charge of the division's artillery and was busy allocating artillery units to support the various defensive 'boxes' that had been created by the infantry using barbed wire and minefields. As he moved between one unit and another he encountered German tanks conducting a probing attack and was forced to flee. Vallentin then found himself isolated with only his command car, his personal staff and driver. Gathering some stragglers from a company of the Duke of Cornwall's Light Infantry, he tried to make his way back to divisional headquarters. His diary captures the events which followed and gives us a sense of the dangerous confusion that attended mobile war in the desert.

I took my cap off and chucked it into the car – it was practically a new one with a somewhat conspicuous red band – and as I was doing so, spotted two tanks about fifteen hundred yards ahead and apparently in or just beyond our main minefield immediately South-East of the Baluchis' box. We pulled up and a quick look through glasses made me suspicious of their silhouette, more than ever as two gun flashes from them were followed by a shell arriving about twenty yards away! We moved on rapidly swerving left . . .

Clear of the minefield, and with no sign of more Germans, I halted to collect my thoughts; while doing so I got Cutler to lug out my bottle of whiskey and we all had a small tot. Macnamara, clicking his heels and saying 'Best respects, Sir' with a quiet twinkle in his eye as he downed his, was worth a guinea a minute; nothing could ever rattle him. The truck, with Balls my orderly and my second driver was also 'up', and halted a hundred yards or so away.

I decided that there was nothing more of use that I could do on my own and with no wireless touch; we had collected some definite and some negative information about the enemy, and it seemed best to take it back direct to Battle Headquarters and fit it into the general picture. We therefore moved off again and, topping a slight rise, saw the mound of BIR HARMAT about a mile to the East of us . . .

I next saw about twenty-five infantry moving in my direction from the south. They were wearing British steel helmets so I drove to meet them and found a Captain and some men of the D.C.L.I. [Duke of Cornwall's Light

Infantry]. The officer, and the men in chorus, told me that they were all that were left of one of their companies which had been guarding gaps in the minefield belt; they had been putting down their own mines in the gaps when Bosch tanks appeared and over-ran them, causing heavy casualties; they claimed to have seen three tanks knocked out by one of the 2 pdr anti-tank guns with which they had been issued the previous day, and were now trying to find their battalion headquarters but were not sure where it was.

The men were in a bad way, they had lost all organization, were thoroughly shaken, and – as usually happens in such cases – as soon as they halted started babbling about their individual experiences . . .

It was no good bully ragging them unmercifully, but firmness was necessary. I told them that I was making my way towards my Battle Headquarters, that I would take them with me, but first they were to organise quickly as three sections based on their Bren guns, and so one platoon. The officer and sergeant responded, and fairly soon we had a platoon of sorts ready to move off. We started off with two sections in line led by myself . . . By now it was about eight o'clock and the sun was just going down. There was not much more than half an hour of daylight left . . . about a mile to our North I could see a leaguer [defended encampment] forming round a burning vehicle . . . We therefore started off towards the leaguer . . .

We had not gone far before a carrier, closely followed by a fifteen hundredweight, came towards us. 'That's all right' I said to the D.C.L.I. captain, 'a patrol to check who we are'. They approached us at about fifteen miles per hour, the carrier with the familiar rocking motion fore and aft. When they were about a hundred yards away I shouted 'Halt, friend!' They did not halt but put on pace. The carrier swung to my right, the fifteen hundredweight to my left, and then halted forty yards away. The 'carrier' was a German half-track with a machine gun in it pointing at us: the fifteen hundredweight was a British vehicle but with a machine gun mounted in front with two visored caps manning it; and previously concealed close behind the fifteen hundredweight was one of those German semi-armoured tracked vehicles with the silhouette of a tank, and mounting a forty-seven millimetre gun which seemed to be pointing straight at my stomach. As I realised this in a split second, a German non-commissioned officer with a tommy gun jumped out of the half-track shouting 'Hands up'. 'B—, they're Bosch' I said, and – there was not much time to think – 'it's no good, pack in'.

It was a neat bit of work just as dark was falling, and, in the state most of us were in I honestly do not think that an attempt at fighting would have been any use. My first re-action was one of intense anger, my next – immediately afterwards – to turn round, tear off my rank badges and medal ribbons, and drop them with my field glasses and revolver in a hole I scuffled in the sand with my foot. Remembering Frank Messervy's experience on the 27th May, I felt certain that provided I could conceal the fact that I was an officer – my cap was still in the car – I would get a chance of escaping that night.

Soon shouting and gestures from the German non-commissioned officer made us collect in a bunch to our right, and while doing so, I was able to whisper to one or two of our men, who started to commiserate with such remarks as 'Bad luck, Sir', not to call me Sir or to let on that I was an officer, and to remind them that Name, Rank, Number was all they should say. We were then filed past a German who carried out a superficial examination of pay books by the light of an electric torch. This rather worried me, as of course I had not got a pay book, however I pulled my identity disc out of the front of my bush shirt and held it towards him. He glanced at it, and after peering into my face remarked 'Ah – old man!' I grunted and passed on, feeling that though I might have a few grey hairs and had not shaved that morning his remark was unnecessary to say the least of it. We then moved off in three's at a fairly rapid walk . . .

About midnight we were moved on again for three quarters of an hour, still with many changes of direction, and here I think that I missed a possible chance of escape. We were made to walk quite quickly, and suddenly and un-expectedly came on two or three old slit trenches which we stepped across. I was in the middle of our little column, and had I only thought fast enough should have dropped into one of them in hopes of not being spotted doing so. The idea only occurred to me as I was crossing the last one and so too late.

We arrived in the middle of a big open leaguer of lorries and tanks, where periodic white lights were being sent up, and lay down while our guards remained standing and extremely wide awake. I then began to realise how very inaccurate was the man who used the expression 'till the sands of the desert grow cold' as a picturesque way of saying 'never', for seldom if ever have I felt so cold as I did at two o'clock on that June morning in the desert. Balls and Macnamara had sensibly collected their greatcoats when we were captured, they got under one and very kindly produced the other for Cutler and myself. Poor Cutler had on desert boots, stockings, shorts, and a thin shirt; I had drill trousers and bush shirt with aertex vest and pants underneath; we huddled together for warmth, but tired as we were found it quite impossible to sleep.

At four o'clock we were again moved on, and nearly an hour later fetched up near BIR HARMAT at what seemed to be a German headquarters, for in the bright moonlight one could see a couple of command vehicles of sorts. What depressed me most, however, was to find a sleeping and muttering mass of British prisoners, at a guess I should say quite a thousand, including a very large proportion of D.C.L.I. We were obviously not the only ones who had been captured.

As the first faint tinges of dawn began to show in the sky, signs of German activity and the starting up of engines became apparent. A German general, a fine looking man, appeared and stood talking for a few minutes to the Colonel of the D.C.L.I. I had a certain temptation to declare myself, the more so as I saw my own car on tow, and apparently still containing a good deal of my kit. However, much as I would have liked to collect a few things, I still had hopes of getting away, so decided to remain quietly among the men, and, if possible, not to catch any German officer's eye. Shortly after five word was passed round for us to get into three's ready to move off, so with Cutler, Macnamara and Balls, I put myself about the middle of the column and stood waiting . . .

At about half past five in the morning we started, a long column of dishevelled figures escorted by single German infantrymen on each flank every thirty or forty yards, and with two fifteen hundredweight trucks mounting machine guns either at head and tail or moving up and down. We were led past the German general, and then down a line of some fifty tanks closed up in column of route ready to move. I counted thirty Mark IVs among the tanks, and from the state of their tracks, bodies and crews, placed many of them as being reinforcements which had certainly not been in the battle since 27th May. There were a fair number of expensive looking Leica cameras among the panzer crews and we were subjected to quite a barrage of snapshots. As we finished this morale raising parade – for the Germans – the tanks moved off due East, leaving me in considerable doubt as to the course of the battle and wondering if the next phase would be an attack on Denys Reid's box at EL ADEM [the 29th Indian Infantry Brigade].

Claude Vallentin appears to have written up his diary shortly after capture. He was one of many staff officers taken prisoner during the desert war. The combination of rapid mobility, vast featureless tracts of desert and the resulting confusion made it easy for commanders to become disorientated and to be over-run by the enemy. His own immediate commander, General Frank Messervy, had been taken prisoner the previous month. Slipping off his badges of rank, Messervy passed himself off as a cook and then managed to escape. Vallentin was not so lucky; he was marched away to Benghazi and spent the rest of the war as a POW.

Wednesday 10 – Thursday 11 June 1942

George Orwell watches the European war from inside the BBC where he works on propaganda

George Orwell was born Eric Blair in Bengal in 1903. He had served in the Burma police in the 1920s and by the 1930s had become a well-known socialist writer and commentator. He fought and was wounded in the Spanish Civil War. Like many writers he worked for the BBC during the Second World War, broadcasting to south-east Asia. His war diary was published in 1968 as part of a three-volume series of collected correspondence and so is not well known.

10 June

The only time when one hears people singing in the BBC is in the early morning, between 6 and 8. That is the time when the charwomen are at work. A huge army of them arrives all at the same time. They sit in the reception hall waiting for the brooms to be issued to them and making as much noise as a parrot house, and then they have wonderful choruses, all singing together as they sweep the passages. The place has quite a different atmosphere at this time from what it has later in the day.

11 June

The Germans announce over the wireless that as the inhabitants of a Czech village called Lidice (about 1200 inhabitants) were guilty of harbouring the assassins of Heydrich, they have shot all the males in the village, sent all the women to concentration camps, sent all the children to be 're-educated', razed the whole village to the ground and changed its name. I am keeping a copy of the announcement, as recorded in the BBC monitoring report.

It does not particularly surprise me that people do this kind of thing, nor even that they announce that they are doing them.

On 10 June 1942 the population of the village of Lidice was forcibly removed. Many of these civilians were systematically shot in groups of ten behind a farm building: 192 men and boys and 71 women were murdered. Other women were sent to concentration camps. The younger children were also removed, some being sent to concentration camps while a few who were considered sufficiently 'Aryan' in appearance were sent to Germany. Afterwards the village was obliterated and all traces of habitation were removed. The name of Lidice was erased on maps and in official records. Predictably, the Czech people now viewed resistance activities with a jaundiced eye. The killing of Heydrich was so controversial that the Czech government-in-exile in London would refuse to take any responsibility for it, even after the war. SEE ALSO PP. 460–2.

Monday 15 June 1942

Chaim A. Kaplan, educationalist and journalist, on profits and smuggling in the Warsaw Ghetto

There is no system to the Nazi killing, but nevertheless the most obvious objective of this carnage is to purge the ghetto of smuggling. In the main, the victims of the shootings are smugglers. The smallest shadow of suspicion that So-and-so is engaged in smuggling is enough to make him a candidate for murder. Jews are not judged, they are merely punished, and there is no lighter punishment for them than death by shooting.

There is continuous war between the cruel, dim-witted Nazis who have condemned us to subsist for a whole month on two kilos of bread apiece and the members of the ghetto who want to live. Even the death penalty has not reduced smuggling. If you can afford to pay twenty-five zloty for a loaf of white bread, someone will throw it into your mouth any time, at any hour you wish. And the same is true of any other delicacies you may crave. The victims among the smugglers fall like barley behind the reapers, but the quantity of smuggled produce in the ghetto does not decline. Every crack is being sealed up; every hole filled in – and the miserable Nazis are dissipating their energies on chaos and vanity. The smuggling doesn't stop. There are even instances of Aryans sneaking into the ghetto to buy produce that is lacking in the Aryan quarter.

And now for the clincher! The Nazis themselves are engaging in smuggling, because it is worth their while. The mice of smuggling, the miserable creatures who smuggle small quantities of produce through the wall, are put to death by the tens, and their death is their penance. This is not the kind of smuggling the Nazis abet. The real smugglers sit at home and no danger awaits them. The Nazi gendarmes receive vast sums of money from them when no one is looking, and the smuggled goods are brought in on loaded trucks through the four entrances that these selfsame gendarmes are guarding. Both sides benefit, and the third side, the ghetto, pays. But it too benefits.

The administration in Warsaw sealed off the ghetto by walling it in on all sides with barbed wire and broken glass. The walls and the passages were guarded by some Germans but mostly Polish police and Jewish police. Smuggling had been widespread since the initial construction of the Warsaw Ghetto in 1940. Average rations were well below subsistence level and so dependence on official food supplies alone would have resulted in the death from starvation of all the population in a short period of time. Consequently, despite repressive measures, food smuggling could not be stamped out.

It was owing to a courageous success in smuggling in the opposite direction that we still have Kaplan's diary. A few days before he was transported to Treblinka in 1942 he arranged for it to be secretly taken out of the ghetto by friends. It was carefully hidden in a kerosene can on a farm outside Warsaw – but was then forgotten, to be discovered, still in its hiding place, only in 1963.

Kaplan was hanged by the Nazis at Treblinka in 1942. SEE ALSO PP. 229–31.

Monday 15 – Tuesday 16 June 1942

James Ambrose Brown, a South African officer, with the retreating 8th Army

James Ambrose Brown was one of the great diarists of the desert war. A South African artillery officer and a veteran of the Abyssinian campaign, he recorded the human experiences of those around him, rather than the course of campaigns and battles. It was now two years since he and his unit had sailed from Durban on a troopship 'cheering like kids at a cricket match'. Their enthusiasm was now somewhat dimmed.

15 June

I am writing this at Bir Hafid, in Egypt. All day elements of the division have streamed, nose-to-tail, along the narrow roads, through the passes and across the desert. Many vehicles from the company have not yet reported in, Captain Rodda's included. Late arrivals report that our rearguard was engaged at the pass but this is not confirmed. It is 16h00 now and I am waiting to go to an Order Group. This may decide our fate and much more . . . the fate of the campaign. I'll give odds that we re-cross the frontier and engage the enemy. Before today I never realised that a division has so much transport – masses and masses of it stretch even to the far horizon where the mirage and heat distortion reflects the mass into the sky so that it appears to be multiplied into infinity. Already there is washing hanging to dry on the old frontier barbed wire erected by Mussolini and canvas lean-tos erected against trucks. Strange how a strand of barbed wire and a canvas overhead gives the illusion of security.

1600 hrs We are temporarily attached to the 10th Indian Division. This is due to the absence of General Pienaar. We are standing by to move as a mobile column. Rumour is rife and upsetting. We hear that Matruh has been attacked – far in our rear! Also, that yesterday the Scots Guards counter-attacked and drove the enemy back to Acroma, somewhat retrieving the situation.

'They always call on our poor bloody Guards,' I hear someone comment, as we stand round the wireless van for the nine o'clock news, 'That's what they're paid for!' comes the answer. Later, as I walk about the immense laager, I see men huddled together in little groups chilling one another's blood with gruesome stories. I hear some unknown man telling that Grant tanks are pouring into Tobruk by night . . . then laughing grimly. 'The rumour is we have no crews to man them.' Now I realise how easily a retreat could be turned into a rout.

16 June

Sergeant Cowan, immaculate even in retreat, was with our rear party. He told me that no sooner had the main body left the old lines at Gazala than the enemy attacked the Cape Town Highlanders' rear party. Our lines including the company areas were heavily shelled by big guns rushed forward for that purpose. Our minefields apparently held them up and the rear party escaped intact to reach the pass at 21h00 where they spent the night anxiously watching the flares of the approaching enemy. Cowan said the rear parties from the 2nd and 3rd Brigades were not so lucky. They were cut off and it is believed they were captured, although some may yet fight their way through. In the bombing of the pass one horrific story stands out. Vehicles were clustered thickly around the bottleneck at the mouth of the pass and two trucks filled with artillerymen plunged to destruction over the sheer cliffs.

Here, on the frontier wire, trucks of all descriptions have poured unceasingly in . . . like a vast cattle stampede. Already the retreat is being called the Gazala Gallop. Some are in tow and many have just made it in an extreme state of dilapidation. Artillery, signal vans, workshops, Bren carriers, staff cars – all the four-wheeled and tracked paraphernalia of a mobile division. What a wonderful target for Stukas! Tomorrow we expect to move to Buq Buq. Today morale is high and steady once more. I feel confident that all will be well, although yesterday I felt that all was lost. A truck has been sent to Matruh for beer – perhaps this has something to do with our recent actions . . . heroism, chivalry, cowardice and brutality. A troop of heavy artillery pieces were attacked by German tanks which closed in under the range of the guns. The men stood to attention by their pieces after the guns were spiked and awaited capture. They were shot to a man. The only men who escaped were the ammunition files some distance behind the guns. Whether this deed was committed out of sheer savagery or because of the inability to take prisoners no one knows. A hospital plane was attacked by an Italian fighter. Suddenly a Messerschmitt flashed out of the sky, shot the Macci to pieces and machine-gunned the pilot who has taken to his parachute. The German pilot then saluted the hospital plane and disappeared. The apocrypha of a lost battle!

Our division has lost 300 men in the withdrawal. Captain Rodda is still missing and Mr Manson and his armoured cars are still unreported. Two sections of 5 Platoon and one of 6 Platoon are still not in. It is hoped they are in Tobruk. Our orders to move to Buq Buq have been changed. We are going to El Hamra, some 27 miles from here to take over prepared positions.

James Ambrose Brown's diary captures the chaos of an army in rapid retreat. The South African Division pulled away from its defensive positions on the Gazala Line and fled down the main road to the east of Tobruk at breakneck speed, knowing that it was within hours of being cut off by the German 15th Panzer Division. Brown's diary also captures the diverse attitudes towards prisoners during rapid advances or retreats, which were often dictated by circumstance and could be very cruel. Nevertheless, the desert war was renowned for being conducted with chivalry, and the shooting of the artillerymen described here was uncharacteristic. This was in stark contrast to the Eastern Front, where troops witnessed the barbarization of warfare. SEE ALSO PP. 439–40, 443–4, 455–6 AND 490–1.

Sunday 21 – Thursday 25 June 1942

Oliver Harvey, Anthony Eden's private secretary, observes
Cabinet panic over the retreat into Egypt

21 June

4 p.m. I've just heard Tobruk has fallen. I'm telephoning to
A.E. in the country to tell him. How right Beaverbrook was
when he said the Germans were fighting here against the
Second Front! I fear this must put us back a lot and even
Egypt itself be endangered.

A.E. much worried, fears there wasn't sufficient garrison
left there. He had had doubts about it. There is to be a
Defence Committee tonight.

22 June

This morning he told me that the Defence Committee had sat
till 2 a.m. not very usefully as Attlee had asked all the War
Cabinet to attend and much time had been taken up by
Bevin declaiming 'We must have a victory. What the British
Public wants is a victory!' As if we didn't all want one! A.E.
spoke to P.M. [in the USA] on the telephone and told him he
ought to come back at once. P.M. appeared peevish and
reluctant and implied he was doing most important things
over there. Very little information yet about the disaster but
A.E. thinks we were both outmanoeuvred and outweaponed.
Yet this was the situation which Auchinleck wanted; he
wanted to be attacked, not to attack . . .

24 June

Auck, I hear, has offered the P.M. his resignation to facilitate
re-organisation. I think both he and Ritchie will have to go.
P.M., I believe, rather favours Alexander to succeed. He is a
fine fighting general who did very well in Burma, but
A.E. says he has no armoured warfare experience or local
knowledge, no great brain. An alternative, I hear, is
Montgomery, a most ruthless man, with pale steel blue eyes

who would clean up Cairo and put the fear of God into the
staff . . .

25 June

We have abandoned Sollum and are falling back slowly on
Matruk lines. Reinforcements are being hurried out from
here and America. But Egypt is in jeopardy . . .

I don't like the news tonight. A most unhappy evening full
of bitter anticipations.

Oliver Harvey was ideally placed to watch the panic that overtook min-
isters in London as Rommel advanced into Egypt and British ships
began to flee the naval base at Alexandria. Churchill was in the United
States and hurried home, bringing with him promises of armoured re-
inforcements from Roosevelt. Meanwhile Attlee and the rest of the War
Cabinet seemed unsure of what to do. Harvey, rightly perhaps, ascribed
the failures to poor leadership and even poorer British tanks. He mused
upon why Britain had produced some of the best aircraft in the world
but the worst armoured fighting vehicles. On 1 July he would note in his
diary: 'We are now back on the Alamein position, the last line before
Alexandria.' SEE ALSO P. 15.

Sunday 28 June 1942

James Ambrose Brown passes local Arabs while fleeing
east into Egypt

28 June

I write this at Abu Mena, near Amiriya – after a slow tedious
journey over the desert, travelling some miles inland from
the main road. The heat today has been terrific and with a
following wind the temperature in the cab of the truck was
almost unbearable. The gauge on the dashboard seldom fell
below 180° and the confined cab, reeking of hot oil, was like
the engine room of a ship. We passed many Arab encamp-
ments on our way, some of them pitched close to ancient
stone buildings. I thought it amazing how primitive these

people still are. They were threshing grain by driving a camel-drawn sledge round in a circle while a man continually fed the grain into the path of the sledge. Watching this primitive exhibition, probably unvaried for thousands of years, I wondered why these people did not utilise the good stone for grinding. Later I watched a family mount and trek away with all their worldly goods and realised that they would not get far with stone mills. The group consisted of three women, a man and a few children. A goat skipped alongside the caravan of a weary donkey, four camels and a yellow dog. The camels, loaded high with tentage and carpets, which bulged far out on either side, swayed slowly past us, noses high in the air, in the usual supercilious camel sneer. I could not help thinking that Arabs lives are, at any rate, their own. They paid us no more attention than if we had been Romans or other conquerors of the past. War or no war they followed their habitual pattern of movement – even through minefields, often with fatal results. As they passed us Bullock raised his hand and shouted a guttural 'Allah akhbar!' To our astonishment the Arab raised his hand [and] came back with the affirmative, 'Allah il Allah!' 'Bull' flushed with pleasure. 'I read it in a book,' he admitted.

Abu Mena was close to Alexandria in Egypt. Brown's unit was continuing to flee from Rommel's attack, which was devastating in its boldness and speed. All of Libya as well as the fortress town of Tobruk had fallen. Although Rommel entered Egypt, his offensive was now slowing. His supply line was very extended and suffering badly from Allied air attack. SEE ALSO PP. *435–7, 443–4, 455–6* AND *490–1.*

Sunday 28 – Tuesday 30 June 1942

Private G. C. Bateman, a British POW, in transit from Tobruk to southern Italy

George Bateman was one of the many British soldiers captured after the fall of Tobruk.

On the 28th June we left for Benghazi airfield. My steel helmet was taken from me with the remark that I should need it no more where we were going! For some time we were left under the wings of a Savoia bomber while the tanks were filled and eventually we embarked. A very fat pilot wearing a 'Mae West' life jacket entered the cockpit. All the Italian Officers waved to us as we took off and for us it was farewell to Africa. There were no seats in the bomber apart from the benches round the sides of an empty bomb rack at our feet. One Italian guard was in charge of every two or three prisoners. Mine remarked that 'Italia e bella e freda' which was of course true compared with Libya and Egypt. He then gave me a small section of lemon which he was eating, followed by an aniseed ball. In payment he asked me to give him my watch and took my refusal with a cheerful shrug of his shoulders. Our flight over a mass of cloud with glimpses of the sea below lasted six hours during which we heartily hoped that the R.A.F. would not spot us. Eventually we saw land, circled over orchards and villages and landed at Lecce in the heel of Italy. We were met by a British Brigadier, who asked us for any British stamps we might have to give to the Italian Colonel who collected them! As we drove through the streets of Lecce there was little sign of hostility on the part of the civilians and we arrived at a hospital outside which were crowds of interested sightseers. We were given soap and led to dormitories with iron beds. In our dormitory was an Italian sentry armed with rifle and bayonet. At our request, and after running to the door to see that no officer was about, he sang 'O Sole Mio' . . .

Although captured by the Germans, these soldiers were technically in Italian territory and therefore prisoners of the Italians. The sea lanes between Tobruk and Italy were increasingly hazardous and so some prisoners went to Italy by air – and some even by submarine! Although the Italians were sometimes visibly short of essential supplies, their treatment of POWs was always good. The first transit camp the POWs encountered was 'comparatively luxurious': they were offered wine and cigarettes and the Italian comandante was very friendly, telling Bateman that his own son was a prisoner of war in England. SEE ALSO PP. 629–30 AND 734–5.

JULY 1942

D URING EARLY JULY, Italian and German forces under Rommel reached heavily defended Allied positions around El Alamein, some 100 kilometres from Alexandria. The defence was initially something of a scramble, and many of the reinforcing units arrived in their positions only just ahead of the German advance. Although there was fierce fighting the Germans were halted by 4 July. Throughout the middle of the month Auchinleck concentrated on attacking weaker Italian formations and some of them were destroyed, forcing Rommel to reorganize and go to their aid. Despite the capture of Tobruk the previous month, Axis forces were still desperately short of supplies and the Italians even diverted some of their submarines to carry supplies across the Mediterranean. Rommel informed Berlin in early July that he did not have the resources to launch any further offensives, and later in the month sent very precise details of his acute shortages of supplies and equipment. The codebreaking efforts of Bletchley Park allowed the British to read all of this communications traffic. In early July, Oliver Harvey noted in his diary that he knew from 'most secret sources' that this was Rommel's last push. The stalemate in the desert would last through August and September. But the balance of the desert war was shifting. While attacks on German convoys in the Mediterranean were gradually starving Rommel of supplies and reinforcements, British losses were being fully replenished with better-quality American equipment, especially tanks. Nevertheless, Allied troops were exhausted after their retreat in unbelievable temperatures, and commanders would take their time before launching a counter-offensive.

By now Churchill badly needed a victory. On 2 July he confronted a censure motion in the House of Commons on the running of the war, suggesting that it was too subject to personal direction by the Prime Minister. Although the motion was heavily defeated, the fact that it had been put at all was a warning. At the end of July Churchill flew to Egypt to oversee radical changes of command. Roosevelt was by now keen to get the United States involved in the ground war in Europe, but at successive

Anglo-American conferences – in Washington in June, in London in July – the British succeeded in persuading the Americans to agree to a north African landing, in the western sectors occupied by Vichy France, as the principal operation of 1942. This would allow Roosevelt to claim some progress towards meeting his earlier rash promise to the Russians that a second front would be opened up in the west in 1942.

On the Eastern Front the Germans continued to make steady gains. On 4 July the siege of Sebastopol came to an end and the Germans took 93,000 prisoners. German forces in the south began to enter the Caucasus and reached the Baku oilfields. By 19 July they had captured Kamesk and secured substantial areas of the banks of the River Don.

In the Arctic the *Tirpitz* had identified the doomed convoy PQ-17 and thirteen of its ships were sunk on 5 July, mostly by U-boats and aircraft. By 9 July it was clear that a total of twenty-four ships from this convoy had been sunk. This disaster called into question the scheme to resupply Russia by Arctic convoy, and for a while these efforts were halted.

Saturday 4 – Monday 6 July 1942

James Ambrose Brown is pulled back from his leave to defend El Alamein

4 July

Red caps waved us through the check posts into the western outskirts of Alexandria. We passed POW areas where bronzed, fit-looking Germans idled in the sun . . . no doubt hoping their captivity was nearly over. To our incredulous joy our new positions are on the sea shore. This is the luckiest break we have ever had. We are stumbling about like kids seeing the ocean for the first time. Imagine . . . a Maginot line on a Mediterranean beach.

We are barracked in concrete rooms below ground level, cool and whitewashed, with bunks for the men. It is marvellous. As I write I hear the surf roaring on a silver beach. Between the pillboxes are budding fig trees and in some places huge bunches of grapes are ripening beneath straggling vines. It is the nearest approach to heaven yet.

5 July

A delightful morning. We swam before breakfast and leisurely organised hygiene. Then suddenly the bottom was knocked out of our little paradise. There is a frantic order for all mortars to return to the front. I felt physically ill. Back to the front! Just as our nerves are beginning to relax.

To have been so close to the outskirts of Alex hoping for a few hours leave, a bath, a haircut, a few good meals and who knows, some of the refreshing incidentals. To be sent back was plain purgatory. To add to it, nearly half our strength has already taken leave. Our own officer and three others have simply disappeared! With this depleted strength I got the men packing frantically, and left for Battalion HQ. As usual we waited. It seemed an age, nervously pacing up and down, cracking jokes we did not feel, and leaking like nervous dogs . . .

6 July

The men who 'escaped' to Alexandria returned this evening looking like the cats which got the cream. George regaled us with some ooh-la-la! He says the famous Berka is in a panic. All the girls are brushing up their German and Italian. 'Gharri drivers draw their fingers across their throats when they pass a British uniform.'

During the desert war substantial efforts were made to provide 'appropriate' rest and relaxation facilities for those on leave. Traditional army practice during leave had been to head into the nearest town, take cheap board and lodgings and then sample some of the earthly delights offered by local bars and clubs. Cities like Cairo and Alexandria had vast areas that catered for this sort of activity, and, although 'off limits' and patrolled by the military police, these places were still much frequented. By 1941 the army had begun to construct rest camps with swimming pools, reading rooms and sports facilities. James Ambrose Brown was able to sample one of these new facilities on the coast – but only briefly. SEE ALSO PP. 435–7, 439–40, 455–6 AND 490–1.

Sunday 5 July 1942

Dwight D. Eisenhower visits Winston Churchill at Chequers

Dwight David Eisenhower, the son of a small farmer, was born in Denison, Texas, on 14 October 1890. He had served in the First World War and specialized in tank warfare. Appointed as an assistant to General Marshall in 1941, his career accelerated and he was picked out to head the US army's European operations. In July 1942, when Churchill and Roosevelt decided on an autumn landing in north Africa, Eisenhower was chosen to command it.

Most of the day in the office, going to Chequers in the evening . . .

The house at Chequers dates from about 1480 and is on the site of an earlier building of which records are kept dating from 1060. It is rather unpretentious but a very good type of English brick architecture of that time. The principal feature of the house is an enormous living room with the ceiling running completely to the roof, around which are built various offices, dining rooms, and dens. On the second floor is a nice movie theater at which the prime minister entertains not only his guests, but all of the retainers of the household. Dinner was at nine with Lady Portal as another guest and Mrs Churchill present. General Ismay and Commander Thompson [Churchill's naval aide] were the only other persons at dinner.

In the evening we saw a movie, *The Tuttles of Tahiti*, an American picture starring Charles Laughton. Fortunately it was in the lighter vein and was hilariously funny. All of us, including the prime minister, had a thoroughly good time.

After the movie, the prime minister and the rest of us talked until about 2:30 AM. We were interrupted frequently to receive reports coming from all corners of the world, principally the Middle East and naval reports concerning the convoy of north Norway. Whenever these reports were of a favourable nature the prime minister's conversation would glow for the next thirty minutes or so. Conversely, a pessimistic report would get him in the dumps. Upon going to bed at 2:30, I found in my room a book that dealt exclusively with the history of Chequers, together with the furniture and objects of art all over the place. I could not go to sleep without reading that part applying to my own room. I slept in an enormous oak bed, four poster, with enormous bulges on the posts at intervals, each elaborately carved, the whole surmounted by a canopy, which instead of being of fabric was solid oak, apparently about six inches thick. The oak was black, either from coloring or from age, and elaborately carved as well. This room was supposed to have been frequently used by Cromwell, whose daughter had married the then owner of the house. Cromwell's picture hung in the room where I slept. Also there was a desk of inlaid wood that was reported to have been one of his favorites.

We rose at 7:45 in the morning, went downstairs to a breakfast that was typically American. Wayne and I each had two fried eggs and plenty of fried ham. Immediately after breakfast I inspected a guard of honor made up of a detachment of the Coldstream Guards. General Clark accompanied me, and both of us were impressed by the very elaborate drill, manual of arms, and ceremonies that the British have set up for this kind of performance. They were a magnificent body of men, the shortest being at least six feet.

We left Chequers at ten o'clock and arrived in London a bit after eleven.

Eisenhower's encounter with Churchill was not untypical and revealed the Prime Minister's prodigious appetite for films and also his love of talking late into the night. Eisenhower did not share Churchill's absolute confidence that the Vichy French in north Africa would not oppose an American landing, or that such a campaign would draw German resources away from the Eastern Front, thus helping the Russians. North Africa had been chosen in preference to a landing in France, which Churchill believed would be 'slaughter' at this stage of the war given the absence of Allied air superiority. SEE ALSO PP. 449–50 AND 659–60.

Monday 13 July 1942

The Countess of Ranfurly, working for the British
administration in Jerusalem, is taught instinctive shooting
by the Palestine police

*On General Wavell's departure from Egypt in late June 1941, the
senior officers decided to attach Hermione Ranfurly to Sir Harold
MacMichael's staff in Jerusalem. By now her husband Dan had been
taken prisoner and so being located near his unit was no longer of great
importance to her.*

*At a party at the King David Hotel in Jerusalem on 12 July the
Countess became embroiled in an argument about the current German
successes and what would happen if the Germans over-ran all of the
Middle East. On learning that she did not know how to use firearms, a
Palestine police officer suggested that he teach her. The next evening she
began training on one of the first 'close quarters battle ranges' to be set
up in the Middle East. Although these elaborate ranges, with their
moving targets and hidden traps, are commonplace today, they were an
innovation in 1942.*

This evening I went straight from the hospital to the police
station on the Jaffa Road. Red Face was waiting for me in a
bare Arab room. I asked his name. 'Call me Abercrombie,' he
said, 'it's as good as any other. Now, sit down,' he continued,
'I shall tell you all I know. I was taught in America by "G"
men and I am a bloody fine shot. Make the gun part of your
arm. You must get so accustomed to it that when you point
at anything you damn well hit it. What do you do when you
eat? You put your fork in your mouth, not in your cheek.
See? When you wipe your nose, you find it first shot. So it is
with shooting. It must be. Now. Take this gun. Don't be
afraid of it: it won't bite.' He showed me how to hold it
easily in my hand, how to cock it and recock it without moving anything but my fingers and wrist. 'Never pull the
trigger,' he said, 'Your gun is like an orange in the palm of
your hand. You must squeeze that orange.' He strode up and

down the small room jerking out his directions, telling me to think of my gun as a pencil with which I must learn to write, neatly and indelibly, in bullets.

He took me over to his range. It was dark inside and after the stark Palestinian sun I could not see. 'There are six dummy men in here,' he said, 'Stay where you are and use your eyes. Kill them.' He was unsparing. I shot with my right hand, with my left hand, and with both hands. I hated the noise and blinked my eyes. My wrist wobbled; my mind wobbled. He made me go on. Sometimes I shot in the dark. Sometimes he turned on the light. He bawled. I shot. 'One, two. One, two. Now left. Now right. Now both together. Squeeze that orange. Keep your eyes open.' Sweating and shy I plugged on, standing close to and then far from his life-size dummies. After an hour he told me to return at the same time tomorrow.

In early July 1942 the desert war had continued to sweep eastwards along the north African coast. This moment represented the high tide of Rommel's success as he advanced to within 75 miles of Alexandria in Egypt. Hermione Ranfurly had worked for SOE in Cairo and knew many senior commanders. Her diary records that British officers working at GHQ Middle East in Cairo were outwardly bullish, but privately nervous. Some had secretly purchased bicycles which they kept in their apartments as a guarantee of swift exit in case Cairo was over-run, confident that so equipped they could escape with ease alongside roads that they knew would be choked with refugees. In reality Rommel's supply lines were now hopelessly over-stretched and the tide would soon turn again. Although Rommel was halted, the episode signalled the end of Wavell's command of the Middle East. SEE ALSO PP. 289–90 AND 721–2.

Wednesday 22 July 1942

Eisenhower records arguments over a projected invasion
of France in 1942

The last few days have been tense and wearing. We have had
numerous conferences with General Marshall and Admiral
King on the subject of the Sledgehammer attack [plans for an
amphibious operation to invade the continent through
France in 1942]. The British have placed themselves on
record time and again as being definitely against this attack.
First, because they believe it would have no beneficial effect
on the Russian situation, and second, because the chances of
tactical disaster are very great. The chances for tactical
disaster arise out of the disparity between ourselves and the
Germans in available military formations and out of the
terrible weather conditions that prevail over the Channel
during the fall.

The burden of stating, for the American side, whether or not
the capture of Cherbourg is a feasible military operation has
been placed upon General Clark and myself. It is a tough
decision to make because so many imponderables are
involved and because the time required for mounting the
attack is so long. We had always understood that the British
staff believed they could mount an attack of this description
within sixty days after receipt of notice – they now demand
four months, with an absolute minimum of three. This makes
the earliest date for the attack October 15. We feel that in many
respects the October 15 attack is a much more highly dangerous affair than the September 15; this due to weather and to
strengthening of German defences as well as to the possibility
of their transferring troops from the Russian front. Moreover,
if the attack is to help the Russians, it ought to be delivered at
the earliest possible date.

Clark and I finally told the general that if he thought the
Russians were in bad shape and that an attack on the French
coast would have a material effect in assisting the Russians,
we should attempt the job at the earliest possible date –

regardless. We do not say that the thing will be a tactical success, but we do say that with wholehearted co-operation all the way round we have a fighting chance. As a result, we advised to fight for the proposition and to insist on making the attack. This was a tough recommendation to make, and I sincerely hope that it works out with reasonable success.

We have sat up nights on the problems involved and have tried to open our eyes clearly to see all the difficulties and not to be blinded by a mere passion for doing something. However, this last factor alone is worth something. The British and American armies and the British and American people need to have the feeling that they are attempting something positive. We must not degenerate into a passive mental attitude.

General Marshall, Roosevelt's Chief of Staff, favoured the idea of an immediate invasion of the continent and a drive for Berlin. The British, however, had real doubts. They knew that the Germans had thirty divisions waiting to oppose them in Europe and that the Allies lacked enough landing craft and air cover to effect a successful landing. SEE ALSO PP. 445–6 AND 659–60.

AUGUST 1942

BY AUGUST 1942 the 'wizard war' was becoming increasingly important. In an unseen conflict, scientist was fighting scientist with new electronic weapons that were being hurried into service. The Allies had made some advances in radars designed to search for submarines, but in August 1942 the Germans began to fit their U-boats with radar detectors. Similarly, in the air the British were using an electronic navigational bombing aid called 'Gee', but by August 1942 the Germans were able to jam its transmissions, making it more difficult for the RAF to find its targets.

Partly as a result of this, the RAF brought in 'pathfinder squadrons' whose job was to mark targets ahead of the main bombing force.

On 3 August Churchill and Alan Brooke arrived in Cairo on an investigative tour of the 8th Army. They had concluded, quite rightly, that leadership was uneven and that, given the Allies' material superiority, more should have been achieved. This review coincided with the death of General Gott, one of the few competent British desert commanders, in an air crash. As a result, on 15 August Montgomery took charge of the 8th Army and immediately began to strengthen defences. Rommel launched a further attack at the end of August, but was still short of supplies. His tanks ran into elaborate minefields, and as British air superiority took its toll the attack petered out.

Closely connected to the desert war were desperate Allied naval operations aimed at continuing to resupply Malta with vital fuel for its aircraft. This was essential if Malta were to continue to interdict Rommel's supply lines. On 11 August a massive convoy led by two battleships, four carriers and seven cruisers escorted fourteen merchant ships towards Malta. A carrier – HMS *Eagle* – a cruiser and a destroyer were sunk, but vital supplies, including the vital tanker *Ohio* with its cargo of aviation fuel, reached the port of Valletta.

On 19 August 6,000 Allied troops conducted a raid on the heavily fortified port of Dieppe. The majority of the forces were from the 2nd Canadian Division, who were joined by British Commandos, together with some American and French forces. The operation was an unmitigated disaster. Very little damage was inflicted and over half the force was lost. The experience underlined the difficulty of amphibious operations against a defended coast and fed into deep British anxieties about opening up a second front in Europe prematurely.

Sunday 2 – Saturday 15 August 1942

Commander Blundell sees the HMS *Eagle* sink while escorting a convoy to Malta

2 August

During Monday we had a damage control exercise, put back the Pom-pom ammunition into 'D' magazine which now has a 'box' welded over the crack in the ship's bottom, got the P.U.'s and exercised night emergency procedure.

On Tuesday 4th we had about 14 destroyers screening us and each one tried to pretend there was a submarine. For an emergency turn, one long blast is given, followed by short blasts to indicate direction. We had a great day working fire extinguishers whilst doing damage control and gunner drills . . .

I read the orders for the operation. It makes me sweat reading the bit about the poor convoy getting through the last bit. Otherwise it is just one of our usual club runs through the Med, leaving the poor blighters in the Skerki Channel. The last party that tried it got rather badly beaten up, and I suppose, this time we are doubling our stakes. For we have 2 battleships, 3 aircraft carriers, and a hoist of destroyers, not to mention the 14 merchantmen. With us we have a cameraman called Ewins and an RAF W/T Intelligence officer called Grum – and a Constructor Commander Skinner who is a reported expert on Damage Control . . .

9 August

At 23.00 I went to the flag deck. A perfectly clear sky, with the Milky Way banded across it and every star shining good-will upon our enterprise. Cape Spartell light to starboard and Cape Trafalgar to port. [This was the western part of the Straits of Gibraltar.]

I felt indeed that some of our party were entering the narrow seas on a desperate venture and prayed to the Ruler of Destiny for his favour on our venture.

11–15 August

So much has happened during these days and the Commanders life in a ship like this is so busy that it is impossible to do much writing. And what a tragic failure this convoy has been! Nine ships out of the fourteen [merchant ships] lost, and great damage and loss to warships. The first terrible thing happened about 13.15 on Tuesday. A submarine got inside the screen, and the first anyone knew about it was to see 'Eagle' listing over to starboard as far as her flight deck. No noise, nothing was heard. One minute there was serene blue sea with peaceful ships and hardly a cloud in the sky or ones mind. Next moment there were some billows of smoke from 'Eagle', mostly funnel gas, I thought, and she had gone in eight minutes. I've never before seen such a thing. It makes one tremble. If anyone took good film of it, it should be shown throughout the country and especially to the Director of Naval Construction and his department. She rolled over bottom up and left her bow jutting up in the air before plunging. One couldn't believe that was the Eagle, or had been the Eagle. I remember thinking of the trapped men. I saw Skinner, the constructor looking like a man who had seen a horrible nightmare; he was sweating and white and I heard him say 'They couldn't have had anything closed' . . .

That night I was planning to give a final pep talk to the ship's company, but it was not to be, for at 20.30 we sounded off, 'Alarm to Arms', followed by the alarm rattlers. Then followed two of the most exciting hours of my life. At about 21.00 we were missed by two torpedoes as near as any ship has ever been; one passed for'ard, its bubble track actually went under us, and the other passed aft. It can hardly have missed us by more than a few feet. Bombs fell all over the place. When it got darkish, about 21.15, the barrage put up by the fleet and its screen was aesthetically one of the weirdest, most beautiful and wonderful I have ever seen: the purple sea, black sky, red in the west, pearls and rubies of the tracer necklaces, lurid bursts in the sky, and the dark little ships. People who had seen it all had a look on their faces as if they had seen a vision, the sort of expression a man would have on his face as if he had looked on the Almighty.

On Wednesday we were closed up at 1st degree AA stations all day. These days, this includes the 16-inch turrets, because we fire 16-inch shells set to burst at 3,000 yards. Our 16-inch barrage was very effective against torpedo bombers appearing low over the horizon. It spread and threw up a curtain of spray through which the planes seemed loath to fly. Our fighters were up and back the whole day, and broke up most of the enemy formations before they got to us. Those that got through got a good dusting from our destroyers. Nothing came near us all day, except three planes which got within fair range of our close-range weapons and were all shot down.

The 'Deucalion' got a near miss and dropped astern. Poor 'Deucalion', who has had such former adventures in the Med, was ordered off to try and creep along inshore, but she was sighted by a U-boat who finished her off. We had three near misses on our port side from one bomb attack, and later on several fairly near the port bow. Incidentally the only 'wounds' we received in the whole trip were two bits of deck with small tears in them starb'd side of the foc's'tle. Just after 7 p.m. there was a fierce air attack. I counted about a dozen torpedo planes coming in on the starboard bow, but they were beaten off by our 16' barrage. Just after this, about 14 Stukas caught 'Indomitable' just at the wrong angle, coming down on her out of the sun.

'Indomitable' disappeared, for all we saw of her for minutes was columns of spray. Finally the maelstrom subsided, and there was 'Indom', still there, but blazing both for'ard and aft of the island, with great columns of smoke pouring from her flight deck.

'Nelson' and 'Rodney' were ordered to leave the convoy and turn back to shield her, the Admiral feared that torpedo planes would try and finish her off. So we said goodbye to the convoy, and shortly after we left, they got beaten up pretty badly – it's a pity we couldn't have stayed a little longer.

We paddled away out of the area as usual at about 20 knots with 'Indomitable', 'Victorious', 'Rodney', 'Scylla', 'Phoebe' and destroyer screen. The convoy going through the Skerki Channel had a terrible time, submarines doing most of the damage. 'Cairo' and 'Manchester' were sunk. 'Nigeria' and 'Kenya' torpedoed, and eight of the surviving merchant ships were destroyed. Only 'Port Chalmers', 'Brisbane Star', 'Melbourne Star', 'Rochester Castle' and 'Ohio' (although the latter was torpedoed) got into Malta. What a price to pay!

Operation Pedestal was mounted to resupply Malta in the full knowledge that the losses were likely to be severe. During July 1942 the 8th Army had fought off significant attacks by Rommel and was holding the Africa Korps out of Egypt at El Alamein. The Germans were now known to be over-extended and had insufficient supplies to push further. Meanwhile Montgomery was building up supplies for a renewed effort to push the Axis back into Libya. Malta had to be resupplied at all costs. Accordingly, the convoy escort was immense, including two battleships and three aircraft carriers, accompanied by seven cruisers and four destroyers. The loss of the Eagle *typified the navy's problems with old ships, for she was in fact an ancient 'convert', having been laid down as the cruiser* Almirante Latoire *for the Chilean navy in 1914 and taken over at the start of the First World War by the Royal Navy. Later she was converted to an aircraft carrier and renamed* Eagle. *So old a ship had severely limited internal strength and thus equally limited chances of survival.*

Although George Blundell, the second-in-command of the Nelson, *saw this part of the battle, he did not witness the last phase of the convoy, as the escorts turned back. Spitfires from Malta battled to protect the* Ohio *and, against all odds, she would eventually be nursed into the harbour at Valetta on 15 August.* SEE ALSO PP. 337–40.

Friday 7 August 1942

James Ambrose Brown, a South African officer, on the problem of 'bomb happiness' in the western desert

This evening I have a feeling of weakness in the small of my back, with headache and slight nausea. I don't know whether I am going to be ill or not, but I am not going to report sick. I haven't had a day off duty in the regiment so far and I do not want to break my record. Many men are going daily down the line. Those who are more fatigued than ill are sent to a rest camp at a pleasant spot near the sea, back at Division, to give them some relief from the continuous gunfire. We all admit to a degree of 'bomb happiness'.

After our first action in Somaliland in December 1940, the term was unknown to us. No man in those heady days of success against the Italians in East Africa would have applied it to himself – and yet, peculiarly enough, we were more afraid of gunfire in those days, those far-off days of our inexperience, than we are now. The shock to the system is more mental today, more delayed, deeper.

Formerly we felt an instinctive physical longing for cover. Today we know only a dull mental desire to be 'right out of it!' Yes, though we grow more and more habituated, more attuned to fire of all descriptions and our personal reactions less apparent on the surface, the shock has a deeper and more lasting effect.

Today the element of chance plays a tremendous part in our lives. We sit on our bedrolls calmly and impersonally watching comrades only a few hundred yards away running and dodging through the smoke and dust of shellbursts. We have arrived at a stage, we old timers, where we can judge to a near thing just where shells will land. Further away than say, 300 yards, we can ignore them. To duck and dive away would be an admission of fear. It is not *done*! Yet we joke about being 'bomb happy!'

The issue of psychological exhaustion, battle fatigue and shell shock was a serious one in the desert war. Some troops serving in Ethiopia had been under bombardment on and off for two years. By early 1942 desertion had become a problem. Some were 'temporary deserters' who lay low or ran away when the fighting started, but returned to their units hours or days later, claiming to have been separated from them in the confusion of battle. The rate of surrender was also high. Auchinleck was so alarmed that he asked London for permission to reintroduce the policy of shooting deserters; but the War Office realized that even if the problem were serious, they dare not admit it, either at home or to their enemies. SEE ALSO PP. 435–7, 439–40, 443–4 AND 490–1.

Friday 14 – Friday 28 August 1942

Padre J. Ellison Platt meets Douglas Bader in Colditz prison camp

British army Methodist chaplain J. Ellison Platt had refused to leave his wounded men at Dunkirk and was captured in June 1940. He was one of the first people to arrive at Colditz Castle, a special camp built to house repeated escapers. He had not in fact been an escaper, but had made a nuisance of himself by badgering to be transferred to camps where his work as a padre could be more useful. Once he arrived at Colditz, he focused on maintaining the spirits and sanity of his fellow POWs. He kept his own spirits up by writing an 800-page diary.

14 August

I may be mistaken, but I see it as one more sign of prison-weariness. I cannot imagine the British officers who were in the IVc [prison camp] twenty-one months ago giving their parole for anything. They were escape-minded, hating enemy detention and discipline as a wild bird hates the bars of its cage. This was the tough guys' camp, and to escape was the first and last duty of a British officer POW. 'No trucking with the enemy so long as a state of war exists' was the oft-repeated maxim.

Parole was first given for certain additions to theatre equipment; next for Red Cross cases in which to store clothes. Today about twenty-five officers – some belonging to the original seventeen of the early days – have given their parole to play football on a piece of ground outside the *Schloss* boundary.

17 August

Wing Commander Bader – the legless air ace – has arrived. He is as vital as a naked electric wire. He walks well without the aid of any stick or crutch. All nationalities are thrilled by his presence, and doubly so when they have felt the pep of his conversation . . .

24 August

Bader continued his talk today when he spoke in the theatre about the Battle of England. The 'Battle of London' he thought would be a better name.

Bader had a command in southern England at the time, and possessed complete information about the strength of the defence. Some of us were almost incredulous when he told us how small the British fighter strength was, and how few the pilots after the losses at Dunkirk . . .

28 August

Dickenson received fourteen days' *Stubenarrest* [solitary confinement] for his escape from the cooler. Rumour has it that the *Posten* whose negligence made the escape possible received an exemplary sentence of six months' *Strengarrest*. Poor devil!

Dickie had escaped by leaping the eight foot wall surrounding the enclosure in which he was given daily exercise. And, three hours after receiving sentence, he made another – unhappily abortive – attempt to escape. By a clever ruse, and just under a *Posten*'s nose, he slipped under a motor-van delivering bread, and stretched himself flat under the body of the car, his feet and legs over the covered-in propeller shaft towards the big end, and his hands and head on the back axle. The van drove out of the *Hof*, and we thought he was all set for a rough journey to the bakery and a reasonable chance of escape. Alas! the doors at the rear of the van bounced open just outside the main gates, and drew the eyes of the *Posten* on duty. Dickie was hauled out.

Douglas Bader commanded No. 242 Squadron, a Canadian unit within the RAF. He soon proved to be an inspiring if unorthodox leader. During fifteen months of operations he accounted for more than twenty-two enemy aircraft. On 11 August 1941 he had bailed out of his Spitfire leaving one of his artificial legs (the right) behind. He became a POW and, having made two attempts to escape, was moved to Colditz Castle in August 1942. Within Colditz, Bader could be temperamental and enjoyed teasing the guards – a pursuit known as 'goon baiting'. Other British officers looked upon 'goon baiting' as childish and counter-productive.

Ellison Platt remained a prisoner until Colditz Castle was over-run by American forces in 1945. Bader left the RAF in July 1946 and returned to his pre-war employers Shell Oil. In 1976 he was knighted. SEE ALSO PP. 22–3.

Monday 17 August 1942

Elena Skrjabina experiences German occupation in Pyatigorsk

Elena Skrjabina was born on 13 February 1906 in Gorky. She had spent her childhood in St Petersburg, where her father was a representative in the last Russian parliament before the 1917 Revolution. In 1925 she married Sergey Scriabine, an engineer, with whom she had two sons. When the Germans had invaded Russia in June 1941 her husband was drafted into the Red Army, while the rest of the family endured the siege of Leningrad until they were evacuated in early 1942. There followed an arduous journey to Pyatigorsk in the Caucasus mountains, during which Skrjabina's mother died and her son Sasha suffered a severe illness.

Our greatest worry was the [Jewish] students living in our pantry. They could not stay there forever. Yesterday evening when the office was closed they came and told us that they had decided to leave. They knew someone in Essentuki whom they could count on. It's difficult to give advice under such circumstances. When it had become completely dark, they left their refuge. I hope everything comes out alright. It does not appear that the German units which we saw are very interested in the Jewish question. The 777 Column which has set itself up in our orchard and in the basement is for the most part favourably disposed toward us. The soldiers begin washing early in the morning. This is an endless procedure and takes place in the yard by the well pump. After that they have breakfast in the garden. Watching them through the window we are amazed at the abundance of food and by the prevailing cleanliness and order.

Elena Skrjabina's family were hiding two Jewish students in their pantry when German troops were suddenly billeted upon them. The pair quickly moved on, and the German troops proved to be amiable; indeed, they restocked the pantry of her near-starving family. She noted: 'There were heaps of food on the tables and the shelves.' In early 1943 when the Red Army advanced, Elena and her family would flee to Bendorf, near Koblenz in the Rhineland. There she worked in German munitions plants until the city was over-run by the Allies in March 1945. Now hopelessly separated, Elena Skrjabina and her husband Sergey each thought the other dead. Sergey would remarry, but died in 1946. In 1950 Elena moved to the United States and was asked to teach at the US Air Force Language Training Program at Syracuse University. She completed her doctorate in 1962 and taught at the University of Iowa until she retired in 1974.

Wednesday 19 – Saturday 22 August 1942

George Orwell, working at the BBC, hears about efforts to cover up the failure of the Dieppe raid

19 August

Big commando raid on Dieppe today. Raid was still continuing this evening. Just conceivably the first step in an invasion, or a try out for the first step, though I don't think so. The warning that was broadcast to the French people that this was only a raid and they were not to join in would in that case be a bluff.

22 August

David Astor [*Observer* editor] very damping about the Dieppe raid, which he saw at more or less close quarters and which he says was almost a failure except for the very heavy destruction of German fighter planes, which was not part of the plan. He says that the affair was definitely misrepresented in the press and is now being misrepresented in the reports to the PM and the main facts were: – something over 5000 men were engaged, of whom at least 2000 were killed or prisoners. It was not intended to stay on shore longer than was actually done (i.e. dawn till about 4 pm), but the idea was to destroy all the defences of Dieppe, and the attempt to do this was an utter failure. In fact only comparatively trivial damage was done, a few batteries of guns knocked out etc. and only one of the 3 main parties really made its objective. The others did not get far and many were massacred on the beach by artillery fire. The defences were formidable and would have been difficult to deal with even if there had been artillery support, as the guns were sunk in the face of the cliff or under enormous concrete coverings. More tank-landing craft were sunk than got ashore. About 20 or 30 tanks were landed but none were got off again. The newspaper photos which showed tanks apparently being brought back to England were intentionally misleading. The general impression was that the Germans knew of the raid beforehand. Almost as soon as it was begun they had a man broadcasting a spurious 'eye-witness' account from somewhere further up the coast, and another man broadcasting false orders in English.

In retrospect the idea of raiding an objective that was as well defended as Dieppe appears bizarre. Surrounded by cliffs and high sea-walls, a more unlikely target could not be imagined. The results were predictable and the Dieppe raid, which lasted less than a day, cost the Allies severe losses. The planners of the operation, who included Montgomery and Mountbatten, would later assert that vital military information was gained. They certainly learned that more sophisticated amphibious equipment would be needed in the future. However, some historians have questioned the purpose of the raid, claiming that it was merely a political gesture designed to please Roosevelt and Stalin. The Canadians bore the brunt of the casualties at Dieppe, losing 907 killed, 2,460 wounded and 1,874 taken prisoner by the Germans. Of the 2,210 who returned to Britain, only 236 were unhurt – and 200 of these were men who had not been landed.

In 1943, Orwell's work took a different turn and he began to write a column for the socialist weekly magazine Tribune. *During the latter years of the war he also completed a novel that satirized Soviet-style communism, which he had seen at close quarters during the Spanish Civil War. His usual publisher, Victor Gollancz, rejected it and, because it effectively attacked one of the major wartime allies, he was unable to find a pubisher for the book before the end of the war. Entitled* Animal Farm, *it was finally published in late 1945 and proved extremely popular. After the war Orwell's health began to fail, and he died in 1950.* SEE ALSO PP. 432–3.

Wednesday 19 August 1942

Anne Somerhausen, resistance worker and mother, sells a portable Corona typewriter

Anne Somerhausen was married to Mark, a Belgian member of parliament who had served in the First World War and rejoined the Belgian army in 1940. He had been taken prisoner, leaving Anne to provide for their three boys, John, Matthew and Luke. She rented out rooms, worked in an office and also assisted the Belgian resistance. But the cost of black-market food was also forcing the gradual sale of their material assets.

Two plus two equals four. Official rations plus black market food equals bankruptcy. The arithmetic of it is all very simple. I am broke again; or rather, I was till this afternoon. Having sold two paintings at bad prices in recent months, and, for a good price, two asthmatic old vacuum cleaners stored away in the attic, I had finally advertised that I was willing to sell a portable Corona. It was Mark's ten-year-old typewriter. The advertisement was published this morning. At noon, when I returned from the office, a young man was coming for the third time to see me about the typewriter. I told him my price, 5000 francs, trembling inwardly lest he find it too exorbitant. He pulled out a fat wallet, put down five one-thousand-franc notes on my desk, grabbed the typewriter and walked out. I ran to the door, saw him get into a motor car with engine still running (an insane waste of precious gasoline), and drive off with two heavily painted and marceled blondes nestling against him.

When one's capital has dwindled to 200 francs, and 5000

francs drop into one's lap for a mere typewriter, life seems pretty good. I told my tale this afternoon at the office – and got a thorough scolding from Monsieur Pottieuw, our buyer. 'Your typewriter is worth 10,000 francs. The Germans are buying up all the typewriters they can find in Brussels, and they prefer portables to all other types. They send out Belgian men to make the deals. Your young man will get paid the German standard rate for your typewriter: 12,000 francs. He would have made a reasonable profit of 2000 francs if you had held out for 10,000. You are' – he swallowed – 'a goose'.

'How long has this raid on our typewriters been going on?' I asked.

'For about a week. When they have the number of typewriters they need they'll stop buying and then the price will go down again. They'll start buying vacuum cleaners next.'

I am a goose, and this is the strangest war there has ever been. Are the Germans shooting with typewriters and bombarding with vacuum cleaners? Or are they simply emptying our country, in exchange for bad banknotes, to fill up theirs?

The drawing away of Belgium's typewriter stock was a classic example of how Germany bled the economies of neighbouring countries. In the inter-war years, German companies such as Mercedes had manufactured typewriters. But now these factories were busy producing vehicles and armaments. With typewriter production in Germany at a standstill, so neighbouring countries were stripped bare to supply German needs. SEE ALSO PP. 13 AND 857–8.

Monday 31 August 1942

Captain L. T. Tomes escapes over the wire at Warburg POW camp

Captain Tomes served in the Royal Warwickshire Regiment and had been captured in northern France in May 1940. He was then moved to a holding pen at Trier with many thousands of other prisoners, mostly from the French army. A few weeks later he was moved to an officers-only camp at Mainz where he met a number of senior French and Belgian generals. In August 1942 he was moved again, to a POW camp at Warburg.

9.30 p.m. saw us waiting in a hut near the wire with complete kit, blackened faces, balaclavas, packs on and socks over our boots. It was a stifling hot evening anyway and everyone was dripping with perspiration. At 9.45 the lights went out all around the wire and some 30 seconds later we got the signal to go and each team filed out of the huts carrying their ladders. It seemed all too light and certain that we could easily be seen as our ladder . . . was only 50 yards or less from the nearest sentry. However, all ladders were successfully launched, though A. had a nasty moment when our crosspiece caught on the telegraph wires and teams began to stream over.

The whole operation took such a short time, 40 seconds, from the hut until it was all over that one hardly had time to worry about what would happen if the lights suddenly went on or shooting started. A., F., C., T. and Fred all went over like cats and I was over and had dropped on the far side scarcely before I realised it. I was vaguely aware of a shout and a shot when I was halfway over.

Then began a dash thro' 50 yards of some root crop and for our team a sharp left-hand turn to the north-west. Having run straight into a strand of barbed wire some 3 feet off the ground dividing two fields, I picked myself up somewhat torn and shaken and looked around for Fred who was not more than a few yards ahead and we ran on together. By now there were a lot of shots going off and cries of 'Halt' behind us. Having run about 300 yards through crops of cabbage and beet, we stopped from sheer inability to go on and walked as fast as we could. My pack seemed like several tons, my throat dry and like sand paper and my legs seemed to have lost all their power. At that moment, more than any other during the whole trip, I felt almost incapable of going on and that my six weeks in hospital [with diphtheria] had made it physically impossible. I was however revived by [sound of] the puffings and blowing of Fred and by emerging into more easy going.

Captain Tomes and his friends would stay on the run until 10 September 1942, when they were spotted by German civilians. Although Tomes spoke good Serbo-Croat, without identity papers the escapees failed in their efforts to pass themselves off as volunteer Croatian railway workers. They were handed over to the police. Tomes spent the rest of the war in captivity.

SEPTEMBER 1942

IN AUGUST AND September 1942 the US 8th Air Force launched its first major bombing operations over Europe. As yet its attention was focused on Belgium and France and it was not yet flying penetration missions into Germany. At this stage of the war much US air strength was being held in reserve for the planned invasion of French north Africa, which would take place in November under the overall command of Dwight Eisenhower.

On the Eastern Front the Germans reached Grozny in the Caucasus. Although they had hoped to reach Afghanistan and even prompt a revolt in India against British rule, in fact this was as far east as German forces would go during the Second World War. Major fighting continued to the north of the city of Stalingrad and the Germans began to close in around the city. The Germans hoped that this would be another episode in which a long siege would be followed by a mass Soviet surrender. However, here the Russians proved to be masters of the art of urban warfare and turned the tables on their opponents.

Attention was beginning to be focused on the scale of German atrocities against the Jews. During the previous month the British section of the 'World Jewish Congress' asserted that one million Jews were already dead in occupied Europe.

Tuesday 1 – Sunday 6 September 1942

Dr Paul Kremer, an SS doctor, records the comforts of his life at Auschwitz

Before the war SS-Obersturmführer Johann Paul Kremer had been an academic. He had received his PhD in 1914 and by 1927 he was a professor and head of the anatomical institute at the University of Münster in Westfalen. He joined the Nazi party in 1932 and secured a place in an SS reserve unit as early as 1934. He arrived at Auschwitz at the end of August 1942 to replace a doctor who had fallen sick.

1 September
Have ordered SS officer's cap, sword-belt and braces from Berlin by letter. In the afternoon was present at gassing of a block with Cyclon B against lice.

2 September
Was present for the first time at a special action [gassing] at 3 am. By comparison Dante's Inferno seems almost a comedy. *Auschwitz* is justly called an extermination camp! . . . .

5 September
This noon was present at a special action in the women's camp ('Moslemes') – the most horrible of all horrors. *Hschf* Thilo, military surgeon is right when he said to me today that we are located here in *'anus mundi'*. In the evening at

about 8 pm another special action with a draft from Holland. Men compete to take part in such actions as they get additional rations – 1/5 litre vodka, 5 cigarettes, 100 Grammes of sausage and bread. Today and tomorrow (Sunday) on duty . . .

6 September

Today an excellent Sunday dinner: tomato soup, one half of chicken with potatoes and red cabbage (20 grammes of fat), dessert and magnificent vanilla ice-cream. After dinner we welcome the new garrison doctor, *Obersturmführer* Wirths from Waldbröl. *Sturmbannführer* Fietsch in Prague had been his regimental surgeon.

One of Kremer's tasks at Auschwitz was to carry out assessments of anyone attempting to gain admission to the hospital. The weaker individuals were almost all killed by phenol injection. He then chose from the remainder those prisoners who struck him as particularly good experimental material. He would question them about such personal details as their weight before arrest and any pills or medicines they had used recently, before conducting horrible experiments upon them. Kremer would eventually be arrested by the British and in 1947 gave testimony before a Polish court in Krakow. Although he was sentenced to death, his sentence was later reduced to life imprisonment. He would be released in 1958 on the grounds of advanced age and good conduct. In 1964 he was still giving evidence at trials and inquests at the age of eighty. His diary is regarded as one of the more important documents of the Holocaust and is much discussed. SEE ALSO PP. 759–61.

Early September 1942

Neil McCallum disembarks at Suez and meets his first Egyptian

Neil McCallum was born near Edinburgh in 1916. In 1942 he was a junior infantry officer in the British army in Egypt. His diary, like so many desert war diaries, is elegant, philosophical and punctuated by occasional black humour. Although McCallum is one of the finer diarists of this conflict, almost nothing is known about him.

The disembarkation was at Port Teufig, Suez, and there was my introduction to the wog, a generic word covering every person of swarthy colour in the Middle East, applicable to all indigenes but reserved especially for menials. It is a portmanteau word, a word of reference, and a word of contempt. Its usage indicates that the wog is one of the lesser breeds, one of the naturally under-privileged, who has had the misfortune not to be born a European, and the particular bad luck not to be born British.

The first Egyptian I saw in Egypt was a baggage man who climbed up the companion-way that had been dropped from the liner to the first of a series of lighters. He arrived at the top and his ragged bulk blocked the light in the square hatch. He was pounced on by a staff officer who cuffed his ears, kicked him, swore at him in English and pidgin Arabic, cuffed him again and then ordered him to lift some baggage. The incident suggested a relation of white to coloured people that does not often receive attention outside the countries where it is normal. One saw at once that the occurrence was normal, both in the way the officer delivered the blows and the way the wog accepted them. It was the correct way of getting things done.

It took some days to absorb this fact, that in Egypt the casual servant works when he is beaten. It took some further days to absorb the deeper truth, that the wog will not work without being beaten or threatened, that otherwise nothing will be done, not out of laziness but out of contempt.

McCallum, along with Cecil Beaton, is one of the few diarists to reflect upon the impact of war on the indigenous peoples of the countries in which the combatants fought. He defined the relationship of the European to the menial Egyptian servant as one of 'mutual distrust' that was 'degrading to both parties'. He added that matters were made worse in Egypt by the massive wartime influx of Europeans who had never been abroad and had 'quaint' ideas about foreigners. These people, he noted, quickly became arrogant and tyrannical.

The origins of the term 'wog' are not clear, but it may well have originated in Egypt during the nineteenth century, where 'Working On Government Service' was a label displayed on the clothing of non-British workers during the construction of the Suez Canal. Others have suggested that it originated in India and meant Westernized Oriental Gentleman. In either case the initial meaning was probably not derogatory, but it became so over time. SEE ALSO PP. 14, 528–9 AND 541–3.

Monday 7 September 1942

Harry C. Butcher, personal aide to Eisenhower in London, loses a page of the headquarters diary – and records his anxiety in his own

Harry C. Butcher was born in 1901 and developed a career as a leading radio manager. By 1929 he was director of the CBS office in Washington, which offered him excellent contacts in the Washington establishment. By 1934 he was president of WJSV (later WTOP) radio in Washington. In 1939 he joined the naval reserve as a lieutenant commander and spent the period 1942–5 as Eisenhower's personal aide. In early September 1942 he was working for Eisenhower in London as they prepared for the Allied invasion of north Africa, codenamed Operation Torch.

The planners may be perplexed, but no more than I, and I'm worried as well. A page of the [headquarters] diary is missing; *it's the page of the first TORCH directive to Ike to clean up the North African coast*. If some enemy spy has managed to get that sheet, all our hope of attaining surprise is already in vain. In merging the official and personal items into one set of pages, many pages had to be recopied and renumbered. This the faithful Miss Jaqua has been doing for many long days. The loss was discovered during the process of microfilming. I had sent Miss Jaqua, Corporal Marshall (General Ike's personal stenographer), and Mickey, with side arms, to the Army's film laboratory to do the job. In the process, page 117 was discovered missing – just wasn't there.

Although there seems no other conceivable way for the sheet to get out of our offices, which are guarded not only by the Marines at the entrances, but by guards in the Commanding General's outer office day and night, the darn page is gone.

We have searched and re-searched, but no page 117. It must have been discarded and burned in the secret stuff Miss Jaqua had finished copying, but that's not definite.

Had to tell Ike today, though I hated like poison having to add to his worries. He was considerably upset but was so considerate I could have wept. Said not to tell anyone outside the office, as there is no need of alarming the whole headquarters, but to continue the search. After all, I'm responsible and probably should be sent home on a slow boat, unescorted, to use one of Ike's favorite expressions.

Butcher helped to keep the headquarters log or diary, which also contained key orders and directives. This stayed within the secure confines of his own office, where sensitive material was usually kept in a safe or a steel press. The loss of a single page could cause havoc.

Security problems raised by diaries of all kinds would not end in 1945. The Allies were keen to keep all sorts of clandestine techniques – including codebreaking and deception – a carefully guarded secret long after the war was over. The British and Americans quickly came to an agreement to screen all memoirs and diaries that were prepared for publication in order to ensure that references to the secret war were removed. Butcher's own personal diary, published in 1946, was thought remarkably candid at the time, but in reality it was one of the first high-level wartime diaries to be subjected to this process whereby the darkest secrets of the war were sanitized before publication. SEE ALSO PP. 27, 544–6, 561–3 AND 712–13.

Thursday 10 September 1942

Anne Brusselmans of the Belgian resistance hides Allied airmen in Brussels

Anne Brusselmans, an Anglo-Dutch woman in her thirties with a family, was an extraordinary heroine of the Belgian resistance, assisting downed Allied airmen to evade the German occupation forces. Her escape line was always busy: at one time she had some fifty airmen under her care hidden in various parts of Belgium.

The other night I had to fetch in two Americans, Hank and Martin. Hank hails from Chicago but is far from looking like a gangster. Mart comes from Ohio.

Martin still bears the marks of the heavy burns he sustained when he jumped out of his 'plane in full daylight. All his clothes were on fire everything he had on was burning except his parachute.

The two Americans landed near a river, which Hank helped Mart to cross by swimming beside him. He then took him to shelter amongst the bulrushes. Meanwhile, the Germans had seen the men come down and were searching the countryside for them, so they hid in this swamp for nine hours. At night they were helped out of their uncomfortable hiding-place by members of the Belgian underground movement who, in a boat rowed by the young son of the local farmer, brought a doctor and a nurse with them to give Mart morphia and attend to his burns before taking them both off to the nearby farm.

After staying in the district until Martin's burns were healed the two men came to Brussels. There was then the usual procedure first, at Mr P's house, where it was decided that as it was late Martin should stay the night but that I would take Hank to stay at my house.

It is now dark, and as we walk part of the way home we stumble, for we can't see very much. The Brussels streets have cobbles which date back to the 16th century, or at least they feel as if they do. I know the way pretty well, as I have done this journey often in the heavy black-out, but Hank, poor man, I pity him . . .

Half-way home we took a tram and it so happened that the two carriages were filled with Germans. I jumped in first and saw Hank hesitate, just for a second. Then he got on after me. We were the only civilians in this tram. Hank's face was not expressive.

There was no hesitation, however, when I went to get off. Hank jumped up double quick and followed me at once. He heaved a sigh of relief, and as a matter of fact, so did I. If those Germans had only known what a bundle of medals they were missing.

The following day I took Hank down town again to have his photo taken for his French identity card.

The Brusselmans family apartment was known to the underground resistance movement simply as 'Rendez-Vous 127'. With a British mother and a Belgian father, Mme Brusselmans' loyalties and languages made her an ideal guide for downed Allied airmen as they sought to escape Hitler's security troops. From 1940 through to Belgium's liberation in 1944, Anne would assist more than 130 airmen in avoiding capture. She gradually developed a network of 'safe houses' across the city, always checking that the occupants were not planted by the Gestapo. The pilots who came to stay at 'Rendez-Vous 127' were introduced to her own children as their 'Flemish cousins'. This arrangement was decided upon because the pilots didn't speak French and the children couldn't speak Flemish, and it provided a reason for speaking in English. As she later explained, eventually her children found out the real identity of their many 'cousins' and realized the danger that their activities involved. SEE ALSO PP. 738–40.

Wednesday 30 September 1942

Field Marshal Sir Alan Brooke, Chief of the Imperial General Staff, in London

During afternoon Harker and Lennox from MI5 came to see me with reference to a conversation between Kenneth de Courcy and Raikes which they had intercepted on a concealed microphone in their room. It went very near having discovered all about the North Africa attack and evidently had been obtained from someone in possession of plans. They did not dare show it to Duff Cooper their legitimate boss as they were uncertain how much he knew about this plan of attack. I discussed it with Pug Ismay and decided that it was safe for Duff Cooper to see, but that he should let P.M. see their conversation.

Alan Brooke's diary records a conversation with Brigadier Harker, Deputy Director General of MI5, and one of his colleagues. The people whom they had placed under microphone surveillance were two British Members of Parliament, Kenneth de Courcy and Henry Raikes, who had gained unauthorized and early knowledge of Operation Torch, the Allied attack on north Africa scheduled for 8 November 1942. The MPs were certainly not privy to this very sensitive information and it was Duff Cooper's job, as the minister responsible for MI5, to find the person who had leaked the information, by deploying 'his agents'. Duff Cooper told Churchill and Brooke that he suspected the Army's Director of Military Operations, John Kennedy (whose diary is also included in this anthology), but the source would eventually prove to be an SOE officer who had been 'talking too freely'. SEE ALSO PP. 26 AND 720.

OCTOBER 1942

HITLER HAD BEEN greatly aggravated by the Dieppe raid of August 1942. He was even more annoyed by a Commando raid on Sark in the Channel Islands, launched on 4 October. The Commandos took five soldiers prisoner but, as they were being escorted to the beach, they began to struggle and scream for help. Fearful of being discovered, the Commandos killed some of the prisoners, their hands still tied behind their backs, and abandoned them. As a reprisal Hitler ordered that all prisoners taken from Commando or other special forces were to be shot immediately. He also ordered all the British populations of the Channel Islands to be deported to concentration camps in Europe.

In the air war, RAF bombing of the continent continued to intensify. Targets in Germany included Flensburg, Essen, Cologne and Munich. The RAF also began to bomb Genoa, Turin and Milan. These operations involved the dropping of over 4,000 tons of bombs. By contrast, on the British home front October saw fewer and fewer night raids, which were now occurring as infrequently as once a fortnight. Although the Luftwaffe were trying to mount reprisal raids, they were increasingly ineffective and involved heavy aircraft losses. The war on the Eastern Front had eaten into German bomber reserves, with over 1,000 aircraft being deployed around Stalingrad alone. On the home front in both Germany and Britain the shortage of labour was beginning to tell. On Thursday 22 October the British government reduced the call-up age from twenty-one to eighteen.

Just before midnight on 23 October Montgomery launched his attack on Rommel's forces at El Alamein. This desert offensive depended on extensive artillery bombardment and elaborate deception measures. He was assisted by the fact that the Germans were, as ever, short of fuel. Moreover, Rommel himself was back in Germany and his deputy commander, General Stumme, died of a heart attack just as the offensive began. Although British losses were high, they were affordable because of good reinforcements and supplies. Rommel's troops had neither, and German retreat was inevitable.

Sunday 18 – Monday 19 October 1942

R .L. Crimp, rifleman and former bank clerk, on taking care of yourself in the desert war

18 October
Nobody knows exactly-when the 'party' is booked to come off. But there's a full moon towards the end of the month.

19 October
Letter from home: 'Do take care of yourself.' Good Lord, as if I ever do anything but! Of course I always take all the cover that's going, and keep my swede down as long as possible. But what's the good? Bill Vole moved heaven and earth to get a job with Rear Echelon, but when a stray Jerry strafed his convoy miles back he got his lot just the same. On the last Jerry push, six weeks ago, there was Johnny Gussett in 'A' Company carriers, wireless operator. He'd only just joined us from the base, where, his old 'Terrier' Batt having been broken up, he'd been sitting pretty for nearly a year. Yet in that one night's skirmishing a Breda shell went through his carrier, through his set and through him. Even Stingo Carstairs (the bandit of 'S' Company), speeding by truck into Cairo on leave, hit a tram, then a tree, and finished up in the military cemetery.

So using your loaf doesn't get you far in keeping it safe. You can only wait – and see. The odd man can't wait, and clears off (not without sympathy). But that wouldn't solve much either, with the thought of letting them down at home, pay stopped, and other complications.

'Do look after yourself.' Rather a problem, eh, chum?

Last letters home today. You shove them under the cushion of the driving seat of the colour sergeant's truck and wonder whether they'll ever get there.

Crimp's diary reveals the sense of foreboding among the ordinary soldiers as the 8th Army approached the launch of its new offensive at El Alamein. It also captures the feeling of frustration on the part of soldiers who realized that real war was far removed from the conflict depicted on cinema newsreels for those back home. Even at the time, military research increasingly showed that soldiers in battle rarely aimed their weapons or tried to kill the enemy. Instead they often 'kept their swedes down', pointed their weapons in the general direction of the opponent, and fired them to give some semblance of activity or to give themselves comfort. As Crimp had learned from his own experience, most deaths occurred as the result of the use of heavy support weapons; those hit by rifle fire were unlucky. SEE ALSO PP. 362–4.

Friday 23 – Saturday 24 October 1942

Andy Fletcher, an Australian soldier at El Alamein, discovers the problem of taking prisoners under fire

I found this fellow who I believe was a Doctor and a Jerry with most of the skin blasted off his back, so what was I to do with them. The Dr indicated that the fellow could not be moved. There were telephones – quite a few of them – a switch board etc which should not be left there and capable of sending back reports to Jerry.

Should I have shot them or not, (we would not be allowed to go for the tanks I feel sure). I did not know what to do, but whether it was right or wrong I disconnected the switchboard and left them. I know they could hook a couple of wires together to make calls but it was shoot them in cold

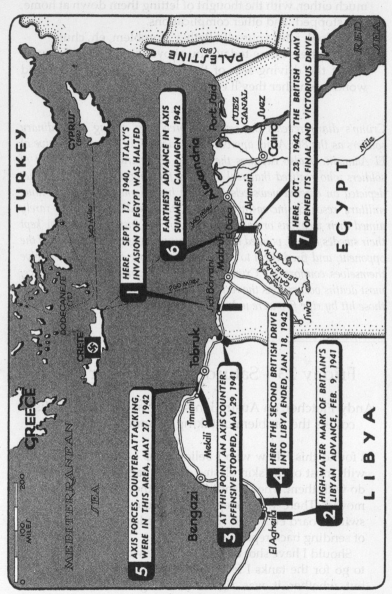

1 HERE, SEPT. 17, 1940, ITALY'S INVASION OF EGYPT WAS HALTED

2 HIGH-WATER MARK OF BRITAIN'S LIBYAN ADVANCE, FEB. 9, 1941

3 AT THIS POINT AN AXIS COUNTER-OFFENSIVE STOPPED, MAY 29, 1941

4 HERE THE SECOND BRITISH DRIVE INTO LIBYA ENDED, JAN. 18, 1942

5 AXIS FORCES, COUNTER-ATTACKING, WERE IN THIS AREA, MAY 27, 1942

6 FARTHEST ADVANCE IN AXIS SUMMER CAMPAIGN 1942

7 HERE, OCT. 23, 1942, THE BRITISH ARMY OPENED ITS FINAL AND VICTORIOUS DRIVE

The War in the Western Desert, 1941–2

blood or leave them – so I carried the switchboard in front of me, it was more uncomfortable than heavy and had gone about 100 yards when swoosh-bang. One of the tanks had fired a 50mm armour piercing shell at me at a range of 400–500 yards. 'Well that's put the cat among the pigeons – what do I do now?' It wasn't very close I guess he missed by 4–5 feet but should I run, go right, go left, go to ground, drop the switchboard or what? So I just walked on, went about another 40–50 yards and swoosh-bang 'Bloody hell – I'd better do something now'. Then I remembered Dick Hall in the battle of Tel El Esia in July knocking out a tank and three fellows were running away. He blew one fellow's head off as they were running and the other fellows came back and surrendered. I just walked on.

Another 30–40 yards and so on – swoosh bang. I do not know if it touched my trousers at knee height or the wind off it, but I felt something on my leg. The shell hit the ground a few feet in front and screamed away.

'Well that's torn it – the bastards mean business now' – had better do something. Left, right, down or run . . . I just walked on why I do not know surely the next one he could not miss. I was not frightened, but fully expected to be hit with a shell weighing 5lb solid steel – could imagine my chances.

Fully expecting everything, I just walked – NOTHING HAPPENED – why – still nothing – why. I feel that if I had run, veered off or gone to ground they would have kept on firing. I don't know why he did not use his machine gun. (I would not mind meeting him to find out his reasons).

When I got back our position was not good – guns not dug in properly and while we were digging in, Jerry opened up with machine guns. Reckon he kept following me but just couldn't hit me.

We had taken over 2 Jerry anti-tank guns, we had one gun knocked out and one truck out by then and 4 chaps wounded. At about 8.30 I heard that another fellow was wounded so went to see him and had just left him to come back to the wireless when the machine gun out of the tank opened up again. I was standing up in a hole and reckoned he was a crook shot [severely injured], but he wasn't quite as bad as I thought. I managed to get a luger [a German pistol].

He started a burst which was hitting about ten yards to the right of me and kept on firing and he could see where the bullets were hitting and just traversed his gun over onto me. All I felt was a thud in my leg and just sat down. Told a fellow I had been cracked. Yanked the pants down and was bandaged up, could not feel much, could not move much. Jerries had us pretty well taped then and every time we put our head up there was a burst. The Shermans [tanks] could not get onto him properly.

Going into the show I was pretty well equipped. I had a great coat, bottle of whisky in each pocket – reckoned they would see me through the stunt, but early in the morning it got too hot so just threw the coat in the hole, reckoned I'd be back later – but did not get back there. Forgot to tell anyone about it so guess there is still a great coat with a couple of bottles of black label in a hole out there.

About 4.00pm that arvo a truck came up to take five of us out who were wounded. No red cross flag or anything. I was put on first and had to sit on the top of the truck while they loaded the other chaps for about 5 minutes. To make matters worse, I was sitting on top of a box of sticky bombs [improvised grenades] so was not too happy.

The shelling and sniping stopped for a while. Went back to the RAP [Regimental Aid Post], had a TT injection and shoved straight on. One of my drivers was there giving a hand and gave me two snorts of whisky, so from then on did not care about any shelling – slept a fair bit. On the way back to the MO's, we pulled up a few times on the way, usually there was a cup of tea or two waiting. From the MO's we went to the CCS [Casualty Clearing Station] at Burg El Arab, and were to go into Tommy's CCS but they were so full of New Zealanders and Indians so we ended up in the Australian CCS luckily. Arrived there at 10am with all the dope – slept pretty well. Woke up there was only one other Australian in the place. Porridge for breakfast. A sister came and asked for Australians to go right to the 7th Australian General Hospital. As the other fellow had to have a dressing or some such thing, I was lucky and sent there. There were 5 of us in the ambulance, mostly broken bones so was a slow trip, about 10 miles/hr. Did not think we'd ever get there. Was an AT driver and she could drive, extra careful so the fellows were as comfortable as possible. Called into the British hospital to put one chap off as he was too crook to go any further. Then the road was much better, but did not arrive at the 7th until 5pm so was extra pleased to get there. Was carted to a ward. The first bloke I saw was Les MacLarn, he had been hit earlier in the shoulder. Bert Sheldon was also there. It was pretty well a continuous stream coming in. Everyone asked for news from the latest arrivals. Ron Leach came just after me, the CO Lt Col Turner was still at the mds [main dressing station]. The 13th copped it pretty heavily. For a start and all through. Curly Wilson of the 17th came through and told me Jim had been hit but not seriously and came into hospital that day. All the fellows we knew seemed to be getting cracked.

Andy Fletcher's diary has the 'stream of consciousness' feel of diaries kept under fire, and captures many of the realities of life on the battlefield. Prisoners often surrendered at the most inconvenient of times – halfway through a long patrol, or on a battlefield where escorting them to the rear area was impossible. The alternatives were often to shoot them or to ignore them, and in the desert the latter option was usually taken. Fletcher's diary also refers to the importance of alcohol on a battlefield. Here many of the Australian troops had been under continuous shell-fire for almost a year in conditions that were sometimes not dissimilar to those of the First World War. Battle fatigue was also an increasing problem.

Andy Fletcher survived the war and returned to Australia, where he married and went into sheep farming.

Wednesday 21 – Saturday 31 October 1942

Dr Zygmunt Klukowski watches the killing of Jews in three Polish villages

Dr Zygmunt Klukowski was the youngest of three children in a Polish family from Odessa. At the turn of the century he had attended medical school in Moscow, but also spent time in gaol for Polish underground activity. During the First World War he fought in the Russian army, but after returning to Poland in 1918 found himself serving in the Polish army against the Russians through to 1921. In the inter-war years he became the long-serving superintendent of Zamosc country hospital near Lublin in eastern Poland. After a month as a medic in the Polish army against the Germans in 1939 he returned to his post in the hospital at Zamosc. Klukowski had always been fascinated by history and assembled a unique collection of books on regional history. He also maintained a daily diary, secreted within the hospital, at some risk to himself.

21 October

Today I planned to try to go to Zamosc again. I woke up very early to be ready, but around 6am I heard noise and through the window saw unusual movement. This was the beginning of the so-called German displacement of Jews, in reality a liquidation of the entire Jewish population in Szczebrzeszyn.

From early morning until late at night we witnessed indescribable events. Armed SS soldiers, gendarmes, and 'blue [Polish collaborationist] police' ran through the city looking for Jews. Jews were assembled in the marketplace. The Jews were taken from their houses, barns, cellars, attics, and other hiding places. Pistol and gun shots were heard throughout the entire day. Sometimes hand grenades were thrown into the cellars. Jews were beaten and kicked; it made no difference whether they were men, women, or small children.

By 3pm more than 900 Jews had been assembled. The Germans began moving them to the outskirts of the city. All had to walk except for members of the *Judenrat* and the Jewish police; they were allowed to use horse-drawn wagons. The action didn't stop even after they were taken out of town. The Germans still carried on the search for Jews. It was posted that the penalty for hiding Jews is death, but for showing their hiding places special rewards will be given.

All Jews will be shot. Between 400 and 500 have been killed. Poles were forced to begin digging graves in the Jewish cemetery. From information I received approximately 2,000 people are in hiding. The arrested Jews were loaded onto a train at the railroad station to be moved to an unknown location.

It was a terrifying day. I cannot describe everything that took place. You cannot even imagine the barbarism of the Germans. I am completely broken and cannot seem to find myself.

22 October

The action against the Jews continues. The only difference is that the SS has moved out and the job is now in the hands of our own local gendarmes and the 'blue police.' They received orders to kill all the Jews, and they are obeying them. At the Jewish cemetery huge trenches are being dug and Jews are being shot while lying in them. The most brutal were two gendarmes, Pryczing and Syring . . .

While I was gone, the gestapo, local gendarmes, 'blue police,' and some street people in Szczebrzeszyn again started the hunt for Jews. Particularly active was Matysiak, a policeman from Sulowo, and Skorzak, a city janitor. Skorzak had no gun, only an ax, and with the ax he killed several Jews. The whole day people hunted and killed Jews, while others brought corpses to the cemetery for burial.

24 October

In Szczebrzeszyn the hunt for Jews is still on. Additional gestapo agents came from Bilgoraj. With the help of gendarmes, 'blue police,' and some citizens they looked everywhere for Jews. All cellars, attics, and barns were searched. Most Jews were killed on the spot, but some were taken to the Jewish cemetery for public execution.

I witnessed a group of Jews being forced to march to the cemetery. On both sides of the prisoners marched gendarmes, 'blue police,' and so-called Polish guards dressed in black uniforms. To speed things up the Jews were beaten on their heads and backs with wooden sticks. This was a terrible picture.

Around noon the gestapo ordered that all men over the age of fifteen be ready by 2pm, with shovels, to start the burial of the Jews. The sale of alcohol to Polish people was stopped. All restaurants are now off limits . . .

26 October

Yesterday, on Sunday, the hunt for Jews was still on. Approximately fifty people were killed and their bodies transported to the cemetery. Approximately one hundred more were taken to the cemetery in two groups, women and children in one, men in another. All were killed.

I witnessed how Jews were removed from a hiding place in the rope-maker Dym's house. I counted approximately fifty Jews as they were taken to the jail. A crowd looked on, laughing and even beating the Jews; others searched homes for more victims.

26 October, 6 p.m.

People coming from town are talking about more German cruelties. My niece Zofia Karolakowa witnessed two gendarmes halt a young Jewish girl. She was beaten, kicked and finally when she was unable to walk she was pulled by her hair to the cemetery and shot. Medic Matuszewski witnessed as Majewski, gestapo agent from Bilgoraj, shot five young Jewish girls.

On all sidewalks there are numerous blood stains. At the city jail every so often there are executions. No one works at city hall except the secretary, Babiarz, who in the absence of the mayor is running the city, and a few clerks who are directly involved in murdering the Jews. Some employees ran home, unable to stand it anymore, but others have become completely apathetic.

Now the robbery of Jewish homes is on the increase. To

prevent this the 'blue police' shot a young boy and a young woman, Felka Sawicowna. Throughout the entire day horse-drawn wagons hauled Jewish households to warehouses for storage.

This is so difficult to describe. I am making these notes on the spot, without any literary elaboration.

27 October
This is not the end. Action against the Jews continues, but there are not many Jews left. People walking on the street are so used to seeing corpses on the sidewalks that they pass by without any emotion. The body of a Polish boy, killed for robbery, lay on the street for more than twenty-four hours.

28 October
I went to town twice and both times I observed a group of Jews being taken to their death. I saw an old Jewish woman unable to walk anymore. A gestapo man shot her once but she was still alive; so he shot her again, then left. People see this now as a daily event and rarely react. I do not know why, but my reaction to these crimes is different from before.

29 October
No change. Horse-drawn wagons are still bringing Jewish goods to the marketplace. The gendarmes sort everything out. Some bedding and household items were given to the hospital; the same as in other cities. I am not at all pleased with this, but with a complete lack of supplies I decided to take them and register them into the hospital inventory.

30 October
Today there were still some more Jews executed at the cemetery, but most of them were from nearby villages. The gestapo arrived from Zamosc and brought with them a few trucks. They confiscated the best furniture from Polish apartments.

31 October
Still some Jews are hiding. Besides the gendarmes and the

'blue police,' four members of the Jewish police are very active in hunting the Jews. They know the hiding places, and they hope they will survive. One thing is sure: they will be the last ones shot.

Zygmunt Klukowski's diary provides a remarkable record of the German and Ukrainian efforts to exterminate the region's Jews in 1942. He was well aware of the fate of the Jews who were taken away, noting as early as April 1942 that they were killed with either gas or electricity and their bodies burned. More than 90 per cent of Poland's 3 million Jews died during this period. Throughout this terrible time Klukowski remained at his post offering medical treatment to all without discrimination. SEE ALSO PP. 649–51.

Saturday 24 – Monday 26 October 1942

Evelyn Waugh referees an army cadet field exercise at Sherborne School

The novelist Evelyn Waugh joined the Royal Marines in 1939 and by 1940 was a captain in command of a company. During 1941 he had served in the Commandos in Crete under Colonel Robert Laycock, who later led a famous raid on Rommel's headquarters in north Africa and whose diary is also included in this anthology. Later that year, on the long sea journey back from the Middle East via the Cape, Waugh had written Put Out More Flags, *a novel set in the period of the phoney war of 1939.*

24 October

Brian, Basil [Bennett] and I, also Tom Churchill and Johnny Atkinson went to umpire a field day at Sherborne School. The exercise, needless to say, was in withdrawal: the boys correspondingly pusillanimous and protection-minded. I spoke to some, asking what regiments they hoped to join; they all wanted to be government chemists or public health officers. The exercise dragged on without incident until nightfall, when all the umpires quietly slipped away to their dinners. Basil and I drank a bottle of Dows 1920 before dinner and another after it. Then we remembered we had been asked to 'sandwiches and beer' with Colonel Randolph the Commanding Officer. We found him sitting behind mountains of food none of which, having cigars in our mouths, we attempted to eat. I was full enough of wine to believe the evening a success but the general opinion is the reverse ...

25 October

... A beautiful day of overeating and overdrinking. In the afternoon we went to Melbury. That evening I was very drunk indeed and enjoyed myself enormously. When I left the house at about 2 I fell down some steps ...

26 October

Called at 6.30. Still very confused with drink and smelling of 'orange gin'. Drove as far as Camberley in a stupor where we had a collision which destroyed the car. Got a lift to Combined Operations HQ where I arrived four hours late ...

Waugh spent 1942 in Britain as a unit intelligence officer and by October had been posted to Sherborne, where the castle was employed as a services headquarters. Quarrelsome and bibulous, Waugh was not a particularly professional soldier, and his commanding officers soon learned to keep him well away from front-line operations, directing him instead towards the labyrinthine world of liaison and staff intelligence work. Waugh's diary chronicles his prodigious alcohol intake in minute detail: he was certainly not unique in drinking on a vast scale, but few recorded their consumption so obsessively. SEE ALSO PP. 24–5, 692–4 AND 768–9.

Friday 30 October 1942

Friedrich Reck-Malleczewen, Prussian aristocrat and anti-Nazi, watches the first bombing of Munich

I watched the first bombing of Munich from a hotel room in Alt-Otting, where I have come to examine the material on

Tilly located here: a hideous red glare, transforming the autumn night and its full moon. I heard in the distance the muffled booms, and it was calculated that since the bombs were dropping eighty kilometers away, it had taken three minutes for the sound to carry – three minutes during which the victims at the scene had been gasping and gagging and dying. Finally, the whole of the sky to the west was a gigantic sheet of fire.

In the days that followed, people spoke of fantastic losses, largely due to suffocation. People were still being dug out five days later, wedged in among fallen beams and rubble, where they had been unable to move. And then there were the dead, whose faces still bore the marks of their last agonies.

Since many high-ranking Nazis have private and luxuriously appointed residences in Solln, which the English evidently know, that unlucky suburb was bombed three times in succession. Werner Bergengruen, who lives there, lost all his manuscripts, his collections, the whole of his possessions when his house went. He was seen the next day in a state of shock and despair, perched on the pile of ruins that had been his house, offering passersby the few things that had survived the holocaust: a Latin primer, a small bronze, a couple of Chinese objets d'art. Alongside was a hand-lettered placard announcing that this was a special sale by [a] German writer of the remains of his possessions. The police tried to drive him off, but he defended himself so energetically, and the crowd standing about was so sympathetic, that the gendarmes had to retreat.

Herr Hitler happened to be in Munich the night of the air raid, and before the alarm had been sounded for the *misera plebs*, he was already safely tucked away in a private shelter complete with rugs on the floors, baths, and reportedly, even a movie-projection room. Thus, while hundreds and hundreds of people buried under rubble struggled horribly to breathe, he might well have been watching a movie . . .

Munich, the birthplace of Nazism, was a favourite RAF target. By the end of the war more than half the city's buildings lay in rubble, many having been badly damaged as early as 1942. Almost all its fine Renaissance and neo-classical buildings were literally bombed off the map, although these depredations have since been disguised by the extensive restoration and reconstruction of the city's many monuments. Munich would suffer badly during the war: 22,000 men of military age died in campaigns, while the civilian population of the city was reduced by almost a quarter of a million by the end of hostilities. These statistics reflect a growing trend throughout the twentieth century: it was increasingly dangerous to be a civilian in wartime.

Reck-Malleczewen lived through some of Germany's worst times only to die in a concentration camp on the eve of the armistice, executed by a shot in the neck in Dachau in February 1945. SEE ALSO PP. 334–5.

NOVEMBER 1942

IN NOVEMBER 1942 the Allies made significant progress. British forces were victorious at El Alamein, although they were slow to capitalize on their success and could have advanced more quickly. On 4 November Rommel told Hitler that he must retreat, and on 12 November British units re-entered Tobruk. Montgomery's victory had not only changed the course of the desert war but had also salvaged Churchill's reputation as a war leader. Convoy supplies to Malta were improving, with greater air cover and reduced losses to shipping. In practice the 'siege of Malta' was now over.

Operation Torch, launched on 8 November, involved the landing of 35,000 American troops on a wide front on the north-west coast of Africa near Casablanca. Germany began to fly troops into Tunisia to bolster the Vichy French regime there.

The growing atmosphere of crisis in Vichy French territories was reinforced on 11 November when German forces began the occupation of those parts of France hitherto controlled by the Vichy government. Hitler assured Marshal Pétain that the purpose of this move was to protect France against the Allies. German troops took control of key points such as the naval base of Toulon. Meanwhile Churchill urged Italy to rise up against Hitler and Mussolini.

German forces were now dangerously over-extended on the Eastern Front. The focal point of this vast military confrontation was the gruelling fighting around the city of Stalingrad. Here Germany's General Paulus launched another major offensive on 11 November – but it was to be his last, soon petering out into a number of small and disconnected operations. The best German forces had been drawn into a weary struggle in the city of Stalingrad itself, while the armies either side of them were thinly spread and included unreliable units of Romanians and Bulgarians. On 19 November the arrival of serious cold weather signalled the onset of the Soviet winter offensive which was intended to encircle the German forces that had been drawn to Stalingrad. By 23 November 300,000 German troops from the 6th Army were cut off in the city. Hitler refused to allow them to break out and instead gave the improbable order that they should be supplied by air.

With the Luftwaffe fully engaged on the Eastern Front, Germany found it harder to retaliate against the RAF's growing raids on German cities. Accordingly, Hitler now gave a very unpopular order to German fighter pilots. Conventional fighter units were now to begin *Terrorangriffe* (terror attacks) on the southern areas of Britain and to strafe civilian targets.

Although Churchill was now politically more secure, anxieties remained about the lack of progress in the Battle of the Atlantic. Most German naval efforts were now focused on U-boat operations in the North Atlantic, and in all 119 ships were sunk in November. During the autumn of 1942 there were heated arguments in London about the way in which the naval war was being managed, but in the end it was technical breakthroughs that would determine the outcome of this struggle in 1943.

Sunday 1 November 1942

Ursula von Kardorff witnesses arguments on the German
home front

*Ursula von Kardorff was a young woman living with her family in
Berlin and working as a journalist on the* Deutsche Allegemeine
Zeitung, *the city's most prestigious paper. In October and November her
two brothers, Jürgen and Klaus, were fortunate to have leave at the same
time. The mood at home was both festive and strained.*

On Saturday we had fifty people to the house and they
stayed half the night. A wartime party. We merely provided
the empty glasses and our guests brought plenty of bottles
with them and saw to it that they were filled. Six badly
wounded officers came – indeed the party was given for
them. One had an arm amputated at the shoulder, another
hobbled on crutches. Schwab-Felisch even managed to
dance, although he has lost half each foot from frostbite and
has not yet got proper orthopedic boots.

It was a strange evening. Many of the guests did not feel
like dancing and instead sat in my room and argued. This
was not a very safe thing to do, because at the last minute Q,
who is an SS-man and a journalist, turned up. I don't suppose he often hears people talk as frankly as they did that
night in our house. Yesterday he told Mamma on the telephone that he had been horrified at so much defeatist talk.
The most violent criticism came from the soldiers, and was
mostly concerned with the Government's religious policy.
Josel mentioned a place in Posen where all the churches had
been closed down. 'Aren't there two sides to an oath of
allegiance?' he demanded. 'Isn't the man to whom allegiance
is sworn bound to keep his side of the bargain?' Somebody
said, 'We're all like rats on a sinking ship, the only difference
being that we can't get off it any more.' 'You mean that it's
like the Nibelungen?' Adelheid asked. Werner Haeften, a
nephew of von Brauchitsch, who has been in the hospital for

months with severe wounds and who had to sit on an air cushion while he was with us, said ironically to Q, 'The only thing we'd like to do with you is to put the lot of you on a desert island and make you listen to your own speeches over the loudspeaker from morning till night.'

By the winter of 1942 it was clear that the German army in Russia had fallen into a morass and the numbers of dead and wounded could not be disguised from a domestic population that had hitherto felt little pressure from the war, even in 1941. Soldiers, particularly the wounded, brought raw reports from the front and felt free to speak their minds. For Ursula von Kardorff the best part of the evening was before the guests arrived when she took turns in dancing with her brothers in the empty room cleared for the party. Jürgen's leave would last only another two days and he told his sister quite frankly that he believed both he and his brother would soon be killed. It was only then that she realized that neither of her brothers believed that Germany would win the war. Jürgen would be seen off on 9 November 1942 with a cosy family lunch that was characterized by 'desperate gaiety' and talk of trivialities. SEE ALSO PP. *525–6, 533–4 AND 807–8.*

Wednesday 4 November 1942

James Ambrose Brown, a South African officer, inspects battlefield debris on the morning after El Alamein

After a night during which the beaten enemy fired machine-guns and mortars as if in a last frenzy of hate, we woke to something new. A strange atmosphere was about us. It was silence – just sweet silence. The first silence since 21h40 on the night of the twenty-third [October]. I felt that, for us, the battle was over.

This afternoon I walked far over the deserted battlefield in order to satisfy a morbid curiosity. I was more than satisfied; I was sated and disgusted, and not a little saddened. All those men and all those fine machines utterly destroyed. More than a score of heavy tanks stood dotted over the plain. Most of them had been rendered helpless, losing their tracks in the minefields and then being pitilessly pounded by anti-tank shells.

To know the truth about tanks, one must see them after the battle, pitted with holes where shells have penetrated the armour, covered with scores where shells gouged out the steel as a spoon gouges out cheese. Some of them had side armour pushed completely in, so that they resembled battered tins. Others, turretless, seemed to kneel with their heads in their hands. The guns pointed to the sky and the guns pointed to the ground. The interiors of the tanks were for the most part masses of twisted steel, shattered and blackened by fire. But others, unburned, were filled with flies, scraps of bloody clothing, spilled oil and pieces of flesh. Dark blood splashes marred the cool white-painted interiors. Telephones, bullets, half-eaten food, pathetic rubbish. I read a fragment of a letter I picked up. It was from a girl to the now meaningless thing which lay in the wreckage. A pitiful document it was, full of love and hope. I used to glory in war: now I am beginning to understand.

On 4 November the British finally achieved a breakthrough at El Alamein and began to push forward towards Tobruk, retracing the steps of their retreat during the first half of the year. Previously held up by complex minefields and anti-tank guns, they were now finding open ground and advanced rapidly. Their most formidable opponents, the 21st Panzer Division, ran out of fuel during the retreat and were overtaken and completely destroyed. By the end of the battle Rommel had only about forty tanks left, all of them low on fuel and ammunition, and was forced to withdraw.

Having survived the desert war and returned home to Cape Town, James Ambrose Brown went on to a successful post-war career as a writer. He was still writing in 1997, the year he published A Year in a Cottage Garden, *which follows the enjoyment of two people in creating a garden at the Cape, and the changes through the seasons.* SEE ALSO PP. *435–7, 439–40, 443–4* AND *455–6.*

Sunday 8 – Thursday 12 November 1942

Corporal John Green of the military police mops up
German prisoners after El Alamein

8 November

I am sent to Fuka, 25 miles west of Darba, this morning, with
a detachment to take charge of water point. This job is a little
quieter than the ones I have had lately. Jerry is flapping &
only fighting rear guard action. Our troops are advancing
& doing fine. The RE [Royal Engineers] are busy all day &
work through the night to get water.

9 November

Start pumping water at 6.30am. I learn that this is the only
water point for miles. 14 Italian soldiers come in from across
the desert & give themselves up.

Later nine Germans come & surrender. I keep filling
batches of prisoners all day. They are all short of water &
look hungry. They say they have been drinking water from
pools left by the recent rains.

10 November

OC visits me today & says we have to take it easy, the whole
Company have been pulled out to rest. The Coy is 25 miles
behind us.

11 November

I go for a look around to-day & find dozens of enemy tanks
knocked out on the desert. The bodies are still in some of
them. There are about 30 German planes all knocked out on
Fuka landing ground.

Prisoners still coming in. Enemy aircraft visit us during
the night, & few shells from very long range guns.

12 November

Our rest doesn't last long, we are on a half hours notice to
move. Jerry is going back faster now & we are to follow up.

We move off at 11.30 hoping to make Mesa Matruh & if Jerry keeps running we shall be in Tobruk in a day or two.

Rommel had retreated from Fuka on 5 November. Most remaining Italian units were destroyed during the battle of El Alamein. Over 40,000 German prisoners were taken after the battle, including General von Thoma, who had been commanding the Afrika Korps while Rommel was on sick leave in Germany. By 6 November heavy rain had turned the roads into a quagmire and advance was possible only in the coastal areas. This probably saved Rommel from further losses. Taking care of very large numbers of prisoners in extreme conditions placed strains on the supply systems of all countries.

Wednesday 11 November 1942

Curt Prüfer, a senior German diplomat, notices the inexorable rise of the black market and its effect on Berlin society

The last two days in BB [Baden-Baden] were especially ruined for us because of the news from the new front in French North Africa. It appears that reconnaissance and the intelligence services of the Axis failed completely, otherwise the surprise attacks of the English and Americans could not have been possible in so many places in Algeria and Morocco simultaneously. In any case, the result is a bad situation for the already hard-pressed Rommel, and it is a further weakening of Italian strategic and moral positions. Today, in order to defend the coast ourselves, we invaded previously unoccupied Southern France. It is also planned to occupy Corsica before the Allies do. They have had their first great success, and the Jews are rejoicing.

The mood here in Berlin appears to be even a shade worse than in Baden, although this is not meant to imply that it is very good there, either. Particularly noticeable here are the edginess of the people and the impoliteness, even rudeness, in the way they behave towards one another. This lack of

patience and friendliness is particularly noticeable among
the personnel at the hotel. The tone in the Hotel Adlon defies
description, it is so vulgar and odious. Although the prices
are extremely high, the guests are treated by the waiters as if
they were beggars. The only person well-served is the black
marketeer who appears at the table with numerous boxes,
tin cans, and tiny packages, full of rare foodstuffs. From this
illicit wealth the waiter hopes for some leftovers and scraps
for himself. In contrast, I was badly treated today by the
maitre d'hotel, an overfed 'gentleman' in a black jacket, who
had me wait, with unmistakable contempt, until a table was
free. This, although I am an ambassador and live in the hotel.
To be sure, the sleeves of my coat have taken on a question-
able sheen, which is not to be found on the clothes of the
black marketeers. After half an hour, when I again modestly
asked the man in the black jacket for a place, I still had no
luck.

We are again on the surest road to disaster because of
internal decay, hoarders, black marketeers, and grumblers.

*In November 1942 many Germans for the first time faced the possibility
that they might lose the war. Losses on the Eastern Front had been
enormous, and the reverses in north Africa came as a great shock. The
Allied successes were in fact attributable not – as Prüfer believed – to
bold strategy, but to patient planning and logistics. Having won the air
war, Montgomery advanced knowing that his supplies were much better
than Rommel's. On the home front in Germany food supplies were
increasingly short, with the war economy finally beginning to bite inside
the German homeland. Wartime Germany saw new privileged classes
emerge. The old aristocratic elite of the foreign office and the army were
already annoyed to find themselves overtaken by the new political elite
of the Nazi party; now both were outranked by the economic elite of the
black market. SEE ALSO PP. 29–30.*

Saturday 21 November – Saturday 12 December 1942

Corporal Schaffstein, a German soldier, surrounded at Stalingrad

Little is known or recorded about Corporal Schaffstein. His diary was captured and translated by the Russians in early 1943.

21 November
All's quiet. We're surrounded.

22 November
Russian attack repulsed. Bad news. The Russians are trying to surround us and have already said so over the radio.

23 November
The situation is becoming critical. We really are surrounded. The Führer takes command of our sector. Retreat.

24 November
The tension is becoming more acute. We prepare to retreat. We are getting ready to destroy everything. We are surrounded for certain.

25 November
We must hold our position to the last man. Heavy fighting to the right and left.
 What is going to happen?

26 November
The situation continues to be tense.

27 November
Increased activity of Russian airmen.

28 November
Our fighter planes have arrived. Soon the Russians will

laugh on the wrong side of the face.

29 November
The rations are running shorter and shorter. Quarter of a loaf per man . . .

30 November
We are still encircled.

2 December
Snow, snow and nothing but. The food is horrible and we are hungry all the time.

3 December
Still encircled . . .

4 December
Mighty torrent of shells belched forth by Russian artillery.

5 December
Again heavy snowfall. What can Manstein be doing? We are getting no mail. The whole supply system is paralysed.

6 December
Our rations are cut still more.

8 December
We are in a sad plight for lack of food. One loaf must do for seven men. We shall now have to tackle the horses.

9 December
All enfeebled horses are slaughtered and eaten.

10 December
Horse-meat is not so bad at all. It's a jolly sight worse to go hungry.

11 December
No immediate prospects of improvement. We are now learning the value of bread.

12 December

To-day I found a piece of stale, mouldy bread. No dainty morsel I had ever eaten tasted better. We now eat once a day – when they dish out the food. Then twenty-four hours of starvation.

Hitler's decision to order the German 6th Army under General Paulus to fight on in Stalingrad, rather than attempt to break out, proved to be a disaster. Although the Luftwaffe made valiant efforts to resupply the beleaguered garrison by air, it could achieve less than a third of the level of supply required to keep the forces fighting. In order to reduce the amount of food that had to be flown in, the 6th Army agreed to eat the 10,000 horses that belonged to its transport components. The Russians used the trapped invaders' plight as an opportunity to bleed German air resources as well as their army. Medical supplies and basic foodstuffs were soon in short supply, and the only hope for the German soldiers was a breakthrough by General Manstein's forces who were trying to relieve them.

DECEMBER 1942

DECEMBER 1942 SAW A marked decline in U-boat attacks. Four-fifths of Allied shipping losses during the year to date had occurred as the result of submarine activity. Now there were greater successes against the U-boat communication system consequent on the breaking of the Triton cipher. Although reading these messages could be painfully slow work, it allowed some convoys to be directed away from the attackers. More importantly, Allied air power was increasing in the Atlantic and the manufacturing capacity of the United States simply began to outstrip what the Germans could sink. 'Liberty ships', built on an assembly-line principle, were pouring out of American shipyards.

Stalingrad remained the focus of fighting on the Eastern Front. During mid-December the forces under Generals Mannstein and

Hoth sent to relieve the besieged 6th Army made good progress, but on 19 December they ground to a halt. The surrounded German troops in Stalingrad could hear the fighting of the relief forces – but their rescuers got no closer. Soviet forces were making progress elsewhere, too: many of Germany's allies, including the Italians, had sizeable units serving on the Eastern Front and the Soviet commanders had chosen these points as soft targets where they could easily push forward.

Despite the débâcle of the Dieppe raid, daring attacks by Allied special forces continued. On 7 December British Commandos made a remarkable raid on Bordeaux harbour, rowing 50 miles up the River Gironde and attaching limpet mines to German shipping. The attack was successful, but few of the Commandos escaped. On 23 December Admiral Darlan, the Vichy leader, was assassinated by Bonnier de la Chappelle, a royalist and a Gaullist. He had received training from a variety of Allied secret services but a direct line of responsibility for the attack still remains unclear.

By the end of 1942 prisoners on all sides ran into millions. The Red Cross was spending £375,000 per month on food parcels for Allied POWs. Vichy France had successfully negotiated the release of some but not all of its prisoners; elsewhere there was no exchange. On 17 December 1942 Eden stated clearly in Parliament that the Germans 'are now carrying into effect Hitler's often repeated intention to exterminate the Jewish people in Europe', and the matter was then debated. It was declared in both London and Washington that these crimes would be avenged.

In December 1942 the Germans set up a unit of anti-Soviet Russians under General Vlasov in the hope of winning over Russians to their cause, but German trust of their Russian protégés was limited. The Russians were strategically further ahead and had already begun to train communist Germans to form the government of a future East Germany.

Tuesday 1 December 1942

A German gunner from the 12th Company, 3rd Battalion, 131st Regiment waits in Stalingrad

This anonymous diary was captured by Soviet forces after Stalingrad fell; the author remains unknown.

We are surrounded. From the 21st of November to this day has been the most frightful period of my life. All that time we were out in the open fighting as we retreated. Always only a hair's breadth removal from captivity or death. Both of my big toes are frost-bitten. All of our belongings were burnt as we could not take them along. The Führer is among us. This stiffens our backs and we find the pluck to carry on. Our hands are covered with a layer of dirt and we have grown beards of enormous size. We marched until we almost dropped. We then occupied a position and are holding it as we were ordered to by the Führer.

It goes without saying that the Russians are not letting us off lightly. Incessant artillery fire that reduces us to the point of exhaustion, but we do not yield to their pressure. We shall stand fast. Three armies have been dispatched to our aid. Let us hope that they will be able to set us free. In any event, I would not like to go through the horror of these days again. We slept on the snow with just one blanket. When we awoke we were too weak to stand on our legs. But everything comes to an end and so will this, either a good end or a bad one. For God and Führer, onward! Between three and half-past four the fire poured into our positions exceeded anything I had yet seen.

The German 6th Army at Stalingrad had effectively been surrounded since 23 November. It had already lost its entire supply organization, its reserve stocks and almost all of its supply personnel during the fighting west of the River Don. The Luftwaffe continued to attempt to fly supply missions in temperatures below minus 30 degrees Celsius, but the weather was often too bad for them to take off. As the area held by the Germans shrank, so the Soviet troops were able to bring a greater density of artillery fire to bear on them. Although Hitler was well aware of the terrible state of the units besieged there, he continued to refuse to allow either a withdrawal or an evacuation by air.

Wednesday 2 – Monday 14 December 1942

Moshe Flinder, a Dutch Jewish boy aged 16, visits the cinema in Brussels

Moshe Flinder was a Jewish boy from The Hague who had fled with his family in 1942 when the Germans began to move the Jews of Holland into concentration camps. Together with his mother, father, five sisters and a brother, he moved to Brussels. The family spent the majority of their time in a large apartment, which they left only occasionally, and to pass the time Moshe began a diary.

2 December, morning

I shall now write about our house and our family. Shortly after we arrived in here, in Brussels, there were disagreements between my mom and my dad about whether we should stay or move on. First it was to non-German France (now all France is inhabited by Germans), and then to Switzerland. My dad has been trading here for twenty years or more now and has been there almost every week, and he said it will be better to stay here until the end of the war and until salvation comes, because Brussels is a big city and it is not too difficult to hide here. Many Jews hide here . . .

14 December, midnight

Yesterday I went with my sister to the cinema. When I was in the days before the German occupation I did not use to go there a lot. When the Germans were in Holland after a while the Jews were forbidden to visit the cinema. Later they started showing anti-Semitic films in the cinemas. I really wanted to go and see these films, but I couldn't because my identification card has a 'J' on it to show I'm Jewish, and if they were doubtful they could ask me to show this card, and I believe that for this offence the punishment was six months in prison. But now in Belgium I have registered as non-Jewish I can visit the cinemas and as they are not very strict here. When I first came here there was nothing in the windows, only in those houses where the owners were anti-Semitic, it said there is no entrance for Jews. But now it says in every single cinema: by German order, Jews are not allowed in cinemas. Despite this I went to see the film *Jud Süss*. What I saw there made me furious. When I left my face was red. I saw there the conspiracy of evils, their tricks and how they do whatever they can to infuse antisemitic venom into the gentile blood. Seeing this film I suddenly remembered the words of the evil [Hitler], in one of his speeches: anti-Semitism will spread until the complete annihilation of the Jews. These were his words. And here I saw the tricks with which he wants to reach his targets ... How deep are his schemes, I don't have enough words to describe this either. I know this though, that if we are not saved by a miracle from above then our doom is as certain as these words I am writing now ...

In 1944 Moshe and his family, denounced by a fellow Jew, would be taken to Auschwitz. Moshe and his parents died but his brother and sisters survived. After the war they returned to their old apartment in Brussels and found the diary that Moshe had been keeping in 1942. It was published in 1958.

Sunday 13 – Monday 14 December 1942

Erich Weinert, a German communist, works on radio propaganda for Russia at Stalingrad

Erich Weinert was born in 1890 in Magdeburg and by the 1930s was a famous cabaret poet and labour activist in Berlin. He was a contemporary of Thomas Mann and Bertolt Brecht. In 1931 the government

had attempted to prosecute him for subversive lyrics and by 1933 the
rise of Hitler had prompted him to flee to Switzerland. Had he remained
in Germany he would not have survived, for as early as 1935 he had
been singled out for attack in speeches by Goebbels as a Jew and a com-
munist. In 1937 he fought in the International Brigade in Spain and
then went to Moscow, where for a while he made a living dubbing
German films in Russian. During the war his main work was to try to
persuade more German soldiers to join the Russian cause. By December
1942 a huge opportunity was presented to him by the German 6th Army
under Paulus, cut off at Stalingrad.

13 December

Yesterday at dusk we drove up to the front line with our loud-
speaker van for the first time. We had tested the apparatus
during the day, and found out that when there is no wind the
human voice can be heard quite distinctly up to a distance of
half a mile. The difficulty is to approach the enemy lines as
close as possible in our tall van without being seen.

The night was clear and starlit. A bright moon shone over
the white steppe. This made our approach even more difficult. There was no wind at all, and as there was no gunfire
the enemy must have heard our motor from far away, and
become alarmed. As we were driving behind our frontline,
taking advantage of all the depressions in the ground, they
nervously began to fire their machine-guns on the other side.
White Verey lights were rocketing up all over the place. Our
van drove cautiously down a hill into a thick little shrubbery.

The bullets whistled in the twigs. The technicians quietly
started their work in the van. A patrol, returning from the
front, reported that the distance to the enemy's line was a
quarter or a third of a mile at the utmost.

There was no shelter in the neighbourhood. We had to
speak from a dug-out which protected us from rifle fire but
hardly from mortar and gun fire. The announcer, who had
had some experience, said, 'We don't get much mortar and
gun fire here as a rule. Probably only when they are
expressly ordered by their HQ. Mostly they interrupt us
with their machine-guns, but apparently only when they
aren't interested in a transmission. The other day, before we

put a [German] prisoner on, we announced [it]! And then they stopped.'

'That means,' said U, 'that they want to listen, but to something substantial, not empty phrases which they can't understand.'

'They listen to what the [recent German] prisoners say,' remarked one of the [Russian] reconnaissance patrol. 'I'm sure they discuss whether they really risk their lives by coming over to us. The day before yesterday, after the prisoner had finished talking to them, they shouted across: "Anybody can pretend to be a German. You just show us a live [German] prisoner, and we'll come over, too!"'

The dynamo began to hum. They seemed to have heard that. The firing became more intense. More Verey lights soared up.

We took the microphone into the dug-out. The announcer introduced the speaker. Then U began his address. 'Fellow countrymen over there! Let's talk plain German. There are Germans here too, on this side, not prisoners, but Free Germans. We have come to you to the front for a single reason: to save the lives of tens of thousands of our countrymen. We want to tell you nothing but the truth which your unscrupulous Nazi officers are hiding from . . .'

After the first words the shooting stopped. The night grew very quiet. No more Verey lights.

'They're listening,' said the Major.

I spoke after U. Our addresses were not short. But nobody over there fired a shot. They were listening. But we had hardly finished and got out of our dug-out when something came howling through the air. We knew that sound.

'Mortars!' cried the Major. 'Take cover!'

Now they burst right in front of us, in the depression. They were aiming at the [loudspeaker] van. But they did not shoot far enough. The last one 100 yards from the van.

We cleared out from our 'trough' as quickly as possible. Again the bullets were whistling through the shrubbery. The Verey lights went up.

14 December
This morning we had an assorted collection of prisoners.

At Stalingrad the Russians and their German protégés began to experiment with battlefield loudspeaker vans to try to persuade entire units of the Wehrmacht to capitulate. One group held out to the end, but others surrendered, and some of the captured Germans soon became Weinert's colleagues. One of them was Heinrich von Einsiedel, who joined Erich Weinert and the Free Germans after Stalingrad; extracts from his diary are also reproduced in this collection.

Weinert's diary is itself a work of propaganda. First published in Moscow in German in 1943, by 1944 it had been translated into English and published in London. Although genuine, it also includes some rather tedious political dialogues. By 1944 Erich Weinert would be promoted to president of the Russian-sponsored Free German National Committee in Moscow. Although this group contained a smattering of Catholics and social democrats, for the most part it was made up of communists like Erich Honecker who were already preparing to form the new government of East Germany after the war.

Wednesday 16 December 1942

Myrtle Wright, a dedicated humanitarian, smuggles Jews from occupied Norway to safety in neutral Sweden

Myrtle Wright was an English Quaker who had recently completed her degree at Cambridge University when the war broke out in 1939. In 1940 she set out for Denmark, where she planned to help evacuate Jewish refugees escaping from Germany. Travelling via Norway, she found herself stranded by the German invasion of that country and remained there for four years. She quickly found plenty of humanitarian work to undertake and was soon smuggling Jews away from German-occupied territory into neutral Sweden. This was dangerous work, but the religious network to which she belonged, in which everyone knew everyone else, offered mutual reassurance against the possibility of betrayal.

Sigrid taken up with getting Israel's Mission to ask for permission to send parcels to Jews at Bredtvedt and Tonsberg (where Jews married to Ayrans [sic] still are). The

Swedish consul is still working, not only to get into Sweden those who have connection with that country, but every one of them, including refugees from Germany and Czechoslovakia. This is a fine gesture from Sweden, if only it can be managed from the Norwegian NS [quisling Nazi party] side. The negotiations are with the Norwegians, and cannot include the Jews who are at Grini under German control.

(The following is entirely to do with arrangements for Jews [comment by Myrtle Wright]). Arthur (*Rondan*) rings up as he has a message for Sigrid; I go down to see him as Sigrid is already in town. He told me that two boys would be arriving tonight; I assured him that Ingebjorg would meet them. *(Later: they were met and have gone on a transport to Sweden.)* Also news of two children from Bergen who come tomorrow evening to stay with friends in town. Sigrid is asked to meet them at the station and take them from the lady and gentleman with whom they are travelling. Arthur has five coming out of hospital and one already out. These are the ones Ingebjorg already knows about. Went with the message to Ingebjorg.

Myrtle's diary was initially hidden beneath some hen coops, and later in a university library, disguised among some Tibetan manuscripts. Even there it was not safe. The Germans eventually raided the university library looking for hidden radios, and so a librarian had to smuggle the diary out under his shirt.

The Nobel Peace Prize Committee made no awards during the Second World War, but in 1947 they awarded the Peace Prize to two Quaker organizations – the Friends Service Council of London (FSC) and the American Friends Service Committee (AFSC) of Philadelphia. It was the sort of work that Myrtle Wright had conducted in occupied Norway during the Second World War, smuggling Jews to safety, that they wished to recognize.

After the war Myrtle married Philip Radley and together they went to South Africa, before becoming part of the team representing the Quakers at the United Nations in 1963–4.

Wednesday 23 December 1942

Flying Officer W. S. Large of the Royal Canadian Air Force
watches the impact of aerial innovations

*William Sydney Large was born at Cambrose, Alberta in 1916. He had
worked for a mining company at Kirkland Lake and had taken some
private flying instruction to get ahead of the queues when the RCAF
began recruiting at the start of the war. He was shot down during the
Dieppe raid and survived that ordeal, before being posted to Tunisia in
the autumn of 1942 as part of Operation Torch. His short diary largely
concerns his life as a fighter pilot located at Bone during December
1942.*

I must tell you about some of the aerial innovations in the
Bone district. When we first arrived here, we did not have a
ground control for radio, nor did we have any means of
detecting the approach of hostile aircraft many minutes
before they are within striking distance. Many times during
the day, the telephone would ring wildly and some French
Naval type would jabber excitedly over the wire about
'avion allemande.' There was not a man amongst us who
spoke French fluently enough to understand him, but we did
know that he had a telephone connection with spotters who
were located thirty miles up the coast, and that when the
mad Frog called us up, there was something approaching.
Almost invariably his reports were confirmed by an attack
within five minutes time. So we learned to respect his warnings. Now, after three weeks, we have a powerful ground
control station, as well as an R.D.F. [Radio Direction-Finding
unit] that has proven invaluable to us, and deadly to the
Hun. During the first two weeks, the enemy dropped in on
us during the night, dropped their parachute flares, and
bombed us at their leisure. Now we have a terrific barrage of
heavy and light ack-ack, as well as fully equipped night
fighters, and a night operational staff. During the first three
nights after their arrival they shot down fifteen Hun

bombers, the result of which has been a decided decline in the number and strength of Jerry night raids. The conquests of the night fighters since that time have been numerous and their lessons have been two. One of these, the first, closed in on a He.111, gave him a burst and his aim was so accurate that he found himself surrounded by pieces of flaming Heinkel. His machine caught fire, one aileron was burned completely off and his windscreen was covered with oil and smoke. Nevertheless he made a remarkably fine attempt to bring her down in one piece and crash-landed on the aerodrome without injury to himself or his observer.

'Gus' Large's diary records the impact of the 'wizard war' upon combat in the air and at sea. Increasingly, effectiveness in these realms was coming to depend on radar, radio direction-finding and the accurate and timely provision of intelligence. Staying ahead in these areas was of increasing importance, and bringing together operational commanders, scientists and production engineers to solve technical problems quickly often proved significant in determining who would win in battle.

Large's diary stops in mid-sentence on 1 January 1943. He was writing up his diary when he scrambled for a mission – from which he did not return.

Christmas Eve, Thursday 24 December – Monday 28 December 1942

Kathleen Church-Bliss and Elsie Whiteman, lathe-turners at Morrison's, record the arrival of Christmas in their factory

The joint diary of Elsie Whiteman and Kathleen Church-Bliss is a remarkable, almost unique, document of wartime social history. It is a journal which the two women kept together from February 1942 until November 1944. Giving up a tea-shop that they owned and ran in Surrey, they trained on lathes and then later went to work in the Morrison factory in Croydon, which specialized in light engineering. Although the mobilization of female labour meant that thousands of women were working on factory shop floors by 1942, almost none of them seem to have kept diaries. In this joint diary, the women wrote in turn and referred to themselves in the third person.

24 December

Sad to learn on arrival that the day and night staff do not change over on Monday after all. This because the night shift men made a tremendous fuss as they didn't see why they should have their places altered 'just to suit Rapley', as they said. This means we shall have to come home on Sunday evening in order to start work at 7.45 am on Monday. Everyone very gay and high-spirited today. About 10am we were invited by Lou to have a swig of cocktail out of a medicine bottle so we crept up behind her machine, which was mercifully in a corner, and had our secret drink feeling very guilty. However, she assured us that the odour of sanctity had been put on it, as the chargehand, George Baker, had had the first drink. There were several quiet little bottle parties going on and the atmosphere got gayer and gayer. We were due to finish at 4pm and after lunch K and E set to work once more like smug girls. But some of them seemed settled down and Muriel got hold a piece of mistletoe and started kissing the bridegroom-to-be George Baker, then Bob Slade (who was not amused) and finally Stan and then Peters. This kissing has become pretty general throughout the factory and there were clinging matches going on all over the place in a most haphazard way. The Peccadillo was visited by about 8 different men who clasped her in a long embrace, which she seemed to submit to like a dummy. Beyond tidying her hair between each onslaught [she] appeared quite unmoved. Laurie got furious with all this passion and finally pulled one man off the Peccadillo muttering 'Disgusting! Disgusting!!' Muriel, being rather above herself after all her kissing pecks, was suddenly set on by Reg Green and kissed in good earnest, which left her flushed and panting. In the other factory we heard that an impromptu band and dance was held and when Mr Overton (who is much feared normally) arrived to protest, he was told to go to hell! Altogether everyone was out of hand and not a scrap of work was being done. Finally, at about 3pm Captain Lines arrived looking very angry, and said everyone was to be out of the building in five minutes. So off we went and felt very glad to get a little more time to pack and tidy up. All the workers had been annoyed that the factory hadn't closed at lunch time as nearly all the other Croydon factories had done so. [Xmas break follows].

27 December
We both arrived back having had a pleasant 3 days, and the thought of no more holidays for we don't know how long cast rather a gloom upon us.

28 December
Nobody would have known to look at the concentrating workers, quiet and rather tired, that they were the same people who created the orgy on Christmas Eve. The kissers and huggers seemed quite oblivious of one another and no one has referred to it. In common with everyone else, we were inexpressibly tired and were thankful to hear that we were closing at 5.15, though we shan't relish having to make it up tomorrow.

The conscription of men from 1939 had inevitably created a severe labour shortage. With the advent of 'global war' in December 1941 the government passed the National Service Act, which called up all un-married women aged between twenty and thirty. Many went into the women's armed services. By 1942 call-up had been extended to married women, although pregnant women and mothers with young children were exempt. One vital need was for women to work in munitions factories. Other women were conscripted to work in tank and aircraft factories, civil defence, nursing, transport and other key occupations. Women also flew RAF aircraft, although not in a combat role. By 1943 almost 90 per cent of unmarried women under forty would be in a war-related occupation. Elsie Whiteman and Kathleen Church-Bliss were shocked by the poor conditions for women at Morrison's, despite the large numbers employed there, and, through the various factory committees, worked to bring about welfare reforms inside the factory. Being both middle-aged and middle-class, they seem to have proved to be more confident and more determined in addressing the management than many of their colleagues. SEE ALSO PP. 598–600.

New Year's Eve, Thursday 31 December 1942

James Chuter Ede, Education Minister, senses the turning of the political tide

Government changes are announced this morning . . . Jowitt really keeps the same job but has a higher status. The choices of Morrison and Macmillan for their respective new posts is good, always on the assumption that the two posts must be filled by Tories. The *Star* tonight says Labour MPs are disappointed that both the Minister and Parl[iamentar]y Sec[retar]y for Town and Country Planning are Tories . . .

This is the end of one of the great years in the history of mankind. It has seen great changes in the mood of Englishmen. Its early months became successively more and more depressing with the spread of Japanese domination over the possessions of Britain, the Netherlands and the USA in the Far East and the Pacific. Then came the defeats of the British in North Africa. I do not think even the collapse of France made me as miserable as did the fall of Tobruk. The faith of everyone was sorely tried and though the Vote of Confidence only had 25 supporters in the lobby misgivings were profound. The Communists' constant demand for a Second Front in Europe and their insinuations that we were failing our Allies added to the feeling of frustration. Then followed months of stagnation, disturbed only by the raid on Dieppe. This apparent inaction still further tried our faith. Had anyone seen an alternative to Churchill the Government would have fallen. Then on the 21st October came the speech by Smuts to both Houses in which he said we were passing to the offensive stage in the war. I noted on 25th October . . . 'In the 1 o'c news today it was announced that the 8th Army had started an offensive in Egypt.' After so many previous disillusionments one received the news and the next few days with every caution . . .

Then the news became outspokenly cheerful. A great revulsion of feeling occurred and the PM's patient and skilful planning became manifest. Even the Darlan incident failed to shake the confidence newly reposed spontaneously in him by the House, especially after hearing him in Secret Session. The tremendous hammer blows since struck by the Russians have confirmed the view that the Allies have in Europe and Africa the initiative. The road ahead may yet be long but in these theatres we can glimpse the summit of the pass.

Admiral François Darlan had been deputy Prime Minister to Pétain when the Vichy collaborationist regime was set up in France in 1940. In November 1942 the Allies had avoided fighting the Vichy French in north Africa by doing a controversial deal with Vichy whereby Darlan became the first civilian leader in Algiers – the so-called 'Darlan incident'. Although the deal worked, the Germans retaliated by taking Vichy areas of metropolitan France under direct German control; meanwhile, in Algiers, Darlan was assassinated on 24 December 1942. Few mourned his passing.

James Chuter Ede's diary was a barometer of the political mood at Westminster and captures the feelings of many, if not most, in the House of Commons in 1942. Although the prospect of England being invaded had begun to lift by the spring of 1942, with German forces clearly bogged down on the Eastern Front, a question mark still hung over Churchill's leadership through much of the year. Some areas of Britain continued to take a pounding from the Luftwaffe and the Battle of the Atlantic was taking a terrible toll on the merchant fleets of Britain, the United States and Canada. More than any other single event, Rommel's advance as far as Egypt in the summer of 1942 had caused a public outcry. There can be little doubt that El Alamein saved Churchill politically, and the symbolic importance of that victory cannot be overestimated. Nevertheless, the real shifts were occurring elsewhere: American forces began to engage the Germans in north Africa in November 1942, while Germany's beleaguered forces at Stalingrad were about to surrender. The end of the war in Europe, though still years away, at last seemed like a realistic prospect. SEE ALSO PP. 391–2.

1943

'IF THESE NOTES of mine one day see the light, it will be because I took precautions to put them in safety before the Germans, through their trickery, made me a prisoner. It was not my intention, while I was writing these hasty notes, to release them for publication just as they are . . . If Providence had granted me a quiet old age, what excellent material for my autobiography! . . . But perhaps in this skeleton form and in the absolute lack of the superfluous are to be found the real merits of a diary. Events are photographed without retouching, and the impressions reported are the first, the most genuine . . .'

Count Galeazzo Ciano, 23 December 1943, nineteen days before his execution

JANUARY 1943

O N 10 JANUARY THE Russians began a major offensive at Stalingrad. A day later the siege of Leningrad was lifted as a partial corridor was opened up to the beleaguered Russian defenders. Elsewhere on the Eastern Front Soviet forces made spectacular gains, partly by attacking non-German units such as the Hungarians, who quickly disintegrated. Against Hitler's orders, General Paulus surrendered the southern pocket of Stalingrad to the Russians on the last day of January. To the north of him General Strecker continued to hold out.

In north Africa German troops launched a major offensive in Tunisia, and by the end of the month had driven the Americans and the British out of the Faid Pass area.

In both Britain and Germany, growing economic pressures meant further mobilization. In Britain the call-up age for single girls was lowered to nineteen. In Germany the whole of the work-force was mobilized for production: this meant that all men aged sixteen to sixty-five and all women aged seventeen to fifty were ordered to register themselves. The war also began to set its own style, with the appearance of substantial lines of 'Utility' clothing and furniture in the shops in Britain. The production of anything other than 'Utility' styles by British manufacturers had been banned by the government in the previous November, along with the production of private cars.

In mid-January Churchill and Roosevelt met up in Casablanca for wide-ranging discussions about the conduct of the war. The Americans were concerned about the delay in opening up a second front in Europe and the British were concerned about a growing American focus on the war against Japan, rather than Germany. There were also disagreements about the relative value of attacking Germany through Italy or through France. At the end of this conference the Allies announced the doctrine of un-conditional surrender, whereby the Axis would not be allowed to bargain for surrender terms or surrender to one country only.

On Wednesday 27 January, the US Army Air Force made its first raid on Germany. Two days later the Nazi party's tenth anniversary celebrations were disrupted by the RAF's first low-level daylight air attack on Berlin with Mosquito aircraft, timed to coincide with the speeches. Although the numbers of aircraft available to RAF Bomber Command were not much greater than a year before, the quality was entirely different. The main aircraft was now the Lancaster, and navigational aids, including new forms of airborne radar, were better. At sea too, Coastal Command began to make use of an improved radar that allowed much more effective searches for U-boats and could not be detected by the Germans.

Tuesday 5 January 1943

Grete Paquin, a German anti-Nazi living in Göttingen, traps an invader in her cellar

Each autumn some mice invade my cellar to make their winter camp there. They enjoy the potatoes, apples, carrots, all the things I have stored away to keep for spring. If they would concentrate on a few pieces I would not mind, but they try here and there and everywhere and leave the rest to me. Well, in desperation I bought a trap and caught them fairly regularly. A miserable business, for I am afraid even of dead mice, and I always look back after I have thrown the small carcass on the compost heap hoping an owl or some other animal will do the rest.

Last night when I went down to fetch something the trap had disappeared, and as nobody had been in, it was absolutely clear that the mouse itself must have removed it. The situation bound me to the Convention of the Red Cross in Geneva – how to treat a wounded prisoner of war. I fixed a candle on a bottleneck and started the search. I looked on each apple shelf, behind each box, but no mouse, no trap. I emptied the box of carrots – nothing – the potato box – and there he was, the poor little fellow, pressed into a corner and looking at me as frightened as I was looking at him. The trap was dangling from his hind legs which seemed to be badly hurt. And funny, at this very moment all fear left me. I ran upstairs to find a box, lined it with cotton and put a cover over it with holes so that the PW could get fresh air. Then I removed the trap carefully, holding him at his neck; and put him in the small military hospital, with a piece of carrot to give him vitamins. It seemed useless and hopeless to fix a bandage to the tiny legs, the best healing is always done by nature herself. Next morning he was dead and stiff, he had not touched the carrot. So I finished by giving him a good military funeral with his deathbed as a coffin. From now on I stop setting traps; let the mice do as they like.

Grete Paquin kept her diary as a record of the situation in Germany for her four children to read after the war, which they did. Grete herself was still alive in the 1960s. SEE ALSO PP. 245, 301–2 AND 383–5.

Friday 8 January 1943

Hannah Senesh, a young Jewish poet and Zionist from Hungary, now living in Caesarea, contemplates a rescue mission to Europe

The long pauses between entries are indicative of my situation. Sometimes there's no ink on my pen; sometimes I don't have a light; sometimes it's noisy – there are others in the room besides me – and sometimes I have no reason to write. Sometimes I don't have time to write, and sometimes I don't feel like writing. Not because nothing happens – on the contrary, there has been plenty happening both inside and out. But I've simply been apathetic to everything that's been going on.

I've had a shattering week. I was suddenly struck by the idea of going to Hungary. I feel I must be there during these days in order to help organize youth emigration, and also to get my mother out. Although I'm quite aware how absurd the idea is, it still seems both feasible and necessary to me, so

I'll get to work on it and carry it through. For the time being this is but a sudden enthusiasm, a hopeful plan to get Mother out and bring her here, at any cost. I spent three days in Tel-Aviv and Jerusalem trying to arrange the matter. At the moment chances are slim, but who knows . . . ?

In 1941 Hannah Senesh had moved from her agricultural college to a kibbutz at Sdot Yam. Here she continued to write poetry and also The Violin, *an autobiographical play about a writer joining a collective. Many Palestinian Jews shared her concern both for the plight of Jews encountering restrictions on immigration into Palestine, and for those suffering growing persecution in Europe, and some were considering the creation of a Jewish force to ally itself with the British against the Axis.* SEE ALSO PP. 236–7 AND 526–8.

Tuesday 12 January 1943

James Webb Young on Soviet spies in Washington

James Webb Young was one of the main figures behind the creation of the famous J. Walter Thompson advertising agency, and indeed one of the principal intellectual influences on the science of marketing in general. During the 1930s he had frequently lectured at the University of Chicago's Business School and in 1941 he proposed the creation of a War Advertising Council. This brought him into contact with wartime propaganda agencies and government officials in Washington DC.

Talked with one of our high officials who has an intimate knowledge of the Russians. Asked him why we were not permitted military observers on the Russian front. The answer, he said, is very simple: The Russians have secret agents in every department in Washington. Knowing how easy it is to place them there, they assume that the Germans have them, too. Thus they figure that reports from their front would sooner or later fall into German hands. I was so astounded I forgot to ask why we couldn't stop this.

Young visited Washington regularly to liaise with the Office of War Information. Recent releases of intelligence material from the 1940s have confirmed the extraordinary scale of Soviet espionage inside the United States during this period, although this was something to which Roosevelt was inclined to turn a blind eye for the duration of the war.
SEE ALSO PP. 534–5.

Monday 18 January 1943

Michael Zylberberg observes the first uprising in the Warsaw Ghetto

Michael Zylberberg had been a teacher of history and literature in a Jewish high school before the war. His diary records life in the Warsaw Ghetto in late 1942 and early 1943. The 11 square miles of the ghetto were being used as a vast factory complex for manufacturing war materials; conditions were terrible and Jews were being periodically deported to the death camp at Treblinka. In mid-January 1943 rumours of impending further deportations created a mood of restlessness and rebellion.

We slept five to a room, warmly covered with a sea of bed-clothes left behind by the deportees. One of the five was a Jewish policeman who left to go to his place of work at six in the morning. Half an hour later he was back shouting, 'Save yourselves; they are already in the street. Two SS-men have been shot in the courtyard of this house.' In seconds we had crawled into the attic through an aperture in the wainscot, and lay flattened between the cavity walls. Until six that night over a hundred people, men, women and children, lay there lethargically, awaiting the worst that could happen. We heard the firing increase in volume and distinguished the sound of marching feet. Suddenly the Germans were in the attic searching and not finding anybody. A deadly silence reigned within the cavity walls. We heard the officers direct commands at the Jewish police. They were to hack down the beams, as our presence was more than suspected. The

SS-men went downstairs, saying they would return shortly, and the Jewish policemen did as they were told and chopped away the woodwork. They knew, of course, that we were hidden there, and even who we were. They quickly gave us the latest news. We were told that one resistance worker, a Miss Landau, had been shot while throwing grenades at some Germans who were leading a group of Jews to their execution. She had managed, nevertheless, to aid the escape of a few hundred. We also heard that Yitzhak Giterman had been shot in the street and that a running fight was going on between some Germans and one man who had escaped on to the roof of our house. We lay silently, waiting for a miracle.

The Germans returned. They inspected; they pried; they did not find us. The day dragged by slowly with cold and hunger. When darkness fell, the Germans withdrew, afraid of a new attack from the Jews. We crept out slowly one by one to find, unfortunately, that some of our number were dead, having succumbed to the shock and the horror of the enforced hideaway . . .

Friends intervened for me, and so I found myself hidden there with several others for the next seven days. Those days in the bakery were horrific. It was like being entombed, and even now, when I think of it, it still has a nightmarish quality. It was said to be a secure bunker, with hiding space for thirty people; in actual fact, a hundred people crowded in. The entrance was a long narrow tunnel opening alongside the oven door. When everyone was inside, a mountain of coal was heaped up to hide the tunnel mouth, so that no one could suspect that there was anyone there. One had to be very agile to get into the tunnel, and then one had to continue along it on one's stomach, using hands and knees for propulsion. It took at least ten minutes of strenuous pushing to get into the actual bunker at the end. The bunker was made up of two tiny rooms, better described as cupboards. They were so airless that one could not even light a cigarette. The overcrowded conditions can be imagined. Sitting or lying down was out of the question. People were pressed together, supporting each other, all standing . . .

Though the place seemed safe enough, the danger of

discovery was considerable. The SS-men directing operations in the street would stop in the bakery above us, since the bakers had to provide them with food and drinks every day. The slightest noise would have betrayed us. We were terrified because of the children. Everything was done to pacify and soothe them while they stood as wearily and silently as the adults. We had had the unusual good fortune of finding among the belongings, hurriedly thrown together, of the baker's family, a Hagada [Passover prayer book] published by Schocken in Berlin. This book was lavishly illustrated, and we used the pictures to amuse and quieten the children while the Germans were eating above us.

The increasing tension was also apparent to the German patrols, and they avoided the darkened snowbound streets of the ghetto after nightfall. Some of those Jews whose relatives had already been deported were determined to exact revenge upon the SS and did so as soon as the new wave of deportations began.

Many diaries and notebooks have recorded the suffering of the Jews in the ghettos of Lodz and Warsaw. Arguably the keeping of a diary was itself an act of resistance: not only was it forbidden, but it was also a symbolic act of permanency at a time when all traces of the Jews in Poland were being obliterated. Michael Zylberberg had decided to begin his record at the end of 1942: as he observes, by then over half of Poland's 500,000 Jews had been exterminated. Among those killed were his parents and three younger brothers, as well as his wife's parents and her three younger sisters. He would continue his diary until May 1943, when he escaped from the ghetto and found refuge working as a gardener for a Catholic family, the Piotrkowiczes of Skolimov. In May 1943 he would leave their house in great haste but managed to hide his diary there. It was then forgotten, but came to light twenty years later during extensive building work on the house. The diary was then returned to its owner in London and later published.

Wednesday 20 – Tuesday 26 January 1943

Mrs Henry Dudeney endures the bombing of Lewes

Alice L. Dudeney (Mrs Henry E. Dudeney) was born in 1866 and had been an established writer of popular fiction at the turn of the century. She was also a stalwart supporter of the Sussex Archaeological Trust. Her husband was a popular mathematician and a founder member of the British Chess Problem Society, created in 1918.

20 January

The Big Raid on Lewes. At 12 when I was peaceful in bed [with flu], the most terrible bangs. The bed and the house shook. I was stunned and so defenceless undressed. Winnie [the maid] came rushing up with some loving incoherence about 'dying together'! A plane rushed past the window, flying very flow. The black shadow of it shut out the light. I shall always think of the Angel of Death and the 'beating of its wings'. I shall never see a blackbird fly past my window without remembering. Three more followed, very close and low, they seemed to be at the window pane. More bangs, rushings, vibrations. I expected the house to go. Then silence. We learned later that 2 people were killed and many injured . . . We, and the Lucas's, have escaped with broken windows. Winnie came up with the supper at 9 and the news that they 'couldn't dig out poor old Mrs Digweed'. (They did in the end.)

21 January

People were so kind . . . all called to see if I was all right. I insisted to Dr Irvine that I must dress and come down, that to lie up there and be buried alive was *too* ghastly a thought. So I am down here, feeling an awful rag.

22 January

The most awful devastation in the town, especially in North Street, New Street and New Road. The 'Stage' Hotel burnt to the ground and Stevensons the Corn Chandler has lost his windows with almost the last lovely fanlights left in Lewes. All the people have got to clear out of St Martin's lane, which also was hit. I sat in my chair all day, half asleep, but jumping like a shot rabbit if even a cinder dropped out of the fire . . .

26 January
Went and slept on the spare room bed after dinner and would gladly have stayed there but Mrs Brough had proposed herself to tea. She says that when the bombs fell last week, Margaret Hills' parrot lay flat on its back at the bottom of its cage and *Swore!*

Alice Dudeney's diary records the impact on the elderly of the bombing of the south coast. It also underlines the destruction of archaeological heritage. Many old houses made 'unsafe' by bombing were pulled down during the war or in the following decade, and Lewes would be no exception. The Blitz resulted in the loss of many smaller vernacular medieval buildings in British towns. SEE ALSO P. 565.

FEBRUARY 1943

DURING FEBRUARY LOSSES to U-boat attacks remained severe. In an effort to counter this, many of the RAF's operations were directed at German submarine construction and servicing facilities on the Atlantic coast, and the experienced Air Marshal Slessor was moved from the Middle East to take control of Coastal Command.

On 2 February the final elements of the 6th Army surrendered at Stalingrad. Of the 280,000 Germans surrounded there, 150,000 were killed, 40,000 were wounded and evacuated and the rest were taken prisoner. Conditions for POWs under Russian control were bad and only 5,000 of the Germans captured there would eventually make it home, some as late as 1955. On Thursday 18 February, following the Stalingrad disaster, Joseph Goebbels, speaking before an enthusiastic audience in Berlin, announced the implementation of 'total war'.

In north Africa Rommel was being pressed by the 8th Army to the east, and also by the new forces under Eisenhower which had landed to the west of him the previous November. He decided to take a chance and attacked the inexperienced American forces in Tunisia by pushing through the Kasserine Pass. Rommel gained a great deal of ground and British and American armoured units only just held off his attack. Despite these successes, German forces were appalled to see the lavish scale of equipment available to the American forces that they had over-run, and it was clear to them that the nature of the war had changed.

Allied scientists were increasingly aware of the possibilities of atomic energy and were worried about German developments in this area. Accordingly, on Sunday 28 February a daring attack by Norwegian special forces, parachuted from British aircraft, destroyed the Norsk Hydro station which was part of the German 'heavy water' atomic research plant at Telemark in Norway.

Tuesday 2 February 1943

Edward D. Churchill of the US army conducts surgery on the front line in Tunisia

Edward D. Churchill was born in Chenoa, Illinois on 25 December 1895. After attending Harvard Medical School he had become a pioneering chest surgeon between the wars. During the Second World War he was commissioned a colonel in the medical corps of the United States army, and served in north Africa and the Mediterranean as a surgical consultant from February 1943.

Beginning at 4:00 p.m. on the 31st, casualties began pouring in. We started operating at once and kept at it through the night, not stopping till 10:30 next am. Just now, 8:00 pm, two more ambulance loads have come in. Frosty reports that casualties are on litters all over the floor of the dispensary. Surely we are taking an awful lacing between here and Maknessey. From one company of over two hundred men, thirty-two are now living.

I certainly have a real operating crew. They are all willing to work until they drop and with never a word of complaint. We have had all types of surgery; sucking chest wounds, abdominal wounds, compound fractures, and amputations of arms, legs, feet, and thighs. Some have had an arm or leg either partially or entirely blown off, so we have no choice. To date we have lost only one case here, a lower one-third thigh amputation with multiple wounds of the left leg and thigh. He was in profound shock in spite of 1,500 cc of plasma, 500 cc of blood and lots of glucose. The operation did not increase his shock, but neither did he improve. More blood might have helped. *Blood is so precious! So urgently needed!* What we do give is being obtained from our own personnel who are most willing, but they really need it themselves after putting in long hours without rest or sleep.

We could not find a donor for a splendid chap from Maine last night. He was in severe shock and needed something in addition to plasma and glucose, so Frosty gave his blood, took a short rest and went back to operating again. We had to amputate his right lower thigh, do a débridement and open reduction on a compound fracture of his left tibia and fibula and then remove a shell fragment from the left temporal region. He was evacuated back in good condition this evening.

They are strafing the road between here and Tebessa every day, killing and wounding our men, burning our supply and ration trucks. Rommel is reported in Gabes, eighty-five miles from here. Our rations are only C and even those are very skimpy. We are often hungry.

During the winter of 1942–3, despite being hard-pressed by the fighting in Russia, the Germans reinforced their position in Tunisia. Field Marshal Albert Kesselring sent fresh troops from Italy and the 5th Panzer Army grew to eleven divisions. In mid-February they attacked

*through the Kasserine Pass, hoping to drive on to Tebessa. The Allies
only just held on.*

Edward Churchill served until October 1945 and was awarded the
Legion of Merit, the Distinguished Service Medal and the European
Theater Service Medal. He had introduced many new procedures for
management of the wounded, and wrote about the problems of surgery
in wartime. After the war he would become chair of the committee on
surgery of the US National Research Council and then president of
the Society of Clinical Surgery.

Saturday 6 – Tuesday 23 February 1943

Ursula von Kardorff, a young German journalist, learns of
the death of her younger brother Jürgen in Russia

6 February
Jürgen's division gets a flattering citation in the Army com-
muniqué. Everyone knows what *that* means. Adelheid rang
up from Elvershagen to express sympathy. Mamma looked
utterly shattered . . .

13 February
Jürgen is dead. He was killed on 2 February, at Slaviansk.
The Dean of the Faculty of Theology brought us the news . . .

16 February
I cannot think, I cannot write or do anything. Today the
notice of his death appeared in the papers, just as I have seen
it in my mind's eye for years past. The Iron Cross was
printed above his name. How did I know already what the
notice said? . . .

23 February
. . . I never realized that I had so many friends, nor what a
comfort sympathy can be. At the office the people are really
touching. I have never known such a feeling of solidarity.
Even Q came to express his condolences. Papa could not

control himself. 'How do you think it's all going to end?' he shouted at the wretched man. 'Do you mean to sacrifice the flower of the nation's manhood uselessly so that your bosses can hang on for a few weeks longer?' Q said nothing. What could he say? Papa was beside himself.

Losing a son like this is especially tragic for people like Papa. For them the sacrifice is quite pointless. A clique of rulers whom they hate, waging war for a cause which they hate, exacts from them what they most cherish.

Jürgen von Kardorff was a lieutenant and a company commander in an armoured regiment. He died fighting on the Donetz on 2 February 1943. His family had suspected his death for a week before they had formal confirmation of it on 13 February 1945. On 28 February his letters were still arriving at home. His personal effects would finally arrive on 15 April, in a parcel stamped 'Died for a Greater Germany'. The tension was unbearable for his family and caused bitter exchanges. Ursula von Kardorff's father was anti-Nazi and saw the war as pointless, while her mother still believed there was some purpose to the conflict. All Ursula's family and friends were already panicking about the arrival of the Russians in Germany and rumours were running wild; it was reported, for example, that the Russians could be in Warsaw in two weeks, though in fact they would not move past Warsaw until the summer of 1944. Meanwhile Ursula's elder brother Klaus was still serving in France. SEE ALSO PP. 489–90, 533–4 AND 807–8.

Monday 22 February 1943

Hannah Senesh, a young Zionist in Caesarea, reflects on her decision to join the Haganah or Jewish underground

How strangely things work out. On January 8 I wrote a few words about the sudden idea that struck me. A few days ago a man from Kibbutz Ma'agan, a member of the Palmach [the active 'strike force' of the Haganah], visited the kibbutz and we chatted awhile. In the course of the conversation he told me that a Palmach unit was being organized to do – exactly what I felt then I wanted to do. I was truly astounded. The *identical* idea!

My answer, of course, was that I'm absolutely ready. It's still only in the planning stage, but he promised to bring the matter up before the enlistment committee since he considers me admirably suited for the mission.

I see the hand of destiny in this just as I did at the time of my Aliyah [emigration to Palestine]. I wasn't master of my fate then either. I was enthralled by one idea, and it gave me no rest. I knew I would emigrate, despite the many obstacles in my path. Now I again sense the excitement of something important and vital ahead, and the feeling of inevitability connected with a decisive and urgent step. The entire plan may miscarry, and I may receive a brief notification informing me the matter will be postponed, or that I don't qualify. But I think I have the capabilities necessary for just this assignment, and I'll fight for it with all my might.

I can't sleep at night because of the scenes I envisage: how I'll conduct myself in this or that situation . . . how I'll notify Mother of my arrival . . . how I'll organize the Jewish Youth. Everything is still indefinite. We'll see what the future brings . . .

In 1943 the British secret services were constantly looking for people with local knowledge and language skills, and recruited a group of Palestinian Jewish volunteers, members of the Haganah or Jewish underground, to cross behind enemy lines into Nazi-controlled Europe. The British were primarily concerned with liberating downed aircrews, but Hannah's priority was to rescue Jews and to free her mother. Hannah joined the Jewish resistance and at the same time also the WAAF, along with several other young Jewish women. Leaving her writings with her friends on the kibbutz, she soon departed for intelligence training in Cairo and was given the codename Hagar.

In March 1944 Hannah would fly with other agents to Bari, Italy, the main special forces despatch point. Shortly thereafter she was dropped by parachute into Slovenia. She made her way into Hungary, only to be denounced the day after her arrival by an informer and taken to a Gestapo prison in Budapest. After four months in captivity, during which she was tortured but continually defied her captors, she was executed by firing squad. During her last days she was allowed to meet her mother, who shared the same prison for a time. Seven of her original team of thirty-two agents died. She was buried in the Martyrs' Section of the Jewish cemetery in Budapest, but was later moved to the Israeli National Military Cemetery on Mount Herzl near Jerusalem. SEE ALSO *PP. 236–7 AND 516–17.*

Tuesday 23 February 1943

Neil McCallum, a junior infantry officer, watches a Messerschmitt come down over the Mareth Line in Tunisia

Still in this restful place. One evening as we were lying idle after supper the sound of a plane was heard. It was the leisurely note of a plane flying low and not very fast. It was almost overhead before we saw it through the trees and what we saw were the large black crosses on the wing. It was a single-engined Messerschmitt, cruising contentedly and quite unaware of us below. It was surprising how many men managed to get off a round or two though there is rarely much hope of rifle shots hitting a plane. It floated over us, just above the tree-tops, and one shot from the ragged fusillade must have hit the engine because we heard later that the plane landed in the salt marshes some miles to the rear and we were officially accorded the kill. It landed quite near a British armoured car which was having trouble in the soft sand. The crew of the vehicle looked on with unconcern as the plane glided to the ground. They watched the pilot get out and walk away to the nearest trees where he vanished. It did not occur to them that the plane might be German and the obvious signs on it did not register with them.

Late that night, before we had news that the plane had come down, I went into the woods to an Arab village to try to get word of it, believing it might have been hit. The Arabs were certain to have a bush telegraph and to know more of what was happening in their country than we did. By some adobe houses in a huddle of palm trees, under a bright moon and surrounded by howling and barking dogs, I tried to converse with an Arab whose few words of French did not match mine. Both the Arab and I got as far as a mutually comprehensible gesticulation for an aeroplane. Beyond that there was no coincidence of ideas. I left him wondering if he knew but pretended to be stupid, or if he was stupid and could not indicate what he did know, or if I was stupid and couldn't understand. It was classic pantomime by moonlight with a chorus of barking dogs, I in battle-dress and he in his white robe, each grinning at the other and making buzzing noises as we held out our arms like wings.

Neil McCallum was at this point serving with the British army in Tunisia, where one of his primary duties was rounding up POWs; as a result he escaped some of the bitter mountain fighting that characterized the final drive through the Mareth Line towards Tunis during early 1943. He did not attempt to disguise his relief. His main concern was being able to carry enough literature and poetry to fill the longer interludes in the fighting. SEE ALSO PP. 14, 467–9 AND 541–3.

Friday 26 – Saturday 27 February 1943

Arthur Dickison, a signaller on the submarine HMS *Safari*, reconnoitres the coast of Sicily for a future invasion

Arthur Dickison joined the Royal Navy on 24 January 1940 and trained as a wireless telegraphist. A few weeks later he was surprised to find himself drafted onto submarines, belying the common myth that even in wartime this was an all-volunteer service. Dickison became the leading telegraphist on the submarine HMS Safari, operating in the Mediterranean. In both the German and British navies, submarine diaries, which were very rare, were most likely to be kept by signallers or senior officers, as they had an excuse to write. This provided a cover for their diary-keeping, which was a court martial offence.

26 February

We sighted a convoy of small ships off Palermo but we were on different business and to attack them would have given away our presence in the area, so they proceeded unmolested. Later when we surfaced we were at boat evolutions [preparing to drop small boats] yet again, but minus me . . .

. . . we were putting out bows close in to the shore in the darkness and then coming slowly back astern away from the shore. With some of the many signals that we were receiving, I found out that this operation was actually called 'Combined Operation Pilotage Parties' (COPP) and, as their name implied, the teams would embark in their boats and slip ashore to survey the layout of the various beaches on the north shores of Sicily. By now we surmised that all this preparation was intended for some future landing in Sicily.

It was quite a hair-raising experience later when we attempted the first landing of the parties, taking the boat in to about 100 yards of the dark shoreline, dropping one folboat and its two occupants, then going back out to sea astern. Then we moved away slightly and dropped another boat and crew in another position before retreating back to sea. I was on the bridge with Bunnie, each of us manning an infrared lamp and special binoculars that would enable one to see the signals, if there were any, from shore. After the parties had left the Klaxon was sounded and we had to dive. An aircraft had been heard buzzing about, so we disappeared down to periscope depth and kept our vigil submerged. The area we were in was called Castellamare and we had been prowling around it for a couple of days. Also there had been heard some explosions to the east of us. There were three other submarines on the same exercise with folboats and their crews at different points around Sicily. We all hoped that they were safe and well.

27 February

We were still working in and around the Gulf of Castellamare and the rehearsals were getting a trifle monotonous. It was a job that had to be done but it was a job that we could have done without, since the amount of enemy shipping that had been allowed to go unmolested, according to the Captain, was in the region of some 16,000 tons. Now we were testing the boat for deep diving, up to periscope depth down to 320 feet. On one occasion while doing this drill, we sighted two tankers with a solitary destroyer as escort; as the song goes 'Pass on By!'. Later we surfaced and let go a couple of officers in a folboat after pushing our bows close into shore at 2000. They left and we retreated to deeper water with the arrangement to return at 2300. This was no exercise. We waited for two hours out about 2 miles distance from the shore, then eased our way back in and got them back inboard safely. We then retreated out to deep water again and charged our batteries. We had been wondering what emblem to sew on the Roger denoting this venture and someone came up with the answer – for every authentic landing we could sew a Commando dagger on the flag.

Submarines were not used only for underwater warfare; they were also used to carry special forces on clandestine operations, including reconnaissance of a coastline preceding a full-scale amphibious invasion. While these missions were important, submarine commanders often resented them because, while they were in progress, for reasons of secrecy, targets of opportunity could not be attacked. In this case the beach investigation was carried out by a Combined Operations Pilotage Party or COPP, a forerunner of the modern Special Boat Service. They employed two-man collapsible canoes, or 'folbots', launched from the submarine. Similar operations were carried out along the coastlines of north Africa, Greece and Yugoslavia. As we have already seen, in mid-November 1941 the submarines Torbay *and* Talisman *had carried Commandos in a failed attempt to assassinate Rommel at his Libyan headquarters. Between March 1942 and September 1943* Safari *sailed more than 31,000 nautical miles, spent almost 140 days underwater and sank 34 ships. Her captain was Commander Ben Bryant, one of the top-scoring Allied submarine aces of the war.*

Arthur Dickison would serve to the end of the war and now lives in retirement in Devon.

MARCH 1943

IN EARLY MARCH 1943 Bomber Harris launched what he called the Battle of the Ruhr with a 1,000-bomber raid on the German town of Essen. This raid employed the new navigational aid codenamed Oboe. The Luftwaffe continued to try to launch reprisal raids, even though its strength was dwindling. On Wednesday 3 March 173 Londoners were crushed to death in an accident caused by panic at Bethnal Green tube station after new anti-aircraft rockets were fired for the first time from nearby Victoria Park, causing a deafening roar.

On 9 March Rommel left Africa for good, believing that the war in the desert was lost. He warned both Mussolini and Hitler that this was the case, but neither could be persuaded to withdraw Axis forces. By 20 March the Americans and units under Montgomery were making a major attack on the Mareth Line – the main Axis stronghold in Tunisia – and by 25 March they had broken through. A key element in the campaign was growing Allied air power in the region. Montgomery was also receiving excellent signals intelligence from Bletchley Park. Although codebreaking had allowed the Allies to detect when Rommel's supplies were arriving, the Allies had to allow some to get through to hide the fact that Axis codes had been broken. Only in March 1943 were the air forces allowed to attack all convoys, closing down Axis shipping completely.

During the week following 14 March the largest convoy battle of the war took place in the Atlantic, with the loss of 20 Allied ships but no U-boats sunk. The war against the U-boats depended heavily on air power, and in March 1943 more small escort carriers were being deployed in the Atlantic.

Wednesday 3 March 1943

Ursula von Kardorff, a young German journalist, notes the
treatment of her Jewish neighbours

Frau Liebermann is dead. They actually came with a stretcher
to carry this old lady of eighty-five off to Poland. When they
came she took veronal. She died next day in the Jewish
Hospital without regaining consciousness. What monstrous
wickedness this is. Why should it be our people who are
guilty of it? What transformation can have taken place, that
normally decent, good-hearted people become servants of
the Devil? Everything is done in a cold-blooded, bureaucratic fashion of these parasites, who began by battening
upon the body of the nation and have now become a part
of it.

Bussy, the compositor, told me that in his neighborhood,
around the Rosenthalerplatz, working-class women had
gathered and protested noisily against the deportation of the
Jews. Armed SS men with fixed bayonets and steel helmets
were dragging miserable figures out of the houses. Old
women, children and terrified men were loaded into trucks
and driven away. The crowd shouted, 'Why don't you leave
the old women alone? Why don't you go out to the front,
where you belong?' In the end a fresh detachment of SS
appeared and dispersed the crowd.

One never sees that kind of thing in our neighborhood.
There the Jews are fetched away at night. If it were not for
Bärchen, who works tirelessly for the Jewish families in her
apartment house, I should not even know what was
happening. How quickly we have all got used to seeing the
Jewish Star.

Most people's attitude is one of complete indifference –
like that of T, who said to me the other day, 'Why should I
care about the Jews? The only thing I think about is my
brother, at Rshev, and I couldn't care less about anything
else.' I think that the ordinary people are behaving much
better than the so-called educated classes or the half-educated.

There is a typical story of a workman who got up and gave his seat in a tram to a Jewess, wearing the Star. 'Come on, have a sit-down, my old doll'! he said. When a Party member protested, the workman simply said, 'I'll do what I like with my own ass, if you don't mind!'.

Ursula von Kardorff and her family were devout Catholics and were increasingly appalled by the activities of the Nazi regime. The large-scale deportation of Jews from Berlin in early March coincided with a particularly heavy air raid on the city, and most of the population muttered that the recent air raid was a direct reprisal for the deportations. Ursula's virulently anti-Nazi father criticized his wife and daughter even for carrying buckets to help with the putting out of fires during air raids. By late 1943 Ursula von Kardorff would begin to meet people involved in the German resistance and knew many on the fringes of the bomb plot against Hitler in July 1944. Ursula's brother Klaus was being sent to Tunis in an increasingly hopeless Axis attempt to hold on to north Africa, and she feared the worst 'every moment of the day'. SEE ALSO PP. 489–90, 525–6 AND 807–8.

Friday 12 March 1943

James Webb Young, advertising executive, on deodorants in wartime

Thirty years ago I had something to do with the introduction of one of the first products for checking and deodorizing perspiration. Shortly thereafter the *Journal of the American Medical Association* pilloried it as a dangerous preparation; and Samuel Hopkins Adams, in a series of muckraking articles, cited it as a flagrant example of the harm done to the public by ad men. Indeed, for many years the whole field of personal grooming preparations has been a happy hunting ground for the advertising reformer. But now the War Production Board lists deodorants and other cosmetics as among the essentials of a bedrock economy; and the most hard-bitten industrial managers have suddenly discovered what color, clothes, and cosmetics mean to the morale of women workers. Thus does *Time* confound the views of men.

Young had thought up some of J. Walter Thompson's greatest campaigns. In 1919 he had developed a campaign under the slogan 'Within the Curve of a Woman's Arm'. This was the first advert to deal with the delicate issue of female underarm perspiration and advertised the product Odorno. The numbers of women workers in factories now ensured that such products were considered essential rather than peripheral to the war effort.

Young would retire from J. Walter Thompson in 1964; he died in New Mexico in 1973. SEE ALSO PP. 517–18.

Saturday 20 March 1943

Philip Jordan watches the beginning of the battle for Tunis

Philip Jordan had reported on the Spanish Civil War and was the News Chronicle's *most experienced war correspondent. He ran a feature called 'Advanced Column' between 1939 and 1942. At the end of 1942 he was sent to cover the Anglo-American landings in north Africa.*

For perhaps the first time in the history of modern war men to-day were able to watch a battle from beginning to end, to watch the forces gathering, deploying, attacking and going through. I was one of those men, for I sat on a hill-top over-looking the wide plain and I could see everything that happened there. All morning the Americans put up a barrage from the batteries behind and in front of us; and there can have been no minute when shells were not flying over. You don't actually *hear* shells going over, but your ears *feel* them; and you *feel* the sound of silk being shaken in the wind. At 12 a vast quantity of armour, of self-propelled guns and tank busters (perhaps 100 of each) were massed behind us, and they came through the low sandy pass into the open plain. This tidal wave rolled out over the plain. It was empty at one moment, except for the advanced batteries and the shattered vehicles of the battle last week and then suddenly it seemed full. The enemy shelled the road just below us and hit a jeep. Its occupants were running for shelter when the burst came and one went flat and you knew he was dead, while the others crumpled in a co-ordinated way and then got up and ran. It was like seeing animated dolls knocked over. You knew when the shells were coming because suddenly men would drop for no reason and then a moment after the burst came near them; and they would get up and go, more slowly than they need have done.

At 1.30 the leading tanks went over a small fold and dashed for the pass through the hills beyond. The right flank was held up by a superb mortar barrage, but the left crashed through what at times must have seemed a walls of shells. When the enemy opened up he let them have everything he'd got and the ground rose about them in evanescent walls that looked solid for a moment and then became dust and smoke. One Sherman was hit. A halo of smoke, blue as periwinkles, hung round it for a few moments and then flames came from it, bright as scarlet flowers in a slum, and its crew went on firing with vigour. They jumped out just before it exploded. There was none of the usual confusion of battle; the whole was as orderly as a rehearsed play and not as good, for it aroused no pity in those who watched it. In a peculiar way this fearful thing lacked all dramatic essence, yet it was one of the most dramatic spectacles that human eyes have ever witnessed.

In March 1943 the Americans deployed their 'tank busters' for the first time. Unlike the British, they had taken the threat of heavy German armour seriously and had sought to counter it with superior equipment. In 1941 they had begun to design an effective anti-tank vehicle, and in Tunisia the new full-tracked M-10 tank destroyer saw its baptism of fire. It had an open turret and was armed with a high-powered, long-barrel 3-inch gun, providing a serious challenge to the German panzers. By June 1944 the Americans would have produced the M-18 'Hellcat': designed from the ground up as a tank destroyer and armed with a high-velocity 76mm gun, it was the fastest armoured fighting vehicle of the war. The Americans were also superbly equipped with heavy artillery and by March 1943 they had begun to develop finesse in using it on the battlefield.

Tuesday 23 March 1943

Nella Last, diarist for the Mass-Observation Archive, comforts the mother of a Wren in Barrow-in-Furness

A lovely day again; but oh dear, such a tiring day. Mrs Woods is away spring-cleaning this week, and so much came into the shop, needing to be looked over and priced. Also, a woman came in and upset me for the rest of the day. She was a stranger, a drawn-faced woman with a cultured accent and beautiful clothes. She bought a little cart for her granddaughter, and we got chatting about the war and prisoners and the worry of mothers with lads in the Services. I think I said something about women with daughters being, on the whole, happier today. Suddenly she started to cry so bitterly. I got her to sit down on the little stool by the radiator, fetched her a drink of water and gave her two aspirins. She looked up and said, 'I feel I'm going out of my mind with worry,' and she told me such a pitiful tale of her daughter of twenty-three, who is a Wren, and whose husband has been a prisoner-of-war since Dunkirk. She 'loves life and dancing', her mother says, and goes off night after night in a clique of girls and Naval men from the Depot, both married and single. She has had 'flu this week, and it's been discovered she can expect a baby within four to five months. Her story is that she knows nothing about it – it must have happened when she was 'tight' some time: at all the parties she goes to there is 'everything to drink'.

Her father, an officer at the Fort, says she is a slut, and that he'll be hanged if he'll 'believe that damn-fool tale'. Her mother says, 'I don't know *what* to believe.' I said, 'You *must* believe her, and if that is too much, don't tell her you doubt her story.' The poor woman said, 'Her husband – a prisoner – who is to tell him, or that proud family of his?' I said, 'Well, if it was my girl, I'd find some way to shield her; and that poor lad in Germany should never know till he is back and she can tell him herself. What *good* will it do to torture him while he is so helpless?' Her grief was distressing when she had let go. I persuaded her to go into the passage behind the shop, and rest. I dropped the latch and went for a taxi to come the back way.

The Wrens (Women's Royal Naval Service) had been created during the First World War, and although it was then in existence for less than two years, it proved highly valuable. As a result it was quickly re-formed at the outbreak of war in 1939. During the Second World War the number of Wrens would reach a peak of 74,000 in 1944, with women engaged in over 200 different naval trades and occupations. Women played an important role in planning and organizing major operations and were vital to the smooth running and maintenance of headquarters and intelligence centres. However, some parents were reluctant to allow their daughters to join the women's services, believing that they would be vulnerable to the concerted attentions of their male colleagues. One of the immediate challenges for the authorities in re-creating or expanding the women's services in 1939 had been the building of separate and secure accommodation. SEE ALSO PP. 130–1, 235 AND 593–4.

Friday 26 March 1943

Mollie Panter-Downes, writing for the *New Yorker*, comments on weak beer and enforced sobriety

All in all, the drink situation is bad and will probably become so much worse that most Britons will have to celebrate the armistice, when it arrives, with nothing more festive than beer, perhaps diluted even below its present strength, which is fifteen per cent less than what is was before the war. In spite of the agitations of the temperance groups, which frequently demand that Parliament explain why barley should be diverted from hungry hens to iniquitous breweries, the authorities have so far steadfastly refused either to cut the beer supply or to introduce the no-treating legislation which was put into effect during the First World War. This is because high prices and limited supplies are to a large extent achieving the results for which the dry elements are crusading. The official attitude seems to be that there's no good setting up regulations which might bring about high words in the corner pub and a sullen slacking-off in the workshops when the same end can be quietly attained without any drastic action by Westminster. Police records show that the country as a whole is becoming, maybe unwillingly but certainly steadily, more sober; the number of arrests in London for drunkenness, for instance, swooped down from the twenty-thousand mark in 1937 to an estimated nine thousand in 1942. Maybe this is because more and more Britons, obliged to drink nothing but weak beer, are finding intoxication a rather expensive and difficult state to achieve . . .

There were sad faces in Scotland on the day that a lone raider came over and dropped a bomb, apparently by mistake, smack on top of seventy thousand gallons of whisky which had been stored in a hideout on a wild and lonely moor. Finding suitable billets for evacuated whisky stocks is a sizeable headache, since the liquor must be kept at an even temperature. Owners of warehouses in vulnerable areas are not allowed to keep spirits on the top floors because of the inflammable nature of the stuff, and must take special precautions to prevent burning alcohol from flowing through the streets. All air-raid shelters uncomfortably close to whisky reserves have been closed.

As the conflict wore on, ever more goods were added to the list of things that were rationed. Sweets, chocolate and soap had been put on ration in 1942. Certain goods, however, were never rationed during the war years, and these included bread, potatoes, tobacco, beer and spirits. However, beer was watered down and its price inflated by excise duties. Suppliers tended to favour old customers, and establishments that catered for the upper echelons had little difficulty obtaining supplies.

Mollie Panter-Downes would continue as the London correspondent of the New Yorker *magazine until 1987.* See also pp. 65–6, 81–2 and 106–7.

APRIL 1943

THE NORTH AFRICAN campaign was drawing to a close in April 1943. By 14 April the Germans had retreated to their final defensive positions in the hills around Bizerte and Tunis. The Axis supply situation in north Africa was now desperate and the Luftwaffe decided to mount an extraordinary aerial relief effort, employing over a hundred massive Gigante transport aircraft. However, Allied intelligence got wind of the operation and more than half the aircraft were destroyed. Between 22 and 29 April there was heavy fighting as forces commanded by General Bradley and General Montgomery attempted to overcome carefully prepared defensive positions.

On 12 April the Germans announced that they had found a group of mass graves at Katyn Wood, containing the bodies of 4,100 Polish army officers. On 18 April the Russians blamed the Germans for the massacre. Although the Polish government-in-exile in London requested an inspection by the Red Cross, the German reputation for atrocities ensured that it was decades before the crime was attributed to its real perpetrators, the NKVD or Russian secret police.

By now the activities of the Special Operations Executive were gathering pace and becoming increasingly militarized, as it turned into more of a 'secret army'. Substantial supplies were making their way to partisans in locations as far afield as Greece and Norway. Large partisan forces in the Balkans were making the lives of the German and Italian occupiers particularly difficult. However, the SOE also had its security problems. In April 1943 two SOE agents in France, Peter Churchill and Odette Sansom, were arrested by the Gestapo operative Hugo Bleicher. They would not be the last ones to be betrayed.

On the last day of this month the British submarine HMS *Seraph* initiated Operation Mincemeat. This involved quietly dropping a corpse, which purported to be the body of a Royal Marines officer, 'Major Martin', off the Spanish coast. Major

Martin, who had supposedly been killed when an aircraft was shot down over the sea, carried in a briefcase chained to his wrist vital plans for an Allied invasion of Greece, which were in fact a deception. This was an attempt to persuade the Germans to deploy their reserves to defend Greece rather than Sicily – the real Allied target for invasion in the summer of 1943 – and it succeeded.

Monday 5 April 1943

Neil McCallum, an infantry officer, reflects on hatred and killing in the hills near Tunis

All day the prisoners have been streaming down from the hills. They come in long straggling lines, very slowly. They have a lost helpless look, not at all as though they had recently been conducting a purposeful war. They are very pleased and tired and full of a sort of dumb relief.

One of us recently received a letter saying, 'How you must hate these bastards'. We don't. It is as easy to say as that. We don't hate them. There is anger, but not at anyone in particular. The whole thing is too vast for so personal an emotion as hatred. In a sense, the more deeply you become involved in war, the more impersonally you regard it. That may be a sort of native caution: an excess of emotion such as hatred is very unbalancing. In any case there are plenty of other things to hate – the flies, the heat, the cold, the grub, or not having enough sleep, and all that. But not the enemy, or very rarely.

Hatred belongs at home, with the civilians. This has all been said before – 'spinsters in the suburbs mewing for blood' – but it is permanently true. The feelings of soldiers in action must be fairly standardised, unless they have been whipped by such obscenities as concentration camps, or deliberate sadistic practices, the bestial treatment of civilians. Such things exert no immediate influence on us, and there is little positive hatred to be drawn from the theoretical. There may be a reason for killing someone in

Africa because of mass-murder in Poland, but it does not involve hatred. There was something significant in the proclamation of Stalin during the siege of Leningrad when he exhorted his people to hate the enemy. That was the politician speaking, not the soldier. It is probably necessary for civilians to hate the enemy; it is a disadvantage for the soldier to do so.

Sometimes, when newspapers arrive from Britain, we read of churchmen commanding people to hate the enemy, 'the evil things' and all that. We grunt or laugh and wonder how the reverend gentlemen would feed their spiritual hatred if they stood in a trench up to their gaiters in sand and had no congregation except bored blaspheming soldiers.

You cannot hate the bastard who is trying to kill you and who you are trying to kill. When war was brief and hand-to-hand hatred might have been possible. But I doubt it; it was even more of a mercenary business than it is now. Certainly hatred is an emotion one cannot sustain when war is very dreary and uncomfortable and everlasting. We shoot at the enemy on the basic grounds of fear and self-preservation. If you don't shoot first he will shoot you. That is a state of moral putridity and is also the justification for a world crusade. Shoot first or be shot. If your nerves are not jangled by fear – as common an emotion as hatred is uncommon – you can only be amazed at the vast silliness of it. You are aware that the shooting only takes place because two sets of people in different uniforms have got themselves into the ridiculous position of not being able to do other than shoot. Instinct is against reason, discipline against emotion – and the war goes on.

When asked to reflect on how they escaped the civilian inhibition against killing a fellow human being, most soldiers gave similar answers. First, they explained that they mostly fired their weapons at targets they could barely see. The enemy were just dots in the distance and the effect was barely visible. Second, if they came closer to the enemy, it became a matter of 'kill or be killed'. Third, close-quarter combat was relatively rare, and so few had to look their enemy in the face as he died.

Neil McCallum would go on to fight in Italy in 1944. His diary –
published in 1959 but largely ignored – is, in my opinion, one of the
finest pieces of writing to emerge from the war. It is now almost un-
obtainable, except from charity shops. McCallum noted in his preface
that he had forgotten his desert notebooks and when he rediscovered
them in his forties he found the young man who had written them
twenty years earlier was almost a stranger – 'someone who had dis-
appeared'. He left the story as it was 'without correction or amendment'.
SEE ALSO PP. 14, 467–9 AND 528–9.

Monday 12 April 1943

Georgi Dimitrov of the Moscow Comintern hears of German policy in Ukraine

Colonel *Starinov* returned to Moscow (he is at Khrushchev's
disposal for Ukrainian work). Described the situation in the
south in detail, particularly Krasnodar and Rostov. Typical
facts: on the *Don* and *Kuban* the Germans successfully in-
gratiated themselves with the locals. They have permitted
no gross excesses. The populace thought that the Soviet
Union was now done for, and people started reconciling
themselves with the Germans. All kinds of girls married
Germans . . . The prevailing attitude – the Germans have not
done anything wrong! During the German withdrawal, a lot
of Don and Kuban locals withdrew along with them. The
Germans play chiefly on the *kolkhozy*. The dissolution of the
kolkhozy was celebrated like a major holiday . . . The Jewish
populace, however, was destroyed en masse by the Germans
under the guise of *reselllement*. Twelve thousand Jews were
destroyed in Krasnodar . . . *Starinov* recounted terrible facts.

As Secretary-General of the Soviet Comintern, Georgi Dimitrov mixed
with a variety of intelligence personnel. Colonel I. G. Starinov was one
such figure, a larger-than-life Red Army intelligence and special forces
operative who had begun his activities in the Spanish Civil War. He had
been tasked with staying behind to blow up key buildings in Kiev after

the Germans took the city in 1942. If anyone knew what real conditions were like in German-occupied areas then it was Starinov. Moscow was anxious about German efforts to win over the captive nations of the Soviet Union, and its policy towards minorities softened noticeably during the war.

Dimitrov would survive the war and become Prime Minister of postwar Bulgaria. SEE ALSO PP. 306–7.

Saturday 17 April 1943

Harry C. Butcher watches Eisenhower and his generals tour the battlefield in north Africa

On Thursday morning left Ike's tented Advance CP, Generals Ike and Tooey in one car, General Porter and I in another, with jeeps and their .50's fore and aft, on roads dusty with the rapid movement of elements of II Corps from its old sector to its new battleground in the north. Ike was intent on calling on General Anderson of the First Army, whom he had not seen for several weeks, as his dealings had been with Alexander since the latter had been given command of the battle front. After thorough exploration of the situation with General Anderson, Ike accepted his invitation to drive fifteen miles north of Beja to see three Mark-6, or Tiger, tanks. These were three of twenty-seven destroyed by the British when the Germans made a push March 26. While Ike was interested in seeing the tanks, he was more concerned with familiarizing himself with the terrain over which American troops soon would operate.

We changed from staff cars to jeeps at Beja, the road eastward being subject to strafing and bombing.

General Anderson himself drove the jeep for Ike. I rode in another and 'manned' the .50-caliber gun. Captain Samuelson, one of Anderson's aides, sat in the front seat to guide. We were told that if we were strafed, we had the choice of staying in the jeeps or dashing off the road into the fields, many of which still had mines left by the Germans. When we reached the scene of destruction of twenty-seven tanks, many of which could still be seen on the hillsides, we had to take a one-way dirt track across a field. The track was marked by white tape and along it were signs, 'Mines-Verges.' Because of possible presence of booby traps, there was a noticeable reluctance to prod into the innards of the Tiger tanks or to touch the articles lying around them. We could hear artillery fire, judged by the experts to be about 2000 yards away. There had been no enemy aircraft that we had seen, although we had seen antiaircraft bursts above and to the right of us. I filled my pockets with burned-out machine-gun cartridges from one of the tanks, pilfered a seven-foot copper whip antenna from another, and got away with an 88-mm. projectile. The size of the Tiger, its armament, and especially its 88 gun were impressive. General Anderson said the British had laid a heavy pattern of artillery fire on this turn of the road when the tanks came charging along. The barrage was so heavy, and so many tanks were hit, that the crews of the Tigers abandoned their mobile fortresses. Clothing was still strewn about and, no doubt, there had been many killed . . .

General 'Tooey' did not tell Ike, but he told me that he had been on a Flying Fortress raid of Palermo and Sicily the day before. Some forty-eight Fortresses took part, but three had been lost, two by fighters and one by flak. Tooey had seen eight of the crew of one Fortress bail out close to the Sicilian coast but over water. He said it wasn't a pleasant sight.

Tooey's trip on the bombers (it wasn't the first by any means) brings to mind that I haven't seen any criticism of American general officers failing to take risks with their men. Quite the contrary. Patton is a notorious front-line kibitzer, Eaker and Doolittle have flown innumerable missions with their crews, and General Ike has not sought the safety of Algiers, nor has he stayed there from choice. But every time he wants to get where the shooting is, every front-line officer tries to discourage him. Then if he insists, so much protection is thrown around him, the party becomes too large and too many lives are needlessly endangered. So most of the time he just growls at his job in this war.

In April 1943 Allied forces closed in on Rommel's last stronghold at Bizerte. Everyone was looking forward to the final phase of the Tunisian battle, with the British 8th Army moving in from the east and the Americans arriving from the west. Patton was given the job of planning the invasion of Sicily and General Bradley took over his role commanding the 2nd Corps in the final push against Rommel. Eisenhower, like so many other generals, enjoyed getting out of his HQ to engage personally with his field commanders and also to get a feel for the terrain. In the desert, where air attack was a constant threat, the risks of doing this were not small. Such battlefield tourism was dangerous because a minor error in map-reading could result in encounters with the enemy. Moreover, the possible capture of senior officers who had knowledge of future invasion plans, or of special techniques such as deception or signals intelligence, represented a real security hazard. SEE ALSO PP. 27, 469–70, 561–3 AND 712–13.

Saturday 17 – Wednesday 21 April 1943

Major David Smiley of the SOE parachutes into occupied Albania

David Smiley was born in 1906 and went to school at Hawtreys and then Pangbourne before joining the Royal Horse Guards in 1936. In 1939 he was still serving in the cavalry in Palestine, but in 1940 had transferred to the SOE in search of adventure, which he certainly found. By 1941 he was already behind Italian lines in Albania.

17 April

Left Derna [in Libya] in a Halifax piloted by Wing-Commander. Party consisted of [Bill] Maclean, Duffy, Williamson and self. Left 8.30 p.m., read 'Horse and Hound' in the 'plane. 11.00 p.m. started to put on parachutes. 11.30 p.m. jumped. Bill first, self second, Williamson third and Duffy fourth. The first time we had jumped out of hole instead of a door. Dropped between 2,000 and 3,000 feet, nearly collided with Bill on the way down, landed very badly and tore a muscle. Dropped within five yards of one of the guiding flares. Warmly greeted by guerrilla with a beard, who kissed me on both cheeks and lifted me up. About fifty guerrillas on the ground and John C. Only two parachutes failed to open and one case of ammunition was lost, otherwise the operation was 100% successful . . .

18 April

Loaded the stores on to a mule train and walked 1½ hours to join Bill and the rest of the party at Romanon Monastery . . .

21 April

Left monastery at about 8.30, with all our stuff less the wireless kit, as the wireless broke on dropping so we had to leave Williamson behind until a new set arrives. Party consisted of ten mules, plus andartes and guides. Walked for nine hours, spent the night in a village called Vowshu, which had been bombed by the Italians a week before. The people were therefore very windy and rather unfriendly. We paid 2,000 dr.[achma] for mules and 15,000 dr.[achma] the night before for one sheep.

In 1943 the SOE was establishing parties with various guerrilla groups, primarily the communists, in both Albania and Yugoslavia. Everything arrived by special duties aircraft that flew to north Africa and then on to Cairo, and later to Italy. In the Balkans time was spent negotiating with disputing local warlords, awaiting further drops of stores and periodically mounting chaotic attacks against increasingly terrified Italians and Germans. The Italians and Germans directed ferocious reprisals against the local population and, unsurprisingly, Smiley and his guerrillas were met with varying enthusiasm by the locals. We will read more of his adventures in May, June and October 1943. SEE ALSO
PP. 554–6, 577–8 AND 610–11.

Sunday 18 April 1943

Hugh Dormer leads an SOE sabotage mission in occupied France

Hugh Dormer was a young Irish Guards officer who, like David Smiley, had volunteered for behind-the-lines work with the SOE. He was twice parachuted into occupied France before the Normandy landings.

First landing in occupied France

The evening sun was glowing on the brick walls of the kitchen garden and on the wild daffodils under the chestnut trees, as we made the final preparations for our journey that night. I sat in a chair outside and read Shakespeare's *Henry V* while the wind ruffled my hair. The tranquil atmosphere of an English country house provided a perfect prelude to our journey. The wind sang in my blood and this mellowness was of ancient times and of an ancient land, for which one would be proud to die.

After an early dinner we left for the aerodrome some few miles distant. Here in a hut we were helped into our parachute equipment which gave us finally the swollen air of some creatures from Mars. Then in closed cars with the blinds drawn we were driven out onto the tarmac runway of the airfield. Our Halifax was warming up and the Polish crew were having a final check up of the controls. The sun was just setting behind the trees. A last handshake all round and the six of us clambered up into the fuselage.

The interior was spacious and, as we were not due over the target area for some four hours, our parachute harness was not hooked up and we were able to walk about inside. We taxied up into the wind and took off, and for the next hour flew south over the coast. The Channel was silver as we droned steadily over it. As we approached the French coast we dived sharply down to tree top level and crossed the line swerving to confuse the defences. Flak glowed up at us from either side a long way distant. As we flew low over the roads

and fields and valleys – as clear as day in the brilliant moonlight – I watched every detail of the country with an
enormous sense of detachment. So we flew on hour after
hour into the heart of France as smoothly as if it were a
peacetime pleasure cruise. During this time I had crawled
forward past the pilot and down into the cockpit of the
plane. And here I crouched looking over the shoulders of
the navigator, who knelt with his maps around him by
the windows. He had a red cushion under his knees and,
Pole as he was, he might have been praying in some prie-
dieu in some cathedral. Below us all the time flashed the
ever changing panorama.

At midnight we saw in the distance two great fires, perhaps the work of earlier bombers. I crawled back into the
fuselage where the others were drinking hot coffee and rum
and eating sandwiches; then curling up in their sleeping-
bags they went to sleep on the floor. I sat and read some
more of *Henry V*. About one o'clock we were approaching
the target, so we were all made to sit down in our places and
our static lines were hooked up. Then the doors over the hole
were uncovered and sitting on the rim I gazed down at the
fields and hedges five hundred feet below. I could see cars
moving on the roads and cattle in the fields. Down in the
cockpit the navigator must have been feverishly busy with
his maps and wind speed indicators, working out his last
minute calculations for it is a tricky business to drop men not
bombs. As we came in over the target, the dispatcher
shouted, 'Action Stations'. I swung my legs into the hole and
waited tensed up for the order to go. Next to me crouched D
wrapped up like a round baby in all his clothes and looking
rather frightened.

The dispatcher knelt on the side holding the package
which he was going to throw out immediately before I was
to jump. As the pilot presumably intended to circle again
over the dropping point, the dispatcher gave me the cancel-
lation signal with his hands and waved to me to take my legs
out of the hole again, which I did, presuming we should get
the order 'Action stations' again before jumping. So for the
next ten minutes I relaxed, sitting on the edge of the hole and
looking down at the ground beneath trying to identify

landmarks. It was fortunate that I did so, for suddenly to my amazement I heard a loud bang and saw the container dropping away to earth, which was the first warning I had that we were going to drop. I knew if I did not jump like lightning after that we should probably never see the container again, which in fact nearly happened. At the same time the thought flashed through my mind that perhaps they had changed the plan at the last minute, after seeing the ground, and that we were going to make two runs – dropping first the containers and packages and then us. However, I swung my legs into the hole and jumped instinctively. As I went out I heard the dispatcher shout something; I was not sure whether it was 'Go' or 'Stop', but in either case it was too late.

All then was peace and complete silence save for the soft rustle of silk above. It was with some relief that behind me I saw the rest of the stick floating against the moon. I drifted down over a hill past a wood and came to earth just short of a hedge. I saw next to mine John's parachute crumple and fall past me on the ground. He landed on his back and bruised his spine and I learnt later that higher up the hill L had a badly twisted ankle.

I don't think I shall ever forget the silence of those few moments after landing. I looked around and found myself alone in a small field about a hundred yards from the main road and some houses. The moonlight was flooding down and I could see for miles. The grass was drenched in dew. Of my companions not a sight or sound. It seemed impossible to realize that one was in the middle of France; the night was of peace; it had nothing to do with war.

Although the existence of the SOE would be known to the public by the end of the war, information about its undercover activities seeped out only gradually. Hugh Dormer's diary, published in 1947, was one of the first autobiographical publications and was cautious, replacing some of his compatriots' names with letters. However, by the 1950s the story of the SOE in France would have become the least secret of the wartime clandestine operations and a matter of public debate. The French resistance were keen to tell their side of the story and play up their contribution. Moreover, a number of SOE operations in France and Holland had gone wrong as a result of German infiltration, leading to the controversial capture and torture of a number of women agents.

Hugh Dormer would not survive the war. He rejoined his regular unit before D-Day and was killed in July 1944 while serving with his tank battalion.

MAY 1943

A S THE EYES OF the Allies turned to Italy and Sicily, the SOE and its American sister service, the OSS, tried to step up the pace of resistance throughout the Balkans in order to convince the Axis that the main focus of Allied strategic planning was an invasion of Greece. British officers were dropped by parachute to liaise with Tito in Yugoslavia and to offer more support. The Germans and Bulgarians responded by applying serious military pressure, forcing Tito and his whole headquarters staff to fight their way out of an attempted encirclement.

In north Africa the Axis collapsed, the last two towns in their possession falling on the same day, 7 May, when Tunis was captured by the British and Bizerte by the Americans. By 13 May 200,000 Axis troops had surrendered in this area, half of which were high-quality German forces. Churchill was keen to make the Mediterranean the focus of future Allied strategy. In part this reflected his desire to move through Italy to occupy southern and central Europe before the Russians did.

In the air, the bombing of Italy and Sicily intensified in the prelude to the coming invasion. The US 8th Air Force was also increasing its attacks on Germany and undertook a daylight raid on Kiel with over 100 aircraft. On Sunday 16 May Guy Gibson led the Dam Busters raid, which used bouncing bombs against the dams of the Ruhr valley. The resulting flooding did not interrupt industrial processes as much as had been expected. The Luftwaffe continued to be a serious menace and on 17 May replied with a heavy raid against Cardiff. The Germans increasingly turned to science to address their problems and on 22 May they tested a formidable jet-propelled fighter – the Messerschmitt ME-262 – which flew at 520 miles per hour. The introduction of this excellent machine had been delayed because of Hitler's obsession with bombers.

At the end of May Churchill flew from the United States, where he had been talking to Roosevelt about strategy, to Algiers for a conference with Eisenhower. He was accompanied by Roosevelt's Chief of Staff, General Marshall. Here they discussed the forthcoming Italian campaign. The Americans were anxious to avoid any commitments in Italy on a scale that might prevent a cross-Channel invasion of France in 1944.

During May the scale of Allied shipping losses continued to decline and forty-one U-boats were sunk, largely as a result of intensified Allied air operations. U-boats could no longer risk travelling on the surface by day and so could no longer reach their positions with any speed. The German navy decided that it must withdraw its submarines from the north Atlantic.

The month of May was also a reminder of the perils of air travel for VIPs. In the latter part of the month the Germans appeared to attempt to shoot down Churchill's aircraft as it passed Gibraltar. Earlier, on 3 May, the US commander in Europe, Lieutenant-General Frank M. Andrews, was killed in an air crash in Iceland. Fourteen of his fifteen officers, including his personal staff, were also killed, with only a sergeant escaping.

Sunday 2 May 1943

Iris Origo describes a visitation by 'Liberators' to Grosseto in Italy

Iris Origo was born in Italy in 1902 to Anglo-American parents and had lived the life of an expatriate society luminary in Florence in the 1930s. She moved in literary circles and would eventually become a renowned writer herself. She was also a local reformer and philanthropist, building up local agriculture and working with children.

Within the last month a new factor has been introduced into Italian warfare: the day-bombing by the 'Liberators'. Already after Cagliari, Naples and Trapani, the Italians had begun to realize that new daylight air-raids were different, not in degree, but in kind, from any experienced before. And now, Grosseto. On Easter Bank Holiday, at two pm, a squadron of twenty-six Liberators flew over Grosseto. Having dropped some bombs on the airport, they then proceeded to fly very low over the main street of the little town, leading from the central square to the 'amusement park'; this was already crowded, with the merry-go-rounds in full swing. Owing to the suddenness of the attack, the alarm did not sound until the planes were already overhead, so that the street was full of people in their Sunday best, and all the way down the street the crowd was machine-gunned. The planes then went on to the amusement park, and machine-gunned the tents containing the merry-go-rounds, where children were riding, and even pursued some people who tried to escape into the surrounding wheat-fields, two cars racing down the road, and four children in a field, herding some geese. Then, wheeling back over the town, they again swooped over the square. There a small crowd had gathered round the parish priest, who was giving absolution to the dying under the church porch – and this crowd was machine-gunned once again. One of the bombs fell upon the surgery of the hospital, destroying most of the first aid kits, so that as the wounded began to pour into the hospital the surgeons and nurses found themselves without bandages, swabs or ligaments. Subsequently the wounded were moved to the hospital at Montepulciano; and their photographs (especially those of the wounded or mutilated children) have been published in the papers.

These tales have done great harm. Yet I do not think that, when all is over, the dispassionate historian will be able to maintain either the Fascist thesis – that these air-raids have at last aroused the Italian people to hatred of the enemy – nor certainly the Allied one, that they have only awakened resentment against Fascism. I have met, of course, individuals who have bitterly felt one or the other of these emotions. But in the great mass of the nation, the keynote

still appears to be a dumb, fatalistic apathy – an acceptance
of the doom falling upon them from the skies, as men living
in the shadow of Vesuvius and Fujiyama accept the torrents
of boiling lava. All this, they seem to feel, is merely part of
war – of the war which they did not, do not want. But they
are not ready to do anything about it – not yet.

*Although daylight raids were intended, in part, to make bombing more
accurate and to minimize civilian casualties, in practice collateral
damage was often heavy. In the prelude to the Allied invasion of Sicily
in the summer of 1943 the bombing of airfields and ports in Italy was
very heavy and the damage extensive. Throughout April and May the
Strategic Air Force attacked airfields at Bo Rizzo, Bocca di Falco, Milo,
Castelvetrano, Decimomannu, Monserrato, Elmas and Villacidro.
Grosseto and Alghero were added as targets at the end of April, in which
month 3,675 tons of bombs were dropped.*

Thursday 13 – Tuesday 18 May 1943

David Smiley of the SOE joins a guerrilla attack on
Leskovik in Albania

13 May
Slept on the floor in a room by myself and woke next morning with a stinking cold. I left the breakfast and did a close
reconnaissance of Leskovik. I drew a sketch. I saw very
plainly the Italian barracks and soldiers walking about,
transports etc. I had lunch with a famous character, known
as Osman Gazeppi. He used to be a Colonel in the Turkish
Army and was a great friend of King Zog [the ex-King of
Albania]. He was delighted to see me and killed the fatted
calf. We had an enormous lunch and all got rather tight . . .
After lunch I moved on to the village of Polishte. We had an
alarm in the middle of the night, woke up, put on our boots,
pistols, etc. and some shooting took place, rather in-
discriminately. It only turned out to be six deserters from
Fafet Butke, the local leader of the Balli Kombetar [the

Royalist faction], who wanted to come over and join the Partisans.

14 May

... In the evening the other cheta [guerrilla band] leaders came in from the neighbourhood ... discovered that a large-scale operation was about to take place against Leskovik by the neighbouring partisans. I asked to go with them, but they would not let me. Finally, however, they agreed to let me accompany their H.Q. as a spectator. At 3.00 a.m. the operation against the Italians started. My bodyguard, who had been promised, arrived in the early hours, amongst whom was a girl about twenty years old, complete with rifle, revolver, bandoliers, etc. This was the first female partisan I had seen ...

15 May

The battle was by now in full swing. I saw three [Italian] RO.37's which circled Leskovik and dropped bombs on the outskirts. The Italian soldiers are still in the town. Their morale was very low since the fall of Tunis. Later that evening much shooting in all directions ...

16 May

Up till now the chetas attacking Leskovik have killed thirty Italians for the loss of two partisans. They also captured much food, but failed to capture the magazine. They ambushed the convoy bringing reinforcements from Korca and inflicted casualties without loss to themselves. They captured all Leskovik with the exception of one room in the barracks and held it for fifteen hours, but were then driven out by the aerial bombing ... The same evening I had the pleasure of watching the chetas ambushing an Italian convoy. This was the one returning to Korca from Leskovik. It was most amusing and as a result the chetas got thirteen Italian prisoners ...

17 May

... Left at 5.30 in the evening and managed for the first time to get a mule ride. It was a great relief. Have since heard that the village of Germenj, where I spent the night previously, had been burnt by the Italians as a reprisal. On the way I found a good [parachute] dropping ground. By now I was dressed in civilian clothes like a partisan. With the red star in my hat and giving the communist salute to whomever I met. I consider this very infra dig for an officer of His Majesty's Royal Horse Guards!

18 May

I arrived at Vithkuq at 2.00 in the morning and slept until 11.00 next day, when I heard that the Italians had burnt the village of Vodice where I had spent the previous night. I seem to leave a trail of fire behind me.

After the Axis defeats at El Alamein and Stalingrad the political climate in Albania had begun to change. The youth of the country, who were mostly of a left-wing inclination, took to the mountains in the south and Enver Hoxha emerged as their leader. The Yugoslavs to the north encouraged them to form a partisan movement. Some of the more liberal landowners and middle classes began to form a resistance movement, the Balli Kombetar, and other tribal leaders became restive. Colonel Neil McNeil and Major David Smiley had been sent by the SOE to investigate the potential of these movements. They found the Hoxha partisans and suggested that support could be sent to all the factions.

A small part of Smiley's diary for Sunday 16 May is still closed under section 3(4) of the Public Record Office Act by the Foreign Office, which exercises control over SOE records. It is not unreasonable to suspect that this material concerns the fate of Italians from the ambushed convoy. SEE ALSO PP. 546–7, 577–8 AND 610–11.

Friday 21 May 1943

Gerald Wilkinson of MI6 in London

Gerald Wilkinson was born in India, the son of a civil servant. Educated at Winchester, he had become a prominent member of the business community in the Philippines. By the 1930s he was also working for the British Secret Intelligence Service or MI6. His wartime work was especially sensitive: he was instructed to watch American commercial ambitions in the Pacific and to send reports directly to Churchill. For this purpose he would also regularly return to London and visit No. 10 Downing Street.

Dined with [Noel] Coward alone at Le Perroquet and on this closing up at about 10.30 p.m. went to his studio somewhere in the Chelsea neighbourhood for about 1½ hours talk . . . For the first year (or 1½ years?) of the war, Coward was working for H.M.G., firstly as Campbell Stuart's P.W. [political warfare] man in Paris and then under the auspices of the Ministry of Information in the United States. Owing to lack of clarity and conservatism by Lothian [the British Ambassador], for whose abilities Coward does not seem to share the general extremely high opinion, he found himself more or less a free lance and obliged to spend his own money on his subsequent tours across the U.S. and to the Far East, Australia etc. he said he paid out of his own pocket at that time approximately £11,000 . . .

He says that while away he was vehemently attacked by certain sections of the Press in London for being away during the 'blitz' and owing to the indefinite nature of his instructions and the secrecy required by the fact that Little Bill [Head of the MI6 station in the United States] was also in negotiations with him for employment, he was unable to defend himself. That on returning from Australia Little Bill was very keen to employ him but was finally and completely turned down from London, to Little Bill's own surprise . . .

There is rather a persistent rumour in London's upper circles that poor Noel is a roaring 'fairey', but taken by and large I should regard him not only as a brilliant but [also] as a most useful citizen of the Empire with a great deal of sound sense and a wide knowledge expressed most potently through the great medium of his plays, provided that, as he gets older, he does not, like Oscar Wilde, let any abnormal personal tendencies in his private life get the better of his sense and discretion. I should think he would be all right . . . Certainly his behaviour this evening has been entirely proper.

Both Wilkinson and Little Bill Stephenson, Head of the MI6 station in New York, known as British Security Co-ordination, thought Coward would be a good recruit to MI6. But their superiors thought otherwise and the move was vetoed at a higher level. Instead, he undertook propaganda-related work both in Britain and in the United States, as well as morale-boosting tours through Africa and the Middle East, performing his famous songs in one-man shows. Access to much of Wilkinson's MI6 diary would be prohibited by the authorities in the 1990s.

Friday 28 May 1943

Vladimir Dedijer at Zablak on rival resistance groups in Yugoslavia

Vladimir Dedijer was born in 1914 and served on the staff of Tito's resistance headquarters throughout the war. At an early stage Tito and one of his commanders, Kardelj, had suggested that he keep a diary. Vladimir Dedijer would be one of the most outstanding partisans of the war in Yugoslavia.

At three this morning the roar of four-engined Halifaxes wakened us, and announced the arrival of the British mission. Lay awake a long time, thinking of all that this day means . . . There is no doubt that the coming of this Mission, albeit exclusively military, means a great victory . . . Truly, great injustice has been done us in the past two years. What foul things the refugee government in London has done, how hard it has been to have Radio London talking about Mihailovic as a Robin Hood and second in this war to Timosenko, when he is in reality the most perfidious traitor of all time. We have needed tremendous energy to convince our men, our vanguard, not to let themselves be provoked – the enemy desiring nothing more than the splitting of the anti-fascist coalition – and that they should not confuse the attitude of reactionaries with that of the British government. Our Party has constantly fought stoutly against any sectarian diversion on this question, constantly pointing to the Anglo-Soviet-American Alliance as one of the bases of victory in this war . . . The English are realists. We should be realists too. We must bear the bitter insult of the recent past with resignation – not let the trees hide the forest from us . . . The consolidation and extension of the British-Soviet-American alliance is the basic task of all patriotic forces in the world. We . . . shall continue to play our part in this.

Vladimir Dedijer (left, with Tito)

In this particular parachute drop Captain W. Stuart and Captain Bill Deakin of the SOE arrived to join Tito's headquarters. The 'in-country' resistance groups who were assisted by the SOE were a source of endless political trouble. Everyone knew that wartime military leaders were likely to be the top post-war politicians. Accordingly, in many Balkan countries, especially Yugoslavia, the resistance groups spent as much time fighting each other as opposing the Axis. In London each local faction had its supporters and detractors. Matters were made worse by poor co-ordination among the SOE, the Foreign Office, the BBC and regional commanders in Cairo and later at Bari, in Italy. Divergences of view among the British agencies, or between the British and Americans, were always taken to be signs of plots, and often were. SEE ALSO PP. 572, 575–6, 583–4 AND 594–5.

John Mitchell, RAF navigator, flies with Churchill in the Mediterranean

Churchill's air travel was recorded by John Mitchell, who served as the RAF navigator on his aircraft and who also maintained an excellent diary. In late May 1943 he recorded waiting in Gibraltar to meet Churchill, who was being brought in from a conference in Washington DC by BOAC flying boat on a flight that took seventeen and a half hours. Churchill's own aircraft was waiting to take him on to meet Eisenhower in Algiers and then take both men on a tour of recently conquered north Africa. John Mitchell's other distinguished passengers included General Marshall, Anthony Eden, Alan Brooke, Arthur Tedder and Hastings Ismay.

We had positioned the York at the end of the runway nearest the flying boat base, in the event that the party would transfer for immediate departure with a minimum of exposure to public gaze. But as they were to stop overnight at the Convent, the Governor's Residence, and the Prime Minister was in no mood to heed security advice to conceal his presence, he was seen by a large number of locals and Service personnel.

The use of Gibraltar for VIP transits to Algiers and points East was always open to security criticism. The Duty Spy, as he was known, was said to be situated on the high ground above La Linea at a site known as Queen Catherine's Chair; with binoculars he could count passengers and take aircraft numbers with the greatest of ease – for transmission to the German Embassy in Madrid and on to Berlin. Also, the Reina Christiana Hotel in Algeciras (even then still British-owned) has a whole wing occupied by Italian and German intelligence staff.

... Our first flight with 'The Owner' was to Algiers (Maison Blanche), a two and a half hour trip with a fighter escort. To our discomfort, the US P38 Lightning Interceptors from their base at Oran cavorted about altogether too close for safety. The RAF Spitfires from Gibraltar had kept a more discreet and useful distance and height from us, from where they could in fact 'defend' us. These Lightnings were in no position to do this and only wanted to get near enough for their pilots to see the Prime Minister giving them the 'V' sign from his state room window.

Churchill was a fanatical traveller and was never happier than when close to the real action. He had his own special aircraft – one of the first of the new Avro York passenger aircraft produced in 1943 – for visits to conferences. However, he was somewhat cavalier about his personal security. Much of Gibraltar was visible from Spain and the border was a favourite haunt for German spies. There were fears of German action against his aircraft, should he be spotted. SEE ALSO PP. 566–8, 617–18 AND 783–5.

Saturday 29 – Sunday 30 May 1943

Captain Harry C. Butcher, Eisenhower's aide, joins Churchill and Eisenhower at Maison Blanche in Algiers

29 May

Although Ike had the Prime Minister driven to the Admiral's house, the PM didn't even stop there to rest. He immediately trundled with Ike down the driveway to our house. There, with General Marshall and the Admiral, they gathered on the front porch, the PM finding a comfortable chair and seeming settled for the duration. An informal conference, pleasant to kibitz upon, continued until time to get ready for dinner.

General Marshall has taken Ike's room again, this time with only a mild protest . . . The Chief of Staff expects to be at our house a few days and will visit American units from Tunis back to Port Lyautey, time permitting. The Prime Minister, still known as 'the man who came to dinner,' is going to stay for numerous dinners, his visit being expected to run a week or ten days.

General Marshall is accompanying the Prime Minister this far, at the PM's request to the President, because the PM openly and avowedly is seeking to influence Ike to pursue the campaign in the Mediterranean area until the Italians are out of the war. Presumably, he then wants the Allied effort to continue in the Mediterranean area rather than across the Channel as already agreed by the Combined Chiefs at their Washington meeting. He makes no bones of his point of view and apparently regards the decision already taken as quite open to review and change. The Prime Minister had told the President he felt it only fair for General Marshall, as the representative of the American point of view to the contrary, to be present. During the trip, especially at Gibraltar, the PM has shown every courtesy to General Marshall, making certain that he was accorded all honors meant for the PM, and, in general, looking after the little details of courtesy.

The PM recited his story three different times in three different ways last night. He talks persistently until he has worn down the last shred of opposition. Ike is glad to have General Marshall on hand. A meeting in our dining room is laid on, starting at 5 this afternoon . . .

30 May

Before dinner, I received a call from Commander Thompson, the PM's aide, inquiring if the General could see the Prime Minister at our house at 10:45 that night. Of course, Ike could, although the date jolted the free and easy lounging he needed so badly.

We returned to the villa in town in time for the PM's late visit. Ike and I sat reminiscing while waiting for the Prime Minister. Ike was growling because of the necessity of spending another night, probably until 1:30, going over the same ground, ie, 'Keep on until you get Italy,' which the PM had already covered, recovered and uncovered – and there were really no serious questions of difference between the two.

'Would you ever have thought a year ago or, certainly, two years ago that you would be in Algiers, in far-off Africa, the Allied Commander of a great and victorious army, sitting in a villa, awaiting a late night call from the Prime Minister of His Majesty's government and growling because the PM was fifteen minutes late?' I asked.

Ike enjoyed the picture, upon which he elaborated, going back to his boyhood days when he had been variously a cowboy, a boiler stoker in a creamery, and a semipro ballplayer . . .

I have used a variety of schemes to hustle visitors away at night. On occasions, I have yawned openly and loudly. On others, I have paraded in my bathrobe before the lingering guest or guests. Neither of these seemed appropriate for this occasion, so I found my flashlight and walked in front of the door. This was at 1 o'clock. The PM left at 1:10, trudging up the driveway to the Admiral's house with a Scotland Yard man who, I found, had waited outside our front door.

Harry Butcher, Eisenhower's personal aide, enjoyed a front seat at many of the most important top-level decision-making confabulations of the European war. His personal diary offers extraordinary insight into the personal relations between the top commanders, which were not always smooth. On the afternoon of Friday 28 May Churchill, General Marshall, Sir Alan Brooke, General Ismay and various staff officers all flew into Maison Blanche outside Algiers to meet with Eisenhower. Butcher noted that such large parties always stretched their VIP facilities. Marshall and Alan Brooke were put up in Eisenhower's house while Churchill lived 'next door' in the house usually occupied by Admiral Cunningham. Together with their aides, he complained, the visitors were 'filling all the beds and overcrowding the bathroom facilities'. There was a clear pecking order, and Marshall evicted Eisenhower into temporary accommodation without hesitation.

Butcher noted 'a feeling of discord lurking between the two countries' which had increased in recent months. There were arguments over the rival leaders of the Free French, and over the invasion of Europe. The Americans wished to launch a cross-Channel invasion into France as soon as possible. The British wished to take more time and to explore the possibility of pushing up into the 'soft underbelly' of the Axis by invading Italy. Churchill pronounced that Italy was ready to collapse and pressed his case, employing his usual tactics of late-night talking and endless repetition. Eisenhower agreed that the invasion of Sicily would be the test case. Everyone breathed a sigh of relief when Churchill left for Tunis on the morning of Tuesday 1 June. SEE ALSO PP. 27, 469–70, 544–6 AND 712–13.

JUNE 1943

TOUGH RESISTANCE FIGHTING continued to accelerate in the Balkans, where the Germans were making a concerted effort to defeat Tito's partisans. In France, the Michelin tyre factory was badly damaged in operations by the resistance, assisted by the SOE. Meanwhile, on the Eastern Front, the Germans were forced to devote more and more resources to dealing with attacks behind the lines by partisan groups which sometimes reached battalion strength, making the confrontations more like pitched battles rather than guerrilla actions.

Remarkably, only twenty ships were lost to U-boats in June 1943. British cipher security had been improved, cutting off a valuable flow of signals intelligence to the German naval high command. At the end of the month, many U-boats were recalled to defend the seaboard against an anticipated invasion of Europe. By contrast, fear of invasion in Britain had completely evaporated, and work now began on the restoration of thousands of road signs that had been removed to make things as difficult as possible for enemy invaders during the dark days of 1940.

Inside the Third Reich the campaign against the Jews continued. On 11 June Himmler ordered that all the Polish ghettos should be completely destroyed and on the 19th Goebbels declared Berlin 'free of Jews'. At the end of the month 20,000 Jews were rounded up in Poland and transported to Auschwitz and Belzec, where they were murdered. Across Europe knowledge about the Holocaust was spreading, and many Jews resisted valiantly.

The US 8th Air Force was now raiding German cities by day while the RAF attacked by night. Münster, Düsseldorf and Bochum in the Ruhr were hit. In retaliation the Luftwaffe carried out night attacks against Plymouth and other locations along the south coast. In Whitehall and Washington arguments about the effectiveness of strategic bombing continued, since German war production was not being as badly affected by it as many had hoped.

Wednesday 2 June 1943

Mrs Henry Dudeney, novelist and local conservationist, on refugees and rumours of enemy agents in Brighton

Emily told me about the raid at Brighton, the worst they've had. A big bit of the railway viaduct broke, so no trains through London Road Station. In Springfield Road many houses with broken windows, damaged roofs, ceilings down and so on. Her house escaped. People machine gunned in the streets. The official list of killed 24 and injured 51 . . . one woman stuck her head out of her window – her head instantly blown off! Brighton full of Germans, especially women married to Englishmen. People are saying that – by the Morse Code – they tell the Germans when the weather and other factors are suitable for raids. Altogether there are too many aliens in this country. Poles, trying to widen the breach between Poland and Russia. And Jews with their Black Markets and dog racing! Eden himself admitted that it would not be wise to admit more Jews as there is, already, a strong anti-Semitic feeling.

Although Nazi atrocities against the Jews were well known by the end of 1942, this did not necessarily result in a decline in anti-semitism; nor did the knowledge that the Nazi state was a racist state result in a decline of racism generally in Britain. In 1946 George Orwell wrote an essay arguing that, although from the mid-1930s there had been conscious suppression, by all thoughtful people, 'of anything likely to wound Jewish susceptibilities', anti-semitism had probably grown during the war. SEE ALSO PP. 521–2.

Wednesday 2 – Friday 4 June 1943

John Mitchell, Churchill's navigator, returns with the Prime Minister from Tunis

The PM came forward on the return journey and enjoyed sitting in the sunshine in the co-pilot's seat. He announced that he would like to try the controls. He did so, and when Collins attempted to smooth out some of the resulting attitudes of the aircraft with discreet use of the tail trimmer, the Owner admonished him. He soon conceded that he would share the controls: Collins to work the rudder and he, the PM, would try climbing and diving. He clearly enjoyed himself, much to the consternation of the passengers (including Tedder) who were thrown about in the back, and to the astonishment of the USAF fighter escort of P38 Lightnings which were then keeping a more sensible distance from us. CIGS commented in his Diary: 'The PM gave us somewhat of a swaying passage for a bit'. On landing at Maison Blanche, 'Dad' Collins explained to our escort commander who was doing the driving.

It is of interest that Mr Churchill is said to have flown with 24 Squadron as a pilot under training at Hendon in 1928, at the same time as Lord Londonderry. He was not successful in his flying lessons, though the noble Lord did qualify. The Prince of Wales (later Edward VIII) and his brother, later George VI, also went through a form of flying training with No 24 in the 1920's.

... After two more pleasant nights in Algiers, we left Maison Blanche for Gibraltar to return to the UK. The US fighter escort was left behind at Oran where we picked up a Spitfire Wing, much to the PM's pleasure. The VIP passengers in addition to the PM were Eden, Alexander and the CIGS. The PM enjoyed the flight deck and wished to stay up front for the landing in order to get a good aerial view of the Rock. As the Flight Engineer was able to take the necessary landing actions from his position between the two pilot's seats, the Captain felt it was OK to leave the Owner in the 2nd Pilot's seat. All went well until the Captain was 'holding off' for a three point landing when he realised he could not pull back the control sufficiently to get the tail down. Gibraltar runway at that time was none too long – it was in the process of being lengthened with the debris from tunnelling within the Rock itself. We all thought the aircraft took a long time to settle, but it was not until the PM dismounted from the cockpit the Captain told us that the 'banjo' was hitting the PM in the stomach and that no effort on his part could get it back far enough! The Captain resolved that if the PM wanted to stay up front in future for the landing, he had better sit at the navigator's table with more comfort and safety for all. The PM was keen to continue home in the York, although we learned later that Higher Authorities had in fact retained the flying boat 'Bristol' on stand-by for the purpose; we guessed this was in case he did not take to the York. It was perhaps just as well that he did not then know that while we were still in North Africa, the regular UK–Lisbon–UK service, operated by an unarmed DC3 of KLM (PH-ALI) and flown by Captain Tepas and an all-Dutch crew, had been shot down by a German night-fighter when homeward bound over the Bay of Biscay. This service had been operated regularly by KLM on behalf of the British Government for the previous two and a half years, to the advantage of the Neutral and Axis Powers as well as the Allies. There had been four KLM DC3's employed, all survivors of the bombing of Schiphol Airport, Amsterdam, in 1940, which had been flown out by their crews to the UK. Leslie Howard [a famous British wartime actor] was one of the passengers in the Dakota. There was a theory at the time that another passenger, Alfred Chenhalls, who was Leslie Howard's accountant, resembled Mr Churchill. Sceptics of course scorned the idea that the PM would fly home via Lisbon in a relatively uncomfortable, slow aircraft. Nevertheless, there had been intensive German night-fighter activity over the Bay all that week and numerous RAF Coastal Command anti-submarine aircraft came under unusually intensive attention. Presumably the Luftwaffe policy had been to shoot at all and everything crossing the Bay while the PM was known to be abroad.

We left Gibraltar at 2200 hours for Northolt, taking our route as far out into the Atlantic as the longitude of 12 W. Such a route kept us well clear of the Spanish coast, and beyond the range of night fighter patrols from the Brest Peninsula.

Churchill's party spent three days at the Aletti hotel in Algiers. Officials arranging the visit had found that they had no choice but to 'throw a certain amount of the PM's vicarious weight around' to evict various brigadiers from the hotel in order to make way for the prestigious party. After three days they returned to Gibraltar bound for London. The active efforts of Axis intelligence in neutral Spain presented a clear threat to VIPs moving through Gibraltar, and also to Allied shipping moving through the neighbouring straits. A number of senior commanders were lost in aircraft, as the result of either deliberate attack or aircraft failure. The death of Leslie Howard, one of the top three leading British actors at the time, was a severe blow to British morale. Howard had won an Oscar before the war and had appeared in some of the more famous wartime propaganda films, including In Which We Serve *(1942).* SEE ALSO PP. 560, 617–18 AND 783–5.

Wednesday 2 June 1943

Noel Coward reacts to the death of the film star Leslie Howard

Was telephoned after the matinée by the BBC asking me to do a broadcast to America immediately, as Leslie Howard had been shot down in a plane coming from Lisbon. This really is a horrid shock. Refused the broadcast as obviously there was not time.

Went down to the cottage. Had supper and went to bed early. Had a long think about death. Imagined all too vividly poor Leslie's last moments. Such a horrible way to die, cooped up with a dozen people in a plane and being brought down into a rough sea. It can't have been so very quick. There must have been lots of time to think and be frightened unless, of course, he had the luck to be hit by one of the bullets. Obviously they were trying to get Winston, who isn't back yet. I must say I have occasional qualms when I think of the amount of flying ahead of me.

For years, rumours have persisted that the plane in which Howard was travelling was serving as a deliberate decoy to protect Churchill, but it is much more likely that his death was a mere coincidence. However, it is possible that the Germans mistook Howard's accountant for Churchill and so mounted a fighter sweep over the area. Another possibility is that the Germans were attempting to eliminate Wilfred Israel, a courageous rescuer of European Jews, who was also travelling on the aircraft and who was in the Gestapo's blacklist. The loss of passenger aircraft on this route was not infrequent, and it would claim other victims before the war ended. SEE ALSO PP. 580, AND 603–4.

Sunday 6 June 1943

William Friedman, an American codebreaker, travels from Bletchley Park to Corpus Christi College, Cambridge

Codebreaking and signals intelligence had a major impact on the course of the war. The leading American figure in this field was William F. Friedman, originally called Wolfe Friedman. He was born in 1891 in Kishinev in Russia. When the family emigrated to Pittsburgh the same year his name was changed to William. As a student he undertook a genetics course at Cornell University, which led to an interest in codes and ciphers. By the end of the First World War he had become a senior American codebreaker. In the 1920s he stayed in this field and tried to keep up with developments in the new mechanical ciphering machines, most of which had multiple rotors. Prior to 1941 he played a leading part in the successful 'Magic' operation to break Japanese codes. He was based at Arlington Hall – the American equivalent of Bletchley Park. In June he visited Bletchley Park or 'BP'.

Up early (7:30), finished packing, breakfast, bus at 8:35 and now at B/P. Winding up affairs. Tel from AH [Arlington

Hall] yesterday which I've not seen yet but general contents of which phoned Tel by A1. Elizabeth [his wife] says won't write any more in view my imminent return. I am to get data for research started on E – Had talk with [Nigel] De Grey on this point and am to see [Gordon] Welchman [two leading codebreakers at Bletchley Park] this am – (Following being written on train enroute to Stoke-on-Trent, Tuesday morning.) [Friedman's note] – Had a quick conf[erence] with Welchman and arrived at tentative agreement re co-op[eration] on E work for AH [Arlington Hall]. He asked me to draw up brief on it, which I rushed through in a few minutes before lunch, at which Tel and De Grey present. – Immediately after it Prof Vincent and I started in BP private car for Cambridge, despite ominous weather and dark clouds – it had been raining pretty hard all morning and it was still not finished. The car is a quite old one but was among the most expensive models in its day. I was a bit apprehensive at Vincent's handling of it, as the road was very wet and the car did not steer too well and Vincent kept driving at high speed – sometimes as much as 60 and for considerable stretches 50–55. The roads are seldom straight, often very narrow, and you can't see more than 100 yards ahead. However, he didn't get us ditched or in a wreck and we got there safely, passing through some of the loveliest of English countryside. Cambridge is 50 miles from BP, and we were on 1½ hours en route. – One of the places we slowed up to see is 'Byron's Pool' – a small pool in the village of Grantchester [just outside Cambridge] by an attractive old bridge. Here Byron used to come often to bathe. An old house at the edge of the pool was occupied much later by Rupert Brooke, whose poem 'Grantchester' tells all about the village, the vicarage, the pool in which Byron played, etc – one of Brooke's best. – En route also we saw one or two concentration camps for Italian prisoners and it is curious to see these P/W walking about on the roads, quite unattended or perhaps with a guard far off in the distance. Vincent, who has the chair in Italian at Corpus Christi College, stopped for a moment to talk with a group of 3 nice looking Ps of W and startled them very much, they being quite shy. – When we reached CCC [Corpus Christi College] Vincent drove into a court (having a key to the gate), we parked the car and went directly for a walk to see the various sights. Cambridge comprises some 22 separate colleges (just like Oxford) many of which were founded as far back as 1250 or 1260. Some were founded after the Great Plague by the Guilds in gratitude for the survival of at least a few in the community. Oxford is a bit older than Cambridge and Vincent laughingly told me that current gossip at the former tells that Cambridge was founded by those who were expelled from Oxford. – The atmosphere of Cambridge, which I drank in in great gulps, gives one a feeling of 'solidity' – the solidity that is England. Here stand in quiet dignity and great strength buildings devoted to learning and democratic institutions and the dignity of man – for nine centuries – still going strong. I could hear Barbara's voice saying, in the current slang, 'solid', with the 'cluck cluck' after it! How she would love it. The colleges are scattered over miles of territory but most of them are adjacent to the river Cam – a quiet, clear, narrow little river with the most charming banks of grass on both slopes, and quaint bridges connecting the college buildings with the playing fields directly across, or connecting two main buildings belonging to the same college.

William Friedman was in Britain to work with the top codebreakers at Bletchley Park, including Gordon Welchman and Nigel de Grey, and also to negotiate the BRUSA treaty – an intensely secret agreement that governed co-operation between London and Washington over code-breaking and security. This treaty was the foundation of the modern Western intelligence community. Bletchley Park was a very unmilitary place, staffed to a large degree by academics, particularly linguists and mathematicians, who spent the war wrestling with German cipher systems such as Enigma. After the war most would return to their peacetime professions in the colleges of Oxford and Cambridge.

Thursday 10 June 1943

Vladimir Dedijer's diary comes under fire during a
German offensive in Yugoslavia

Dawn found us beyond Lucke Kolibe, when we climbed up
the Katunisce, which seemed endless. The sun was high in
the sky when we reached a plateau ... Olga was tired, and
we had just taken her from the horse when orders came to
continue without delay ... During the night the Germans
had brought up strong reinforcements and were now attacking Kosuta and Ljubin Grob with all they had ... points
protecting our line of withdrawal. Olga lay under a tree and
had me lie down beside her ... at eleven, aircraft appeared
and began a terrific bombing ... I took out the bag with this
Diary and tried to protect Olga's head from flying splinters
... She held my hand; when the bombing was over, she said:
'It will be all right!' ...

Before dark there was another raid. There cannot have
been a patch of ground from Kosuta to Ljubin Grob not
spattered with splinters. Whole trees were torn up by the
roots, and when all the bombs were dropped, that terrible
machine-gunning began ... and when they had fired the last
round, the Germans came down as low as possible and
flew by, leaning through their windows giving the Hitler
salute ...

*Vladimir Dedijer was among Tito's forces when they were encircled by
vastly superior German and Italian forces during May and June 1943.
The partisans ran out of food and the packhorses, which were normally
used for hauling supplies and ammunition, were themselves eaten.
Dedijer was serving alongside his wife, Olga, who was the
senior surgeon to the 2nd Brigade. Despite his best efforts his wife
received a serious leg wound from a piece of shrapnel and would later
have to undergo amputation. Captain W. Stuart, who had been dropped
in by the SOE, was killed during the fighting and Major Bill Deakin was
wounded. Tito's forces would break out of the attempted German
encirclement ten days later. SEE ALSO PP. 558–9, 575–6, 583–4 AND 594–5.*

Thursday 17 June 1943

The diplomat Joseph P. Kennedy hears of the real Roosevelt–Churchill relationship from Max Beaverbrook

I asked him [Max Beaverbrook] how Roosevelt and Churchill really got along and he said 'I will tell you a secret if you won't repeat it,' so I am just having this for my own file. He said 'Churchill is a terrible bore. I have known him for 33 years and while he is a great vitality of the nation he is still a hell of a bore. When Roosevelt and he went to Camp Rapidan together and he kept repeating or talking Roosevelt opened the stamp book and started to work on the stamps, letting Churchill continue to talk. This annoyed Churchill so much that he stalked out of the room in a huff and sat outside and smoked his big black cigar, peeved, while Roosevelt continued to work on the stamps. Finally I came along and went into the room and, of course, I understand how to handle Roosevelt, I think, better than Churchill and can get him talking and so all I have to say is "Now, who do you think represents the best ideal of Democracy, Jackson or Jefferson" and, of course, with that he closes the stamp book and talks on that and while that discussion is going on Churchill walks back into the room.' This is an interesting and only side light I have on how the two boys are getting on together, but where the opinion of the world is that every visit is spent in big discussions you have a general idea of what is going on. Beaverbrook said 'I had two fights with him while on the ship going over, when he didn't speak for a day and one in Washington when he didn't speak to me until the following morning when he opened up the conversation by remarking that we haven't changed much, we still argue and fight, but it only shows that we are vital people and we must continue in our regular way.'

The aftermath of the story was that when Roosevelt sent for Beaverbrook last Thursday for a week-end party to go traveling somewhere, as they got in the car Roosevelt said to Beaverbrook 'Well, on this trip I am not taking my stamps.'

Believe me, there will be a row between Churchill and
Roosevelt one of these days and I can imagine what they say
about each other.

I asked him about the China situation and he was
rather bitter. He confirmed the Madame Chang Kai-Shek,
Roosevelt and Churchill discussion about the meeting, but
he was indignant that she should ask Churchill to come to
New York. He said it was a hell of a gall for her to consider
as after all she was not an official representative and why
should Churchill call on her. Anyway, he thought very little
of her. In fact he said she was a Lesbian and her girlfriend
was a 26 year old girl, Soon, who she had with her. I thought
to myself that it certainly didn't portend any great feeling
between two countries if the top-side people feel the way
they do.

He also talked about that he thought neither Roosevelt nor
Churchill ever had any affairs with women, as was being
discussed about Princess Martha. She was at the week-end
party with them and he thought that they like to have
women around and talk to them and all that sort of thing,
but that was as far as it went. They have had nothing in their
head but power.

*By 1943 Joseph Kennedy was taking a back seat in American politics.
His old friend Beaverbrook was trying to persuade him back into public
life. Kennedy was keen to ask Beaverbrook about the mysteries of the
Roosevelt–Churchill relationship. Historians have constructed a myth of
personal sympathy between the two wartime leaders, reading much into
factors such as Churchill's half-American parentage and their shared
love of naval matters. The hundreds of letters and telegrams they sent to
each other during the war certainly bear testimony to their remarkable
co-operation. However, their ways of doing business were radically
different and they found each other's company annoying. Churchill liked
a meandering conversation that allowed him to sound off for hours on
anything he chose. Underlings had to tolerate this tedious habit, but
Roosevelt did not, so personal meetings could be difficult. Running at a
deeper level were fundamental disagreements about how the post-war
world should be organized. One of the issues that divided them was
China and the American support for the Chiang Kai-shek regime. It was
perhaps unfair to say that both men were only interested in power.*

Roosevelt was interested in lofty ideals while Churchill liked pragmatic agreements, and as the war progressed this divergence of approach would make for an atmosphere of growing suspicion and discord.

Despite Beaverbrook's blandishments, Joseph Kennedy remained on the sidelines of US public life, devoting his energies to promoting the careers of his sons Jack and Robert. SEE ALSO PP. 53–5 AND 64–5.

Sunday 20 June 1943

The fate of Vladimir Dedijer's wife after a field amputation in Yugoslavia

On the move. – I went to Medakovic. My temperature was tormenting me. It was 39C. Mitar called me aside around noon. I saw he wanted to tell me something:

'Olga's condition is very serious. We'll give you a horse. Go to her at once.'

'I knew that yesterday. The amputation was too late. Doctor Pavletic said she had only a 5 percent chance of surviving . . .'

I rode for two long hours . . . We found the Second Proletarian. They were carrying Olga on a stretcher along Romanija. She was fully conscious.

'Yesterday was horrible. I heard you were wounded. Have you had a tetanus shot?' I did have to take a shot. Later, Stanojka Djuric came to give Olga a camphor injection, but Olga refused:

'Don't waste valuable medicine Stanojka. Keep it for others whose lives it may save!' The comrades put the stretcher down to rest for a while. Olga called me to her:

'Take care of Milica. Bring her up well. Don't let her become an army doctor. When you get home, tell her to remember her mother.'

These were her last words. We had to find new comrades to carry the stretcher. I went to the battalion commander. Olga died ten minutes later, conscious to the last.

I stood on the edge of Romanija, on the rocks, on the path

which led from Stojno-Medakovic to Mokro. Night had already fallen, the wind was gusting, bending the large juniper trees. We dug Olga's grave with our bare hands and knives, because we did not have any shovels. A platoon was with me, our column's guard. All the rest had gone ahead. We were two hours from the village where the Germans surely were. Olga lay wrapped in the white blanket. Her black hair nearly covered her entire face. The wind beat the junipers over even more, and Laza, a miner, by birth from Sekovik, a fighter in Serbia already in 1941, tore at the ground with his fists:

'Vlado, we have reached stone.'

A comrade on whom Olga had operated dug out the last bits of earth:

'She saved my life; we all loved her.'

We placed her in a shallow grave, piled up the clods of dirt and stones, made a marker, eight metres from the Romanija path, beside the very cliffs on the Southeast side. Sasa Bozovic, Stanojka Djuric, three comrades from the platoon, and myself all took off our hats.

'Glory be to comrade Olga' shouted Laza, and after him the rest of us.

We all set off into the dark forest, and reached one of the Second Proletarian Brigade in the dark, silent, walking through the dense swampy forest. Olga died for her people. She had died a member of our Party. I held in my hand her watch which I had taken for Milica. Tears began to well, first one, then two – and then an entire stream. I had much to cry for.

It was not until ten days after being wounded that Olga Dedijer, herself a skilled surgeon, was able to receive any significant medical attention. At the headquarters of the 2nd Dalmatian Brigade she underwent a hurried amputation in a 'dark, dirty little room'. Soon after the operation the partisans were on the move again to avoid a further German offensive. Vladimir, too, had been wounded in the head by shrapnel during the same forced withdrawal and although the injury seemed slight, he would develop blood poisoning. Nevertheless he fought on during the summer, despite repeated fevers. SEE ALSO PP. 558–9, 572, 583–4 AND 594–5.

Tuesday 22 June – Wednesday 23 June 1943

SOE operative David Smiley distributes gold sovereigns in Albania

David Smiley (right)

22 June
Bill left to go north . . . while I remained behind to organise the sorties. Bill left with me the local political commissar, by name Ramiz Aranitas. Ramiz was going to organise the reception of the stores and provide all the labour and the mules. He had dinner with him and left about 8.00. Shortly afterwards I heard a shot.

23 June
At 2.00 a.m. I heard aeroplanes. Quite unexpected, as Cairo never said they were coming. Rushed out in my pyjamas and bare feet and three of us eventually got eleven fires going, and the 'plane dropped the stores. It was a complete nightmare; the fires were damp, my feet were stung all over

by nettles, the aeroplane circled for at least half-an-hour before we had lit all the fires. I sent a runner to Ramiz, but he shortly came back saying that his body was about a mile away with a bullet through his back. It later transpired that my guard, Ali, had shot him and stolen from him 200 sovereigns which I had seen Bill give to Ramiz. It was lucky he did not know that I had 4,000 sovereigns under my bed, as he had been my only guard for about a week. Ali escaped to a neighbouring and rival cheta [guerrilla group].

In the early morning collected all the stores which were dropped accurately, but unfortunately the wind took the majority down a ravine about 400 yards from the fires and it was very hard work carrying all the stuff up to our hut. It was a terrible sortie, as we never got any warning from Cairo, but later in the day another warning came through telling us to expect more that night.

Further supplies arrived the following night. They contained materials intended to help in training and equipping an organized brigade of guerrillas rather than the rag-tag group or 'cheta' that had been operating hitherto. The ultimate objective was to attack positions held not by the Italians, but by the Germans, altogether more serious opponents. SEE ALSO PP. 546–7, 554–6 AND 610–11.

JULY 1943

BY 5 JULY BOTH Germany and the Soviet Union had concentrated very large armoured forces at Kursk on the Eastern Front. Hitler personally ordered the delivery of the latest Tiger and Panther tanks, the most formidable armoured vehicles existing at the time. There was no element of surprise, the battle proved to be a slogging match rather than a test of operational manoeuvre, and it was superior Soviet artillery which eventually tipped the balance. By 13 July the Soviet Union had won the largest tank battle of the war. A day later the Russians held the first war crimes trial and put eleven Germans on trial in

Krasnodar for the murder of Russian Jews, whom they had killed in mobile gas vans.

In July the Allies celebrated as Italy was knocked out of the war. At the start of the month General Antonescu of Romania suggested to Mussolini that Romania, Hungary and Italy should all surrender together. But Hitler had psychologically bullied Mussolini, and when they met at Feltre on 19 July the Italian leader took no initiatives, only orders. During July the Allies completed the successful invasion of Sicily and at the end of the month the leading Fascists in Rome turned against Mussolini. Il Duce was imprisoned.

On Saturday 24 July the RAF launched Operation Gomorrah. This was the first in a week of air attacks against Hamburg with explosives and incendiaries. In the first attack 750 bombers dropped over 2,000 tons of bombs on Hamburg in less than an hour. The resulting firestorm could be seen more than 100 miles away. The RAF bombers also began to use a technique code-named Window, which involved the dropping of millions of tiny aluminium foil strips which jammed German radar. As a result RAF losses were low and repeated attacks could be mounted. On 29 July, after seven heavy air raids in six days, the evacuation of Hamburg was ordered, and on 31 July 'Bomber' Harris ordered the massive incendiary bombing of what remained of the city. Over 40,000 people were killed and Hitler, seeking revenge, ordered the acceleration of the V-1 rocket bomb programme.

Luftwaffe raids against the south-east of England continued, although now on a smaller scale. On 9 July ten German bombers carried out a raid on London. One aircraft became detached and sought a 'target of opportunity', which happened to be a train pulling into East Grinstead station. One of the bombs hit the Whitehall Cinema where 184 people were watching *Hopalong Cassidy*. In 1943 air raids were thought of as a diminishing threat and so the audience in the cinema, mostly children, had not heeded the sirens. Over 100 people were killed.

VIP casualties from air crashes continued. General Sikorski, along with several other Polish leaders of the London-based anti-communist Polish government-in-exile, died in a plane crash shortly after take-off from Gibraltar and some made accusations of foul play.

Sunday 4 July 1943

Noel Coward entertains the Churchills at Chequers

At twelve o'clock the Prime Ministerial car fetched me and drove me to Chequers. Found Mrs Churchill alone and played a little croquet with her. The PM was very amiable and charming. I played 'Don't Let's Be Beastly to the Germans' over and over again, and he was mad about it.

After tea I had a long talk with him about [Wendell] Willkie and de Gaulle (whom he doesn't like and suspects of being a potential little French Fuehrer). Sarah Churchill appeared on leave. A little more general conversation, then an hour closeted with the PM, during which we played six-pack [bezique] and I took ten shillings off him. At dinner he was very gay and sang old-world Cockney songs with teddy bear gestures. In the course of the day, he admitted that he had been mistaken over the abdication. Mrs Churchill added later that his mistake had been providential because it had kept him out of office at a moment when it would have been compromising. After dinner we saw a news-reel and I played the piano for hours and then left.

Although Churchill was now almost seventy and found war work tiring, nevertheless things were looking up. The tide of the war had visibly turned and his political problems were over. On the personal front his finances had undergone a remarkable transformation. He had begun the war in an impoverished state, but the last few years had transformed him into one of the most sought-after writers in the world. He was already signing advance book contracts for very large sums. He could well afford to lose ten shillings to Noel Coward at bezique. SEE ALSO PP. 568–9.

Thursday 8 July 1943

John Steinbeck watches a mixed anti-aircraft battery in action in southern England

John Steinbeck was born in Salinas, California on 27 February 1902. He had studied marine biology at Stanford University but opted to work as an agricultural labourer while writing novels. Much of his work was set in farming communities, but it was a novel about Monterey, Tortilla Flat, *that brought him national recognition in 1935. During the war he became a reporter for the* New York Tribune, *first based in England and then moving to Italy to cover the difficult amphibious landings in Salerno in September 1943.*

John Steinbeck

The countryside is quiet. The guns are silent. Suddenly the siren howls. Buildings that are hidden in camouflage belch people, young men and women. They pour out, running like mad. The siren has not been going for thirty seconds when the run is over, the gun is manned, the target spotted. In the control room under ground the instruments have found their target. A girl has fixed it. The numbers have been transmitted and the ugly barrels whirled. Above ground, in a concrete box, a girl speaks into a telephone. 'Fire,' she says quietly. The hillside rocks with the explosion of the battery. The field grass shakes, and the red poppies shudder in the blast. New orders come up from below and the girl says, 'Fire.'

The process is machine-like, exact. There is no waste movement and no nonsense. These girls seem to be natural soldiers. They are soldiers, too. They resent above anything being treated like women when they are near the guns. Their work is hard and constant. Sometimes they are alerted to the guns thirty times in a day and a night. They may fire on a marauder ten times in that period. They have been bombed and strafed, and there is no record of any girl flinching.

The commander is very proud of them. He is fiercely affectionate toward his battery. He says a little bitterly, 'All right, why don't you ask about the problem of morals? Everyone wants to know about that. I'll tell you – there is no problem.'

He tells about the customs that have come into being in this battery, a set of customs which grew automatically. The men and the women sing together, dance together, and, let any one of the women be insulted, and he has the whole battery on his neck. But when a girl walks out in the evening, it is not with one of the battery men, nor do the men take the girls to the movies. There have been no engagements and no marriages between members of the battery. Some instinct among the people themselves has told them trouble would result. These things are not a matter of orders but of custom.

The girls like this work and are proud of it. It is difficult to see how the housemaids will be able to go back to dusting furniture under querulous mistresses, how the farm girls will be able to go back to the tiny farms of Scotland and the Midlands. This is the great exciting time of their lives. They are very important, these girls. The defense of the country in their area is in their hands.

During the Blitz the shortage of personnel to operate searchlights and guns forced the authorities to introduce women from the Auxiliary Territorial Service (ATS) into the many anti-aircraft batteries that ringed major cities and strategic sites. Much discussion preceded this decision because it effectively brought women into the front line, a place from which they had hitherto been excluded. Because of determination to maintain the non-combatant status of women, a line had to be drawn: females were forbidden to load the ammunition or to fire the guns. The work of women was carefully restricted to tracking, plotting and aiming. Curiously, the principal source of resistance to the suggestion of mixed batteries was not the Royal Artillery, but the higher echelons of the ATS itself. SEE ALSO PP. 626–9.

Thursday 15 – Friday 16 July 1943

Vladimir Dedijer, a partisan with Tito's headquarters staff, observes an SOE supply drop from a special duties aircraft

15 July

Ponjerka – We do not have a radio receiver with which to listen to the news. We are using the english radio. That is why Tepavcevic and I went with Captain Deakin and Veljko Illic to the village of Draapnici where the allies were to have air-dropped two loads . . .

The allied planes set off early tonight from their bases in North Africa and reached us sometime after ten . . . Suddenly, white parachutes opened up and things began to fall all about. We were almost killed. The airplane dropped ten bales without parachutes, which fell directly by us. The Liberator then fired some rockets and left. Our company began collecting the containers, which resembled bombs. It was long past midnight by the time we settled down on the edge of the forest to sleep. I stretched out in this empty Bosnian village on a bale with a blanket, which was full of desert sand. Four hours earlier the bale had been in Africa.

16 July

Drapnici – The Seventh Croatian Division has sent fighters to gather and guard the supplies. All through the morning small black barrels were passed under the tall firs. We then began opening them. Captain Deakin and Valjko noted what had arrived. Mostly explosives. Over 800 kilograms of Nobel 808 explosives were heaped in a pile in front of us. The allies sent them to us to destroy the railroad lines with. This would greatly help them. For example, they requested through the Main Staff for Croatia that we destroy Zidani Most. There were very few medical supplies. They did not send us what we had asked for: digitalis, antipyretics, antidiarrheal medicine.

The soldiers shook their heads scornfully at a pile of shoes. The little English telegraph operator, Walter Rothen, also felt this, and began to blush.

Vladimir Dedijer had remained ill as the result of the shrapnel wound to his head and spent much of his time listening to the radio with the British mission at Tito's headquarters. The news of the fall of Mussolini greatly helped the partisan cause in Yugoslavia, for the local population took it as a clear sign of the way the war was moving. Dedijer took a cynical view of SOE supply drops. The quality and quantity of supplies were poor, but the demonstrable ability of Tito's headquarters to conjure supplies from the sky was 'politically useful', especially in areas where they were competing with Tito's rival Mihailovic. Arguments about these supply problems continue: some have attributed them to foul play, pointing to rival communist and right-wing factions within SOE Cairo. In fact these problems occurred everywhere: in Malaya, for example, an SOE party asking for food and medicine were sent a batch of jungle boots, all for the left foot. SEE ALSO PP. 558–9, 572, 575–6 AND 594–5.

Sunday 18 July 1943

Dr Theo Morrell is kept busy by Hitler's abdomen as the Führer prepares to meet Mussolini

Dr Theodor Morrell served as Hitler's doctor for nine years. Hitler was undoubtedly a hypochondriac, but he was also resistant to the business of detailed medical examination and proved to be a most difficult and demanding patient. Hitler's choice of Morrell as his doctor was, and remains, controversial. Morrell was an enthusiast for all sorts of strange and unusual treatments, and injected Hitler with a regular cocktail of amphetamines and opium-based painkillers to which the Nazi leader seems to have been addicted. Theo Morrell had enjoyed a thriving private practice in Berlin where he used electrical stimulation to treat prostatitis.

Fuhrer had me sent for at ten-thirty A.M., said he has had the most violent stomach pains since three A.M. and hasn't slept a wink. His abdomen is as taut as a board, full of gas, with no palpation pains anywhere. Looking *very* pale and exceptionally jumpy: facing a vital conference with the Duce in Italy tomorrow. Diagnosis: *Spastic constipation* caused by overwork over the last few days – three days with virtually no sleep, one conference after another and working far into the night. – Last night he ate white cheese and roll-ups (*Rolladen*) with spinach and peas.

As he can't duck out of some important conferences and decisions before his departure at three-thirty P.M., no narcotics can be given him; I can only give him an intravenous injection of one ampoule of Eupaverin, some gentle stomach massage, two Euflat pills and three spoons of olive oil. Last night he took five Leo pills.

Before leaving for the airfield I gave him an intramuscular injection of an ampoule of Eukodal. He was looking very bad and rather faint.

In the Condor airplane Reichsmarschall Göring wanted to give me a few final tips (Ondarza was standing just behind him): 'You must give him Euflat. That once helped me a lot.'

'Yes, two tablets three times a day. I'm doing it already.'

'But you've got to keep doing it over a long period. I took them for eighteen months. And then you must give him Luizym too!'

'We're already doing that too!' (He got the name wrong at first but Ondarza corrected him.)

During the actual flight Hitler let off wind, which resulted in some improvement. Upon reaching the Berghof I gave him another body massage, with more Euflat followed by the Luizym I have been giving him now repeatedly for some time.

In the evening he had some quite easily digestible nutrition and went to bed around twelve-thirty, after taking a Phanodorm-Calc and half a Quadronox tablet.

When Hitler met Mussolini in July 1943 Italy had been thrown out of Africa, its army had melted away and it was facing invasion from the south. At the end of July Mussolini was overthrown by his own Fascist Grand Council, and thereafter Victor Emmanuel III, the King of Italy, appointed Marshal Badoglio Prime Minister. Mussolini was arrested and Italy changed sides. SEE ALSO PP. 758–9.

Friday 23 July 1943

David Scholes of the RAAF waits to join a squadron in England

Born and educated in Melbourne at Scotch College, in 1940 David Scholes left medical school to serve as a pilot in the Royal Australian Air Force. He undertook his initial pilot training at Western Junction in Tasmania, where he met his future wife, Pat. In 1943 he was posted to Europe and travelled across the United States, arriving in Scotland and then travelling to southern England for further training.

I have been before a Selection Board for the purpose of deciding what aircraft I am to fly and after pleading for half an hour for Mustangs in Tactical Air Force and being given daylight spits in Fighter Command, I am not very displeased because a lot of chaps who trained on singles, have been put on multies [multi-engined aircraft]. The demand for bomber pilots is acute and if they can see any way out, then you're a gonner and a bomber pilot! . . .

We have had numerous raids and alerts, but no bombs have fallen close enough to me yet to scare the daylights out of me. I enjoy these raids very much! Especially when they begin pumping the flak up. There is no better way of describing the noise it makes, than the word 'crump'! I have taken several more bus rides, a little further afield than before, and visit Alfriston a beautiful little place with a tumbled down church and a handful of people, Lewes, Berwick, Pyecombe, Worthing, Peacehaven and others all of which I find very interesting and beautiful in their own little way. I take numerous photographs, but can see that soon I shall be up the spout for film.

Out towards Berwick, Stan Silver and I find ourselves near a little church one sunny afternoon. Inside we find the vicar and have a long talk with him. It is not bomb-blast that has shaken the building, but about six months ago the field artillery had been practicing in the neighbouring fields and the shock from the guns had caused some damage. The church had been first built in about 1400, but in true English fashion additions here and there had taken place including the spire some 800 years ago! This *is* old – I have seen many churches and all of them are very old.

At times I have been a little browned off with things in general. I am sure a bit of mail would help matters. I frequent the Regent Dance Hall and the various cinemas to pass time.

One afternoon I met a girl named Helen and we talked on a wooden seat before having fish 'n chips in the park. Towards evening she showed me an air raid shelter. After a while I go to check on some kids outside and on return find her lying on the low flat table naked from the waist down. This is my first encounter with a prostitute and having just been lectured a couple of days ago about the risk of catching a dose, I tell her I have to get back to camp where I get pretty

mad on finding my wallet stolen from my tunic top pocket
while I was checking outside.

David Scholes

*David Scholes was anxious to fly single-engined fighter aircraft but, as
the balance of the war shifted from defence to offence during 1944, he
would find himself on the latest Lancaster bombers with 5 Group, a unit
famous for the 'Dam Buster' and 'Tirpitz' raids. He was awarded the
Distinguished Flying Cross. A high proportion of the 'British' air contribution during the war was made by the Commonwealth, either by the
Commonwealth air forces as distinct units, or by their pilots on attach-
ment to the RAF. Bomber crews were often multinational. Like so many
pilots from the Commonwealth and the United States, Scholes was
fascinated by the opportunity to explore historic Britain, a country of
which he had heard much from relatives, but had never seen himself.
SEE ALSO PP. 19–20 AND 670–3.*

Wednesday 28 July 1943

Heinrich von Einsiedel of the Wehrmacht decides to join the Russians

Heinrich von Einsiedel was born in Germany in 1922 and had joined the Hitler Youth in his teens. Later he became an officer in the Wehrmacht, and by December 1942 he had found himself in Russian hands in a POW camp outside Stalingrad. There he converted to Marxism and joined the political cadre that eventually formed the core of Stalin's protégé East German government, the National Committee for a Free Germany. This was a substantial organization with its own magazine, called Free Germany. *In 1943 he was already mingling with the future communist leaders of East Germany, including Walter Ulbricht.*

'We' are a delegation of the National Committee consisting of Friedrich Wolf, the doctor and German writer, known for his plays *Zyankali* and *Professor Mamlock* and for his fight against Paragraph 218; Major Homann, Captain Stolz, Lieutenant Colonel Baratov from the political headquarters administration of the Red Army, and me. In addition we have two German officers with us who want to prepare the way for starting a league of German officers. The idea for this came from Professor Arnold, that is from the Russians, and from the officers of the committee. It is clear that our propaganda will have a chance of success in the Wehrmacht only if Paulus and the majority of the higher Stalingrad officers back it. But along with their other scruples these gentlemen are unwilling to sit down with party politicians, especially Communists, to recognize a pacifist poet-agitator as president, or to sign anything like our appeal to found illegal fighting groups in preparation for the coup d'état against Hitler. But an officers' league would give them the opportunity of expressing themselves in the beginning in much more moderate and 'officer-like' terms. They would be under the impression that they were playing an independent role and would gradually get used to our way of thinking. This is our means of making the decision to take part in our plan easier for them.

All these ruses would hardly have been necessary if the Communists were not so horribly clumsy and unacquainted with the German mentality. There are Communists like Bredel, Wolf, and Wilhelm Zaisser who are quite good at dealing with the officers. But party hacks such as Ulbricht with his wooden 'dialectical' monologues are insufferable. Yet Ulbricht seems to have the most influence with the Communists. One of the students at the antifascist school compared him with a union big shot who is always arranging something behind the scenes and then presenting the workers with a fait accompli.

In the wake of the Battle of Kursk, Heinrich von Einsiedel's wartime task was to try to persuade other officers to join him, but while many German officers hated the Nazis, they would not work with the communists either. Eventually the Russians would have to set up another organization called the 'Officers' League', which was anti-Nazi but not so explicitly communist, in order to persuade some of the German officers to come over. Even then only a minority of them did so. At a special German officers' prison camp at Yelabuga they were treated to long political speeches by Walter Ulbricht, despite interruptions from senior German officers shouting 'Even if there are only twelve million of us left we will fight on to final victory!' to thunderous applause from their comrades. SEE ALSO PP. 605–6 AND 631–2.

AUGUST 1943

ON MONDAY 2 AUGUST the RAF made its ninth attack in eight days on the city of Hamburg. By September the Air Ministry in London would be proudly boasting of the most complete destruction visited upon any city in history. On Friday 6 August the Germans announced the partial evacuation of Berlin. Two weeks later the Luftwaffe Chief of Staff, Colonel General Jesehonnek, committed suicide after receiving biting criticism from Hitler. Nevertheless, the German air force was attempting to hit back against the Allies. In mid-August Portsmouth suffered its heaviest raid for two years when it was bombed by almost 100 aircraft. Britain had received intelligence that revealed Hitler's programme to develop missile 'revenge weapons' and test sites were already being attacked. On 17 and 18 August the RAF bombed Peenemunde on the Baltic coast, the main test site for the 'V' weapons. As a result, the development of these weapons was delayed and they would not be used against Britain until the summer of 1944.

Sicily fell to the Allies on 17 August. Two days later the Italians began surrender negotiations through their representatives in Lisbon. Eisenhower's representatives were his Chief of Staff, General Walter Bedell Smith, and his intelligence officer, General Kenneth Strong. Eisenhower had ordered Patton to apologize personally to the shell-shocked soldiers he had struck in the notorious 'face-slapping incident' during a hospital visit, when he had refused to accept that they were psychologically damaged and instead accused them of cowardice.

In mid-August there was a historic uprising by the inmates of the Treblinka concentration camp. Sixteen German guards were killed and 150 inmates escaped. In retaliation the guards murdered a further 550 prisoners.

By 1943 the shortage of manpower had become the key problem in the British war effort. The changing role of women was absolutely critical in meeting the need for workers in every area. Of a 2.8 million increase in people employed in Britain during the war, 2.2 million were women. The working day was lengthened far more drastically in Britain than in America. There was also ruthless channelling of the British labour force, so that under half those working were now employed in activities not war-related.

Sunday 1 August 1943

Mathilde Wolff-Mönckeberg views Hamburg on
'the day after'

Mathilde Wolff-Mönckeberg was born in Hamburg in 1879, daughter of the Lord Mayor. In 1925 she married Emil Wolff, Professor of English Literature at Hamburg University. Both of them loathed the Nazi regime and most of their children left Germany before the outbreak of the war. By 1937 her daughter was married to Ifor Evans, principal of the University College of Wales at Aberystwyth.

Driving through the devastated town was so frightful that I shall never forget it. The little car shuddered over mountains of debris, we had to navigate around piles of rubble and stones, torn-out waterpipes, blocks of concrete and in between the charred corpses of human beings and horses, ghastly sights. And then suddenly we were in open country, heather-covered fields, and we stopped in Sprötze in front of the small railway post-house, where the Hahns had found asylum. It was crowded and primitive, but oh so good to be with helpful, sympathetic people who gave us all a good plentiful evening meal and allowed us to camp down in the actual post office. We were so exhausted that after a short walk we retired. Streams of refugees came and brought reports that it had been given out on the Moorweide during a food distribution that a vast reprisal raid had been made on London, a thousand aircraft had rained down bombs for hours on end. Totally untrue, of course! No sooner had we drifted off to sleep than the siren started to scream and we were witnesses to the fourth enormous terror raid on Hamburg. We stood outside the front door for two hours watching wave upon wave of heavy bombers droning their way towards the unfortunate city, listening to the distant crashes of continuous thunder, marvelling at the never-ceasing rockets of fire, the falling of burning, shot-down aeroplanes in a night sky dotted all over with millions of

stars. What was left of Hamburg? We were told the following day that all Winterhude was razed to the ground and
gave up all hope of ever seeing our home and our belongings again.

*Between August and November 1943 there would be thirty further
major raids on Hamburg. SEE ALSO PP. 651–2.*

Nella Last, a volunteer diarist for the Mass-Observation
Archive in Barrow-in-Furness, reflects on women who
have gone into pants

I suddenly thought tonight, 'I know why a lot of women
have gone into pants – it's a sign that they are asserting
themselves in some way.' I feel pants are more of a sign of
the times than I realised. A growing contempt for man in
general creeps over me. For a craftsman, whether a sweep or
Prime Minister – 'hats off'. But why this 'Lords of Creation'
attitude on men's part? I'm beginning to see I'm a really
clever woman in my own line, and not the 'odd' or 'un-
educated' woman that I've had dinned into me. Not that
in-laws have bothered me for some time now. I got on my
top note, and swept all clean, after one sticky bit of interference and bother. I feel that, in the world of tomorrow,
marriage will be – will *have* to be – more of a partnership,
less of this '*I* have spoken' attitude. They will talk things
over – talking *does* do good, if only to clear the air. I run my
house like a business: I have had to, to get all done properly,
everything fitted in. Why, then, should women not be looked
on as partners, as 'business women'? I feel thoroughly out of
time. I'm not as patient as I used to be, and when one gets to
fifty-three, and after thirty-two years of married life, there
are few illusions to cloud issues.

*Military styling and lines influenced the cut of both men's and women's
clothing from the outset of the war. Increasingly, women wore trousers,
or a one-piece 'siren suit', which could be put on quickly when an*

air-raid warning siren sounded. The siren suit was popularized by Churchill, who enjoyed being photographed in his. Headgear became much more streamlined and practical, seen as a means of keeping hair out of the way. Clothing was often exchanged, and there were endless schemes to give advice on recycling or making clothes last longer. Top designers developed the Utility look, trying to make the best use of limited materials. For many the change in women's clothing was not just a matter of economy but was also symbolic of political and social change. SEE ALSO PP. 130–1, 235 AND 537–8.

Monday 9 – Tuesday 10 August 1943

Vladimir Dedijer observes a further SOE supply drop to Tito's headquarters

9 August
Petrovo Polje

At last the local peasantry are convinced we were not deceiving them when we said that the allies would drop supplies by air. There was great rejoicing when two Liberators appeared about one am ... The British have dropped six anti-tank rifles, excellent weapons – but with very little munitions for them. Otherwise, in place of 400 uniforms, we got 70!

... They also sent us two barrels of little shovel-like instruments for killing flies! ... Veljko and I examined these peculiar implements – and laughed. A British officer who was with us went scarlet. I said to him: 'We asked for anti-aircraft machine-guns, and we've got little fly-swatters – it won't be easy bringing down aircraft with these.'

10 August
Petrovo Polje

An aircraft came to-night, five anti-tank guns, 320 hand grenades, 70 uniforms and some under-linen. All five guns were broken in dropping them – we shall mend them somehow ...

Vladimir Dedijer passed the time between supply drops enjoying political discussion with the SOE officers in Tito's headquarters. The officers observed that throughout Europe the young people leading the resistance in the various occupied countries were in conflict with the old politicians in exile in London. They observed that Greece looked particularly troublesome and vulnerable to faction-fighting, although for the time being the various resistance groups had agreed not to fight each other.

By October 1943 Dedijer was incapacitated by the effects of his wound. He was probably saved by the improving military situation, which allowed Tito to request his evacuation by the SOE to Cairo for an operation. He would return to the fray in July 1944 and kept his diary until Belgrade was liberated in October 1944.

After the war Dedijer would became editor-in-chief of the Communist Party newspaper Borba, and published what became the standard biography of Tito. He was appointed Yugoslavian ambassador to the UN and later became a visiting professor of history at Cornell, Brandeis and Harvard Universities and the University of Michigan. He died in 1990. SEE ALSO PP. *558–9, 572, 575–6* AND *583–4.*

Mid-August 1943

Edward Ardizzone, an official war artist, helps to oversee the surrender of Italian soldiers at Taormina on Sicily

Born in 1900 at Haiphong in the French colony of Indochina, Edward Ardizzone was the son of Italian and Scottish parents. He spent much of his childhood in England, where he attended the Westminster School of Art, and had already exhibited by 1928. Domiciled in Britain, he was appointed a full-time official war artist in 1940 after serving for a while as a lieutenant in anti-aircraft artillery. He served with the British Expeditionary Force in France and then moved to the Mediterranean. Working in north Africa, he heard of the impending invasion of Sicily and, ignoring guidance that he should travel with the rear echelons, he joined friends from the 50th Division and landed with the first wave of troops in July 1943. By mid-August they had reached Taormina, situated at the eastern end of Sicily, between Messina and Mount Etna.

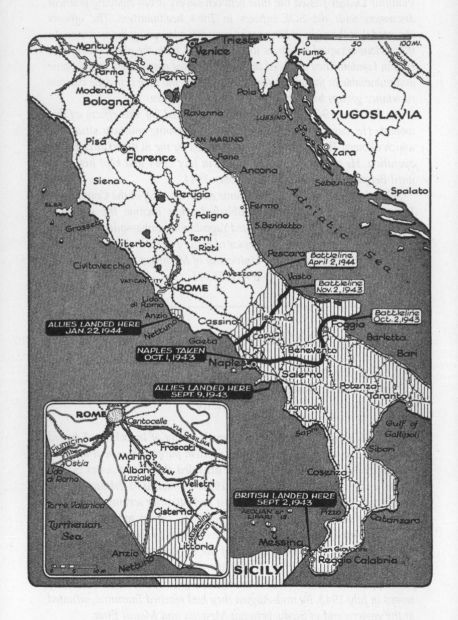

The War in Italy, 1943–4

Now begins our incredible adventure. Geoffrey, with enormous coolness and sang-froid and myself, slightly panic stricken, and both unarmed, capture the town of Taormina plus a Colonel and four hundred Italian troops.

Our route was through Giardini which was completely silent, deserted and shuttered, though one could hear snatches of conversation from behind the closed doors. Four very old men and one old woman were sitting under a tree but paid no heed to us. We walked cautiously and slowly as there were many mines and there was every possibility of being fired on. Climbing into the town we heard a shot fired but as it did not seem to be at us, we went on.

Turning a corner we came almost face to face with half company of Italian infantry with Spandaus. We hailed them and walked up to them, asked for the Commanding Officer. A *Tenente* and *Soutenente* pushed their way through the soldiers, we demanded their revolvers, which they rather unwillingly handed over. After a minute it transpired that they thought we were Germans. When they discovered that we were English they broke into smiles. The men cheered, shook us by the hand and offered us wine and food. Some rather dirty men and women with them. Frightful smell of shit.

We ordered the *Tenente* to collect his men and march them, disarmed, down the hill towards Giarre. Before doing so he took us to some large caves where there were some more of his Company, fifty in all. Surrounded by a mob of smiling women and children there. We then ordered the *Tenente* off with his troops and climbed some steps to an hotel, where we lunched in style on pasta and champagne. In the meantime Geoffrey had sent a message by the hotel manager to the Italian commander, an Alpini Colonel, telling him to report at once to us alone with his Adjutant. I was on tenterhooks in case he should call our bluff and know more of the situation than we did, we had learned that he had four hundred men under his command. To my surprise he turned up with the Adjutant. We told him that the town was surrounded and that he must surrender and ordered him to disarm his troops and march them away southward. Over a glass of champagne he meekly and sadly complied.

We then borrowed his car and, in company with the hotel manager and a comic proprietor of the Water and Electricity Co, made a tour of the town, visiting the Greek and Roman ruins. Passed through some barracks and ordered the men away.

Leave the car and were met in street by the Chief of Police and his two assistants, ceremonial dress, much shaking of hands. We give them instructions about maintaining order in the town. Drink Veuve Cliquot with them at the Police Station. Demand two bicycles. Sundry characters, the violent anti-Fascist who burst into our room at the hotel, Madame Vanderveldt, supposedly Dutch. Drink vermouth at the canteen of a barracks, smiling populace. Back to the hotel, our bicycles arrive. We gingerly ride off, threading our way past the mines, two Sappers blown up on the road, my back tyre flat. Have to lie down in the dirt when the RES fire a charge. Wade the river and arrive, half dead with fatigue, at the place where we had left the jeep . . .

By 17 August 1943 Messina had fallen and all of Sicily was in Allied hands as the result of a panic evacuation by German and Italian troops. Over 100,000 Italian troops surrendered. Although the invasion of Sicily went very smoothly and Allied casualties were quite low, some Axis forces were allowed to escape to the mainland more or less unmolested. After Sicily fell Edward Ardizzone would take part in the invasion of Italy and spend most of the rest of the war there, before travelling to Germany in April 1945 to observe the final stages.

Friday 20 August 1943

Kathleen Church-Bliss and Elsie Whiteman, two women lathe-workers at Morrison's factory, attend a dinner-hour factory concert

Another amateur concert during dinner hour today. The place was packed and Mr McGiveney, Lines and Proctor came and leant against the wall to listen. One man played the *Warsaw Concerto*, but it was largely drowned in the clatter of crockery. Then a wild girl played the mandolin, but she looked very anxious and was still in the counting stage. Then Mr Biffo announced that Mr Lavender would play another of his song compositions and that this time the chorus would be sung by Sally Fillingham. Sally is the true factory type, bursting with high spirits, completely unself-conscious, and with the wild, free gestures of the very rough. Most of the girls are at great pains to doll themselves up for their public appearance, but Sally rose from her seat in her filthy white overall, with the usual grease marks all over the backside and walked onto the platform giving the double-handed boxer's salute. She is a tall, fair girl, with thin, stringy, loose limbs and a long, thin face which lights up. We have always been interested in her since we heard her singing like a lark in the shelter one day during an alert. She has the roughest gin-and-fog voice and was one of the firm's first girl employees. When she began her song there was an almost immediate breakdown, as Lavender's songs seem utterly tuneless and quite unsingable. Everyone roared with laughter as this had happened last week with the other chorus singer. Sally had an altercation with Lavender, accompanied by much arm slinging while the audience shrieked. She started off again and there was another break-down. Finally Mr Biffo said 'Never mind – sing something next week instead', but Sally said 'Oh! No I don't. I came up here to sing and sing I'm going to' and she broke into a mod-ern dance hit and the orchestra joined in. She sang awfully well and was received with thunderous applause. The double bass and the pianist had tears streaming down their faces at Sally's altercation and the directors were also howl-ing with laughter. Even the grim Capt[ain] Lines, who has never before been seen to smile, was purple in the face and mopping his eyes. Sally really is a find and has all the makings of Gracie Fields.

The concert then ended with some dire crooning and a very young girl, Pansy Williams, playing the piano with wonderful rhythm. She played popular dance music and quite spontaneously the workers gradually joined in, until the whole room was singing with her. It is quite evident from the packed room and the vociferous applause, that the workers much prefer to come and see what talent there is amongst themselves than to listen to the grand professional orchestra provided to the firm.

Kathleen Church-Bliss and Elsie Whiteman had definite views on music. After the war they would become involved in societies that promoted both American and British traditional folk songs and folk dancing. They would also publish scores and settings still in use today. SEE ALSO PP. 507–9.

SEPTEMBER 1943

ON 3 SEPTEMBER General Castellano signed the Italian surrender at Cassibili in Sicily. Allied landings went smoothly at Taranto but met with stiff resistance at Salerno. The surrendered Italian fleet sailed for Malta but was attacked by the Luftwaffe en route and the battleship *Roma* was sunk. In Corfu there was heavy fighting between German forces and Italian troops who had changed sides. On the Italian mainland the Allies advanced slowly, delayed by demolitions and booby-traps. Mussolini was rescued from his place of captivity at Gran Sasso by German paratroops led by Otto Skorzeny. This was a difficult mission and constitutes one of the most notable special forces coups of the Second World War. Mussolini proclaimed a new government on 23 September, but parts of northern Italy were now under direct German rule.

On the Eastern Front Soviet troops advanced steadily towards Kiev. On 25 September the Red Army took Smolensk and Roslaval, while the German army fell back to make a stand behind the Dniepr river. Hitler's stubborn refusal to allow organized withdrawals to well-prepared positions resulted in additional losses for the weary legions of the Wehrmacht.

Six British midget submarines were sent to attack the *Tirpitz*, the last major German warship that was still operational; based in Atenfiord in Norway, it continued to pose a threat to Allied convoys sailing to Russia. Only two submarines managed to attack the target but the *Tirpitz* was seriously damaged and would be unable to operate again until March 1944.

Despite the good weather the Luftwaffe were almost completely absent from British skies during this month, in stark contrast to July and August, when Portsmouth and Grimsby had been heavily attacked. Only five people were killed in air raids, the lowest number since May 1940. This encouraged more people who had evacuated to return to the cities, placing an almost unbearable burden on public services such as schools. Public relief at the decline in bombing was visible, and many concluded – quite wrongly – that the period of German air attack was drawing to a close.

Friday 3 September 1943

George Beardmore, writer and rate-collector, reflects on war damage to the fabric of human society in London

On this, the fourth anniversary of the outbreak of war, here are two indications of how it is affecting society.

I was sent to Golders Green on the track of a defaulting rent-payer, one of our rehoused. His name appears on the books as Leamington. At the address given me by the Food Office (nobody can go into hiding these days) he was living as Mr Ford together with a Mrs Ford. Furnished rooms. The landlady said that he had been absent for about a fortnight and that he had reappeared with a beard and broken fingernails. By the face she made I understood prison, particularly as he had subsequently had letters readdressed to him from Brixton. I met Mrs Ford, who is really Miss Ford, a plump blond girl four years older than Leamington. By coincidence she has been a typist employed by my friend, the Welfare Officer at Napier's at Borehamwood. She (the Welfare Officer) told me that Miss Ford had been fired for 'carrying-on' – with anyone she took a fancy to, a labourer, a clerk in the cashier's office, and now Ford. Leamington himself has a legal wife in whom pregnancy has brought on TB. She now lies at Redhill Hospital and he was given his term at Brixton for failing to maintain her. Between his wife and Miss Ford there had been another woman who had come and gone from our requisitioned flat in Stonegrove.

None of this would have arisen in pre-war days when neither of them, Ford or Leamington, would have dared to risk losing a well-found job.

The other indication found its way into our own home when Jean [George's wife] stood at Pinner in the same bus-queue as Mrs Flaxton, who lives with her pretty daughter Sharon down the road. Out of neighbourliness Jean brought her home to tea. A remark about nerves and ill-health brought out the information that two years ago Mr Flaxton, a corporal with the AA, handed her a wrong letter betraying the traditional 'other woman'. Eighteen months ago he told her that he could no longer live with her, she must realise that she was getting on (she's thirty-three) and that he could, and did, pick up any girl he fancied simply by leaning across in a cinema and asking for a light. Later he went on (out of cussedness, I should think) to describe his latest girl's underwear. Six days of his last leave he spent with his mother and in the short space of five hours spent at home he knocked Sharon spinning and called his wife a hag. Last year she had tried to do away with herself. She is ashamed, she says, to show anyone inside of her house because she can take no pride in it. The garden, too, has been allowed to run wild. (In this she's not unique: the number of gardens I come across that had once been their owners' pride and joy and are now only dreams in the minds of men in Italy or on the high seas.) She paid her husband's CO a visit but was told only that her case was one of hundreds like hers. She is still devoted to him, certain that he will come back. His behaviour, she said, was quite out of character, formerly he had been withdrawn and shy.

The Second World War was an enormously powerful engine of social change in Britain. One of the clearest indices of changing social attitudes to sex was the fact that of the 5.3 million British children born between 1939 and 1945, over a third were illegitimate. Dislocation as a result of the war was a tremendous stimulus to extra-marital sexual activity. The highest rate of illegitimate births was not among teenagers, as some had expected, but in women aged between twenty and thirty: in both Britain and the United States women in their twenties gave birth to nearly double the number of pre-war illegitimate children.

After the war Beardmore gave up his local authority work and turned to writing full-time. He was never able to make writing pay well, but had considerable success as an adventure writer for children, contributing to the magazines Eagle *and* Girl *as well as writing several novels. His last book was* Treasure of the Spanish Bay, *published in 1975, four years before his death. His diaries – by then long forgotten – came to light in 1977 when he was moving house. SEE ALSO PP. 85–6 AND 89–90.*

Sunday 5 September 1943

Noel Coward entertains a 'bloody-minded' audience of British troops outside Cairo

Arrived at Lydda feeling not very well so asked Bill Murray if I could go to bed for an hour before my concert which was at six. When I woke up I felt like death, took my temperature which was 101 and sent for the MO. When he arrived I explained that I couldn't possibly not do the concert and that it was also essential for me to do my second one that evening which was at Nathanyia rest camp about two hours away by car. He looked a bit dubious, gave me a benzedrine tablet and said that he would come with me to Nathanyia. Apart from feeling ill I was rather agitated. You never know in these climates what you might have caught! However I bounced on to the stage with a great deal of forced vitality and got through all right and then drove off with the MO to Nathanyia. Here I found several thousand men waiting for me in the open air. They were a little fractious because, owing to us having lost our way, we were late and they had been kept waiting for a half an hour or so. The situation was in no way improved by an idiotic man jumping on to the stage and announcing that I had been detained by the RAF.

This, I need hardly say, is not the ideal introduction to an entirely Army concert. I started singing with the definite feeling that the whole audience was against me. They were not actively hostile in any way and they stayed quiet, but they just sat there sullenly without giving me any response at all. I have known troop audiences be bloody-minded like this before and there is nothing whatever to be done about it but grit your teeth and persevere and behave as though you thought they were the greatest audience in the world. On this particular evening I determined to get them going if it was the last thing I ever did; I also felt that it was highly possible that it might be. I can only assume that black inward rage has astonishing curative powers for by the time I had got through my first three numbers all fatigue and fever had fled from me. About half way through they began to relax and laugh a bit and from then on I knew the worst was over. By the end they were cheering and applauding as though they really had been the best audience in the world and, flushed with triumph, I went off with the commanding officer and had the strongest and most welcome whisky and soda that ever crossed my lips.

Noel Coward agreed to keep a diary of his 1943 tour of the Middle East for immediate publication. Unlike Joyce Grenfell, he was not permanently engaged in this sort of concert touring work, but like her he found that audiences and venues varied enormously. To deal with his illness the MO gave him benzedrine, the Second World War's standard 'pep pill'. At this time the American, British, German and Japanese armed forces all issued amphetamines – usually benzedrine sulphate pills – to their men to counteract fatigue, elevate mood and heighten endurance. In particular, they were often given to tank or submarine crews who had to sustain action for more than twenty-four hours at a time without resting. Although they were popular, prolonged use could result in short-term bouts of psychotic aggression or, in the long term, addiction. SEE ALSO PP. 568–9 AND 580.

Thursday 9 – Sunday 12 September 1943

Heinrich von Einsiedel records the diary of
Wolfgang Heinz, a captured German officer, within the
text of his own diary

Heinrich von Einsiedel was attached to Russian troops close to the front line, and was engaged in attempting to bring recently captured POWs over to the Russian cause. On 10 October 1943 his party would come upon a horde of abandoned German documents. Among them was the diary of Wolfgang Heinz, a young officer cadet from Nürnberg. Heinrich von Einsiedel was unsure whether the author of the diary had been killed or taken prisoner, but found his diary fascinating and so copied a section of it into his own diary. It is reproduced here.

9 September

We run into so many people here, one gradually gets a view of many areas of life and learns to look at things differently. I can't write freely about all this yet. The end of the war will clear up everything. But one thing is plain to me now: one of the reasons for the great defeats which our army has suffered is the false official communiqués. Everything is lied about, embellished, improved on, touched up, so that a tank division which had say twenty tanks still at its disposal suddenly has two hundred again. I wonder whether head-quarters realizes what the troops are going through in the Mius retreat; that they have no blankets to cover them at night in zero temperatures; not a tent, nor a spade to dig in with; nor clean underclothes nor sweater nor socks, since everything has been burned during the retreat!

10 September

It is often terribly difficult to carry out some of the orders. We have had to burn down a village today. The poor people who had so laboriously built it all were in despair. 'But you are a civilized people,' one woman said to me, and one can only shrug one's shoulders. They went down on their knees to plead with us, offered us all their money and held up icons to us. But what could we do? Orders! And while the women wept, we burned the village down. 'C'est la guerre!' . . .

12 September

Why does one stand all this? Is it for the Führer, the Fatherland, and one's people? No, no, a thousand times no. It is only because one's comrades are in the same boat and one mustn't forsake them. That is the reason, nothing else! Out here we want a quick end to all this mess where our comrades get killed while the high and mighty at home grow fat. And we want to get home!!! Why give one's bones for a regime which isn't worth it? This war has proved its unfitness for life. We should put an end to this murder of young people now while there may still be time. But the gentlemen at the top have no conscience. They are afraid to stand up for their actions. I must stop. The Russians have begun to attack. Goodbye. No doubt it will soon be over.

It was not unusual to find abandoned diaries on the battlefield, even though all sides forbade diary-keeping. Heinz recorded that he had only been at the front for fourteen days but remarked that it felt as if it had been fourteen years. He was tired of being ordered to hold his position to the last man, only to find that his battalion headquarters had slunk away in retreat. He confessed himself stripped of all ideals – Nazi or otherwise – and commented: 'Isn't the war just a swindle?' He correctly observed that most soldiers who fought tenaciously were motivated not by ideals, but by a desire to defend their comrades. This was common to all armies. SEE ALSO PP. 589–90 AND 631–2.

Friday 10 September 1943

Anthony Eden is exasperated with Winston Churchill, absent in Washington

Felt depressed and not very well all day. Partly I think, because of exasperating difficulty of trying to do business with Winston over the Atlantic. Two telephone calls during the day. Roosevelt has had his way again and agreed to Moscow for his Foreign Secretaries conference with alacrity. His determination not to agree to London meeting for any purpose, which he says is for electoral reasons, is almost insulting considering the number of times we have been to W[ashing]ton. I am most anxious for good relations with the US but I don't like subservience to them, and I am sure that this only lays up trouble for us in the future. We are giving the impression, which they are only too ready by nature to endorse, that all the military achievements are theirs and Winston, by prolonging his stay in Washington, strengthens the impression. Now I am to go to Moscow on a par with an American Under Sec who is known to be anathema to Hull [American Secretary of State]. I don't like all this and said so in telegram to W[inston], which won't please him. Busy with boxes all day . . . Wrote to congratulate Simon who has been chosen to train for a pilot.

In September 1943 Churchill went on a long trip to Canada and the United States to discuss future strategy and to be presented with an honorary degree at Harvard University. His acceptance speech captured an important Churchillian sentiment: the theme of Anglo-American unity. He was talking not only about war aims but also about values and culture. Being himself half American, he spoke easily about what he called the 'gift of a common tongue' – a priceless inheritance. Anthony Eden was never so convinced of the benefits of Atlanticism. The previous year he had chaired a meeting in the Foreign Office about the United States after which one of his officials who was present had written, 'We talked on the United States as if she was the enemy.' Eden's last sentence here refers to his son, Simon, training as an RAF pilot, who two years later would be killed fighting in the war against Japan.

Eden would wait until 1953 to follow Churchill as Prime Minister, and would have liked the job sooner. In 1957 he resigned because of ill health and began his memoirs. In this latter task his diaries were not much help, for he was not a diligent diarist, making entries only sporadically – often when Churchill had seriously annoyed him. SEE ALSO PP. 298 AND 420–1.

Saturday 25 – Sunday 26 September 1943

Alison Uttley, children's author, hears that her son John has been reported missing

Alison Uttley was a famous writer for children, perhaps best known as the creator of The Little Grey Rabbit. *Born in Cromford in Derbyshire in 1884, she had shown early promise at school, with a particular enthusiasm for scientific subjects. Later she was awarded a scholarship to study physics at Manchester University and became the second woman honours graduate of the university in 1906. She turned to writing because of financial hardship after her husband died in 1930 following a long illness resulting from service in the First World War.*

25 September
Missing. I cannot write the words. God help us both. Oh John, my darling John. Can you reach him! Oh John. I love you. John. Missing on Sept 9. Please God, let him be alive. Please God help us.

26 September
To have stood in the breach and kept the way open for the vast future.

I went to church. I read 'Rock of Ages' and was comforted. I went back with Mrs Rankin for a little time. Then out to lunch with Miss Collins, who I helped in the kitchen, and the action helped me. Then home, I lighted the fire and wrote to my dear friends the grievous news. Mrs Harrap came after this, then kissed me, and sat with me. So the day has gone by, I dare not think, but I pray ... I listened to the service tonight and the prayers [on the radio]. People say the Germans took many prisoners, so I hope still for John's life. Oh God, hear my prayer and save him.

Alison Uttley kept a constant diary. Her forty notebooks of stories, thoughts and material gathered for her writing capture her literary life, including frequent contact with other writers such as Walter de la Mare, and also aspects of her personal life, including her close relationship with her son, John Corrin Taylor Uttley, who was reported missing while serving in the Army in 1943, aged twenty-eight. Her diary captures the agony of uncertainty into which so many were plunged. She would wait another month for news of her son's fate. SEE ALSO P. 622.

OCTOBER 1943

ON THURSDAY 14 OCTOBER the US 8th Air Force attempted to deliver a heavy attack against the ball-bearing plant at Schweinfurt. The plant was well defended and losses of aircraft and crews were severe. Of the original force of 291 B-17s, 198 were either shot down or damaged beyond repair, whereas the Germans lost only about 40 fighter planes. The belief, widely held by American aviators, that well-armed bombers could defend themselves on daylight raids by flying in close formation had now been disproved. Protection from long-range fighters would clearly be essential to the future of American air operations.

In Italy, Naples fell to the Allies on 1 October and on the 15th Marshal Badoglio's government formally declared war against Germany. The pace of the Allied advance in Italy was accelerating and Hitler ordered the local German commander, General Kesselring, to construct formidable defensive positions south of Rome, which became known as the Gustav Line.

In Russia, the Red Army crossed the Dniepr. On 31 October

the remaining German forces in the Crimea were cut off when their last rail link was severed by the Soviet advance. Anthony Eden went to Moscow for a foreign ministers' conference with his American and Soviet counterparts. As well as receiving more complaints from the latter about the lack of a second front in western Europe, he was increasingly anxious about the scale of Soviet ambitions in eastern Europe and realized that these would pose a problem when the time came to make a post-war settlement.

Friday 1 – Thursday 7 October 1943

David Smiley of the SOE blows up a bridge in Albania

1 October

Sgt. Melford returned from an ambush . . . Seven Germans killed and three prisoners.

5 October

Reached main Librasht–Kapathanos road, near Premergjios. Saw large convoy coming, so I put the three prisoners on the road and left them. They all seemed very grateful, as they certainly should have been, as I had much difficulty to prevent the Partisans shooting them. In five minutes I saw them all picked up. I was sitting about 100 yards from the road and they did not give me away, as they had promised not to say anything until they had gone. Reconnoitred the road all the way as far as Xhyra where I spent the night. Saw many Huns.

6 October

Continued along the old Klasasn road which runs parallel and overlooks the new main road used by the Huns. Saw more Huns in convoys and barracks and guarding bridges. Also saw large fortifications at Babie and went inside them. The Germans also did a recce of these the day before. At night after the mules had crossed the main road near Mirakaj, I blew up the bridge leading to these fortifications.

I worked alone and after lighting the fuse found that I could not cross the bridge and had to swim the Shkumbi [river]. It was very frightening as I thought I could ford across it and I was being dragged towards the bridge which I knew was going to blow up any moment. It blew up just as I reached the far side. The Germans then started firing from all sides as there were German barracks a mile up and down the road and they never stopped firing all night. Both [guerrilla] bands who were waiting for me were terrified and made me walk for eight hours up the mountains when I wanted to go into the nearest village and get a mule.

7 October
Reach Labinto, the staff there were furious I had blown up the bridge, as I had not asked for their permission . . . .

In the Balkans, the mountainous countryside cut by deep gorges made Axis communications very vulnerable to ambush and the blowing up of bridges, as well as the cutting of telephone and power lines. David Smiley's diary captures some of the confusion and anxiety attendant on these special operations. One recurrent problem for the SOE and the American OSS in all theatres was persuading guerrillas to follow the normal customs and usages of war. In July 1943, after Mussolini was overthrown, the fragmented Albanian resistance groups had come together and launched a general insurrection; it had been brutally crushed by the Germans, and because the Germans and Italians had committed brutal reprisals against so many Albanian villages, the partisans routinely liquidated prisoners after interrogation. The three Germans here were most fortunate to escape this fate.

Smiley would survive his hazardous service with the SOE in the Mediterranean and the Far East, and after 1945 worked for MI6. SEE ALSO PP. 546–7, 554–6 AND 577–8.

Monday 4 – Sunday 10 October 1943

Frances Partridge, translator, editor and pacifist, on Noel Coward's tour of the Middle East

Nick Henderson, back from Cairo came to see us, bringing messages from old friends – Bryan Guinness and Michael MacCarthy are both miserable and longing to be home. Eddie Gathorne-Hardy says Ham Spray 'is the only civilized house in England'. Nicko is attached to Lord Moyne in some capacity which involves entertaining visitors from England. He gave an amusing account of Noel Coward, wanting to swim but having no bathing trunks, so he had to accept a long, unbecoming pair of underpants belonging to Lord Moyne. Then he asked Nicko, 'is there such a thing as a lav about?' Nicko pointed vaguely to some large trees. N.C.: 'No, no, old chap; big stuff, very much so.' So Nicko took him indoors and found a lavatory for him. Soon afterwards Coward came out clutching Lord Moyne's pants, half on and half off, and ran into Nicko with a lady visitor. Nicko rather maliciously introduced them, and N.C. said 'Simply amazing meeting you like this. Definitely no sign whatever of toilet paper.'

During 1943 Frances Partridge continued to sit out the war in the safety of her house, Ham Spray in Wiltshire. However, the war was never far away and a constant stream of visitors from quite elevated circles seeking respite from the conflict made their way out to visit, either from London or returning from service abroad. One such figure was 'Nicko' (Nicholas) Henderson: then a very junior diplomat attached to Lord Moyne, Deputy Minister of State in the Middle East, based in Cairo, he would go on to an illustrious career in the Foreign Office.

Noel Coward's diary of his Middle East tour does not mention the borrowed bathing trunks.

Frances Partridge would publish many volumes of her diaries, continuing to work right up until her death in February 2004 just short of her 104th birthday. Her son Burgo, aged nine in 1943, would continue the family tradition of writing, publishing in 1958 his celebrated book A History of Orgies, *which went through many impressions. SEE ALSO PP. 19, 176–7, 211–12 AND 348–50.*

Tuesday 12 October 1943

Henry A. Wallace on arguments over the opening of the second front

Henry A. Wallace had graduated from Iowa State College with a degree in agriculture in 1910 and became editor of a number of farmers' newspapers. He also developed several high-yielding strains of hybrid corn and made his fortune by successfully selling it through his own company. He was Secretary of Agriculture during the first two Roosevelt administrations and an ardent supporter of the New Deal. In 1940 Wallace was elected Vice-President and between 1942 and 1943 spent a good deal of time on goodwill tours to Latin America and the Far East.

Ralph Ingersoll told me he had been working with some of the generals in London, especially with Lieut. General Jacob Devers. These men have been working especially on the opening up of a genuine second front in France. Ingersoll was greatly concerned about two things and both of these items he had gotten effectively to Harry Hopkins. First, the British have been strongly against a second front, and in case there were a second front, they wanted to have control of it themselves, even though the United States were furnishing two or three times as many men as the British. Part of their plan was to get General Marshall over to England serving on a very high level, while the British generals of the 21ˢᵗ Army really ran the show. Ingersoll found, in talking with Harry Hopkins, that he had been aware of this maneuver on the part of the British and it seemed as though effective steps had been taken to prevent General Marshall from becoming a mere figurehead in the stratosphere. It seems that General Marshall will go to England but on an effective and not an ineffective basis. Everyone seems to be agreed that Marshall is the only one who has the necessary combination of real knowledge, guts, and front to handle Churchill. Churchill has enough military knowledge and front so that he is able to talk down most American generals.

Ingersoll had also talked with Hopkins about the shocking lack of landing craft. He told Hopkins that he had briefed the minutes of the Quebec Conference for the American generals in London and he knew that both the British and American natives had in effect lied about landing craft. They claimed there were a certain number, which was correct, but did not mention that one-third of them were out being repaired or that another third could not be used for other reasons. Ingersoll said that if it were not for the shocking shortage in landing craft, the landing could have been made in France this fall and the war could have been terminated this year . . .

At one time the expectation was that the landing would be made in France about the middle of September. It is now put off until next spring. Arrangements have now been made with the Russians so that they can stage a powerful drive at the same time that we start our landing. Ingersoll is convinced that if we had foreseen the need for landing craft and had staged an invasion of France at the same time that the Russians were pushing in the East, the war would have been over in a month or two. Ingersoll mentioned that the United States admiral in charge of landing operations looks on his position as a demotion instead of a unique opportunity. The only way Ingersoll can explain the Navy's singular blindness with respect to the situation is that the Navy has concentrated on the idea of doing a complete job in the Pacific; also, the Navy has never been properly interested in landing craft. Ingersoll apparently feels that while the Navy has apparently been an extraordinarily efficient organisation in many respects, in other particulars it is unbelievably blind. Churchill told Devers that the Italian Show was important to give the people some victories to cheer them up.

Admiral Royal Ingersoll was Commander of the US Atlantic Fleet and General Jacob Devers was commander of the US 6th Army. Most American generals wanted to invade France in 1943 but faced substantial obstacles in a lack of complete air superiority and a shortage of specialized landing craft. Operation Torch in 1942, and the various operations in Sicily and Italy in 1943, meant that the invasion of France – codenamed Overlord – was in practice bound to be much delayed. However, Churchill was wrong to think that Italy could ever have been the main battlefront for the Allies in the west, since by 1944 it would have effectively become a strategic dead end, proving the Americans had been right to focus their attention on the planned amphibious invasion of western France.

Wallace would be replaced as Vice-President by Harry Truman in 1944.

Saturday 16 October 1943

Ernst Jünger, German officer in Paris, learns of the Nazi death camps

In the 1920s and 1930s Ernst Jünger had been a writer whose works were popular with the Nazi party. The work that found particular favour was his First World War memoir, The Storm of Steel: From the Diary of a German Storm Troop Officer on the Western Front. *He had participated in the invasion of France in 1940 and a year later had joined the staff of the German army commander for France, General Otto von Stülpnagel. He was based at the Hotel Majestic and worked on plans for Operation Sealion, the invasion of Britain. As an intellectual, a theologian and a philosopher, his role as an officer in the Third Reich became increasingly repellent to him as he learned more of the atrocities in the east. He published* Jardins et Routes *in 1942 and gained admirers in Parisian intellectual circles.*

In the evening Bogo came by. He spoke of his travels. In this connection, certain secrets. I was especially shocked by details he reported from the ghetto in Lodz or, as it is now called, Litzmannstadt. He had gained admittance there on a pretext and conferred with the headman of the Jewish community, a former Austrian lieutenant. One hundred and twenty thousand Jews live crowded together in this cramped enclosure, toiling for the armaments industry. They have built up one of the largest factories in the east. That means, as long as they are indispensable they enjoy a certain reprieve. Meanwhile increasing numbers of deported Jews stream in from the occupied territories. To eliminate every trace of them, crematoriums have been built near the ghettos. The victims are brought there in vans that are alleged to be an invention of the head nihilist Heydrich – the exhaust fumes are funneled into the interior, which within seconds becomes a death chamber.

It seems there exists yet a second manner of slaughter: before incineration, the victims are lined up naked on a huge iron plate that is then charged with high-voltage current. One had recourse to these methods because it turned out that the SS men who had been assigned to shoot the victims in the back of the neck were suffering nervous disorders and finally refused. To run these crematoriums one requires little personnel; evidently a breed of diabolical masters and attendants ply their trade there. So that is where the multitudes of Jews disappear who are deported from Europe for 'resettlements.' This is the setting in which Kniébolo's nature reveals itself perhaps most clearly and which even Dostoevsky did not foresee.

Those destined for the crematoriums must be named by the headman of the ghetto. After long deliberation with the rabbis he picks out the old people and the sick children. Among the old and the infirm many are said to volunteer – in the end, such atrocities always redound to the glory of the persecuted.

The Litzmannstadt ghetto is closed off – in other, smaller towns there are ghettos that consist merely of a few streets inhabited by Jews. There, evidently, Jewish policemen who were charged with the capturing of victims also seized some Germans and Poles who were passing through the ghetto and turned them over without anyone ever hearing from them again. Above all, this is reported of Volga Germans who were waiting there for allotments of land. Of course

they assured their tormentors that they were not Jews, only
to hear in response: 'That's what they all say here.'

*'Bogo' was a codename for Jünger's friend Frederick Hielscher, a mystic
who moved on the fringes of the Nazi party and who had recently been
to Poland.*

*Ernst Jünger remains a controversial figure, revered by many for his
vast writings on culture and philosophy, but seen by others as typifying
the cynical way in which conservatives believed they could use the Nazis
to destroy the despised Weimar Republic and restore Germany as a
power, yet without allowing Hitler and his henchmen to take full control.
During the war the conservatives found themselves trapped inside the
Hitler machine and tried to avoid thinking about the consequences by
retreating to the sidelines of war. The extent of Jünger's genuine opposition
remains a matter of discussion, but what his diary does make clear
(notwithstanding inaccuracy in a few details) is the considerable extent
of the knowledge of many middle-ranking German army officers by 1943
of the sorts of atrocities being committed.*

*Jünger would be dismissed from the army in the aftermath of the July
bomb plot and was lucky not to be arrested. His son would be killed at
Carrara in Italy on 29 November 1944 after being sent to a punishment
battalion for organizing subversive discussions in his unit. Jünger
survived the war and died on 17 February 1998, aged 103.*

Tuesday 19 October 1943

RAF navigator John Mitchell recalls an overnight incident
on Churchill's aircraft

We set the same time for take off as before, leaving Cairo
West with our passengers at 2230 hours GMT or 0230 local
. . . the York flew as well as ever – a smooth nine hour flight.
   During the night when all was relatively still, if not exactly
quiet, Jack Payne would often walk aft just to check for any
smouldering cigarette end or other oddities and have a word
with the steward. He heard a rattle which annoyed him and
tracing it to a tooth mug in one of the forward toilets he

found that it was not stowed properly in its holder. He flung the contents into the Elsan can with no more ado and stuck the mug firmly in its stowage. Some hours later, about two hours out from Maison Blanche [Algiers], the passengers were woken with tea and invited to dress for breakfast before landing – always eggs and bacon. The steward was accosted by a somewhat agitated Admiral: 'I've lost my false teeth'. Jock Duncan, the chef, reported the loss to Jack Payne – everything except the navigation was referred to Jack (even when Churchill's Elsan became blocked with too much paper – 'Am I now the Sanitary Engineer?'). Jack immediately realised what was in the tooth mug when he threw the contents into the can – with a rattle!

There was nothing for it but to search the can of Elsanol, and other fluids, with his sleeve rolled right up: Jock Duncan the steward keeping the Admiral occupied with more tea. 'Have you found them yet?' Was the admiral more concerned than poor Jack? Anyway, they were quickly retrieved from the can, whittled to galley under towel, and then 'treated' under the tap etc. 'Here they are sir, just dropped on the floor behind the basin'. The Admiral snapped them into place . . .

Churchill's aircraft was waiting at Cairo for a new engine to be fitted after a serious fire in mid-air. Once fitted with a new engine, it carried the Colonial Secretary, and his unlucky ADC Rear Admiral Bromley, from Cairo to Algiers. Commander Tommy Thompson, ADC to Churchill, would later enjoy telling Admiral Bromley exactly where his teeth had been.

Improvements to comfort in aircraft were being made all the time. By 1944 engineers from GEC would have provided a special electric-powered 'hot-seat' to take the chill off the Elsan toilet at high altitude. Churchill complained that it was too hot, fearing the possibility of shocks from its powerful 50 watt circuit, and Jack Payne was eventually ordered to disconnect it. SEE ALSO PP. 560, 566–8 AND 783–5.

Sunday 24 October 1943

Marie Vassiltchikov, an anti-Soviet Russian in Berlin, prepares German files on Katyn Wood for President Roosevelt

Marie Vassiltchikov was a Russian émigré princess, born in the year of the Bolshevik Revolution. She came to Berlin soon after the outbreak of the Second World War. Her diary describes the experience of a Russian who had chosen to join the Germans and who worked for the foreign ministry. However, she secretly joined the conspirators against Hitler responsible for the July 1944 bomb plot.

I have a new urgent assignment: the translation of the captions for a large number of photographs of the remains of some 4,000 Polish officers found murdered by the Soviets in Katyn forest near Smolensk. The mind boggles.

This is all very hush-hush. I have seen the confidential report sent by von Papen, the German Ambassador in Ankara. He had authorised a member of his staff to become chummy with a Polish diplomatic representative in Turkey who, in his turn, is a friend of Steve Early's, President Roosevelt's special representative there. [Steve Early was actually Roosevelt's press secretary.] Roosevelt has expressed the wish to receive the full, unadulterated story – a thing he is, apparently, unable to do in the States because his entourage (Morgenthau?) intercept and suppress any report unfavourable to the Soviet Union . . .

The translations must be ready in two days. I feel very strange when I think that my prose will land on President Roosevelt's desk in less than a week. What a responsibility! It is also hard work. But above all the detailed evidence that has come to light is harrowing.

Although Britain and the United States received growing amounts of evidence that pointed to the Russians as the perpetrators of the Katyn Wood massacre of Polish officers, they bent over backwards to keep this

*quiet during the war for reasons of Allied solidarity. In the United States,
the Office of War Information routinely censored reports that pointed to
atrocities committed by the Russians. During the Nuremberg war crimes
trials the Soviet representatives were allowed to make unsubstantiated
allegations about the Germans and Katyn Wood without correction. It was
not until 1951 that the mood of international events had changed
sufficiently for it to become politic for the United States to investigate the
matter. SEE ALSO PP. 633–4 AND 716–17.*

Thursday 28 October 1943

Norman Lewis, an intelligence officer responsible for
interrogating prisoners, observes the habits of the
Neapolitans with interest

*Norman Lewis was a travel writer, novelist and journalist. He was also
a sometime military intelligence officer, racer of Bugatti sports cars and
grower of lilies. He was born in 1908 in Enfield in north London, but
spent much of his youth with relatives in Wales. Before the Second
World War he had published books on Spain and on Saudi Arabia.
During the war his geographical knowledge, languages and superb
writing ability took him into the Intelligence Corps. He served in north
Africa and Italy, and in 1943 was stationed in Naples.*

Neapolitans take their sex lives very seriously indeed. A
woman called Lola, whom I met at a dinner-party given by
Signora Gentile, arrived at HQ with some denunciation
which went into the waste-paper basket as soon as her back
was turned. She then asked if I could help her. It turned out
she has taken a lover who is a captain in the RASC [Royal
Army Service Corps], but as he speaks no single word of
Italian, communication can only be carried on by signs, and
this gives rise to misunderstanding. Would I agree to interpret for them and settle certain basic matters?

Captain Frazer turned out to be a tall handsome man
some years Lola's junior ... She wanted to know all about
his marital status and he hers, and they lied to each other

to their hearts' content while I kept a straight face and interpreted.

She asked me to mention to him in as tactful a way as possible that comment had been caused among her neighbours because he never called on her during the day. Conjugal visits at midday are *de rigueur* in Naples. This I explained, and Frazer promised to do better.

When the meeting was over we went for a drink, and he confided to me that something was worrying him too. On inspecting her buttocks he had found them covered with hundreds of pinpoint marks, some clearly very small scars. What could they be? I put his mind at rest. These were the marks left by *iniezione reconstituenti*: injections which are given in many of the pharmacies of Naples and which many middle-class women receive daily to keep their sexual powers at their peak. Frequently the needle is not too clean, hence the scars.

She had made him understand by gestures one could only shudderingly imagine that her late husband – although half-starved, and even when in the early stages of tuberculosis from which he died – never failed to have intercourse with her less than six times a night. She also had a habit, which terrified Frazer, of keeping an eye on the bedside clock while he performed. I recommended him to drink – as the locals did – marsala with the yolks of eggs stirred into it, and wear a medal of San Rocco, patron of *coitus reservatus*, which could be had in any religious-supply shop.

Sex with local women was a matter fraught with anxiety for Allied troops. They were frequently subjected to terrifying lectures and films about the consequences. Perhaps the most memorable contribution was made by the eminent director John Ford. In his 1942 film Sex Hygiene *several servicemen relax by playing pool, but one of them goes off with a prostitute. Later, he discovers he has contracted a venereal disease, and the film offers graphic presentations on the types and treatment of these conditions. Those who saw this widely shown film recall that it contained close-ups of syphilitic penises, discussion about 'clap' and 'blue balls', and a nightmare scene in a brothel.* SEE ALSO PP. 669–70.

Friday 29 October 1943

Alison Uttley, author, hears news of her son John

John is safe! Thank God! Tonight a phone message from [relatives of] Captain Jock de Gooreynd, (Pusey-Farrington, Berks), saying that John was a prisoner in Germany, in the same hospital, in the next bed to him. John was suffering from shrapnel wounds in his back, but only slight, they were taken out and he was recovering. They had played bridge together. I must write at once, and send a parcel of clothes and shaving brushes . . . Oh how thankful I am, I feel dazed with the good news.

My prayers, my supplications of St Jude answered. Yesterday was St Jude's day . . . it was a special day. I've written a long letter to John, now I'm going to bed. Oh God, thank you . . .

John Uttley was a gunner and had been taken prisoner on the beaches outside Salerno in Italy on 9 September 1943. Here the Allies had landed on a 20-mile front but had encountered stiff resistance. He was eventually incarcerated in Stalag VIIB at Memmingen, near the Austrian border in southern Germany, and would survive the war.

Alison Uttley had already added a wartime theme to her own writing with Hare Joins the Home Guard, *published in 1941. By the time of her death in 1976 she would have written over 100 books. Her diaries have never been published but are preserved in the John Rylands Library at the University of Manchester, together with her own personal library. SEE ALSO PP. 608–9.*

NOVEMBER 1943

NOVEMBER WAS AN important month in the air war. The US Army Air Force had changed its policy to provide fighter escorts for its bombers over Germany, and on Wednesday 3 November no fewer than 600 fighters escorted a 400-bomber daylight raid on Wilhelmshaven. The primary target for the British during this month was Berlin, and they began on Thursday 18 November by dropping 700 tons of bombs on the city. On Monday 22nd the RAF attacked Berlin again, dropping more than 2,300 tons of bombs in under 30 minutes. Only twenty-six planes were lost in this attack, allowing for further sorties. On Tuesday 23rd Berlin was hit again by the RAF, making it the most heavily bombed city in Germany at this point in the war: 12,000 tons of bombs had been directed at this target over the course of 1943, resulting in the deaths of perhaps 10,000 people.

In Italy the British met severe opposition from the 16th Panzer Division in the south, but eventually the Germans had to withdraw this crack unit to refit it for service on the Eastern Front. The American 5th Army met stalwart resistance at the Reinhard Line about 40 miles north of Naples, so their front-line units were withdrawn and rested for a while. Difficult terrain and deteriorating weather favoured the German defenders, and the Italian campaign slowed to a crawl.

On 6 November Soviet forces took Kiev, one of the most important cities in the Soviet Union. However, the Germans were becoming more skilful at withdrawal and their losses were not great. In the Arctic, British convoys to Russia now sailed with impunity.

Hitler's attitude to the progress of the war was unclear, but on Monday 8 November he gave what proved to be his last speech to a full assembly of the Nazi party. It had a doleful quality that seemed to acknowledge the downturn in Germany's fortunes, for he asserted: 'We shall go on fighting past twelve o'clock.'

On 22 November Churchill, Roosevelt and Chiang Kai-shek

met in Cairo to discuss Allied strategy. This conference also served as a preparatory base for talks with Stalin scheduled to take place in Tehran in December. In the second half of the month a storm of protest erupted in Britain over the release of Sir Oswald Mosley, the British fascist, on health grounds. Many internees had been released in 1943 as the danger of German invasion had largely disappeared.

Tuesday 2 – Tuesday 30 November 1943

Gwen Wansborough ploughs the fields at St Albans in Hertfordshire

Gwen Wansborough had joined the Women's Land Army in February 1940, probably in her early twenties, and worked on the land throughout the war. During that time she was variously a milker, a tractor driver and a general farm worker near St Albans in Hertfordshire. She also became engaged in fund-raising efforts for various wartime relief causes.

Gwen Wansborough and friends take a break

2 November

Ploughed little field – 2 acres

Oiled and greased the Drill in readiness for 'Canham's' tomorrow.

Received my 120 extra coupons – I shall use them for more woolies.

6 November

Too wet to drill or plough – sorted potatoes until 3 p.m.

Did the cattle and helped Fred to litter the yard.

Good editorial in the 'Farmer's Weekly' re W.L.A's equipment for the winter, also a report of Mrs. Hudson's visit to Hertford.

9 November

Finished ploughing 'Dickenson's' meadow, Jim drilled it in Essex blue coned rivet.

After lunch I carted swedes and litter for the cows. Started the calves on crushed oats.

Mrs. Roosevelt mentioned the L.A. in her diaries 'My Day', glad we are getting some publicity.

I was sent to plough a field of 23 acres of ley at Nast Hyde, a contract job.

Wrote to the area Organiser of the Y.F.C. [Young Farmers' Club] re starting a club in this district. Jim tells me we are getting an international track layer soon [a tracked farm vehicle] – Hope I am to drive it.

15 November

Church Parade at North Mymms; inspection by Lord Claussen. He shook hands with me, as I was the only female in the 'Farming Section' of the parade.

21 November

Ploughing at Bell Bar with the 'Big Case'. There is a lot of watergrass which won't bury properly. I have a streaming cold. Jim the Foreman and Head Tractor Driver has enteritis, so I have plenty to do.

27 November

Finished ploughing the kaleground, it has done well, considering that last year it was just part of Tollgate Wood. I must put a new mouldboard on my front plough. My nose bled for nearly two hours this evening. I often wonder what I should do if it happened when I was working miles from anywhere.

30 November

Ploughing potato ground 9" deep, dung is long and the boy has to poke it into the furrow after each bout, so that the plough keeps clear. I went to a Home Guard dance this evening at Welham Green, and was initiated into the mysteries of the 'Hokey Pokey' or some such name.

During the war vast areas of land that had not previously been under cultivation were turned over to food production. This involved not only parks and recreation grounds in towns, but also marginal land that had not previously been ploughed over in the countryside. In this and other ways, the war changed the landscape of Britain. Although Gwen Wansborough was in the 'country', her diary also recorded that by 1944 St Albans and the surrounding area would feel the effect of V-1 rocket bombs that had over-shot London. She would continue to work on the land until 1945, when she met her future husband.

Wednesday 3 November 1943

Writer John Steinbeck, with the US army in Italy, on soldiers and lucky charms

A great many soldiers carry with them some small article, some touchstone or lucky piece or symbol which, if they are lucky in battle, takes on an ever-increasing importance. And being lucky in battle means simply not being hurt. The most obvious magic amulets, of course, are the rabbits' feet on sale in nearly all gift stores. St. Christopher medals are carried by

Catholics and non-Catholics alike and in many cases are not considered as religious symbols at all, but as simply lucky pieces.

A novelty company in America has brought out a Testament bound in steel covers to be carried in the shirt pocket over the heart, a gruesome little piece of expediency which has faith in neither the metal nor the Testament but hopes that a combination may work. Many of these have been sold to parents of soldiers, but I have never seen one carried. That particular pocket is for cigarettes and those soldiers who carry Testaments, as many do, carry them in their pants pockets, and they are never considered as lucky pieces.

The magic articles are of all kinds. There will be a smooth stone, an odd-shaped piece of metal, small photographs encased in cellophane. Many soldiers consider pictures of their wives or parents to be almost protectors from danger. One soldier had removed the handles from his Colt .45 and had carved new ones out of Plexiglass from a wrecked airplane. Then he had installed photographs of his children under the Plexiglass so that his children looked out of the handles of his pistol.

Sometimes coins are considered lucky and rings and pins, usually articles which take their quality from some intimacy with people at home, a gift or the symbol of some old emotional experience. One man carries a locket his dead wife wore as a child and another a string of amber beads his mother once made him wear to ward off colds. The beads now ward off danger.

It is interesting now that, as time in action goes on, these magics not only become more valuable and dear but become more secret also. And many men make up small rituals to cause their amulets to become active. A smooth stone may be rubbed when the tracers are cutting lines about a man's head. One sergeant holds an Indian-head penny in the palm of his left hand and against the stock of his rifle when he fires. He is just about convinced that he cannot miss if he does this. The employment of this kind of magic is much more widespread than is generally known.

As time goes on, and dangers multiply and perhaps there

is a narrow escape or so, the amulet not only takes on an increasing importance but actually achieves a kind of personality. It becomes a thing to talk to and rely on. One such lucky piece is a small wooden pig only about an inch long. Its owner, after having tested it over a period of time and in one or two tight places, believes that this little wooden pig can accomplish remarkable things. Thus, in a bombing, he held the pig in his hand and said, 'Pig, this one is not for us.' And in a shelling, he said, 'Pig, you know that the one that gets me gets you.'

But in addition to simply keeping its owner safe from harm, this pig has been known to raise a fog, smooth out a high sea, procure a beefsteak in a restaurant which had not had one for weeks. It is rumored further that this pig in the hands of a previous owner has commuted an execution, cured assorted cases of illness, and been the direct cause of at least one considerable fortune. This pig's owner would not part with him for anything.

The association between a man and his amulet becomes not only very strong but very private. This is partly a fear of being laughed at, but also a feeling grows that to tell about it is to rob it of some of its powers. Also there is the feeling that the magic must not be called on too often. The virtue of the piece is not inexhaustible. It can run down, therefore it is better to use it sparingly and only to call on it when the need is great.

Novelty companies have taken advantage of this almost universal urge toward magic. They turn out lucky rings by the thousands and coins and little figures, but these have never taken hold the way the associational gadgets do.

Whatever the cause of this reliance on magic amulets, in wartime it is so. And the practice is by no means limited to ignorant or superstitious men. It would seem that in times of great danger and great emotional tumult a man has to reach outside himself for help and comfort, and has to have some supraprofessional symbol to hold to. It can be anything at all, an old umbrella handle or a religious symbol, but he has to have it. There are times in war when the sharpest emotion is not fear, but loneliness and littleness. And it is during these times that the smooth stone or the Indian-head penny or the wooden pig are not only desirable but essential. Whatever atavism may call them up, they appear and they seem to fill a need. The dark world is not far from us – from any of us.

Men in every branch of the services were superstitious. During the war the Royal Navy continually improved the quality of torpedoes, and by the end of the war they would be deploying the Mark XVII. There had actually been only sixteen variants – but the sailors had not wanted to handle a Mark XIII torpedo, so this number was missed out.

After the war John Steinbeck would move to New York City, although he later returned to his native California to research East of Eden. *In 1962 he was awarded the Nobel Prize for Literature; he died six years later.* SEE ALSO PP. 581–3.

Mid-November 1943

G. C. Bateman, a British POW, visits the dentist in Moosburg, Germany

During our time at Moosburg I had severe toothache and was taken to the hospital where a German dentist with the rank of Gefreite filled one tooth but said that I must see the German civilian Zahnarzt. Apparently the dentist was a technician qualified to drill and fill but not to extract. So I was taken to another surgery by a guard who waited for me. While I awaited my turn, the surgeon-dentist was merrily extracting teeth without any anaesthetic from Italian and Yugoslav prisoners, teeth flying about the room which was filled with shrieks and groans. When my time came, as I was British, I was given an anaesthetic and in due course he extracted the tooth, breaking the root which he then proceeded to dig out. Later I was told he had taken out the wrong tooth! My guard then took me back, but before doing so, wrapped a scarf around my face to keep out the cold. This is one single act of kindliness that I like to remember and it came to mind two years later when we were relieved by American troops, who were none too gentle with our guards.

Bateman had been in a POW camp at Chieti until the Italian surrender in 1943, when he was transferred to the German camp at Moosburg. During his time in captivity he kept himself busy. A trained optician, he set up treatment rooms, examining eyes and writing prescriptions – initially on cigarette packets, because of lack of paper. The prescriptions were initially fulfilled using second-hand glasses provided by the International Red Cross in Geneva. Remarkably, by 1944, he would be prescribing glasses sent out from Britain to order via the Red Cross and providing 'a very quick service'. In his spare time, he diverted himself with elaborate amateur dramatics. SEE ALSO PP. 440–1 AND 734–5.

Thursday 18 November 1943

Adrian Secker, a British teenager interned in Germany, appreciates Red Cross parcels

Adrian Secker was born in Iver, Buckinghamshire in 1924. He had been studying at the University of Rome when Italy entered the war in May 1940. The authorities decided that an enemy alien of near military age in Rome was an embarrassment. However he was allowed to go and live in Merano as long as he reported to the authorities regularly. In 1943, when northern Italy was taken over by the Germans, he was interned at a special Straflager (prison camp) at Innsbruck–Reichenau.

After washing up . . . I go down for a turn in the Courtyard where we assemble later for counting by rooms. It usually means standing around getting ones feet frozen for about 20 minutes. Then most days, we go to the parcel office to draw tins, as the parcels are handed over intact, but unpacked so that the Germans can open and check the tins as they are drawn.

Each parcel always contains a tin of margarine, a condensed milk, a piece of chocolate, a slab of sugar, a tin of Crackers, tea, cocoa, jam and then tins of fish or meat or vegetables and a bar of soap. But it varies from parcel to parcel, sometimes one gets a Canadian parcel, which I have not yet had, which is supposed to be better. At 11.30 the German rations come up to the floor. Sometimes it is barley, which we eat as porridge and keep for next morning's breakfast. Other times soup etc. Some people forgo the rations altogether and only live on parcels. Bread is distributed every day and is bad but alright toasted for strong teeth. If one does eat the rations one might have a snack of toast and meat paste for example. The main meal one might say is high tea at four. Each floor has a kitchenette where two internees prepare what each person has available. Potatoes also come with the rations and generally make the basis for high teas . . .

Adrian kept his diary hidden by writing inside a copy of Horace's Satires and Epistles – in Italian, in the hope that if it were found the German censors would not be able to read it. At the end of November he would be moved to Poland and was eventually released at the end of the war.

Monday 22 November 1943

Heinrich von Einsiedel, a German working for the Russians, wins over a captured German officer

A small village immediately behind the front line near Perekop, the approach to the Crimea. The Russian commander led us to a house where we met a first lieutenant and battalion adjutant who had been captured only a few hours before.

The tall, thin student from Dresden looked at us disconcertedly from behind his spectacles. In a faltering voice he told us how he had been taken . . .

[The prisoner recounted] In ten minutes we were overrun. We were able to hold our command post a little while; then the tanks shot it to bits. The last four men of the battalion and three officers, the commander, the artillery man, and I, were sitting in a deep dugout. The Russians blew the entrance open and told us to come out. Then they threw hand grenades in. We squeezed ourselves against the walls. In a quiet moment while I was burning papers and cards a sergeant major suggested we give ourselves up. The two other officers didn't want to. A Russian shouted: 'Two more minutes and you're dead.' A private jumped toward the entrance shaft and tried to climb out. There was a shot. I turned round and saw the lieutenant staring at the private who was collapsed and moaning. Before I could move, he put his pistol to his head and shot himself. The other soldiers climbed out of the dugout. I looked at the commander. He just nodded. So I went to the entrance too. A private gave me a hand to pull me up. Another shot. The commander had killed himself.

I found myself standing among the Russians. One of them pointed at the dugout:

'Any more in there?'

'Three dead,' I said and put my hand to my head as if shooting myself.

'Dead – why dead?' he asked. 'No good. You live, go home. German soldiers live in Russia. Hitler dead – good. Germans live – good.'

The captured young lieutenant explained to Einsiedel that their battalion was down to thirty men (a mere platoon) but had nevertheless been told to stand and fight. They had been promised artillery and air support but neither had materialized. They were finally over-run by Russian T-34 tanks. In response to questions the lieutenant conceded that he had heard of the Russian-sponsored Officers' League, but considered the existence of such a group impossible. This came as a surprise given that the National Committee for a Free Germany had its own radio station and was regularly broadcasting messages from prisoners back to a domestic audience in Germany. It now became clear to Einsiedel and his colleagues that the Russian propaganda message about the Officers' League was not getting through.

After the war Heinrich von Einsiedel would join the SED, the Communist Party of East Germany. In the 1950s he defected to the West. By the mid-1950s he was, in his own words, 'persona non grata' almost everywhere. In communist countries he was now an anti-communist defector; yet he had difficulty entering the United States, for he enjoyed the remarkable distinction of having been a member of both Nazi and communist organizations. Even in West Germany many reviled him for having worked for the Russians during the war. SEE ALSO PP. 589–90 AND 605–6.

Tuesday 23 November 1943

Marie Vassiltchikov, an anti-Soviet and anti-Nazi Russian, endures a heavy raid on Berlin

The streets were full of people. Many just stood around, for the visibility was so poor on account of the rain that nobody expected the raid to last long or cause much damage. At home I was met by Maria Gersdorff who told me that her husband Heinz had just telephoned from his office at the Stadt-Kommandantur [HQ of Berlin's garrison] to warn her that the enemy air formations were larger than usual, that the raid might therefore be serious and that he was staying on at the office for the night. Having had no time for lunch, I was ravenous. Maria asked old Martha the cook to warm up some soup while I went upstairs to change into slacks and a sweater. As one does now in such cases, I also packed a few things into a small suitcase. Papa was in his room, giving a language lesson to two young men. He told me that he did not wish to be disturbed.

I had just finished packing when the *flak* opened up. It was immediately very violent. Papa emerged with his pupils and we all hurried down to the half-basement behind the kitchen, where we usually sit out air-raids. We had hardly got there when we heard the first approaching planes. They flew very low and the barking of the *flak* was suddenly drowned by a very different sound – that of exploding bombs, first far away and then closer and closer, until it seemed as if they were falling literally on top of us. At every crash the house shook. The air pressure was dreadful and the noise deafening. For the first time I understood what the expression *Bombenteppich* ['bomb carpet'] means – the Allies call it 'saturation' bombing. At one point there was a shower of broken glass and all three doors of the basement flew into the room, torn off their hinges. We pressed them back into place and leant against them to try to keep them shut. I had left my coat outside but didn't dare go out to get it. An incendiary flare fell hissing into our entrance and the men crept out to extinguish it. Suddenly we realised that we had no water on hand to put out a possible fire and hastily opened all the taps in the kitchen. This dampened the noise for a few minutes, but not for long ... The planes did not come in waves, as they do usually, but kept on droning ceaselessly overhead for more than an hour.

In the middle of it all the cook produced my soup. I thought that if I ate it I would throw up. I found it even impossible to sit quietly and kept jumping to my feet at every crash. Papa, imperturbable as always, remained seated in a wicker armchair throughout. Once, when I leapt up after a particularly deafening explosion, he calmly remarked: 'Sit down! That way, if the ceiling collapses, you will be farther away from it ...'

The all-clear came only half an hour after the last planes had departed, but long before that we were called out of the house by an unknown naval officer. The wind, he told us, thus far non-existent, had suddenly risen and the fires, therefore, were spreading. We all went out into our little square and, sure enough, the sky on three sides was blood-red. This, the officer explained, was only the beginning; the greatest danger would come in a few hours' time, when the fire storm really got going. Maria had given each of us a wet towel with which to smother our faces before leaving the house – a wise precaution for our square was already filled with smoke and one could hardly breathe.

SEE ALSO PP. 619–20 AND 716–17.

DECEMBER 1943

DURING THE LAST days of November and the first few days of December Churchill, Roosevelt and Stalin met in Tehran. Stalin always insisted on remaining on Soviet-controlled territory, and Iran – jointly occupied by the British and the Russians – was one of the few viable venues. Partly because of Stalin's anxieties about travel, this was the first time that the 'Big Three' leaders had met. At this meeting the planned invasion of western Europe in 1944 was confirmed by Roosevelt and Churchill, while Stalin promised to join the war against Japan once Germany was defeated. Roosevelt was aware that the British and Americans had met many times and was anxious not to present Stalin with a united Anglo-American front.

Allied bombers resumed what 'Bomber' Harris had called the Battle of Berlin, but German air defences were better co-ordinated in December and the RAF lost forty-one aircraft in one raid. On Thursday 16th a further attack on Berlin brought the Allied total of explosives dropped on the city up to 18,500 tons. The pressure was unrelenting now, and on Wednesday 29th the RAF made a further major raid on Berlin, marking the third anniversary of the fire-bombing of London.

The fight for France was already being anticipated with a major battle between an increasingly well-supplied resistance and German troops in Bernex in eastern France. On Sunday 12 December it was announced that Rommel had been made Commander-in-Chief of Army Group B, which placed him in charge of all the coastal defences from Holland to Spain. Eisenhower was given the job of Supreme Commander Allied Expeditionary Force and Montgomery was made Commander-in-Chief of the 21st Army Group.

In Italy an American ammunition ship moored in Bari harbour was hit. It exploded, destroying eighteen other ships and vast quantities of supplies. Experienced units were now being withdrawn from Italy in order to rest and re-equip them for Overlord.

In both Britain and Germany, the remorseless demand for labour was now a grave problem. On Thursday 2 December Ernest Bevin, Minister of Labour, announced conscription to the mines as coal output continued to decline. In the same month Hitler ordered the conscription of German youth for active service at the front. On 16 December the British government announced the Education Bill, which would radically change schooling at the end of the war.

Tuesday 7 December 1943

Sergeant C. E. S. Tirbutt bails out of his tank on the Gustav Line in Italy

Sergeant Tirbutt was serving in the 44th Royal Tank Regiment, a territorial unit from Bristol that was part of the 4th Armoured Brigade. He had fought in the Sicilian campaign in August 1943 and spent late August and September reorganizing and training on his unit's Sherman Mark III tanks. In late September the unit had been moved to the west coast of Italy, arriving at Taranto on the 29th. After being visited by Montgomery on 9 October they had begun to push up the roads along the west coast against heavy German resistance.

Caught up with the tanks at midnight and found I was to be Tug Wilson's operator/loader and what a day we had. Moved off in the dark at 0530 hrs following the Moro river for some time until we found a suitable crossing place. Then up a very steep slope to the village and only six tanks made it. Major Forster [actually Foster] was grand going forward on foot repeatedly for personal recce. We threaded our way through the village meeting only one badly frightened Hun who crept out of a building with his hands up. Canadian infantry very glad to see us. We halted at the far end of the village and fanned out hull down to watch and wait. Suddenly the peace was shattered by Gray Boyce's voice over the air saying vehicles had been heard from the road, and next moment a Mark IV danced into view. Hell for leather, actions automatic, load, fire, reload. Hit it with probably third shot and pumped in a few more until it brewed up. Tug was bloody good, a trifle excited but did not let it affect his judgement. Pleased as a schoolboy. Having disposed of one we were at once fired on by another, and had to scuttle behind a house. Observation bad and we could only see A.P. [Armour Piercing] and Browning [machine gun] flashing back and forth between two invisible opponents. We thought he was behind a haystack so we waited with the gun pointing over the rear of the tank. He moved out and we fired together and felt a thud and the engines cut out. Driver reported engines refused to start again so we were sitting meat. Baled out and nipped behind cover as there was plenty of dirt flying about. We did not find out till much later that our first shot had knocked out the Mark IV. Tug had his Tommy Gun and ordered me to take the crew to safety. I took them into the village and left them in a building and rushed back to Tug borrowing a couple of grenades en route from the Canadians. Tug not there so tried engines but failed to start. A great deal of small arms flak around so took shelter in doorway of a house. Through window I could see two dirty big Mark IVs stationary and both still alive. I tried to get Dusty Miller in the nearest tank to fire through the window but the angle was too great. Suggested brewing up a haystack to use as a smoke screen but we eventually decided not feasible. Remained there for some time spotting for Dusty Miller then Tug turned up and we immobilised the guns on our tank. While Tug went looking for an ambulance for Capt. Hunniball and Hugh Bishop I tried the engines again and this time one responded. The Major turned up and together we went over and looked at Graham Boyce's tank. One shot through the bottom of the driver's compartment and one through his headspace and the gun mounting badly knocking about jamming the gun solid. Feeling pretty low we climbed up to look into the tank wondering what kind of horrible sight we should find but were relieved and amazed to find nothing. Apparently all crew had managed to get out. Inspected the Mark IVs. Our first shot must have killed the co-driver, the other two smashed the track and bogies. We reorganised and left a guard tank and leaguered at the top of the track up which we had climbed from the valley. The Major held a short pow-pow and congratulated us all on a bloody good show and we retired to bed but were heavily shelled all night and got little sleep.

Tirbutt had been involved in heavy fighting during early November as his unit advanced towards the River Sinello near Scerni, and then the River Sangro. Here the unit moved through the village of Rualti. Many of their Sherman tanks were lost and after this engagement Sergeant Tirbutt would be awarded the Military Medal. In January 1944 the unit would return to Taranto, embarking for Britain on the 27th on the SS Ranchi, after being overseas for more than three years. Once back in Britain they would begin working up for D-Day.

Thursday 30 December 1943

General Bernard Montgomery gives his opinion of his superior, General Alexander

In July 1942, with German forces only 70 miles from Alexandria, Churchill and Alan Brooke had made an emergency visit to the Middle East. The Prime Minister had appointed General Alexander as Commander-in-Chief in the Middle East and, under him, General Bernard Montgomery as Commander of the 8th Army. Even then, Montgomery was regarded by his colleagues as 'difficult', even 'ruthless', and his appointment had been a measure of Churchill's desperation. By 1943 it was clear that Montgomery would never be an easy subordinate: he regarded all officers alongside him or above him as a problem.

If you want to wage successful war, you have got to have a commander who understands the business.

Alexander is my very great friend. But he does not understand the business, and he is not clever; he cannot grasp the essentials. The plain truth is that so far he has been 'carried', from inclusive ALAMEIN onwards, by the Eighth Army, and he has never failed to take its advice. This time he has failed to do so, and as a result, we are now having very great troubles.

I think we can very probably pull the thing out of the fire for him; but we have lost valuable time and the bad winter weather will soon be on us at the Adriatic side.

What happened, of course, was that in the discussions at AFHQ Alexander was 'seen off' by the other C in C's. He did not really know what he wanted so the others got what they wanted. He is not a strong man and gives way too easily.

In any future set up the Prime Minister wants to be very careful as to the job given to ALEXANDER, he has definite limitations, and has not got that sure and certain hand on the helm that indicates the true professional touch.

By December 1943 Montgomery and Alexander were embroiled in the Italian campaign. Eisenhower was in overall control, with Alexander in command of the land forces, which included armies commanded by both Montgomery and Patton. Montgomery's ego was colossal and it is unlikely that his diary provides an accurate account of events within his own command. However, it does provide some insight into his psychology.

Friday 31 December 1943 – Saturday 1 January 1944

Gustave Folcher, a French POW working on a German farm, reflects on 1943

Before being mobilized in September 1939 Gustave Folcher had been a French peasant in the Gard. His diary offers a record of the war as viewed by an ordinary French soldier, rather than an intellectual. Folcher was drafted at the age of thirty and kept notebooks in order to counter the boredom of military life. Taken prisoner in 1940, he spent most of the rest of the war near the village of Schorstedt, north of Magdeburg in Germany. He avoided being cooped up in a POW camp by volunteering for farm work, where he enjoyed comparing German farming practices with those of his own locality.

31 December

And so the year 1943 is coming to an end without bringing any great change in our situation. We expected a lot of the year that is ending, during which we have been counting on the war ending and our return home. True, the Russians have advanced a good deal, they are nearly back at their frontiers almost everywhere, having almost thrown the formidable German armies completely out of their country. In Italy the Allies have been marking time outside Rome for quite a while already, after the great effort of the previous summer.

1 January

Once more it is New Years Day. What will this year hold for us? We do not even dare any longer to form plans for the future, when we have been so disappointed. Our New Year wishes are no less fervent than before, but we have so often been disillusioned in the year which has just gone that we can no longer make predictions. We have moments when we doubt the future completely and seriously wonder whether we shall ever see France again, our towns, our villages. The villages of which we think night and day. This long captivity where there is no way of seeing the end, after 42 long months of life as prisoners, affects the most determined, above all because there is nothing, absolutely nothing on the horizon to make us think that it might all end one day. There are times when we are seized by despair and when we seriously ask ourselves if we are to finish our days in this miserable life, in the midst of this great forest, in a strange land.

We can't complain physically, to be sure. The work, although sometimes very hard, isn't beyond us. Most of us are peasants, used to working on the land all our lives. Naturally some of the blokes tire much from the work, it not being their line, and they take the more credit for it. For example, Simon a teacher from near Agen, and some others, Parisians or men from the North, employed in banks, offices or small factories, had to work harder than us, but all things considered they come out of it pretty well. Of course when we first arrived some of them talked about arranging sport, in the summer evenings after work at the Camp, football and other things. But they quickly came to understand that after turning over manure with a pitchfork or labouring behind a horse for 10 or 12 hours, or having loaded heavy logs for the whole day, or kneeling for days on end harvesting potatoes, or moving tons of sugar beet, they understood for themselves that sport, however enjoyable, was not too sensible for arms and legs which had just been on the go for 12 hours at a time.

The food was always the same. The same things appeared on the table every day from 1 January to New Year's Eve, and there were times when frankly it became nauseating. But it was at least sufficient to keep us in more or less normal health. No one, it should be pointed out, suffered from hunger, far from it. If anything it was thirst we suffered from, but it was not really thirst because there was plenty of water to drink, even if it was not particularly good in this area. But most prisoners are lads from the South, and being good southerners they adored their wine, something precious that we have seen nothing of for coming up four years. Four long years without seeing the colour of wine, which is only present here in our endless discussions on winter evenings around the stove. There were amongst us some great experts on the most celebrated vineyards and interminable discussions took place on all the colours and tastes of the great wines of France. Sometimes minor quarrels even broke out on the subject of wine, which was thoroughly debated. But it all stopped there, for there was never any tasting, all that we had from time to time was a few small glasses of a beer which was low in alcohol and poor in taste, a real cow's piss which provoked no discussion on the subject of beer.

The German war economy made wide use of forced labour. There were remarkable variations in the way foreign labourers were treated. Many Russians were employed on industrial projects where they were often worked to death within weeks of arrival at the relevant location, but the experience of many French and Polish POWs who were put to work on the land was rather different. In many cases POWs were treated no differently from the way in which German landowners had always treated agricultural workers down the ages. They enjoyed a good diet, recreation and even access to recent newspapers. The Vichy government had negotiated the repatriation of some French POWs at the end of 1941, but most would remain in Germany until the end of the war. SEE ALSO PP. 812–14.

1944

'NO POSSIBILITY OF reading, of keeping up the diary, of reflection. Slavery in the factory and domestic chores, lack of sleep, deadly tiredness . . . The war is stagnating bloodily . . .'

Victor Klemperer, in a factory near Dresden: diary entry for 4 March 1944

JANUARY 1944

BY JANUARY 1944 THE scale of air attack on Germany was enormous. The British Air Ministry announced that the RAF had dropped 157,000 tons of bombs on Germany in 1943, while the Luftwaffe had dropped only 2,400 tons on Britain. The so-called Battle of Berlin continued. On Sunday 2 January Hitler's Reich Chancellery was badly damaged, with many trapped in its shelters after a direct hit during an RAF raid. On Thursday 20 January the RAF made its heaviest raid yet on Berlin. Hitler was now completely obsessed with retaliation, and on Friday 21 January the Luftwaffe launched a large raid on south-east England with about 100 aircraft. Hitler had insisted on the pro-duction of bombers rather than fighters; nevertheless, fighter defences over Germany remained strong and were now equipped with air-to-air rockets, so it was not uncommon for an Allied raid to result in the loss of fifty aircraft.

On the Eastern Front, Soviet forces were making good progress in bad weather, and on 6 January they crossed over the Polish frontier. The Red Army was also advancing into the Ukraine. Initially Leningrad remained under partial siege by the German army, although it was receiving supplies from across a frozen lake, but by the end of January the area around Russia's second city was clear. Once again the Russians had shown that they were better equipped than their enemies to fight in the winter weather.

By contrast the Italian campaign was going badly for the Allies. The US 5th Army launched fresh attacks along significant sectors of the Gustav Line south of Rome, but these were in fact distractions and deceptions designed to shield an amphibious attack at Anzio on the west coast of Italy, not far from Rome, designed to outflank German defences. The Anzio operation began on 22 January and on the first day 35,000 men were landed for only thirteen casualties. They had taken the Germans entirely by surprise. However, the Allied commanders pushed forward only slowly, good defensive positions in depth were not secured, and the operation eventually developed into a bloody stalemate. By the end of January the forces at Anzio were facing twelve German divisions. At this point Montgomery escaped the stalemate of Italy and came back to Britain to take command of the British elements of the Allied forces being marshalled for the Normandy invasion in June 1944, referred to as 'D-Day'.

Meanwhile, Mussolini's rump government in the German-occupied north – the Italian Socialist Republic – put numerous 'traitors' on trial. Those convicted and executed included De Bona, who had once been one of Mussolini's enforcers, and Mussolini's son-in-law Galeazzo Ciano, one of the great diarists of the Italian Fascist regime, who had resigned in February 1943 after a number of heated arguments.

Early January 1944

Guy Sajer, a Frenchman fighting on the Eastern Front, discovers army bureaucrats

Guy Sajer was a French national who had joined the German army at the young age of sixteen. The son of a German father and a French mother, he was not under any obligation to fight. His first days with the Wehrmacht, on basic training in Poland, were pleasant. However, he was soon serving in the elite Gross Deutschland division and was plunged into the horror of the Eastern Front. His account is one of the most remarkable descriptions of the misery and desperation of the retreating Germans as they were pushed out of Russia.

The piercing cold was a continuous element we could never forget, even during moments of strong emotion, as in our recent clash with the partisans. A short time later, we rejoined the division in a town of a certain size and importance called Boporoeivska, if I remember correctly. Between the trenches and the barbed wire, the engineers and the Todt organization were busy mining the area. Other infantry regiments and an armored unit equipped with

Tigerpanzers had also reached this point. A dozen of these motionless monsters seemed to be grinning at us as they watched the passage of our battered equipment. The presence of the Tigers reassured everyone. They were like steel fortresses, and no Russian tank could equal them.

Several Wehrmacht civil servants had been billeted at Boporoeivska. These gentlemen were surprised and displeased to find themselves suddenly at the center of a battlefield. They all seemed to be in an extremely bad humour, and their attitude toward us seemed tinged with a certain distrust. Perhaps their bureaucratic minds resented our fighting as we retreated. For them Russia meant this organized town where one could shelter from the cold and eat one's fill, provided one had established the proper connections with Supply. Perhaps there were also charming evenings with the charming Ukrainian women who seemed to abound in these parts. These ladies and girls seemed to be preparing for a hasty departure in the company of their gentlemen friends, to look for a distant and more tranquil spot. We, it seemed, would be given the honor of defending these bureaucratic love nests. This attitude infuriated us, and many brawls began, but were quickly stifled. In the end, we were too exhausted and hungry to bother with these people, and occupied the warm isbas [huts or log cabins] we were given with the greatest satisfaction. In the isbas we found food and drink and the opportunity to wash. Our cabins were rarely equipped with candles or lamps, but the flames in the fireplaces, which we fed with every combustible substance we could find, brilliantly lit these fragments of paradise. Within a few hours of our arrival, several cubic yards of snow had been melted in each billet, and we were all stripped naked, scrubbing off our filth as best we could. We soaked our trousers, underwear, shirts, and tunics with feverish, almost panicky haste. Our opportunity would certainly be brief, and everyone wished to make the most of it. Someone had even found a box full of small cakes of toilet soap. These were mixed into the water of the largest tubs.

In turn, timed by a stop watch, we plunged into the warm, foaming bath: two minutes each and no overtime. We joked and larked as we hadn't done for months. The water spilled over the edge of the tub, and flooded the big room, where some thirty shadowy figures cavorted. We kept pouring water into the tubs, to keep the level up. The dim light prevented us from noticing that the foam which so delighted us had turned gray with filth. However, our lice died a scented death: Marie Rose.

When we had finished washing, we emptied the tubs into a hole we had dug inside the isba. There was no question of going outside. The thermometer registered twenty degrees below zero, and everyone was naked. When the water was gone, we broke up the tubs and burned them. The fire had a voracious appetite, which was difficult to satisfy. Hals was exultantly chewing a fragment of soap, laughing and shouting that he had to clean his innards too, as they were probably just as filthy and overrun with lice as his skin.

'Now the Popovs can come whenever they like,' he shouted. 'I feel like a new man.'

The door suddenly opened, letting in a blast of astonishing cold. Everyone howled in protest. Two soldiers stood on the threshold, their arms loaded with delicacies for the table. We gaped at this gift from heaven as the soldiers laid down their burden on a pile of damp overcoats: a string of spicy wurst, several loaves of gingerbread, several boxes of Norwegian sardines, a brick of smoked bacon. There were also eight or ten bottles – schnapps, cognac, Rhine wine – and cigars. The fellows kept right on emptying the huge pockets of their coats, and our shouts of astounded delight seemed to shake the flimsy walls.

'Wh . . . where did you find it?' someone asked, almost sobbing with joy.

'Those goddamn bureaucrats were really living it up: Grandsk [our company cook] never saw anything like this. Those bastards were keeping it all here. They were ready to run off with it, too. This is just a small sample, but they're all as mad as hornets; said they'd report us for stealing personal possessions.'

Sajer's account is an unusual one. Relatively small numbers of men from conquered European countries, including Belgium, France, Holland and even Britain, volunteered to fight for the Wehrmacht. His own account focuses upon the issue of why young men volunteer to fight and deals with his romantic vision of war and his subsequent disillusionment. SEE ALSO PP. 820–1.

Tuesday 18 – Thursday 20 January 1944

Major Hardy Parkhurst experiences stalemate near Castelforte on the Gustav Line in Italy

Major Hardy Parkhurst was born in 1914 in Newhaven, where his father was a doctor. He had been commissioned into the Royal Northumberland Fusiliers in 1941.

18 January

Tonight the Boche still holds Castelforte, and after a pretty bloody crossing it looks as though we may find ourselves down that way before long. Air activity has been on an increased scale of late, and this morning I had the best view of a plane crashing that I've ever had in my life. It was a Jerry FW 190, I'm pleased to say. There had been a lot of aerial machine gun fire and we looked out of the window of Group H.Q. and there was the plane falling down, slowly like a leaf, very unreal, very toy-like as a child's glider, and impersonally, impassively, we watched it crash on to the hillside not far away. It did not catch fire. As it was in our area, I went over to see what the results were and, of course, by the time I had reached the spot there were already a lot of soldiers there. The pilot was dead, had been killed in the air I believe, his body terribly lacerated, almost unrecognisable. Already his boots had been taken off as booty, his parachute too for a table cloth, his maps to the Y. & L.H.Q [York and Lancaster Regiment Headquarters]. It was an unpleasant sight, a mass of twisted machinery, a mangled body; the scene typified war and civilisation today, a messy bloody twisted sort of existence. Already the soldiers, quite unconcernedly, were digging the pilot's grave.

20 January

So, as often happens in war, the plan went awry; the 128 Brigade attack was a failure, a failure not so much due to the enemy as to nature. The river, at the points selected for the crossing, was too fast running, and the boats were swept away and ropes broken.

On the left only a few men managed to get across; on the right about three-quarters of a company succeeded. Then the Boche got wind of it, poured small arms fire and threw grenades onto the boats as they struggled to get across. It was a heroic effort, which had to be called off. I heard later that the 'little company' was still fighting on the other side and had even counter-attacked when surrounded. Let us hope that some of them manage to get back under cover of darkness tonight. I cannot help feeling that the attack in this particular area was based on faulty appreciation, especially as all patrol reports had stressed the difficulties of crossing the river here. However, such is the confusion of war.

Sant' Angelo and Castelforte were outposts on the strongly held Gustav Line that barred the road to Rome. British and American forces would pound away at these mountain defences for months before breaking through in May 1944. One of the greatest problems was that Italy presented an interminable series of mountains overlooking rivers, which in effect were difficult barriers overlooked by excellent fire positions. The early months of 1944 were strewn with costly attempts to cross such obstacles. SEE ALSO PP. 687–8.

Wednesday 19 January 1944

Victor Klemperer, a Jewish slave labourer, on a heroic attempt to rescue a mother

Heroic hoax. Among the many death notices of the fallen (swastika inside the iron cross at the side of the notice), *Dresdener Zeitung*, 19th January, '44: 'Ordained by fate, my only dear son, student of chemistry, Lance-Corporal Horst-Siegfried

Weigmann, volunteer, holder of the Iron Cross, Second Class, participant in the Polish and French campaigns, was suddenly and unexpectedly taken from this life in the midst of his studies at only 24 years of age. In deep sorrow Bruno Weigmann, Master Musician Munich.' – Paul Lang, the physician and Dr Katz both knew the dead man personally; his fate, which at first I thought to be a legend, is confirmed from several sources. His mother, divorced from his father, was Jewish and was one of those arrested in the last *action* . . . The son (like Erich Meyerhof's sons a soldier at first) went to police headquarters, [said] he was a Gestapo officer, wanted to speak to the prisoner and take her somewhere. He actually reached the entrance of the headquarters with her; once outside he would have got her to safety. (There are said to be many Jews in hiding, particularly in Berlin . . .) There he ran into a Gestapo man, who knew him. The mother is now in Theresienstadt, the son hanged himself in his cell. 'Hanged himself' – was it really suicide? – And on top of that the death notice with the military decoration! But he had truly fallen on the field of honour and has shown more courage than any soldier in battle. He will undoubtedly go down in history and literature, will be the hero of plays and novels.

Klemperer sought to write down the minute details of his experience in the hope of creating a 'cultural history of disaster'. He was especially interested in the fate of people in so-called 'mixed marriages', having himself been saved from deportation because he was married to a non-Jewish woman – a Nichtjüdin. In Germany many non-Jews had divorced their Jewish spouses in an attempt to protect themselves from increasing persecution; others remained loyal. There were some remarkable stories of resistance. In February 1943 Jewish men married to non-Jews began to be imprisoned at a Jewish community centre at Rosenstrasse 2–4, Berlin. This would become a focal point of a protest led by as many as 6,000 women. In order to avoid the embarrassing problem of open dissent, propaganda minister Joseph Goebbels released the men, including twenty-five who had already been sent to Auschwitz.

In February 1945 Victor Klemperer avoided deportation to a death camp by chance when the bombing of Dresden disrupted rail communications. Together with his wife Eva he survived the war and

became an enthusiastic communist citizen of the new East Germany.
There he resumed his academic work in philology. When Eva died in
1951 he married one of his students, the 25-year-old Hadwig. He died
in 1960 at the age of seventy-eight. SEE ALSO PP. 381–2 AND 643.

Thursday 20 January 1944

Mathilde Wolff-Mönckeberg, daughter of the Mayor of
Hamburg, views the city in the fifth winter of the war

But I must talk about this, the fifth winter of the war. Only
sad, horrid visions pass before my inner eye, grey and dull,
like a bad film-show. Nothing but heaps of rubble wherever
one looks, hollow ruins of houses, empty windows, lonely
chimney stacks, charred remnants of furniture, high up on a
bit of wall a bath-tub, a forlorn bed-frame, a radiator or even
a picture clinging precariously to the bombed-out shell of
what was once someone's home. In this dismal weather it is
a devastating scene. In the streets mountains of rubbish are
piling up. The big metal dustbins are never emptied and
garbage is bursting out all over the place. Paper, potato-peel,
cabbage leaves, the muck-containers open their lids like
gaping throats, vomiting out their evil contents. Then the
wind takes it all and scatters it over the wet roads, leaving a
stale, foul stench. We are told that every street must dig its
own rubbish pit to avoid further contamination. And this in
our super modern and clean Hamburg! But it isn't our
Hamburg any longer. Grandfather Mönckeberg would never
recognize it. We are told that it will be rebuilt 'more splendid
than ever'. On goes the film-show. Dark shadowy creatures
creep towards the mountains of leftovers and stir them up
with greedy hands, looking for something to salvage, something to eat. They are Italians in long brown coats, their caps
still somewhat coquettishly perched on their dark hair. They
are supposed to clear away the mess in hand-carts, but first
they try to find something to still their hunger, chewing
ancient potato and apple peel. They are members of the
'Badoglio Clique', so one is told, lazy devils who shun work,

that is why they are ravenous. One is not allowed to speak to them, but I feel sorry for them. The other day I gave one of them bread coupons for 500 grammes and he touched his cap at least twenty times.

There are children everywhere, hordes of them. There is no school and they roam the streets all day long. Like the foreigners they forage in the garbage, dig tunnels in the rubble and imitate the siren to perfection. Women, their tired faces half-hidden in head shawls, climb over the debris. They have official permits to collect what is still usable. They cart away what they can, to build new homes somewhere outside town. Thousands sleep in the bunkers every night, not having a roof over their heads. It is amazing how these poor human beings manage to create something, some kind of homestead, out of the rawest of materials, charred wooden boards and broken bricks. Everybody lends a hand: the husband if he is at home, the wife and all the children. And they are so proud of their achievement, preferring to live like Robinson Crusoe in one single room on the lonely heath, rather than be billeted out amongst strangers.

Hamburg was bombed continuously through 1944 because of the proximity of key oil refineries. Oil and lubricants had been identified as a weak link in the chain of the German war economy and associated plants were attacked remorselessly. However, bombing was inaccurate – even with the newer target-locating devices that were coming into service in 1944 – and Hamburg had become a wasteland.

Mathilde survived the war and in June 1945 received news of her daughter Ruth, who had married the Principal of the University College of Aberystwyth, Ifor Evans, in 1937. Ruth had been desperate for news of her mother, knowing how heavily Hamburg had been bombed, but censors on neither side would allow civilian correspondence into or out of Germany. In 1974 Ruth found the manuscript of her mother's diary, written in tiny characters on a scarce supply of wartime paper, in a forgotten chest in her sister's house near Hamburg. SEE ALSO PP. 592–3.

Saturday 22 January 1944

Signalman P. J. Lovett comes ashore at Anzio with the 46th Royal Tank Regiment

P. J. Lovett was a signalman attached to the 46th Royal Tank Regiment, which was equipped with Sherman Mark III tanks. He was part of the second wave of forces being sent from Naples to reinforce the units hemmed in at the Anzio beachhead.

Dawn – whole fleet at anchor a mile or two off the coast – a balloon floated from every boat, a wonderful sight. A mine floated past – corvettes pot at it and sink it. Initial assault seems to have gone well – seems to be a bit of delay landing us. Through field-glasses I could see the beach from which a steep track made the same morning by 'bulldozers', rose up to wooded slopes. At the top of a track a scammell was waiting with winch ready to assist any vehicle that failed to climb the steep sandy incline, Bofors guns were already in position against expected dive-bombing, but not a plane did we see. DUKWs (steel boats on six road-wheels, that can drive down the beach and straight into the water) were plying to and fro down the track and up to the sides of lighters to collect fuel, stores and ammo, and blokes on the shore were already digging slit-trenches and bivvy-holes. About midday we moved further in, ready to discharge vehicles on to pontoons stretching to the beach, the water being too deep (seven to nine feet) to permit an attempted wet landing. Then the shelling began – German batteries got the range of the beach and sent over air-bursts and shells, most of which whistled over and landed in the water sending up a shower of spray, but some of them were near misses, bursting with an ear-splitting crack near the boat; if you were below on the tank-deck it seemed like inside a huge bell as shrapnel clanged against the hull. Later a plane dived with lightning suddenness – machine-gun bullets spattered on the deck and two bombs dropped in the woods above the beach. Our boat had to have two attempts at ramming its keel over a sand-bar to get up against the pontoons, and finally at 5 pm we crawled slowly over the pontoons; every vehicle was preceded by a tank which pulled and dragged it across the soft wet sand and up the slope, to the wood. A batch of German prisoners stood at the top of the slope silently surveying the scene – tall youths in field-grey and some wearing those grotesque tin hats.

The landings at Anzio in Italy were an attempt to outflank the stalemate at Monte Cassino. The operation was conceived by Churchill and was codenamed Operation Shingle. Initially it went well and a diversionary attack to the south ensured that the Germans were taken completely by surprise. However, the commanders were somewhat cautious after their rough experience at the landings at Salerno in the summer of the previous year and because their force was relatively small. Instead of pushing inland, they were keen to secure a beachhead and began to dig in only four miles inland, despite the fact that no enemy had yet been encountered. By the afternoon the beaches were under sporadic artillery fire and air attack. The German commander in Italy, General Kesselring, reacted rapidly and by the end of February the Allies were still penned in not far from the beachhead. In May 1944 Lovett would still be fighting in the same area of Italy.

FEBRUARY 1944

ON TUESDAY 8 FEBRUARY the agreed strategy for D-Day – the invasion of France – was finalized and the date was set for late May or early June. The commander of the operation, General Dwight D. Eisenhower, had already identified the weather and the tides as critical factors. The following week Eisenhower set up his headquarters in Britain. One of his biggest headaches was liaison with de Gaulle and the Free French.

On Tuesday 15 February the RAF carried out its heaviest raid yet on Berlin, dropping 2,500 tons of bombs. In retaliation, on Friday 18th the Luftwaffe launched its heaviest night raid on London since 1941. Londoners had become unaccustomed to taking air-raid precautions and this attack came as an unpleasant surprise. Although British public opinion mostly regarded RAF attacks on German cities as a matter of Hitler 'reaping what he had sown', nevertheless there were protests in the House of Lords during February about the scale of destruction in Germany.

In Italy there was fierce fighting throughout February around Monte Cassino, a fortified hill in German hands which included an ancient monastery. Despite a controversial decision to begin heavy bombing of this historic building it was not possible to dislodge the Germans. Repeated German attacks on the Anzio beachhead stronghold also failed to make progress. Further south, the Americans and the British had already restored Italian civil government in Sicily, Sardinia and the mainland southern provinces of Salerno and Potenza. Hitherto these areas had been ruled by the Allied Control Commission and the Allied Military Government. These were among the first areas of Axis territory to return to something approaching normality.

On 20 February a second attack was carried out on heavy-water production in Norway by the Norwegian resistance, assisted by the SOE. A ferry carrying a large stock of heavy water to laboratories in Germany was sunk. This was part of a widespread programme to slow the German development of atomic weapons.

On the Eastern Front a large pocket of Wehrmacht forces was surrounded at Korsun in western Ukraine. The Battle of the Korsun Pocket, also known as the Battle of Cherkassy, was a grinding confrontation where the last German offensive strength was drained away, preparing the way for the victorious Soviet advance into Poland, Romania and the Balkans in the summer and autumn of 1944. This vast battle – little known in the West – involved more than a million men fighting along the banks of the Gniloy Tickich. Some 50,000 soldiers of the Wehrmacht were encircled here by early February 1944. The most stalwart defenders of this outpost were a Belgian SS brigade, which consisted of a curious mixture of Belgian fascists and Walloon separatists, fighting alongside a Scandinavian SS unit. Less than half of these soldiers would escape the pocket.

In Britain there were already signs of the future direction of post-war politics and leading figures were increasingly inclined to make party political points in the House of Commons. The coalition government suffered a heavy by-election defeat when C. F. White won the West Derbyshire seat for the Common Wealth Party – a fringe party well to the left of the Labour Party – with a majority of 4,561. Meanwhile the government published proposals for a comprehensive National Health Service to widespread public approval.

Thursday 3 – Friday 18 February 1944

Michael Hoskin, aged thirteen, monitors air raids on London

Michael Hoskin was a schoolboy living in the East Sheen district of west London during the last two years of the war. He had initially been evacuated during the Blitz but had returned to his home in London by 1942. Two years later, aged thirteen, he began his diary as one of an army of volunteer observers and recorders of the air war against London.

AIR RAIDS FOR 1944: FEBRUARY: OFFICIAL R.D.C.C. FILES

DATE	DAY	TIME S.	TIME F.	VVV	REMARKS
3: 2	Th	20:50	21:40	7	No activity after 20:10 Very little gunfire,
4: 2	Fr	05:00	06:15		in first raid. In second gunfire heavy and flares. Big fire. 70 planes came over in two raids of which 20 reached London
6: 2	Su	06:00	06:15	1	Just one or two planes. Medium gunfire.
11: 2	Fr	19:50	20:35	0	Slight gunfire at 20:10, Nothing else.
13: 2	Su	20:35	21:30	8	To-day Tudor and I fitted up a

18: 2 Fr   00:45   02:00

bell on which I could signal different stages in air raids. This was tried out for the first time in this raid.

20:40 Raiders in sight.
20:55 Danger imminent.
20:58 Danger past.
21:05 Danger imminent.
21:10 Danger past.
21:30 All clear.

This raid was the heaviest for three years, and the worst I have ever experienced. I was woken up at 01:15 by the roar of the greatest barrage ever put up. Bombs were whistling down in the ne[a]r distance, and I was debating with my mother whether to get up, when a stick of bombs whistled past. I dived under the bedclothes, but my mother just stood there, not knowing what to do. It sounded as though the end of the world had come, at least as far as I was concerned. However, there was a big bang and a rush of blast, but fortunately the windows did not come in. That settled the argument – I got up! We rushed down-stairs into the cubby-hole. We were surprised to here [hear] shots, apparently from rifles. We deduced this to be Home Guards firing at flares overhead. Soon we crept upstairs to see what was doing. The sky was lighted up by a terrific fire about 200 yds. away towards N.E.E. Ammunition was going off at intervals, sending showers of sparks in all directions, and clouds of smoke was billowing past my window. The fire, a certain target for any Jerries, was soon got under control, and I was able to return to my interrupted sleep.

It was not until the following afternoon that I learned how near had been my escape. I wandered down towards the direction of the fire. As I began my walk, the Upper Richmond Road was covered in the glass from the shops on either side. As I neared the dentist's, the houses were practicably untenable. When I reached the Barnes Council's official offices I received a conciderable [sic] shock. They were completely in ruins, and among the wreckage were visible forms of almost every colour. What was once a fine building was once a mass of ruins. But what was even worse was the destruction which lay all around. For a quarter of a mile to the N. everything was a mass of ruins. That morning the S.R. [Southern Region] line was blocked and everywhere, people were sweeping up debris, and emptying buckets of brick into the road. It was amasing [*sic*] that two or three bombs, even heavies, could wreak so much destruction. The ammunition had come from small firebox store-house cum factory, which had gone up in flames. Mobile canteens were serving tea to the workers even then searching the debris for people who might even be alive.

Michael recorded raids by night, but by day he undertook the long journey to his school, which had been evacuated to the relative safety of Old Windsor. He continued to live at home in London and travelled there each day by train and bus. He left the house at 7.20 a.m. in order to reach his desk by 9.00 a.m. As bombing disrupted the trains operating in the Southern Region, his journey became ever longer. Shortly after this diary entry, on Sunday 20 February, the Luftwaffe would mount a raid with about 100 aircraft and followed this in the early hours of the next Wednesday morning with a 175-aircraft raid. The next morning Michael had to take four trains, two rides in army lorries and one bus ride to reach his school. SEE ALSO PP. 703–5.

Monday 7 February 1944

Dwight D. Eisenhower, Supreme Commander in Europe, reflects on press evaluations of command personalities

Much discussion has taken place concerning our command set-up, including newspaper evaluations of personalities and abilities. Generally speaking, the British columnists (not the chief of staff or the prime minister) try to show that my contributions in the Mediterranean were administrative accomplishments and 'friendliness in welding an allied team.' They dislike to believe that I had anything particularly to do with campaigns. They don't use the words 'initiative' and 'boldness' in talking of me, but often do in speaking of Alex and Monty.

The truth is that the bold British commanders in the Mediterranean were Admiral Sir Andrew Cunningham and Tedder. I had peremptorily to order the holding of the forward airfields in the bitter days of January 1943. I had to order the integration of an American corps and its use on the battlelines (if I had not done that, Tunis would have evaded us a much longer time). I had to order the attack on Pantelleria. And, finally, the British ground commanders (but not Sir Andrew and Tedder) wanted to put all our ground forces into the toe of Italy. They didn't like Salerno, but after days of work I got them to accept. On the other hand, no British commander ever held back when once an operation was ordered. We had a happy family, and to all the commanders in chief must go the great share of the operational credit. But it wearies me to be thought of as timid, when I've had to do things that were so risky as to be almost crazy. Oh hum.

Eisenhower was regarded almost universally as an affable, easy-going, softly spoken individual who, if anything, attempted to disguise his penetrating intelligence and critical eye. He enjoyed the business of commanding units in the field but had nevertheless spent most of his early career as a staff officer. At West Point, both he and Patton were early advocates of mobile armoured warfare and anticipated many of the developments of the 1940s. Both Roosevelt and Marshall recognized Eisenhower's unique talents as a team-builder, staff co-ordinator and planner, and began immediately to groom him for ultimate command in the European theatre. Having advanced his career so rapidly, he clearly regretted missing the opportunity to command troops more directly and closer to the battle. SEE ALSO PP. 445–6 AND 449–50.

Thursday 10 February – Wednesday 1 March 1944

Peter Moen's diary offers consolation during interrogation in Norway

Peter Moen, born in 1901, was brought up by deeply religious parents at Drammen in Norway. Between the wars he had worked as an actuary for a life insurance company in Oslo. When Norway was occupied by the Germans he became involved in the resistance and helped to run underground newspapers. For a long time he helped to run the London News *(so called because some of its contents were culled from the BBC), the most widely read of all illegal papers in Norway, and just before he was arrested he had become head of all underground newspapers in the country. On 3 February 1944 he was taken to Oslo's main police station at 19 Møllergaten. There was also a large concentration camp in the suburbs of Oslo where many of Norway's leading intellectuals were held. Moen most feared being taken to a third location, the Gestapo headquarters at Victoria Terrasse or 'VT'.*

10 February
19 Møllergaten
Have been to two cross-examinations. Was whipped. Betrayed Vic. Am weak. Deserve contempt. Am terrified of pain. But not afraid to die.

This evening I am thinking of Bella. Wept because I have done Bella so much harm. If I live Bella and I must have a child . . .

16 February
I cannot bear my guilt. I should have been ten times more careful with other people's safety. Because of my carelessness and weakness many must suffer and the free press in Norway is destroyed. Oh comrades – I deserve all your contempt. Life's fruits are bitter. I cannot do otherwise than weep – God help me.

A quarter of an hour's fresh air. That is to say alone in the courtyard. The command is bawled – *Los* – *Los* – much worse than to a dog. But things are done in an orderly fashion here. During the fortnight I have been here I have not seen anything but decent treatment of the prisoners – from a material point of view. The law of war and prison is strict, but not inhuman here at 19 M. So much have I seen from my solitary cell. I see very little.

It is VT which is the great terror. I was broke – physically and morally – in thirty hours there. I dread . . .

24 February
21st Day

Shall probably be called to VT during the morning. It is horrible. I am terrified of torture. I beg God to help me. Now He is my only support.

Donnerwetter made an inspection of the cells!! He did not find my diary. It is hanging tidily on the nail with the toilet paper. He didn't find my pen. It is a tack in the blackout window. My 'chess game' lay in the stocking on the peg right under his nose. Cell inspection in a naked cell – that is also the Gestapo . . .

I am thirsty and pass water. Fear and excitement. VT!! Lord my God! It is becoming a habit to be afraid . . .

1 March
27th Day at 19 M

The interrogations are a consistent terrorizing. One is perpetually threatened with torture. If one refuses to reply – if one is caught in a lie – or if they *think* one is concealing something – then one is tortured. This is the Gestapo's 'secret'. Police work with proofs and witnesses does not exist. One proves one's own 'guilt'. The 'accomplices' and their helpers are found in the same way. It disgusts me to go into detail about this. The whole theme of Gestapo methods makes me vomit morally.

Against this background the loneliness of the cell is a refuge to be coveted. I am tired in spite of 10 hours sleep last night. Yesterday evening I prayed to God with many tears. I see no light of faith shining before me.

Peter Moen's diary was written on toilet paper by painstakingly picking out each letter using a tack removed from a blackout curtain. When each sheet was completed he wrapped it in an unmarked sheet and dropped it through a ventilation grille into a small, dry, hidden space. Moen would die en route to Germany in September 1944 when the ship in which he was being transported hit a mine, but a fellow prisoner whom he had told about the location of the diary survived and the journal was later recovered from its hiding place. SEE P. 17.

Monday 14 February 1944

Bernard Berenson, an American Jewish art historian hiding out in northern Italy, observes the violent remnants of Fascist rule in Florence

Bernard Berenson was an American Jew born in 1865. He had been one of the most important and influential cultural historians and critics of the early twentieth century. His main specialism was the Italian Renaissance and he lived outside Florence. By 1939 he was a very old man and reluctant to leave his adopted homeland. During the war he was hidden from the Italian authorities by aristocratic friends. Jewish but also possessed of extremely right-wing views, he was ambivalent about the war, abhorring especially the level of destruction visited upon Italian culture.

When the resurrected Fascists returned here, as a cynically transparent mask for a Nazi occupation, they could trust neither the militia, nor the *carabinieri*, nor the police to do their bidding. They proceeded to empty out of the reform school boys of criminal propensities, armed them to the teeth, mounted them on cycles, and ordered them to act as police. These are having a grand time, ordering people about, insulting, threatening, and at times carrying out their threats.

It seems that the other day they had been banqueted and came out the worse for drink. While marching through one of the principal thoroughfares, some of them fired off guns and pistols, upon which the others, in their booze, concluded that they were being shot at from the houses they were passing. A general *fantasia* succeeded, and some of the cheery lads rushed into the houses to discover who might be shooting at them. In one they found a most respectable professional man in his bath and killed him outright, shouting as they left: 'We have done for him.'

It appears that the German commander of the district asked the specter-Fascist general of the same district how many troops he could dispose of. 'Seven thousand,' was the answer, 'but they are unarmed and unless you supply them with guns and ammunition they are of no use.' The Germans, for fear that they might turn against themselves, will not trust them with arms.

In early 1944 Berenson continued to be hidden by his Italian friends in northern Italy. This was one of the most distasteful periods of Fascist rule. Groups of irregular political police attacked Jews and crushed resistance activities on the orders of Mussolini, who had returned to 'power' in the small town of Salò on Lake Garda. Large bands of deserters and brigands also roamed the countryside. In Florence and Padua much of the terror campaign was conducted by a security force led by Mario Carità.

Monday 21 February 1944

The artist Käthe Kollwitz reaffirms her pacifism and world socialism

The artist Käthe Kollwitz was born Käthe Schmidt on 8 July 1867 in Königsberg, East Prussia. Her father, who was a stonemason, had encouraged her to draw, and she studied under the engraver Rudolf Mauer. At seventeen she enrolled at the Berlin School for Women Artists, and went on to study in Munich. In 1891 she married Dr Karl Kollwitz and they lived in one of the more deprived sections of the city where she found the tragic subjects depicted in her work. The first woman elected to the Prussian Academy, she had been expelled in 1933 on account of her political beliefs.

The strength [the German sculptor] Gerhard Marcks has summoned up remains almost incomprehensible. Not only has his son fallen, but all his work has been destroyed; everything is gone and yet the man starts a new life. Where does all this strength come from? It is almost incomprehensible to me, what degrees of endurance people can manifest. In days to come people will hardly understand this age. It must have been like this after the Thirty Years' War. What a difference between now and 1914, when the severest blow of my life struck me. Then I thought I had the right to go on living for the sake of my Roggevelde sculpture. That was why the father and mother figures were done. Now, so few decades later, all that once more appears in a different light. People have been transformed so that they have this capacity for endurance. Germany's cities have become rubble heaps, and the worst of all is that every war already carries within it the war which will answer it. Every war is answered by a new war, until everything, everything is smashed. The devil only knows what the world, what Germany will look like then. That is why I am wholeheartedly for a radical end to this madness, and why my only hope is in a world socialism. You know what my conception of that is and what I consider the only possible prerequisites for it. Pacifism simply is not a matter of calm looking on; it is work, hard work.

Whatever my old head works out is very fragmentary and unsatisfactory.

Kollwitz was one of many artists whom the Nazis considered politically undesirable and she was prevented from exhibiting. Ironically, during the war, the Nazis used some of her famous images for their own propaganda purposes.

Kollwitz's home had been bombed in 1943 and some of her work destroyed; she had lost her son in the First World War and her grandson had already been killed in this war. Käthe Kollwitz would live only until 22 April 1945, but by then she had the satisfaction of knowing that Hitler was headed for defeat.

MARCH 1944

IN ITALY FIERCE FIGHTING continued on all fronts, with increasing amounts of bombing and damage to civilian areas. On 15 March the Allies launched another major offensive against Monte Cassino, defended valiantly by the German 1st Paratroop Division, but could not capture the redoubt. The major psychological objectives of Monte Cassino and the Gustav Line remained the main obstacles on the road to Rome.

By now the RAF was turning its attention away from Berlin, where losses had been heavy, and instead focused on a bombing offensive against railways and communications over northern France in preparation for D-Day. Other areas of Germany continued to be bombed heavily. The largest raid of the war so far was launched against Stuttgart on 15 March. Attacking Germany continued to be hazardous, and in a single attack on Nuremberg on Thursday 30 March the RAF lost 96 bombers and 600 aircrew. This reflected improved German scientific developments in airborne radar and direction finding.

On the Eastern Front the Soviet army was pushing into Poland, while in the south the Germans had all but been driven out of Ukraine. On 29 March Soviet troops entered Romania. Hitler was incensed by this defeat and dismissed two of his most senior and experienced commanders, General Manstein and General Kleist. Hitler had now dismissed or arrested more than thirty generals. The success of the Red Army in the east prompted the German government to send troops into Hungary on 23 March to establish a pro-German puppet government. Doeme Sztojay became the new Prime Minister.

Unusually, the home front in Britain was the scene of industrial unrest. Unofficial strikes for higher wages began on 6 March and very soon the whole Welsh coalfield was on strike. Scottish miners soon joined them. By 9 March it was estimated that the loss to coal production was running at a third of a million tons per week. Miners' leaders persuaded most of the miners to go back to work by the end of the month and began working for a negotiated settlement in London.

Sunday 5 March 1944

The collective diary of the Lodz Ghetto records how Jews
seek to evade transportation to the camps

Sketches of Ghetto Life: Peculiar Bravery

A woman is standing in the crowd of people waiting outside
Central Prison. Her husband is inside waiting to be shipped
out of the ghetto. He appears at the second-story window of
the building in which his group is quartered. Apparently, he
has arranged with her that he will contrive to make himself
unfit for labor. He is about to leap out of the window; he
hesitates. But his wife shouts to him (in Yiddish): 'Hob nisht
keyn moyre!' (Don't be afraid!). She herself goads him to
jump. And he actually does jump; he sustains minor injuries
and is, in fact, exempted from conscription. The adventure
could also have ended more unpleasantly.

6 March

News of the Day: The 1,710 Workers

The first group, 750 men, has already reached its destination.
Although it is physically impossible, people would like to
have received messages from the workers in the first transport, which left in the direction of Czestochowa. Naturally,
this is quite out of the question.

The roundup continues. Last night was yet another night
of terror. Men and women, mostly the latter, were forcibly
removed from their apartments – approximately 350 persons,
most of them unmarried. The lists were drawn up by the
Bureau of Labour and not, as the ghetto grapevine has it, by
factory managers.

*During the spring of 1944 the Germans decided to liquidate the Lodz
Ghetto, and in order to achieve this they reactivated the Chelmno
extermination camp, just over 37 miles away. Deportations to Chelmno
were often disguised as the transfer of forced labour to Germany. By the
summer of 1944 over 7,000 people would have been sent to Chelmno to*

be killed there. *From early August the destination would change to Auschwitz. The Lodz Ghetto diary records that there was little active resistance to the deportations. By August 1944 only 1,200 Jews were left at Lodz in two assembly camps. A small group of survivors, perhaps 800, would finally be liberated by the Soviet army in January 1945. About 200,000 people passed through the Lodz Ghetto; fewer than 10,000 survived. SEE ALSO PP. 251–2 AND 320.*

Tuesday 14 – Friday 17 March 1944

Sergeant Harry Schloss flies on missions to bomb Rome and Monte Cassino

14 March

Made mission 15. Target – Rome marshalling yards. 100 per cent concentration of bombs. Good job. Made 5.05 time. Cook's tour of Italy.

15 March

Made Mission 16. Flying almost every day is tough. Target – Cassino. Right on front line. We were only one of 16 Bomb Groups to hit the town. When we got over it, there was nothing left of [the town of] Cassino. Only a hole in the ground. Loads & loads of trucks going to the front. It was a sight I'll never forget. The town was only dust. Captain Tate asked me to write up my impressions of the raid for the squadron book. I did so. Capt Tate said I did swell. Tonight is my first broadcast on the group radio program. Made the broadcast. Quite successful except that I read the news too fast, but with a little experience might do right well.

16 March

Flew spare. Saw two ships collide and explode. Chet Angell, VE Miller & Wise. My buddies all dead. Flew back to field. Sick. 13 good men dead. Can't stand it much more. Guess I'm a sissy.

17 March
Went on Mission 17. Dropped 1000 lb bombs on Orvatello marshalling yards. 34th did good job. On return we were given speech by Lt General Baker. He can't get over our record. He says in England they say that if a B-26 does half as good as a 17 it's OK. Here it's the reverse. He watched the Cassino run, says it amazed him. On mission today, piece of flak cracked window over Gates' head. If it had come through we'd all be in bad shape. Especially Gates. On primary target, couldn't make it. Overcast.

On 15 February 1944 the Allies had begun to bomb the monastery of Monte Cassino, supporting a renewed assault on the mountain by Indian and New Zealand troops of the 8th Army. The combined aerial and ground attack was unsuccessful but the heavy bombing did badly damage the monastery, which dated from AD 524. Arguably the bombing was counter-productive because the Germans did not make use of the abbey until after it had been bombed. Some bomber crews were told that they were justified in bombing the monastery because during the north African campaign the Germans had hidden artillery in mosques to avoid air attack, although in reality there was little evidence of this practice.

Wednesday 15 March 1944

Intelligence officer Norman Lewis watches as Italy suffers bombing by its former ally

A bad raid last night with heavy civilian casualties, as usual, in the densely populated port areas. I was sent this morning to investigate the reports of panic, and frantic crowds running through the streets crying, 'Give us peace,' and 'Out with all the soldiers.' In Santa Lucia, home territory of the Neapolitan ballad, I saw a heart-rending scene. A number of tiny children had been dug out of the ruins of a bombed building and lay side by side in the street. Where presentable, their faces were uncovered, and in some cases brand-new dolls had been thrust into their arms to accompany them to the other world. Professional mourners, hired by the locality to reinforce the grief of the stricken families, were running up and down the street, tearing at their clothing and screaming horribly. One man climbed into the rubble and was calling into a hole where he believed his little boy was trapped under hundreds of tons of masonry, begging him not to die before he could be dug out. 'Hang on, son. Only a few minutes longer now. We'll have you out of there in a minute. Please don't die.' The Germans murder only the poor in these indiscriminate raids, just as we did.

Allied bombers had wrought havoc on Naples during late July 1943 at the time when Italy was changing sides in the war. With that transition completed, Naples began to be bombed by its former allies, the Germans, and it suffered particularly badly in early 1944. When the Germans retreated they destroyed the water and sewage systems, helping to provoke a typhus epidemic. To add to Italy's troubles, Mount Vesuvius erupted on 18 and 19 March, causing considerable economic devastation to the area and also damaging an entire wing of Allied B-25 bombers stationed on the eastern side of the volcano.

After the war Lewis would spend time as a war correspondent; he also published many more books, including a study of the Mafia entitled The Honoured Society. *He died in July 2003.* SEE ALSO PP. 620–1.

Thursday 16 – Friday 17 March 1944

David Scholes of the RAAF witnesses the crash of bomber 352 'K-King' near Beachley

16 March

Tonight is not very brilliant at all yet we fly. We have quite a hair-raising time and I am quite glad to get down again. It is around 1245 when we are waiting for the bus at our dispersal. An aircraft comes over and overshoots. As I watch it pass by at some 200 ft I sort of wonder somehow just how things are inside and who is in it, feeling happier still inside

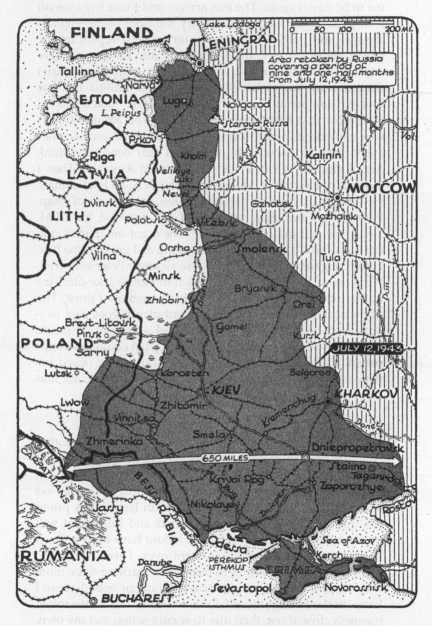

The Russian Advance, Late 1943 and Early 1944

me to be down again. The bus arrives and I take my eyes off it to pick up my things. Suddenly the note of the engines changes and I am just in time unfortunately to pick up the nav lights as the A/C dives vertically into the ground near Beachley with full motor, and explodes with vivid scarlet flames. I am somewhat stunned because amidst the few blurred comments I hear, someone says, 'that's 352'. I remember that Peter took 352 K-King. The ammunition is now exploding the sky is brightly lit and black smoke comes away from the awful sight on the hill near Beachley. I think first, I thought of Pat, Peter's girl back in Australia. Then I thought of the crew – 'Moose', and the B/A, an Englishman. He always used to be mending bikes, funny sort of chap. P/O Dennis the other pilot. He'd just received the DFM. Small, the rear gunner, I wonder if he'd get out. Surely not, not out of this blaze. My mind is blank as I get into the bus. I light a cigarette. Nobody talks. We all knew Peter very well. We were in the Crew Room with him before take-off. I try not to look out on the way back, but somehow I must. The sky is still an orange colour. The ambulance goes past us – not much need for that, I think. I feel a little upset inside – quite natural I suppose. I try to think what could have happened. Only one thing I'm sure. He must have raised his flaps in one go. Horrible business. We have supper, not that I feel like it, and go to bed. Somehow I go to sleep.

17 March

I get down to the Flight at about 1.30pm to find that another crate has gone in, this time a ditching. All have got out, I am told, except the WOP, an English chap (also from our hut). They were picked up in the Wash by a destroyer. Thank God some are safe. Small, the rear gunner, in last night's prang has got out. He is very badly injured and burnt, but will probably live poor devil. I think it would have been better if he had gone too. All the rest went over. There will be no funeral as there is nothing to bury. I am learning to be more than careful. I am learning to trust nothing or nobody until I have checked things myself. I want to come out of this rotten business alive, if not, then due to enemy action, not my own.

ABOVE: POWs at Stalingrad in January 1943. Some surrendered Germans, such as Erich Weinert (p. 501), chose to work for the Soviets, broadcasting propaganda.

BELOW: The hanging of suspected partisans in a Russian village: diarists on the Eastern Front testified to the barbarization of warfare.

OPPOSITE: In May 1943 Churchill stayed with Eisenhower (left) in Algiers. See p. 561.

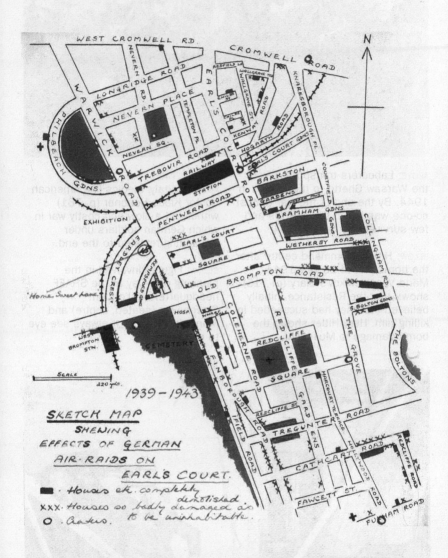

ABOVE: Veronica Goddard's beautiful diary contains this map of the bombs dropped on her neighbourhood in Earl's Court. See p. 209.

ABOVE: Labourers transported from the Warsaw Ghetto to the camps in 1944. By the end of the war almost no-one was left in the ghettos and few survived the camps.

BELOW: Hitler's command centre after the bomb plot of 20 July 1944. Marie Vassiltchikov's diary (p. 716) shows that the Resistance initially believed that they had succeeded in killing him. Here Hitler shows the bomb damage to Mussolini.

OPPOSITE PAGE

ABOVE: In Italy, medics like American doctor Klaus Huebner (p. 761) witnessed a slow and costly war in which German soldiers under Kesselring resisted to the end.

BELOW: Figures involved in the planning of D-Day at the SHAEF headquarters in London. Eisenhower (seated, centre) and Monty (right) did not always see eye to eye.

RIGHT: US officers like David K. Bruce (p. 732) and John Maginnis (p. 740) had great difficulty controlling the resistance fighters or 'FFI', who were temporarily the new rulers in large parts of provincial France in the summer of 1944.

BELOW: The USS *Mason*: James A. Dunn (p. 763) served on this American naval vessel crewed largely with black sailors, who had hitherto been restricted to shore duties. The ship served with great distinction in the summer of 1944.

LEFT: Allied soldiers quickly established good relations with the local population in towns such as Aachen, the first German town to be occupied. See Richard Crossman's diary, p. 774.

BELOW: The German HQ on Guernsey, located in a hotel in St Peter Port. Baron von Ausfess's diary (p. 730) records good relations between Germans and the occupied Channel Islanders during 1944.

LEFT: Germany deployed soldier children in the spring of 1945; Guy Sajer (p. 820) noted how some still carried their school satchels.

BELOW: Catastrophic damage from a V-2 rocket: Vere Hodgson (p. 744) recorded the climate of deep fear created by the first wave of V-2 attacks on London in September 1944. Initially there was no official information on these mysterious new weapons.

In March 1944 David Scholes was still converting to Lancasters at 17 Operational Training Unit, based at RAF Turweston in Northamptonshire. His diary records the numbers of crew who died, not on operations, but as the result of accidents and mishaps. Although these casualties were surprisingly numerous, the Lancaster was much more reliable than other aircraft types, and accident rates were being reduced as they were used more widely.

After the war, David Scholes would settle in Tasmania as a successful commercial artist and Australia's premier fly-fishing writer. SEE ALSO PP. 19–20 AND 586–8.

Saturday 18 – Sunday 19 March 1944

Dr Zygmunt Klukowski, hospital surgeon and local historian, watches the German settlers retreating from Poland

18 March

Around 3pm all Germans in town received instructions to pack and be ready to move out. Naturally all the settlers and *Volksdeutsch* are in a panic. They are trying to sell whatever they can – crying, cursing, shouting, and running around without any purpose. No one has any real information about what is happening and what is behind the sudden German evacuation.

19 March

Since early morning the traffic in town has been heavy. From every direction horse-drawn wagons carrying Germans settlers have been arriving. Here in town Germans are look-ing for wagons and horses . . .

The Germans are burning the files at city hall. The local *Volksdeutsch* have not yet been ordered to move out. If they decide to escape on their own, they must supply horses and wagons. So far only a few have begun packing. The Germans are selling their belongings, even cows and pigs, for very low prices. Our own people are busily buying. I am sure the Germans will not survive the road without big surprises.

Now they are to travel to Radom, and later to Lodz. Today's picture of German misery makes us all feel good. We have come to the day when we can see Germans escaping from Neue Deutsche Stadt Szczebrzeszyn (new German city of Szczebrzeszyn).

Zygmunt Klukowski had witnessed appalling horrors in eastern Poland during the war years. In March 1944 he noted that overall 'there is a happy feeling here', for the inhabitants of Zamosc felt that the days of their slavery were numbered. Many Germans had come east as pioneering settlers, exploiting their status as the master race in Hitler's new Lebensraum policy. However, by 1943 they had fallen prey to the very active Polish underground and had to stay inside their protected towns and new settlements. By mid-March 1944 the local German population was fleeing of its own accord, fearing that they would be surrounded and cut off by the Russians. Klukowski realized that he was now likely to survive the war, but his trials were not over. From 1944 there followed a longer period of Soviet occupation during which both he and his son would work in the Polish resistance. The enemy had merely changed from the Gestapo to the Russian NKVD. In July 1952 Zygmunt's son Tadeusz would be sentenced to execution for partisan activity, and he himself was imprisoned for years in Wronki gaol before being rehabilitated.

Zygmunt Klukowski would survive to see the publication of his diary in 1958. This remarkable record of barbarity, resistance and invasion won a Polish literary award for the best account of the Second World War. SEE ALSO PP. 480–4.

APRIL 1944

IN MID-APRIL 1944 the British Foreign Office forbade the sending of coded messages from most foreign embassies in London and thereafter insisted that diplomatic bags be censored. Only the major Allies were excluded from the ban. Such draconian measures were a major breach of diplomatic privilege. Telephone services to southern Ireland were also stopped. The purpose of these measures was to reduce Axis intelligence operations during the run-up to D-Day. At this point, personnel, arms and equipment were flowing into Britain from North America at an unprecedented rate in preparation for the invasion. The Allies were trying to sell a deception story to the Axis – pretending that they intended to invade the Calais area with a force called FUSAG, which was in fact entirely fictional. De Gaulle had now established himself as head of the Free French armed forces, replacing General Giraud.

The RAF continued to focus on attacking targets in France, while the Americans attacked aircraft factories in Germany. During this month the USAAF also accidentally bombed the town of Schaffhausen in neutral Switzerland. The Swiss protested strongly and the Americans offered reparations. Throughout the war the highly efficient Swiss air force made a point of shooting down most of the intruding aircraft that made incursions into the country's neutral airspace.

In Italy Allied forces ceased their attacks to rest and recuperate in preparation for a major offensive in May that was intended to precede the amphibious landings on the coast of France a few weeks later. In Rome the Cabinet of Marshal Pietro Badoglio resigned, signalling the end of the regime; however, King Victor Emmanuel III then invited Badoglio to remain as Prime Minister and form a new government which would negotiate with the Allies.

On the Eastern Front Soviet forces continued to make good progress and recaptured Yalta, but the Germans were becoming more skilful in their withdrawals and managed to rescue many of their troops from the Crimea.

April also saw a final resolution of a series of unofficial miners' strikes in Britain, with the signature of a miners' pay agreement in London. The wages of railway workers also went up by five shillings per week. The laws of supply and demand had worked in the favour of both agricultural and industrial workers throughout the war. During the Chancellor's budget speech it was announced that since the start of the war prices had risen 28 per cent against a rise in wages of 37 per cent. This had largely benefited manual and semi-skilled workers.

Thursday 6 April 1944

Colonel D. K. Reimers, commander of the US 343rd Field Artillery Battalion, arrives in Britain

Colonel Reimers was one of 500,000 additional American servicemen pouring into Britain in early 1944 during the build-up to D-Day in June.

I went to Birmingham to see the sights. Birmingham is only 25 miles from our camp but it took over an hour to get there. By American standards the roads are only one car wide and it's impossible to go more than 30 miles an hour. It rained most of the way and that didn't help. The first place we hit was the Queen's Hotel, the best in the city. We visited the bar, in the basement, and for the first time I was able to meet some of the English people. For a while we were the only Americans in the place but after about an hour three more officers came in. George had been there before so he already knew the bar tender. It's a good thing too. If you are a stranger there isn't much chance of getting a drink. If the bar tender doesn't know you you might get, 'Sorry, I just sold the last'. I found out the secret for getting service. Each drink costs a shilling on the side, a tip. From there we went to two other places ... Dance halls close at 2200 so there is nothing else to do except go home.

The streets are absolutely black. If you are not careful you can be run over by an English car or an army vehicle. Both tear around with only black out lights. In some dark areas you also have to be careful not to interrupt some soldier and his girl friend intent on making love ... It's scary. Going to Birmingham and on our return also introduced me to left hand driving. I was petrified both going and coming back. Every time we rounded a curve and met a car coming in the opposite direction I was positive we would have a collision ...

Yesterday morning I went to Colport to meet 'B', 'C' and Service Batteries. Captain Ingram was my guide and this time took me on a roundabout way to get to the station so I could see some of the surrounding country. On the way we drove through Bridgenorth, a quaint little village about 4 miles west of our camp. It's a historical place having a castle of red stone built on a hill overlooking the village. Our troops will be allowed to go to Bridgenorth or any other town within 50 miles of our camp. Right now, Bridgenorth is 'Off Limits' to all troops. Recently there was a fight there between white and colored soldiers. Mingling of the two creates a serious situation. The English allow colored soldiers in the pubs, dance halls, hotels and private homes. The soldiers also take out English girls who do not believe in discrimination. Some have even married colored men. Most of the time our soldiers, especially the southern ones, resent this bitterly and openly. The situation creates a problem in our division because the majority of the men come from southern states.

The social adjustments required of American troops arriving in Britain were considerable. Some struggled with the British currency. Racial problems were considerable and there was often public disorder when white American troops tried to insist that their black colleagues be ejected from pubs and hotels on racial grounds. Where large numbers of American soldiers were stationed, the US army attempted to persuade the British government to introduce the policy of segregation and discrimination that was universal in the United States at this time. The British government refused. SEE ALSO PP. 843–5.

Saturday 22 April 1944

Actress Joyce Grenfell talks to Brigadier Clark at Maqil about messages from home

Joyce Grenfell spent much of the war with her friend Viola Tunnard, entertaining the troops as part of an ENSA team. ENSA stood for Entertainments National Service Association, but was commonly translated as 'Every Night Something Awful'. She had worked in Britain during the first few years of the war, then toured the Middle East in 1944.

Brigadier Clark told us about a Londoner in his unit who asked if he could have a word with him concerning a cable he'd just had from home. It read: 'Son born both doing well love Mary.' The brigadier said how splendid, and the private said it wasn't, because he hadn't been home for two years. 'Oh,' invented the brigadier wildly, 'perhaps the cable has been a long time coming?' The man wasn't to be comforted and went away very low. Sometime later he came rushing back with a letter in his hand: 'I've got a letter from my wife sir, and it's all right, it's not her it's my mother. She's a widow. Must have been playing around with some man.' He was fully comforted and indeed delighted. So was the brigadier.

Although this incident was a light-hearted one, the war had a serious impact on marriage in the UK. In the period 1936–40 there were 30,903 divorces; between 1941 and 1945 the total increased to 51,944, but in the period 1946–50 the number shot up to 199,507. It is hard to resist the conclusion that war was a major motor of social change.

In 1944 Joyce Grenfell shuttled backwards and forwards through Algiers, Malta, Sicily, Italy, Iraq and Egypt; she would undertake a second tour through Asia in 1945.

Joyce Grenfell

Monday 24 April 1944

Harold Macmillan visits General Anders and the Polish Corps in Italy

Born in 1894, Harold Macmillan was the grandson of the publisher Daniel Macmillan and had been educated at Eton and then Balliol. After serving with distinction in the Grenadier Guards during the First World War he joined the family publishing company, but found it uninteresting and instead went into politics. A quintessentially Edwardian figure, he always seemed older than his years. Accordingly, in 1942 he was singled out at a relatively young age to be Britain's Minister of State resident in north Africa, with the task of resolving political problems that occurred first in Algiers and later in Rome. His diary is also Edwardian in its determinedly outward gaze, recording interesting details that Macmillan observed, but capturing little of his inner feelings.

We lunched with General Anders, Commanding the Polish Corps. I thought him very attractive – a keen soldier and a powerful political controversialist. Fortunately, for the time being the former interest is uppermost in his mind. But naturally memories of Poland, fear for his fate, and equal hatred of Russians and Germans are never far removed from his thoughts.

We saw an exercise, some way from the line, by one of their battalions. It consisted of an attack on a hill, covered by smoke-screen for mortar and machine-gun fire. It was most realistic, live ammunition was used throughout.

After the exercise, we were given tea at battalion H.Q. It consisted of 'zakouski' – various *hors d'oeuvres* – and scrambled eggs, with red wine and tea. We had then some songs and recitations – a very good show indeed, with most talented playing of mandolins and accordions.

We arrived at General Anders's H.Q. just at noon. The trumpeters played a curious and appealing call, which ends suddenly – broken off in the middle of a musical phrase. We were told that this is always played at noon. It commemorates a trumpeter who was calling the people of Cracow to muster against the Tartars. As he was playing, an arrow pierced his throat. Ever since, for six or seven hundred years, this call is played at noon, in memory of the Poles' long struggle against barbarism and urging them still to fight in the same cause. It always ends on this broken note.

This Polish Corps has had an extraordinary history. It is almost entirely recruited from the Polish population *east* of the 'Curzon Line' – Vilna and such places. Therefore they were imprisoned in Russian internment camps in 1939 (subsequent to the Stalin–Ribbentrop pact – and the defeat of Poland by Germany). After Germany attacked Russia, we pleaded with the Russians to let them free. After incredible adventures they walked (like the Greeks in Xenophon's *Anabasis*) all the way eastwards, till they finally reached Persia and Palestine. Now they have re-entered Europe in Italy.

One of the officers told us that when they were in Turkestan they gave a concert in the market place of some town. The people asked for the trumpeters of Lukistan (Poland) of whose musical powers they had heard. So they played every conceivable tune. But the people asked if they knew no more – so at last they played the noon-day call. This was recognised by the delighted crowd who knew the legend of the Tartar's arrow. They had a story that only when this trumpet call was played by a trumpeter of Lukistan in Turkestan itself, would peace and freedom come to all the people of the world. *Prosit omen!* [An auspicious sign]

The Polish Corps were an army in exile. Some had fled to Britain in 1939, but most were captured labourers who had been transported from Poland into Russia when Stalin, in league with Hitler, occupied part of their country in 1939. However, when Hitler had attacked Russia in 1941, Moscow allowed many Poles to march south from Ukraine through the Caucasus and into the Middle East, where they formed one of the toughest fighting units to serve in that theatre. This was an epic journey that truly paralleled the march of Xenophon's account of the 'One Thousand'. As part of the 8th Army, they were commanded by General W. Anders. Having fought with distinction in the desert, they landed in Italy between December 1943 and January 1944. One of the more remarkable soldiers serving in the Polish Corps was Wojtek, a brown bear adopted in Iran as its mascot. Wojtek actually helped in the fighting by carrying ammunition for the guns.

Harold Macmillan would succeed Anthony Eden as Prime Minister in 1957.

MAY 1944

MAY WAS THE BREAKTHROUGH month for Allied forces in Italy. On 11 May a major offensive was launched and the German defenders retreated, finding themselves outnumbered by more than two to one. Nevertheless, Polish forces took particularly heavy casualties around Monte Cassino. Another major breakthrough was achieved by the French on 14 May at Ausonia, and this precipitated the collapse of the German defence along the whole of the Gustav Line. By 17 May the Germans had opted for a general retreat. A week later the Allied forces further north finally began their breakout from the Anzio beachhead and began to move towards Rome.

Allied air power was now directed almost exclusively at softening up the invasion areas in northern France. A record 5,000 bombers raided railway targets and airfields in northern France and Belgium. On 20 May Eisenhower's secret orders were broadcast to European underground armies in an effort to cause distraction and dispersal of German forces immediately prior to the landings. The Free French estimated that their numbers had swelled to 100,000. The Germans had redoubled their efforts against the resistance right across Europe and were increasingly engaged in large-scale repressive actions. On 25 May they dropped a special commando unit in Yugoslavia close to Tito's headquarters in an attempt to capture him and his staff. Tito and Randolph Churchill, his British liaison officer, narrowly escaped.

German atrocities against Commando forces, pilots and escaping prisoners continued to be a matter of concern. On Friday 19

May Anthony Eden informed the House of Commons that forty-seven RAF officers had been shot while 'escaping' from Stalag Luft III. Despite this grim news, on the home front London continued to edge back towards normality, and one sign of this was the increasing amount of public sport taking place. Football had continued throughout the war in some form or other, but cricket had been badly interrupted. In May and June 1944, test match cricket enjoyed a substantial revival.

Thursday 4 May 1944

Tony Benn is entertained by Noel Coward in Rhodesia

Tony Benn's wartime ambition was to join the RAF. His father had previously served in the air force and rejoined at the remarkable age of sixty-nine. Having followed in his footsteps, Tony Benn was busy training in southern Africa. With the ring closing in on the Germans in Europe, many thought they would end up fighting in Asia against Japan. Benn applied to be posted direct to a unit fighting against the Japanese, but instead was sent to Cairo and Jerusalem.

In the evening Noel Coward came to the camp to give his one-man show. John, Les, Ken and I queued up between 6 and 6.30. The doors opened at 7.30 and from then until 8 the 'Hillside Scamps' played. Then the great moment arrived and Coward came on with his pianist Norman Hackforth. He was very smartly dressed in a khaki shirt and tie, light brown soled suede shoes. His programme which lasted a little over an hour long was absolutely first rate. He sang
'Don't put your daughter on the stage Mrs Worthington'
'Let's fly away'
'London Pride'
'Don't let's be beastly to the Germans'
'I'm in love'
'Senorita Nina'
'Always be nice to the gentlemen'
'Let's do it – let's fall in love'
'Epilogue from *In Which We Serve*'

After the interval it carried on well, the best of all being the last song, 'Grandpa ate a large apple and made a rude noise in the Methodist Chapel'. I admire Noel Coward for being so low despite the ladies present. He used the words 'bloody, bitch, Christ, bastard, short arm inspection, sexy' and so on despite them.

In 1944 Noel Coward gave a great number of performances to entertain troops in South Africa, India, Burma and France. Noel Coward's work was often risqué and his song 'Don't Let's be Beastly to the Germans' was banned by the BBC because it contained flippant lines such as: 'Though they've been a little naughty to the Czechs and Poles and Dutch – But I don't suppose those countries really minded very much'. Notwithstanding this, it was Churchill's favourite.

In June 1944 Tony Benn would lose his brother Michael who was fighting in the Middle East. He returned home in 1945 in time to participate in the June election campaign and was elected to the House of Commons in 1950.

Friday 5 May 1944

An unknown victim of the Holocaust confesses his own misdeeds

Avraham Benkel was released from the concentration camp at Auschwitz in May 1945. He had been deported there with his wife and family but only he had survived. Before being placed in the concentration camp, the family had been incarcerated in the Lodz Ghetto, and so he returned there to try to locate other relatives. He failed to find any of his family and all the houses had been vandalized by the local population. However, in a neighbouring apartment, now abandoned, he found a diary which had been written between May and July 1944. Benkel took the diary with him when he emigrated to Israel in 1949 and in 1970 handed it to the Yad Vashem museum in Jerusalem, where it is now preserved in the archive. Written in a mixture of four different languages including Hebrew and English, it is a remarkable and poetic

*reflection on the state to which human beings were reduced when
incarcerated in the Lodz Ghetto.*

I decided to write a diary: though it is a bit late. To re-
capitulate the past events is quite impossible so I begin with
the present. I committed this week an act which is best able
to illustrate to what degree of dehumanisation we have been
reduced – namely – I finished up my loaf of bread at a space
of three days, that is to say on Sunday, so I had to wait for
the next Saturday for a new one. [The weekly ration was
approximately 33 ounces of bread.] I was terribly hungry
and I had a prospect of living only from the resort soups (the
soup ladled out to forced labourers) which consisted of three
little potato pieces and two dkg. [decagrams; 1 dkg = three-
quarters of an ounce] of flower [*sic*]. I was lying on Monday
morning quite dejectedly in my bed, and there was the half
loaf of bread of my darling sister . . . To cut a long story
short I could not resist the temptation and ate it up totally.
After having done this – which is at present a terrible crime,
I was overcome by terrible remorse of conscience and by a
still greater care for what my little one would eat for the next
five days. I felt a miserable helpless criminal. I suffer terribly
by feigning that I don't know where the bread has gone and
I tell people that it was stolen by a supposed reckless and
pitiless thief. And for keeping up appearances, I have to
utter curses and condemnations on the imaginary thief. 'I
would hang him with my own hand had I come across him'
and such like hipocritic [*sic*] phrases – indeed I am nervous,
too exhausted for literary exertion at the present moment.
All I can say is that I shall always suffer on the remembrance
of this 'noble' deed of mine . . .

*The name of the diary writer and his sister are unknown, although the
girl was twelve years of age. She was working in a neighbouring
German textile factory attached to the Lodz Ghetto; she had arrived with
her father, but he had already died of hunger by 1944. The brother did
not have access to a notebook and so kept his diary by writing in the
margins, and even across the text, of an old French novel. His sister also
kept a diary which is now lost. Her brother copied a few passages of this*

into his own diary. One of them was in verse and began: 'Childhood, dear days – Alas, so few they were.'

Tuesday 9 May 1944

Peggy Ryle keeps a diary for her husband, reported missing

Peggy Ryle had divorced in the 1930s. Her second husband Georgie had changed his date of birth on his RAF papers to ensure that he could go into active service with the air force rather than simply do a desk job. He had taken part in the first raid over Berlin and reached the rank of squadron leader. Peggy had married Georgie in 1942 and they lived close to London with her two daughters from her first marriage – Day and Sally. In late April 1944, serving with an elite pathfinder squadron, Georgie was reported missing. Peggy was convinced he was alive and started a diary to record all the things she wanted to say to him, but could not.

11 South Bank

Your birthday, darling, and I don't know where you are or even if you are alive, although all this week I have had a premonition that you are, and are trying to get to me to feel that you are not dead. Please God I am right.

As I can't give you a birthday present, I thought at least I could keep a diary telling you all I have done since that ghastly morning, Friday 28th April.

That night I slept more deeply than I usually do, but woke up with a start at 2.45am. From 4am until 8.25 I walked about the house waiting for you. You had said you were going to be very late so until 7.30am I did not really start to worry. I still had some comfort from the fact that no one from Oakington had phoned and you had said they would if you were one hour overdue! By 8.25am however, I could bear it no longer, so I phoned the Mess. The Scots telephonist answered and I asked for you. I waited ages and knew then something had happened. I kept saying to myself, 'This is it.

This is it.' Then Dickey came to the phone and I asked where you were. He said, 'Haven't they phoned you, Peg?' – so I knew. He had only just come down and heard himself. I went upstairs and told Sally. Then I went down on my knees and prayed and prayed . . .

All that first week, darling, I could not feel anything one way or the other as to whether you were alive or dead, but *everyone* genuinely has the feeling that you are OK. This week I feel as if you are willing me to know you are trying to get back to me.

On Sunday night Judy Lockhart phoned to say they now have all the names of the planes that came down in Switzerland and that yours was not among them. I was so frightened you might have come down in Lake Constance without your Mae West. But only one crew did that and they swam ashore – Australians and Canadians. I try to keep my mind off all the awful things that may have happened to you, because if I think too much, I shall go off my head.

When I was a little girl, and anything awful had happened, I used to go to sleep and wake up cheerful and then the memory of the awful thing would suddenly flood all over me. With this, I never lose the pain or worry, waking or sleeping – though I don't seem to sleep much. The doctor had given me some sleeping pills (would not let me have the Neurinase you left in the bar!).

Throughout May 1944 Peggy Ryle was confident that her husband was a POW and kept up long entries in her diary for him, noting: 'I wonder how many months it will be before you read this, darling.' SEE ALSO PP. 718–19.

Thursday 18 May 1944

Major Hardy Parkhurst, with the Royal Northumberland
Fusiliers, witnesses a costly victory at Monte Cassino

It is a great and memorable day. Cassino has fallen and the
Gustav Line has been completely broken. We were not able
to close the gap entirely by joining hands with the Poles on
Route 6, and so a lot of the Parachutists were able to get
away. Hence the fury with which they fought against both
Poles and 4 Division. By keeping the jaws apart they were
able to thin out to a large extent. Nevertheless, they have
suffered terrific casualties. But the day is ours and a great
victory has been won. Last night we received an operation
order for the attack on Cassino in which we were to take
part. It was to be supported by two squadrons of N.Z. tanks.
But when the infantry probed the outskirts they found little
opposition, and many Germans gave themselves up. There
was some sniping and some machine gunning, but this was
soon overcome, and in due course the place was mopped up.
Some casualties were caused by time bombs left by the Hun.
Later we learnt that the Polish flag was flying over the
Monastery. It was very fitting that this should be so, for the
Poles have suffered dearly. Georgi, the Polish liaison officer,
told me that the hills behind the Monastery were absolutely
indescribable. Hundreds of dead lay all over the hillsides.
Americans, French, N. Zealanders, and now Poles. The
Germans were dug in in steel emplacements and they would
not give up.

I went down into Cassino at about 1100 and they were still
mopping up. It was a phantom town, stark and horrible, the
epitomy of war. I went straight down Route 6 with its green
fields and lovely trees on either side. On approaching the
Rapido bridge, the green stopped. All the trees were naked,
stark and leafless. The bridges we had managed to get up
were almost totally wrecked. Route 6 dwindled into a 'sheep
track' which wound its way through shell craters, bomb
craters, and the gaunt remains of houses.

All the way up this track was a mass of kit, blankets, bits of clothing, boots, steel helmets. The whole of the area in front of the town was a ghastly marsh, caused by the lack of drainage and the bombs and shells which had blown everything to pieces. All the craters have filled with water, which stank horribly and were very often a watery grave. Down this grim avenue were many bodies, which had been untouched for weeks, a grim spectacle. The town itself was a shattered wilderness of rubble. I cannot describe the destruction. I looked up at the Monastery, a mass of jutting rubble. Every single tree on the shell-shattered mountain face below the Monastery was stark and naked. The war-mongers should see the place, they should leave it as it is as a warning to all future Dictators, to all future generations. I saw some German prisoners coming back; they looked like ghosts. The town has been heavily mined and booby-trapped, so a complete inspection was not advisable. The stench was horrible and I cannot imagine anyone coming back to live there. It is hard to imagine a few months ago, this was a beautiful town. It has made an indelible mark on my memory.

In May 1944 the Allies launched yet another offensive – named Operation Diadem – in which units from the 8th Army finally overcame the German paratroop division that was holding Monte Cassino and punched a hole in the Gustav Line. A leading role in this achievement was played by the remarkable Polish Corps, most of whom had marched to the Middle East from captivity in Russia to join the Allied war effort. In the last week of May, assisted by the pressure that this operation created, seven Allied divisions would also break out from the Anzio beachhead. Then, on 4 June 1944, shortly before Operation Overlord began, Rome would fall to the Allies. The Germans moved back to the next natural defensive position, called the Gothic Line, close to the open-ing of the Po valley. Bitter fighting would continue in Italy until the end of the war, with the two sides collectively losing 600,000 men.

Major Parkhurst, having served with the 2nd Battalion the Royal Northumberland Fusiliers for six years, returned after the war to his former career in banking. He rediscovered his diaries after they had sat in the back of a cupboard for forty years. SEE ALSO PP. 648–9.

Tuesday 23 May 1944

Robert S. Capps, south of Rome, on the unexpected hazards of bomber operations

As the pace of the Italian campaign stalled, the Allies tried to address the problem by applying more and more air power. Robert S. Capps was one of the pilots involved in these operations and served with 456th Bomber Group. He was the first pilot in his group to reach fifty missions.

Only 16 bombers, planes in 1st Unit of the formation of which my plane was a part, were able to see the target sufficiently through the clouds to drop their bombs, and we dropped 39 tons of 500 pound general purpose bombs . . .

The rest of the bombers, the entire 2nd Unit of the formation consisting of 18 bombers, were unable to find the target through the clouds by the time their Unit flew over it, and they returned to our base with their bombs. This turned out to be hazardous . . .

Our landing procedure after we arrived over the home base was for each box to fly over our runway, then peel off one Box at a time, in order to enter the traffic pattern . . .

After I had landed my plane, parked the B-24 on the steel matted hardstand, cut the engines and got out of my plane, boxes from the 2nd Unit were still landing. I saw our plane's crew chief pointing excitedly into the air. I and the rest of my crew looked up in time to see two B-24s that had collided and both began to tumble down to the ground, out of control, in a horrible flaming crashing in front of us. One plane, with its tail almost gone, made a wide sweeping turn, and we didn't know where it would hit the ground around us. The other crashed down in front of us. Both planes hit the ground going almost straight down, in a huge fiery ball and explosion. There were some very anxious moments until we were certain the planes would not land on us because we were not near. One of the planes crashing injured a ground crewman . . .

I didn't know at the time that my two close buddies, 2nd Lt Gail J Scritchfield and bombardier 2nd Lt Edward J Heffner, both on Van Dyke's plane, were on board one of the aircraft that I was watching, nor did I know that both planes had their full load of bombs on board because they didn't drop on the target. There was only one survivor of the crash, S/Sgt Robert Gullet, tail gunner ... Gullet miraculously survived with only bruises and a broken leg.

Robert Capps flew the Consolidated B-24 Liberator. Although a slightly odd-looking aircraft – sometimes called the Flying Boxcar – it could carry a heavier load faster, higher and further than the famed B-17 Flying Fortress. Later in the war more armour and weapons were added for daylight operations over Germany. The problem of not finding a target was serious, confronting the pilots with the dilemma of either dropping their bombs at random to get rid of them or taking them back to base, with the possibility of accidents.

Sunday 28 May 1944

Lance Bombardier C. Morris faces the security clamp-down before D-Day

Lance Bombardier C. Morris served with No. 3 Troop of No. 6 Commando and kept a journal immediately before D-Day and during the landings. After the war he donated his journal to one of his commanding officers, Brigadier Derek Mills-Roberts, who was collecting historical material about the unit. It is now preserved in the Liddell Hart Centre for Military Archives. About Morris himself little is recorded.

At Southampton we were taken by troop transports to what turned out to be our final grouping center. This was a mass of tents on either side of the main road around which was a heavy barbed-wire fence. On entering we were shown to our troop areas and explained the whereabouts of the NAAFI and cinema, etc. The whole affair was organized and run by Yanks and seemed very good, the food being excellent. All the lads were amazed at the amount of white bread and other luxury foods that were available.

On the day of our arrival everyone was allowed out of camp, much to the dismay of the local inhabitants, for all the lads were walking around armed to the teeth with guns, knives, hatchets, and everything imaginable. The general direction appeared to be the beer houses, which soon ran dry, for they had not been prepared for anything like this. After all interest in the town was finished, everyone made tracks for camp again, where we found quite a change. During our absence it had been sealed and surrounded by security police, who now informed us of the camp orders which had been put into force, the most important of which was that we were not allowed to converse with any passing civilians and if any of the latter were caught they would be thrown into jail. Also we were not allowed to talk to any of the camp staff re any of our training, and the camp was filled with security personnel in many guises whose job was to catch you out if possible. All this could only mean one thing – that was It.

The weather was sweltering, and in a nearby park equipped with a swimming pool the local beauties were tripping around in swimsuits in full view and looked very tempting indeed. Three of the camp staff soon tired of this confinement and jumped it. They were missed on the evening roll call. A net was immediately thrown over the locality and a search made. The missing men were found in a beer house, which was immediately closed, and customers, proprietors, and deserters were thrown into jail, likewise a woman talking through the wire to her husband.

No chances whatever were being taken. On several occasions the Yankee guards, who were armed with .22 rifles, opened fire on civvies loitering near the wire.

In the approach to D-Day a great security blanket was thrown over southern England. Information was passed out to officers on a 'need to know' basis only. Those who needed to know were given a special clearance, codenamed Bigot. These regulations were policed by 'Bigot security officers' who watched for security slips. Their greatest scare was provided by the London Daily Telegraph, whose crossword puzzles contained repeated oblique references to D-Day information. During May its answers included both 'Utah' and 'Omaha', two of the code-names of landing beaches. This was followed by other key codenames including 'Mulberry' and 'Neptune'. The schoolmaster who had prepared the crosswords was arrested, but investigators eventually concluded the names had appeared by coincidence. In 1984 one of his pupils would reveal that the boys from his school hung around nearby camps and listened to the soldiers; when the schoolmaster had asked the boys for suggestions for the crossword, he'd been offered titbits from their amateur eavesdropping.

Tuesday 30 May – Thursday 1 June 1944

Evelyn Waugh, having recovered from a parachuting injury, reports for duty with the SAS

Evelyn Waugh had suffered an injury at the SOE parachute training school at Ringway airport outside Manchester and had been released on long leave to convalesce. He had used the time to write Brideshead Revisited, *which would be a huge success. Having recuperated, he now reported for duty.*

30 May

Today I returned, being assured by Bill Stirling that I might rest assured of as long as I needed to finish the book. I wrote in the afternoon during a refreshing storm of rain but in the evening came a telegram ordering me to Windsor to report before proceeding to my new unit. It is a great waste of time, energy, and money.

31 May

Travelled to London and thence to Windsor in order to be told the address of 2SAS Regiment to which I had written daily for weeks, which the Life Guard adjutant said was too secret for the post. I saw Basil [Bennett] for one minute in which he told me that Bill [Stirling] had been sacked [as commander of 2SAS] and succeeded by Brian [Franks]. It was hot and I was tired. I went to White's dined with Bill; the wine went to my head. I joined Hugh Sherwood. He had a drunken row with Kenneth Campbell, each saying to the other 'You're no gentleman, sir.' Then Hugh and I went to Pratt's where I was given some poisonous port, had great difficulty in walking home, fell down in my bedroom and was sick.

1 June

Woke half drunk and had a long, busy morning – getting my hair cut, trying to verify quotations in the London Library, which is still in disorder from its bomb, visiting Nancy. At luncheon I again got drunk. Went to the Beefsteak, which I have just joined, with Christopher and Freddy. Basil Dufferin stole my cab and made me miss my train to Chagford. Back to White's – more port. Ed Stanley arrived. Went to Waterloo in an alcoholic stupor, got the train to Exeter and slept most of the way. Arrived in poor shape at the Rougemont where I was well received and slept ill. I should add that I saw Brian who gave me leave to finish my book.

Evelyn Waugh

Although the place of the SAS in history is now assured, during the war most regular officers regarded it as a temporary and troublesome outfit. Its charismatic leaders, although brilliant on the battlefield, tended to feud when not actively employed, and relations with higher command formations were often tempestuous. Many SAS officers were former Commandos and former mess-companions of Evelyn Waugh, who accordingly secured a position with 2SAS. However, while they enjoyed Waugh's friendship, they did not rate him as a brother officer. Brian Franks was therefore happy to grant him extended leave, and even happier when Waugh received an offer of secondment to a mission to Yugoslavia, led by Churchill's irascible son Randolph. SEE ALSO PP. 24–5, 484–5 AND 768–9.

JUNE 1944

ON TUESDAY 6 JUNE, in the early hours, paratroops and gliders began to land behind enemy lines in France. The USAAF and RAF bombed coastal defences while British, Commonwealth, French and American troops landed along a 60-mile stretch of the Normandy coast. The initial D-Day invasion force consisted of 4,000 ships and 10,000 aircraft. By nightfall, 156,000 troops had landed. The following day British forces had reached Bayeux, about six miles inland from the Normandy coast, and all beachheads were reported as secure.

Deception measures had confused the German defenders, who were expecting an attack at Calais rather than Normandy. American forces were therefore able to cut the main road and rail links on the Cherbourg peninsula with ease. It was only on 9 June that Rommel finally ordered all German forces in Normandy onto the defensive. By mid-June the Allies were flying from French airfields for the first time since 1940.

By Wednesday 14 June the front was wide enough and deep enough for extensive battlefield tourism. King George VI and General de Gaulle made separate tours of the Normandy front.

Many other dignitaries wished to have their photos taken on the beachhead and the rush had to be restrained. The active support given by the French resistance prompted German reprisals, and on Saturday 10 June SS troops murdered most of the population of Oradour-sur-Glane. This inflamed the resistance who then made counter-reprisals against the Germans in the coming weeks and months. By July many resistance units – often known as the French Forces of the Interior or FFI – had declared open season on Germans, even those trying to surrender.

The first V-1 flying bomb flew over Britain on 13 June just after four in the morning, landing at Swanscombe in Kent at 0418. Three days later the V-1 offensive began in earnest as almost 100 were fired across the Channel. Whitehall panicked and responded to this event with an uneasy silence, the resulting lack of public information causing anger and anxiety. It was a week before the authorities released official details of the new rocket weapons. V-1s could be shot down by anti-aircraft fire and the AA gunners decided to christen them 'doodlebugs'.

At the end of the month the last sections of Cherbourg surrendered, together with 6,000 prisoners on the Cherbourg peninsula. Heavy bombing had damaged the port and it was three weeks before it was operational and could receive supplies. Nevertheless, by then the Allies had contrived to land half a million vehicles, 2 million men, and 4 million tons of supplies to support the invasion of northern France.

In Italy the Allies had already captured Rome and began advancing towards Florence. The Red Army was pushing through Belorussia towards Minsk; assisted by the Normandy invasion which was draining all the German reserves, its rate of advance increased.

Sunday 4 – Monday 5 June 1944

Admiral Sir Bertram Ramsay watches the weather before D-Day

Admiral Sir Bertram Ramsay was the Allied Naval Commander for Operation Overlord, the naval operation that would culminate on D-Day – which eventually proved to be Tuesday 6 June. Ramsay was an ideal figure to head such a massive naval operation: a meticulous planner and also a sophisticated operator who tended to smooth over command difficulties rather than generating friction. This was a rare skill among the top Anglo-American commanders, where ego was often a problem.

4 June

Commanders met here at 0415 to hear the latest weather report which was bad. The low cloud predicted would prohibit the use of airborne troops, prohibit the majority of air action including air spotting [for naval bombardment]. The sea conditions were unpromising but not prohibitive. I pointed out we had only accepted a daylight assault on the understanding that overwhelming air & naval bombardment would be available to overcome the enemy coast and beach defences. S.A.C [Eisenhower] therefore decided to postpone assault for 24 hours. Forces U & O would have started and must be recalled. The weather got progressively worse from midday, having been lovely at 0415 making the decision to postpone more difficult. As the day went on the forecast became more fully justified. Force U had a bad time regaining shelter & will have suffered great discomfort. No enemy reactions. At 2100 held another Comd[rs] conference at which the weather prophets were more optimistic & we decided to continue with the operation as ordered. The grounds were not too good and we were obviously taking a big chance but it seemed to be Tuesday or not this week at all. When informed, all Naval Force Comdr[s] showed great concern.

5 June

Held a final meeting at 0415. This time the prophets came in smiling, conditions having shown a considerable improvement. It was, therefore, decided to let things be and proceed. The wind was still fresh and it is clear that Forces will have an uncomfortable initial journey, improving as the day proceeds. Thus has been made the vital and crucial decision to stage and start this great enterprise which will, I hope, be the immediate means of bringing about the downfall of Germany's fighting power and Nazi oppression and an early cessation of hostilities. I am under no delusions as to the risks involved in this most difficult of all operations and the critical period around H Hour when, if initial flights are held up, success will be in the balance. We must trust in our invisible assets to tip the balance in our favour and to allow the landings to proceed without interruption. We shall require all the help that God can give us and I cannot believe that this will not be forthcoming.

The last days of May 1944 had been 'boiling hot', but on Thursday 1 June, as D-Day approached, the mercury was falling and Ramsay noted that this was probably the precursor 'of the storm to follow'. On Friday 2 and Saturday 3 June the weather was fair 'locally', but looked worrying over the landing beaches. Ramsay noted that Eisenhower knew that the consequences of postponement would be 'frightful' and so decided not to call off the preparations but instead to call a conference for the next day, Sunday 4 June at 0415. As we can see, things improved through the Sunday and the Monday. Tuesday 6 June was indeed D-Day and Ramsay wrote in his diary, 'The sky was clear, thank God,' noting that this would allow the crucial bombing of enemy positions to go well. The intriguing mention of 'invisible assets' was undoubtedly a reference to the secret services' elaborate deception plan Fortitude, designed to persuade the Germans that the real attack would be focused on Calais, and also to check via Allied signals intelligence whether the German commanders had taken this carefully prepared bait.

D-Day – Tuesday 6 June 1944

David K. Bruce of OSS watches the shore bombardment off Utah Beach

David Bruce was the London head of the Office of Strategic Services, the American wartime intelligence service. He had spent the early months of 1944 building up his organization ready for the Normandy invasion, and in May and June escorted General William J. Donovan, the overall head of OSS, during his visit to Britain. On 30 May 1944 they had travelled to Plymouth, where the harbour was brimming with American vessels, and boarded an American destroyer, part of Task Force 122 under Admiral Kirk. On Tuesday 6 June Bruce found himself on board the USS Tuscaloosa, with 1,200 officers and men, moored off Utah beach.

At 6:30 am the bombing of the Utah beachhead ceases; our troops start ashore, and land at 7:00. Of this phase we can see little, except that once a small ship was hit near the beach and thrown about 200 feet into the air. Meanwhile there is cannonading on all sides as well as from the shore. Spouts of water rise from near the ships as German long-range batteries try to reach them. The Black Prince is bracketed and hit, and calls for a smoke screen, 2 planes skim the water and interpose a billowing blanket of cloud between it and the shore. One of the planes, however, is hit and seems to skid along the water's surface until it bursts into a glowing ball and then disappears. Closer in, one sees the darting red tongues of the destroyers' guns. Bilious yellow clouds of smoke shoot forth above the mouths of our guns. Aboard the Tuscaloosa, the air is acrid with powder, and a fine spray of disintegrated wadding comes down on us like lava ash. Everywhere there is noise. When we fire, the deck trembles under our feet, and the joints of the ship seem to creak and stretch. When a whole turret is discharged the teeth almost rattle in one's head. At 7:10 am the US Destroyer Corry has been hit and may have to be beached. She had previously been damaged on her way to her station by dropping a depth charge in shallow water against a suspected submarine. At the same time, a periscope was reported seen 1,000 yards from the Tuscaloosa. Some landing craft, having put their troops ashore, are returning – a good sign. A beach fire control party, or parties, has sent conflicting messages to the Shubrite, one that it is firing into our own men, another asking that it maintain its present attack. The Corry has now partially sunk, and will be replaced in her hot spot by the Butler. Communications between the ships are constant, by radio, telephone, by electric lamp signalling, by key, and even by wig-wag [flag signals]. For security reasons, the radio is used as little as possible. At 8:30 am the Tuscaloosa had run out of targets for the time being. Four heavy enemy guns are shelling our troops on the beaches, but a landing has been effected and reinforcements are pouring in. The Hawkins, as well as the Black Prince, received direct hits early in the engagement, but have continued firing, and each has knocked out at least two enemy batteries. The most serious casualty thus far on the Tuscaloosa has been a direct hit by something on General D's water closet, adjoining the Admiral's cabin – at any rate, it is completely shattered and in ruins on the floor. When our own guns are discharged the noise is terrific, and without cotton in one's ears would be deafening. We have undergone thus far no attacks by enemy planes, nor have we seen any. There is now, at 9:50 am, a complete lull as far as this ship is concerned, and we have not been under enemy fire for sometime – the last salvo against us was distant about 2,000 yards. The Tuscaloosa is beginning to look rather forlorn in the officers' quarters. Repeated concussions have driven screws out of their sockets, shattered light bulbs, thrown articles all over the floors, and generally made an awful mess. 10:00 am. A Spitfire in trouble lost altitude, gliding down to what seemed a perfect landing but, after a second, nosed under water and disappeared. 10:30 am. We are again being fired upon. The first shell was at 2,500 yards and then successively they hit at 2,000, 1,500, 1,000, 500 and 50 yards. After the last, and just in time, for the next shell fell in our anchorage, we shifted position and shelled them back.

The ship had been sealed since leaving port in Belfast for security rea-
sons. Large numbers of transport aircraft, returning from dropping their
paratroops in France, passed overhead. They opened fire at 5.45 a.m.
and exchanged fire with shore batteries. Most of the ships were only
2,000–3,000 yards offshore and well within enemy range. Their task
was to silence no fewer than thirty-eight batteries of 75mm guns, and
they fired for most of the day. By the end of 6 June Tuscaloosa *had*
suffered minor damage as a result of structural pressure caused by the
continual firing of the guns, and the crews were completely exhausted.
SEE ALSO PP. 701–3 AND 732–3.

Anne Frank, aged fifteen, hiding in the 'secret annexe' in Amsterdam

Anne Frank was born in Frankfurt into a Jewish family, with whom she
had fled Germany for Holland in 1933 in order to escape the Nazi
persecution. She was thirteen years old when she joined her sister and
parents and four other people hiding from the Germans in a 'secret
annexe' at the back of an Amsterdam office building. They hid there
successfully for two years. In June 1944 their spirits were lifted by news
of the Allied invasion of Europe.

'This is D-Day,' came the announcement over the British
radio and quite rightly, 'This is *the* day.' The invasion has
begun!

The British announced the news at eight o'clock this
morning: Calais, Boulogne, Le Havre and Cherbourg, also
the Pas de Calais (as usual) were heavily bombarded.
Moreover, as a safety measure for all occupied territories,
everyone living within a radius of 35 kilometres from the
coast has been told to prepare for bombardments . . .

Great commotion on the 'Secret Annexe'! Would the long-
awaited liberation that has been talked of so much, but
which still seems *too* wonderful, *too* much like a fairy-tale,
ever come true? We don't know yet, but hope is revived
within us: it gives us fresh courage, and makes us strong
again. Since we must put up bravely with all the fears,

privations, and sufferings, the great thing now is to remain calm and steadfast. Now more than ever we must clench our teeth and not cry out. France, Russia, Italy and Germany, too, can all cry out and give vent to their misery, but we haven't the right to do that yet!

Oh, Kitty, the best part of the invasion is that I have the feeling that our friends are approaching. We have been oppressed by those terrible Germans for so long, they have had their knives at our throats, that the thought of friends and delivery fill us with confidence!

Now it doesn't concern the Jews anymore; no, it concerns Holland and all occupied Europe. Perhaps, Margot says, I may yet be able to go back to school in September or October.

In August 1944 Anne Frank's family would be betrayed and taken by the Germans. Anne and her sister were separated from the rest of their family and would die of typhus in Bergen-Belsen concentration camp in February 1945. Their father, Otto Frank, was the only member of her family to survive, released when Russian troops liberated the camp where he was interned at the end of the war. When he returned home he was given his daughter's diary by Miep Gies, one of the family's helpers, who had salvaged papers from the house after they had been arrested. It was published in Dutch two years later. It has since been republished countless times and is perhaps the most widely read book on war and persecution.

D-Day + 1 – Wednesday 7 June 1944

David K. Bruce lands on Utah Beach and discusses capture with William J. Donovan

The Quincy is going back to England this afternoon to reload with ammunition. This afternoon at 4pm General D and myself clambered down a swinging ladder on the Tuscaloosa and boarded a launch. We were accompanied by the aviators who were picked up this morning, by Shadel, and by the 3 corpses. We boarded a Destroyer Escort vessel (the 695,

Captain Michel) which took us near the convoy concentration point. There an LCV (Landing Craft Vehicle), conducted by a swarthy boy from Chicago, was persuaded to take us near the Utah beach, where we transshipped to a Duck which took us ashore. As we reached the middle of the beach there was the drone of airplane motors and almost immediately afterwards machine gun fire as they swept immediately over us down the beach. The General, accustomed to such emergencies, rolled nimbly off the hood where we were sitting, onto the sand. I, with slower reflexes, followed, and fell squarely on General D, gashing his chin with my helmet. As the machinegun bullets spattered the Duck's hood, the General grinned happily and said, 'Now it will be like this all the time.' ... At this time he wore, and it was the only occasion when I knew him to do so, the ribbon of the [Congressional] Medal of Honor, in those days everywhere recognizable.

We sauntered inland to an American antiaircraft battery, the farthermost position occupied by our people in that sector. Beyond was a huge open field, enclosed at the far end by a tight hedge. In the field, three presumably French peasants approached the battery and he said he was going forward to question his three French agents, who were expecting him. The captain, looking at his bloody throat and the Congressional medal, warned him this was dangerous, but let him proceed.

As we progressed, our alleged agents disappeared; Donovan and I came to a halt in the lee of a hedgerow that was being subjected to intermittent German machine-gun fire. Flattened out, the general turned to me and said: 'David, we mustn't be captured, we know too much.' 'Yes, sir,' I answered mechanically. 'Have you your pill?' he demanded. I confessed I was not carrying the instantaneous death pellet concocted by our scientific adviser. 'Never mind,' replied the resourceful general, 'I have two of them.' Thereupon, still lying prone, he disgorged the contents of all his pockets. There were a number of old hotel keys, a passport, currency of several nationalities, photographs of grandchildren, travel orders, newspaper clippings, and heaven knows what else, but no pills. 'Never mind,' said Donovan, 'we can do without them, but if we get out of here you must send a message to Gibbs, the hall porter at Claridge's in London, telling him on no account to allow the servants in the hotel to touch some dangerous medicines in my bathroom.'

This humanitarian disposition having been made, Donovan whispered to me: 'I must shoot first.' 'Yes, sir,' I responded, 'but can we do much against machine guns with our pistols?' 'Oh, you don't understand,' he said. 'I mean if we are about to be captured, I'll shoot you first. After all, I am your commanding officer.'

By 7 June William J. Donovan had become restless. Dressed in an olive-green skullcap and rubber-soled shoes he wanted to see the battlefield and insisted on going ashore. During the First World War Donovan had been America's most highly decorated soldier and so relished the sound of gunfire, but his escort, David Bruce, was less sure that being shot at was enjoyable. Getting ashore was not difficult because things had gone well at Utah and resistance had been light, but limited numbers of enemy fighters were still active. American forces were already some miles inland. SEE ALSO PP. 698–700 AND 732–3.

Tuesday 13 – Tuesday 20 June 1944

Michael Hoskin, schoolboy aged thirteen, observes the new V-1 raids on London

Michael Hoskin observed the beginning of V-1 attacks in mid-June 1944. Although his school had been evacuated to Old Windsor, one of the first V-1 rockets overshot its target and damaged the Bells of Ouseley public house close by. Many teenage boys performed a vital observing and warning role at this time. Stationed on factory roofs and vantage points, they scanned the sky for V-1s, and if they appeared to be on course for their location they pressed a buzzer or rang a bell to warn people to take cover. On this basis life could continue with a degree of normality, despite the frequent buzz of approaching V-1s. Michael recalled that he did his homework every evening in a bedroom with a window looking out towards the south-east, the direction from which the

V-1 attacks came. Because they flew straight it was possible to tell at a glance whether they posed any danger to his immediate vicinity. Those who could only hear the V-1, but could not see it, were left in a state of anxiety. So Michael kept a bell by his desk which he rang to alert his family and neighbours if they needed to take cover. At night they all retreated to a neighbour's purpose-built underground shelter which had an additional emergency exit in case the main exit was blocked by rubble.

On Tuesday, 13 June, 1944, the Germans used for the first time one of their most successful 'secret weapons'. It was a crewless, jet-propelled bomber, and it flew so fast that no fighter could keep up with it and no gun fire at it accurately. Londoners rushed for the tin-hats, gas-masks and shelters. Through the night flew these purring ghosts, with no guiding hand at the controls, and no crew with human frailties.

Then, in the morning, emerging dog-tired from the shelters, when we saw the damage done, and the lives lost, we made a resolution to spend the next night in the shelter. All day the sirens wailed, and all day these untouchable ghosts. Loaded with bombs, flew in a straight line over our head to there [*sic*] targets.

DATE	DAY	TIME S.	TIME F.	VVV	REMARKS
13: 6	Tu	04:00	04:15	?	No incidents
		04:30	04:45	?	No incidents
15: 6	Th	23:40	09:25	?	Longest raid since the blitz. Very heavy gun-fire.
					Bells of Ouseley destroyed. Streatham and Croydon hit . . .

By 20 June Michael was recording the arrival of a 'large number of planes in the early hours'. V-1 attacks were soon occurring round the clock, and the long journey home from school in far-away Windsor was filled with anxiety. Had his house been hit? As he made his way home through the streets, still at some distance from his own house, he would begin to look for newly broken glass which would tell him if his area had

been hit by a V-1 during his absence that day. In June alone Michael recorded, with his customary precision, that there had been 28 raids lasting a total of 80 hours and 55 minutes, with each raid lasting an average of 2 hours and 53 minutes. In fact V-1s were vulnerable to fighters and gunfire, and many were being destroyed over the south coast. SEE ALSO PP. 656–9.

Friday 16 – Friday 30 June 1944

Katherine Moore, a teacher, sees exams being taken under fire from doodlebugs

Katherine Moore was an English teacher who lived in a rented house in a pleasant eighteenth-century street in Sevenoaks, Kent. Her children had just left school and her husband worked in London.

16 June

Discovered that the row last night was from the Germans' new weapon – pilotless planes. Found chaos at school: no one had slept much. It was decided not to send the boarders away for half term and it was given out that no one was to leave the school buildings without permission. Completely by chance my first lesson was 'Julius Caesar' and the first speech to be read was from Act 2 Scene 2:

'Nor heaven nor earth have been at peace tonight.
. . . Think you to walk forth?
You shall not stir out of your house today.
. . . Fierce fiery warriors fight upon the clouds
In ranks and squadrons and right forms of war
The noise of battle hurtled in the air.'

. . . Slept in shelter from 1.30 am not very well. Sleeping under the Morrison shelter is very oppressive . . .

30 June

Raids have been going on pretty continuously. It is very tiring at school and difficult teaching underground in the stuffy dark trenches crouched on the wire bunks. A good many of the children have now been sent away to safer districts. The poor School Certificate and Higher Certificate candidates had to do their exam papers either in the trenches or, if in the classrooms, to get down under their desk tables each time a bomb came over – sometimes five times in one paper! I was invigilating for an art exam when the form had to disappear several times beneath the desks and I saw one arm after another stretch out and up, grab their paper and paint brush and continue on the ground.

The continual spotting duty is very trying – air raid warnings are often too late for doodle bugs and so a member of the staff is always outside in the grounds on guard. It is anxious work, especially when there is a high wind, for what with that and our own aircraft it is hard to distinguish sounds. I gave the alarm the other morning and everyone rushed for shelter and it turned out only to be the motor mower on the recreation grounds nearby!

The whole of June has been a month of deep, grey gloom and oppression. At school the staff are getting curt and short-tempered: poor Miss Ramsay, responsible for all those children, is noticeably and understandably so. There have been only three fine days in the whole month, none of which I wasted I am glad to say for on one I biked to lovely Penshurst, on another walked to Magpie Bottom and on the third I had tea with Mary and the babies in the garden. The consistent bad weather has been the best possible for the doodle bugs and the worst for our invasion operations.

By 1944 many had given up on the old Anderson shelters which had sprung up in over 2 million gardens in 1940. Although they provided a good level of protection they could be cold and damp, and in low-lying areas tended to fill with water. The preferred form of protection became the indoor Morrison shelter.

Katherine Moore would survive the war and publish several novels.

Saturday 17 June 1944

Charles Ritchie, a Canadian diplomat based in London,
reaches the Mulberry temporary harbour at Arromanches

It was my first experience of the machine-like precision of the
landing arrangements about which we read in the newspapers. The troops in the end were landed but there was
nothing very machine-like in the process. By hollering from
the bridge at every passing small craft asking for aid and by an
exchange of insults with those who refused it, some craft
which should no doubt have been taking troops off another
landing craft was pressed into our service. Eventually, however, in the midst of shouts, orders and counter-orders, we
reached a pontoon bridge and remained stuck there until
night-time when we got free and tied up to the bridge.

There is no natural harbour at Arromanches. The artificial
harbour which has been constructed is known as the
Mulberry and was full of small shipping – the bigger ships
ride at anchor outside. It was crowded with troopships, a
variety of landing craft, tankers, munition and supply ships
and small tugs in which are seated majors with megaphones
who are supposed to have some control over the movements
of the shipping. They dash about like sheepdogs. The majors
shout down their megaphones in gloomy authoritative tones
at the small craft which crowd the Mulberry telling them
they must move out of this berth or tie up to that ship and
above all keep a safe distance from their precious pontoon
bridge which is their chief concern. The captains and crews
of the hounded small craft curse and protest but in the end
do as they are told.

*During 1942, when the Allies had started to think about the future
invasion of mainland Europe, they realized that they could not be sure
to capture a port in the early stages of the campaign. Accordingly, it was
decided that two artificial harbours would be developed near the
Normandy beachhead, one for the British at Arromanches and the other
for the Americans at St Laurent. Codenamed Mulberry, the mobile*

harbours were constructed from metal-framed concrete caissons called Phoenixes. These huge sections had been towed by tugs across to France and, once laid out, had been sunk to provide a firm foundation on the seabed. Eventually some 150 caissons were built. On 4 June tugs began towing the completed sections towards Normandy, travelling at about 3 knots. On 7 June – D+1 – the Phoenixes were brought to about a mile of the shore and turned over to a fleet of harbour tugs. However, both Mulberries were badly damaged by dreadful storms which swept the Channel during late June.

Ritchie had travelled to Arromanches to report on the circumstances of the many Canadian troops – a sensitive matter after the heavy losses suffered by Canada in the Dieppe raid of 1942. He continued his diplomatic career after the war, becoming Canadian ambassador to the United States in 1964. SEE ALSO PP. 33–4 AND 223–4.

Monday 26 June 1944

Sergeant Richard Greenwood, British tank commander, at Cheux

Sergeant Richard Greenwood commanded a Churchill tank in 'C' squadron, 9th Royal Tank Regiment, supporting the 9th Cameronians in an attack near Cheux twenty days after D-Day. He discovered that the lanes, woods and hedgerows of Normandy provided the Germans with good defensive positions, and their 88mm anti-tank guns took a heavy toll.

We took up our position in a large field below the crest of the hill: 5p.m. Our infantry were in position too – some hundreds of them. A sturdy looking crowd – mostly Scotties – all smiling and cheerful. They asked us to swipe the hell out of Jerry. We were thoroughly conversant with the plan of attack and ultimate directive. We also had a pretty good idea of where enemy's main anti-tank guns were, from previous reconnaissance. Close to our zero hour, word came through that 60 Panthers had appeared within a few hundred yards of our line of advance. Hell's bells! Poor little 'C' Squadron.

Before we started the Panthers advanced on our position and were engaged by some fairly heavy stuff – 17 pounders. After about an hour Jerry retired. He certainly didn't get through. We commenced our delayed start at 6.15 p.m. Infantry ahead, rifles at the ready. By 7 p.m. the battle was on. A/Tk guns were firing like hell and so were we. Very soon I saw one crew bale out, tank on fire. They crawled away in the long corn avoiding jerry snipers and MG. Advance proceeded. Infantry kept 'going to ground' because of Jerry MGs. We sprayed those woods with BESA. Tons of it and HE and Smoke. Impossible to see A/Tk guns in woods. Could only find there 'flash'. Advance proceeded slowly. Two or three Jerry tanks appeared, all were engaged. They disappeared. More of ours were hit. Some burning, crews bailing out. Found myself behaving rationally and quite calm. Was really terrified just prior to 'going in'. Eventually, we retired waited. It seemed like hours to me. We were on the battlefield all the time.

Even in the summer of 1944 the Allies were still struggling to produce armour that equalled the German tanks, and the 'up-gunned' Sherman Firefly with a 17-pounder was one of the few vehicles that proved effective. Allied air superiority helped to tip the balance.

Sergeant Greenwood survived the war but little is known about him thereafter.

JULY 1944

D URING JULY ALLIED forces broke out of the Normandy beach-head and advanced into northern France. After an extremely heavy pre-bombardment by aircraft and by the battleship HMS *Rodney*, British and Canadian troops captured Caen. Good German defensive positions made these operations very costly. Tanks broke through the German lines at St Lo and fanned out across northern France, capturing Rennes; on 6 August they would reach Nantes. As the dreadful weather gradually improved, Allied air attacks prevented the Germans from reinforcing their lines. Orléans fell to the Allies on 17 August.

The Allied governments, now more optimistic about the outcome of the war, held a conference at Bretton Woods in New Hampshire to seek agreement on the post-war international financial system. Some of the building blocks of the post-war world economy were laid down here, notably in proposals for an International Monetary Fund and an International Bank for Reconstruction and Development (later called the World Bank) to avert currency problems and liberalize constraints on the world economy.

A group of dissident military officers in the German army attempted to kill Adolf Hitler at his East Prussian headquarters in Rastenburg. Senior staff officers in Berlin, such as General Halder and General Beck, were actively involved, and many others were aware of what was afoot. On 20 July a bomb was planted at his military headquarters by Count von Stauffenberg. The bomb exploded but by chance Hitler escaped the full force of the blast and suffered only slight injuries. In response he mounted a major purge against the German resistance. Thousands of officers were shot, arrested or retired.

On 3 July Soviet troops captured Minsk. At the end of the month Moscow rejected the claim to legitimacy of the Polish government-in-exile in London and officially recognized the Polish Committee of National Liberation – the so-called 'Lublin Poles' – as the official Polish government. The Russians helped organize this new government in Moscow and concluded an agreement with it for the administration of liberated Polish territory.

On 6 July Churchill finally made a statement explaining the phenomenon of the V-1 'doodlebugs', and admitted that over 2,700 had been launched, causing 11,000 dead and injured so far.

Remarkably, despite the growing pressure on transport and other resources, operations at Germany's concentration camps continued. In July all the Jews living on Corfu were sent to the Greek mainland and placed on trains to Auschwitz. The conditions of travel were so terrible that only half of those sent arrived alive.

Wednesday 5 July 1944

Harold Nicolson talks with Anthony Eden about Churchill and de Gaulle

Harold Nicolson was born in 1891 and was the son of a serving diplomat. He too entered the Foreign Office and attended the Versailles peace conference in 1919. After the First World War he married Vita Sackville-West and began a career as a biographer. In the 1930s he toyed briefly with Oswald Mosley's 'New Party'. During the war he was an MP, a junior minister at the Ministry of Information and a governor of the BBC. This work brought him into close contact with the Free French in London.

Anthony begins by telling me about his bitter battles on behalf of de Gaulle. The Prime Minister had invited de Gaulle to come over here for the big battle of France. On 4th June, Winston and he [Eden] had gone down in a special train to near Portsmouth. De Gaulle and his own party came there by car and Anthony went to meet them. Then they lunched in the train and Winston produced champagne and drank to health of France. Roosevelt had said that de Gaulle was not to be told the plan of operations, but Winston ignored that, told him everything, took him across to see Eisenhower and forced the latter to show him the maps. Not one word of thanks from de Gaulle. Winston, feeling rather hurt, said, 'I thought it only fitting that you should be present with us today.' 'I see' said de Gaulle glumly; 'I was invited as a symbol.' Viénot and Béthouart were in despair. Anthony was almost beside himself, feeling that Winston was deeply moved emotionally by the thought of the occasion, and that de Gaulle's ungraciousness would make him dislike the man all the more. Finally Winston asked de Gaulle to dine with him. 'Thank you. I should prefer to dine alone with my staff.' 'I feel chilled', said Winston to Anthony.

Nicolson was perfectly placed to observe the appalling relations between Charles de Gaulle and his Anglo-Saxon allies. Churchill and Eden found de Gaulle infuriating but both recognized that he was vital to the reconstruction of western Europe and also to the defence of the European empires against American plans for their dissolution. By late 1944 Franklin D. Roosevelt, who liked de Gaulle even less than Churchill did, would agree to meet him in Washington – a sign of France's reviving power.

Monday 10 July 1944

Harry C. Butcher records discussion between Eisenhower and his chief of staff, Walter Bedell Smith, on what to do with German leaders after the war

Ike repeated his views that the German General Staff regards this war and the preceding one as merely campaigns in their dogged determination first to dominate Europe and eventually the world. He would exterminate all the General Staff. Or maybe they could be concentrated on some appropriate St Helena.

Beetle [Bedell Smith] chimed in that imprisonment would not accomplish anything. It would simply lead to eventual release of the prisoners because in six or eight years our own publics again would grow softhearted and conciliatory. Halifax asked Ike how many officers are on the German General Staff. Ike guessed about 3500. He added he would include for liquidation leaders of the Nazi party from mayors on up and all members of the Gestapo.

There was agreement that extermination could be left to nature if the Russians had a free hand. Ike added that justice would be done if zones of influence in Germany could be temporarily assigned to the small nations overrun by Hitler. He would give Russia the largest portion and other areas to the Czechs, Yugoslavs, Poles, Danes, Norwegians, Greeks, and the French.

*A vigorous debate was beginning to develop about what to do with or
'to' Germany when it had been defeated. This curious outburst on the
part of Eisenhower, while talking to Bedell Smith, seems out of character.
In fact, Eisenhower had something of an obsession with destroying the
German military staff, its training and its records. During the Potsdam
conference of August 1945 he would advocate very strong measures in
this area to Truman, intending to make it impossible for the German
military machine ever to function again. Others would argue for
'pastoralization', which would have meant removing all heavy industry
from Germany and rendering its economy largely agricultural. SEE ALSO
PP. 27, 469–70, 544–6 AND 561–3.*

Tuesday 18 July 1944

Robert Boscawen's tank unit joins Operation Goodwood outside Caen

*Robert Boscawen was the fourth son of the 8th Viscount Falmouth and
had been educated at Eton and Trinity College, Cambridge. As one of the
youngest officers in the elite Guards Armoured Division, he recorded
the bitter battles in the bocage, the densely wooded countryside of
Normandy.*

It was a clear grey dawn with no mist. I woke up about six
and lay waiting for the day to start. Suddenly the silence was
broken by the crash of a nearby medium battery, followed by
a rising crescendo of guns, soon breaking into a roar all along
the line. A minute or two later the heavy drone of bombers
could be heard. And there they came, hundreds of them,
sweeping in from the coast in an endless untidy stream, protected by a few Spitfire, flashing and wheeling like hawks
high above them. Soon they were over their target, red sparks
and white puffs of flak were going up all round them, and
then one heard the muffled crumps of their bombs. The air
boomed and the ground shook as these showered down,
while a dense cloak of grey dust rose slowly over the battlefield. Soon nothing but a continuous roar could be heard. The
game was on, the umpire had said 'Play'.

For a few minutes I lay and watched them going over, and then threw my blanket off and got up, encouraging my crew to make some breakfast and wash. I saw Hugo and the Sergeant-Major, all slightly staggered at the size of the bombardment. On and on came the bombers, Lancasters and Halifaxes, then one fell victim to the flak; with an orange flame and black smoke it fell like a stone to the ground . . .

Breakfast of two sausages and tea, then we cleared up and got the tank ready. At a quarter to eight we broke wireless silence and 'netted' the sets. Whittle, my operator, had switched on and I could hear Oliver H checking the battalion net. Then came the familiar whine of the starter-motor, one or two coughs, a bang, and a roar as Jepson warmed her up.

Around eight the 11th Armoured moved forward and the barrage slowed down. A couple of shells landed quite close, so we mounted our tanks ready to go. Soon after eight the battalion moved off in a long column line-ahead.

We crossed the Orne on a pontoon bridge called 'Pegasus' and made across country for our start line. Even on a large-scale map I found it hard to know exactly where we were then, but we just followed blindly. Through the wrecked gliders of the 6th Airborne Division where they had landed on D-day we moved up to the start line . . .

We eventually crossed the start line through our own minefield and, still line-ahead, moved south. To our left was a battalion of the 11th, the Fife and Forfar Yeomanry, in Shermans, firing at some houses. What at I do not know, but they were all milling around firing shots at a blazing farm, so I traversed my gun vaguely in its direction. We passed over a lot of slit-trenches and pits full of dead and 'bomb-happy' Germans offering no resistance, though I had a grenade ready in hand to chuck in if anyone was truculent . . .

We passed Cuverville and Demouville on our right and crossed a railway line running east to west, having done about two miles advance . . .

Then we stopped. The Grenadiers in front had been held up somewhere, no one knew quite what was happening.

Later we discovered about eight of their tanks had fallen victim to 88 mms and other anti-tank guns, and Sir Arthur Grants, their No 2 Squadron Leader, had been killed. Our No 1 Squadron spread out in front and No 2 to the left flank. On our right was a blazing Sherman and a little further on some German Mark IVs, the most numerous and reliable of the enemy tanks. Oily black or white smoke poured out of the turrets and every joint in the armour . . .

No 1 Squadron came up with reports of three Panthers moving on the left. I scanned carefully with my binoculars but could see no movement in the trees about eight hundred yards away. Then Malcolm Lock reported a Panther opposite him and he got it with his Firefly, the 17-pounder Sherman. He did very well getting it, I heard afterwards, having stalked close; with one shot it 'brewed up' nicely.

Operation Goodwood was a disastrous British armoured offensive launched around Caen under the direction of Montgomery. After massive air bombardment, British tanks were deployed rather slowly and were delayed further by a bottleneck at the three bridges over the River Orne. Once they reached the battlefield, they ran into difficulties with extensive enemy and Allied minefields. The terrain was difficult and filled with little villages, each of which had a small German garrison of infantry, armour and artillery. The area was thus divided into a series of German strong-points overlooking the Allied line of advance, often deploying German 88mm anti-tank or AA guns pressed into the anti-tank role. Montgomery failed to achieve a breakthrough and the Germans lost just 100 tanks to an Allied loss of 413 tanks and over 5,500 men.

Robert Boscawen would fight from the beaches of Normandy to the battles deep inside Germany in April 1945. He suffered severe burns in this last stage of the war when his tank was destroyed but, having escaped from four such destroyed tanks in the course of less than a year, was awarded the Military Cross. After the war he would join the Red Cross civilian relief organization in Europe and later became a long-serving Conservative MP.

Thursday 20 July 1944

Marie Vassiltchikov, a Russian working in the German
foreign office, hears the first news of the July bomb plot
against Hitler

Could it be the *Konspiration*? (all that with the receiver in my
hand!) She whispered 'Yes! That's it! It's done. This morning!' Just then Percy replied. Still holding the receiver, I
asked: 'Dead?' She answered: 'Yes, dead!' I hung up, seized
her by the shoulders and we went waltzing around the
room. Then grabbing hold of some papers, I thrust them into
the first drawer and shouting to the porter that we were
'*dienstlich unterwegs*' ['off on official business'], we tore off to
the Zoo station. On the way out to Potsdam she whispered
to me the details and though the compartment was full, we
did not even try to hide our excitement and joy.

Count Claus Schenck von Stauffenberg, a Colonel on the
General Staff, had put a bomb at Hitler's feet during a conference at Supreme HQ at Rastenburg in East Prussia. It had
gone off and Adolf was dead. Stauffenberg had waited outside until the explosion and then, seeing Hitler being carried
out on a stretcher covered with blood, he had run to his car,
which had stood hidden somewhere, and with his ADC,
Werner von Haeften, had driven to the local airfield and
flown back to Berlin. In the general commotion nobody had
noticed his escape.

*Princess Marie Vassiltchikov was close to the anti-Nazi resistance. On
10 July 1944 she had dined with one of the key conspirators, Adam von
Trott, and afterwards he told her of the plans to put a bomb in Hitler's
Rastenburg HQ and explained that they were 'imminent'. In the hours
after the attack, the plotters were all convinced that Hitler had been
killed and were sure the dissident elements of the army were marching
on Berlin. In fact Hitler had been saved by part of a table which shielded
him from the bomb blast. Gradually the reality dawned on the hunters,
who became the hunted as the SS began the search for the plotters.*

Later that year Marie Vassiltchikov would leave her job at the Foreign

Office to become a Red Cross nurse in Austria, although she maintained her contacts with anti-Nazi Germans. Evading the advancing Red Army in 1945, she survived the war and lived until 1978. SEE ALSO PP. 619–20 AND 633–4.

Monday 24 – Tuesday 25 July 1944

James A. Dunn arrives in Belfast on the USS *Mason* and is made welcome

James A. Dunn was one of the four signalmen on the USS Mason, *a destroyer escort that worked with convoys in the Atlantic and the Mediterranean in the closing years of the war. The* Mason *was unique in that most of its crew were African Americans – indeed, it was the only American wartime ship to employ them in roles other than cook or mess-mate. Nevertheless, all the officers were white.*

In the winter of 1943–4 Dunn had been sent to destroyer escort school in Norfolk, Virginia. Norfolk was a segregated base and typically the black crewmen were denied entrance through the front door of the base movie theatre, being forced to enter through the back door. Their commander reversed the policy.

24 July

Early this morning we finished delivering the rest of the convoy and proceeded to a port close by. We arrived in Belfast, Ireland, about seven thirty this morning and it is really a beautiful seaport town. I've often read of towns like these but this is my first time of ever seeing it. It looks like something you see in movies. I don't know if we will get liberty here or not but all of us sure need it. We have been out to sea for forty-four days without seeing a person or land. We would like to pick up some souvenirs if possible. They finally granted the second section of our crew liberty this afternoon from one o'clock until eight Tuesday morning and the boys really deserve every bit of it and more. I think the ship is getting worse all the time, because some of the officers try to run their departments and others too. Some of them don't want to give you credit for knowing anything at all. Most of the crew have gone ashore. Our ship pulled up in the City of Belfast and some of the Irishmen came alongside of our ship and talked for quite a while. They wanted American cigarettes and candy. They say that the city is fine. They are very friendly. I know why people come to Europe: because of the beautiful scenery and things are rather cheap. So the night passes away.

25 July

About five of us went out on liberty today and had a nice time. Everyone treats you very nice. Colour doesn't mean a thing to them. In fact they like all of the coloured soldiers and sailors far better than the white. Quite a few of the coloured soldiers have married girls over here. The white sailors and soldiers from the states have tried to poison the minds of the Irish people against the Negro but they found out that they had lied and now the people won't hardly speak to a white sailor. All of the coloured soldiers have moved into France for the invasion, and the people hated to see them leave. The Negro is treated better anyplace but the United States.

Although African Americans had served in the US navy from the Revolution of 1776, they had been excluded from all but the lowliest positions on ships during the early twentieth century. This changed in June 1942, partly in response to pressure from civil rights campaigners but also because of a shortage of men. SEE ALSO PP. 763–4.

Thursday 27 July 1944

Peggy Ryle copes with a family crisis alone and begins to lose hope that her husband, a missing RAF pilot, is alive

A terrible day, dearest. I left Andover at 7.21 am and arrived at Hampden House [boarding school] at 12.30. Mrs Robley Browne [headmistress] was very charming but says there is no doubt Day has told two girls in her bedroom all about lesbianism. Half the school seems to know about it and she can't keep her. She apparently was told by a girl who left last term. Isn't it too ghastly? Mrs RB thinks she should be at home with me and go to a day school. Goodness knows how I shall manage, but I cannot go to town until the Doodles stop she cannot start school until then. Oh, Georgie, I am so miserable, I did not sleep a wink last night. I do so wish you were here to help me through this. The great difficulty is going to be keeping it from Don and the family. Mrs RB has agreed to say anything that will help Day, because she also agrees that it would be dreadful for her if anyone found out.

Had a letter tonight from Group Captain Combes. He is not hopeful about you now darling, after three months. Please dear God they are all wrong. I think if anything else happens I shall not be able to stand it. If I was sure you were dead I would try and come to you.

Tomorrow I pick up Sally. I have had a talk with Day and told her I will try and do all I can for her, but she must not let Sally know or say anything about the whole business ever again. Wouldn't it be dreadful if she did tell Sally? Oh I feel so sick about it all.

Goodnight my own and God bless you. I forgot to tell you we caught the 5 pm train back from Waterloo. Doodles overhead twice while we were at the station.

Peggy Ryle's elder daughter, Day, attended a small boarding school that was temporarily based in Hampden House, an Elizabethan country house close to the Prime Minister's residence at Chequers in Buckinghamshire. Paranoia about lesbianism was not unusual during the 1940s, especially within educational establishments. Day seemed none the worse for her expulsion from boarding school and the next day went to the pictures with her aunt. She was 'laughing and talking away' as if nothing had happened. Nevertheless, Peggy Ryle felt the burden of dealing with these issues alone and on 29 July she wrote: 'Missing you more and more every day and hope is getting less and less.' Two months later, on 26 September, still maintaining her diary, Peggy would note, 'I feel a little scrap of hope tonight.' But the next day she was told that the wreckage of Georgie's aircraft had been located and that he was one of 'five unidentifiable bodies'. Her diary ends here with the words 'God help me'. SEE ALSO PP. 685–6.

Field Marshal Sir Alan Brooke, Chief of the Imperial General Staff, thinks about the next war

I have earned my pay today! Started with a very rushed hour from 9.45 to 10.45 examining telegrams and being briefed for COS [Chiefs of Staff meeting]. At 10.30 COS attended by Planners at which we discussed many papers of importance. Back to WO to have an hour with S of S [Secretary of State for War] discussing post war policy and our policy in Europe. Should Germany be dismembered or gradually converted to an ally to meet Russian threat of 20 years hence? I suggested that latter and certain that we must from now onwards regard Germany in a very different light. Germany is no longer the dominating power of Europe, Russia is. Unfortunately Russia is not entirely European. She has however vast resources and cannot fail to become the main threat fifteen years from now. Therefore, foster Germany, gradually build her up and bring her into the federation of Western Europe. Unfortunately all this must be done under the cloak of a holy alliance between Britain Russia and America. Not an easy policy and one requiring a super Foreign Secretary!

By 1944 senior circles in Whitehall were buzzing with secret talk of early planning for what would soon become known as the Cold War. That summer Whitehall's joint military–diplomatic future strategic planning committee tore itself apart over the issue of whether to revive Germany against Russia. Despite efforts to keep this controversy secret, the arguments between the military and the diplomats were so bitter that gossip about it was soon all over Whitehall. The military feared the worst – an expansionist Russia – while the diplomats considered anti-Soviet planning a self-fulfilling prophecy that was bound to provoke Moscow.

Sir Alan Brooke was ennobled in January 1946 as Lord Alanbrooke. He remained Chief of the Imperial General Staff until June 1946 and so participated in some of the volatile debates over Britain's early Cold War strategy and the future of British possessions in the Middle East. Once retired, he had more time to pursue his lifelong interest in ornithology. He died in 1963. SEE ALSO PP. 26 AND 472–3.

Monday 31 July 1944

The Countess of Ranfurly visits Evelyn Waugh and
Randolph Churchill in a hospital at Bari after an air crash
in Yugoslavia

Yesterday I was given three days' sick leave so I drove over
to stay with Dan who is working at Fitzroy's Headquarters
in Bari. The journey took seven hours. From Caserta the road
winds through the mountains. In the little towns and
villages, which are perched on the summits, peasant women
sat in the streets in front of vine-trellised houses watching
their children play in the gutter. In the valleys the corn was
golden. Great white oxen pulling high-wheeled carts, and
ponies gaily in painted floats, moved along the roads.
The only signs of war were the bridges which had all been
blown up. Temporary Bailey bridges spanned the streams
and rivers. Towards evening I reached the coastal plains and
saw one of Mussolini's greatest achievements: collective
farming. The farmhouses are built on the same pattern. The
farms all have the same acreage. I saw hundreds of them.

Today Dan and I went to see Evelyn Waugh and Randolph
Churchill in hospital. The plane that was taking them to
Yugoslavia crashed on landing and nearly all the passengers
were killed. Randolph did not seem in the least subdued by
the accident and was busy distributing propaganda posters
in the hospital. Periodically he and Evelyn had arguments
about nothing in particular and shouted at each other. They
are very funny.

*Hermione Ranfurly was now at Caserta in Italy, working with General
'Jumbo' Wilson and the Minister of State for the Middle East, Harold
Macmillan. She was preparing quarters for a forthcoming visit by King
George VI and Winston Churchill, and was using the apartment
designated for Churchill on his arrival; she worried that the bed was
'very nobbly'. Hermione Ranfurly's husband Dan (the Earl of Ranfurly)
had been taken prisoner by the Italians at an early stage in the desert*

war, but in 1944 he was released into the company of an ecstatic Hermione. Dan Ranfurly was now working at Bari in the headquarters of Brigadier Fitzroy Maclean, who was responsible for Britain's missions to Tito's forces in Yugoslavia. By 1944 Britain enjoyed liaison missions all over the Balkans with the various competing guerrilla groups. Churchill's son, Randolph, had been chosen to lead one of these and had taken Evelyn Waugh with him. However, their aircraft crashed on arrival and they had both been lucky to survive.

In 1953 Hermione Ranfurly's husband was appointed Governor of the Bahamas. She was dismayed by the lack of books in schools and libraries there and asked her friends in London to send out unwanted volumes. When she returned to London in 1957 she founded a charity called Book Aid International. She was awarded an OBE in 1970, and in 1994, at the age of eighty, she published her diary to great critical acclaim. Hermione Ranfurly died on 13 February 2001. SEE ALSO PP. 289–90 AND 447–8.

AUGUST 1944

IN THE FIRST DAYS of August, with Soviet troops approaching Warsaw, Polish resistance forces led by General Bor (Tadeusz Komorowski) decided to stage an uprising against German occupation forces in anticipation of the Red Army pressing forward. The Germans ruthlessly suppressed the rebellion, although fighting would carry on until early October. The Red Army did not come to the assistance of the Poles.

On 15 August, the Allies conducted another amphibious invasion of France, landing troops on the Mediterranean coast between Marseilles and Nice. The landing was relatively unopposed, although some fighting with the German garrison at Marseilles would later develop.

Diplomats from the United States, the British Commonwealth and the Soviet Union came together once more during the third week of August at Dumbarton Oaks, in Washington DC, to discuss the replacement of the League of Nations with a more effective organization dedicated to world peace and security. The scheme they came up with would serve as the basis for the Charter of the United Nations. The main obstacle, however, was the veto issue: the Soviet Union, unlike the other Allies, did not want to bar members of the Security Council from voting on matters in which they were themselves involved.

On 19 August Allied forces approached Paris and its citizens rose up against the German occupation forces. The FFI, who controlled the resistance and had been liberally supplied with arms by the Allies, launched an onslaught against the retreating Germans. Paris was quickly liberated, and on 29 August Eisenhower turned over the administration of the French capital to General Charles de Gaulle and the French Committee for National Liberation. In the last days of August American troops liberated Soissons, some 60 miles north-east of Paris, while other American forces reached the River Meuse. Montelimar was taken by the French, who were delighted to have crossed the Rhône in several places. Meanwhile Canadian forces entered Rouen and the British 11th Armoured Division captured Amiens, taking the key bridge across the Somme in a surprise attack.

Sunday 6 – Tuesday 8 August 1944

Jack Hugill of 30 Assault Unit works alongside the resistance near Brest

John ('Jack') Hugill was born in 1916, the son of Engineer Rear-Admiral R. C. Hugill. Just before the war he went to Magdalen College, Oxford where he obtained a first class honours degree in chemistry. With the outbreak of war he found himself assigned to work on protection against gas attack. In 1942 he joined the weapons division of the Admiralty; later in that year he began to gravitate towards scientific intelligence work and served as assistant naval attaché in Lisbon, the capital of neutral Portugal, and one of the great spy capitals of the war. A year later he moved to 30 Assault Unit, which was led by Ian Fleming, a naval intelligence officer who would later become famous as author of the James Bond novels.

6 August

... it's been a slightly nerve-racking business. There are no troops except a tank arm'd division, near Brest. We are alone, but have made contact with the Maquis who have warned us of 5,000 Germans 9 km. away down the road. So we're camping in a farm ready either to fight it out or move away. It's most amusing being a pocket of resistance surrounded by Huns . . .

Jack Hugill

My God these Bretons are lads! They're all in the Maquis, & are the Huns frightened of them? So frightened that they won't surrender to anyone except us or Yanks. But if they knew how few we were – and what we are, it might be nasty.

Funny thing, they were going to drop either me or Pat to make contact with these Maquis and instead of that we've come by road. Well, Pat Jobs made contact with one Maquis chief; and Peter with another, and a third has come to see us.

7 August

They live an extraordinary existence, one or two Englishmen & yanks living with 1,000 or 1,500 Frenchmen and having the whole countryside at their command. The Germans are scared stiff of them for they take no prisoners – or if they do, merely interrogate and then shoot them. They also shoot collaborators. The one Pat went to sounds most impressive, a sort of Robin Hood party, in constant W/T [radio] contact with London.

It is of course, criminal of me to go on with this diary now. We are about 100 and shall be 150 miles from the nearest large body of troops, and the Germans have numerical superiority over us . . .

We are off in ½ an hour skirting round Corliax where there are 5,000 young Huns belonging to the Crete SS parachute Division. A very bloodthirsty crowd. Self amused at finding myself in such an odd position, and at the same time scared. Our troops are about half grassy-green and talk a bloody sight too big about what they'll do to the fuckin' Germans. My bleeding oath!

I wish I had more leisure time to write of what one sees each day. Some time, perhaps, if I can still remember these things as vividly as I see them now, I will write of . . . Of how yesterday was Sunday, and all the people in all the towns were in their Sunday best, the girls chic and attractive, the older women in their enchanting lace butterfly caps, the men lithe, wiry, fair or vividly dark and active as befits good Bretons . . . Of the way the people babble in Breton and then break into French for our benefit . . .

Of how we are getting short of food, petrol and oil, having far outrun the lines of supply. Of the young Patriots who crowded in to see us, offered us brandy, got drunk themselves out of joy that we were there, and apologised – 'But tomorrow we shall take up our rifles and kill more Bosche. You are – we are of the same race, you English – Our Comrades'. Of how when we stop in a small village, perhaps, everyone crowds out and out of their meagre pittances of food – the Germans have taken all they could at the point of a pistol – offer us cider and bread and butter and are offended if we say 'no'!

Of the swarthy Resistance man in an unspeakable pair of trousers, a black battle dress jacket with corporal's strips and an American Captains' helmet. A villainous, lantern-jawed taciturn creature always sucking a cigarette end and very loyal and helpful, who keeps popping out of a hedge and jumping on to one of our cars to guide us . . . We are going to make for Brest (the last lap) starting at 0930 [tomorrow]. But we shall have to siphon the petrol from the 15cwts to the small cars and leave our gear here.

8 August

Off early towards Brest. On the way captured 5 Huns in a very useful truck, containing 2 bidous of 20 gallons each of petrol – of which we are short. They surrendered after two shots had been fired. Brest still uncaptured but we caught up with the yanks at Pulaniel who were very surprised to see us.

Maquis most helpful but appear more and more brutal. They have shot three Huns who gave themselves up in the village here today. Made them dig their own graves first.

Last week they got 34 and burnt them alive. They are also shaving the heads of all the collaboratrices [women collaborators], as usual. Apples are falling and two have had direct hits on my head and the light is fading. Goodnight.

30 Assault Unit was known as Fleming's 'private army'. The unit was a group of specially trained Commandos who were sent on specific intelligence missions, often targeting German specialist equipment. As part of 30 Assault Unit, Jack Hugill had arrived in Normandy during the D-Day landings. During this campaign, Hugill was awarded the Croix de Guerre by the French, was mentioned in despatches, and won the Distinguished Service Cross for taking the surrender of 280 troops under a Luftwaffe officer at a radio station near Brest in August 1944. SEE ALSO PP. 735–6.

Tuesday 8 August 1944

Walter Musto, recently retired civil servant, views the impact of a V-1 attack on suburban East Molesey in Surrey

To entertain visitors from more peaceful parts of the country just now is a responsibility not lightly to be undertaken, and this morning I knew that I had done well to advise Bobby's brother at Muirfield to postpone his holiday with us at

Shieling and the agreeable prospects it offered for us all. The relative immunity of our immediate neighbourhood of East Molesey from the Flying Bomb came to an end this morning just after dawn with a reverberating crash that seemed to shake the whole district when one of these horrors fell nearby. Already partly dressed, I spring from my mattress-bed first to do the rounds of the house – which had suffered nothing worse than the flinging open of already unlatched doors – and admit my opposite number, neighbour Ward, himself still in his pyjamas, who had called for emergency instructions. However, in the absence of any immediate call for help from the adjoining sector, we could only stand by until the all-clear released us from our own. By 6 am I was at the scene of the action, less than ten minutes' walk from home, the trail blazed by the steadily mounting numbers of dislodged tiles, shattered windows, burst doors and piles of ceiling plaster and presently, the wreckage of whole houses with the stricken occupants already sorting from the indescribable confusion of debris such articles of clothing and furniture as were still recognizable. US soldiers from their nearby Hurst Park Camp were first on the scene with every sort of rescue appliance for the succour of victims, closely followed by the regular wardens, WVS, and first-aid parties. It was indeed a sorry spectacle, which, to me, seemed the more grimly ironic because of the bright sunshine of a perfect summer morning as the rescue squads moved slowly to waiting ambulances with the dead and injured. Not the least inconspicuous and useful of the rescue equipment from the camp was a large mobile canteen, which introduced a specially welcome and friendly note into the story with its inscription 'Presented to the US Army by the town of Honolulu, Hawaii', and was supplying much-needed refreshment to helpers and victims alike. Falling between two streets direct on to a double Anderson shelter full of people, it devastated these and wrecked many of the houses in two other streets, turning into a heap of rubble the adjacent homes and making uninhabitable many more. Partly dressed, unwashed and still a little dazed, men, women and children were trying to make something of the wreckage, not moaning about their calamitous experience, and I was proud of my countryfolk's fine spirit. Of two tousled, elderly, half-dressed women in a front garden standing almost knee deep in ceiling plaster, broken furniture, torn bedding, curtains, etc, one, as I passed, said to the other, 'I wouldn't care a damn if only I could find my other skirt.' Later, on my way home to breakfast, I took particulars of damaged roofs, windows and doors in my own sector, to pass on to the authorities for attention when the more urgent matters had been dealt with, myself doing certain small neighbourhood repairs later in the day.

The V-1 flying bomb was initially despatched from the Pas-de-Calais on the northern coast of France, though military operations gradually pushed back the German launch areas. The arrival of this terrifying new weapon prompted a new wave of evacuation, with over a million people leaving London and the surrounding areas. The British employed double agents to send the V-1s off-track by falsely reporting their point of impact, causing the Germans to adjust their aim until many V-1s fell short of target. However, this had consequences for the populations of the admittedly less densely populated areas in the suburbs and the home counties. By August only about a fifth of the V-1s despatched were reaching their targets.

Musto's remarkable wartime diaries were recently discovered by his great-nephew in a family attic. Hidden in a dusty pile of notebooks filled with neat handwriting, the reflections of a sixty-year-old civil servant living in Surrey comprise one of the most outstanding examples of sustained social commentary and capture life during the Blitz on the suburban front. SEE ALSO PP. 214–15 AND 242–3.

Friday 11 August – Thursday 7 September 1944

Sergeant Pieter Kahl, platoon leader from the German 202nd Mountain Battalion, begins to lose heart

Pieter Kahl and his unit were from Salzburg in the Tyrol. In previous weeks they had been all but cut off and surrounded in the difficult terrain

of the Vosges in northern France. The battalion was decimated over a
period of three days, after which the remnants were rescued in a frantic
operation by their sister unit, the 201st Mountain Battalion. Kahl then
accompanied the battalion's transport column in a disorderly retreat
through the Franco-German border areas of Alsace-Lorraine. They were
continually ambushed by members of the French resistance – whom he
deemed 'terrorists'.

11 August

... You just don't know what's going on any more. Some
people have already lost their head. We're supposed to
retreat and take up position on the southern bank
of the Loire ... Caution is necessary; the terrorists are no
joke.

12 August

The guessing game again: Where will we end up now? The
population is calm and has behaved peacefully. There have
been no clashes. All of us can understand that they'd rather
see us leave than arrive. But you only have to imagine if the
situation was reversed. It remains to be seen whether the
new occupying forces – the English and Americans – will
treat them so humanely. Perhaps 'de Gaulle' will make his
presence known by conscripting all the able-bodied French
and sending them against us ...

13 August

... Circulating stories, as always. I don't want to quote any
of these rumours because they're too absurd ... Why are we
stopping? Perhaps we're doing it for tactical reasons that I
don't have an overview of and so I can't make a judgement.
We do our duty to the very end and are ready for action as is
demanded of us, as that's why we're soldiers and everyone
knows what we're fighting for ...

26 August

... Shortly before evening terrorists are reported. There are
losses on both sides. 100 Italians defect with a captain to the
terrorists ...

7 September
In the meantime a large company has gathered. In addition to us (infantry), scattered soldiers from all arms of service have joined us, including O.T. Reichsbahn [railway troops] etc. They endeavour, under pressure, to retreat as quickly as possible. We, however, are still a unified whole. The French in Fulande (?) are a terrible people. You seldom see a person when passing through villages. Closed doors and windows, a sign that they do not have a clear conscience . . . We're in a gorge being shot at by terrorists who have their hiding place above us. Two are caught and shot dead on the spot. One of them is silent and resigns himself to his fate. The older one calls out before the bullet hits him: Vive la France. Actually they should have been hanged but the leader of the [battalion] transport column train doesn't want to. The units following behind have lost 50 out of 80 vehicles . . .

Pieter Kahl's diary offers a glimpse into the bitter war fought between demoralized elements of the German army and the French resistance, emboldened by the advance of the Allies. Kahl was helping to escort his unit's transport column, but even though he was not in the front line, he was subjected to constant attacks by Frenchmen who wished to offer a parting shot to the departing occupiers. The precipitous mountains and forests of the Vosges region were ideally suited to guerrilla tactics. When members of the resistance were caught they were shown no mercy. SEE ALSO PP. 751–3.

Saturday 12 – Monday 14 August 1944

Baron von Aufsess on fraternization and repression in the Channel Islands

Baron von Aufsess was born on 4 August 1906 and went to school in Bayreuth in Bavaria. Always interested in the countryside and animals, he studied forestry, but eventually became a lawyer. From 1942 to 1945 he was one of the key German administrators on the Channel Islands. A gentle and cultured individual, he disliked some of his fellow officers whom he considered Nazi zealots.

12 August

On the beach complete amity still reigns between the German soldiers and the local girls. With a few exceptions the girl will surrender to her partner readily enough, provided this can be effected in proper privacy. The Englishwoman is astoundingly simple, effortless and swift in her lovemaking. While the Frenchwoman involves herself totally in the game, which she likes to be conducted along intellectual lines, for the Englishwoman it is a surprisingly straightforward physical matter. This direct and uncomplicated fashion of making love is not to be underrated; in its openness and honesty it precludes all that is wanton or furtive. If the Frenchwoman, after prolonged kissing, would murmur some word of love or quote a romantic couplet, the Englishwoman would surely only laugh at such tactics . . .

14 August

We discuss the delicate question of reprisals against the civilian population for sheltering escaped prisoners. I am the only one in favour of restraint. We should not, on account of a couple of unimportant escapees, drop the velvet glove which we have used with success in the past. We exhaust our strength prematurely on trifles.

In the morning the medical corps brought the horses down onto the beach again. I first rode Toni, an elegant little horse which at the gallop bounds along like a hare. Then came Froni, the white mare, wild, intractable and never tiring. I rode her bareback in my bathing trunks and managed to keep her, if with difficulty, under complete control. A marvellous feeling, with a mettlesome horse beneath one and miles of beach ahead. We varied the procedure by riding into the sea. Froni swam out to deep water and balancing above her, I gave her free rein. There was an occasional very high wave, bringing her muzzle under water, so that only her pink distended nostrils showed, poking up like the snout of a hippopotamus. Then she quickly drew a deep breath and surfaced again, snorting and baring her teeth, evidently disapproving of this salty taste. I sometimes take small boys up on a horse and give them a ride, which they vastly enjoy, but Froni is too untamed to take such liberties with.

It seems that Froni and I were quite a sensation on the beach. B. told me afterwards that people were asking 'Who is it?' but most knew well enough that it was 'the Baron'. I have become thus known everywhere and am never, like my colleagues, addressed by my military title.

Relations between the Germans and the population of Jersey were more civil than under many occupations elsewhere. The local police continued to use their normal uniform but had to salute German officers when they came across them; if they did not, then a fine was levied. A fierce communications blackout was imposed. Radios were forbidden and many were put in prison for breaking this rule. The occupation was a multinational affair, with many slave labourers from Russia brought in to work on the massive emplacements built to defend the islands. SEE ALSO P. 798.

Saturday 19 August 1944

David K. Bruce of the OSS watches the resistance extending its control over Chartres

Bill Jackson appeared this morning, and it was arranged that he would deal with the matters discussed with General Gaffy. We then started off and lunched at Nogent-le-Rotrou, arriving at Chartres in the afternoon. We found the town quiet, and all the hotels closed. All was not quiet, however, at the Prefecture where a constant drama took place in the courtyard. When we arrived there, a row of women, with their faces pressed to a wall, presented their backs to the crowd. They were individually interrogated and taken away to an upstairs room. I went there and found them in process of having their heads shorn – first with scissors and then with clippers. Most of them were very unattractive, but there was one good-looking girl of about twenty, who faced the situation almost gaily.

Members of the French Forces of the Interior were much in evidence, and very careless with their weapons. They, like some of our own soldiers, are 'trigger happy,' and while we were standing there at least one piece was discharged by accident, an occurrence that has become familiar to us. We went to the cathedral, which is essentially undamaged. Its wonderful stained glass windows were placed in storage long ago, so the interior had lost its pristine soft luminosity. Leaning over the parapet of the cathedral Close, and looking into the terraced gardens and shrubbery below, we witnessed what seemed to be a rabbit hunt. A Senegalese, a Gendarme, and several civilians, carrying an assortment of weapons, were poking about in the weeds, vegetables, and under-brush, looking for German soldiers. They could not have anticipated that any German they might encounter would offer fight, for from time to time they would turn their backs on as yet unexplored terrain to smoke and chat together. At the Prefecture, prisoners were being brought in from time to time, tired, dusty and apathetic.

By mid-August David Bruce was passing through the cathedral city of Chartres and moving towards Paris. He was helping to command a range of OSS units that were working behind the lines in support of the invasion forces. These included Jedburgh teams – heavily armed units drawn from the OSS, SOE and SAS – designed to bolster their resistance in attacks on Axis command and communications. The diaries of some Jedburgh operators feature elsewhere in this anthology. Everywhere the resistance seemed to be in control and was dealing with surrendered Germans and collaborators. In some places this was a mild and almost matter-of-fact affair, but elsewhere the settling of accounts was more brutal. In either case Allied officers rarely intervened, but allowed the French to carry out their own business.

Bruce's career blossomed under Truman's post-war administration, during which he held a succession of senior positions culminating in his appointment as Under Secretary of State (1952–3). Throughout this period he was mostly concerned with implementing the Marshall Plan to foster European recovery and encouraging European unification. SEE ALSO PP. 698–700 AND 701–3.

Thursday 24 August 1944

George Bateman, a British POW at Brunswick in Germany, is bombed by Allies

Many activities, such as art exhibitions, lectures and gardening continued as at previous camps ... First Aid classes continued and First Aid posts were established in every basement. These proved very useful on the 24th August when we had the 'massacre of St Bartholomew's Day'. A few days earlier two American pilots who had been shot down were brought into camp and seemed surprised that we mostly took cover when American aircraft were flying overhead, always during the daytime. They told us there was no need as their bombing was so accurate that they could never miss the target. First they dropped a marker on the target and this sent up a column of smoke and then the bombs were dropped exactly on the marker. However, on the 24th August the target happened to be the aircraft factory which, with the German H.Q. and our camp formed a fairly close knit triangle. The marker was dropped into our compound by mistake and a bombardment of incendiary and anti-personnel bombs followed. Most of us had taken shelter in the basements, but a few remained outside to watch. Seven were killed and more were wounded by the anti-personnel bombs which also wounded some of our number who were trying to put out fires caused by the incendiaries. The wounded were brought down to the cellars where the M.O. and anyone trained in First Aid were kept hard at work. After the raid was over, the German mess was on fire with only one man trying to put out the flames, which proved too much for him. The German Mess and our cookhouse were burned out. High explosive bombs were also dropped and left large craters, but luckily missed our buildings.

The main impact of these raids on George Bateman was inconvenience. He had been running an eye clinic in a room which he shared with a dentist but had to stop because his optician's equipment was now covered in dust and broken glass. Water pressure in the camp dropped, rendering the latrines unusable and forcing them to use a more primitive system outside. The camp at Brunswick, to which Bateman had been sent from Moosburg, had an especially elaborate theatre with 'luxurious' space for green rooms, wings and even drop sets. Here drama, 'radio plays' (with performers behind sheets) and symphony concerts were performed. But the increasing number of bombing alerts caused the theatre to close for a period towards the end of 1944.

George Bateman published his diary privately in 1986; like so many circulated in this way, it remains virtually unknown. SEE ALSO PP. 440–1 AND 629–30.

Monday 28 August 1944

Jack Hugill of 30 Assault Unit advances through the countryside beyond Caen

I was going to say that the Caen plain is hideous and uncomfortable and a more suitable terrain for war than any other I have seen in France. A measure of what the resistance has been can be gauged by the number of burnt-out tanks (German & British) . . .

10 miles or so before Lisieux the country becomes more undulating and interesting. You see many little half-timbered houses nestling in orchards. And after Lisieux moving East and South you are on a high and placid plain.

In Lisieux itself I was surprised by Marine Powell. We saw three old women sitting on their bundles by this pile of rubble that had been their home. They'd just got back. Powell, who is normally talkative and keeps up a string of cockney wisecracks suddenly stopped and said 'That sort of thing always wrings me yer know' pointing to the old women.

Nor is he the only one I've met who gives way to bursts of sympathy in that way. The average English soldier is rather like that.

On the road today, when we'd paused for a 10 minute halt,

the M.P. corporal in charge of all the D.R.'s also surprised me by a sudden show of humanity.

A Frenchman was driving a couple of horses in front of a large shay [a two-wheeled cart], on which were perched all his household goods and his family, in the opposite direction to us. Two large Army lorries came hooting along and tried to get past him. The M.P. went straight out, stopped the lorries and waved the Frenchman ahead of them. As he came back he said in a slightly shamefaced way 'don't see why they shouldn't be allowed to drive on their own fuckin' roads, do you?' . . .

The Canadian 4th Div. has been moving along the road continuously since 1800 yesterday. It's now 1450 p.m. and I don't think we shall move yet . . . There's nothing for me to do, so I shall just scribble in this book . . .

Jack Hugill clearly found his diary to be a helpful release for the more emotional aspects of war. At times he felt a degree of self-rebuke from what he called his own 'public school conscience' for writing in an overtly emotional – perhaps 'unmanly' – way about what he saw. At one point he remarked – 'I'm gushing, I can't help it'. He was clearly pleased to note that he was not the only person, even in his tough special forces unit, to be affected by sentimentality and compassion; indeed, he valued these feelings as a mark of humanity which he saw as lending additional character to the English soldier.

Jack Hugill would survive his adventures with 30 Assault Unit in France and advance on into occupied Germany. There he would stay in scientific intelligence work, a growth industry in Germany at the end of the war. From 1945 to 1946 he was in charge of the Forward Interrogation Unit in Hamburg, one of the front lines in the emerging intelligence struggles of the Cold War. In 1947 he eventually wrote up some of his war experiences in a memoir called The Hazard Mesh, *before beginning a long career with the Tate & Lyle Sugar Company. SEE ALSO PP. 723–6.*

SEPTEMBER 1944

IN THE FIRST days of September the British had reached the Somme and the Americans were at Verdun. The Canadians had captured Dieppe and surrounded Calais. Comparisons with the First World War were inevitable. At this stage of the war the British Commonwealth had suffered about 250,000 personnel killed, compared with 800,000 in the period 1914–17.

Britain suffered no further raids by conventional bombers and so the blackout was lifted. This was partly a matter of safety, for nearly 6,000 people had been killed on Britain's roads the previous year, more than half of them during the night-time blackout. The return of street lighting to British cities also made a big difference psychologically. The Germans had lost their last V-1 launch site in France; however, they launched a new V-1 campaign, firing the weapons from aircraft. Added to this was the new menace of the V-2, a ballistic rocket, larger than the V-1 and with a longer range, which gave no warning because of its trajectory and supersonic speed. It was used against both London and Paris in September.

With their troops firmly established in France, many of the Allied leaders were increasingly optimistic and some hoped that Germany might capitulate by the end of the year. On 11 September Roosevelt and Churchill met in Quebec City to discuss strategies for the final victories over Germany and Japan. Although the war was still being fought, political and military leaders were increasingly concerned with the occupation zones after the conquest of Germany and the policy of post-war administration. It was at this point that the US Secretary of the Treasury, Henry Morgenthau, pressed for the 'pastoralization' of Germany, hoping to reduce it to a purely agrarian economy. The plan was initially approved but later dropped.

American forces crossed into Germany on 12 September. They moved over the German frontier near Eupen and by 21 October had reached the historic town of Aachen. Here the strong German defences on the Siegfried Line slowed the Allied advance. Hoping to outflank German defences by moving further north, Montgomery was given authority to launch a major airborne operation in Holland, designed to seize crucial bridges.

Operation Market Garden began on 17 September, when the 1st Allied Airborne Army dropped troops at Eindhoven, Nijmegen and Arnhem to secure bridgeheads. Meanwhile the British 2nd Army pushed north into Holland from Belgium to link up with them. German resistance was fierce, and parachute units had to pull back from Arnhem after a week of intense fighting. On 22 September the 2nd Army, which was trying to relieve the parachutists, was only six miles away but could get no closer. Some 7,000 troops were lost or taken prisoner during this battle, which ended on the last day of September. The Canadian 1st Army managed to secure many of the Dutch ports such as Antwerp and Middelburg.

By the third week of September the Red Army had consolidated its position in the Baltic states, capturing Tallinn in Estonia on 22 September. Early the following month it would capture Riga in Latvia. Further south, Soviet forces had moved through Romania and were now on the borders of Hungary. The Red Army was now ready to begin its advance into Germany.

V-1 attacks on England were still occurring, but their frequency had diminished. At the end of September Whitehall decided that the National Fire Service could be stood down and informed its members that they were likely to be sent into the armed services or into industry. Compulsory Home Guard parades also ceased in September 1944.

Saturday 2 September 1944

Anne Brusselmans, a key figure in the Belgian secret army, hides a resistance worker in her house and outwits the Gestapo

'Who is there?' I heard him call out.
'German police. Open!'
The reply came in stern, threatening tones.

This is it. We are for it, I thought.

Rushing back into the sitting-room – I had crept out into the passage without knowing it, to listen at the door – I went round frantically picking up all my papers, and then dumped them down under a heavy stone on the terrace and put the dustbin on it.

After this I returned to the sitting-room and turned the wireless on to a German programme.

When Julien walked in, with three policemen behind him, I was sitting there, knitting and listening quietly to the 'Blue Danube' played by a German band.

The Germans glanced round at this domestic scene, made no comment, and then went on to search the rest of the flat.

It was only then, stunned as I was, that I remembered we had a young Belgian member of the Secret Army staying with us in Jacques' room. He had gone to bed early, and had been so quiet, that for the moment I had forgotten completely about him.

Forcing myself to be calm, I strolled out after the Germans into the hall . . . and after a thorough look round, the two men came out, and made towards me as I retreated in front of them down the passage. They were coming towards Jacques' room, the room with the man in it.

I must stop them getting in here somehow, I thought. If they find the man in there, we're done.

So, I stood firmly in their way, trying to think of something to say.

'Excuse me, madame,' one of the men said. 'We want to go in there.'

'You'd better not, Monsieur,' I replied, still searching for something effective to say.

He looked at me suspiciously, and in that moment inspiration came.

'Oh, and why not, madame?'

His tone was faintly threatening, though still polite.

'I am afraid my little boy is very ill and the sight of you might upset him.'

They were not too much impressed at this, and still looked as if they would go in.

'He's got typhoid.'

I added this casually, as if it were a secondary consideration, but in reality it was my trump card, for if there is one thing that Germans are afraid of, it is infectious illness.

As I hoped, this information worked like a charm, and the Germans now went on into the kitchen again.

Anne Brusselmans' house was the first link in a very long chain that spirited downed Allied airmen away to the south and to freedom. Pilots had to make their way south into France and then, before the arrival of the Allies in the summer of 1944, down to one of the several secret escape routes over the central Pyrenees into northern Spain. It was not only aircrew who took this route, but also hundreds of Frenchmen and also Jews being hunted by the Nazis. Escaping aircrew were passed from link to link in the chain by a succession of local 'helpers' who clothed, fed and hid them, usually at great personal risk to themselves.

Anne Brusselmans was later made a Member of the British Empire by the British government. She also received the Medal of Freedom with Silver Palm from General of the US Army Dwight D. Eisenhower, and in 1987 was given permission to live permanently in the United States. SEE ALSO PP. 470–2.

Thursday 7 – Friday 8 September 1944

John J. Maginnis, a civil affairs officer from the US army, talks with the resistance in the Ardennes

7 September

Since the advance on the V Corps front had now moved into the wooded, hilly country of the Ardennes, the local disposition of German forces, especially along the Meuse to the north, was of great interest to the corps commander. Colonel Maroney asked me to discuss this with the FFI, to learn what information they might have. Later, I called on the FFI chief for the Ardennes, Commander Fournier, and met his staff for the first time. Jacqueline, the adjutant, impressed me as the most forceful of any of the group. They told me that the Germans were getting out of the Ardennes as quickly as possible, but that they would check it further and give me the latest information in the morning.

I had observed the FFI about town. They were having a high old time, tearing through the streets in captured or seized cars, always carrying arms, and taking liberties almost at will. This was their day in the sun, the day they had been working toward for so long. I felt that they were entitled to this moment of power and glory while the flush of liberation lasted – provided they did not get out of hand. Their attitude of being above the law, however, did not sit well with some of the citizens of the community (Fournier previously had been a barber and Jacqueline had worked in a store in town). The fact remained that they had suffered, put their lives in jeopardy, and battled the Germans to the full extent of their limited capacity.

Because Charleville-Mézières had been cleared of the enemy did not mean that there were not Germans still in the vicinity. I learned that, until today, Germans in some force had been at Nouzonville just three miles down the river. Some enemy forces were making a stand of sorts along the east bank of the Meuse river just north of Charleville. Many hundreds of them had been by-passed and were now in our rear. FFI people were combing the countryside for them; sometimes they brought them in as prisoners of war and sometimes they simply liquidated them.

8 September

I was invited to the secret rendezvous of the FFI to have dinner with the people who had operated French under-ground activities in the department of the Ardennes. This meeting place was no longer a secret, but it certainly looked and felt secret – a dark, dimly lit room in the basement of a small hotel near the Meuse. Almost everyone was carrying a weapon of some kind. There seemed to be a good supply of wine and spirits on hand, and it was gay in a bizarre and murky way. The food was simple – a stew of sorts. Commander Fournier, Jacqueline, Vice-commander Beaufort, Lieutenant Dervien, and other members of the staff were there. These persons did not seem to have the tough look of the Maquis that I had expected, but as we talked it became evident that these underground operators were a dedicated and capable band. They had hidden out in the hills and forests of the Ardennes for months, constantly harassing the enemy and providing valuable information to the Allies. Those here now were the lucky survivors, for more than one hundred of their organization had been tortured and shot by the Germans. The real leader and moving spirit was Jacqueline. She was probably the toughest of any of them. I was to see quite a lot of her and, although we had our difficulties, I became very fond of her. I could see that these people were pleased and a little flattered to have the American commander at their *popote*, but I also realized that they were studying me closely and that our future relations might well be colored by their assessment.

At the end of the war John Maginnis found himself working for General Floyd Parks, who chaired the committee overseeing the joint Allied occupation of Berlin. We shall hear more from him in the second volume of this collection. He served in Berlin until March 1946 and retired from the army in 1957.

Friday 8 September 1944

Claude Mauriac, de Gaulle's private secretary, savours a liberated Paris

Claude Mauriac, aged twenty-four, helped to liberate Paris and then greeted the arrival of Allied tanks in his khaki shirt and Free French armband. He then met up with his friend Claude Guy, who was an aide-de-camp to General de Gaulle. Claude Guy gave him 'an enormous carton of American cigarettes' and two tins of food – and then quickly and unexpectedly pressed him into service in the General's private office.

I have seen liberated Paris today for the first time. By that I mean for the first time since peace descended on the city, I have been out at an hour other than the first or last of the day. It was at 7.00 this evening, at the end of an exhausting day's work at the office. I decided to walk and get a breath of fresh air. A downpour had cleared the sky, in which three French fighters were flying at low altitude – yes, French, with good and true tricolour markings – oh, what a miracle! And over those beautiful buildings by Gabriel, damaged but already in the process of being restored, floated our three colours. And all along the rue de Rivoli, only a few days ago still besmirched with Nazi swastikas, hung our own blue, white and red flags, I wanted to kneel down right there, in the middle of this magnificent square, so small under an immense sky, and yet greater than the world. I would have done it had I been alone.

In the rue de Royale, decorated with various Allied colours, I saw the first British soldiers and even more Americans – on leave, I mean walking, strolling along, out of their vehicles. Am struck by the free and easy carelessness of their attire, not actually untidy but so unmilitary. Their uniforms resemble civilian workmen's clothes, anyway. 'It's a war of garage-hands,' de Gaulle is supposed to have said, though he denied it hotly when my father reminded him of it the other day.

As the General was dining in town I was able to leave the Cabinet early (9 p.m.). I went to the Sphinx, certain of finding all the American expatriates there. There were so many soldiers and so many of them drunk that there were very few women in the noisy crowd. One or two however, moved about, with naked breasts, from hand to hand and mouth to mouth. Under their inelegant helmets (possessing none of the tragic beauty of the German variety), in their mechanics overalls, chewing gum and keeping their heavy jaws in motion, gay as children, the American soldiers shouted to each other in their half-incomprehensible and wondrous language . . .

On my way home, pedalling in the dark night of the blacked-out city, I whistled – for the first time as a liberated man.

Claude Mauriac's diary captures all the mingled joy and sadness of the first days of liberation. At the Pont Neuf, he notes that people were dancing on the pavement between an American armoured vehicle and the barricade, while shooting went on in the next street. De Gaulle's Cabinet Office was overflowing with work generated by the first days of liberation and Mauriac was soon buried in paperwork. It was only in the first days of September that he had free time to savour a liberated Paris returning to normality.

Wednesday 13 – Tuesday 26 September 1944

Vere Hodgson, a charity worker in Notting Hill, hears rumours about the first V-2 attacks on London

13 September

We have heard a lot about the big explosion heard all over London on Friday night. There is nothing about it in the papers ... word is just going round. But we fear it is the V2 which has arrived. On Tuesday morning about 6.15 a.m. all London was aroused from peaceful slumber by a further terrific explosion, bigger than the last, in that the murderous rumbles went on after the explosion.

I had been fast asleep. There was no Warning. I felt sure it was no Gas Works exploding, as we thought when we heard it on Friday. It was something the Germans were sending over! It is the great topic of conversation as soon as people meet. But neither radio nor newspapers speak. But we feel if many more come the truth must be told. Rumour says this last fell on a motor factory near Kew. Many were killed. It is all hush-hush. They seem to be Rockets which drop from the stratosphere. You may be out peaceably walking and one drops. Nice prospect!

I was dreaming of robots last night. Dozens of us in a room – all with a Fly Bomb attached to our shoulders waiting for them to go off! ...

26 September

I have been to Brum for a week. But to return to Friday Sept

15th. At 4.15 a.m. another mysterious terrific explosion. It quite unnerved me, and I could not sleep again. We gather it had fallen at Staines – or in that direction. The Pig Breeder had felt it badly at Hounslow. All Londoners were looking at one another as if they had a disgraceful secret to hush up. We all have a covert look – a dreadful secret – a skeleton in the cupboard.

Saturday I set off for Paddington at 8.15 a.m. Had to queue a long way round. Just as we were half-way another huge explosion rent the air. We, waiting, looked at one another – another!

Got a seat and was only an hour late. They have been doing some painting and distempering at home. There are no workmen, so you just do what you can yourself. A programme was arranged for me of taking down the Black-out, mending cushion covers, sheets and towels. You can buy none of these things, so I interspersed such good work with seeing a few friends.

The sun shone, and the garden looked very nice. They do not expect any more raids. There are lights on the Hagley Road. After five solid years of blackness what a joy to move without a torch. The spiders have been having a lovely time, and are rather sorry the war is nearing a close.

Had a tea on Tuesday with Elsie and Neville, and he told me as much as was allowable about the super supers on London. I was comforted to learn that the Government do know where they are coming from. They are said to be fifty feet long and five feet wide. Like an enormous Pencil . . .

All the week the liberation of Holland has been going on, but it has not been so easy as Belgium. Our airborne men are in a tight corner [at Arnhem].

Returned to London – mobs of people – but got a corner seat!

Vere Hodgson correctly identified the first V-2 hit on London on Friday 8 September. Why she was so well informed about the weapon is not clear. The V-2 was successfully tested in October 1942 and production began in 1943. The existence of the weapon had been known to Allied intelligence for a long time and its introduction had been successfully delayed by bombing raids against testing centres. Like the V-1, it carried a warhead that weighed 1 ton, yet this was a wholly different kind of weapon that travelled at supersonic speed and could attain an altitude of over 50 miles. Accordingly there was no effective defence, and its arrival was completely silent, so Londoners regarded it with complete horror. Although over five thousand V-2s were fired at Britain, fewer than a quarter reached their target and the attacks ended in March 1945, when Allied troops in Europe over-ran the last launch sites.

In retirement Vere Hodgson would live in Church Stretton in Shropshire and spend some of her last years editing her voluminous diaries, which were then published in 1976. She died in 1979. SEE ALSO PP. 371–2.

Sunday 17 – Monday 18 September 1944

Captain 'Lech' Zagorski on fear and civilian resistance in the Warsaw Rising

Captain Waclaw Zagorski of the Polish Home Army kept a diary for seventy days, between 30 July and 7 October 1944, which chronicled the intense fighting with the Germans around the Grzybowska Street area of Warsaw. He had been an important socialist political leader before the outbreak of war, and spent much of the early wartime period procuring forged documents to assist Polish Jews in escaping detection by the Germans.

17 September

I went back to my reports: as usual 'All positions held'. It was already quite dark when Wislanski handed a note to the runner, Pataszon.

'Take it to Group HQ and bring a receipt back.'

A few minutes later Wanda came into the office.

'What's the matter with Pataszon?' she asked.

'He's gone over to Group HQ with a message.'

'He must have come back then, or something must have happened, for he's sitting on the stairs and crying.'

I went out and saw him there, sobbing.

'What is it, Pataszon? Why haven't you taken the message?'

'I'm ... afraid.'

'You've never been afraid before, so why are you now? What is it? Listen, they're not firing any longer.'

'It isn't the firing that I'm afraid of. Only it's so dark out there, and quiet. And the chaplain, and Turek, and Lieutenant Tadeusz ...'

'Yes, I see,' I said, trying to sound kind and putting my arm around him. 'All the same, that's no reason for crying, is it? You're a big boy now. Still, don't worry, I'll get someone else to go.'

'No!' Pataszon exclaimed. 'I'm not crying because I'm afraid, but because I haven't taken the message! I've *got* to take it.'

'Good for you, Pataszon. But hold on a minute. Wanda has to go in that direction; you can go together, and you'll both feel better. And you take this revolver. I've got a Mauser, and can manage without it.'

He stood speechless for an instant. His eyes gleamed as he took hold of the revolver tightly.

18 September

... Okularnik's comrades were making fun of him in the position in Ceglana Street. Two German officers, who clearly didn't know the terrain, had missed their way and gone past the ground floor window at which Okularnik was stationed with a Sten gun. He let them go past towards our barricade, and not until they wanted to get back again did he open fire at them at some twelve paces range. He'd missed.

'I was too sure of myself and my hands were shaking like a jelly,' Okularnik protested. 'But I'll make up for it.'

In July 1944, with Soviet forces approaching Warsaw, the Polish government-in-exile in London had called for an uprising in the city, so that they could return to a liberated Warsaw and attempt to prevent a communist takeover. The Polish resistance began the uprising on 1 August. The Soviet army was only 18 miles away, but refused to assist in the aerial resupply of the insurgents. The resistance fighters believed that the Germans had all but abandoned the city and expected to fight only for a few days, but after sixty-three days of bitter conflict the leaders of the rising agreed a conditional surrender with the Wehrmacht. The 15,000 remaining Home Army soldiers would be treated as POWs, and remnants of the remaining civilian population expelled.

Sunday 17 – Tuesday 26 September 1944

Lieutenant Peter Baillie, Airborne Division, lands by glider at Arnhem

Peter Baillie was based in Lincolnshire during 1944. His unit had been stood to for operations six times during the D-Day landings of June 1944, but each time had been stood down again. They were being kept in readiness for a major airborne operation to capture key bridges ahead of Montgomery's advance into Holland. They were told of this operation two days in advance, and on Saturday night he noted they 'wrote a few last letters and went to sleep'. They boarded their gliders at ten o'clock the next day.

Our pilot slightly misjudged it, and we overshot somewhat and found ourselves heading straight for a thick wood, doing about 80 m.p.h., but due to his masterly piece of flying he remained on full flap, raised the nose, and stalled it, and we hit the deck with such force it smashed the tricycle undercarriage, and we spun round and crashed into a bank. No one was hurt except for my Sgt. and myself who were slightly grazed.

D+1 . . . About 1.30 the second lift came in. What a sight that was. I doubt if any of us will see such an incredible sight ever again. The total aircraft in the air at that time, including fighters, bombers etc, was over 2,000! The sky was black with gliders, tugs, parachutes, fighters, bombers. Parachutes were dropping everywhere. How could any German stop and fight all this we thought, little knowing what a tough and disastrous time we had ahead of us. In just over 2 hours the whole area was clear and all that was left was broken gliders and discarded parachutes . . . We moved off . . . and we eventually had to cross a large open ploughed field to a thick wood on the other side. We did this in arrow head [formation] with my pln [platoon] as the van[guard], for the coy[company]. When my leading section was about 40 [yards] from the wood, a shot was fired, killing one of my men instantly. We went to ground and unfortunately couldn't locate the position where the fire came from, so had no alternative but to get up and advance again. When we had gone about 10 [yards] fire opened up all along the wood. We hit the ground again and machine gun bullets were wizzing everywhere. My leading section cmdr [commander] happened to see a badly sighted M.G. 34 [German machine gun] nest just in front of him. He immediately got up, and with a 36 grenade in each hand, doubled forward toward it, screaming and shouting at the top of his voice. He threw both grenades in, killing the crew, and putting the gun out of action. (I have recommended him for the M.M. [military medal]).

D+4 Things were now looking pretty bum. We had no water, ammo running short and casualties were mounting up . . .

D+5 This was probably the worst day of all. They shelled and mortared us to blazes at rapid rate non-stop . . . Flame throwers were causing a lot of casualties and it was awful to see men burnt alive and screaming in agony . . .

D+6 Mortared all night and as dawn broke they let go at a rapid rate again . . . a mortar bomb exploded just in front of me. How I wasn't killed is still a miracle to me. It blew me off my feet and I received five small pieces of shrapnel. I can remember the stretcher party coming, and then the next thing I knew I was awake in the RAP [regimental aid post], crying like hell! I was struck dumb for nearly two days, and this scared me to death as I thought I would be dumb for life. The RAP was crowded out. Dead were lying outside, their bodies rotting and stinking to hell . . .

[Baillie was then moved to a new aid post in the cellar of a house.]

D+9 *8.30 in the morning*. Everything was so quiet you could have heard a pin drop. Eventually we heard voices and they arrived. Bob and I went up first with hands up, to explain that there were many wounded chaps below . . .

The sight we then saw has continually preyed on my mind ever since, has given me bad dreams and kept me awake every night since I was captured, and I have also prayed every night that I *never* see that *bloody* awful sight again. There were dead bodies by the *dozens*, lying about and stinking – not just lifeless corpses that you must expect to see on the battlefield, but bits of bodies. Bodies without heads, arms or legs. Bodies burnt, riddled with bullets. Smashed up jeeps and houses and everything smashed to smithereens. The stench of the rotting bodies filled the air. The sudden shock of seeing all this and I suppose the condition I was in, I'm not ashamed to confess that I just knelt down and cried. All these poor swine killed – for what! For what! For what! I kept asking myself this over – over again. We crossed the road and sat down on the pavement. I felt as weak as a kitten, and terribly tired. One by one, the Germans brought the wounded out and laid them on a grass bank. Then a strange thing happened. The Germans drove up in one of our own jeeps, and gave out food and cigarettes to us. Admittedly, they were our own cigs and food, that had been captured by them, but it was more than welcome. Then Bob and I tried to get a few things organised, to get the badly wounded off straight away to a German or Dutch Hospital. During the whole time, the Germans did everything they could to help us up and in no way did they treat us harshly or badly . . .

Peter Baillie was captured at Oosterback in Holland on 26 September. He was taken by ambulance to a hospital and given bread and jam. He wrote up his diary shortly after capture. Eventually, those in reasonable condition would be marched to the station and transported to Stalag XIB. Baillie would move through several camps before being liberated at the end of the war.

Saturday 23 September – Friday 27 October 1944

Sergeant Pieter Kahl, with the remnants of the 202nd Mountain Battalion, retreats through Alsace towards the German border

By 23 September Pieter Kahl's platoon had just passed through Willgottheim, a small village about 14 miles north-west of Strasbourg. They were now about 30 miles from the German border. Here, the local French population were reserved but at the same time reasonably obliging. The punishing attacks the French resistance had launched against them a few weeks ago were less in evidence. However, they now faced a new threat: ever-harsher German military discipline, designed to prevent men from retreating too hastily, engaging in defeatist talk or surrendering.

23 September

... Many wounded are being brought back. They're mostly soldiers [drafted] from the Luftwaffe who are still young and so they lack infantry training. They often had to be taken up to the front ...

29 September

... (Near Bruyeres):

... Just before evening a few comrades go to the front. NCO Jainz is staying here with his men because they have no footwear ...

2 October

... It's no exaggeration if a unit suffers 80% losses in one day. Both of our battalions are still 120 men strong. An order from the front: today 50% of the men and NCOs from the [battalion] transport column train are going to the H.K.L. [*Hauptkampflinie* – front line]. Is it that far gone? Do we have no more reserves? When will the new weapons be deployed? People say that at the moment it can possibly take up to another ½ a year. Some comfort! At the moment ½ a year is a lifetime. Relief is simply unthinkable, even if people continually talk about it. They are hollow phrases and props of hope that no one can hold onto, with which he sinks into the abyss.

3 October

The enemy flying activity has eased up due to the bad rainy weather. Instead of that the artillery has increased its fire . . . On top of that we're becoming ridden with lice.

5 October

. . . They've now laid mines behind our own lines. For what purpose? Probably so that no one can retreat any more. Today that's caused 3 deaths and 4 wounded. As well as that two officers are supposed to have been shot [for cowardice] by the court-martial.

7 October

. . . I'm being sent with a letter to the regimental command post in order to obtain a signature from the commanding officer which will entitle me to go to St. Die for delousing as there's a danger of typhus fever . . .

26 October

. . . Post from home on top of that, that makes me happy. The only thing lacking is that the damn war would end. Even the best idealism gets lost in the length and in hard, very hard combat (the losses are unbelievably high).

27 October

. . . NCO Keuzian and four men are sitting by me and listening to Dr. Goebbels' speech [on the radio]. Even they can't be inspired any more by well-delivered words and speeches. War-weariness is becoming noticeable. They say: 'If only the war would end, no matter "how" . . .' You're made guilty even by just overhearing them . . .

(Back over the German frontier)

Pieter Kahl is a classic example of why front-line forces were not allowed to keep diaries. He is thought to have surrendered at the end of November 1944 near the German town of Aachen, which is close to the border with Belgium. His diary then fell into Allied hands and, in common with so many personal journals, it was seized on as a valuable source of intelligence. In this case, Kahl's diary would be analysed by Richard Crossman, at the time a psychological warfare officer keen to assess the morale of retreating German forces. Comments written in the diary in early November 1944 about men aged sixty going to the front line and exclamations such as 'Those who retreat are shot dead without mercy' were extremely illuminating in terms of the overall cohesion of German units. Within days Kahl's diary would become the substance of an intelligence report to Eisenhower's Psychological Warfare Division. Richard Crossman's own diary of his visit to Aachen is also reproduced in this anthology. The ultimate fate of Pieter Kahl is unknown. SEE ALSO PP. 728–30.

Thursday 28 September 1944

John J. Briol, a ball-turret gunner in an American B-17 bomber, flies over Germany

John J. Briol was a ball-turret gunner with the 457th Bomb Group, 748th Squadron, based at Glatton airfield in England. His diary is a testimony of the extraordinary losses suffered by Allied aircrew over Germany and the horrific effect of watching one's comrades plunging to their death. A religious man, he often caught himself praying out loud when the flak began to burst around him on a dangerous mission.

Today, as the British would say, 'We had it,' again, we were the only one ship of our element of three to return alive. Our squadron only put up twelve ships today (part of another squadron). Only two came back. We were in a box of twelve ships. We bombed the Krupp works of Magdeburg. Waves of twenty enemy fighters attacked our box of twelve ships. There were a couple hundred enemy fighters in the area. I never expected the Luftwaffe to come back but it did, as I've seen with my own eyes. I also know God is definitely with our crew. I'm pretty sure I got a fighter today. I claimed it but I don't think I'll get credit for it because I didn't actually see it fall; I was too busy. I think Ozzie, our toggalier, got one too.

We got up about three o'clock this morning. Got our pass to briefing, went down to the theater, received Communion and went to breakfast.

I've never seen such a nice priest in my life. He's so concerned about the men. He keeps a list of all the men that are lost and also compares the names with those that receive before every mission. He asks us how missions are etc.

At briefing, as usual we groaned. This target was right next to Berlin. We were over Germany from early this morning till six tonight. We met some flak on the way to the target but it wasn't so bad, the worst was to come. As we got to the I.P. [initiation point – beginning of bomb run] we opened the bomb bay doors. We were 40 miles from the target. We had five bombs, each weighing 1000 lbs. We had 2700 gallons of gas because this was a long trip. We had about 30 miles to the target when we sighted the enemy off in the distance at 3 o'clock level. It's impossible to describe the feeling. There seemed to be hundreds of them. They went around in back of us to 7 o'clock. Then they seemed to break into groups of 20. I don't know where our fighter escort was. They came for us low. I thought we were all lost but we responded automatically. I guess I was fighting like a cornered rat but somehow I wasn't thinking of myself. There were so many I didn't know which one to shoot at. I got my sight on the nearest one and blasted away at him. All of his guns were firing at us. I tracked him all the way up along side our ship still blasting away. I forgot all about short bursts. As he came alongside, the German crosses were plain as day. I saw fire and smoke starting to come out the right side of his engine. I may get credit for shooting down that fighter. Our navigator verified it. He saw it fall in flames. I could see the dead pilot. His oxygen mask was torn off. The ship looked as if it were hanging in the air for a second, then I turned my guns away from him onto another ship just coming up on our tail. My left gun went out but all this time I was still blasting away with my right one. The other plane went off to the left without attacking. There was another going under. I tracked him all across the sky underneath getting in a few shots but he was pretty far away. The whole ship was vibrating from everyone shooting.

I was too busy but I saw most of our planes blazing and burning alongside of us. Further back I saw one blazing Fortress spinning down and breaking up. I only got in a glance at that. All of a sudden our fighter escort was there and the enemy planes scattered with P-51s on their tails. That was really a show to see the FW-190s get it instead of our Fortresses.

Our interphone had gone out on us and we could hardly talk to each other. These Fortresses are like a flying tomb without an interphone. Our no. 2 engine was shot up from the bandits but it was still pumping away.

We made it to the target with the two ships we had left. Our formations were all broken up. Planes were scattered all over. We got our bombs away in the middle of the flak. At first only two bombs went, so we salvoed the other three to hit part of the city anyway. Again our bomb bay doors wouldn't come up, so Haynes, our engineer, had to start cranking again. These doors hold the ship back a lot when open. In the process he busted the hose on his mask and almost passed out from the rarefied air. He was trying to hold his breath while someone dug out the extra mask we bring along. His face was starting to get purple and we couldn't leave our positions. The navigator came back and helped him.

Before the fighting started I was in misery because I couldn't leave the turret to relieve myself. When the fighting started I had worse to worry about, so I didn't notice it again until we were headed for friendly territory. Another thing from being in one position all the time, my legs and back ache to beat the Dickens.

Our whole squadron was shot down except two of us.

Some have compared the experience of bomber crews over Germany in 1943 and 1944 to that of the infantrymen of the First World War. Despite the arrival of P-51 Mustang fighters that could accompany the bombers all the way to the target, casualties were still very heavy. In the autumn of 1944 the Luftwaffe were still putting up substantial numbers of Focke Wolfe 190 fighters. Bomber crews would wake before dawn and begin to draw equipment. This included parachutes, harnesses and Mae Wests. The crews would carry .45 Colt automatic pistols in a shoulder holster. Flying at up to 40,000 feet in an attempt to reduce the impact of flak, they required electrically heated clothing and shoes. They also put on an oxygen mask, helmet and goggles, and a flak suit, and carried a personal escape kit in case they had to bail out. Once dressed and equipped, the crews would move to the armoury to draw machine-guns. All surplus oil had to be carefully cleaned off the guns because it would freeze in the intense cold of high altitude.

On 30 November 1944 John J. Briol and his crew would be badly hit by flak near Leipzig, losing an engine, the radio and all their landing gear. Remarkably, they managed to crash-land in a field in Belgium inside Allied territory, and the whole crew walked away from the landing. On 3 February 1945 Briol completed his last required mission and realized that he had made it safely through his tour as a ball-turret gunner − one of the most dangerous occupations of the Second World War.

OCTOBER 1944

ON 2 OCTOBER the resistance forces of Warsaw, led by General Bor (Tadeusz Komorowski), surrendered to the Germans after two months of remarkable and bitter urban warfare. During the fighting the US air force dropped supplies to the resistance, but pinpoint dropping was difficult and their situation became hopeless.

In the second week of October Winston Churchill and Anthony Eden flew to Moscow to meet with Stalin. Churchill assured Stalin that he was 'not sentimental' and suggested a realistic bargain over the future of eastern Europe. Accordingly, the two leaders settled on a 'percentages deal' by means of which they divided the Balkan region into spheres of influence. On the basis of a single piece of paper passed backwards and forwards between Churchill and Stalin, the Soviet Union would take the lead in Bulgaria, Hungary and Romania, while Britain would be the dominant power in Greece. Somehow both countries were to share influence in Yugoslavia. The awkward issue of Poland's geographical extent, together with its often changed borders, was also discussed. The ailing President Roosevelt, when learning of these agreements reached in Moscow, announced that he would take no account of them.

On 13 October the Allies liberated Athens from German rule after four years of harsh occupation. However, rival factions previously involved in resistance work against the Axis were already fighting for control of the country, which was heading towards civil war. German units in the Balkans were fleeing north at a rapid rate for fear of being cut off as the Russians moved into Czechoslovakia.

In western Europe during mid-October the US 1st Army had completely surrounded Aachen, and on 19 October Field Marshal Model gave up his attempts to relieve the city. However, as the Nazis departed they warned of vengeance against any Germans who collaborated with the new occupiers. Aachen finally fell to the 1st Army on 21 October. On 18 October Joseph Goebbels, the German Minister of Propaganda, called up the Volkssturm. These were Germany's answer to the Home Guard, but in contrast to the British, these units would actually have to fight. All able-bodied men from sixteen to sixty were now conscripted.

The German population was now fully aware that the Axis was losing the war, both in Europe and in Asia. In the Pacific during mid-October the Americans won the crucial naval battle of Leyte Gulf and began the reconquest of the Philippines. Nevertheless, the Nazi grip on Germany itself was not weakening but instead tightening. Heinrich Himmler was made Commander-in-Chief of the Forces of the Interior. On Saturday 14 October, Field Marshal Rommel committed suicide after he was implicated in the bomb plot of 20 July.

Sunday 1 October 1944

Dr Theo Morrell, Hitler's doctor, worries about the Führer's physical deterioration

One P.M. There have been two bowel movements since last night, containing disintegrating fragments. He looks better but limp. Pulse 96, temperature 36.8, blood pressure 140 mm, heart examination shows second heartbeat accentuated as usual. No epigastric tension, some tenderness still, deep down near the left flexure and deep in the pit of the stomach, but that in the gall bladder region is virtually gone. The yellow color has also largely vanished.

For lunch he had oatmeal gruel made with water, steamed fruit and an Acidol-Pepsin tablet as an experiment. Still confined to bed. Massage with Franzbranntwein lotion would seem called for but is not desired. The positive effect of the chamomile enemas is recognized, but the patient wants to continue to perform them by himself . . .

I again proposed most urgently a change of air (to Berlin) either for two or three days and then the mountains for twelve or fourteen days or just Berlin for eight to ten days. He rejects the Berghof out of hand and says Berlin is unsuitable as he (the patient) would have to keep going down to the bunker, and he cannot walk much at present, he is too weak. I referred to the unsuitability of the new bunker for him, the living and sleeping quarters are tiny and despite the ventilation system there is far too little oxygen. He is much too undemanding as the top man and leader of the Reich. He gave me a promise that he would go on more walks. 'You say that but then you don't,' I argued, and said: 'I consider it vital that you build up a physical reserve by taking in as much oxygen as possible, thereby creating better food-combustion conditions for the likely exertions of the coming months.' As I went, the Führer suddenly sat bolt upright, and said he had painful wind and stabbing pressure on his heart.

Hitler's medical condition remains a subject of substantial debate. The conventional view is that he had contracted syphilis in Vienna just before the First World War and by the 1940s was suffering extensively from its effects. Certainly the mania which he displayed during his last years would be consistent with the mental effects of the disease. He also suffered an abnormal heartbeat that was suggestive of syphilitic aortitis. The diary kept by Dr Theo Morrell offers some circumstantial evidence but no conclusive material. Hitler was vulnerable to encephalitis, dizziness, flatulence, neck pustules, chest pain, gastric pain and restrictive palsies, which are all symptoms of syphilis. Indeed, the appointment of Dr Morrell, one of Germany's experts on the disease, as Hitler's physician in 1936 is itself telling. Morrell would be dismissed by Hitler in 1944 when his medical rivals gained the upper hand. At the end of the war he would bury his diaries near his private bunker at Bad Reichenhall. He was then captured by the Allies but never prosecuted, and died in 1948. SEE ALSO PP. 585–6.

Thursday 5 October 1944

Paul Kremer, an SS doctor, watches the destruction of Münster in Westphalia, where he had previously been a professor in the medical school

Today, just before noon, when the sky was slightly clouded one of the most shattering air-raids upon Münster that I have ever experienced took place. Its duration, also the shattering effect of the screaming engines and the detonations, were exceptional. I had gone to the cellar shortly before and there I had to endure this horror alone with the three 'children of spring'. Here I had the opportunity to grasp what the fear of death really means. It would not and would not end, and with every fresh approach of the enemy's bombers one believed one's last moment had come. Tortured, shocked and exhausted, one could only press into a corner of the cellar to await the end of that hell. Smoke came over the town, driven from the east, and covered it with a thick mantle. The town had again suffered dreadfully. Especially hard hit were the Mauritz quarter and Warendorferstrasse,

including the St Francis Hospital. The railway crossing at
Bohlweg is no more, so that trains from Warendorf cannot
reach the station. On the other side passengers travelling in
the direction of Hamm are obliged to get in and out of trains
at Stille, as the Main Railway Station can no longer be used.
The situation of the Westphalia railway is similar; the trains
get only as far as Graumendorf, for the railway tracks along
Loddenheide are completely ruined. The *Landesbahnhof*
has again ceased to exist. Many soldiers have lost their
lives in the covered trench in Fürstenbergerstrasse (County
Archive). The entire harbour district stood in flames. The
Domplatz and Überwasserkirchplatz look like fields full of
bomb craters. The organ loft of the Überwasserkirche has
had a direct hit and nothing is left of it. The Spiekerhof is
impassable on account of the ruins of the houses in it.
The staircase of the University had a direct hit and is completely ruined. And only fragments are left of the backs of
the old college buildings, so that a continuation of studies in
Münster is now not possible, if only for that reason. The
university library had not been damaged very much, having
only a broken roof and windows; I met the head librarian as
he personally swept the debris from the pavement with a
broom. Opposite, the *Landesversicherungsanstalt* (County
Insurance Company) has been badly hit again, while in
Pferdegasse several houses have been completely razed to
the ground. In Ägidiistrasse there is a huge, gaping bomb
crater in front of Kolpinghaus and the street is therefore
closed to traffic. However, the arch has suffered most. After
a bomb had dislodged great quantities of earth from in front
of the *Stadtweinhaus*, both the balcony and the decorations of
that building for the most part disappeared. The old City
Hall has immense cracks in its walls, and two angels have
fallen from its top. *Kiuxen*, not far from St Lambert's Church,
was obliterated during the attack, and so was the third house
beyond the City Hall at the corner of a small street (a hat
shop). The former Englischer Hof, now Petzold, had its left
façade substantially damaged, while Stuhlmacher close by is
now quite ruined. On the other side of the arch one can see
the exteriors of houses with historical gables, but one can
look through most of them as the back parts of them have

been extensively ruined by the bombs which fell on Cathedral Square. The photographer Heinkele has lost his entire laboratory. The old historical café 'Mädendorf' (*Rombergkaffee*) is destroyed; the region of the clinics was again spared this time. The nearest bombs fell into the mounds of rubble in Hindenburgplatz and onto the back of the *Landgericht* [Law Court], tearing away a huge part of the building. Right in front of my tailor's (Hülsmann) there is a tremendous bomb crater. His flat was, of course, very heavily damaged. But my overcoat, which I had brought there to be repaired, luckily remained intact. We are again without water and there has been no electricity since September 12.

Münster had perhaps suffered the most continual bombing through the war of any German city. It had been selected for a particularly heavy raid by the RAF in July 1941, after which perhaps about a quarter of the city was destroyed. In October 1943 it was the subject of a major American daylight raid, which also produced one of the most spectacular aerial battles of the war. In 1944 the city continued to be bombed. Most of its beautiful medieval quarter was destroyed and, although this can be seen today in some splendour, almost all of it consists of restoration and reconstruction. Like Munich and Warsaw, little of the original has survived. SEE ALSO PP. 466–7.

Friday 6 October 1944

Klaus Huebner, an American army doctor, attends to American and German wounded on the Gothic Line in Italy

Klaus Huebner was a field doctor with the 3rd Battalion of the 349th Infantry Regiment – the 'Blue Devils', part of the 88th Division. He had accompanied American infantry on their long slog north through the Gustav Line towards Rome in the spring of 1944.

Several Germans are among our congregation of wounded

awaiting us. The most seriously wounded is a German who insists that he is a walking case and not badly hurt. He has a hole in his back big enough for me to see parts of his lung expanding with each breath. He states that his company has had a rough night. When only four men were left, something hit him in the back and he fell. He shouted all night but no one came to his rescue. By morning he saw our medics using this church, so he decided to walk over, give himself up, and be treated. Since he seems to be breathing better with the hole in his chest wide open rather than closed, I cover it only with a very loose dressing and fill him up with sulfadiazine pills. He says his pain is not severe enough to require morphine . . .

Frequently the narrow road crosses and recrosses the creek over small wooden bridges. These are usually de-molished, and we cross the stream on debris strewn around them. I witness the entire battalion cross over one such obstacle, except for the last man, who is unfortunate enough to have his foot blown off by a shoe mine. How 450 men have crossed over the same path and avoided stepping on that mine is almost unbelievable! . . .

By 8:00pm I am in a barn on a mountain ridge. There is no defilade, but at least I have a roof over my head. I wouldn't stay here if the weather were clear. Visibility today is only about two hundred yards, and if the Krauts want to shoot us up, they must do so by map. I am directly behind our troops, which are once again having a rough time. Progress is very slow. Sometimes they advance less than two hundred yards all day. Consequently, I remain here for three days. We treat at least fifty casualties per day. The arriving wounded are mud covered and rain soaked. The majority of wounds are gunshot and mortar shrapnel. Our station is constantly harassed by mortar fire, shells exploding outside both day and night. There are almost as many German wounded as GIs. One German non-commissioned officer is brought in with a palm-sized hole in his buttock. He had been lying in the woods for forty-eight hours. His wound is filled with leaves, sticks and dirt. What he desires most is a swig of cognac. I offer him my canteen filled with whiskey, and he empties one-half of it without drawing a breath between gulps. I loosely suture his buttock together without any anesthesia. He never says 'ouch.'

Churchill was wrong about Italy being a 'soft option'. He was right in suggesting that the Italian forces would crumble easily, but their German allies did not. The Germans exploited the excellent defensive country with skill, using the mountainous terrain to build fortifications that had to be eradicated yard by yard. The cost to both sides was high, as the crowded war cemeteries of northern Italy witness. Medics faced appalling difficulties, having to move through defensive areas infested with mines and operating in filthy conditions, usually in farm out-buildings. In early October Huebner made his way towards the heavily fortified Mount Bernadini and set up in the basement of a ruined church near the village of Pezzola about 1,000 yards behind the front line. Unfortunately, any building that provided good clean shelter for medical teams and patients became an obvious target for German artillery. SEE ALSO PP. 766–8 AND 772–3.

Monday 16 – Thursday 19 October 1944

James A. Dunn on the USS *Mason* encounters heavy weather in the English Channel

16 October

This morning found us a little closer to our destination. The sea is still raging and pitching our ship from side to side. All of the ships of the convoy are scattered about and we are try-ing to round them up just like a shepherd rounding up his sheep. The North Atlantic really lives up to its name. The rough Atlantic. Late this afternoon a call came over the PA system for all signalmen to report to the signal bridge, and all of us were there in nothing flat. We were changing course and the message had to be sent to every tug in the convoy. We were waiting for something like this anyway. And the four of us sure did lay it on them. It was fast and short. It is now 6:45 pm and I am listening to Amos and Andy (a popular radio program). However it is only 2:45 pm in the states. So I am signing off until tomorrow.

18 October

We sighted the beacon light last night and are now heading up the English Channel. We have a lot of responsibility taking all of these boats into Falmouth, England. They are hard to keep together because of the sea being so rough. We sighted the coast of England about 11:30 am and it really looks good after being out here one month today without stopping. The rest of the convoy is about forty miles behind us. They ran into a storm last night and lost one ship and seven men. We might have to go back after them . . .

19 October

We took our group of ships into England yesterday evening safe and sound. Two British ships met us in the Channel to help us the rest of the way. The weather is still very bad and a terrific storm is coming up. Around about six o'clock we received word from the commodore to come back out to sea to help escort the other ships in. The two British ships started back with us but later turned back because the sea was too rough. But we had to keep going. It didn't look as though we were going to make it but with the help of the Lord we made it safely. We have never been in a storm as rough as that one. It has calmed down a little now and we are searching for lost ships and survivors. We should reach Plymouth, England this evening or in the morning.

On 16 October 1944 the USS Mason *was escorting convoy NY-119 in atrocious weather, with seas running between 30 and 50 feet. She persevered and delivered her section of the convoy, which consisted of seventeen small oil-tankers, safely into port at Falmouth. The ship had her radio antennae blown away in the storm and suffered structural damage, such was the battering from the waves; nevertheless, after emergency repairs she heroically headed out again to bring in more ships. The* Mason *finally arrived at Plymouth on the night of 20 October. The* Mason *was recommended by the convoy commander for a formal commendation at the time, but this would not be awarded until 1995. SEE ALSO PP. 717–18.*

Wednesday 18 October 1944

Brigadier Dudley Clarke watches victory celebrations in Athens

Brigadier Dudley Clarke was the father of organized strategic deception during the Second World War. Along with signals intelligence, this was probably one of the most valuable, and certainly one of the most closely guarded secrets of the conflict. Dudley Clarke had helped to create the Commandos in 1940. Thereafter he served as General Wavell's deception planner during 1941 and created a unit known as 'A Force' to implement his complex deceptive schemes. The unit assisted Wavell in defeating a force of 250,000 Italians with an Allied force of only 50,000. Dudley Clarke's pioneering efforts resulted in the creation of a similar unit in London, which by late 1944 had already scored a notable success in effectively masking the D-Day landings in Normandy, drawing German attention instead to a fictional 'plan' to invade via Calais.

I was shown up to a magnificent suite of rooms with balconies overlooking the main square with the Accropolis [*sic*] towering behind it. All the buildings were gaily beflagged and everywhere hung banners of WELCOME. There were many strange home-made variations of the Union Jack, the Stars and Stripes and the Red Flag of Russia with many EAM banners and of course the Greek national flag. Speeches were being related over loud-speakers to cheering crowds, and I witnessed one very dramatic scene. At the end of the speech the Greek national anthem was played and the crowd stood bareheaded to attention. Just as they were moving away the band played 'God Save the King'. Only a few people recognised it, but in a few seconds all were once again strictly at attention. Opposite my window a ragged old man stood at attention cap in hand when two peasant women passed him. He said something to them as they drew abreast, and they too stood immediately beside him. It was a simple but moving scene.

Later on I went for a stroll through the streets and found myself an embarrassingly conspicuous figure. A small girl pushed a white carnation into my hand, the crowd cleared a passage for me everywhere and there were many smiles and salutes as I walked along.

Little clusters of people surrounded every British soldier who was ready to talk of his adventures – most of them were paratroops – and every lorryload of soldiers was clapped as it passed. All the streets were gaily lit with some flood-lighting, and the cinemas and theatres were going full blast. At many points crowds stood to listen to speeches or music from loudspeakers. Everywhere there was a surprising profusion of flags and . . . pictures of the Allied leaders and Papandreou as well as victory slogans and posters on all the walls.

The British liberated Athens on 14 October 1944. Although Clarke was charmed by the happy scenes that marked victory celebrations in Athens that month, by December much of Greece would have already descended into bitter civil war. The Greek Civil War was fuelled by the arms and training that had been distributed to the various underground groups in an attempt to encourage resistance to the Germans. Churchill would visit Athens in December 1944 in the hope of negotiating some sort of settlement, but sadly this cruel conflict dragged on until 1947.

Tuesday 24 October – Saturday 4 November 1944

Klaus Huebner, a US army doctor, endures pouring rain and boredom on the Gothic Line in Italy

On October 24 I move further up Mount Grande into the small town of Frassineto. Our lead companies are trying to probe the terrain beyond and extend the spearhead. I move into another shack in a gully, which is worse than the one I just left. This one still has three rooms left, namely, a pig stable, a larger former kitchen, and a living room. This is a concrete house, but the walls are cracked and the roof leaks; the cement floor is covered with mud and water. Headquarters Company will occupy the rooms and allocates the pig stable to the medics. We clean out our ten-by-six-foot pig sty and convert it into an aid station. It never becomes very liveable, however. Whenever it rains, water pours through the cracks in the walls and ceiling. All our bandages and food remain rain soaked. Muddy water seeps through the concrete floor and through the door. Every crevice and ditch on Mount Grande has turned into a muddy stream, and every stream engulfs all in its path. We usually have at least three inches of water on our aid station floor.

The next two weeks are a trying ordeal. Our troops are not advancing but are holding Mount Grande and patrolling the ridges . . .

My chief occupation is looking for food and thinking up some new menus. There isn't too much you can prepare in a pig stable. For several days my diet consists of only dehydrated egg yolks and apple flakes. Whenever a PX ration arrives, I partake of nothing but peanuts and beer until that supply is exhausted. I've eaten all the other stuff so long that it nauseates me. One day a loaf of bread is received but in our eagerness unwrapping it, we allow it to fall into the water on the floor, and it is wasted. Whenever I receive a quart of whiskey, I mix it with lemon juice powder, sugar, and water, and live on nothing but whiskey sours for another two days. On November 1 one of the men in Headquarters Company spots a cow lost on the hillside. He fells it with a bullet from his carbine. It is butchered and divided. On November 3 I eat steak fried in Barbasol shaving cream; on November 4 I have fried liver followed by a week's session of diarrhea. I will be glad when all the meat is out of my sight.

The men begin to annoy one another. Everyone is grouchy and in a bad mood. Everyone is sick and tired of wet feet, damp clothes, and early morning rheumatism. Everyone has heard the other fellow's funny story a hundred times before. No one thinks that anything is funny anymore. Even the company sergeant's famous last warning words to the nightly outgoing patrol is no longer humorous, but he nevertheless persists in saying, 'Now, any of you guys that owe me money be careful and don't get killed.'

By late October Huebner's unit were engaged in a holding operation on Monte Grande in northern Italy. Unlike the campaign in France, the war in Italy continued to move slowly. Incessant rain had set in; at least the low visibility offered some protection from shellfire. Along with the often futile quest for dry, secure accommodation, Huebner and his medics were also searching for something that would vary the monotonous diet of C rations. Quite often they would chase livestock out of an outbuilding in order to turn it into an aid station and then eat the livestock. The result was often illness from food poisoning. SEE ALSO PP. 761–3 AND 772–3.

Friday 27 October 1944

Evelyn Waugh spends a rainy day with Randolph Churchill in Croatia

A day of continuous rain. We did not leave the house. Further 'tiffs' with Randolph resulting in his making a further appeal to me for kinder treatment. It left me unmoved for in these matters he is simply a flabby bully who rejoices in blustering and shouting down anyone weaker than himself and starts squealing as soon as he meets anyone as strong. In words he can understand, he can dish it out, but he can't take it. However, as we are obliged to live together I must exercise self-control and give him the privileges of a commanding officer even though he shirks the responsibilities. I have felt less inclination to hide my scorn since his loss of self-control during the air-raid on Sunday. The facts are that he is a bore – with no intellectual invention or agility. He has a childlike retentive memory and repetition takes the place of thought. He has set himself very low aims and has not the self-control to pursue them steadfastly. He has no independence of character and his engaging affection comes from this. He is not a good companion for a long period, but the conclusion is always the same – that no one else would have chosen me, nor would anyone else have accepted him. We are both at the end of our tether as far as war work is concerned and must make what we can of it.

Evelyn Waugh's initial journey to Yugoslavia had been calamitous. He had set off from Gibraltar with Randolph Churchill on 16 July 1944 but had crashed in Yugoslavia, narrowly avoiding death, and had had to be flown back to Bari in Italy for treatment. Both men recuperated in Corsica, returning to Yugoslavia in September. Almost immediately it began to rain torrentially. Waugh found himself cloistered with Randolph Churchill and 'Freddy', the 2nd Earl of Birkenhead, for whom Randolph had fagged at Eton. Freddy's father was the famous politician F. E. Smith and Freddy was also Churchill's godson. This threesome were cooped up together for weeks on end while the rain poured down. The monotony was punctuated only by air raids, during which Randolph was inclined to panic. Waugh spent his time going to Mass (Croatia was the centre of Roman Catholicism in Yugoslavia), taking baths and arguing. In December he would be posted away to Dubrovnik, on the Dalmatian coast, as a liaison officer between British and local forces, but he was later withdrawn at the request of the Yugoslav authorities. SEE ALSO PP. 24–5, 484–5 AND 692–4.

NOVEMBER 1944

IN EARLY NOVEMBER the British Royal Marines and Commandos began a major operation to capture the island of Walcheren off the Scheldt estuary, in pursuit of the British aim of clearing the entire coast of Holland in order to use the ports for resupplying British troops as they pushed north. The operation went badly: poor weather prevented the effective use of air support and some of the assault craft were sunk. The Canadian 2nd Division was forced to withdraw from a narrow bridgehead in Walcheren. Nevertheless, on 9 November the last Germans on the island ceased resistance. The Canadians also took Zeebrugge, the last substantial area of German-occupied Belgium, on the Channel coast; and on 6 November Middelburg in southern Holland also surrendered to the Canadians, but only after heavy bombing.

By Saturday 18 November the city of Metz had been cut off

and effectively surrounded by the US 3rd Army's XX Corps. The US 95th Division then pushed its way into the suburbs, but some of the fortifications continued to hold out. In late November, in some cases fighting in the snow, the French 2nd Armoured Division took Strasbourg and also Belfort in the mountainous area of France near the Swiss border. The French were now pressing Roosevelt and Eisenhower to allow them an occupation zone of Germany. With the Allied forces well inside Germany, all eligible Germans were now ordered to enrol in the Volkssturm on pain of court martial.

At sea, many of Germany's remaining U-boats had been sunk during efforts to impede the invading forces, and they now lost most of their Channel bases and refuges. On 12 November the RAF caught up with one of the last major prizes of the naval war and attacked the *Tirpitz* with 12,000lb bombs. After several direct hits the ship capsized.

By early November the Red Army, flushed with victories in Romania, Bulgaria and Yugoslavia, reached the gates of Budapest. Hungarian and German troops mounted a savage defence of the city and the last troops would not capitulate until 13 February 1945. Operational German forces were still active in Albania.

General Scobie in Athens was given the difficult task of trying to disband the guerrilla armies in Greece. Not only here, but also in locations as far distant as Burma and Palestine, the civil wars and insurgencies that would plague the early post-war years were already beginning to gain momentum, often fuelled by large amounts of small arms left over from the major conflicts.

Winston Churchill, who was seventy years of age in November, visited Paris and received a rapturous reception. Churchill, Eden and all their entourage were now beginning to show the signs of exhaustion from a war that had already been going on for a full five years.

Sunday 5 November 1944

'Baffy' Dugdale hears of the assassination of Lord Moyne in Cairo

Lady Blanche Dugdale, the niece of the Conservative politician Arthur Balfour, was born in 1880. She was politically well connected and had been an important figure in League of Nations circles in the inter-war period. She was also a keen supporter of the Zionist cause and a close friend of both Chaim Weizmann in London and Ben Gurion in Palestine.

In the evening Linton rang me up with the dreadful news that Lord Moyne has been murdered in Cairo. Oliver Stanley [Colonial Secretary] asked Chaim to come to the Colonial Office to see him this evening (sending his car) and told him it is suspected that the assassins are Palestinian Jews. I fear it may be so, but there is as yet no certainty, and Stanley's manner of imparting the news gave Chaim a terrible shock. Linton, who went with him, reported that he came out of Oliver's room as white as a sheet. It is indeed a dreadful disaster, all the more cruel because it follows on a very satisfactory talk Chaim had with the PM when he lunched with him at Chequers last week. The PM set his mind at rest about rumours of a bad partition and assured him that no decision would be come to without consulting him. We had been very happy about this for the first time in months; and Chaim starts for Palestine on Friday. But this more than spoils all. Chaim will however be more needed than ever in Palestine, for if this murder is really committed by the Stern Gang, the Yishuv [Jewish community in Palestine] *must* now take action against them, which may well plunge the country in civil war. Also there is the risk to Chaim's life. It is a dreadful tragedy.

Lord Moyne was a prominent member of the Guinness family and had been a politician in the 1930s. In 1941 he had returned to government, becoming Secretary of State for the Colonies and Leader of the House of Lords. In August 1942 he went out to Cairo and in January 1944 was made Minister Resident in the Middle East. On 6 November 1944 he was assassinated. The premeditated attack was designed as a clear protest by various Zionist terrorist organizations operating inside British Mandated Palestine directly to the highest echelons of the allegedly pro-Arab British Foreign Office. Their anger stemmed from the refusal of the British to allow large-scale immigration of Jews into Palestine. The assassins, Eliahou Bet-Zouri and Eliahou al-Hakim, were members of the Stern and Lehi Jewish terrorist groups. They would be caught and executed shortly afterwards. SEE ALSO PP. 856–7.

US army doctor Klaus Huebner and his unit are relieved by the British

On November 5 we have exciting visitors. A British lieu-tenant and sergeant, on an advance reconnaissance mission, stop in to look over our house. They intend to relieve us in several days. Now, this is good news! The relievers will be the 11th Lancashire Fusiliers.

During the next three days our troops are gradually relieved by the British, and we have an excellent opportunity to observe their actions and manners. They are indeed dif-ferent from us. Walking in battle column, the men appear chubby and pink cheeked; one fellow smokes a pipe, the other carries a cane; the next man looks quite scholarly wear-ing horn-rimmed glasses, and carefully scrutinizes all the surrounding scenery. All seem very nonchalant and un-concerned, yet all appear very solid. The ever-present white enameled tea cup dangles from the corner of every man's field pack.

Jeeps follow the rear of the column. The British will ride in jeeps as far along as possible, no matter how horrible the trail. The vehicles are loaded to the roof with equipment; nor is seven men to a jeep an uncommon sight. Contrary to our rules and regulations in a battle zone, the roofs and windshields of the vehicles are all up. No one seems to care. The jeeps always seem to get stuck. They are either being driven off the road or into a creek, where they just remain standing upended, all four wheels off the ground. Some day they will retrieve them.

The British officers are all well groomed. Their faces are clean and their moustaches waxed. They are never without a necktie . . .

The carefree attitude of the British continues to amaze me. At night they strike matches, build fires, or sing. They will stop their vehicles in the middle of the road in broad daylight and have a spot of tea with the Krauts watching them.

They never seem to be in a hurry. They admit that war is just another big game that may last either one year or four. It makes no difference how long it takes, as long as you win.

By early November Huebner's unit was exhausted and many of the cases he was treating were battle fatigue or disease. On 5 November they were relieved and rotated out of line for a well-deserved rest. Huebner moved south to Montecatani and Rome. One of the fascinations of the Italian campaign was the diversity of units with their own curious uniforms, habits and modes of operation. Canadians, Indians, French, north Africans, rearmed Italians and many other nationalities joined British and American units pushing north. Huebner was particularly charmed by Indian units, who managed trains of African mules and sang melodiously as they made their way forward through the tough terrain. SEE ALSO PP. 761–3 AND 766–8.

Friday 17 November 1944

Richard Crossman enters the first occupied area of Germany at Aachen to examine the new problem of ruling Germans

Richard Crossman's post-war political diaries are famous, even notorious. They would chronicle his life as a rather outspoken backbench Labour MP in the 1950s, and then as a minister and Leader of the House of Commons in the 1960s. They were published amid great controversy only a decade after he retired, in the late 1970s. However, his first effort at diary-keeping has remained hitherto unknown. It captured a short period of his time as a psychological warfare officer working for Eisenhower during the invasion of Europe in 1944.

Richard Crossman

We arrived at Spa at 5.15 p.m. in driving rain. Our P.M. people were reluctant to send us on into Aachen so late at night, but the General was determined to go on. So a staff car was ordered and we pushed on up slippery roads coated with mud by the tanks. We got to Karnelimuenster as darkness was falling, and stopped at a beautiful old abbey near by where must have been originally the eighteenth century palace. It had been made into a local museum; and after the heavy bombing of Aachen had become the Nazi Party headquarters for the area. It had now become the Corps Headquarters. There we waited until the General gave the word and we went in to see General Collins. He was sitting telephoning in what was previously, I suppose, the Abbot's private sitting room, surrounded by junk from the museum and working by the light of a candle. He immediately invited us to mess and stay the night . . .

After dinner we spent the evening with General Hardin and his number two . . . They reinforced General Collins' warning that food was the central problem. So far there has not been a single case of sabotage or sniping in the 7th Corps Area. The population has been docile and ready to work. His impression in Aachen was that here too there were no problems. The population, who had refused evacuation, were overwhelmingly Catholic and anti-Nazi and their sole interest was to save what little they possessed and get their town going again. The chief problem [in Aachen] so far had been to persuade people to take responsibility. Everyone was terrified of reprisals. In Aachen they finally persuaded the Bishop's lawyer to become Burgomeister. (General Collins stated that even Colonel Wilck who had taken over the last ditch defensive at Aachen, had stated after capture that he had been warned of what would happen to his family if he did any funny business. This applies universally. Everyone is terrified of reprisals . . .

Here a note of personal observation . . . the crossing of the German frontier is something of a shock. Even in Nazi Germany the cows have four legs, the grass is green and children with pigtails stand round the tanks. Self-indoctrination by years of propaganda makes it a shock to re-discover these trivialities. All the officers we spoke with reinforced them. The people left behind in this area are human beings with a will to survive. Just because we are conquerors, and they know it, they are in certain ways easier to handle than liberated Belgians or French men. They know they must obey our orders, and, if they are allowed to survive and reconstruct their lives by self-help, they do not of themselves cause any trouble. Behind the front line, for instance, every road and by-way is littered with cables, telephone wires, etc. Minor sabotage would be child's play. It has not happened because the people are not interested in the war but in looking after themselves ...

In November 1944 Crossman, together with other officers from the Psychological Warfare Division of Eisenhower's HQ, was sent to investigate issues of morale and resistance in the first area of Germany to be occupied by the Allies. This was a pocket of western Germany around the Catholic town of Aachen, which quickly became a laboratory for the Allies. Soon they would occupy all of Germany; what would this task entail? Would the population co-operate or resist? Aachen offered the first opportunity to discover these things at first hand and was the source of endless fascination for Allied officers.

Well aware of how the Russian front had oscillated, the population of the city was very conscious that any co-operation might mean reprisals if the front moved back again. Although Aachen would not fall back into German hands, die-hard Nazis were determined to make an example of the first area of Germany lost to the enemy. On 24 March 1945 they would send in an undercover 'Werewolf' unit by parachute; landing on the outskirts of Aachen, they located the hapless Burgomeister and executed him in a garden near his house. On 1 April 1945 Reichsminister Joseph Goebbels gave a radio broadcast in which he gloated over this incident and warned that he would reach out to any other collaborators.

Crossman would return to England with several captured German diaries, one of which, that of Pieter Kahl, is reproduced in this anthology.

Tuesday 21 November 1944

Odd Nansen, a Norwegian humanitarian, watches the 'pill patrol' at Sachsenhausen concentration camp

Just now a singular patrol is marching round and round the parade-ground interminably. All are kitted up and sing and whistle as they walk. That's the 'pill patrol'. They're being used to test out a new energy pill. How long can they keep going full steam on it? After the first forty-eight hours it's said that most of them had given up and collapsed, although the theory is that after taking this pill one can perform the incredible without the usual reaction afterwards. Well, no doubt the Germans could use a pill like that now. The guinea-pigs are arrested SA men, so they say. Anyhow they sing and carry on like most Germans – so it needn't have anything to do with the pills.

The concentration camp at Sachsenhausen, a little to the north of Berlin, contained many categories of prisoner. In early November 1944 Odd Nansen watched a group of German conscientious objectors being hanged. Each was offered a last chance to serve the Fatherland but each was 'steadfast to their faith' and was executed in turn. In late November he witnessed bizarre medical experiments with an endurance drug called D-IX, which contained cocaine and other substances. The drug had been created by a research team led by a Kiel pharmacologist on the orders of Hitler's headquarters in Berlin. Eighteen Germans carrying packs of 20 kilograms ran in a circle around a barrack square for two days before collapsing from exhaustion. Wartime conditions would prevent the manufacture of D-IX on any scale.

At the end of the war Odd Nansen would be evacuated to Neuengamme ahead of the advancing Russian army and returned to Norway with his secret diary, which was published in 1949. SEE ALSO PP. 401–3.

DECEMBER 1944

DURING DECEMBER 1944, despite continued air attacks, the home front in Britain began to demobilize. The Home Guard was stood down at a major parade on Sunday 3 December where their Colonel-in-Chief, King George VI, announced that they had fulfilled their task. Over 7,000 Home Guard then marched through the centre of London prior to disbanding.

During the first week of the month Allied troops continued to advance steadily on a broad front, with significant gains in the

Saar region on the Franco-German border. The US 3rd Army was pushing into Germany beyond Aachen along a 30-mile front. On Tuesday 12 December they over-ran a large underground V-weapon factory at Wittring. Its construction in a series of deep tunnels helped to explain why Hitler's V-weapon production had been relatively immune to Allied bombing.

On 16 December the Germans began a surprise winter offensive that pushed through the thinly held American lines in the Belgian and Luxembourg sectors, hoping to drive to the coast and cut Allied forces in two. Initially the Germans did well, breaking through the American line, advancing on a 70-mile front, and pushing the Americans back to the Meuse river. However, the Americans held Bastogne and did not collapse under this sudden pressure. Bad weather had prevented the attack from being identified in advance by aerial reconnaissance, so that Allied troops on the ground had little air support as the fighting got under way. The German forces created a 'bulge' in the line but could go no further and eventually lost even that ground. This effort cost the Wehrmacht key units that would have been important in the final defence of Germany.

On Christmas Day Winston Churchill and Anthony Eden were in Athens to try to quash the emerging Greek civil war, with bitter fighting continuing between leftist and royalist factions. Churchill's intervention facilitated the creation of a regency care-taker government under Archbishop Damaskinos, who was sworn in as regent on 30 December by King George II. However, peace did not last and the factions would soon be fighting again.

Saturday 2 December 1944

Edith van Hessen on the difficulties of having escaped the Holocaust

Edith van Hessen had started a diary in 1938 when she was aged thirteen. Her reason for doing so had little to do with the gathering clouds of war, of which she was blissfully unaware, and was simply a desire to 'freeze' the happy moments that she experienced within her loving and creative family at their house in The Hague. The German invasion of Holland in May 1940 did not impinge dramatically upon her existence at first. However, being Jewish she noticed the growing network of restrictions. By 1942 repression had turned to obvious threat. Supplied with forged identity papers, she was sent to spend the war hidden away with a Christian family in a small town in the south of Holland. Having survived the war to late 1944, she was then confronted with the fate of friends and family who had not escaped.

It is strange, but I can't stand it any more when people ask me about my family. From now on I just won't tell them much. I will just say: 'Poland.' That's all. Because, of course, they feel sorry for me, and then they want to do something for me, something friendly, something cheering and consoling, but I don't want people to feel sorry for me, I feel the need to cheer up others, to give others courage, rather than to be the recipient of the same. I would so like to *do* something – for the Netherlands – for our people – for all the Dutch who have suffered. I want to roll up my sleeves and work, really work – and to show my foster parents that I am good for something. Because I *can* do it and I *want* to do it. But what?

I don't know anything about nursing. I can't go to England to be trained for the army, too young, and besides, here they would not let me go. Dammit, why isn't there anything that I can do? I have been passive for two and a half years, I just let everything come to me, even Ineke – just accepted everything, love, consolation, a home – but now, now surely the time has come for me to give something back? Now wait a minute, Edith, don't do anything hasty, take your time, think everything through first.

Sometimes I'm so afraid that Guus [her brother] is not alive. Still, I hope fervently that he is fighting for us, that he is helping all our men – for the liberation of the Netherlands, of the East Indies, for the freedom of Mother, Jules, all our friends.

Most of the time you can stay cool inside, and calm – but then again you get such a terrible longing for home, and the home you left behind, with Mother and Father and the boys. That you may never have that again – it's hard to accept. Strange, it hurts at the bottom of your skull, in the back of your throat – is that your heart that you feel aching? Silly girl.

By December 1944 Edith van Hessen was enjoying the benefits of liberation, including her first taste of Belgian chocolate for several years. She had been blessed with a kind foster family throughout the war and Edith had been pleased to discover that this family had a daughter of a similar age, Ineke, who became a close friend, almost a sister – though Edith was less pleased when Ineke began reading her diary. By December 1944 Edith was having to deal with a flood of information about life inside the concentration camps, where her mother, grand-mother and brother Jules had been taken, and uncertainty about her other brother, Guus, who had joined the Allied forces and was fighting in Germany. SEE ALSO PP. 808–9.

Monday 18 December 1944

Sergeant Henry Giles of the US army is put on the front line in the Battle of the Bulge

Sergeant Henry Giles served in A Company, 291st Engineer Combat Battalion. This unit had arrived in England in October 1943 and was initially involved in constructing bases and facilities for the large numbers of additional American troops who would follow on behind. However, in March 1944 the unit had changed over to a concentrated programme of combat training conducted at Highnam Court, Gloucester. Everyone knew this was in preparation for the invasions of Europe. By December 1944 the unit had reached the Ardennes.

Late yesterday afternoon we were called together and told as much of the situation as is known here. The Krauts *are* attacking in a very strong offensive and they have pene-trated as far as Malmédy and Stavelot and it is believed they are heading for Liège. *That* kind of news gives you the real jitters. To think they're headed right at you and in strength enough to overrun everything in their way so far. Gave me the shakes so bad I found myself lighting a cigarette and wondering why I was so awkward at it, looking down and found I already had one going . . .

They loaded a bunch of us on trucks and hauled us out, dropping two or three off at each outpost, until two other guys and myself were left and we were taken to a roadblock out on the main road west. The Krauts are expected to come from that direction and the south. The Lieut told us to position our own guns and stay till relieved. He said every position was a 'hold fast.' In other words, get killed but don't fall back. Said they'd try to relieve us in the morning.

The roadblock was nothing but some mines across a paved road and some logs and not even a damn bush to hide behind. I sort of took over, being a Weapons Sgt and got the guns in position, on either side of the roadblock and one a little farther back, but it was a naked position. A .30 cal can mow down a line of infantry but against a tank it wouldn't be much better than a rifle.

Cold, my Lord! Snow and ice and slush underfoot and a drizzle of sleet falling. The sleet fell down your neck even with your collar up and you just hunched up and tried to keep the wind and the wet out the best way you could. Gloves too short and checking the guns every now and then soon get wet, then froze. Feet were soaked inside of half an hour. I don't have any overshoes and my shoes leak like a sieve.

All we could do was stamp around trying to keep some feeling in our feet and my hands got so numb if anything had happened. I don't think I could have fired the gun. All tensed up, looking and listening, thinking every vehicle we heard – and what a hell of a lot of them there were – was a Kraut. Everything that moved scared the living hell out of us. Don't know whether I took worse from cold or fear.

One of the gunners was just a kid and he got to crying. He had been in the hospital from trench foot and said his feet were still swollen and sore and were killing him and if the Krauts came he was going to get killed anyway. His name was Logan. I felt so sorry for him I told him and the other fellow, Swain, to hang on and I'd see if I couldn't find some planks or boards or rubbish of some kind for us to stand on. Rummaged around and found a sack in a ditch but that was all. Told Logan to fold it up and stand on it and get his feet out of the slush for a while – till it soaked through the sack.

When the Germans attacked in force Henry Giles was moved up out of a reserve depot and into the front line armed with a .30 cal machine-gun. Many of the units thrown in the path of the Germans were under-experienced. On 20 December Giles was moved onto a two-man Bazooka team, but neither soldier had fired the weapon in their lives. Giles wondered aloud in his diary how the 'big brass' had allowed them-selves to be caught out so badly. The answer was that the Allies had been stretched thin by offensive action. SEE ALSO FOLLOWING EXTRACT.

Thursday 21 December 1944

Sergeant Henry Giles on German special operations behind Allied lines

But it's a hell of a mess and it makes me madder than hell for the brass to have goofed this way. All we do is take orders, but they are supposed to know. I don't see how they could have been caught short like this. Nobody knows where the Krauts are. All we know is that this whole end of Belgium is crawling with them. And they say a whole bunch have been parachuted in dressed in American uniforms, with American vehicles, all speak English and are running around behind our lines.

We have to stop every vehicle, everybody, and ask questions only a real, genuine American would know the answers to. It's real screwy and makes you jumpy as hell. Some of the questions we are told to ask, such as what is the capital of Iowa, what is Bob Hope's theme song, etc., I wouldn't know the answers to myself. They say these Krauts even have GI identification and have been briefed on the outfits they're supposed to belong to. I imagine a few real Americans will get taken in, but it's better to do that than let these spies get by.

Since the summer of 1944 Otto Skorzeny, one of the most talented German special forces commanders, had been training a unit to masquerade as Americans. They not only mastered American accents but also learned some of the finer details of American mannerisms and behaviour. Equipped with captured American uniforms and vehicles, they were sent behind the American lines. The presence of these saboteurs caused panic behind the lines and the military police rounded up anyone who could not answer questions about American football teams – including Brigadier General Bruce Clark, who proved unable to answer a question about the Chicago Cubs. Later the matter turned more serious, with numbers of the captured German commandos being tried and shot for their activities. SEE ALSO PRECEDING EXTRACT.

Christmas Day, 25 December 1944

John Mitchell, RAF navigator, visits war-torn Athens with Churchill

Airborne at 0500 on Christmas morning we set course for Selsey Bill, over the Channel to Barfleur and so south to Toulouse at 8,000 feet; the standard transport route across France. The Party had been served with their drinks soon after the aircraft settled down to its climb. The PM himself came forward soon after crossing the French coast, and thoroughly enjoyed his new aircraft's cockpit ... Into the RAF Staging Post at Pomoigliano just before 0900 hours local time, the passengers breakfasting in flight as we were scheduled for a short stop only. We were met by Admiral Sir John Cunningham and Air Marshal Sir John Slessor.

Off again at 1050 hours for Athens, routed via Cape Otranto, Cephalonia and the Gulf of Corinth. An excellent lunch served en route. Warned by the local RAF control that intermittent small arms firing was occurring in the city and the outskirts, especially towards the airfield, there was little we could do but land with the minimum of hanging around low down in the circuit. We found it bitterly cold on arrival.

Met by the Ambassador, Rex Leeper, and General Scobie, the local GOC, we found that General Alexander and Mr

[Harold] Macmillan had arrived separately from Italy. They all entered the aircraft and conferred for three hours with the PM's party in the main cabin. With the engines switched off the cabin soon cooled down and Elizabeth Layton recalls that, when summoned to take down a statement for the Press, her fingers were so cold that she could scarcely use her typewriter.

Just before dark, the PM's party set off for Piraeus to embark in HMS Ajax which was anchored offshore in support of the army. This gave them secure accommodation and enabled the PM to have preliminary talks with M. Papandreou and the Orthodox Archbishop Damaskinos: the latter was later to be dubbed a 'scheming medieval prelate' by the PM. The party drove through ELAS-controlled areas in armoured cars – the PM sitting with a giant 45 Colt revolver on his knees and a look on his face that suggested he would love to fire it . . .

Local Greek employees were not to be trusted. Some worked for us by day and for ELAS at night. The women were reported to carry hand grenades in their shopping baskets or under their black skirts. There were various alarums and excursions: the Duty Officer being called to the phone frequently. A burst of gunfire was heard but the CO said it was only someone in the Guard Room playing the fool with his Sten gun. Moral: never let the RAF have their hands on loaded small-arms. However, we had to trust the protection of the aircraft to the local RAF, for the army had no troops to spare. Even so, a stray bullet had made a hole in one of the undercarriage doors, but we did not tell the Owner until we were on our way home. Politically, the PM made surprisingly successful progress in the conspiratorial atmosphere of an Athens cellar. Grounds for a cease-fire and settlement seemed to have been arranged, with Damaskinos taking the title of Regent. On the second day of our stay at Hassani, Bill and I were summoned into the Embassy in the centre of the city to hear the plans for departure. There was no question of an armoured car for us; we were driven into town in the back of an open RAF truck, 'guarded' by an evil looking local desperado with a Sten gun on his lap. These weapons were notoriously light on the trigger. The vehicle bounded around horribly. I was much more afraid of being shot by the guard than by ELAS.

In December 1944 Churchill took delivery of a new personal aircraft. This was a luxurious Skymaster, an enormous plane with the unusual benefit of a level cabin floor. The flight crew no longer had to travel in a cockpit cluttered by despatch boxes and crowded with other staff, such as Churchill's own bodyguard. Sawyers, Churchill's valet, now had room to lay out all of Churchill's uniforms. Athens, the first destination for this new 'aerial yacht', was a strife-torn city where the communist ELAS guerrillas had ceased to fight the Germans and had turned their attentions on the British, who favoured the royalist factions.

Mitchell continued to serve in the RAF after the war, retiring as an air commodore. He later moved to Canada. SEE ALSO PP. 560, 566–8 AND 617–18.

Christmas Day, 25 – Boxing Day, 26 December 1944

Bruce Bain, soldier and poet, endures a reflective Christmas on a troopship from Tripoli to Aden

Christmas Day has been pathetic. The morning service was genuine and moving; at the foot of the stair the popular C.O. shared a hymn book with a young erk. Afterwards Father Neptune toured the ship, but we missed it. We played cards. Dinner was fatty pork, which I couldn't finish. We had a Christmas present of six mintoes and two bars of chocolate. In the afternoon we played cards, and we played cards after tea. Then we sang, very deliberately, hearty community songs, but the act wasn't very convincing. Self-pity was rife. Somehow we were cheated. Some of the last delusions vanished, and we were a little more alone. Comfort and Christmas and easy comprehensible worlds were far behind. We were, I think, growing up. The alliterative bitterness is involuntary.

Walked on deck before breakfast to find Port Said. It was,

of course, like any other port, except for some gigantically irrelevant greenery on the starboard side. Palms and evergreens grew incongruously together. They looked new and awkward, as if they had just been painted on the wrong set. The bumboats were already alongside, and all day there has been a brisk traffic in wallets, fezzes and handbags. The Egyptian police row about in small boats delightfully dressed in cavalry breeches and riding boots. There is an unpleasant smell. We talk about the end of the war and our release. Every morning we start this discussion and we say the same things. We never get tired of talking about it.

The limitation of space at sea gives a curious sense of personal freedom. Your walks are restricted – fore and aft, backwards and forwards – till you know the decks 'by heart.' Knowing the ship as an entity gives a point of departure. This is the perfect opportunity for the contemplative life. Somehow, this restricted *completed* world gives scope for self-completion. There is no new sensual experience to delay the reluctant conscious mind . . . But there are too many men. There is no privacy. You cannot be alone for a minute. Even the lavatories lose their power of sanctuary; they have no doors, and we sit with artificial nonchalance, carefully avoiding each other's eyes. Eating, we use our knives and forks with difficulty, and at night, leaning over the rail in the warm night, we press against each other, silently, and look out to sea. There is a lighthouse. A tiny answer on the horizon. We look, and then stumble below deck, where the hammocks swing in rows, in a thick heavy sweaty heat. Crouching and ducking, we reach our own and swing ourselves in.

Harry leans over and recites Rupert Brooke and asks me if I like Baroness Orczy.

We are slipping down the canal by moonlight. Doug and I stood on deck, singing with three boys playing mouthorgans, while the ship rolled lazily onwards, under a sky choked with stars.

By December 1944 many newly recruited soldiers were destined for Asia rather than Europe. The group in which Bruce Bain sailed left England in mid-December and passed through Gibraltar and the Mediterranean.

After a few days' rest at Port Said, they were moved by troopship through the Suez Canal towards Aden. From there they were taken across the Indian Ocean to Bombay and Trincomalee, where Mountbatten's forces were building up for a major offensive against the Japanese. Many believed that the Far Eastern war would drag on into 1946 or 1947. The journey was long and there was ample time for literary pursuits, both reading and writing. Some immersed themselves in the writings of a previous generation of soldiers who had fought in the First World War.

1945

'I FOUND THIS DIARY in a couple of exercise books in the blue cupboards at Neauphlé-le-Chateau.

'I have no recollection of having written it.

'I know I did. I know it was I who wrote it. I recognise my own handwriting and the details of the story. I can see the place, the Gare d'Orsay, and the various comings and goings. But I can't see myself writing the diary. When would I have done so, in what year, at what time of day, in what house? I can't remember . . .'

Marguerite Duras comments on her diary for 1944 and 1945

JANUARY 1945

IN JANUARY 1945 the Red Army, led by General Zhukov, began a major offensive in Poland. Warsaw fell to Soviet forces on 17 January, followed by the cities of Lodz, Tarnow and Krakow a few days later. More importantly, the Germans were being pushed back from their defensive lines along the major rivers. By the third week of January they had abandoned their positions on the Vistula and then the Oder. On 28 January the Red Army began to move into German Pomerania. Russian soldiers treated the German population with extreme brutality, expressing a wish for vengeance for previous German activities inside Russia. A wave of panic passed through eastern Germany. An army of more than 200 Soviet divisions now began to move towards Berlin, which was less than 50 miles away, and would start to chew its way through the city's outer defences in February.

Meanwhile, on the Western Front during early January the American 1st and 3rd Armies began to push the Germans back on either side of the Ardennes salient with vigorous offensives. On 3 January the US 1st Army made good progress with counter-attacks on the northern side and by the 21st had driven the Germans back from the Ardennes 'Bulge' to their earlier positions. Hitler now began to direct German forces at the divisional level and below, issuing orders even to small units. Further south, the French 1st Army under General de Lattre de Tassigny was attacking the Colmar Pocket in northern Alsace. At the end of the month the town of Oberhausen, well inside the Rhineland some 10 miles north-east of Duisberg, fell to the Allies. The operations against Germany meant that the flow of Allied supplies to the Italian front had all but halted and so no major offensive was attempted there.

The Allied air forces were primarily involved in supporting the ground offensives in the west, as well as attempting to damage communications targets and also oil supplies. The 2nd Tactical Air Force, composed of RAF, Commonwealth and Free

European squadrons under British command, was extremely active in the Ardennes when weather permitted, and the remorseless search for V-1 and V-2 weapons sites went on. The latter efforts were assisted by Danish saboteurs who attacked a V-2 factory in Copenhagen. The Luftwaffe continued to put up a substantial defence, not only with fighters but also by attacking Allied airfields in Belgium, Holland and France – airfields that until recently it had itself occupied. These attacks caught the Allies off guard and over 300 aircraft were lost on the ground. However, this was the last major initiative attempted by the Luftwaffe, and by the end of January it had lost about a quarter of its remaining 800 planes, and in any case had little fuel for those remaining.

At the end of the month Roosevelt and Churchill came together on the island of Malta – now somewhat restored after its years of siege in the early part of the war – to discuss the final phase of the campaign against Germany with their commanders. Both of them were unhappy with the obvious scale of Soviet ambitions in Europe, but Roosevelt expected this problem to be resolved over time through the United Nations. Roosevelt's primary objective was to ensure a unified commitment to a working United Nations, as would become clearer when the Allied leaders moved on to the Yalta conference with Stalin in the first days of February 1945. Roosevelt began a fourth term of office as US President on 20 January, but was looking increasingly frail.

Behind the front line it was possible to detect a creeping restoration of normality. On 16 January the London to Paris boat-train service resumed after a hiatus of more than four years.

Monday 1 January 1945

Hans Ulrich Rudel, Stuka pilot, is decorated by the Führer at his Western HQ

Hans Ulrich Rudel was born during the First World War in Silesia, the son of a priest. Hans showed no academic prowess and did not do well at school in activities other than sport. In 1936 he joined the Luftwaffe and proved to be an outstanding pilot who specialized in ground attack missions on the Eastern Front. By the spring of 1943 he had flown over 1,000 missions and was firmly established as a national hero. In that year he was moved to a new elite 'Panzerjagdkommando Weiss' unit created at Briansk and converted to a new tank-busting version of the Stuka aircraft, armed with two 37mm cannon. In late March 1944 one of his comrades was shot down and could be seen on the ground behind enemy lines. Rudel decided to land to rescue his comrade, but could not take off again because of the boggy ground. His party swam the icy River Dniestr to escape; only Rudel survived. Then, in November 1944, during missions against Russian ground forces in Romania, he had been shot in the thigh, but flew in combat a few days later with his leg in a plaster cast.

A fairly long drive through the forest brings us into a town of huts and chalets, the Führer's Western HQ. Over coffee I tell Wing Commander von Bülow about the latest happenings on the Russian front; after twenty minutes he leaves me, comes back at once and briefly asks me to follow him. Quite unsuspectingly I follow him through several rooms, then he opens a door, stands aside for me to pass and I am face to face with the Führer. All I can think of is that I have not put on a clean shirt; otherwise my mind is a blank. I recognise the other persons standing round him: the Reichsmarschall, beaming – very unusual of late – Admiral Dönitz, Field Marshal Keitel, the Chief of the General Staff, Lieutenant General Jodl and a number of other military notabilities including Generals from the Eastern front. They are all grouped round an enormous table spread with a map showing the present situation in the field. They look at me and this scrutiny makes me nervous. The Führer has noticed my embarrassment and regards me for a while in silence. Then he offers me his hand and praises my last operation. He says that in recognition of it he is awarding me the highest decoration for bravery, the Gold Oak-leaves with Swords and Diamonds to the Knight's Cross of the Iron Cross, and is promoting me to the rank of Group Captain. I have been listening to his words in a semi-daze, but when he says with marked emphasis: 'Now you have done enough flying. Your life must be preserved for the sake of our German youth and your experience', I am on the alert in a twinkling. This means

I am to be grounded. Goodbye to my comrades!

'My Führer, I cannot accept the decoration and promotion if I am not allowed to go on flying with my wing.'

My right hand is still clasped in his, he is still looking me in the eyes. With his left hand he gives me a black, velvet lined case containing the new decoration. The many lights in the room make the diamonds sparkle in a blaze of prismatic colours. He looks at me very gravely, then his expression changes, and he says: 'All right, you may go on flying', and smiles.

At this a warm wave of joy wells up in my heart and I am happy. Afterwards von Bülow tells me that he and the generals nearly had a stroke when I made my proviso; he assures me that the sheet lightning in the Führer's face does not always resolve into a smile. Everyone offers his congratulations, the Commander in Chief of the Luftwaffe with especial cordiality; he gives me a hefty pinch in the arm from sheer delight. Admiral Dönitz's congratulations are rather qualified, for he adds a trifle snappishly:

'I consider your persuading the Führer to allow you to go on flying unsoldierly. I have also had good U-boat captains, but sooner or later they have had to give up.'

It is a good thing he is not my C-in-C!

For his bravery in March 1944 Rudel had been awarded Diamonds to his Knight's Cross with Oak-leaves and Swords, the highest German military award. For his efforts in November 1944 the German authorities had found it necessary to create a new decoration, having run out of top medals. In February 1945 Rudel would again be seriously wounded, by anti-aircraft fire near Frankfurt. He landed in German-held territory, where his leg had to be amputated. A hospital in Berlin quickly fitted him with an artificial limb so he could be returned to his squadron. In the last days of war on the Eastern Front he would offer to fly a suicide attack with his squadron, but instead he was kept back – some believed, so that he could fly Hitler to safety. In May, when Germany surrendered, he took his aircraft west to surrender to the Americans and was interrogated at length before being sent to a hospital in Bavaria to recover. In 1946 he began working as a haulage contractor; however, in 1948 he emigrated to Argentina, where he was employed by the aircraft industry and where he also set up a local branch of the Nazi party.

Saturday 20 January 1945

Guy Liddell, Head of MI5's B Division, discusses a possible merger of MI5 and MI6 with Peter Loxley, Cadogan's private secretary

Guy Liddell

I saw Peter [Loxley] at the Club. I asked him what had been the result of the conversation between Cadogan [senior official at the Foreign Office] and Grigg [Minister of State for War] a propos of the enquiry into the relations between ourselves and Section V [of MI6]. He said that Grigg had been worried about Bridges [the Cabinet Secretary] conducting the enquiry since his absence would undoubtedly have come to the notice of the PM who would have wanted to know all about it and moreover he felt that as much of the material was very delicate, particularly Roger Hollis's work, it would be undesirable to have the papers relating to the enquiry floating around 10 Downing St. where they might be seen by the Beaver [Lord Beaverbrook]. He thought it would be infinitely preferable if the enquiry were conducted by somebody away from Cabinet Secretariat circles. In this connection Findlater Stewart [Head of the Home Security Executive] had been suggested though no final solution had been reached. Peter inclines to the view that anything in the nature of total amalgamation will not be acceptable though it may be desirable. I said that in my experience once things of this sort reached Cabinet level it was the toss of a coin whether they went right or wrong. Peter entirely agreed and mentioned off the record the atmosphere in which SOE's future was being discussed. There had been several minutes by Eden and by the Chiefs of Staff and the papers had come up to the PM at the end of a rather tiring day. He had written across them 'let Major Morton look into this and advise. SIS I know but who are SOE? I know S. Menzies. He is head of MI5'.

Sir Stewart Menzies was in fact Head of MI6 not MI5. This diary entry underlines the extent to which senior figures at Cabinet level were exhausted by 1945. Churchill in particular increasingly tended to make policy on the basis of what he read in the newspapers rather than reading his detailed briefs. Churchill had traditionally taken a very strong interest in intelligence, but now could not even recall the identity of the SOE, the legendary wartime sabotage service that he himself had helped to found. Guy Liddell and MI5 had little confidence in the senior management of MI6, which was undoubtedly weak. Earlier that month Liddell had told Peter Loxley that while a merger made sense organizationally, MI5 would need a guarantee that 'all the hopelessly dead wood in SIS [MI6] would be removed' as they could not work under such people. The individuals they wanted to see go in MI6 were the whole top echelon of management, including Sir Claude Dansey and Colonel Valentine Vivian. This top stratum was not removed and the merger did not proceed. On 27 February 1945, Liddell's diary records that he shared these thoughts 'quite frankly' with one of his contacts in MI6, Kim Philby. SEE ALSO P. 20.

Thursday 25 – Saturday 27 January 1945

Robert Buckham, a Canadian POW, evacuates in a panic to escape the Russians

Robert Buckham was born in Toronto in 1918. He served as a pilot with the Royal Canadian Air Force and flew Wellington bombers with 428 Squadron over France and Germany. Shot down near Bochum in Germany in April 1943, he had been imprisoned north of Dresden at Stalag Luft III, the famous site of the 'Great Escape'. Buckham recorded his time as a POW in different ways: he kept an excellent diary and also painted portraits of his fellow prisoners. He preserved these paintings in two tubes made out of food cans, which he carried with him at all times.

25 January

The camp is tense tonight. The Russians are but forty-six miles distant at Steinau, west of the Oder River. This morning a long low rumble lasting for a half-minute was identified as gunfire.

Our most recent news broadcast at 4 pm today is likely twelve hours old, and the Russian pace is fast. Tomorrow could be our day.

We are prepared to pack immediately. Backsacks and packboards are in major production throughout the camp, the latter being supervised by ex-mountie Rod Ball, who became thoroughly familiar with them in the Arctic. Iron ration is being prepared as well. This is a 'dry' cake, made with finely ground pilot biscuits, chocolate powder, raisins, prunes (pitted), and black-bread crumbs. These ingredients are mixed with warm margarine which hardens as it cools. The finished product not only has the appearance of chewing tobacco but resembles it in other ways also.

We ate potato peelings for lunch, once again, although the selection has narrowed considerably, after which we received a further bread ration. This is considered to be significant. Apart from the tension, our energies have been spent by trudging seven circuits. Twice around is considered to be about a mile.

A near-panic was caused tonight by an unconfirmed rumour that the goons were actually pulling out and leaving us behind. There are an estimated 15,000 to 20,000 Allied Airforce POWs in the several compounds in this area and some conjecture has arisen that the Russians will arm us and order a common advance against the Germans. As Eliza said, 'Not bloody likely!'

27 January

It is 1:30 pm. We have been waiting to leave camp for over two hours.

A breathless runner read the German order to us at 8:30 pm. We were to be ready to march in one hour. A moment of disbelief was immediately followed by a reaction verging on panic. Lockers were stripped. Duffle bags were stuffed to the overflow, unpacked, and packed again. At 9:30 a runner announced a delay of half an hour . . .

Two hours later the room is a shambles. Torn bedding, broken glass, splintered bunks, discarded clothing and boots, overturned stools, chairs, and table . . .

Buckham began marching away from the Russians on 27 January 1945. After several days of walking in bitter weather, he was put on a train to a POW camp at Tarmstedt, south of Hamburg. Many of the prisoners and the guards suffered frostbite on the journey. Keen to record the experiences of his fellow prisoners, he now exchanged cigarettes for paper, brushes and watercolours. He would undertake a second march in February to a new camp at Lübeck, from which he was liberated on 3 May 1945. Subsequently he returned to Canada and began a career in advertising in Montreal; on retirement he moved to Vancouver.

Monday 29 January 1945

Baron von Aufsess, a senior German administrator on
Jersey, observes the ironic use of 'Heil Hitler' among
German officers

The way people greet each other reflects the disorder of the
times. 'Heil Hitler' has never really caught on. To the
General, I say 'Heil Herr General' and he says 'Heil dear
Aufsess'. In speaking to Helldorf on the 'phone, I omit any
form of greeting, which conforms to his undercover method
of transacting business. Lt-Colonel Lindner and I are on
friendly 'Grüs Gott' terms. Colonel Heine I greet, with
proper caution and circumspection, according to the other
people present; not with 'Heil Hitler' if this is possibly
avoidable. With the younger officers and with Schade 'Heil
Hitler' is expedient; with the Geheime Feldpolizei [secret
field police] the iron rule. Almost a pity when this special
greeting, reserved for people one dislikes or distrusts, falls
out of usage.

*War conditions had toughened and the Channel Islands had begun to
endure a siege after the D-Day landings cut them off from German-
occupied France. At this point, in June 1944 the relatively relaxed Oberst
Graf von Schmettow, the Commander-in-Chief, had been replaced by the
hard-line Vice-Admiral Huffmeier. Aufsess's diary is a delightful
comment on the gradual subversion of Nazi values in the German army
as the war progressed. After the war he would be held in Britain until
1947 before returning to a law practice in Bamberg. An admired and
respected supporter of the arts, museums and culture, he died in 1993.
SEE ALSO PP. 730–2.*

Late January 1945

Maureen Stuart-Clark accompanies Churchill to Malta, en route to the Yalta conference

Maureen Stuart-Clark was born into a colonial family in Singapore in the 1920s. She was serving as a Wren officer and in 1945 became one of the first female 'flaggys', or flag lieutenants, to a senior officer attending the major end-of-war conferences – in her case Admiral Sir James Somerville, with whom she had worked in Washington during 1944. This was an unusually elevated role for a female officer during the war and accordingly her diary contains interesting observations on both gender and class. Female facilities were rarely provided for officers at her level, so she often found herself billeted with female clerks and typists.

Maureen Stuart-Clark

Breakfast ... was rather a strain with the 1st Sea Lord, Admiral Sir John Cunningham, and U.J. ['Uncle' James – her nickname for Admiral Somerville] all feeling equally cheerful at one end of the table and making innumerable jokes at our expense at the other end. After dinner the first night, Gerald Paul, J. Cunningham's Flaggy, and I thought it would be tactful to disappear so we ... drove round Malta for about an hour returning rather pleased with ourselves. However, we were greeted with rather anger-torn faces in his office as there had been a flap in our absence owing to the P.M. giving an early E.T.A. [estimated time of arrival] and there was no-one to do the necessary phoning etc. The P.M. eventually arrived at 2 a.m. in his plane, and drawn up on the freezing airfield were all the nobility in the land and all the half-perished Chiefs of Staff. The bitter blow fell when his plane taxied to a standstill and the door was opened by Commander Thompson [Churchill's aide], saying 'Oh, dear, didn't you get the message – the P.M. is asleep in bed and doesn't intend to get out until tomorrow morning – he didn't want anyone to meet him!!'. They were all quite infuriated and I don't blame them.

In January 1945 Maureen Stuart-Clark joined the British delegation to the Yalta conference. Yalta was a resort in the Crimea on the edge of the Black Sea, and various parties travelled out via Malta in late January. Although VIP aircraft equipped for this purpose had improved greatly during the war, the problems of long-distance air travel were still all too apparent. It was not only slow and arduous by modern standards, but also perilous. Another aircraft carrying a number of Foreign Office officials to Malta became lost in the gathering dark of early evening and could not find land. Running out of fuel over the sea, it was forced to ditch, killing most of the occupants. One of those killed was the young Peter Loxley, Alexander Cadogan's private secretary and one of the key unseen figures involved in the management of Britain's expanded wartime intelligence community. Peter Loxley appears in this anthology in Guy Liddell's diary entry for 20 January 1945, a week before his death. SEE ALSO PP. 803–7.

FEBRUARY 1945

A T THE BEGINNING of February the 'Big Three' – Roosevelt, Churchill and Stalin – met in Yalta, a seaside location on the Crimean peninsula which had recently been liberated from the Germans. Their main business was post-war planning and the dividing up of reclaimed territories. The discussions at Yalta, which involved substantial changes of national borders, have remained controversial ever since, and details of the meeting would remain secret long after the end of the war. The Soviet Union agreed to declare war against Japan and was offered in return the southern half of Sakhalin Island, the Kurile Islands and an occupation zone in Korea. Plans for the final surrender of Germany, for post-war occupation and for reparations were also agreed. One of the most awkward issues was the future of Poland, which was effectively moved westward, to the benefit of Russia and at the cost of German territory. Poland's western borders were extended to the Oder–Neisse Line – well inside eastern Germany. For his part, Roosevelt secured an apparently enthusiastic Soviet commitment to support the embryonic United Nations.

In early February the US army captured the first of seven Ruhr dams. Retreating German forces blew up the floodgates of the great river, flooding the area immediately west of Cologne and hampering the use of pontoon and assault floating bridges by Allied troops. Nevertheless, by 11 February the US 1st Army had captured the most important Ruhr dam. By the end of the month the 1st and 9th Armies had made rapid advances on the Cologne plain as the morale of the German army at last began to crumble. By the end of the month the Allies were approaching the city of Cologne.

Belgium was now completely free of German forces. British and Canadian troops continued their northward progress and opened a wide offensive, pushing into Holland to the south of Nijmegen and then into northern Germany to destroy the main

Siegfried Line defence zones. In the south, General de Lattre's French forces had captured over 22,000 German prisoners since mid-January. However, Germans who wished to surrender had to choose their moment and risked being shot by their own side if they were caught merely 'talking defeatism'.

During early February the RAF's Balloon Command, largely staffed by WAAFs, was disbanded because the air-raid threat to Britain had reduced. Balloon Command had managed thousands of barrage balloons that had presented a real impediment to incoming bombers on account of the steel wires that moored them in place. Even in the latter stages of the war the barrage balloon had proved effective in destroying nearly 300 V-1s.

On 14 February the RAF and USAAF launched a massive attack on the city of Dresden. The death toll remains a matter of dispute, but was undoubtedly well over 40,000 – and, taking into account the influx of refugees into the city from the east, possibly higher. One purpose of the bombing was to show the advancing Russian army the scale of the Western contribution to the defeat of Germany. Berlin was bombed for thirty-six nights in a row during February and March, while the communications system in central Germany, including most major railway stations, was effectively destroyed. Advancing Allied forces brought civil affairs units in their wake, and these were already beginning to wrestle with the problems caused by the scale of the aerial destruction wrought by their own side.

Neither Hitler nor Goebbels accepted that they were losing the war. They continued to talk in terms of an absolute victory that simply required one final and supreme effort. Nevertheless, particular reverses required explanation and responsibility was gradually pinned on the German people, who were increasingly portrayed as 'unworthy' of their great leaders. On the Eastern Front a large proportion of the population were fleeing the Russian army, or going into hiding in the countryside. On the Western Front a grateful populace received the enemy with white flags and soldiers had to be coerced into fighting. In all areas of Germany the home front was characterized by a mass exodus from the towns to the countryside. This had begun in 1944, with the intensification of bombing, but was now exacerbated by a breakdown in the system of rationing. In the towns there was little food.

With the end of the war in sight, a number of countries that had hitherto been neutral sought to jump on the bandwagon of victory. On 23 February Turkey, hitherto neutral, declared war on Germany. On 25 February the premier of Egypt, Ahmed Pasha, proclaimed that his country had declared war against Germany and Japan, but ultra-nationalists saw him as a colonial collaborator and assassinated him within hours. Nevertheless, the Egyptian parliament approved the declaration of war the following day. Although these countries were a little late entering the fray they were comfortably ahead of Argentina, which did not declare war on Germany until 27 March.

Saturday 3 – Saturday 10 February 1945

Maureen Stuart-Clark arrives in the Crimea for the Yalta conference

The British delegation to Yalta were to be accommodated at the Vorontsov Palace in Alupka, once the residence of Count Mikhail Vorontsov. This had been designed by the well-known British architect Edward Blore, a major figure in nineteenth-century romantic architecture. With 150 rooms, it incorporated a curious mixture of Tudor and Moorish styles. It is now a museum of Russian and Western art.

On February 3rd we took off at 2 a.m. [from Malta] for the Crimea. They had converted two of the seats in our plane into bunks for Jumbo [General 'Jumbo' Wilson] and U.J. [Admiral Somerville]. They looked too sweet tucked up in bed like two naughty boys whilst we curled up uncomfortably in our seats preparing for a sleepless night. As dawn came we were over the South of Greece, and I actually saw the sun rise over the Black Sea which was a lovely sight. When we came over the Russian coast it was just what we expected – bleak, snowcovered and very flat. We landed at about 11.30 a.m. local time and muffled up in our snow boots etc. climbed out to find an absolute host of uniforms and

Russians to meet us. We were taken to tents where a meal was laid out and invited to help ourselves. We hoped it was breakfast, but were informed it was lunch, and as it consisted of bits of bread and cheese, chocolate biscuits, vodka, champagne, and eggs rolling about in their shells we were by no means satisfied. U.J. hopefully took an egg, banged it on his plate at which it burst spluttering all over him and us as it was raw! I consumed a glass of vodka and champagne and was just about to start eating when I was told the car was ready so I left feeling definitely empty and rather dizzy. I found myself in a Russian car with two Ogpu [KGB] drivers in front, U.J. and Jumbo Wilson in the back and Mark Chapman Walker and I on bucket seats in front of them with the luggage on our laps. We were told the drive was 110 miles so I felt even more miserable. Oh, I should have mentioned that Mr Molotov [the Russian foreign minister] was there to greet us. The Ogpu [KGB] wear black cloth caps and seem to be tin Gods, they professed to understand no English at all, but it was quite obvious that they did. During the whole of the 100 miles there was a Russian sentry every 150 yards, a female soldier at every cross roads and an officer every mile, and we had to salute every one.

The first part of our journey was bleak, flat, snow covered and desolate. The only dwellings we saw were more or less mud huts and the peasants looked extremely gross, hard and healthy but very drab and grim. We drove, drove and drove, getting very cold and weary. Every so often we saw convoys of other cars stopped at the side of the road for a very obvious reason, but the endurance of our travellers seemed to be amazing, and my champagne wasn't feeling at all comfortable.

We then started to climb a pass in the mountains about 3,000 feet up and the scenery became more interesting. Periodically we passed derelict German or Russian tanks and any town we passed through was completely gutted. Finally I could exist no longer so I turned round to Field Marshal Wilson and said 'Do you mind if we stop soon, Sir' to which he replied rather ponderously 'No, No, but *you*'d better choose the place'. I did – one of the derelict Russian tanks to which I plodded through the snow . . .

Eventually ... we arrived at the Voronthov [*sic*] Palace
where the British Chiefs of Staff were going to be accommodated. It was quite the ugliest place I have ever seen –
built in a mixture of Moorish and Gothic styles. The entrance
at either end was Gothic with castle like turrets and gate,
while the centre was Moorish with minarettes [*sic*] and
domes. It had been built for Prince Yusof who killed
Rasputin and had not been destroyed because it had been
promised to the German General who captured the Crimea,
and had left it till too late to destroy it. We found the rest of
us were housed in two sanatoriums between five and ten
minutes drive down the road. They had been old Palaces,
partially destroyed by the Germans and rebuilt especially for
this occasion. We spent the first evening desperately trying
to organise luggage, office papers etc. and tempers were
fairly short. Most of the Kremlin guard had come down to
act as guards and sentries, and they looked very smart in
their khaki uniforms with their high boots, red and blue
caps, gold braid etc. They had sent down hordes of interpreters from Moscow – mainly women – who spoke
excellent English although they had never left the country.
Actually the whole thing was rather superficial and unreal.
Russia is definitely a hard, ruthless country and yet they had
laid on the most terrific show for the British, which includes
maids in caps, aprons and high heeled shoes which they had
never worn before and consequently presented a ludicrous
spectacle wobbling unsteadily around; interpreters in new
suits and stockings so they would not be inferior to us;
vodka, champagne, smoked salmon etc. when the only
ration they themselves are certain of getting is black bread; it
rather disappointed me as one thought they could have
afforded to say 'We've done jolly well on this so you ought
to try it and jolly well like it'. The water was unsafe to drink
and the *only* liquid there was to swallow was the vodka,
champagne etc. so we spent the whole time either very
definitely muzzy or else parched with thirst! They even
brought a lemon tree all the way from Batoum so that there
would be lemon for the drinks, but they never thought to
provide a simple plug for the basins! The sanitary arrangements were the most peculiar thing. In our place there was a

bath and three showers all in a little hut together down the garden. There was a sweet peasant girl in attendance who scrubbed your back vigorously, irrespective of your sex, in fact there was considerable trouble at first as they all bath and swim in the nude together and couldn't understand our reluctance to bath with Major Generals or Naval officers at the same time. You ploughed down the garden in your great coat and hoped you wouldn't get pneumonia returning. *But* – the lavatory situation was the grimmest. In the Palace there was a total of 3, one of which was kept for the private use of the P.M. The other two had to provide for the use of the 3 Chiefs of Staff, General Ismay, F.M.s [Field Marshals] Alexander and Wilson, U.J., Anthony Eden, Lord Leathers, Sir Ralph Metcalf, lots of foreign office boys, typists, clerks, sentries, maids, interpreters, Marine orderlies and *all* the visitors. The result was that we lost all shame and openly discussed the best bushes in the garden which was the only solution.

Conditions at the Yalta meeting were slightly surreal. The Russians had mounted a fantastic effort to provide international conference facilities in a part of the Soviet Union that was still recovering from German occupation. The results were uneven: many of the bathroom fittings in some of the buildings had been torn out of hotels in Moscow and hastily refitted in Yalta. Although the baths and basins were of the highest quality, the result of hasty assembly was that only a trickle of brown mud came out of taps. For decades afterwards, plumbing in some of the best hotels in Moscow failed to work, and the staff would patiently explain that it had suffered from being transported to Yalta and back again for the international conference of February 1945.

Delegations to conferences attended by Stalin were always struck by the intense security of the Soviet arrangements. Maureen Stuart-Clark remarked that the women sentries were 'immense, tough, and had the largest legs I had ever seen'. She was fascinated to learn that women in the Soviet armed forces seemed genuinely the equivalent of men and enjoyed forward combat roles. She noted that they all had weapons, usually tommy guns, and 'you at once realised why the Huns did not spare them'. They were 'very insulted' if anyone suggested that they were 'members of a Women's service'. This was very different from the situation of women in the British and American armies.

Maureen Stuart-Clark continued to serve as flag lieutenant to Admiral James Somerville until the end of the war, when they both left the navy. Shortly afterwards she married Commander Robert Allan who, like her, had undertaken naval liaison duties in Washington. Her husband became an MP in 1950 and thereafter they were both heavily involved in the life of Whitehall and Westminster. In 1973 she became Lady Allan. She now lives in Hampshire and is a patron of the World Community for Christian Meditation. SEE ALSO PP. 799–800.

Sunday 4 February 1945

Ursula von Kardorff and her fellow journalists await the fall of Berlin

The new offices at Tempelhof are a madhouse. It takes two or three hours just to reach them. We all sit in an enormous room with glass walls, like parrots in the Zoo. We are robots, performing functions that everybody knows to be pointless. For example, we have to get out long leaflets every day filled with horror stories about the Russians or with asinine appeals and exhortation. 'Hold fast,' because Goebbels says that we are on the brink of victory. 'We shall win because we must win!' is typical of their convincing logic. Today one of the men in the office who is terribly stuffy, always wears a tie pin with the old Imperial crown and never lets himself go, stood in the door, livid with rage, shouting: 'Even the bloody food is a load of shit!' I could not help laughing.

By February 1945 most of the population of Berlin were making plans to leave, although some of these were quite ludicrous. The air was thick with talk of forged passports and bogus duty trips to areas of safety. Working for Berlin's leading newspaper, the Deutsche Allgemeine Zeitung, *Ursula von Kardorff was particularly struck by the farcical nature of the propaganda that journalists were required to serve up compared with the reality around them. Constant air raids meant that it was not possible to sleep at normal times, but this did not matter greatly as there was little real work to do. Ursula's father had died a*

*month before and the numbers of arrests of people with dissident views
like herself had increased alarmingly. A few days later she resigned from
her job and fled to the country. There she would survive the last months
of the war working on a farm. See also pp. 489–90, 525–6 and 533–4.*

Saturday 10 – Thursday 22 February 1945

Edith van Hessen feels the grief and anxiety of a Holocaust survivor

10 February
Just heard over the radio that 300 Dutch people have arrived
safe in Switzerland, inmates of a Jewish concentration camp
in Theresienstadt . . . Mother?

22 February
Why do you keep hoping, even when you know there's no
hope left? I went to the van Buerens because they have the
list of the freed Dutch Jews from Theresienstadt now in
Switzerland. Mother's name wasn't there – nobody's. Except
Phil Dwinger and wife, and Renée's uncle Louis Kiek, and
Aunt Map's brother. It's not that I had expected anything,
really – but on the way home I almost collapsed. What an
idiot.

I have such a need to cry these days – just for a few
minutes, and then it's over, and I laugh at myself. When I
ride past houses, I think to myself, 'What would it be like to
live there?' and even if they are ugly houses, I know that if
I lived there and I came home and Mother was waiting for
me inside, how lovely it would be! At every house I picture
how it would be, with Mother standing by the window
arranging flowers . . .

*Even for those who escaped the Holocaust the end of the war brought a
growing picture of incarcerations, illness, betrayal and deportations of
which many had been only dimly aware during their wartime period
of hiding. After the war Edith van Hessen would go on to attend
Amsterdam University and in 1949 married Loet Velmans. Qualifying*

as a psychologist specializing in gerontology, she moved to the United States with her husband. She has three daughters and five grand-children. SEE ALSO PP. 778–80.

Mid-February 1945

Bill Goodall, a British POW, on a forced march through the snow in Germany

Bill Goodall was an RAF navigator who had commenced training at Maxwell Air Force Base in Alabama in the United States in the autumn of 1941. In 1943, after a period ferrying aircraft across the Atlantic from their place of manufacture in North America, he was assigned to a bomber unit. He was shot down over Holland by a night-fighter on 25–26 July 1943 en route to an attack on Essen in Germany. Most of the crew managed to bail out, and some met up with the resistance and got as far as Brussels before being captured by the Gestapo. Bill Goodall had not found any civilians who would hide him and was soon arrested by German soldiers. By early 1944 he found himself in a POW camp at Belaria in eastern Germany.

The next day's march began soon after 8am with snow still falling and everyone feeling somewhat worse than the previous day mainly due to lack of sleep for two consecutive nights and a good deal of foot trouble. We had spent such an uncomfortable night that our party of 11 was determined to fare better at our next farm so two of us had their loads lightened and shared between the remainder in order that they could lead the column; in this way they would be able to find a stable or other warm accommodation at the end of the day. We plodded on with short breaks every hour and 30 mins for lunch normally in the middle of a thick wood for shelter. Here I must pay tribute to the German Commandant of Belaria [the vacated POW camp] who accompanied us all the way, usually on foot himself, and always with his magnificent Alsatian police dog. He had no responsibility for the march beyond delivering us from Belaria to Spremberg and I consider that he did try, within the limits of his powers, to act humanely towards us. If the SS had been in charge it would have been a very different story.

This Commandant – a Major in the Luftwaffe – was the not uncommon type in Germany who has to shout loudly even in polite conversation and during the lunch break on this second day he yelled at one of our officers who was sitting on a snow covered milestone; neither party could understand the other's language and we were afraid that our colleague was in dire trouble for some unknown crime. However when an interpreter was found, it transpired that the Major was merely advising the Officer not to sit on the cold snow as there was a danger of contracting piles.

All the way we had no difficulty in getting water from cottages along the route and on this second day we halted after 17 kilometres at a large farm in a village called Gross Selten near Priebus. Fortunately our two front men had found for us a little room adjoining a stable covered with straw on a brick floor and deriving some warmth from the stable. This was a great improvement on the previous night with access to a water tap where we could wash and water was boiled in the farm kitchen so that everyone got a cup of tea. After supper the 11 of us bedded down close together for warmth and we slept like logs until about 6am when we were able to get some cooked potatoes from one of the Polish workmen at the farm.

Quite early in the morning it was announced that no move would be made that day so we busied ourselves in making a small fire in the farmyard from bits of wood which were lying around. Soon the yard was dotted with little fires and crouching figures bending over the smoke endeavouring to do some elementary cooking in the few utensils which we had brought along. I should have mentioned that on the second day we saw many tanks and lorries of Panzer divisions which had been driven back from the battle front and which had become so disorganised that they drove back into Germany as far as their petrol would take them and then stopped, absolutely cut off from their units. Some tanks were quartered with us at this farm on the third day and before long brisk bargaining was going on with the tank

crews for their iron rations – mainly a kind of Ryvita crisp-
bread called 'Knackebrot'. It really was an astonishing
incident, but an even more surprising episode took place in
the evening when the tank commander returned from a day
foraging in the area with his small car; this he unwisely left
unguarded in the yard with a plump goose on the back seat.
Within an hour or so the goose was stolen, plucked, cooked
and eaten [by the Germans] following which there was a
tremendous row when he discovered his loss; all kinds of
dire penalties were threatened but he was finally pacified by
the gift of 200 cigarettes and a bar of chocolate. The third
night was spent in relative comfort for everyone compared
with our first night and we were ready to move out from
Gross Selten early on Wednesday morning. Some attempt
was made each morning at a roll call but it was not very
serious and did not delay our departure. Meanwhile wild
rumours were circulating to the effect that a new
Government had been formed in Germany and that our
troops had crossed the Rhine; all this was completely without foundation and in fact we were totally without news
throughout the march although a wireless set had been
smuggled along with us. But this was for use at our next
camp and was not used on the march as its component parts
were carried by several individuals. On Wednesday afternoon the weather improved greatly and the sun made a brief
appearance; unhappily this spell of warm weather coincided
with the first stretch of hilly country which we had to
negotiate and we all suffered considerably.

In addition our route lay along forest tracks which were
very rough and which made sledge pulling very difficult. By
this time the guards were becoming somewhat distressed,
which was not surprising as they were heavily laden and
were older men than us although they had better food
and accommodation at night. Just before dusk we marched
through a fairly large town called Birkenstedt and at the far
end we were directed into another large farmyard, the
biggest and most prosperous we had yet seen.

This time we were not allowed to commandeer quarters in
the first come first served principle but we were all lined up
in the yard before being released to find billets in the barns

and stables; however we were again fortunate and found a warm corner with the horses in their stable. Also we quickly made friends with the Polish stableman who brought us potatoes and in general helped us during our stay with him; in his case it was not bribery but a genuine friendly feeling which we reciprocated to the full.

By January 1945 it was known that Soviet forces were close and Bill Goodall and his friends had hoped that this would prompt their guards simply to flee, leaving them to be liberated by the Russians. Instead, on 27 January, orders came from the German high command that the whole camp at Belaria was to be evacuated and moved to Spremberg, just south of Berlin. This meant a forced march through the snow, sometimes alongside retreating German forces. Once the prisoners reached Spremberg they were taken by train to Stalag Luft III, from which the famous 'wooden horse' Great Escape had been made earlier in the war. The Russians would catch up with them here on 21 April, but were slow to release British and American POWs, and Bill Goodall would not be flown home to Oakley airfield in Oxfordshire until 30 May.

Thursday 22 – Saturday 24 February 1945

Gustave Folcher, a French POW working on a farm in Germany, witnesses the bombing of Stendal station

The month of February saw some terrible days of bombing, now it is all the railway lines which are for it, morning, evening, night, dawn, twilight, every second fighters and bombers are streaking across the German sky. On Thursday 22 February, at midday, there is a most violent attack, a wave of 40 bombers escorted by countless fighters, apparently heavily-loaded, aim right for Stendal, describe a huge circle over the town and then in three minutes empty their frightful cargoes on the main station where huge damage results. On Saturday 24 February we are called to Stendal to give assistance to the clearing of the station. We left the village at four in the morning and do eight kilometres in a cart and the rest, 15 more, in a tractor-drawn vehicle. At seven o'clock we are at the main station square which is strewn with debris of all kinds. The big buildings surrounding it, despite being badly hit, are still proudly upright. But when we get into the huge station it's totally different. How can I describe the spectacle which confronts us? I give up for I cannot do it and I am not capable of finding the words necessary for such a description, so far has what we call the inferno of Stendal station gone beyond my comprehension. Human imagination could never have come up with such a cataclysm. First of all we go onto the platform for travellers. All kinds of rubble is lying on the various platforms. But, continuing on to the vast marshalling yard and the big locomotive depot we see something other than debris. The first thing, which at first sight affects you most, is the signal bridge which stretches right across the station. The poor bridge, or rather what was left of it, all blackened by fire, has collapsed in various places, leaving a scene of tangled and twisted beams, wires, signals and rubble of all kinds. One part of the bridge has collapsed onto an engine which was immediately underneath. Right after the bridge comes the real disaster. The chaos of equipment mixed up with earth is unimaginable, all twitching, upside down in the most incredible positions among the vast, huge craters that adjoin each other and even in certain places form real ravines where trucks disembowelled of their contents are lying higgledy-piggledy, engines overturned, wheels in the air, wooden debris, sleepers, twisted and intertwined rails. No, what I'm writing does no justice to what I've seen. Of the tracks, there's nothing to be said for nothing of what's left could lead one to suppose that there were in that vast space, 25 or 30 lines of shunting track. Nothing is left except a horrible vision. Some beautiful locomotives, the latest models made for speed, streamlined, these mastodons of the track of 80 tons, have been thrown aside like mere playthings. Fifty engines are there in the station, ripped open, on their sides, overturned in the strangest positions. One of them has even mounted a group of wagons which have themselves been smashed open.

We are 6,000 men confronting this spectacle. How are we to organise the work? Where can you start on such an enterprise? How can it be that there is no discipline in the face of such a disaster? No police, and we can see no officers, no one at all in command. We were used here to seeing all the work in Germany, like everything else, minutely organised, supervised very closely by a swarm of zealous officials! Here, there's nothing, not an order, nothing happens. Of the 6,000 there are a full 5,000 foreigners with no one in charge. And that for the huge station which is nearly the same in size and layout as the Courbesac station at Nimes, is quickly transformed into a vast museum which everyone visits but no-one works. We discuss things a good deal, we meet a lot of friends we have not seen for a long time, and the visit continues among the volcanic landscape with its unimaginable and fantastic sights. This lack of organisation completely astonishes us, the general disorder shows us that right now Germany is being overcome by events which begin to be beyond its powers.

The town of Stendal was a major rail junction lying between Hanover and Berlin. Early 1945 provided very good bombing weather and the German rail network was brought to a standstill on 22 February when some 2,000 bombers attacked key rail targets. Stendal had been the primary goal of the 91st Bomb Group.

The disruption of the railways would make the POWs' own repatriation to France much harder. Eventually, on the night of 11 May 1945, Folcher would return to his family in Aigues-Vives, after five years of separation. SEE ALSO PP. 639–40.

MARCH 1945

BY EARLY MARCH the Third Reich was conscripting fifteen- and sixteen-year-olds into the regular army. Boys of similar age who had been serving as ground staff in the Luftwaffe were also now being transferred into the front line with little or no training.

For some months the Wehrmacht had been suffering a death rate of 5,000 men per day. The Third Reich had already mobilized all available young men in the age group seventeen to twenty-five, so now turned to mobilizing children from the Hitler Youth. Joseph Goebbels, the propaganda minister, was particularly active in this. Although the formal requirement was for youths close to the normal age of recruitment, in practice many local Hitler Youth groups decided to volunteer for service together, taking with them children as young as twelve. Having attracted this youthful influx, the Third Reich found that it had no weapons to issue to its new recruits, and so middle-men were sent to northern Italy to try to buy weapons of any sort on the black market. However, even these desperate measures could not slow the gathering pace of the Allied advance. The Americans reached Cologne on 5 March and Koblenz the following day. Their progress was further accelerated when the US 9th Armoured Division achieved a surprise dash across the intact Rhine bridge at Remagen, establishing a foothold on the eastern bank of the river. This was a crucial breakthrough, and by the end of March the Allied front extending from Remagen into central Germany was 30 miles wide.

Further north, the British 2nd and Canadian 1st Armies started an assault across the Rhine north of the Ruhr. Montgomery's 21st Army Group chose to cross the Rhine 15 miles to the north of Duisberg after a massive artillery barrage. More than 16,000 paratroops landed across the Rhine in this attack, codenamed Operation Plunder; the bitter lesson of Arnhem had been learned and the paratroops were dropped almost within sight of the relieving forces. They soon linked up with advancing British troops and established four bridgeheads over the Rhine.

On 6 March the Germans launched their last offensive in the east. General Dietrich's 6th SS Panzer Army, which had already fought in the Ardennes, began an operation codenamed Spring Awakening. The Russians were forced to give up some ground, but the German objective, to push them back to the more easily defended line of the River Danube, was never achieved. The main problem for the Germans was a lack of fuel for their tanks. In Poland, large numbers of ethnic Germans and more recent German settlers had begun to evacuate, particularly from areas such as Danzig, where there was a mixed population.

The last bomber attack by the Luftwaffe was a night raid on RAF airfields in England which destroyed only twenty-two aircraft. The bombing of German cities continued relentlessly. RAF Bomber Command established a record for the largest tonnage dropped on a single target in a single day at Essen, when 4,661 tons were dropped on the city, but exceeded this the next day during an attack on Dortmund. During March the 1,115th and final V-2 to reach England landed in Kynaston Road, Orpington, Kent. More than 200 people were killed and injured by V-2s in March. The very last enemy action against Britain was achieved by a V-1, probably launched from an aircraft, which landed in Datchworth in Hertfordshire on 29 March 1945.

At the end of March the US 1st Army moved into Paderborn and began a gruelling four days of urban warfare to capture the town. A day later the Germans completed their withdrawal from Holland and a jubilant French army crossed the Rhine for the first time since Napoleon. On 19 March Hitler ordered a vigorous scorched earth policy, arguing that areas of Germany that had failed to resist the invaders did not deserve to exist. Two days later Albert Speer chose to inform Hitler that, in his opinion, they were facing defeat. Hitler insisted that he retract these comments immediately. Speer was already thinking about Germany's rehabilitation and so privately resisted Hitler's scorched earth policy. He had admitted to Goering as early as November 1944 that defeat was inevitable. The last known film of Adolf Hitler was taken during March 1945: it captured him in the garden outside his bunker, decorating members of the Hitler Youth for bravery in combat.

Thursday 1 March 1945

Private Jack R. Blann of the US army comes upon the aftermath of battle on the road to Cologne

We moved out of town a little distance directly toward Cologne and soon came to the top of a hill where there were bodies of dead Germans laying everywhere. There were two German Mark 5 tanks knocked out over on one side of the hill and there were dead German soldiers laying all around the vehicles. We felt that this action must have occurred all day before, although the vehicles were still smoking. Beside one of the vehicles, we noticed that one of the Germans was still alive, even though he had been blown almost in two and his legs were missing. His eyes were open and he was moaning. There was no way that this man could recover from such wounds. In fact, we couldn't understand how he had managed to live this long. We were all disturbed by the suffering that the man must be enduring, so one of the officers walked over and closed the man's eyes, and shot him in the head with his forty five.

From the hill, you could see the battle line still quite some distance in front of us and you could see the bursting artillery in the distance all along the front. The panorama stretching before us reminded me of some of the panoramic drawings of battles that I had seen in *Life Magazine*. The line seemed to bulge out in the direction of Cologne and it looked as if some of our troops must be getting pretty close to the big city. At this time, a big armada of B-26's flew over and began to bomb Cologne and the roads around the city. We were so close to the bombers that we could see the bombs as they left the planes. There was no flack going up against them, probably because the retreat had thrown the anti-aircraft defenses into confusion.

Some of the men looked around the dead Germans on the ground around us to see if there were any valuables that might be worth picking up. As for myself, I never became hardened enough that I could loot the dead. I didn't want to have anything to do with the dead soldiers. It was hard enough to just look at these men, killed at such a young age. One good looking young German boy had long black hair that was usually combed straight back from his forehead. Now it had fallen forward over his face. I could see myself lying there.

We left the hill and went down into a little ravine where we waited for our orders. While we were there, chow came up and we had a hot meal. I picked up some old German and French money laying on the ground in the ravine, probably discarded by some of the looters because it apparently had no value. Then it began to sprinkle, and we began huddling around each other to talk about what the future might hold for us. All of us were hoping that maybe we would never catch up with the front line, but of course, we all knew that sooner or later we would.

Looting the enemy was a time-honoured practice and was almost universal in the Second World War. The search was not only for valuables, but also for souvenirs, including pistols and ammunition. At the end of the war, units were often searched as they came home in an attempt to relieve them of the large number of German weapons that had been acquired as trophies. The amount of loot was also an important military indicator. Where there were few personal effects and papers in an enemy position, it could be concluded that the enemy had withdrawn in an orderly fashion, probably to hardened defensive positions that would be encountered sooner rather than later.

Sunday 4 March 1945

Joseph Goebbels meets with Hitler in Berlin after a visit to the front

This evening I had a long interview with the Führer. In contrast to last time I found him somewhat depressed – understandable in the light of military developments. Physically too he is somewhat hampered: I noticed with dismay that the nervous twitch on his left hand had greatly increased. His visit to the front last Saturday went off very well. The general officers put on a good show and the soldiers cheered the Führer. Unfortunately, however, the Führer refuses to issue a press statement about his visit to the front. Today it is as essential as our daily bread . . .

I tell the Führer in detail about my talk with General Vlasov [leader of the Russian fascist collaborators], especially about the methods used on Stalin's orders to save Moscow in late autumn 1941. The Soviet Union was then in exactly the same situation we are in today. At that time she took decisive measures which various important people on our side have neither the nerve nor the energy to take today. I submit to the Führer my plan to intercept soldiers on the move and form them into new regiments. The Führer approves this plan. He also agrees that we should form women's battalions in Berlin. Innumerable women are volunteering to serve at the front and the Führer is of the opinion that, provided they volunteer, they will undoubtedly fight fanatically. They should be placed in the second line, then the men in the front line will lose all desire to withdraw.

Joseph Goebbels

Even in March 1945 Joseph Goebbels, Nazi Minister for Propaganda, maintained a surreal belief that an increased effort might save the German situation. The German leadership had promised their population that the tide would soon be turned by scientifically advanced 'wonder weapons' that would shock the enemy, but these had not materialized – and Goebbels knew they did not exist. Hitler had been physically and mentally shaken by the 'bomb plot' assassination attempt of July 1944, and his condition was visibly deteriorating. The Allies now enjoyed complete air superiority and Soviet tanks were approaching Berlin. Substantial numbers of German troops had detached themselves from their units and were avoiding front-line duty, sensing that the end was not far off. SEE ALSO PP. 21 AND 822.

Early March 1945

Guy Sajer, a Frenchman fighting with the Wehrmacht, watches young boys of the Volkssturm heading for the front line

In the next street, we found the divisional store, which was still much better stocked than the supply stores of ordinary divisions. Some of our men could be given quite a few of the things they needed. While we waited, we watched a crowd of men, part of a new Volkssturm battalion, swarm into a factory courtyard. When we looked more closely at these men recently called up by the Führer our eyes opened wide with surprise. They all belonged to the last class of reserves and seemed to be an even more extreme case than the Marie-Louise conscripts at the end of the Napoleonic era.

Some of these troops with Mausers on their shoulders must have been at least sixty or seventy-five, to judge by their curved spines, bowed legs, and abundant wrinkles. But the young boys were even more astonishing. For us, who had saved our eighteen-, nineteen-, and twenty-year-old lives through a thousand perils, the idea of youth meant childhood and not adolescence, which was still our phase of life, despite our disillusion. But now we were looking literally at children, marching beside these feeble old men. The oldest boys were about sixteen, but there were others who could not have been more than thirteen. They had been hastily dressed in worn uniforms cut for men, and were carrying guns which were often as big as they were. They looked both comic and horrifying, and their eyes were filled with unease, like the eyes of children at the reopening of school. Not one of them could have imagined the impossible ordeal which lay ahead. Some of them were laughing and roughhousing, forgetting the military discipline which was inassimilable at their age, and to which they had been exposed for barely three weeks. We noticed some heart-wringing details about these children, who were beginning the first act of their tragedy. Several of them were carrying school satchels their mothers had packed with extra food and clothes, instead of schoolbooks. A few of the boys were trading the saccharine candies which the ration allotted to children under thirteen. The old men marching beside these young sprouts stared at them with incomprehension.

What would be done with these troops? Where were they expected to perform? There was no answer to these questions. Were the authorities going to try to stop the Red Army with them? The comparison seemed tragic and ludicrous. Would Total War devour these children? Was Germany heroic, or insane? Who would ever be able to judge this absolute sacrifice? We stood in profound silence, watching and listening to the final moments of this first adolescence. There was nothing else we could do.

Volkssturm units were the German 'Home Guard' and were organized by local Gauleiters of the Nazi party. In East Prussia, Eric Koch was the first local Gauleiter to lead such a rag-tag unit against the battle-hardened Red Army. Hitler Youth boys, who had received a great deal of military training and also indoctrination, along with old men, were the main source for the Volkssturm in the closing months of 1944. Boys of sixteen and above were legally required to join the Volkssturm, but many younger boys joined as volunteers. The older men were veterans of the First World War, but were less keen to fight than the young boys. The best weapon given to the Volkssturm was the Panzerfaust, *a type of lightweight anti-tank weapon with which even a boy could disable a tank. American and British troops regularly reported encountering members of the Hitler Youth as young as twelve in deadly combat.*

Guy Sajer surrendered a few days after making this entry and would eventually make his way back to France, where he later worked as an illustrator. SEE ALSO PP. 645–8.

Thursday 8 March 1945

Joseph Goebbels visits German paratroops at Lauban in eastern Germany

Colonel-General Schörner ... is decidedly a personality as a commander. The details he gave me about the methods he uses to raise morale were first-rate and demonstrate not only his talents as a commander in the field but also his superb political insight. He is using quite novel modern methods. He is no chairborne or map general; most of the day he spends with the fighting troops, with whom he is on terms of confidence, though he is very strict. In particular he has taken a grip of the so-called 'professional stragglers', by which he means men who continually manage to absent themselves in critical situations and vanish to the rear on some pretext or other. His procedure with such types is fairly brutal; he hangs them on the nearest tree with a placard announcing: 'I am a deserter and have declined to defend German women and children.' The deterrent effect on other deserters and men who might have it in mind to follow them is obviously considerable ...

As the soldiers marched past I noticed a lieutenant who proved to be Hägert, one of my old associates who had volunteered to return to the front with the 'Grossdeutchland' Division. He was deeply moved to see me again. On the flank of the troops as they marched past was a member of the Hitler Youth aged only 16 who had just won the Iron Cross.

In early 1945 elite German units, including paratroops, retook the town of Lauban from Soviet forces. However, the numbers of elite units were dwindling and German lines were increasingly bolstered with the Volkssturm. The most brutal measures were taken against stragglers and deserters during this period and so German soldiers tended to surrender only when ordered to do so by their superiors. SEE ALSO PP. 21 AND 818–20.

Saturday 10 – Sunday 11 March 1945

Dorothy Higgs experiences hunger and robbery in occupied Guernsey

Dorothy Higgs lived at Alta Vista, Delancey on Guernsey and endured the German occupation from 1940 through to 1945. She wanted to write letters sending news to her sister Phyllis, who lived in England, but could not. Instead, as a substitute, she kept a diary for her sister to read. Her journal ranged widely over issues including food, farming and morale.

10 March

... BUT – to-day we have each a 2lb loaf of the most perfect white bread ever seen, made from the finest quality Manitoba No. 1 wheat. It is so lovely to look at that we can hardly bring ourselves to eat it. Between you and me, at first I thought England could not realise just how hungry we were, or she would have sent brown flour, which wouldn't have been nearly so thrilling, but would have been much more satisfying. I did not mention that to a soul and then I heard that the reason for the super white bread was to build us up, and the next cargo will be standard bread. That is much sounder reasoning than mine was, in view of the numbers who really have starved.

11 March

– Well, to leave the subject of food for a bit – my favourite goat is due to kid any day now. I had decided not to keep any more kids until the Jerries had gone, but if she has a good nanny, I'll have a shot at keeping it. She is the best goat for quality and quantity and was very well mated. So many goats have been stolen and slaughtered that I scarcely know anyone who has not lost at least one, and some have lost all of them.

The robberies have reached such a pitch that no one has the heart to grow anything at all. The men are leaving all their plots undug. Every greenhouse that has anything edible is ravaged over and over again. Those who have planted potatoes just have them dug up within a few days; and every patch of ground where roots have been grown is dug over and over again by soldiers searching for stray roots that may have been missed.

Quite a number of the robberies have been with violence. On Friday, one bakery had 20 loaves and a sack of flour taken by armed marines. How much longer the poor blighters must hold out I don't know; it is said that many have already died of malnutrition and their hospitals are full to overflowing with cases of collapse. It tears one's heart to see them dragging about with hunched shoulders and arms hanging loose. Ought we to feed them when England is trying to starve them out, and when so many of our own people have barely escaped the same fate? While our own people were really hungry I could harden my heart. But if the Red Cross feeds us really well, I am not sure what I, personally, shall do about this problem.

But we are not out of the woods yet, as there will be no root or potato ration after this week. There was a notice in the paper yesterday to say that no water may now be used for washing clothes, flushing, or even apparently washing one's person. Only drinking and cooking. We are already independent of water-works here, so it will be OK till the rain water gives out. After that we shall have to pump from the well.

At the outset of the war Guernsey and Jersey had reacted differently to the threat of German occupation. Half of Guernsey's population had fled to the mainland, whereas only a fifth of the population left Jersey. In early 1945 the German grip was tightening everywhere. As early as June 1944 Count von Schmettow, the aristocratic nephew of General von Runstedt, had been replaced as Commander-in-Chief of the Channel Islands by the extreme Nazi Vice-Admiral Huffmeier. Nevertheless, by now discipline in the German armed forces was beginning to break down. The German garrison had been cut off from the mainland for many months and increasingly requisitioned what little food supplies the islanders could produce. This was burdensome enough, but the soldiers also engaged in stealing and looting. Islanders in turn hoarded what they could, but growing crops became futile as anything worth eating was stolen before it could be harvested. Even if offenders were caught, they went unpunished.

Friday 23 – Monday 26 March 1945

Sir Cuthbert Headlam, a backbench Conservative MP, reflects on the future of Hitler and Churchill

23 March

The rumour of the Nazi last stand in the Bavarian alps is being spread a good deal – 50 divisions are said [to be] being kept for this job by Hitler – and the stand is going to last for 2 or 3 years, etc. It all sounds rather absurd but then the Nazis are absurd – and the whole of this war has been absurd – and the whole of the immediate future looks as if it were going to be absurd ...

26 March

This crossing of the Rhine has been a splendid performance – the incessant bombing goes on and must be wrecking German concentrations. Winston is reported to have crossed the Rhine – how the man must be enjoying himself and what amazing vitality he has – I only hope that he will live to see the thing through – but if he does, how wise he would be to retire from public life – but he will never do that I imagine of his own free will – he loves the lime light and probably would quickly expire without it.

Disquiet about the possible strength of Hitler's 'Alpine redoubt' in Bavaria had been growing since late 1944. Intelligence officers predicted that as the war drew to a close, fanatical Nazis would move military departments to Bavaria – the original home of the Nazi party – where a last stand would be made with an elite force of 300,000 SS troops and 'special weapons'. By early 1945 there were so many intelligence reports from so many sources about this fantastic fortress with its extraordinary defences that its existence had come to be accepted as a fact. In the event,

after the war, no trace of this fabled 'Alpine redoubt' would ever be found.
SEE ALSO PP. 193–4.

APRIL 1945

DURING THE FIRST days of April the US 1st and 9th Armies met up at Lippstadt, isolating 300,000 German troops in the Ruhr area, most of whom surrendered. Meanwhile the British 7th Armoured Division entered the Rhine region near the Dortmund–Ems canal. The British Special Air Service Brigade prepared to be dropped by parachute into eastern Holland, to help clear the way for Canadian troops who were moving north.

On Thursday 12 April the US 6th Armoured Division over-ran Buchenwald concentration camp. The next day a local ceasefire was agreed at Celle to enable the British 2nd Army to assume control of the Belsen concentration camp. Troops were appalled by what they saw and insisted that the German population from local towns and villages visit these locations to view the crimes that Hitler's regime had perpetrated. A day later, glider troops captured the former German Chancellor, Franz von Papen, at a country hunting-lodge near Stockhausen, together with three senior generals. The French launched a final assault on the trapped German garrison at Bordeaux.

Across Germany large numbers of Allied POWs were being released and on 16 April American troops reached the famous castle at Colditz, freeing 19,000 POWs from this special camp for dedicated escapers. A further 20,000 were liberated at Sandbostel by the British army at the end of the month. Many British and American prisoners were freed by Soviet forces in eastern Germany.

Large numbers of German civilians had fled west in an attempt to escape the torments visited upon them by the Red Army. At the end of the second week of April, Soviet forces began their last offensive against Germany, entering Berlin on the 20th. On the same day, Hitler's birthday, the Allies captured Nuremberg, the location of many Nazi political rallies. After five days of bitter urban warfare, American and Soviet troops met at Torgau, cutting Germany in half.

Representatives of fifty nations gathered in San Francisco on 25 April to finalize the Charter of the United Nations. Cold War tensions were already emerging and the American and Soviet representatives could not agree over the veto process in the Security Council. Nevertheless, Soviet forces were ready to play their part in the Far Eastern war and during April they repudiated a five-year non-aggression pact with the Japanese empire. On 1 April American and British forces in the Pacific had begun Operation Iceberg, the invasion of the island of Okinawa, which formed part of Japan. Resistance was extremely fierce, with numerous attacks by kamikaze aircraft. Accordingly, both London and Washington were keen to see Soviet troops join the final assault on the Japanese mainland.

Benito Mussolini attempted to escape to Switzerland during the last days of April, but was captured by Italian partisans and quickly executed near Lake Como. His body was later displayed with that of his mistress, hanging by their feet in a garage forecourt. This marked the symbolic end of the Italian Fascist movement.

Monday 9 April 1945

Hans von Lehndorff experiences the arrival of the Russians in a German hospital

Living in Königsberg in East Prussia with his wife, Doktora, Hans von Lehndorff had seen his mother arrested in 1944 by the Gestapo for enquiring after the fate of a Lutheran pastor who had been caught listening to the BBC news. In early 1945 he watched German teenagers being press-ganged by the SS into military service in the dying days of the Reich. Shortly after this he was overtaken by a tide of barbarity as the Red Army arrived in the hospital he headed at Königsberg and subjected them to treatment that was worse than they could have imagined.

Towards five in the morning I was wakened by a babel of voices and hurrying footsteps outside my door. I woke Doktora and told her to get dressed. 'What's up?' she asked, drunk with sleep. 'I think the Russians are here', I said, 'I'm just going to see'. 'The Russians? Oh, have they actually come? I'd quite forgotten them.' 'Well, there you are,' I said, 'it [remaining with the hospital staff] was your own choice.' She nodded. I put on my white jacket and went out into the passage.

Czernecki, my Ukrainian assistant, ran up to fetch me to receive the Russians. The patients I went past poked up their heads. 'Two of them have been through here already and taken our watches, and Wally's had a knock-out.' Wally, our plucky White Russian nurse, was lying among the patients with blood streaming over her face, not stirring. The Russians she had tried to intercept had seized her by the hair and dashed her to the floor, face downwards. Her upper jaw was broken and several of her teeth had been knocked out. She was conscious, but made no sound.

Outside the main building two Russians were rummaging in a trunk. There was something frightening in the sight. I felt like someone who'd gone bear-hunting, and forgotten his gun . . .

In the operating theatre Doktora was busy dressing patients' wounds. A crowd of nurses had taken refuge there and were pretending to be hard at work. In the background the Russians were prowling round the patients, searching for watches and wearable boots. One of them, a mere lad, suddenly burst into tears because he hadn't yet found a watch. He held up three fingers: he would shoot three men if he didn't get a watch at once. His despair brought about the first personal contact. Czernecki entered into a long palaver with him, and finally, somewhere or other, a watch was found for him, with which he ran off, beaming with joy.

The arrival of the first officers destroyed my last hopes of coming to endurable terms. None of my attempts to address them was any use; even for them I am only a hall stand with pockets, they see me only from the shoulders downwards. A couple of nurses who got in their way were seized and outraged from behind, and then released again, thoroughly dishevelled, before they realised what was happening. The older ones could hardly believe their senses; they went wandering aimlessly about the corridors. There was nowhere to hide, and fresh tormentors kept falling upon them.

The diary of Dr Hans von Lehndorff is a remarkable testimony of suffering, endurance and faith. It shows clearly that it was not only Germans who fell victim to the activities of the Red Army. There were numerous Russian civilians working in the hospital, and also Russian prisoners being treated there, who feared the arrival of their compatriots. Stealth was an essential characteristic displayed by survivors of this tumult: one Russian theatre nurse quickly acquired the uniform of a Russian riflewoman and thus ensured her safety for a period. Lehndorff was sustained through this terrible period by his profound Christian faith and was never without his bible. Though he was searched literally hundreds of times, his bible was never taken from him. Remarkably, Lehndorff also managed to retain his watch, attached to his ankle and hidden under two pairs of socks. SEE ALSO PP. 830–2.

Monday 9 – Wednesday 11 April 1945

Jock Colville, Churchill's private secretary, on relations with the Russians

9 April
He [Churchill] and Sarah [Churchill] went off to Chartwell for lunch, to profit from the warm sun and to investigate the mysterious theft of the P.M.'s favourite goldfish from the upper pond there. I returned to London.

10 April
A brisk canter in Richmond Park where I examined a large V-2 crater near White Lodge. There have been no V-1s or V-2s for over a week.

Stalin has answered the P.M. both about Poland and the accusations he made about negotiations with the Germans.

He has climbed down, ungraciously, in his own way about the latter. It boils down to this: the Russians are jealous of our rapid successes in the West while, on the Oder at any rate, they are stuck. The explanations are briefly:

i)   Our weapons are better and man for man our soldiers are more efficient;
ii) we have massive air superiority and they have none;
iii) the Germans view our advance with less horror than they do that of the Russians – and not without reason.

11 April

There is a good deal afoot. In the military field we still race towards the Elbe, from which we are not now far . . . Von Papen has been captured in the Ruhr, the first of the war criminals to be taken alive . . . the Americans have reached the Elbe.

By early April 1945 the Allied armies in the east and the west were only 100 miles apart. In London, Moscow and Washington attention was firmly on the post-war settlement and difficult issues such as the future of Poland. The main pressure was off and Churchill was looking more relaxed, spending more time with his family at his private house at Chartwell.

After the war Jock Colville was private secretary to Princess Elizabeth in the late 1940s, returning to the No. 10 private office in November 1951 to serve through Churchill's last premiership. He retired to Hampshire and died in 1987. SEE ALSO P. 153.

Wednesday 11 April 1945

Hans von Lehndorff on further Russian torments in a German hospital

Just as we feared, the Russians had found some alcohol. Right alongside of us in the Menthal liqueur factory lay some thousands of gallons, carefully kept dark, saved up by the irony of fate for this very moment. Then something like a tide of rats flowed over us, worse than all the plagues of Egypt together. Not a moment went by but I had the barrel of a pistol rammed against my back or my stomach, and a grimacing mask yelling at me for 'Sulfidin!' So nearly all these devils must have got venereal disease. Our dispensaries were burnt out long ago, and the huge store of tablets lies trampled to bits in the corridors. It gave me a certain wry pleasure to be reduced to pointing, again and again, to the havoc wrought by their fellows. They broke in from Menthal in flocks – officers, men, riflewomen, all drunk. And not a chance of hiding anybody from them, because the whole neighbourhood was lightened up as bright as day by the burning buildings.

We stood close together, awaiting the end in some form or other. The fear of death, which had hardly played any part since the days of the bombardment, had been entirely dispelled now by something infinitely worse. On every side we heard the despairing screams of the women: 'Shoot me, then! Shoot me!' But the tormentors preferred a wrestling match to any actual use of firearms.

Soon none of the women had any strength left for resistance. In a few hours a change came over them; their spirit died, one heard hysterical laughter, which made the Russians madder than ever. Is it really possible to write about these things, the most frightful things human beings can do to one another? Isn't every word of this an accusation of myself? Hadn't I many opportunities of flinging myself between them and finding a decent death? Yes, it's a sin to be still alive, and that is why none of all this must be passed over in silence.

On my return from the town a major, who seemed more or less in his senses, had sent for me to go to the isolation block. Thirty or forty Russians were rampaging among the patients. I was to tell him who these people were. Sick people, of course, what else? But what sort of sick people, he wanted to know. Well, all sorts: scarlet fever, typhus, diphtheria ... He gave a yell, and hurled himself like a tank among his men. But he was too late: when the tumult had subsided four women were dead.

Rape was a common activity for the Red Army as it entered the eastern provinces of Germany and mass venereal disease followed in its wake. In the German countryside, entire villages attempted suicide – sometimes running en masse into rivers to drown – in order to avoid the fate which they knew was moving in their direction. Many Russian soldiers spoke of a deep desire to visit the same treatment upon Germans that their own families had suffered at the hands of the Germans since 1941, and of a psychological need to see fear on the faces of German civilians. Von Lehndorff tried to limit the predations of the Russians in his hospital by keeping large numbers of nurses in the operating theatre where they 'operated' on a woman who was in reality, long deceased. He was able to assist a number of German officers in escaping Russian attention by supplying them with civilian clothes – an almost unobtainable commodity by now – taken from the dead in the overflowing hospital mortuary. Von Lehndorff would survive because at the end of April he was ordered to an internment camp in nearby Rothenstein. There he set up a primitive 'hospital' but lacked any significant medical instruments or supplies. Essential amputations were carried out with a garden saw.

Von Lehndorff was later awarded the Paracelsus medal by the German Congress of Physicians. SEE ALSO PP. 827–9.

Thursday 12 April 1945

Edward Stettinius on the sudden death of President Roosevelt

Edward Stettinius was born in Chicago in 1900 and spent time there and in New York City before going to the University of Virginia in the 1920s. He did not complete his degree because of his absorbing interest in social work. During the war he was an Assistant Secretary of State until the autumn of 1944, when Secretary of State Cordell Hull resigned due to illness. Stettinius became a popular Secretary of State and threw himself into preparations for the creation of the United Nations.

I was in my office meeting with Forrestal, Biddle and Patterson discussing world intelligence. I received a call

from Steve Early about ten minutes after five. He said to
please come over to the front door of the White House
immediately without being noticed. I told him I was with
three cabinet officers, but he said to come immediately and
that it was an 'order.' I went and was shown to the front of
Roosevelt's bedroom by the head usher. Mrs. Roosevelt was
there and, very composed . . . Mrs. Roosevelt took me by the
hand and said it was her sad duty to announce that Franklin
had died a few moments ago . . .

Everything was completely disorganised and nobody
knew exactly where to turn. I spoke up and said that a
Cabinet meeting should be held immediately, and Anna
Boettiger [FDR's daughter] asked where. I said it should be
in the Cabinet Room at 6 P.M. Truman then asked me if I
would make the arrangements. Anna then said she should
make the arrangements for the funeral . . .

I (then) instructed the chief usher to call the cabinet meeting at 6 o'clock, and I returned to my office, where I met
Forrestal and told him of the president's death. Forrestal said
that he had heard yesterday from someone in the Senate that
the president was very ill and that his death was not a shock
to him . . .

It was then decided that Truman should take the oath of
office immediately and we asked him whom he would like
to give the oath. He said the Chief Justice and he was sent for
. . . Truman took me aside and asked me if it would be
appropriate for him to have a photograph taken as he took
the oath. He said his mother was ninety-two years old and
he wished she could be there. Truman said that Jonathan
Daniels was pressing him to have the photograph taken, and
I agreed that it would be proper . . .

During the time we were waiting for the Chief Justice to
arrive I was sitting next to Truman and we had a rather
intimate talk relative to the fact that he did not believe that
this would happen. He was shocked and startled that he had
been called upon to perform this great task. I told him that
he had a job with the greatest responsibility of any one man
in the world. He said he realised this and that he would do
his best. I said somehow a person is given the inner strength
to arise to any occasion and said that I had full confidence

that the American people would rally round and see us through. I said we were well on the road to the defeat of the enemy and we must win on the world organisation [United Nations] . . .

I talked with Admiral McIntyre [Roosevelt's personal doctor] and he said this was a complete shock to him – it was something absolutely new and came as a complete surprise. The president's blood pressure was all right and had been for sometime, and there was absolutely no apparent cause for the stroke. Henry Wallace walked with me from the office to the White House and said that from the standpoint of Roosevelt as a person in history that this was a good time for him to go. Wallace said that he had won the war and would have to go through a fight with the Senate, and he went out like Abraham Lincoln. He said that it is tragic for all humanity, but from the standpoint of a person, the Good Lord was looking out for him.

Roosevelt's death came as a shock to most people in the US government, even though many had noticed the gradual deterioration in his health over the previous few months. Truman was particularly shocked because he had not taken much part in the direct running of the war. Truman publicly announced that he would be true to Roosevelt's wishes and maintain the course of his foreign policy, but in private he had little idea what this was. As Vice-President Truman had been largely concerned with domestic affairs, and the new President now had to be initiated into the great secrets of which he had hitherto been unaware, including the breaking of Axis codes via Magic and Ultra, and also the Manhattan Project that would produce the first atomic bomb only two months later. Truman made it clear that he did not want Stettinius to stay on. Later, Stettinius would become US representative to the UN, but was disappointed by what the new body could achieve. He died in February 1949, aged only forty-nine.

Saturday 14 April 1945

John T. Bassett of the US army takes German prisoners in the Apennines

*John T. Bassett was an American soldier serving in an infantry platoon.
His unit was engaged in the last offensive against General Kesselring's
stronghold in the Apennine mountains in northern Italy, about 20 miles
south of Bologna.*

Directly behind us was another wooded hill, smaller than
ours. Near the crest were a row of dugouts covered with
trees and leaves. Pfc [Private First Class] Rabideaux and
others begin to get suspicious of them: 'Hey!' he cried, 'Let's
find out if anyone's in them!' We agreed, and began firing.
This went on for several minutes. Then, in one, we saw
something moving. Two Krauts came out cautiously waving
a white rag on a long branch. We all yelled up and down our
hill to hold the fire. Dead prisoners was not policy. There
was an ugly rumor about that Sgt Meier had lined up several
Krauts on Mt Belvedere at the edge of a sheer drop-off, and
then shot them in a fit of rage with one of their burp guns.
They had all disappeared over the edge of the mountain. I
believed the story because I knew a little about Meier. It was
only his face that I knew: it was long, narrow and white and
his eyes were set close together and they leered out at the
world and in this war he found sufficient reason to kill, both
in the heat of battle, and in the cold aftermath. But Luca
Luhaink, my foxhole buddy, had almost done the same
thing. After Mt Belvedere was taken, we walked up on a
large pile of frozen American corpses that had been gathered
for identification and future burial. A single Kraut stood
nearby with his hands clasped tight over his black helmet.
Luhaink suddenly stepped towards him with his M1 thrust
out – 'See! See! You goddamned Kraut, what you did?' It was
close. We grabbed Luhaink and pushed up the gun. He
was very mad, but allowed us to bring him back to his senses
in time.

For many days Bassett's unit had been waiting in their foxholes, hoping that an end to the war would save them from a final push, since no one wanted to die in the last days of the war. As they moved off Bassett noted that 'faces grew taut and white with dread expectation'. The slopes of the Apennines were carefully fortified and fighting was characterized by heavy artillery fire, mortars and a desperate search for cover. Many Germans knew the game was over and were giving themselves up where they could. However, surrendering after an intense fight in which there had been heavy casualties was sometimes hazardous. The shooting of prisoners was not common, but neither was it unheard of; it was usually the result of heightened emotions sparked by the loss of close friends. On the Allied side there is almost no official record of this practice, but it is sometimes captured in the pages of personal diaries. SEE ALSO PP. 850–2.

Sunday 15 April 1945

B. G. Barnett, a British soldier, arrives at Belsen concentration camp

Major Benjamin Barnett was born in 1912 and had joined the territorial branch of the Artillery in 1936 as a lieutenant. By 1945 he was a captain serving in 63 Anti-tank Regiment. In April 1945 he accompanied the commander of his regiment, Lieutenant-Colonel R. I. G. Taylor, into Belsen.

Conditions in Camp I

Meeting with Kramer about 1900hrs – disarming of SS – no records of internees – nos. of internees – (Arrival of Brig.[adier] Hughes DDMS [Deputy Director Medical Services] 2 Army). Reports of rioting in cookhouses all food for tomorrow gone – so we decided to go into the inner camp. The things I saw completely defy description, there are no words in the English language which can give a true impression of the ghastly horror of this camp. I find it hard even now to get into focus all these horrors, my mind is really quite incapable of taking in all I saw because it was so completely foreign to anything had previously believed or

thought possible. I will nevertheless try to give an accurate
description of all I saw . . . Firstly then I will take events as
they unfolded themselves; the smell – the people and their
clothes the wounded – the dead by the gates – the potato
dumps – the kitchens – the spirit of the people – the condition of the people – their clothing – no food for 4 days no
water for 5 days except in a stinking pit – cookhouses
garbage heaps – the mass of fires cooking – pleas from
people to stay there and not leave them – Kramer made to
carry wounded – DDMS message to Army Comdr.– Kramer
under close arrest – riots in food stores – official visit next
morning with Harries, Schmidt and Kramer [senior camp
staff] – the latter not ashamed of all the horrors, the former
definitely so – 1st to cremation the mass open graves – size
30ft deep x 30ft long x 10ft wide others of same size –
obviously filled in – several hundred corpses some very bad,
women's hut also there. Broadcasting van told people what
we were trying to do.

From here on I can only give you a rather jumbled impression – Firstly the *huts* there must have been about 120 all
told capable of holding 50 or at most 100 people some with
500 or 700 people in them (about 40 x 80 [feet]) including
dead and dying – some beds rags for blankets etc.: *Latrines*
NIL – open trench for women no seat – *Hospitals* Typhus –
dead – excreta from dysentery patients – operating room
– *Corpses* – living waking to piles of dead – besides heap by
grave mass pile by children's huts all naked – cannibalism –
Food turnip soup and broth – water old concrete tank
– *Mortuary* – *Internees* class of person, nationality, from
Hanover and Brunswick – children between 500 and 1000 –
2/3 women, old clothes and boots –

Dying Persons walking to die over 200 every day – *Cooks* –
SS arrested on Monday evening and put in cells men and
women and made to work and feed same as internees –
Jewellery etc. – *Gallows and cells 1st Meal* on Monday night by
block and lagers – water carts *Breakfast* bread and sweet milk
– *people lost all sense of civilisation* – *thieving* – spare compo
boxes untouched distributing food – clothing stores – food
stores living took no notice of the dead.

Why did the Germans do this? . . .

Lieutenant-Colonel Taylor was in charge of the unit taking over the civil administration in the general area in which Belsen was situated and does not appear to have known in advance what he had come across. On 13 April he was simply looking for a place to billet his troops and thought he had found a routine military camp. He was immediately presented with the problem of the welfare of tens of thousands of people, many of whom were close to death. Joseph Kramer, the senior SS officer, was interrogated several times by the field security police, then arrested and taken away to Celle. Oberst Harries, the camp commandant, and his deputy, Schmidt, remained to assist in administering the camp. During the following night, three of the SS guards tried to commit suicide, one successfully.

George Barnett would survive the war and in 1986 gave his diary, together with photographs, to the Liddell Hart Centre for Military Archives at King's College London.

Monday 16 April 1945

Giovanni Guareschi, an Italian soldier, is liberated from a German POW camp

Giovanni Guareschi was an Italian soldier who had fought first against the Allies, then later against the Germans when Rome changed sides in 1943. For two years he made copious but highly condensed notes, about everything that happened to him and everything he saw, in three bulky notebooks. These condensed jottings and abbreviations filled over 2,000 pages.

At half past five in the afternoon, everyone began shouting: 'Here they come!' and rushing toward the gate. There were six thousand of us, counting both French and Italians, but I managed to climb up on one side of the posts supporting the barbed-wire fence, and it was from this vantage point that I saw the liberators. They came in a medium-sized black car and all of them were engaging in appearance, especially Major Cooley, who had round, rosy cheeks like those of the jolly drinkers in the multi-colored liquor advertisements of the Christmas issue of *Esquire*. The other two were a Scottish corporal and a Canadian soldier, each armed with a machine gun . . .

After this, all three liberators advanced into the camp, and an incident occurred which the Frenchmen found particularly puzzling. The Gestapo had made frequent inspections and searches, carried out with such meticulous care as to be positively indecent. Nevertheless, after nineteen months of internment, we were able to display cameras by the dozen and an Italian flag twelve by fifteen feet in size, whereas the Frenchmen could not come out with a single cockade. Italians are gifted this way. Once in Poland, when we were being transferred from one camp to another, I saw a Sicilian lieutenant emerge from the search hut clad in nothing but a shirt, which was the only garment they had left on him, and carrying the rest of his clothes in his arms with, hidden among them, a big six-tube radio.

I myself am the least scheming man in the world, and in January, 1945, when we were in the process of shifting from one camp to another and they took all our blankets away because they said the bombed-out inhabitants of Hamburg and Bremen needed them more badly than we, they deprived me of the scarf I had made myself out of a piece of

Giovanni Guareschi

heavy woolen cloth. I came out of the search shivering and groaning, but in my duffel bag I still had my old seven by eight barracks blanket.

Giovanni Guareschi's account captures the sense of an individual adrift in the chaos of war. Above all, it captures the spirit and the essential personal survival skills quickly acquired by anyone who has been a soldier or a prisoner, or both. A prisoner needed to keep his whole world in his duffle bag and then order it carefully on a series of nails hammered into the wall of the wooden railway cars which formed their prison huts during the last months of the war. Above all, he needed to be able to hide anything during repeated inspections from guards or from fellow prisoners, and to learn to peel a potato in his pocket.

When Guareschi returned home he set about deciphering his compressed notes and amplifying his comments into a full diary. Later he would become famous as the author of The Little World of Don Camillo. SEE ALSO PP. *18–19.*

Wednesday 18 April 1945

Major B. N. Reckitt sets up military government at Olpe and Hagen in Germany

Brian Reckitt attended the special civil affairs training school in Wimbledon set up to provide the specialist officers required for the government of occupied areas. The training presumed the existence of a transport and communication infrastructure in Germany which simply was not there when the officers actually arrived. Reckitt recalled that the most useful thing he had learned at Wimbledon was what to do first when taking over a town that was in ruins: create a police force to restore order.

Next morning an American NCO arrived and announced that he was taking over the town. I gave him all the information I could and hoped he was genuine. Within a day or two he was deposed, protesting, by another detachment which was sent from Halver to take over. We came across a case of one American deserter who had sewn on sergeant's stripes and taken over a village as military governor. He had done a roaring trade in passes at so many marks each and lived in the lap of luxury until he was caught.

We now all had German private cars of our own. These had been found mostly abandoned for lack of petrol. (Also to be found, wanting batteries, clocks and luxuries attractive to displaced persons.) The colonel had a dangerously fast six-cylinder machine and I owned a steady four-seater BMW. These cars made our work much easier. Travelling quickly and comfortably helped us to be more efficient and was less exhausting. The army provided only 15 cwt lorries. One officer spent nearly all his time nosing out abandoned cars in distant corners of the forest and our fleet at one time became embarrassingly large. Even our American liaison officer had one, but we couldn't spare him a driver and it suffered endless damage.

We left our surplus stores at Olpe and drove to Milspe where we were given orders to take over Hagen, a large town which had had important iron and steelworks . . .

The Belgian captain found us good French staff and we were soon comfortably installed with offices in one house and mess in the other. A new interpreter turned up; a seedy-looking individual name Pressler, who announced in broad Cockney that he was British and produced papers to show that he had served with the Middlesex Regiment in the last war. He had a German wife and had kept his job as a clerk in the big Accumulator Works right through the war. He turned out to be one of the best interpreters we ever had.

The 21st Army Group had crossed the Rhine on 23 March and Reckitt's civil affairs group was soon called forward. Its first mission was at Olpe, where it was required to assist the inmates of a former concentration camp and move them to a displaced persons' camp at Siegen. Reckitt was soon moved on to the iron and steel town of Hagen since his specialism was industry. In reality, the first thing that they had to do on arriving in any town was not, in fact, to set up a police force, but to find accommodation. Their standard practice was to turn people out of ordinary houses at two hours' notice – 'unpleasant but unavoidable'. Reckitt was always amazed that the inhabitants complied without protest, even though there was a good chance that they would not see their property again.

Friday 20 April 1945

Marguerite Duras sets up a tracing service for returnees at the Gare d'Orsay

Marguerite Duras was born in Saigon, the southern city of the French colony of Indochina. She had arrived in France at the age of eighteen to study. A successful student, she completed a law degree and held an official post with the Outre Mer – the French colonial ministry. In 1939 she married the poet Robert Anthelme and in 1942 suffered a stillborn child. Strongly inclined to the political left, she joined the Paris resistance. Robert, her husband, was arrested along with her sister-in-law, Marie-Laure, who would later perish in the camps.

[Gare d'] Orsay. Outside the center, wives of prisoners of war congeal in a solid mass. White barriers separate them from the prisoners. 'Do you have any news of so-and-so?' they shout. Every so often the soldiers stop; one or two answer. Some women are there at seven o'clock in the morning. Some stay till three in the morning and then come back again at seven. But there are some who stay right through the night, between three and seven. They're not allowed into the center. Lots of people who are not waiting for anyone come to the Gare d'Orsay, too, just to see the show, the arrival of the prisoners of war and how the women wait for them, and all the rest, to see what it's like; perhaps it will never happen again. You can tell the spectators from the others because they don't shout out, and they stand some way away from the crowds of women so as to see both the arrival of the prisoners and the way the women greet them. The prisoners arrive in an orderly manner. At night they come in big American trucks from which they emerge into the light. The women shriek and clap their hands. The prisoners stop, dazzled and taken aback. During the day the women shout as soon as they see the trucks turning off the Solferino Bridge. At night they shout when they slow down just before the center. They shout the names of German towns: 'Noyeswarda?' 'Kassel?' Or Stalag numbers: 'VII A?'

'III A Kommando?' The prisoners seem astonished. They've come straight from Le Bourget airport and Germany. Sometimes they answer, usually they don't quite understand what's expected of them, they smile, they turn and look at the Frenchwomen, the first they've seen since they got back.

Not all the returnees arriving in the Gare d'Orsay were former French POWs from Germany. Some were French citizens who had been sent to concentration camps for their part in the resistance and had been branded 'terrorists' by the Germans. Others were returning French volunteer factory workers who had willingly gone to Germany to assist the Third Reich. A few – like Guy Sajer – were Frenchmen who had volunteered to fight in the German Wehrmacht.

Marguerite Duras was hoping to find her husband, who had been sent to Dachau concentration camp. He survived in very poor health and would eventually be brought back by François Mitterrand, who had headed their section of the resistance in Paris. After the war she became a leading novelist and a prominent member of the intelligentsia. SEE ALSO P. 789.

Monday 23 – Tuesday 24 April 1945

Colonel D. K. Reimers, commander US 343rd Field Artillery, enters the town of Trobes in Germany

23 April
Beau Caudray

The 1st Bn. captured 350 prisoners in Kaimling. A platoon entered the town to find all 350 lined up in parade ground formation and ready to surrender. When asked where their fire arms were they said they didn't have any. I saw a stack of ammunition that could have held up our infantry for a couple of days. Most of the Germans are ready to give up. The only ones still fighting are either fanatics or are being forced to fight by the SS.

Last night Bremer called for a mission on Vohenstrauss. The 3rd Bn. sent a patrol there and it had been fired upon.

We gave him a volley of white phosphorous and a couple of volleys of high explosive. Now the town is on fire and it is lighting up the entire sky. We've found this is the best way to make a town surrender.

24 April
Trobes

This morning I did the reconnaissance with a Red Cross girl in the back seat of my jeep. She said it was the most exciting experience she has had since coming to Europe. I can well imagine it. There aren't many Red Cross girls who have the opportunity of entering a burning town on the heels of the infantry. Just as the 3rd Bn. pulls out of Vohenstrauss we entered and followed the 3rd for a thousand yards or more until I found a good place for the 179th. The German people glared at us with hatred in their eyes as their homes burned behind them. On the outskirts of the town a dead American soldier, who had been killed last night, still lay in the middle of the road . . . my Red Cross companion left me to join her friends and help set up their wagon. They were here long enough to serve everyone coffee and doughnuts before leaving to return to their unit at Division rear.

Captain Bracher discovered a mass grave of about 20 or 30 bodies who had been killed either last night or this morning. They had been stabbed or clubbed to death, layed in a long row and lightly covered with dirt and leaves. They were terribly emaciated and horrible to look at. Three ex-Greek soldiers came out of hiding in a farm we are occupying. They had been in the British Army that had been in Greece and were captured when the Germans parachuted over Crete. They escaped from the Germans three days ago and hadn't eaten for days. We asked them what they knew about the buried dead. They told us the Germans had driven thousands of slave laborers down the road the day before we arrived. Those who became sick or too weak to go on were killed. All three Greeks could speak a little English. We turned them loose in the kitchen and food lockers of the farm and they ate so much they became ill. I watched one of them wolfing down his food and as he ate beads of perspiration began to come out of his face. All of a sudden he turned deathly white and vomited up all he had eaten. Very shortly thereafter he was back eating again.

The fate of both POWs and forced labourers was uncertain in the last months of the war. POWs were anxious that their camps might be mistaken for barracks or military installations and shelled. They often painted large signs on the roofs of their huts to indicate their identity. Forced labourers were marched from place to place but in the final stages of the war they became a nuisance and were often abandoned. Everyone in Germany was desperately short of food.

After fighting at D-Day Colonel Reimers had taken part in some of the savage battles of early 1945, most notably at Lichtenberg. SEE ALSO PP. 676–7.

Friday 27 April 1945

Marta Hillers watches Russian soldiers pursue 'the fat ones' in her communal shelter in a Berlin cellar

This diary records the rape of German women by Red Army soldiers in a large cellar in Berlin which served her, and many of her neighbours, as a communal shelter. The diary was published anonymously in the 1950s, but has recently been identified as the work of Marta Hillers – a German female journalist in her thirties at the time, who had studied at the Sorbonne, travelled extensively in Europe, and written for German newspapers and magazines. She spoke several languages, including some Russian. Her unsentimental diary portrays the Germans as victims of war, as well as perpetrators.

At about 6 P.M. it started. A bull of a man [a Russian soldier] burst into the cellar, dead drunk, brandishing a revolver, and then made a beeline for the distiller's wife. He had evidently singled her out. With his revolver he chased her straight across the cellar, shoving her before him toward the door. She struggled, lashed out, howled – and suddenly the revolver went off. The bullet struck between the props and the wall, without causing any damage. Promptly a cellar panic started. Everyone leaped up, began shouting . . . The 'hero,' evidently scared vanished down the corridor.

Around 7 P.M. I was sitting in the widow's flat over evening soup when the janitor's daughter dashed in. 'Please come at once!' she shrieked. 'You must talk to them in Russian, they're after Frau B. again!' So, the distiller's wife again. She is by far the fattest of us all, with an enormous bosom. It's general knowledge that they are on the lookout for the fat ones. Fat equals beauty because it's more female, more distinct from the male body. Primitive people, after all, revere their fat women as symbols of abundance and fertility. It'll take them some time to find that here. Most of the elderly women who were once so plump are nowadays terribly shrunk. The distiller's wife had actually suffered no hardships: throughout the war she was never without something to barter. Now she has to pay for her selfish fat.

When I came down she was standing in the house entrance whimpering and trembling. She had managed to escape her pursuers, but now she doesn't dare return to the cellar, nor does she dare go up to her fourth-floor flat since German guns have not yet ceased firing. She is also afraid that 'they' might find her here alone. Clawing onto my arm so hard that I can still see the nail marks, she implores me to go with her to the 'commandant' and ask him for an escort or some kind of protection. Imagine!

I accost a passer-by with shoulder stars and try to explain to him the woman's fear, but realize I don't know the Russian word for fear. He immediately waves me away: 'Rot, no one's going to do you any harm. Go home.' The sobbing woman finally staggers upstairs; haven't seen her since, she must be hiding in some corner. Just as well, she's too much of a bait.

I'd hardly reached the widow's flat when the janitor's daughter, who had evidently been chosen as a messenger, came running up again. More men in the cellar. This time they are after the baker's wife who has also managed to preserve considerable corpulence throughout the years of the war. The baker is already swaying towards me down the corridor. As white as his flour, he stretched out his hands towards me, stammers: 'They're with my wife . . .' His voice breaks. For an instant I have the feeling I'm taking part in a play. It seems impossible that an ordinary little baker should move like this, should be able to put into his voice such emotion, look so naked, so exposed – something until now I've witnessed only with great actors.

There's no light in the cellar, the kerosene has evidently given out. By the flickering flame of a little wick in a stearin-filled saucer, a so-called Hindenburg light, I recognise the chalk-white face, the twitching mouth of the baker's wife. Round her stand three Russians . . .

In Berlin alone it is thought that some 100,000 women were raped by Russian soldiers between 1945 and 1948. Many women committed suicide before the Red Army arrived; some did so afterwards, unable to bear the torments that had been visited upon them. The Russian soldiers clearly saw gang-rape as an act of both subjugation and revenge. Some historians now see all war as a misogynist act and interpret rape as the ultimate expression of military activity. SEE ALSO PP. 849–50.

MAY 1945

O N 1 MAY, with the Red Army still fighting in Berlin, German radio announced that the Chancellor, Adolf Hitler, had committed suicide. It appears that the previous day he had his favourite Alsatian dog 'Blondie' poisoned and the two other dogs in the household shot. Later he summoned his two remaining women secretaries and gave them capsules of poison to use if they wished to when the advancing Russian soldiers entered the bunker. Hitler himself and his mistress, Eva Braun, were hurriedly married before killing themselves. Hitler used a pistol and Eva Braun took poison. Joseph Goebbels also committed suicide alongside his Führer, having previously killed his wife and family.

On Thursday 3 May German representatives joined Montgomery at his command centre on Lüneburg Heath, near Hamburg, to agree procedures for surrender. Hitler's successor,

Admiral Dönitz, was asked to surrender all military units facing the 21st Army Group. By the beginning of May the Wehrmacht was disintegrating, and in its place was simply a mass of troops, foreign labourers, civilians, prisoners and refugees fleeing west in an effort to escape the attentions of the Soviet forces. At Hamburg the local commander, General Wolz, had already surrendered to the British 2nd Army. Further south the American armed forces met up with their Russian allies at many points.

On 7 May the German government under Dönitz accepted the Allied surrender terms unconditionally. Thereafter, Field Marshal Jodl, together with a number of senior German military officers, signed the treaty of unconditional surrender in Rheims at 2:41 a.m. This stated that all operations were to cease at one minute after midnight (GMT) on 8 May, which was declared to be Victory in Europe Day or 'VE-Day'. The next day, German forces in the Channel Islands surrendered to a British Commando force on a destroyer anchored off St Helier in Jersey.

Soon the Allies had begun the disarmament of the German forces, issuing orders through the medium of the temporary administration led by Dönitz. This interregnum lasted only a fortnight, at the end of which the temporary government was disbanded; thereafter, Dönitz, Jodl and a number of other officers found themselves and the German general staff under arrest in preparation for an international war crimes tribunal. Goering was arrested by the Americans near Salzburg and Kesselring was captured in Austria. Although the British located and arrested Heinrich Himmler at Bremervorde, he managed to commit suicide while in custody using a hidden cyanide capsule.

The rapid restoration of France to the status of a significant power continued. In mid-May President Harry Truman informed the French that he would relinquish part of the American zone of occupation in Germany to French control. The French were to occupy the Saarland, Rheinland-Pfalz, Baden and Württemberg. Psychologically this was of enormous importance to the French people. The occupation tasks facing all four victorious powers were huge: in the British and American zones alone over 4 million displaced persons were thought to be at large.

In the last week of May Britain's wartime coalition government, led by Churchill and his Deputy Prime Minister, Clement Attlee, came to an end. Political tensions between Labour and

Conservative members of the coalition had already been showing in the House of Commons during February and March. The Labour Party, which had constituted a formidable part of this wartime team, rejected Churchill's suggestion that coalition arrangements be extended until the war against Japan was over. Instead, preparations for an election began and the date was fixed for 5 July.

Tuesday 1 May 1945

Marta Hillers, in Berlin, writes it down 'with a calm hand'

What is rape? When, on Friday evening, I pronounced this word aloud for the first time, an icy shudder ran down my spine. Now, I can already think it, write it down with a calm hand. I say it aloud in order to accustom myself to its sound. It sounds like the last, the ultimate, the end of all things, of life itself. But it isn't.

On Saturday afternoon around three o'clock two of them banged their fists and revolver butts against the front door, bellowed, and started kicking at the door. The widow opened it, she's continually frightened someone's going to smash the lock. Two grey heads entered, reeling. They thrust their guns through the one remaining undamaged pane of the passage window. The glass clinked down into the court-yard. They then tore the blackout blinds to shreds and kicked the grandfather clock.

One of them, having pushed the widow out of the way, grabs me and drives me into the front room. The other takes up a position at the front door, keeping the widow at bay with his gun, without speaking and without touching her. The one who has got hold of me is an older man with grey stubble on his face, he reeks of schnapps and horses. He carefully closes the door behind him and when he finds there is no key in the lock, he pushes an armchair against it. He seems quite unaware of his victim, which makes it all the more frightening when he suddenly throws me on the bed. Shut your eyes, clench your teeth, don't utter a sound.

Paralysis. Not disgust, just utter coldness. The spine seems to be frozen, icy dizziness encircles the back of the head. I find myself gliding and sinking deep down through the pillows, through the floor. So that's what it's like – sinking through the floor.

Once more eye looks into eye. The lips above me open. I see yellow teeth, one front tooth half-broken. Slowly the corners of the mouth rise, tiny wrinkles form round the slit eyes. The man is smiling.

Before leaving he fishes something out of his pocket, throws it without a word on to the night table, pushes the chair away and slams the door behind him. What he has left behind turns out to be a crumpled packet of cigarettes. My fee.

When I got up I felt dizzy and wanted to vomit. I staggered along the passage, past the sobbing widow, to the bathroom. There I vomited. In the mirror I saw my green face, in the basin what I had vomited. I didn't dare rinse it as I kept on retching and we had so little water left in the bucket.

Marta Hillers was remarkably laconic, even casual, about her own suffering, observing in one of her entries: 'I laugh right in the middle of all this awfulness.' Her diary would itself be the cause of grief, for after reading it her partner decided that he wanted nothing more to do with her. When she chose to publish it in the 1950s she was criticized by German women for raising matters which others preferred to leave unspoken. Marta Hillers would eventually marry, move to Switzerland and give up journalism, disappearing into obscurity. After her death in June 2001, at the age of ninety, her diary was republished and spent five months in the German bestseller lists. SEE ALSO PP. 845–7.

Friday 4 May 1945

John T. Bassett, an American soldier in northern Italy, witnesses a training accident at the end of the war

'Come on, John T; wake up.' It was Holman, at the ungodly hour of 6:00am.

'Why? What's up?' I asked.

'We're going out on a hike, weapon nomenclature, the usual training routine. It's to keep us from going soft.' I groaned and rolled over, but I kept my eye on Holman, and when he returned with a slender board in his hand, I jumped quickly off the cot.

Outside, on the street, I saw that it promised to be a fair spring day. We hiked casually, almost gaily, although in formation, out of Riva and then turned off a dirt path that led up a steep wooded hillside. After a mile we left the path and spread out over a grassy slope, each platoon occupying its own separate ground for the purpose of the training exercise. Then the squads formed into separate units, sitting in little semicircles on the ground, looking down at the exercise leaders a few feet below them. Holman put a blanket on the ground below us and asked Crest to take apart his BAR, name each part and explain how it worked, and then reassemble it. Crest did the routine in his low, calm voice.

Without warning a burst of gunfire erupted violently from the area of our neighboring squad to the left, followed by terrible screams and shouting. Automatically, without thinking, I rolled over on my stomach and pointed my M1 down the slope. Some of the squad lay with me on their stomachs; the rest ran up the hill. The screaming, a high-pitched, terrifying sound, continued for a few more seconds. There was no further gunfire. I looked over at the GIs running around like crazy men and I realised that the firing somehow had happened within the squad. Then, out of the milling frenzied group, Cross came limping towards me.

'You're bleeding, Cross,' I gasped, scrambling to my feet. 'What happened? Were you hit?'

'Yes-yes-God-yes, I was hit in the leg, but I've got a tourniquet – 1 can walk – won't wait for medics – God – how awful for this to happen.' He limped past me toward the path. I now realized that the screaming had stopped. I looked around wildly: GIs were still shouting – still running about. No one took charge. We were like a flock of disoriented, devastated sheep. I spied Rabideau coming towards me. Blood was dripping from his left hand.

'Here – wait, Rabideau!' I cried. I pulled out an unused handkerchief from my pocket. 'Let me tie this around your hand. Is that your only wound?'

'Yeah, Bass, I was lucky. I only got one round right through the middle of my hand.'

'What happened?' I asked as I walked with him toward the path. 'Was it your BAR that fired?'

'Yeah. I saw it happen. Hackett took it apart, and when he had it put back together, it was pointed uphill at us, on the bipod. I think he was half asleep, like the rest of us. When it was finished, I heard him say, 'Now the last thing you do is pull the trigger.'

'Who was screaming?'

'Schuck. He got two bullets just below his neck.'

'Is he dead?'

'Don't know. Thanks for the 'kerchief – see you later.' I ran back to the slope to find my squad. I discovered them throwing their ammunition away, into the bushes. Rebel was crying.

'Come on, Bass, throw your bullets away. Schuck may be dead.' . . .

Later that day, I ran across Hackett. We did not speak. His face was as white as snow. He was nervous and he looked wary. For Hackett, as for Schuck, Cross and Rabideau, the war had ended, but then, like the most horrible of all nightmares, it had begun again.

Fighting had effectively stopped in Italy by 1 May, and three days later it had ceased across most of Europe. Only in areas of Czechoslovakia was there still significant conflict. John Bassett's unit – the 10th Mountain Division – had not been involved in combat for some time. After the cessation of hostilities training was continued to keep units occupied. It was still necessary for them to be issued with live ammunition because of the threat from large bands of deserters and bandits, who would become a growing problem in northern Italy in late 1945. Accidents in training with weapons and friendly fire incidents were inevitable in large-scale conflicts, but this did not blunt the extreme sense of horror and waste that such events provoked. In June Bassett's unit would move to Cividale in the north-east Po valley to await return to the United States, passing the time with tours into Austria to see the Alps. John T. Bassett currently lives in Stagecoach, Nevada. SEE ALSO PP. 835–6.

Sunday 6 May 1945

Sir Raymond Streat, industrialist and supply official, on
hopes for the future in Manchester and Wilmslow

What a week! And through all this activity connected with
my job in life, ran a constant background of tense excitement, in me and in everybody else, over the great events
which were happening.

. . . Curious perhaps but true that I do not now remember
as I sit in my chair on which day precisely the various things
happened during this crowded week. I think Berlin fell to
the Russians and the death of Hitler – or his announced
death for there was much scepticism about it – occurred on
Monday, the 30th [April]. Certainly the surrender of Germans
in Holland, Denmark and West Germany to Montgomery
was on Friday. Hamburg fell in between. It must have been
Thursday evening when twiddling the knob of the radio I
stumbled on a low toned German voice on the Hamburg
wave length making an oration about Hitler's place in
history – a peon of praise which surprised me at this hour of
defeat . . .

Happiness was in the air because our own dangers and
troubles were clearly over: because the security and stability
of our British way of life was now assured with the
downfall of the tyrants who would have destroyed it. After
five-and-a-half years it was at last safe to allow the mind to
dwell on the future. Now there is no reason why one should
NOT think of a holiday place for next year, a career for
Christopher, a family for Basil, which rooms to decorate first,
a new carpet in due course. This week has been the first time
I have realised how many chains the war has really put on
the legitimate day-dreaming of the average man and
woman. I have found my day-dreams for the future sprouting again. Previously one dared not look ahead.

But how quietly all this has been taken in Manchester
and Wilmslow. No boisterousness. No clamour – not even
buoyancy – perceptibly at any rate.

Raymond Streat's thoughts on the end of the war were, like those of many, rather mixed. In Britain there was a clear sense of the 'real' war being over, with the implied tendency to forget about those engaged in the war against Japan, which many believed would go on for another eighteen months. By contrast, for most Americans Japan was the main enemy.

The idea that the end of the war would mean an end to privation was soon dispelled by further ration cuts. Britain was victorious, but it was also bankrupt, as Streat knew only too well. His thoughts were tinged with more than a little sadness, for while there were plans for two of his sons, Christopher and Basil, a third son, Tony, had been killed fighting in the war. On VE-Day Sir Raymond attended a service in a small church at Nether Alderley at which there were references to those who had given their lives to purchase victory. He noted in his diary that his wife Doris 'took this stoically'. After the war, Streat would cease working as a Whitehall official and return to the north; he became Chairman of the Manchester Cotton Board, a post he held until 1957. He died in 1979. SEE ALSO PP. 55–6 AND 70–1.

The evening before VE-Day – Monday 7 May 1945

James Sweetland, aged seventeen, watches the victory celebrations with detachment

James Sweetland was a teenager living in Marylebone throughout the war. The Blitz had disrupted his schooling, for in 1940 he had been evacuated along with his entire school to Brackley in Buckinghamshire, where the reception was less than welcoming. On his return, further bombing and an influx of large numbers of refugees into his school had also taken their toll on his academic progress. He was now working as a clerk in the office of the Judge Advocate General, but the end of the war left him with an uncertain future.

On the evening of May the 7th I caught my usual 38 bus from outside Hobart House to Piccadilly Circus. In the Circus itself, groups of people stood around expectantly, and in one spot a newsreel camera was set up and waiting. I thought the war must now be over but preferred to catch my next bus home to the radio to find out for sure. True enough, the news was of the German surrender; and that tomorrow, May the 8th, would be 'V.E. Day', and a public holiday. I was a bit taken aback by this announcement and didn't really know if my employers would close the office. Anyway, in the end I decided not to go in.

So now the long war was finally over, in Europe at least, which to many seemed the *real* war. Locally, as throughout the country, preparations were quickly made for a celebration. Trestle tables magically appeared, placed end to end in the courtyards beneath the blocks of flats, where they could be fitted in between the surface shelters and bicycle sheds, for a grand childrens' party. Similarly, flags and bunting appeared at windows and were slung between balconies, reminiscent to me of my last childrens' party, for the Coronation of 1937. Indeed, it was clear that cardboard cut-outs of their Majesties, together with slogans of 'God Bless the King and Queen', had been safely stored since then. Elsewhere bonfires in the streets were made ready for the evening of the 8th. A huge bonfire was prepared on part of Cumberland Market, the local boys dragging old doors and any timber they could lay their hands on to add to the pile.

As for myself, I had made arrangements with my friend Gus, whom I had known since infant school days, that on that evening, we would make our way to the West End to watch the celebrations. Outragious [*sic*] it may sound, but I didn't feel like celebrating, and it became clear that Gus felt the same. The war had begun when I was eleven and, now being seventeen, the whole of those six years, despite every hardship, had been the only real and normal life that I could recognise, for I was a child before September, 1939. Therefore, peacetime presented a prospect of the Great Unknown, in which the unity of wartime would vanish. So it was that I felt a complete outsider, observing only the dancing, singing and general merrymaking taking place in the West End. Servicemen would now rightly look forward to a return to civilian life, with the promise of a better life than the one they had left; but with the war in the Far East not yet over, Gus and I had to await our call up to the services and I, as a temporary Civil Servant, would be without a job to return to, if and when I did.

Many feared that peace would bring a return to pre-war conditions of widespread unemployment, but in fact there was a labour shortage. For Sweetland there would certainly be plenty of work, as his office became a major co-ordinating centre for war crimes investigation groups.

VE-Day – Tuesday 8 May 1945

Baffy Dugdale, political campaigner and Zionist, listens to Winston Churchill addressing the crowds in Trafalgar Square

To Zionist Office in morning for a Yeshiva, no staff there. Nothing unusual in the streets in the morning. About 2pm I boarded a 77 'bus to go to Parliament Square. Lucky to get a seat on top, for we progressed at walking pace along the Strand. In Trafalgar Square and Whitehall were the densest crowds, and the best-behaved, I ever saw in all my experience of London. Unusually gay and coloured, for it was a warm and sunny day, and the carnival paper hats were many and various and very becoming to most girls. Loudspeakers were on Government buildings all down Whitehall. At 3pm the loud murmur of the vast crowds in Parliament Square were absolutely hushed, to hear the PM. He was very good. I don't think anyone but him could have got away with 'Advance Britannia!' But he did, at the end there was a mighty roar. The cheering for him when the Commons came out to go to St Margaret's was so loud that I could not hear my own voice, though shouting at pitch of my lungs. I stayed to see them come out. With them walked the ghosts of Victor Cazalet and Rob Bernays.

Victor Cazalet had been an MP in 1939 and had left his seat in the Commons to become a major in the British army. He was killed in action in 1943. Rob Bernays had also been an MP and was killed in the Bay of Biscay in the same plane crash as the actor Leslie Howard in 1943. Baffy Dugdale would die on 16 May 1948, four days after the creation of the state of Israel, for which she had campaigned exhaustively. SEE ALSO *P. 771–2.*

Monday 7 – Saturday 12 May 1945

Anne Somerhausen, Belgian resistance worker, learns the fate of Mark, her husband, who had been a prisoner of war in Germany

7 May

Am I a widow? Is my husband dead? Why has no word come through from him these long, long eight months? Must I fight on alone forever? I am as tired as if I had lived for centuries – through centuries of war. How many, many days will this dreadful uncertainty last? Does life mean to crush me flat?

12 May

The miracle has happened. Five years ago to the day, almost to the hour, my husband kissed me goodbye and turned back to his antiaircraft gun. Today he returned, an older, stronger man, tanned by the sun, hale in his battle dress – a very silent man, still somewhat a stranger in his own home. He walked into it, using his own latchkey, which he had carried like a talisman all these five years.

He walked straight into the garden, where Luke and Matthew were playing. He recognized Matthew and asked somewhat shyly: 'Is this Luke?' And Luke asked timidly: 'Are you my Dad?'

Johnny rushed down from upstairs to see who the soldier was. He recognized his father. But Mark was almost shocked. He had left a boy of thirteen; he found a young man, impossible to identify.

Johnny called up my office. I burst into tears. The office staff gathered around me. 'Put your hat on right' 'You must powder your nose.' 'Put a bit of lipstick on.' I ran off in a daze.

There he stood in the doorway – my husband. We fell into each other's arms. No, this wasn't coming home after five years of war. This was Mark, coming home from a somewhat leisurely trip abroad. Surely we had parted only three weeks or so ago? This was all quite natural and normal. Surely it was a little unbalanced to be crying?

... He is asleep now. He does not sense that I am watching him, or that from time to time I am holding his hand. There are many deep new lines in his face, and I am trying to read the story they tell. His hands are harder and broader – no longer the soft white hands of an intellectual. He sleeps profoundly – only, at times there is a nervous twitching around his mouth.

He is asleep. He is here. I am holding my husband's hand at last. The children, too, are having their rest – each healthy boy sound asleep. No more war. My work is done. All, all is well.

For so many people right across Europe, VE-Day brought both joy and trepidation. News of the state of relatives in POW camps was often slow to arrive and intermittent, and news from concentration camps had been almost non-existent. In Germany, Joseph Goebbels had forbidden the civilian population to receive letters from German POWs in Russia for fear that they contained communist propaganda. Everywhere relatives endured an agony of waiting to see if their loved ones were alive and well. SEE ALSO PP. 13 AND 462–3.

JUNE – DECEMBER 1945

AFTER THE THRILL OF victorious conquest came mundane issues of military government. During the first days of June the Allied occupying powers – Britain, France, the United States and the Soviet Union – divided Germany into four administrative zones. With fighting over, the Allies were now able to count the cost of victory in the West. In the eleven months between D-Day and VE-Day the Allies had suffered some 776,967 casualties, of which 141,590 had died. By mid-June demobilization of the armed forces had begun. The British 2nd Army in Germany was to be disbanded and sent back to Britain. In the July general election Clement Attlee and the Labour Party secured a landslide victory. Behind the scenes, major arguments developed between the military and Attlee's new government. The services wished to retain imperial bases and a sizeable army in order to contain the Soviet advances in Europe; Attlee was keen for Britain to demobilize and for Britain to give up its empire. Andrew Cunningham, Chief of the Naval Staff, was horrified and noted in his diary that the new Labour leader was 'past belief'. Remarkably, Whitehall had begun thinking about the Cold War even before the Second World War in Europe had ended.

On 17 July the 'Big Three' met among the ruins of Berlin, which provided a dramatic backdrop for the Potsdam conference. Here the leaders discussed the forthcoming use of the atomic bomb, which had been tested in New Mexico just before the conference. Churchill had been particularly keen to see the atomic bomb used operationally. Truman also looked forward to the dropping of the bomb, noting in his diary on the first day of the conference: 'Fini Japs when that comes about.' During July the Japanese rejected Allied overtures designed to secure their complete surrender. Accordingly, on Monday 6 August an atomic bomb devastated Hiroshima, and on Thursday 9 August a second atomic bomb destroyed the city of Nagasaki. Intense secrecy had surrounded the development of the bomb, and even some senior generals and diplomats were surprised by these events. The Japanese now offered unconditional surrender, although they were allowed to retain their Emperor. On Wednesday 15 August 'Victory Japan Day' or 'VJ-Day' was declared. The Japanese Emperor gave a radio broadcast informing his people that they must now 'bear the unbearable'. The Emperor had never used the radio before: this was the first time that most Japanese people had heard his voice.

Relief at the end of the war was mixed with anxiety over the use of atomic weapons. On Tuesday 7 August Oliver Harvey, who had been Eden's private secretary, noted in his diary, 'I feel shocked and ashamed,' adding that posterity would judge it to have been a bad decision. On Friday 10 August, at her home in Scotland, Naomi Mitchison pondered what atomic weapons meant for the future and recorded: 'All the time one keeps thinking of this bomb ... a perpetual menace over everything.' However, the military, who had been more directly involved in the business of fighting Japan, found their consciences less troubled. On Saturday 11 and Sunday 12 August Alan Brooke went off to spend a 'glorious weekend' at the seaside with his family, bathing frequently and enjoying what he called 'perfect rest and quiet'. Delighted with the imminent Japanese surrender, he noted in his diary: 'All going well.'

At the end of August the final list of major German war criminals to be tried at Nuremberg was drawn up by a Four-Power Commission of Prosecutors in London. In mid-October the first session of the International Military War Crimes Tribunal began proceedings against twenty-one senior figures of the Nazi state. All of them pleaded not guilty. At a lower level many SS personnel, convicted of atrocities at Auschwitz, Belsen and other concentration camps, were also hanged. However, it became clear that minor war crimes were very widespread and the authorities became perplexed about how to dispense meaningful justice without incarcerating a very large number of people for some decades. The second volume of this study will encompass the issue of war crimes in Europe and Asia, the British election of July 1945 and the end-of-war settlements, together with the post-war occupations of Germany, Austria and Japan.

Although the war was now officially at an end, it cast a long shadow. Many people were still waiting for relatives to return from active service overseas, as the Second World War merged seamlessly with some of the 'small wars' of the late 1940s in Greece, Palestine and Indonesia. Others were still waiting for news of family members who were 'missing' and whose fate remained uncertain. Meanwhile, most diary-keepers, having always regarded their journals as a 'special' wartime occupation, stopped writing. This was certainly the case with Helena and Catherine Harrison, two sisters living in Beckenham, close to the RAF station at Biggin Hill, who had worked respectively in the local WVS and in the Citizens' Advice Bureau at Catford.

However, preserved together with their wartime diaries at the Imperial War Museum are their post-war ration books. This underlines the fact that bread rationing did not end until 1948, tea rationing until 1952 and the rationing of meat not until 1954. Everywhere these events continued to touch people personally for more than a decade after the Second World War was 'over'.

SOURCE NOTES

1939

Epigraph: Jean Malaquais, *War Diary* (New York: Doubleday, Doran and Co. Inc., 1944), p. 1.

29 Jan.–19 Mar. 1939: Diary of H. P. L. Mott, 97/14/3, Imperial War Museum.

17–19 Mar. 1939: Emil Dorian, *The Quality of Witness: A Romanian Diary 1937–1944* (Philadelphia: Jewish Publication Society of America, 1982), pp. 60–1.

28–29 Apr. 1939: M. Muggeridge (ed.), *Ciano's Diary, 1939–1943* (Heinemann, 1947), pp. 78–9.

2–9 May 1939: D. Dilks (ed.), *Diaries of Sir Alexander Cadogan* (Cassell, 1971), pp. 177–9.

21 May 1939: Muggeridge (ed.), *Ciano's Diary*, pp. 90–1.

24 June 1939: N. MacKenzie and J. MacKenzie (eds), *The Diary of Beatrice Webb*, vol. 4: *1924–1943, The Wheel of Life* (Virago/LSE, 1985), p. 435.

25–29 Aug. 1939: K. Langhorne, Mass-Observation Archive, University of Sussex. The name of this diarist has been replaced with a pseudonym to preserve anonymity as required by the archive.

25–28 Aug. 1939: A. O. Bell (ed.), *The Diary of Virginia Woolf* (Hogarth, 1984), pp. 230–1.

27 Aug. 1939: Amanda Smith (ed.), *Hostage to Fortune: The Letters of Joseph P. Kennedy* (New York: Viking Penguin, 2001), pp. 363–4.

29 Aug. 1939: Marguerite Dupree (ed.), *Lancashire and Whitehall: The Diary of Sir Raymond Streat*, vol. 1: *1931–39* (Manchester: Manchester University Press, 1999), p. 612.

30 Aug. 1939: K. Vaughan, *Journals, 1939–1977* (John Murray, 1989), pp. 3–4.

——K. Worth, Mass-Observation Archive, University of Sussex. The name of this diarist has been replaced with a pseudonym to preserve anonymity, as required by the archive.

2 Sept. 1939: Diary of Kay Phipps, P/178, Imperial War Museum.

3 Sept. 1939: W. E. Holl, 'A Diary of Civil Defence Goes Through It: Paddington 1937–1945', MSS 9100.c.44, British Library, p. 22.

——Gladys Cox, 'War Diary', 86/46/1 (P), Imperial War Museum.

——Smith (ed.), *Hostage to Fortune*, p. 366.

——William Shawn (ed.), *Mollie Panter-Downes: London War Notes* (New York: Farrar, Strauss & Giroux, 1971), p. 5.

4 Sept. 1939: Diary of Miss D. M. Hoyles, 77/50/1, Imperial War Museum.

7 Sept. 1939: MacKenzie and MacKenzie (eds), *Diary of Beatrice Webb*, vol. 4, pp. 440–1.

10 Sept. 1939: S. Baley, *Two Septembers 1939 and 1940: A Diary of Events* (Allen & Unwin, 1941), pp. 18–19.

——Dupree (ed.), *Lancashire and Whitehall*, pp. 7–8.

11 Sept. 1939: D. Barlone, *A French Officer's Diary 23rd August 1939–1st October 1940* (New York: Macmillan, 1943), pp. 10–11.

19 Sept. 1939: Diary of Kay Phipps.

20–21 Sept. 1939: H. C. Robbins Landon (ed.), *Wilhelm Prüller: Diary of a German Soldier* (New York: Coward-McCann, 1963), pp. 32–4.

22 Sept. 1939: G. Hagglof, *Diplomat* (Bodley Head, 1971), pp. 113–14.

25 Sept. 1939: Robbins Landon (ed.), *Wilhelm Prüller*, pp. 38–9.

1 Oct. 1939: Shawn (ed.), *Mollie Panter-Downes*, pp. 14–15.

8–25 Oct. 1939: J. Phillips, *My Secret Diary* (Shepeard-Walwyn, 1982), pp. 73, 78.

22 Oct. 1939: G. Beardmore, *Civilians at War: Journals 1938–1946* (John Murray, 1984), p. 43.

29 Oct. 1939: Diary of Muriel Green, in D. Sheridan (ed.), *Wartime Women* (Heinemann, 1990), pp. 57–8.

2–16 Nov. 1939: Beardmore, *Civilians at War*, pp. 44–5.

5 Nov. 1939: W. Shirer, *Berlin Diary: The Journal of a Foreign Correspondent 1934–1941* (Hamish Hamilton, 1941), pp. 194–6.

22–25 Nov. 1939: K. Gerbet (ed.), *Generalfeldmarshal von Bock: The War Diary 1939–1945*, trans. D. Johnston (Atglen, Pa: Schiffer, 1996), p. 88.

Late Nov.–early Dec. 1939: G. Stuhlman (ed.), *The Diary of Anaïs Nin, 1939–1944* (New York: Harcourt Brace Jovanovich, 1969), pp. 3–4.

1 Dec. 1939: A. Weymouth, *A Psychologist's Wartime Diary* (Toronto: Longman, 1940), pp. 126–7.

4 Dec. 1939: Axel Heyst, *There Shall be No Victory: Diary of a European* (Gollancz, 1947), pp. 26–7.

12 Dec. 1939: Weymouth, *A Psychologist's Wartime Diary*, pp. 149, 150–1.

18–21 Dec. 1939: P. Roubiczek, *Across the Abyss: Diary Entries for the*

Years 1939–40, trans. George Bird (Cambridge: Cambridge University Press, 1982), pp. 200–2.

20 Dec. 1939: Shawn (ed.), *Mollie Panter-Downes*, pp. 185–6.

21 Dec. 1939: Jean-Paul Sartre, *War Diaries: Notebooks from a Phoney War, November 1939–March 1940* (Verso, 1984), pp. 153–4.

27 Dec. 1939: Diary of Muriel Green, in Sheridan (ed.), *Wartime Women*, pp. 57–8.

31 Dec. 1939: G. Ciano, *Diario 1937–1943* (Milano: Biblioteca Universale Rizzoli, 1980), p. 339, trans. for this edition by Manuela Williams.

1940

Epigraph: Sir Walter Citrine, *My Finnish Diary* (Penguin, 1940), pp. 171–2.

5–16 Jan. 1940: Roubiczek, *Across the Abyss*, p. 254.

18–20 Jan. 1940: Malaquais, *War Diary*, pp. 101–2.

27 Jan. 1940: Citrine, *My Finnish Diary*, pp. 80–1.

Late Jan. 1940: Diary of A. R. C. Leaney, PP/MCR/206, Imperial War Museum.

Mid-Feb. 1940: Anon., *The Bells Go Down: The Diary of a London AFS Man* (Methuen, 1942), p. 60.

17 Feb. 1940: Sartre, *War Diaries*, pp. 199–200.

24 Feb. 1940: Malaquais, *War Diary*, pp. 124–5.

12 Mar. 1940: R. Macleod and D. Kelly (eds), *The Ironside Diaries 1937–1940* (Constable, 1962), pp. 226–7.

14 Mar. 1940: H. Blodgett (ed.), *Capacious Hold-all: An Anthology of Englishwomen's Diary Writings* (Charlottesville: University of Virginia Press, 1992), p. 390.

Mid-Mar. 1940: Anon., *The Bells Go Down*, pp. 62–3.

——H. Bolitho, *A Penguin in the Eyrie* (Hutchinson, 1955), pp. 55–6.

21 Mar. 1940: S. Hedin, *Sven Hedin's German Diary, 1935–1942* (Euphorion, 1951), pp. 121–2.

25–26 Mar. 1940: Barlone, *French Officer's Diary*, pp. 35–6.

9 Apr. 1940: A. Weymouth, *Journal of the War Years (1939–1945) and One Year Later* (Littlebury & Co., 1948), pp. 220–1.

13–30 Apr. 1940: Diary of Arthur Turner, A. H. Turner papers, 92/27/1, Imperial War Museum.

20 Apr. 1940: H. Clegg, *A Canuck in England: Journal of a Canadian*

Soldier (Harrap, 1942), pp. 83–4.

23 Apr. 1940: Diary of J. Davies, 81/2/1, Imperial War Museum.

12 May 1940: J. Wilton (ed.), *Internment: The Diaries of Harry Seidler May 1940–October 1941*, trans. J. Winternitz (Sydney: Allen & Unwin, 1986), pp. 35–6.

14 May 1940: John Colville, *The Fringes of Power* (Hodder & Stoughton, 1985) p. 130.

——Anon., *The Diary of a Staff Officer (Air Intelligence Liaison Officer at Advanced Headquarters North BAAF 1940* (Methuen, 1941), p. 11.

16 May 1940: 'Visit to France and Belgium in May and June 1940 as DDMO', papers of General Sir Otto Lund, MISC 24, Churchill Archives Centre.

20 May 1940: Macleod and Kelly (eds), *Ironside Diaries*, p. 321.

——Diary of Sergeant L. D. Pexton, BEF France and POW, Imperial War Museum.

23–24 May 1940: R. R. James (ed.), *'Chips': The Diaries of Sir Henry Channon* (Phoenix, 1999), p. 254.

29 May 1940: Diary of L. F. Barter, PP/MCR/426, Imperial War Museum.

6 June 1940: Diary of Cecil King, Special Collections, Boston University Library.

7 June 1940: A. Werth, *The Last Days of Paris: A Journalist's Diary* (Hamish Hamilton, 1940), p. 139.

12 June 1940: Unknown diary of an Italian pilot, trans. British Military Intelligence, WO 106/2160, Public Record Office.

——Diary of F. Watt, 03/10/1, Imperial War Museum.

13 June 1940: G. Bilaikin, *Diary of a Diplomatic Correspondent* (Allen & Unwin, 1940), pp. 105–6.

22 June 1940: Shirer, *Berlin Diary*, pp. 328–31.

24 June 1940: F. Partridge, *A Pacifist's War* (Hogarth, 1978), pp. 47–8.

——F. Stark, *An Italian Diary* (Murray, 1945), pp. 2–5.

2 July 1940: Diary of Diana Falla, in B. A. Read, *No Cause for Panic: Channel Islands Refugees, 1940–1945* (Seaflower, 1995), p. 82.

3–15 July 1940: 'Extracts from a Diary of an Interned German Refugee . . .', attached to Lt-Col. D. R. Robertson to Director of POWs, 13 Mar. 1941, HO 215/210, PRO.

14 July 1940: Wilton (ed.), *Internment*, pp. 62–3.

14–16 July S. Ball (ed.), *Parliament and Politics in the Age of Churchill and Attlee: The Headlam Diaries 1935–1951* (Cambridge University Press, 1999), pp. 212–13.

23 July 1940: Clegg, *A Canuck in England*, pp. 132–4.

7 Aug. 1940: T. N. Depuy (ed.), *The Halder Diaries: The Private War Diaries of Colonel General Franz Halder* (Boulder, Co.: Westview, 1976), vol. 1, p. 153.

10 Aug. 1940: Giuseppe Bottai, *Diario 1935–1944* (Milano: Biblioteca Universale Rizzoli, 1989), pp. 220–1, trans. for this edition by Manuela Williams.

14 Aug. 1940: MacKenzie and MacKenzie (eds), *Diary of Beatrice Webb*, vol. 4, pp. 458–9.

15 Aug. 1940: J. Cassington (ed.), *A Metal Man's Wartime Diary* (Egsham: Quinn, 1941), p. 73.

21 Aug. 1940: Ben Pimlott (ed.), *The Second World War Diaries of Hugh Dalton, 1940–45* (Cape, 1986), p. 76.

30 Aug. 1940: J. Wyndham, *Love Lessons: A Wartime Diary* (Heinemann, 1985), pp. 138–9.

7–12 Sept. 1940: Weymouth, *Journal of the War Years*, pp. 320–1.

12–13 Sept. 1940: Diary of V. Goddard, Con Shelf item, Imperial War Museum.

14 Sept. 1940: Partridge, *A Pacifist's War*, p. 60.

15 Sept. 1940: J. Leutze, *The London Observer: The Journal of General Raymond E. Lee* (Hutchinson, 1972), pp. 58–9.

16 Sept. 1940: A. McCulloch (ed.), *The War and Uncle Walter: The Diary of an Eccentric* (Doubleday, 2003), pp. 147–8.

17 Sept. 1940: C. Cross (ed.), *Life with Lloyd George: The Diary of A. J. Sylvester 1931–45* (Macmillan, 1975), p. 278.

2 Oct. 1940: C. Perry, *Boy in the Blitz: The 1940 Diary of Colin Perry* (Cooper, 1972), p. 176.

7 Oct. 1940: Diary of Emily Riddell, 92/25/1, Imperial War Museum.

13–14 Oct. 1940: Perry, *Boy in the Blitz*, p. 192.

20 Oct. 1940: Bell (ed.), *Diary of Virginia Woolf*, pp. 330–1.

26 Oct. 1940: Ritchie, *Siren Years*, pp. 74–5.

27 Oct. 1940: Diary of Mrs Cecilie Eustace, 85/27/1, Imperial War Museum.

Late Oct. 1940: Naomi Royde Smith, *Outside Information: A Diary of Rumours* (Macmillan, 1941), pp. 142–3.

1–11 Nov. 1940: Diary of Edith Kupp (*née* Heap), Liddle Collection, Brotherton Library, University of Leeds.

5 Nov. 1940: A. I. Katsh (ed.), *Scroll of Agony: The Warsaw Diary of Chaim A. Kaplan* (Hamish Hamilton, 1966), pp. 200–1.

7 Nov. 1940: Leutze, *London Observer*, p. 125.

15–19 Nov. 1940: P. Donnelly (ed.), *Mrs Milburn's Diaries: An Englishwoman's Day-to-Day Reflections 1939–1945* (Harrap, 1979), pp. 66–7, 70.

22 Nov. 1940: Blodgett (ed.), *Capacious Hold-all*, pp. 395–6.

27 Nov. 1940: A. Eban (ed.), *Hannah Senesh: Her Life and Diary* (New York: Schocken, 1972), pp. 98–9.

8 Dec. 1940: Diary of Mrs Cecilie Eustace.

25 Dec. 1940: L. Archer, *Balkan Journal: An Unofficial Observer in Greece* (New York: Norton, 1944), pp. 149–50.

Christmas 1940: Diary of Vera Reid, PP/MCR/88, Imperial War Museum.

28 Dec. 1940: Evelyn Jackson, in N. Smart (ed.), *The Bickerseth Family World War II Diary* (Lampeter: Mellen, 1999), p. 259.

31 Dec. 1940: McCulloch (ed.), *The War and Uncle Walter*, p. 163.

—— J. B. Hattendorf, *On His Majesty's Service: Rear Admiral Joseph H. Wellings US Navy* (Newport, RI: US Naval War College Press, 1983), p. 85.

1941

Epigraph: G. Paquin and R. Hagen, *Two Women and War* (Philadelphia: Mughlenberg, 1953) p. 73.

1–9 Jan. 1941: Dilks (ed.), *Diaries of Sir Alexander Cadogan*, pp. 346–8.

11–12 Jan. 1941: A. Danchev (ed.), *Establishing the Anglo-American Alliance: The Second World War Diaries of Brigadier Vivian Dykes* (Brassey's, 1990), pp. 31–2.

14 Jan. 1941: L. Dobroszycki (ed.), *The Chronicle of the Lodz Ghetto 1941–1944* (New Haven: Yale University Press, 1984), p. 9.

26 Jan. 1941: Diary of John Kennedy, 4/2/3, John Kennedy papers, Liddell Hart Centre for Military Archives, King's College, London.

4 Feb. 1941: M. Sebastian, *Journal 1935–1944* (Heinemann, 2001), p. 316.

13 Feb. 1941: D. Lawrence, *Diary of a Washington Correspondent* (New York: H. C. Kinsey & Co., 1942), pp. 106–7.

15 Feb. 1941: War diaries of Private Steve Lonsdale, 7538963, transcribed by Stuart Lonsdale and reproduced here with his kind permission. These diaries may be read at http://www.warlinks.com/memories/lonsdale/index.html.

24 Feb. 1941: Diary of Charles Hutchinson, Hutchinson papers, 66/62/1, Imperial War Museum.

26–27 Feb. 1941: Diary of William Hares, reproduced in Revd S. P. Shipley (ed.), *Bristol Siren Nights: Diaries and Stories of the Blitzes* (Bristol: Redcliffe, 1989), pp. 16–17.

8 Mar. 1941: E. Baume, *I've Lived Another Year: A Journalist's Diary of the Year 1941* (Harrap, 1942), p. 19.

9 Mar. 1941: A. G. Street, *Hitler's Whistle* (Eyre & Spottiswoode, 1943), pp. 139–40.

14 Mar. 1941: E. G. C. Beckwith (ed.), *The Mansel Diaries: The Diaries of Captain John Mansel, Prisoner-of-War – and Camp Forger – in Germany 1940–45* (privately printed, 1977), pp. 27–8.

24–27 Mar. 1941: Wyndham, *Love Lessons*, pp. 232–3.

Late Mar. 1941: Vaughan, *Journals*, pp. 26–7.

7 Apr. 1941: Archer, *Balkan Journal*, pp. 165–6.

13 Apr. 1941: Clement Semmler (ed.), *The War Diaries of Kenneth Slessor, Official Australian War Correspondent* (St Lucia: University of Queensland Press, 1985), pp. 238–9.

14 Apr. 1941: A. W. Martin and P. Hardy (eds), *Dark and Hurrying Days: Menzies' 1941 Diary* (Canberra: National Library of Australia, 1993), p. 112.

17 Apr. 1941: Bolitho, *Penguin in the Eyrie*, pp. 56–7.

25 Apr. 1941: Martin and Hardy (eds), *Dark and Hurrying Days*, p. 118.

26–27 Apr. 1941: Diary of Charles Hutchinson.

28 Apr. 1941: Archer, *Balkan Journal*, pp. 197–8.

30 Apr.–2 May 1941: Diary of Maurice Hankey, HKN 1/7, Churchill Archives Centre, Churchill College, Cambridge.

5 May 1941: Countess of Ranfurly, *To War with Whitaker: The Wartime Diaries of the Countess of Ranfurly, 1939–1945* (Mandarin, 1995), p. 93.

7–8 May 1941: Diary of R. Peat, 97/40/1, Imperial War Museum.

8–22 May 1941: Unknown diary of an Italian pilot.

12–14 May 1941: Baume, *I've Lived Another Year*, pp. 55–7.

14 May 1941: Diary of Anthony Eden, Lord Avon papers, Birmingham University Library, Special Collections.

20 May 1941: M. Pöppel, *Heaven and Hell: The War Diary of a German Paratrooper* (Hippocrene, 1988), pp. 55–6.

27–28 May 1941: Paquin and Hagen, *Two Women and War*, pp. 76–7.

1 June 1941: Sebastian, *Journal*, p. 359.

—— S. M. Ryan, *POWs Fraternal: Diaries of S/Sgt Raymond Ryan – Poems of Pte Laurence (Bouff) Ryan* (Perth: Hawthorn, 1990), pp. 55–6.

21 June 1941: I. Banac (ed.), *The Diary of Georgi Dimitrov, 1933–1949* (New Haven: Yale University Press, 2003), p. 165.

22 June 1941: T. N. Depuy (ed.), *The Halder Diaries*, vol. 2, p. 965.

30 June 1941: Robbins Landon (ed.), *Wilhelm Prüller*, p. 66.

5–20 July 1941: Graves, *Off the Record*, pp. 194, 202.

7 July 1941: J. Offenberg, *Lonely Warrior: The Action-Journal of a Battle of Britain Fighter Pilot* (Mayflower, 1969), pp. 132–3.

12 July 1941: E. Klee, W. Dressen and V. Riess (eds), *'The Good Old Days': The Holocaust as Seen by its Perpetrators and Bystanders* (Old Saybrook, Conn.: Konecky & Konecky, 1988), pp. 96–7.

27 July 1941: Diary of H. E. Harrison, containing diary notes by Catherine Harrison, P/347, Imperial War Museum.

1 Aug. 1941: Dobroszycki (ed.), *Chronicle of the Lodz Ghetto*, p. 70.

2–4 Aug. 1941: Sebastian, *Journal*, p. 389.

7 Aug. 1941: Offenberg, *Lonely Warrior*, pp. 151–2.

8–15 Aug. 1941: Graves, *Off the Record*, pp. 207–9.

9 Aug.–1 Sept. 1941: Klee *et al.* (eds), *'The Good Old Days'*, p. 11.

11 Aug. 1941: Dorian, *The Quality of Witness*, p. 166.

28 Aug. 1941: Vaughan, *Journals*, pp. 28–9.

1 Sept. 1941: Diary of J. S. Gray, 97/29/2, Imperial War Museum.

Early Sept. 1941: F. P. Reck-Malleczewen, *Diary of a Man in Despair*, trans. P. Rubens (Macmillan, 1966), pp. 137–8.

22 Sept. 1941: Ciano, *Diario*, p. 537, trans. for this edition by Manuela Williams.

25–27 Sept. 1941: Diary of George Blundell, 90/38/1, Imperial War Museum.

4 Oct. 1941: Wilton (ed.), *Internment*, pp. 136–7.

6–13 Oct. 1941: Diary of Lt-Col. Ralph Marnham, Liddell Hart Centre for Military Archives, King's College, London.

21 Oct. 1941: R. Mouchotte, *The Mouchotte Diaries* (Panther, 1957), pp. 117–18.

23 Oct. 1941: Partridge, *A Pacifist's War*, pp. 109–10.

25–29 Oct. 1941: Diary of Mrs Trowbridge, in Sheridan (ed.), *Wartime Women*, p. 156.

3 Nov. 1941: Semmler (ed.), *War Diaries of Kenneth Slessor*, p. 303.

10–19 Nov. 1941: Supplementary Report on 'Operation Flipper' by

Robert Laycock, Middle East Commandos War Diary, DEFE
2/205, PRO. See also Ranfurly, *To War with Whitaker*, pp. 117–18,
entry for 1 Jan. 1942.

20 Nov.–5 Dec. 1941: Anon., *True to Type: A Selection from Letters and
Diaries of German Soldiers and Civilians Collected on the
Soviet–German Front* (Hutchinson, 1945), p. 14.

21 Nov.–10 Dec. 1941: Diary of Lt-Col. Ralph Marnham.

30 Nov. 1941: Charles Burdick and Hans-Adolf Jacobsen, *The Halder
War Diary 1939–1942* (Novato, Calif.: Presidio, 1988), p. 481.

——Bowlby (ed.), *The Diary of a Desert Rat*, pp. 57–60.

1–5 Dec. 1941: Diary of Mrs Gertrude Bathurst, Lambeth Borough
archives, Minet Library, catalogue ref. 24/222.

5 Dec. 1941: Diary of John Kennedy.

7–11 Dec. 1941: F. L. Israel (ed.), *The War Diary of Breckinridge Long:
Selections from the Years 1939–1944* (Lincoln: University of
Nebraska Press, 1966), pp. 226–9.

9 Dec. 1941: Vere Hodgson, *Few Eggs and No Oranges: The Diaries*
(Persephone, 2002), pp. 232–3.

10 Dec. 1941: G. Greene, *In Search of a Character: Two African Journals*
(Bodley Head, 1961), pp. 99–100.

——P. Rose (ed.), 'Tommy's War', p. 6. I am indebted to Paul Rose
of 1 Cambridge Terrace, Berkhamsted, Herts HP4 2EH for
kindly allowing me to quote from his typescript version of the
diary.

1942

Epigraph: Graves, *Off the Record*, v.

1 Jan. 1942: Ryan, *POWs Fraternal*, pp. 69–70.

4 Jan. 1942: M. Chalmers (ed.), *To The Bitter End: The Diaries of Victor
Klemperer 1942–1945* (Weidenfeld & Nicolson, 1999), p. 5.

6 Jan. 1942: Nan Le Ruez, *Jersey Occupation Diary* (Seaflower, 1995),
p. 209.

6–13 Jan. 1942: Paquin and Hagen, *Two Women and War*, pp. 96–7.

8 Jan. 1942: J. Guest, *Broken Images* (Longmans, 1949), pp. 72–3.

6–7 Feb. 1942: J. D. Phillip, *Gunner's Diary* (Boston: Meador, 1946),
pp. 36–9.

15–18 Feb. 1942: Diary of James Chuter Ede, Add. MSS 59690–703,

British Library.

19 Feb. 1942: R. Hilberg, S. Staron and J. Kermisz, *The Warsaw Diary of Adam Czernaikow* (New York: Stein & Day, 1979), p. 328.

Early Mar. 1942: R. Buckle (ed.), *Self-Portrait with Friends: The Selected Diaries of Cecil Beaton, 1926–1974* (Weidenfeld & Nicolson, 1979), p. 95.

4 Mar. 1942: Guest, *Broken Images*, pp. 83–4.

9–14 Mar. 1942: Anon., *True to Type*, pp. 51–2.

12–21 Mar. 1942: K. John (ed.), *Day After Day: Odd Nansen* (Putnam, 1949), pp. 43–4, 52.

16 Apr. 1942: D. Sheridan (ed.), *Among You Taking Notes: The Wartime Diary of Naomi Mitchison 1939–1945* (Gollancz, 1985), pp. 194–5.

16–26 Apr. 1942: J. Bright-Holmes (ed.), *Like It Was: The Diaries of Malcolm Muggeridge* (Collins, 1981), pp. 178, 181.

19 Apr. 1942: Diary of Harold J. Dothie, MG 30, E 398, Canadian National Archives.

21 Apr.–17 May 1942: War diary of SOE Italy, HS 7/265, PRO.

29 Apr. 1942: Marion Kelsey, *Victory Harvest: Diary of a Canadian in the Women's Land Army, 1940–1944* (Montreal and Kingston: McGill-Queens University Press, 1977), pp. 136–8.

1 May 1942: Mouchotte, *The Mouchotte Diaries*, pp. 138–9.

2 May 1942: Kelsey, *Victory Harvest*, pp. 138–40.

3–5 May 1942: Dilks (ed.), *Diaries of Sir Alexander Cadogan*, pp. 449–50.

12 May 1942: Diary of Anthony Eden, Lord Avon papers, Birmingham University Library, Special Collections.

25 May 1942: A. Werth, *The Year of Stalingrad* (Hamish Hamilton, 1946), pp. 30–2.

9–10 June 1942: Personal diary of Brigadier Claude Vallentin, CRA 5th Indian Division, FO 217/30, Public Record Office.

10–11 June 1942: S. Orwell and I. Angus (eds), *The Collected Essays, Journalism and Letters of George Orwell*, vol. 2: *My Country Right or Left, 1940–1945* (Secker & Warburg), p. 430.

15 June 1942: Katsh (ed.), *Scroll of Agony*, pp. 269–70.

15–16 June 1942: J. A. Brown, *One Man's War: A Soldier's Diary* (Cape Town: Howard Timmins, 1980), pp. 88, 89–90.

21–25 June 1942: Diary of Oliver Harvey MSS 56398, British Museum.

28 June 1942: Brown, *One Man's War*, p. 100.

28–30 June 1942: G. C. Bateman, *Diary of a Temporary Soldier* (privately published, 1986), pp. 61–2.

4–6 July 1942: Brown, *One Man's War*, pp. 104–5, 107.

5 July 1942: R. H. Ferrell (ed.), *The Eisenhower Diaries* (New York: Norton, 1981), pp. 70–1.

13 July 1942: Ranfurly, *To War with Whitaker*, pp. 137–9.

22 July 1942: Ferrell (ed.), *The Eisenhower Diaries*, pp. 72–3.

2–15 Aug. 1942: Diary of George Blundell, 90/38/1, Imperial War Museum.

7 Aug. 1942: Brown, *One Man's War*, p. 129.

14–28 Aug. 1942: Duggan (ed.), *Padre in Colditz*, pp. 200, 202–3.

17 Aug. 1942: E. Skrjabina, *A Leningrad Diary: Survival During World War II*, trans. Norman Luxemburg (Carbondale, Ill.: Southern Illinois University Press, 1978), pp. 7–8.

19–22 Aug. 1942: Orwell and Angus (eds), *Collected Essays, Journalism and Letters of George Orwell*, vol. 2, pp. 444–5.

19 Aug. 1942: Somerhausen, *Written in Darkness*, pp. 150–1.

31 Aug. 1942: Diary of Captain L. T. Tomes, Liddle Collection, Brotherton Library, University of Leeds.

1–6 Sept. 1942: Klee *et al.* (eds), *'The Good Old Days'*, pp. 257–9.

Early Sept. 1942: McCallum, *Journey with a Pistol*, p. 35.

7 Sept. 1942: H. C. Butcher, *My Three Years with Eisenhower: Captain Harry C. Butcher, USNR Naval Aide to General Eisenhower, 1942 to 1945* (New York: Simon & Schuster, 1946), p. 89.

10 Sept. 1942: A. Brusselmans, *Rendez-vous 127: The Diary of Madame Brusselmans, MBE* (Benn, 1954), pp. 88–9.

30 Sept. 1942: A. Danchev and D. Todman, *War Diaries 1939–1945: Field Marshal Lord Alanbrooke* (Weidenfeld & Nicolson, 2001), pp. 325–6.

18–19 Oct. 1942: A. Bowlby (ed.), *The Diary of a Desert Rat* (Cooper, 1971), pp. 136–7.

21–31 Oct. 1942: Zygmunt Klukowski, *Diary from the Years of Occupation, 1939–44* (Urbana: University of Illinois Press, 1993), pp. 219–23.

23–24 Oct. 1942: A. Fletcher, *NX 20365* (Walcha, NSW: privately published, 1980), pp. 90–4.

24–26 Oct. 1942: Michael Davie (ed.), *The Diaries of Evelyn Waugh* (Weidenfeld & Nicolson, 1976), pp. 529–30.

30 Oct. 1942: Reck-Malleczewen, *Diary of a Man in Despair*, pp. 159–60.

1 Nov. 1942: U. von Kardorff (ed.), *The Diary of a Nightmare* (New

York: Day, 1966), p. 10.

4 Nov. 1942: Brown, *One Man's War*, pp. 184–5.

8–12 Nov. 1942: J. E. Lewis (ed.), *The Mammoth Book of War Diaries and Letters* (New York: Carroll & Graf, 1998), pp. 404–5.

11 Nov. 1942: McKale (ed.), *Rewriting History*, pp. 4–5.

21 Nov.–12 Dec. 1942: Anon., *True to Type*, pp. 74–5.

1 Dec. 1942: *ibid.*, p. 72.

2–14 Dec. 1942: Diary of Moshe Flinder, 0.33/111, Yad Vashem, Jerusalem.

13–14 Dec. 1942: E. Weinert, *Stalingrad Diary* (ING Publications, 1944), pp. 9–10.

16 Dec. 1942: M. Wright, in Blodgett (ed.), *Capacious Hold-all*, p. 419.

23 Dec. 1942: K. B. Conn (ed.), *The Diary of a Canadian Fighter Pilot: Flying Officer W. S. Large* (Toronto: Reginald Saunders, 1944), pp. 41–2.

24–28 Dec. 1942: S. Bruely (ed.), *Working for Victory: Diary of Life in a Second World War Factory* (Sutton, 2001), pp. 101–2.

31 Dec. 1942: Jeffreys (ed.), *Labour and the Wartime Coalition*, pp. 115–16.

1943

Epigraph: Muggeridge (ed.), *Ciano's Diary*, p. 556.

5 Jan. 1943: Paquin and Hagen, *Two Women and War*, pp. 117–18.

8 Jan. 1943: Eban (ed.), *Hannah Senesh*, p. 125.

12 Jan. 1943: J. W. Young, *The Diary of an Ad Man: The War Years June 1, 1942–December 31, 1943* (Chicago: Advertising Publications, 1944), pp. 101–2.

18 Jan. 1943: M. Zylberberg, *A Warsaw Diary, 1939–1945* (Vallentine Mitchell, 1969), 79–81.

20–26 Jan. 1943: D. Crook (ed.), *A Lewes Diary 1916–1944 by Mrs Henry Dudeney* (Tartarus, 1998), p. 227.

2 Feb. 1943: E. D. Churchill, *Surgeon to Soldiers* (Philadelphia: Lippincott, 1972), pp. 113–14.

6–23 Feb. 1943: von Kardorff (ed.), *Diary of a Nightmare*, pp. 32, 33.

22 Feb. 1943: Eban (ed.), *Hannah Senesh*, p. 127.

23 Feb. 1943: McCallum, *Journey with a Pistol*, pp. 85–6.

26–27 Feb. 1943: P. Dickison, *Crash Dive: In Action with HMS Safari* (Sutton, 1999), pp. 66–7.

3 Mar. 1943: von Kardorff (ed.), *Diary of a Nightmare*, pp. 36–7.

12 Mar. 1943: Young, *Diary of an Ad Man*, pp. 128–9.

20 Mar. 1943: P. Jordan, *Jordan's Tunis Diary* (Collins, 1943), pp. 216–17.

23 Mar. 1943: R. Broad and S. Fleming (eds), *Nella's Last War: A Mother's Diary 1939–1945* (Bristol: Falling Wall, 1980), pp. 244–5.

26 Mar. 1943: Shawn (ed.), *Mollie Panter-Downes*, pp. 272–3.

5 Apr. 1943: McCallum, *Journey with a Pistol*, pp. 104–6.

12 Apr. 1943: Banac (ed.), *Diary of Georgi Dimitrov*, p. 270.

17 Apr. 1943: Diary of Harry C. Butcher, Box 6, Butcher papers, Eisenhower Library, Abilene, Kansas.

17–21 Apr. 1943: War diary of Major David Smiley, SOE, HS 5/143, PRO.

18 Apr. 1943: H. Dormer, *Hugh Dormer's Diaries* (Cape, 1947), pp. 13–14.

2 May 1943: I. Origo, *War in Val D'Orcia* (Cape, 1947), pp. 28–9.

13–18 May 1943: War diary of Major David Smiley.

21 May 1943: Diary of Gerald Wilkinson (SIS/MI6), Churchill College, Cambridge.

28 May 1943: V. Dedijer, *With Tito through the War: Partisan Diary 1941–1944* (Alexander Hamilton, 1951), pp. 320–1.

—— Diary of John Mitchell, MISC 59, Churchill College, Cambridge, p. 14.

29–30 May 1943: Butcher, *My Three Years with Eisenhower*, pp. 316–17, 319.

2 June 1943: Crook (ed.), *A Lewes Diary*, p. 232.

2–4 June 1943: Diary of John Mitchell, pp. 15–17.

2 June 1943: G. Payn and S. Morley (eds), *The Noel Coward Diaries* (Macmillan, 1982), p. 21.

6 June 1943: Diary of William F. Friedman, National Cryptologic Museum, Fort Meade, Maryland.

10 June 1943: Dedijer, *With Tito through the War*, p. 331.

17 June 1943: Smith (ed.), *Hostage to Fortune*, p. 557.

20 June 1943: Dedijer, *War Diaries*, p. 312.

22–23 June 1943: War diary of Major David Smiley.

4 July 1943: Payn and Morley (eds), *Noel Coward Diaries*, pp. 21–2.

8 July 1943: J. Steinbeck, *Once There Was a War* (NY, 1958), p. 61.

15–16 July 1943: Dedijer, *War Diaries*, pp. 353–4.

18 July 1943: D. Irving (ed.), *Adolf Hitler: The Medical Diaries, The Private Diaries of Dr Theo Morrell* (Sidgwick & Jackson, 1983),

pp. 130–1.

23 July 1943: D. Scholes, *Air War Diary: An Australian in Bomber Command* (Kenthurst, NSW: Kangaroo Press, 1997), pp. 26–7.

28 July 1943: Heinrich von Einsiedel, *I Joined the Russians: A Captured German Flier's Diary of the Communist Temptation* (New Haven: Yale University Press, 1953), pp. 80–1.

1 Aug. 1943: R. Evans (ed.), *Mathilde Wolff-Mönckenberg: On the Other Side – To My Children: From Germany 1940–1945* (Peter Owen, 1979), pp. 80–1.

—— Broad and Fleming (eds), *Nella's Last War*, pp. 254–5.

9–10 Aug. 1943: Dedijer, *With Tito through the War*, p. 351.

Mid-Aug. 1943: E. Ardizzone, *Diary of a War Artist* (Bodley Head, 1974), pp. 44–5.

20 Aug. 1943: Bruely (ed.), *Working for Victory*, pp. 146–7.

3 Sept. 1943: Beardmore, *Civilians at War*, pp. 142–3.

5 Sept. 1943: N. Coward, *Middle East Diary* (Doubleday, 1944), pp. 101–2.

9–12 Sept. 1943: Von Einsiedel, *I Joined the Russians*, pp. 114–15.

10 Sept. 1943: Diary of Anthony Eden.

25–26 Sept. 1943: Diary of Alison Uttley, John Rylands Library, University of Manchester.

1–7 Oct. 1943: War diary of Major David Smiley.

4–10 Oct. 1943: Partridge, *A Pacifist's War*, p. 171.

12 Oct. 1943: J. M. Blum (ed.), *The Price of Vision: The Diary of Henry A. Wallace, 1942–1946* (New York: Houghton Mifflin, 1973), pp. 312–13.

16 Oct. 1943: J. Peters (ed.), *German Writings before and after 1945* (Continuum, 2002), pp. 28–9.

19 Oct. 1943: Diary of John Mitchell, p. 31.

24 Oct. 1943: M. Vassiltchikov, *The Berlin Diaries 1940–1945 of Marie 'Missie' Vassiltchikov* (Chatto & Windus, 1985), p. 97.

28 Oct. 1943: N. Lewis, *Naples '44: An Intelligence Officer in the Italian Labyrinth* (Eland, 1983), pp. 48–9.

29 Oct. 1943: Diary of Alison Uttley.

2–30 Nov. 1943: Diary of Gwen Wansborough, 86/6/1, Imperial War Museum.

3 Nov. 1943: Steinbeck, *Once There Was a War*, p. 196.

Mid-Nov. 1943: Bateman, *Diary of a Temporary Soldier*, p. 85.

18 Nov. 1943: Diary of Adrian Secker, Imperial War Museum.

22 Nov. 1943: Von Einsiedel, *I Joined the Russians*, pp. 128–30.

23 Nov. 1943: Vassiltchikov, *Berlin Diaries*, pp. 103–5.

7 Dec. 1943: Diary of Sergeant C. E. S. Tirbutt, Imperial War Museum.

30 Dec. 1943: Diary of Montgomery of Alamein, Imperial War Museum.

31 Dec. 1943–1 Jan. 1944: R. Cazals and C. Hill (eds), *Marching to Captivity: The War Diaries of a French Peasant, 1939–1945: Gustave Folcher* (Brassey's, 1981), pp. 197–8.

1944

Epigraph: Chalmers (ed.), *To The Bitter End*, p. 367.

Early Jan. 1944: Guy Sajer, *The Forgotten Soldier* (Weidenfeld & Nicolson, 1971), pp. 340–1.

18–20 Jan. 1944: H. Parkhurst, *Diary of a Soldier* (Durham: Pentland, 1993), p. 73.

19 Jan 1944: Chalmers (ed.), *To The Bitter End*, p. 357.

20 Jan. 1944: Evans (ed.), *Mathilde Wolff-Mönckenberg*, pp. 90–1.

22 Jan. 1944: Diary of Signalman P. J. Lovett, Imperial War Museum.

3–18 Feb. 1944: Diary of Michael Hoskin, MISC 71, Churchill Archives, Churchill College, Cambridge.

7 Feb. 1944: Ferrell (ed.), *The Eisenhower Diaries* (New York: Norton, 1981), p. 111.

10 Feb. 1944: K. Austin-Lund (ed.), *Peter Moen's Diary* (Faber & Faber, 1951), pp. 15, 19, 27.

14 Feb. 1944: B. Berenson, *Rumor and Reflection: The Wartime of the Most Celebrated Humanist and Art Historian of our Times* (New York: Simon & Schuster, 1952), pp. 234–5.

21 Feb. 1944: H. Kollwitz, *The Diary and Letters of Käthe Kollwitz* (Evanston, Ill.: Northwestern University Press, 1988), pp. 183–4.

5 Mar. 1944: Dobroszycki (ed.), *Chronicle of the Lodz Ghetto*, p. 468.

14–17 Mar. 1944: J. E. Lewis (ed.), *Mammoth Book of War Diaries*, pp. 420–1.

15 Mar. 1944: N. Lewis, *Naples '44*, pp. 115–16.

16–17 Mar. 1944: Scholes, *Air War Diary*, pp. 62–3.

18–19 Mar. 1944: A. Klukowski and H. Klukowski (eds), *Diary from the Years of Occupation 1939–1944: Zygmunt Klukowski* (Chicago: University of Illinois Press, 1993), pp. 310–11.

6 Apr. 1944: 'My War': diary of Colonel D. K. Reimers, Reimers

papers, US Army Military History Institute, Carlisle Barracks, Pennsylvania.

22 Apr. 1944: J. Roose-Evans (ed.), *Joyce Grenfell. The Time of My Life: Entertaining the Troops – Her Wartime Journals* (Hodder & Stoughton, 1989), pp. 104–5.

24 Apr. 1944: Diary of Harold Macmillan, Bodleian Library.

4 May 1944: R. Winstone (ed.), *Tony Benn, Years of Hope: Diaries, Letters and Papers, 1940–1962* (Hutchinson, 1994), p. 42.

5 May 1944: Anonymous diary found by Avraham Benkel in the Lodz Ghetto in 1945, Yad Vashem, Jerusalem. Additional information from the *Jerusalem Post*, 3 May 1970.

9 May 1944: P. Ryle, *Missing in Action May–September 1944* (W. H. Allen, 1979), p. 23.

18 May 1944: Parkhurst, *Diary of a Soldier*, pp. 102–3.

23 May 1944: R. S. Capps, *Diary of a Flying Colt: Liberator Pilot in Italy* (Alexandria, Va: Manor House, 1997), pp. 320–2.

28 May 1944: Diary of C. Morris, in R. Miller, *Nothing Less than Victory* (New York: Morrow, 1993), pp. 140–1.

30 May–1 June 1944: Davie (ed.), *Diaries of Evelyn Waugh*, pp. 566–7.

4–5 June 1944: Robert W. Love, Jr and John Major (eds), *The Year of D-Day: The 1944 Diary of Admiral Sir Bertram Ramsay* (Hull: University of Hull Press, 1994), pp. 82–3.

6 June 1944: Diary of Colonel David K. E. Bruce, Virginia Historical Institute, Richmond.

—— Anne Frank, *The Diary of Anne Frank* (Pan, 1947), pp. 203–4.

7 June 1944: Diary of Colonel David K. E. Bruce.

13–20 June 1944: Diary of Michael Hoskin.

16–30 June 1944: K. Moore, *A Family Life, 1939–45* (Allen, 1989), pp. 153–5.

17 June 1944: Ritchie, *Siren Years*, p. 171.

26 June 1944: Sergeant Richard Greenwood, 'One Day at a Time', reproduced in Patrick Delaforce, *Marching to the Sound of Gunfire: North West Europe 1944–5* (Sutton, 1996), pp. 45–6.

5 July 1944: Nigel Nicholson (ed.), *Harold Nicolson: Diaries and Letters, 1939–45* (Collins, 1967), p. 385.

10 July 1944: Butcher, *My Three Years with Eisenhower*, p. 609.

18 July 1944: R. Boscawen, *Armoured Guardsmen: A War Diary June 1944–July 1945* (Pen & Sword, 2001), pp. 28–31.

20 July 1944: Vassiltchikov, *Berlin Diaries*, p. 188.

24–25 July 1944: M. G. Blackford, *On Board the USS Mason: The*

World War II Diary of James A. Dunn (Columbus: Ohio State University Press, 1996), pp. 23–4.

27 July 1944: Ryle, *Missing in Action*, pp. 119–20.

—— Danchev and Todman, *Alanbrooke*, p. 575.

31 July 1944: Ranfurly, *To War with Whitaker*, p. 260.

6–8 Aug. 1944: Diary of John Hugill, HUGL 4, Hugill papers, Churchill College, Cambridge.

8 Aug. 1944: McCulloch (ed.), *The War and Uncle Walter*, pp. 285–6.

11 Aug.–7 Sept. 1944: Diary of Uffz. P. Kahl, 202nd Mountain Bn., Report for PWD DE42.DIS202, 5 Dec. 1944: Crossman papers, MSS.154/3/PW1/190, Modern Records Centre, University of Warwick.

12–14 Aug. 1944: K. Nowlan (ed.), *The von Aufsess Occupation Diary* (Chichester: Phillmore, 1985), pp. 7–8.

19 Aug. 1944: N. D. Lankford (ed.), *OSS Against the Reich: The World War II Diaries of Colonel David K. E. Bruce* (Kent, Ohio: Kent State University Press, 1991), p. 156.

24 Aug. 1944: Bateman, *Diary of a Temporary Soldier*, pp. 98–9.

28 Aug. 1944: Diary of John Hugill.

2 Sept. 1944: A. Brusselmans, *Rendez-vous 127*, pp. 164–6.

7–8 Sept. 1944: R. A. Hart (ed.), *Military Government Journal, Normandy to Berlin: Major General John J. Maginnis* (University of Massachusetts Press, 1971), pp. 105–9.

8 Sept. 1944: C. Mauriac, *The Other de Gaulle: Diaries 1944–1954* (Angus & Robertson, 1973), pp. 27–8 (first publ. Paris, Hachette, 1970).

13–26 Sept. 1944: Hodgson, *Few Eggs and No Oranges*, pp. 530–1.

17–18 Sept. 1944: W. Zagorski, *Seventy Days* (Müller, 1957), pp. 188–9.

17–26 Sept. 1944: Diary of Peter Baillie, Airborne Forces Museum, Aldershot.

23 Sept.– 27 Oct. 1944: Diary of Uffz. P. Kahl.

28 Sept. 1944: Diary extract kindly provided from the original by the family of John J. Briol, courtesy of Marcella M. Briol. See also John F. Welch (ed.), *Dead Engine Kids: World War II Diary of John J. Briol, B-17 Ball Turret Gunner* (Silver Wings Aviation, 1993).

1 Oct. 1944: Irving (ed.), *Adolf Hitler: The Medical Diaries*, pp. 194–5.

5 Oct. 1944: J. Bezwinska and D. Czech (eds), *H. B. Kremer: KL Auschwitz Seen by the SS* (Panstowe Museum, 1978), pp. 257–8.

6 Oct. 1944: K. H. Huebner, *Long Walk through War: A Combat*

Doctor's Diary (Texas A&M University Press, 1987), p. 138.

16–19 Oct. 1944: Blackford, *On Board the USS Mason*, pp. 46–7.

18 Oct. 1944: Diary of Brigadier Dudley W. Clarke, 99/12/1, Imperial War Museum.

24 Oct.–4 Nov. 1944: Huebner, *Long Walk through War*, p. 146.

27 Oct. 1944: Davie (ed.), *Diaries of Evelyn Waugh*, p. 587.

5 Nov. 1944: N. A. Rose (ed.), *Baffy: The Diaries of Blanche Dugdale* (Vallentine Mitchell, 1973), pp. 217–18.

—— Huebner, *Long Walk through War*, p. 154.

17 Nov. 1944: R. H. Crossman, 'Diary of a Visit to Occupied Germany', Crossman papers, MSS.154/2/PW/1/173, Modern Records Centre, University of Warwick.

21 Nov. 1944: Nansen, *Day after Day*, p. 515.

2 Dec. 1944: E. Velmans, *Edith's Story* (New York: Bantam, 1999), pp. 210–11.

18 Dec. 1944: Janice Holt Giles (ed.), *The GI Journal of Sergeant Giles* (Boston: Houghton Mifflin, 1965), pp. 141–3.

21 Dec. 1944: *ibid.*, pp. 144–5.

Christmas Day, 25 Dec. 1944: Diary of John Mitchell, pp. 79–81.

25–26 Dec. 1944: 'Troopship', by Bruce Bain, in S. Schimanski and H. Treece, *Leaves in the Storm: A Book of Diaries* (Lindsay Drummond, 1947), pp. 257–8.

1945

Epigraph: M. Duras, *The War* (New York: Pantheon, 1986), p. 3.

1 Jan. 1945: H. U. Rudel, *Stuka Pilot* (Dublin: Euphorion, 1953), pp. 156–7.

20 Jan. 1945: Diary of Guy Liddell, Head of MI5's B Division, fos 59–60, KV 4/196, PRO.

25–27 Jan. 1945: R. Buckham, *Forced March to Freedom: An Illustrated Diary of Two Forced Marches and the Interval between January to May, 1945* (Stittsville, Ont.: Canada's Wings, 1984), pp. 14–15.

29 Jan. 1945: Nowlan (ed.), *The von Aufsess Occupation Diary*, p. 129.

Late Jan. 1945: Diary of Maureen Stuart-Clark, Admiral Sir Ralph Alan Bevan Edwards papers, RED/W, Churchill Archives Centre, Churchill College, Cambridge.

3–10 Feb. 1945: *ibid.*

4 Feb. 1945: Von Kardorff (ed.), *Diary of a Nightmare*, p. 192.

10–22 Feb. 1945: Velmans, *Edith's Story*, p. 217.

Mid-Feb. 1945: 'Bill Goodall's War Diaries', an edited selection made by Ian Goodall from 'Journal of William Motion Goodall, ordinary member of the RAF during World War II', available at http://www.goodall.net.

22–24 Feb. 1945: Cazals and Hill (eds), *Marching to Captivity*, pp. 219–20.

1 Mar. 1945: J. R. Blann, *A Private's Diary: The Battle of Germany as Seen through the Eyes of an 18 year old Infantry Rifleman* (Houston: J&L, 1997), pp. 39–40.

4 Mar. 1945: Hugh Trevor-Roper (ed.), *The Goebbels Diaries: The Last Days* (Secker & Warburg, 1977), pp. 40–1.

Early Mar. 1945: Sajer, *Forgotten Soldier*, pp. 395–6.

8 Mar. 1945: Trevor-Roper (ed.), *The Goebbels Diaries*, pp. 80–1.

10–11 Mar. 1945: D. Higgs, *Life in Guernsey under the Nazis, 1940–1945* (St Peter Port: Toucan Press, 1979), p. 58.

23–26 Mar. 1945: Ball (ed.), *Parliament and Politics in the Age of Churchill and Attlee*, p. 454.

9 Apr. 1945: Hans von Lehndorff, *East Prussian Diary, A Journal of Faith, 1945–1947* (Oswald Wolff, 1963), pp. 51–2, 53.

9–11 Apr. 1945: Colville, *Fringes of Power*, pp. 372–3.

11 Apr. 1945: Hans van Lehndorff, *Token of a Covenant. Diary of an East Prussian Surgeon, 1945–7* (Chicago: Henry Regnery Co., 1964), pp. 57–8.

12 Apr. 1945: T. M. Campbell and G. C. Herring (eds), *The Diaries of Edward R. Stettinius, Jr. 1943–1946* (New York: New Viewpoints, 1975), pp. 92–3.

14 Apr. 1945: John T. Bassett, *War Journal of an Innocent Soldier* (Hamden, Conn.: Archon, 1989), pp. 10–11. I am indebted to Mr Bassett for additional information.

15 Apr. 1945: Diary of George Barnett, Liddell Hart Centre for Military Archives, King's College, London.

16 Apr. 1945: Giovanni Guareschi, *My Secret Diary, 1943–1945* (New York: Farrar Strauss & Cuday, 1958), pp. 170–1.

18 Apr. 1945: B. N. Reckitt, *Diary of Military Government in Germany 1945* (Ilfracombe: Arthur H. Stockwell, 1989), pp. 36–7. (The diary actually records Wednesday 18 Apr. 1945.)

20 Apr. 1945: Duras, *The War*, pp. 16–17.

23–24 Apr. 1945: 'My War', diary of Colonel D. K. Reimers.

27 Apr. 1945: Anon. [M. Hillers], *A Woman in Berlin*, trans. J. Stern

(Harborough, 1955), pp. 46–7.

1 May 1945: *ibid.*, pp. 53–4.

4 May 1945: Bassett, *War Journal*, pp. 110–11.

6 May 1945: Dupree (ed.), *Lancashire and Whitehall*, pp. 258–9.

7 May 1945: Diary of J. L. Sweetland, 97/21/1, Imperial War Museum.

8 May 1945: Rose (ed.), *Baffy*, pp. 220–1.

7–12 May 1945: Somerhausen, *Written in Darkness*, pp. 150–1.

REFERENCES

The main research for this project was conducted in the following locations. Some of the published material is long out of print and most of this was consulted in the Library of Congress and the British Library of Political and Economic Science. Where the material is unpublished, full archival locations are given in the references.

Airborne Forces Museum, Aldershot
Bibliothèque Nationale, Paris
Birmingham University Library, Special Collections
Bollings Air Force Base, Washington DC
British Library, London
British Library of Political and Economic Science, London
Brotherton Library Special Collections, University of Leeds
Bodleian Library, University of Oxford
Canadian National Archives, Ottawa
Churchill Archives Centre, Churchill College, Cambridge
Dwight D. Eisenhower Library, Abilene, Kansas
Hallward Library, University of Nottingham
Harry S. Truman Library, Independence, Missouri
Hartley Library, University of Southampton
Harvard University Library, Cambridge, Mass.
Hoover Institute on War Revolution and Peace, Stanford, California
House of Commons Library, Westminster, London
Imperial War Museum, London
India Office Library and Records, Blackfriars, London
International Museum of Social History, Amsterdam
John F. Kennedy Library, Boston
John Rylands Library, University of Manchester
Lauinger Library, Georgetown University
Liddell Hart Centre for Military Archives, King's College, London
MacArthur Memorial, Norfolk, Virginia
Mass-Observation Archive, University of Sussex
Modern Record Centre, University of Warwick
National Army Museum, London
National Cryptologic Museum, Fort Meade, Maryland
National Museum of Labour History, Manchester

Nuffield College, Oxford
Public Record Office (PRO), Kew, London
Rhodes House Library, Oxford
St Antony's College, Oxford, Middle East Centre
US Army Military History Institute, Carlisle Barracks, Pennsylvania
US National Archives, Washington DC
US Naval Operational Archives Branch, Navy Yard, Washington DC
Yad Vashem Holocaust Museum, Jerusalem

Unpublished sources

Anonymous diary, May–July 1944, found by Avraham Benkel in the
    Lodz Ghetto in 1945, Yad Vashem, Jerusalem
Baillie, Peter, diary, Airborne Forces Museum
Barnett, George, diary, Liddell Hart Centre for Military Archives,
    King's College, London
Barter, L. F., diary, PP/MCR/426, Imperial War Museum
Bathurst, Mrs Gertrude, diary, Lambeth Borough archives, Minet
    Library, catalogue ref. 24/222
Blundell, George, diary, 90/38/1, Imperial War Museum
Briol, John J., diary extract kindly provided from the original by the
    family of John J. Briol, courtesy of Marcella M. Briol
Brooke, Field Marshal Sir Alan, Chief of the Imperial General Staff,
    Liddell Hart Centre for Military Archives
Bruce, Colonel David K. E., diary, Virginia Historical Institute,
    Richmond, Virginia
Butcher, Harry C., diary, Box 6, Butcher papers, Eisenhower Library,
    Abilene, Kansas
Cadogan, Alexander, diary, A/CAD, Churchill Archives Centre
Clarke, Brigadier Dudley W., diary, 99/12/1, Imperial War Museum
Cockhill, Major J. W. H., typescript memoir, p. 119, 99/85/1,
    Imperial War Museum
Cox, Gladys, 'War Diary', 86/46/1 (P), Imperial War Museum
Crossman, R. H., 'Diary of a Visit to Occupied Germany', Crossman
    Papers, MSS 154/2/PW/1/173, Modern Records Centre,
    University of Warwick
Davies, J., diary, 81/2/1, Imperial War Museum
Dothie, Harold J., diary, MG 30, E 398, Canadian National Archives
Eden, Anthony, diary, Lord Avon papers, Birmingham University

Library, Special Collections

Edwards, Admiral Sir Ralph Alan Bevan, papers, RED/W, Churchill Archives Centre

Eustace, Mrs Cecilie, diary, 85/27/1, Imperial War Museum

Flinder, Moshe, diary, 0.33/111, Yad Vashem Holocaust Museum

Friedman, William F., diary, National Cryptologic Museum

Goddard, V., diary, Con Shelf item, Imperial War Museum

Goodall, Bill, 'Bill Goodall's War Diaries', an edited selection made by Ian Goodall from 'Journal of William Motion Goodall, ordinary member of the RAF during World War II', available at http://www.goodall.net

Gray, J. S., diary, 97/29/2, Imperial War Museum

Hankey, Maurice, diary, HKN 1/7, Churchill Archives Centre

Harrison, H. E., diary containing diary notes by Catherine Harrison, P 347, Imperial War Museum

Harvey, Oliver, diary, MSS 56398, British Museum

Holl, W. E., 'A Diary, Civil Defence Goes Through It: Paddington 1937–1945', MSS 9100.c.44, British Library

Hoskin, Michael, diary, MISC 71, Churchill Archives Centre

Hoyles, Miss D. M., diary, 77/50/1, Imperial War Museum

Hugill, John, diary, HUGL 4, Hugill papers, Churchill College, Cambridge

Hutchinson, Charles, diary, Hutchinson papers, 66/62/1, Imperial War Museum

Kahl, Uffz. P., 202nd Mountain Bn, diary, in Report for PWD DE42.DIS202, 5 Dec. 1944, Crossman Papers, MSS.154/3/PW1/190, Modern Records Centre, University of Warwick

Kennedy, John, diary, 4/2/3, John Kennedy papers, Liddell Hart Centre for Military Archives, King's College London

King, Cecil, diary, Special Collections, Boston University Library

Kup (*née* Heap), Edith, diary, Liddle Collection, Brotherton Library, University of Leeds

Laycock, Robert, Supplementary Report on 'Operation Flipper', Middle East Commandos War Diary, DEFE 2/205, PRO

Leaney, A. R. C., diary, PP/MCR/206, Imperial War Museum

Liddell, Guy, Head of MI5's B Division, diary, fos 59–60, KV 4/196, PRO

Lonsdale, Private Steve, 7538963, war diaries, transcribed by Stuart Lonsdale and reproduced here with his kind permission. These

diaries may be read at
http://www.warlinks.com/memories/lonsdale/index.html

Lovett, Signalman P. J., diary, Imperial War Museum

Lund, Otto, 'Visit to France and Belgium in May and June 1940 as DDMO', papers of General Sir Otto Lund, MISC 24, Churchill Archives Centre

Macmillan, Harold, diary, Bodleian Library, Department of Western Manuscripts

Marnham, Lt-Col. Ralph, diary, Liddell Hart Centre for Military Archives, King's College, London

Mitchell, John, diary, MISC 59, Churchill Archives Centre

Montgomery of Alamein, diary, BLM46 Reel 4, Imperial War Museum

Mott, H. P. L., diary, 97/14/3, Imperial War Museum

Peat, R., diary, 97/40/1, Imperial War Museum

Pexton, Sergeant L. D., BEF France and POW, diary, Imperial War Museum

Phipps, Kay, diary, P/178, Imperial War Museum

Reid, Vera, diary, PP/MCR/88, Imperial War Museum

Reimers, Colonel D. K., 'My War': diary of Colonel D. K. Reimers, Reimers papers, US Army Military History Institute

Riddell, Emily, diary, 92/25/1, Imperial War Museum

Rose, P. (ed.), 'Tommy's War'. I am indebted to Paul Rose of 1 Cambridge Terrace, Berkhamsted, Herts HP4 2EH for kindly allowing me to quote from his typescript version of the diary.

Secker, Adrian, diary, Imperial War Museum

Smiley, Major David, war diary, SOE, HS 5/143, PRO

SOE Italy, war diary, HS 7/265, PRO

Sweetland, J. L., diary, 97/21/1, Imperial War Museum

Tirbutt, Sergeant C. E. S., diary, Imperial War Museum

Tomes, Captain L. T., diary, Liddle Collection, Brotherton Library, University of Leeds

Turner, Arthur, diary, A. H. Turner papers, 92/27/1, Imperial War Museum

Uttley, Alison, diary, John Rylands Library, University of Manchester

Vallentin, Brigadier Claude, diary, FO 217/30, Public Record Office

Wansborough, Gwen, diary, 86/6/1, Imperial War Museum

Watt, F., diary, 03/10/1, Imperial War Museum

Wilkinson, Gerald (SIS/MI6), diary, Churchill College, Cambridge

'Extracts from a Diary of an Interned German Refugee . . .',
enclosed in Lt-Col. D. R. Robertson to Director of POWs, 13 Mar.
1941, HO 215/210, PRO

Unknown diary of an Italian pilot, translated by British Military
Intelligence, WO 106/2160, Public Record Office

Published sources

Unless otherwise stated the place of publication is London.

Anon., *The Bells Go Down: The Diary of a London AFS Man* (Methuen,
1942)

Anon., *The Diary of a Staff Officer (Air Intelligence Liaison Officer at
Advanced Headquarters North BAAF 1940* (Methuen, 1941)

Anon., *True to Type: A Selection from Letters and Diaries of German
Soldiers and Civilians Collected on the Soviet–German Front*
(Hutchinson, 1945)

Anon. [M. Hillers], *A Woman in Berlin*, trans. J. Stern (Harborough,
1955)

Archer, L., *Balkan Journal: An Unofficial Observer in Greece* (New York:
Norton, 1944)

Ardizzone, E., *Diary of a War Artist* (Bodley Head, 1974)

Armstrong, W. (ed.), *With Malice toward None – Cecil King: A War
Diary* (Sidgwick & Jackson, 1970)

Austin-Lund, K. (ed.), *Peter Moen's Diary* (Faber & Faber, 1951)

Baley, S., *Two Septembers 1939 and 1940: A Diary of Events* (Allen &
Unwin, 1941)

Ball, S. (ed.), *Parliament and Politics in the Age of Churchill and Attlee:
The Headlam Diaries 1935–1951* (Cambridge University Press,
1999)

Banac, I. (ed.), *The Diary of Georgi Dimitrov, 1933–1949* (New Haven:
Yale University Press, 2003)

Barlone, D., *A French Officer's Diary 23rd August 1939–1st October
1940* (New York: Macmillan, 1943)

Bassett, John T., *War Journal of an Innocent Soldier* (Hamden, Conn.:
Archon, 1989)

Bateman, G. C., *Diary of a Temporary Soldier* (privately published,
1986)

Baume, E., *I've Lived Another Year: A Journalist's Diary of the Year 1941*

(Harrap, 1942)

Baynes, N. H. (ed.), *The Speeches of Adolf Hitler*, vol. 1 (London: Oxford University Press, 1942)

Beardmore, G., *Civilians at War: Journals 1938–1946* (John Murray, 1984)

Beckwith, E. G. C. (ed.), *The Mansel Diaries: The Diaries of Captain John Mansel, Prisoner-of-War – and Camp Forger – in Germany 1940–45* (privately printed, 1977)

Bell, A. O. (ed.), *The Diary of Virginia Woolf* (Hogarth, 1984)

Berenson, B., *Rumor and Reflection: The Wartime of the Most Celebrated Humanist and Art Historian of our Times* (New York: Simon & Schuster, 1952)

Bezwinska, J. and Czech, D. (eds), *H. B. Kremer: KL Auschwitz Seen by the SS* (Panstowe Museum, 1978)

Bilaikin, G., *Diary of a Diplomatic Correspondent* (Allen & Unwin, 1940)

Blackford, M. G. (ed.), *On Board the USS Mason: The World War II Diary of James A. Dunn* (Columbus: Ohio State University Press, 1996)

Blann, J. R., *A Private's Diary: The Battle of Germany as Seen through the Eyes of an 18 year old Infantry Rifleman* (Houston: J&L, 1997)

Blodgett, H. (ed.), *Capacious Hold-all: An Anthology of Englishwomen's Diary Writings* (Charlottesville: University of Virginia Press, 1992)

Blum, J. M. (ed.), *The Price of Vision: The Diary of Henry A. Wallace, 1942–1946* (New York: Houghton Mifflin, 1973)

Bolitho, H., *A Penguin in the Eyrie* (Hutchinson, 1955)

Bond, B. (ed.), *The Diaries of Lt-General Sir Henry Pownall*, vol. 2: *1940–1944* (Cooper, 1974)

Boscawen, R., *Armoured Guardsmen: A War Diary June 1944–July 1945* (Pen & Sword, 2001)

Bottai, Giuseppe, *Diario 1935–1944* (Milan: Biblioteca Universale Rizzoli, 1989)

Bowlby, A. (ed.), *The Diary of a Desert Rat* (Cooper, 1971)

Bright-Holmes, J. (ed.), *Like It Was: The Diaries of Malcolm Muggeridge* (Collins, 1981)

Broad, R. and Fleming, S. (eds), *Nella's Last War: A Mother's Diary 1939–1945* (Bristol: Falling Wall, 1980)

Brown, J. A., *One Man's War: A Soldier's Diary* (Cape Town: Howard Timmins, 1980)

Bruely, S. (ed.), *Working for Victory: Diary of Life in a Second World War Factory* (Sutton, 2001)

Brusselmans, A., *Rendez-vous 127: The Diary of Madame Brusselmans, MBE* (Benn, 1954)

Buckham, R., *Forced March to Freedom: An Illustrated Diary of Two Forced Marches and the Interval between January to May, 1945* (Stittsville, Ont.: Canada's Wings, 1984)

Buckle, R. (ed.), *Self-Portrait with Friends: The Selected Diaries of Cecil Beaton, 1926–1974* (Weidenfeld & Nicolson, 1979)

Burdick, Charles and Jacobsen, Hans-Adolf (eds), *The Halder War Diary 1939–1942* (Novato, Calif.: Presidio, 1988)

Butcher, H. C., *My Three Years with Eisenhower: Captain Harry C. Butcher, USNR Naval Aide to General Eisenhower, 1942 to 1945* (New York: Simon & Schuster, 1946)

Campbell, T. M. and Herring, G. C. (eds), *The Diaries of Edward R. Stettinius, Jr. 1943–1946* (New York: New Viewpoints, 1975)

Capps, R. S., *Diary of a Flying Colt: Liberator Pilot in Italy* (Alexandria, Va: Manor House, 1997)

Cassington, J. (ed.), *A Metal Man's Wartime Diary* (Egham: Quinn, 1941)

Cazals, R. and Hill, C. (eds), *Marching to Captivity: The War Diaries of a French Peasant, 1939–1945: Gustave Folcher* (Brassey's, 1981)

Chalmers, M. (ed.), *To The Bitter End: The Diaries of Victor Klemperer 1942–1945* (Weidenfeld & Nicolson, 1999)

Churchill, E. D., *Surgeon to Soldiers* (Philadelphia: Lippincott, 1972)

Ciano, G., *Diario 1937–1943* (Milan: Biblioteca Universale Rizzoli, 1980)

Citrine, Walter, *My Finnish Diary* (Penguin, 1940)

Clegg, H., *A Canuck in England: Journal of a Canadian Soldier* (Harrap, 1942)

Colville, John, *The Fringes of Power* (Hodder & Stoughton, 1985)

Conn, K. B. (ed.), *The Diary of a Canadian Fighter Pilot: Flying Officer W. S. Large* (Toronto: Saunders, 1944)

Coward, N., *Middle East Diary* (Doubleday, 1944)

Crook, D. (ed.), *A Lewes Diary 1916–1944 by Mrs Henry Dudeney* (Tartarus, 1998)

Cross, C. (ed.), *Life with Lloyd George: The Diary of A. J. Sylvester 1931–45* (Macmillan, 1975)

Cull, N., *Selling War* (Oxford: Oxford University Press, 1997)

Danchev, A. (ed.), *Establishing the Anglo-American Alliance: The*

Second World War Diaries of Brigadier Vivian Dykes (Brassey's, 1990)

Danchev, A. and Todman, D. (eds), *War Diaries 1939–1945: Field Marshal Lord Alanbrooke* (Weidenfeld & Nicolson, 2001)

Davie, Michael (ed.), *The Diaries of Evelyn Waugh* (Weidenfeld & Nicolson, 1976)

Dedijer, V., *The War Diaries of Vladimir Dedijer: From Nov. 28, 1942 to September 10, 1943* (Michigan: University of Michigan Press, 1990)

——With Tito Through the War: Partisan Diary 1941–1944 (Alexander Hamilton, 1951)

Delaforce, Patrick, *Marching to the Sound of Gunfire: North West Europe 1944–5* (Sutton, 1996)

Depuy, T. N. (ed.), *The Halder Diaries: The Private War Diaries of Colonel General Franz Halder* (Boulder, Co: Westview, 1976)

Dickison, P., *Crash Dive: In Action with HMS Safari* (Sutton, 1999)

Dilks, D. (ed.), *The Diaries of Sir Alexander Cadogan, 1938–1945* (Cassell, 1971)

Dobroszycki, L. (ed.), *The Chronicle of the Lodz Ghetto 1941–1944* (New Haven: Yale University Press, 1984)

Donnelly, P. (ed.), *Mrs Milburn's Diaries: An Englishwoman's Day-to-Day Reflections 1939–1945* (Harrap, 1979)

Dorian, Emil, *The Quality of Witness: A Romanian Diary 1937–1944* (Philadelphia: Jewish Publication Society of America, 1982)

Dormer, H., *Hugh Dormer's Diaries* (Cape, 1947)

Duggan, M. (ed.), *Padre in Colditz: The Diary of J. Ellison Platt MBE* (Hodder & Stoughton, 1978)

Dupree, Marguerite (ed.), *Lancashire and Whitehall: The Diary of Sir Raymond Streat*, vol. 1: *1931–39* (Manchester: Manchester University Press, 1999)

Duras, M., *The War* (New York: Pantheon, 1986)

Eban, A. (ed.), *Hannah Senesh: Her Life and Diary* (New York: Schocken, 1972)

Einsiedel, Heinrich von, *I Joined the Russians: A Captured German Flier's Diary of the Communist Temptation* (New Haven: Yale University Press, 1953)

Evans, R. (ed.), *Mathilde Wolff-Mönckenberg: On the Other Side – To My Children: From Germany 1940–1945* (Owen, 1979)

Ferrell, R. H. (ed.), *The Eisenhower Diaries* (New York: Norton, 1981)

Fletcher, A., *NX 20365* (Walcha, NSW: privately published, 1980)

Frank, Anne, *The Diary of Anne Frank* (Pan, 1947)

Gerbet, K. (ed.), *Generalfeldmarshal von Bock: The War Diary 1939–1945*, trans. D. Johnston (Atglen, Pa: Schiffer, 1996)

Giles, Janice Holt (ed.), *The GI Journal of Sergeant Giles* (Boston: Houghton Mifflin, 1965)

Graves, C., *Off the Record* (Hutchinson, 1944)

Greene, G., *In Search of a Character: Two African Journals* (Bodley Head, 1961)

Guareschi, Giovanni, *My Secret Diary, 1943–1945* (New York: Farrar Straus & Cudahy, 1958)

Guest, J., *Broken Images* (Longmans, 1949)

Guske, H., *The War Diaries of U-764: Fact or Fiction?* (Thomas, 1996)

Hagglof, G., *Diplomat* (Bodley Head, 1971)

Hammond, E., *1941–3: The War Diary of Edward Hammond* (Ixworth: Ixworth Association, 1980)

Hart, R. A. (ed.), *Military Government Journal, Normandy to Berlin: Major General John J. Maginnis* (Amherst: University of Massachusetts Press, 1971)

Harvey, J. (ed.), *The War Diaries of Oliver Harvey, 1941–1945* (Collins, 1978)

Hattendorf, J. B., *On His Majesty's Service: Rear Admiral Joseph H. Wellings US Navy* (Newport, RI: US Naval War College Press, 1983)

Hedin, S., *Sven Hedin's German Diary, 1935–1942* (Euphorion, 1951)

Heyst, Axel, *There Shall be No Victory: Diary of a European* (Gollancz, 1947)

Higgs, D., *Life in Guernsey under the Nazis, 1940–1945* (St Peter Port: Toucan, 1979)

Hilberg, R., Staron, S. and Kermisz, J., *The Warsaw Diary of Adam Czerniakow* (New York: Stein & Day, 1979)

Hodgson, Vere, *Few Eggs and No Oranges: The Diaries* (Persephone, 2002)

Holliday, L., *Children in the Holocaust and World War II: Their Secret Diaries* (New York: Washington Square, 1995)

Huebner, K. H., *Long Walk through War: A Combat Doctor's Diary* (Texas A&M University Press, 1987)

Irving, D. (ed.), *Adolf Hitler: The Medical Diaries, The Private Diaries of Dr Theo Morrell* (Sidgwick & Jackson, 1983)

Israel, F. L. (ed.), *The War Diary of Breckinridge Long: Selections from the Years 1939–1944* (Lincoln: University of Nebraska Press, 1966)

James, R. R. (ed.), *'Chips': The Diaries of Sir Henry Channon* (Weidenfeld & Nicolson, 1967; Phoenix, 1999)

Jeffreys, K. (ed.), *Labour and the Wartime Coalition: From the Diary of James Chuter Ede, 1941–1945* (Historians Press, 1988)

John, K. (ed.), *Day After Day: Odd Nansen* (New York: Putnam, 1949)

Jordan, P., *Jordan's Tunis Diary* (Collins, 1943)

Kardorff, U. von (ed.), *The Diary of a Nightmare* (New York: Day, 1966)

Katsh, A. I. (ed.), *Scroll of Agony: The Warsaw Diary of Chaim A. Kaplan* (Hamish Hamilton, 1966)

Kelsey, Marion, *Victory Harvest: Diary of a Canadian in the Women's Land Army, 1940–1944* (Montreal and Kingston: McGill-Queens University Press, 1997)

Klee, E., Dressen, W. and Riess, V. (eds), *'The Good Old Days': The Holocaust as Seen by its Perpetrators and Bystanders* (Old Saybrook, Conn.: Konecky & Konecky, 1988)

Klukowski, A. and Klukowski, H. (eds), *Diary from the Years of Occupation 1939–1944: Zygmunt Klukowski* (Chicago: University of Illinois Press, 1993)

Klukowski, Zygmunt, *Diary from the Years of Occupation, 1939–44* (Urbana: University of Illinois Press, 1993)

Kollwitz, H., *The Diary and Letters of Käthe Kollwitz* (Evanston, Ill.: Northwestern University Press, 1988)

Lankford, N. D. (ed.), *OSS Against the Reich: The World War II Diaries of Colonel David K. E. Bruce* (Kent, Ohio: Kent State University Press, 1991)

Lawrence, D., *Diary of a Washington Correspondent* (New York: H. C. Kinsey & Co., 1942)

Lehndorff, Hans von, *East Prussian Diary: A Journal of Faith* (Wolff, 1963)

—— *Token of a Covenant. Diary of an East Prussian Surgeon, 1945–7* (Chicago: Regnery, 1964)

Le Ruez, Nan, *Jersey Occupation Diary* (Seaflower, 1995)

Leutze, J., *The London Observer: The Journal of General Raymond E. Lee* (Hutchinson, 1972)

Lewis, J. E. (ed.), *The Mammoth Book of War Diaries and Letters* (New York: Carroll & Graf, 1998)

Lewis, N., *Naples '44: An Intelligence Officer in the Italian Labyrinth* (Eland, 1983)

Love, Robert W., Jr and Major, John (eds), *The Year of D-Day: The*

1944 Diary of Admiral Sir Bertram Ramsay (Hull: University of Hull Press, 1994)

McCallum, Neil, *Journey with a Pistol: A Chronicle of War (from Alamein to Sicily) from a Point of View other than that of Montgomery of Alamein's Memoirs* (Gollancz, 1959)

McCulloch, A. (ed.), *The War and Uncle Walter: The Diary of an Eccentric* (Doubleday, 2003)

McKale, D. M. (ed.), *Rewriting History: The Original and Revised World War II Diaries of Curt Prüfer, Nazi Diplomat* (Kent, Ohio: Kent State University Press, 1988)

MacKenzie, N. and MacKenzie, J. (eds), *The Diary of Beatrice Webb*, vol. 4: *1924–1943, The Wheel of Life* (Virago/LSE, 1985)

Macleod, R. and Kelly, D. (eds.), *The Ironside Diaries 1937–1940* (Constable, 1962)

Malaquais, Jean, *War Diary* (New York: Doubleday, Doran & Co., 1944)

Martin, A. W. and Hardy, P. (eds), *Dark and Hurrying Days: Menzies' 1941 Diary* (Canberra: National Library of Australia, 1993)

Mauriac, C., *The Other de Gaulle: Diaries 1944–1954* (Angus & Robertson, 1973; first publ. Paris, Hachette, 1970)

Miller, R., *Nothing Less than Victory* (New York: Morrow, 1993)

Moore, K., *A Family Life, 1939–45* (Allen, 1989)

Mouchotte, R., *The Mouchotte Diaries* (Panther, 1957)

Muggeridge, M. (ed.), *Ciano's Diary, 1939–1943* (Heinemann, 1947)

Nansen, Odd, *Day after Day* (New York: Putnam, 1949)

Nicolson, Nigel (ed.), *Harold Nicolson: Diaries and Letters, 1939–45* (Collins, 1967)

Nowlan, K. (ed.), *The von Aufsess Occupation Diary* (Chichester: Phillmore, 1985)

Offenberg, J., *Lonely Warrior: The Action-Journal of a Battle of Britain Fighter Pilot* (Mayflower, 1969)

Origo, I., *War in Val D'Orcia* (Cape, 1947)

Orwell, S. and Angus, I. (eds), *The Collected Essays, Journalism and Letters of George Orwell*, vol. 2: *My Country Right or Left, 1940–1945* (Secker & Warburg, 1968)

Paquin, G. and Hagen, R., *Two Women and War* (Philadelphia: Mughlenberg, 1953)

Parkhurst, H., *Diary of a Soldier* (Durham: Pentland, 1993)

Partridge, F., *A Pacifist's War* (Hogarth, 1978)

Payn, G. and Morley, S. (eds), *The Noel Coward Diaries* (Macmillan, 1982)

Perry, C., *Boy in the Blitz: The 1940 Diary of Colin Perry* (Cooper, 1972)

Peters, J. (ed.), *German Writings before and after 1945* (Continuum, 2002)

Phillip, J. D., *Gunner's Diary* (Boston: Meador, 1946)

Phillips, J., *My Secret Diary* (Shepeard-Walwyn, 1982)

Pimlott, Ben (ed.), *The Second World War Diaries of Hugh Dalton, 1940–45* (Cape, 1986)

Pöppel, M., *Heaven and Hell: The War Diary of a German Paratrooper* (Hippocrene, 1988)

Ranfurly, Countess of, *To War with Whitaker: The Wartime Diaries of the Countess of Ranfurly, 1939–1945* (Mandarin, 1995)

Read, B. A., *No Cause for Panic: Channel Islands Refugees, 1940–1945* (Seaflower, 1995)

Reckitt, B. N., *Diary of Military Government in Germany 1945* (Ilfracombe: Stockwell, 1989)

Reck-Malleczewen, F. P., *Diary of a Man in Despair*, trans. P. Rubens (Macmillan, 1966)

Ritchie, C., *The Siren Years: Undiplomatic Diaries, 1937–45* (Toronto: Macmillan, 1974)

Robbins Landon, H. C. (ed.), *Wilhelm Prüller: Diary of a German Soldier* (New York: Coward-McCann, 1963)

Roose-Evans, J. (ed.), *Joyce Grenfell. The Time of My Life: Entertaining the Troops – Her Wartime Journals* (Hodder & Stoughton, 1989)

Rose, N. A. (ed.), *Baffy: The Diaries of Blanche Dugdale* (Vallentine Mitchell, 1973)

Roubiczek, P., *Across the Abyss: Diary Entries for the Years 1939–40*, trans. George Bird (Cambridge: Cambridge University Press, 1982)

Royde Smith, Naomi, *Outside Information: A Diary of Rumours* (Macmillan, 1941)

Rudel, H. U., *Stuka Pilot* (Dublin: Euphorion, 1953)

Ryan, S. M., *POWs Fraternal: Diaries of S/Sgt Raymond Ryan – Poems of Pte Laurence (Bouff) Ryan* (Perth: Hawthorn, 1990)

Ryle, P., *Missing in Action May–September 1944* (Allen, 1979)

St John, John, *To the War with Waugh* (Cooper, 1974)

Sajer, Guy, *The Forgotten Soldier* (Weidenfeld & Nicolson, 1971)

Sartre, Jean-Paul, *War Diaries: Notebooks from a Phoney War, November 1939–March 1940* (Verso, 1984)

Schimanski, S. and Treece, H. (eds), *Leaves in the Storm: A Book of Diaries* (Drummond, 1947)

Scholes, D., DFC, *Air War Diary: An Australian in Bomber Command* (Kenthurst, NSW: Kangaroo Press, 1997)

Sebastian, M., *Journal 1935–1944* (Heinemann, 2001)

Semmler, Clement (ed.), *The War Diaries of Kenneth Slessor, Official Australian War Correspondent* (St Lucia: University of Queensland Press, 1985)

Shawn, William (ed.), *Mollie Panter-Downes: London War Notes* (New York: Farrar, Strauss & Giroux, 1971)

Sheridan, D. (ed.), *Among You Taking Notes: The Wartime Diary of Naomi Mitchison 1939–1945* (Gollancz, 1985)

——*Wartime Women: An Anthology of Women's Wartime Writing for Mass-Observation 1937–1945* (Heinemann, 1990)

Shipley, Revd S. P. (ed.), *Bristol Siren Nights: Diaries and Stories of the Blitzes* (Bristol: Redcliffe, 1989)

Shirer, W., *Berlin Diary: The Journal of a Foreign Correspondent 1934–1941* (Hamish Hamilton, 1941)

Skrjabina, E., *A Leningrad Diary: Survival during World War II*, trans. Norman Luxemburg (Carbondale, Ill.: Southern Illinois University Press, 1978)

Smart, N. (ed.), *The Bickerseth Family World War II Diary* (Lampeter: Mellen, 1999)

Smith, Amanda (ed.), *Hostage to Fortune: The Letters of Joseph P. Kennedy* (New York: Viking Penguin, 2001)

Somerhausen, A., *Written in Darkness: A Belgian Woman's Record of the Occupation, 1940–1945* (New York: Knopf, 1946)

Stark, F., *An Italian Diary* (John Murray, 1945)

Steinbeck, J., *Once There Was a War* (New York: Penguin Putnam, 1958)

Street, A. G., *Hitler's Whistle* (Eyre & Spottiswoode, 1943)

Stuhlman, G. (ed.), *The Diary of Anaïs Nin, 1939–1944* (New York: Harcourt Brace Jovanovich, 1969)

Sulzberger, Charles, *A Long Row of Candles: Memoirs and Diaries 1934–54* (Macdonald, 1969)

Taylor, F. (ed.), *The Goebbels Diaries 1939–41* (Hamish Hamilton, 1982)

Trevor-Roper, Hugh (ed.), *The Goebbels Diaries: The Last Days* (Secker & Warburg, 1977)

Vassiltchikov, M., *The Berlin Diaries 1940–1945 of Marie 'Missie'*

Vassiltchikov (Chatto & Windus, 1985)

Vaughan, K., *Journals, 1939–1977* (John Murray, 1989)

Velmans, E., *Edith's Story* (New York: Bantam, 1999)

Weinert, E., *Stalingrad Diary* (ING, 1944)

Welch, John F. (ed.), *Dead Engine Kids: World War II Diary of John J. Briol, B-17 Ball Turret Gunner* (Silver Wings Aviation, 1993)

Werth, A., *The Last Days of Paris: A Journalist's Diary* (Hamish Hamilton, 1940)

——*The Year of Stalingrad* (Hamish Hamilton, 1946)

West, Nigel, *Counterfeit Spies* (St Ermin's, 1998)

Weymouth, A., *Journal of the War Years (1939–1945) and One Year Later* (Littlebury & Co., 1948)

——*A Psychologist's Wartime Diary* (Toronto: Longman, 1940)

Wilton, J. (ed.), *Internment: The Diaries of Harry Seidler May 1940–October 1941*, trans. J. Winternitz (Sydney: Allen & Unwin, 1986)

Winstone, R. (ed.), *Tony Benn, Years of Hope: Diaries, Letters and Papers, 1940–1962* (Hutchinson, 1994)

Wyndham, J., *Love Lessons: A Wartime Diary* (Heinemann, 1985; pb Virago, 2001)

Young, J. W., *The Diary of an Ad Man: The War Years June 1, 1942–December 31, 1943* (Chicago: Advertising Publications, 1944)

Zagorski, W., *Seventy Days* (Müller, 1957)

Zylberberg, M., *A Warsaw Diary, 1939–1945* (Vallentine Mitchell, 1969)

ACKNOWLEDGEMENT OF PERMISSIONS

The author has endeavoured to identify the current copyright owners of the selections in this book and to obtain permission to include them, whenever necessary. In the event of an error or omission in any acknowledgement, please contact the author through the publisher and, if appropriate, an acknowledgement will be made in future reprints.

Permission for the use of material reproduced in this book was kindly granted by the following archives and individuals with regard to unpublished sources.

From the Peter Baillie diary, with the permission of the Airborne Forces Museum. George Barnett diary, with the permission of the trustees of the Liddell Hart Centre for Military Archives. From the L. F. Barter diary, with the permission of the trustees of the Imperial War Museum. From the Gertrude Bathurst diary, with the permission of Lambeth Borough archives, Minet Library. From the George Blundell diary, with the permission of the trustees of the Imperial War Museum. From the John J. Briol diary, with the permission of John F. Briol and courtesy of Marcella M. Briol. From the Field Marshal Sir Alan Brooke diary, with the permission of the trustees of the Liddell Hart Centre for Military Archives. From the Colonel David K. E. Bruce diary, with the permission of the trustees of the Virginia Historical Society, Richmond, Virginia. From the Harry C. Butcher diary, with the permission of the Dwight D. Eisenhower Library, Abilene, Kansas. From the Alexander Cadogan diary, with the permission of the trustees of the Churchill Archives Centre and the Master, Fellows and Scholars of Churchill College, Cambridge. From the Brigadier Dudley W. Clarke diary, with the permission of the trustees of the Imperial War Museum. From the Major J. W. H. Cockhill typescript memoir, with the permission of the trustees of the Imperial War Museum. From the Gladys Cox 'War Diary', with the permission of the trustees of the Imperial War Museum. From the R. H. Crossman 'Diary of a Visit to Occupied Germany', with the permission of the Modern Records Centre, University of Warwick. From the J. Davies diary, with the permission of the trustees of the Imperial War Museum. From the Harold J. Dothie diary, with the permission of the Canadian National Archives. From the James Chuter Ede diary, with the permission of the British Library. From the Anthony Eden diary, with the permission of Lady Avon. From the Cecilie Eustace diary, with the permission of the trustees of the Imperial War Museum. From the Moshe Flinder diary, with the permission of the Yad Vashem Holocaust Museum. From the William F. Friedman diary, with the permission of the National Cryptologic Museum. From the John Gray diary, with the permission of the trustees of the Imperial War Museum. From the Veronica Goddard diary, with the permission of the trustees of the Imperial War Museum. From Bill Goodall, 'Bill Goodall's War Diaries', with the permission of Ian Goodall. From the Maurice Hankey diary, with the permission of the trustees of the Churchill Archives Centre and the Master, Fellows and Scholars of Churchill College, Cambridge. From the Helena Harrison and Catherine Harrison diary, with the permission of the trustees of the Imperial War Museum. From the Oliver Harvey diary, with the permission of the trustees of the British Museum. From W. E. Holl, 'A Diary of Civil Defence Goes Through It: Paddington 1937–1945', with the permission of the trustees of the British Library. From the Michael Hoskin diary, with the permission of Michael Hoskin. From the D. M. Hoyles diary, with the permission of the trustees of the Imperial War Museum. From the John Hugill diary, with the permission of the trustees of the Churchill Archives Centre and the Master, Fellows and Scholars of Churchill College, Cambridge. From the Charles Hutchinson diary, with the permission of the trustees of the Imperial War Museum. From the Uffz. P. Kahl diary, with the permission of the Modern Records Centre, University of Warwick. From the John Kennedy diary, with the permission of the Liddell Hart Centre for Military Archives. From the Cecil King diary, with the permission of Boston University Library. From the Edith Kupp (née Heap) diary, with the permission of the Brotherton Library, University of Leeds. From Robert Laycock, 'Operation Flipper', Middle East Commandos War Diary, with the permission of the Public Record Office. From the A. R. C. Leaney diary, with the permission of John Leaney and the trustees of the Imperial War Museum. From the Guy Liddell diary, with the permission of the Public Record Office. From Steve Lonsdale, war diaries, with the permission of Stuart Lonsdale. From the P. J. Lovett diary, with the permission of the trustees of the Imperial War Museum. From Otto Lund, 'Visit to France and Belgium in May and June 1940 as DDMO', with the permission of the trustees of the Churchill Archives Centre and the Master, Fellows and Scholars of Churchill College, Cambridge. From the Harold Macmillan diary, with the permission of the Western Manuscripts Department, Bodleian Library. From the Ralph Marnham diary, with the permission of the trustees of the Liddell Hart Centre for Military Archives. From the John Mitchell diary, with the permission of the trustees of the Churchill Archives Centre and the Master, Fellows and Scholars of Churchill College, Cambridge. From the Montgomery of Alamein diary, with the permission of the trustees of the Imperial War Museum. From the H. P. L. Mott diary, with the permission of the trustees of the Imperial War Museum. From the R. Peat diary, with the permission of the trustees of the Imperial War Museum. From the L. D. Pexton diary, with the permission of the trustees of the Imperial War Museum. From the Kay Phipps diary, with the permission of the trustees of the Imperial War Museum. From the Vera Reid diary, with the permission of the trustees of the Imperial War Museum. From the Colonel D. K. Reimers diary, with the permission of the US Army Military History Institute. From the Emily Riddell diary, with the permission of the trustees of the Imperial War Museum. From 'Tommy's War', with the permission of Paul Rose. From the Adrian Secker diary, with the permission of the trustees of the Imperial War Museum. From the David Smiley war diary, with the permission of the Public Record Office. From the Maureen Stuart-Clark diary, with the permission of Lady Maureen Allan. From the J. L. Sweetland diary, with the permission of the trustees of the Imperial War Museum. From the Sergeant C. E. S. Tirbutt diary, with the permission of the trustees of the Imperial War Museum. From the L. T. Tomes diary, with the permission of the Brotherton Library, University of Leeds. From the Arthur Turner diary, with the permission of the trustees of the Imperial War Museum. From the Alison Uttley diary, with the permission of the John Rylands Library, University of Manchester. From the Gwen Wansborough diary, with the permission of the trustees of the Imperial War Museum. From the F. Watt diary, with the permission of the trustees of the Imperial War Museum. From 'Extracts from a Diary of an Interned German Refugee . . .', anonymous, HO 215/210, with the permission of the Public Record Office. From the diary of an Italian pilot, anonymous, with the permission of the Public Record Office.

Various estates and publishers have kindly granted permission to reproduce extracts from the following copyright works.

From *The Bells Go Down: The Diary of a London AFS Man*, anon. 1942, reprinted by permission of the publishers, Methuen. From *The Diary of a Staff Officer*, anon. 1941, reprinted by permission of the publishers, Methuen. From *True to Type: A Selection from Letters and Diaries of German Soldiers and Civilians Collected on the Soviet–German Front*, anon. 1945, reprinted by permission of the publishers, Hutchinson. From *A Woman in Berlin*, 'anon.' copyright M. Hillers 1955, reprinted by permission of the publishers, Harborough. From *Balkan Journal: An Unofficial Observer in Greece*, copyright L. Archer 1944, reprinted by permission of the publishers, Norton. From *Diary of a War Artist*, copyright Estate of E. Ardizzone 1974, reprinted by permission of the Laura Cecil Literary Agency and the publishers, Bodley Head. From *With Malice toward None – Cecil King: A War Diary*, copyright Boston University 1970, reprinted by permission of the publishers, Sidgwick & Jackson. From *Peter Moen's Diary*, copyright Estate of Peter Moen 1951, reprinted by permission of the publishers, Faber & Faber. From *Two Septembers 1939 and 1940: A Diary of Events*, copyright S. Baley 1941, reprinted by permission of the publishers, HarperCollins. From *Parliament and Politics in the Age of Churchill and Attlee: The Headlam Diaries 1935–1951*, copyright Durham County Archives 1999, reprinted with the permission of Cambridge University Press. From *The Diary of Georgi Dimitrov, 1933–1949*, ed. I. Banac, copyright G. Dimitrov 2003, reprinted by permission of the publishers, Yale University Press. From *A French Officer's Diary 23rd August 1939–1st October 1940*, copyright D. Barlone 1943, reprinted by permission of the publishers, Cambridge University Press. From *War Journal of an Innocent Soldier*, copyright John Bassett 1989, reprinted by permission of the publishers, Archon. From *Diary of a Temporary Soldier*, copyright G. C. Bateman 1986, privately published. From *I've Lived Another Year: A Journalist's Diary of the Year 1941*, copyright E. Baume 1942, reprinted by permission of the publishers, Harrap. From *Civilians at War: Journals 1938–1946*, copyright G. Beardmore 1984, reprinted by permission of the publishers, John Murray. From *The Mansel Diaries: The Diaries of Captain John Mansel, Prisoner-of-War – and Camp Forger – in Germany*

the publishers, Macmillan. From *Establishing the Anglo-American Alliance: The Second World War Diaries of Brigadier Vivian Dykes*, ed. A. Danchev, copyright V. Dykes 1990, reprinted by permission of the publishers, Brassey's. From *War Diaries 1939–1945: Field Marshal Lord Alanbrooke*, ed. A. Danchev and D. Todman, copyright Estate of Lord Alanbrooke, reprinted by permission of the publishers, Weidenfeld & Nicolson. From *The Diaries of Evelyn Waugh*, ed. M. Davie, copyright the Estate of E. Waugh 1976, reprinted by permission of Peters, Fraser & Dunlop and the publishers, the Orion Group. From *The War Diaries of Vladimir Dedijer: From Nov. 28, 1942 to September 10, 1943*, copyright V. Dedijer 1990, reprinted by permission of the publishers, University of Michigan Press. From *Marching to the Sound of Gunfire: North West Europe 1944–5*, copyright P. Delaforce 1996, reprinted by permission of the publishers, Sutton. From *The Halder Diaries: The Private War Diaries of Colonel General Franz Halder*, ed. T. N. Depuy, copyright Estate of General Halder 1976, reprinted by permission of the publishers, Westview. From *Crash Dive: In Action with HMS Safari*, copyright P. Dickison 1999, reprinted by permission of the publishers, Sutton. From *The Diaries of Sir Alexander Cadogan, 1938–1945*, ed. D. Dilks, copyright Churchill Archive Centre 1971, reprinted by permission of the publishers, Cassell. From *The Chronicle of the Lodz Ghetto 1941–1944*, ed. L. Dobroszycki, copyright Yad Veshem Memorial 1984, reprinted by permission of the publishers, Yale University Press. From *Mrs Milburn's Diaries: An Englishwoman's Day-to-Day Reflections 1939–1945*, ed. P. Donnelly, copyright Mass-Observation Archive 1979, reprinted by permission of the publishers, Harrap. From *The Quality of Witness: A Romanian Diary 1937–1944*, copyright E. Dorian 1982, reprinted by permission of the publishers, Jewish Publication Society of America. From *Hugh Dormer's Diaries*, copyright H. Dormer 1947, reprinted by permission of the publishers, Jonathan Cape. From *Padre in Colditz: The Diary of J. Ellison Platt MBE*, ed. M. Duggan, copyright J. Ellison Platt 1978, reprinted by permission of the publishers, Hodder & Stoughton. From *Lancashire and Whitehall: The Diary of Sir Raymond Streat*, vol. 1: *1931–39*, ed. M. Dupree, copyright Bodleian Library 1999, reprinted by permission of Dr M. Dupree and the publishers, Manchester University Press. From *The War*, copyright M. Duras 1986, reprinted by permission of the publishers, Pantheon. From *Hannah Senesh: Her Life and Diary*, ed. A. Eban, copyright Estate of H. Senesh 1972, reprinted by permission

publishers, Toucan Press. From *The Warsaw Diary of Adam Czerniakow*, ed. R. Hilberg, S. Staron and J. Kermisz, copyright A. Czerniakow 1979, reprinted by permission of the publishers, Ivan Dee. From *Few Eggs and No Oranges: The Diaries*, copyright V. Hodgson 2002, reprinted by permission of the publishers, Persephone. From *Long Walk through War: A Combat Doctor's Diary*, copyright K. H. Huebner 1987, reprinted by permission of the publishers, Texas A&M University Press. From *Adolf Hitler: The Medical Diaries, The Private Diaries of Dr Theo Morrell.*, ed. D. Irving, copyright Estate of T. Morrell 1983, reprinted by permission of the publishers, Sidgwick & Jackson. From *The War Diary of Breckinridge Long: Selections from the Years 1939–1944*, ed. F. Israel, copyright Estate of Breckinridge Long 1966, reprinted by permission of the publishers, University of Nebraska Press. From *'Chips': The Diaries of Sir Henry Channon*, ed. R. R. James, copyright P. Channon 1999, reprinted by permission of the publishers, Orion Group. From *Day After Day: Odd Nansen*, ed. K. John, copyright O. Nansen 1949, reprinted by permission of the publishers, Putnam. From *Jordan's Tunis Diary*, copyright P. Jordan 1943, reprinted by permission of the publishers, Collins. From *The Diary of a Nightmare*, ed. U. von Kardorff, copyright U. von Kardorff 1966, reprinted by permission of the publishers, Day. From *Scroll of Agony: The Warsaw Diary of Chaim A. Kaplan*, ed. A. I. Katsh, copyright Yad Vashem Memorial 1966, reprinted by permission of the publishers, Hamish Hamilton. From *Victory Harvest: Diary of a Canadian in the Women's Land Army, 1940–1944*, copyright M. Kelsey 1977, reprinted by permission of the publishers, McGill-Queens University Press. From *'The Good Old Days': The Holocaust as Seen by its Perpetrators and Bystanders*, ed. E. Klee, W. Dressen and V. Riess, reprinted by permission of the publishers, Konecky & Konecky. From *Diary from the Years of Occupation, 1939–44*, ed. A. Klukowski and H. Klukowski, copyright Estate of Z. Klukowski 1993, reprinted by permission of the publishers, University of Illinois Press. From *The Diary and Letters of Käthe Kollwitz*, ed. H. Kollwitz, copyright Estate of K. Kollwitz, reprinted by permission of the publishers, Northwestern University Press. From *OSS Against the Reich: The World War II Diaries of Colonel David K. E. Bruce*, ed. N. D. Lankford, copyright Virginia Historical Society, reprinted by permission of the publishers, Kent State University Press. From *Diary of a Washington Correspondent*, copyright D. Lawrence 1942, reprinted by permission of the

The Mouchotte Diaries, copyright R. Mouchotte 1957, reprinted by permission of the publishers, Panther. From *Ciano's Diary, 1939–1943*, ed. M. Muggeridge, copyright M. Muggeridge 1947, reprinted by permission of the publishers, the Orion Group. From *Day after Day*, copyright O. Nansen 1949, reprinted by permission of the publishers, Putnam. From *Harold Nicolson: Diaries and Letters, 1939–45*, ed. N. Nicolson, copyright William Collins 1967, reprinted by permission of the publishers, HarperCollins. From *The von Aufsess Occupation Diary*, ed. K. Nowlan, copyright the Estate of Baron von Aufsess, reprinted by permission of the publishers, Phillimore. From *Lonely Warrior: The Action-Journal of a Battle of Britain Fighter Pilot*, copyright J. Offenberg 1969, reprinted by permission of the publishers, Souvenir Press. From *War in Val D'Orcia*, copyright I. Origo 1947, reprinted by permission of the publishers, Cape. From *The Collected Essays, Journalism and Letters of George Orwell*, vol. 2: *My Country Right or Left, 1940–1945*, ed. S. Orwell and I. Angus, copyright Estate of G. Orwell 1969, reprinted by permission of the publishers, Secker & Warburg. From *Two Women and War*, copyright G. Paquin 1953, reprinted by permission of the publishers, Mughlenberg Press. From *Diary of a Soldier*, copyright H. Parkhurst 1993, reprinted by permission of the publishers, Pentland Press. From *A Pacifist's War*, copyright F. Partridge 1978, reprinted by permission of the publishers, Hogarth. From *The Noel Coward Diaries*, ed. G. Payn and S. Morley, copyright G. Payn 1982, reprinted by permission of the publishers, Orion Group. From *Boy in the Blitz: The 1940 Diary of Colin Perry*, copyright C. Perry 1972, reprinted by permission of the publishers, Cooper. From *German Writings before and after 1945*, ed. J. Peters, copyright J. Peters 2002, reprinted by permission of the publishers, Continuum. From *Gunner's Diary*, copyright J. D. Phillip 1946, reprinted by permission of the publishers, Meador. From *My Secret Diary*, copyright J. Phillips 1982, reprinted by permission of the publishers, Shepeard-Walwyn. From *The Second World War Diaries of Hugh Dalton, 1940–45*, ed. B. Pimlott, copyright British Library of Economic and Political Science, reprinted by permission of the publishers, Jonathan Cape. From *Heaven and Hell: The War Diary of a German Paratrooper*, copyright M. Pöppel 1988, reprinted by permission of the publishers, Hippocrene. From *To War with Whitaker: The Wartime Diaries of the Countess of Ranfurly, 1939–1945*, copyright Hermione the Countess of Ranfurly 1995, reprinted by permission of the Random House Group. From *No Cause for Panic: Channel Islands Refugees, 1940–1945*, copyright B. A. Read 1995, reprinted by permission of the publishers, Seaflower. From *Diary of Military Government in Germany 1945*, copyright B. N. Reckitt 1989, reprinted by permission of B. N. Reckitt and the publishers, Stockwell. From *Diary of a Man in Despair*, trans. P. Rubens, copyright F. P. Reck-Malleczewen 1966, reprinted by permission of the publishers, Macmillan. From *The Siren Years: Undiplomatic Diaries*, copyright C. Ritchie 1974, reprinted by permission of the publishers, Macmillan. From *Wilhelm Prüller: Diary of a German Soldier*, ed. H. C. Robbins Landon, copyright Wilhelm Prüller, reprinted by permission of A. P. Watt Ltd. From *Joyce Grenfell. The Time of My Life: Entertaining the Troops – Her Wartime Journals*, ed. J. Roose-Evans, copyright Reginald Grenfell and James Roose-Evans 1989, reprinted by permission of David Higham Associates Ltd. From *Baffy: The Diaries of Blanche Dugdale*, ed. N. A. Rose, copyright Estate of B. Dugdale 1973, reprinted by permission of the publishers, Vallentine Mitchell. From *Across the Abyss: Diary Entries for the Years 1939–40*, trans. George Bird, copyright P. Roubiczek 1982, reprinted by permission of the publishers, Cambridge University Press. From *Outside Information: A Diary of Rumours*, copyright Estate of N. Royde Smith 1941, reprinted by permission of the publishers, Macmillan. From *Stuka Pilot*, copyright Estate of H. U. Rudel 1953, reprinted by permission of the publishers, Euphorion. From *POWs Fraternal: Diaries of S/Sgt Raymond Ryan – Poems of Pte Laurence (Bouff) Ryan*, copyright S. M. Ryan 1990, reprinted by permission of the publishers, Hawthorn. From *Missing in Action May–September 1944*, copyright P. Ryle 1979, reprinted by permission of the publishers, Allen. From *The Forgotten Soldier*, copyright G. Sajer 1971, reprinted by permission of the publishers, Weidenfeld & Nicolson. From *War Diaries: Notebooks from a Phoney War, November 1939–March 1940*, copyright Estate of J. P. Sartre 1984, reprinted by permission of the publishers, Random House Inc. and Verso. *From Leaves in the Storm: A Book of Diaries*, ed. S. Schimanski and H. Treece, reprinted by permission of the publishers, Drummond. From *Air War Diary: An Australian in Bomber Command*, copyright D. Scholes 1997, reprinted by permission of the publishers, Kangaroo Press. From *Journal 1935–1944*, copyright M. Sebastian 2001, reprinted by permission of the publishers, Heinemann. From *The War Diaries of Kenneth Slessor, Official Australian War Correspondent*, ed. C. Semmler, copyright K. Slessor 1985, reprinted by permission of the publishers, University of Queensland Press. From *Mollie Panter-Downes: London War Notes*, ed. W. Shawn, copyright M. Panter-Downes 1971, reprinted by permission of the publishers, Farrar, Strauss & Giroux. From *Among You Taking Notes: The Wartime Diary of Naomi Mitchison 1939–1945*, ed. D. Sheridan, copyright Naomi Mitchison and the trustees of the Mass-Observation Archive 1985, reprinted by permission of the publishers, Gollancz. From *Wartime Women: An Anthology of Women's Wartime Writing for Mass-Observation 1937–1945*, ed. D. Sheridan, copyright Mass-Observation Archive 1990, reprinted by permission of the publishers, Heinemann. From *Bristol Siren Nights: Diaries and Stories of the Blitzes*, ed. Revd S. P. Shipley, reprinted by permission of the publishers, Redcliffe. From *Berlin Diary: The Journal of a Foreign Correspondent 1934–1941*, copyright W. Shirer 1941, reprinted by permission of Brandt & Hochman Agency. From *A Leningrad Diary: Survival during World War II*, trans. Norman Luxemburg, copyright E. Skrjabina 1978, reprinted by permission of the publishers, Southern Illinois University Press. From *The Bickerseth Family World War II Diary*, ed. N. Smart, copyright Bickerseth Estate 1999, reprinted by permission of the publishers, Mellen. From *Hostage to Fortune: The Letters of Joseph P. Kennedy*, ed. A. Smith, copyright J. F. Kennedy Memorial Library 2001, reprinted by permission of the publishers, Viking Penguin. From *Written in Darkness: A Belgian Woman's Record of the Occupation, 1940–1945*, copyright A. Somerhausen 1946, reprinted by permission of the publishers, Knopf. From *An Italian Diary*, copyright F. Stark 1945, reprinted by permission of the publishers, John Murray. From *Once There Was a War*, copyright J. Steinbeck 1958, reprinted by permission of the Executors of the Estate of John Steinbeck and the publishers, Penguin Putnam. From *Hitler's Whistle*, copyright A. G. Street 1943, reprinted by permission of Miranda Corben on behalf of Pamela Street. From *The Diary of Anaïs Nin, 1939–1944*, ed. G. Stuhlman, copyright G. Stuhlman 1969, reprinted by permission of the publishers, Harcourt Brace Jovanovich. From *A Long Row of Candles: Memoirs and Diaries 1934–54*, copyright C. A. Sulzberger 1969, reprinted by permission of the publishers, Macdonald. From *The Goebbels Diaries: The Last Days*, ed. H. Trevor-Roper, copyright H. Trevor-Roper 1977, reprinted by permission of the publishers, Secker & Warburg. From *The Berlin Diaries 1940–1945 of Marie*

'Missie' Vassiltchikov, copyright M. Vassiltchikov 1985, reprinted by permission of the publishers, Chatto & Windus. From Journals, 1939–1977, copyright K. Vaughan 1989, reprinted by permission of the publishers, John Murray. From Edith's Story, copyright E. Velmans 1999, reprinted by permission of the publishers, Bantam. From Stalingrad Diary, copyright E. Weinert 1944, reprinted by permission of the publishers, ING. From The Last Days of Paris: A Journalist's Diary, copyright A. Werth 1940, reprinted by permission of the publishers, Hamish Hamilton. From The Year of Stalingrad, copyright A. Werth 1948, reprinted by permission of the publishers, Hamish Hamilton. From Journal of the War Years (1939–1945) and One Year Later, copyright A. Weymouth 1948, reprinted by permission of the publishers, Littlebury & Co. From A Psychologist's Wartime Diary, copyright A. Weymouth 1940, reprinted by permission of the publishers, Pearsons. From Internment: The Diaries of Harry Seidler May 1940–October 1941, trans. J. Winternitz, ed. J. Wilton, copyright Harry Seidler 1986, reprinted by permission of the publishers, Allen & Unwin. From Tony Benn, Years of Hope: Diaries, Letters and Papers, 1940–1962, ed. R. Winstone, copyright Tony Benn 1994, reprinted by permission of Curtis Brown Ltd, London on behalf of Tony Benn. From Love Lessons: A Wartime Diary, copyright J. Wyndham 1985, reprinted by permission of the Random House Group. From The Diary of an Ad Man: The War Years June 1, 1942–December 31, 1943, copyright J. W. Young 1944, reprinted by permission of the publishers, Advertising Publications. From Seventy Days, copyright W. Zagorski 1957, reprinted by permission of the publishers, Müller. From A Warsaw Diary, 1939–1945, copyright M. Zylberberg 1969, reprinted by permission of the publishers, Vallentine Mitchell.

Seeking permission to reproduce material that was published some time ago can be difficult because many publishers have disappeared or changed hands and rights often revert to the author after a period. Accordingly, in addition to the above, permission has been sought for several extracts that are not cited here. These were being chased as the book went to press.

ILLUSTRATION CREDITS

The author and publishers would like to thank the following for permission to reproduce illustrations, including the Australian War Memorial (AWM), the Imperial War Museum, London (IWM), and the United States National Archives (USNA).

In-text illustrations: p. 45: Alexander Cadogan, USNA still pictures, OSS box 12, 26-A-11168; p. 64: Joseph P. Kennedy, © Bettmann/CORBIS; p. 144: Arthur Turner, IWM Department of Documents, Turner papers; p. 150: Harry Seidler, courtesy of Harry Seidler; p. 174: William Shirer, IWM MH1926; p. 209: Veronica Goddard, IWM Department of Documents, Goddard papers; p. 222: Virginia Woolf, Barbara Strachey/National Portrait Gallery Picture Library; p. 276: Kenneth Slessor, AWM 001830; p. 332: James Gray, IWM Department of Documents, Gray papers; p. 337: George Blundell, IWM Department of Documents, Blundell papers; p. 349: Frances Partridge, Hulton Archive; p. 354: Lt-Col. Geoffrey Keyes, IWM E4732; p. 421: Anthony Eden, Hulton Archive; p. 559: Vladimir Dedijer, Bert Hardy/Hulton Archive; p. 577: Col. David Smiley, IWM HU65075; p. 581: John Steinbeck, © Bettmann/CORBIS; p. 588: David Scholes, courtesy of David Scholes; p. 624: Gwen Wansborough, IWM Department of Documents, Wansborough papers; p. 678: Joyce Grenfell, © Hulton-Deutsch Collection/CORBIS; p. 693: Evelyn Waugh, Howard Coster/National Portrait Gallery Picture Library; p. 724: Jack Hugill, Churchill Archive Centre, Churchill College, Cambridge; p. 774: Richard Crossman, Bassano/National Portrait Gallery Picture Library; p. 794: Guy Liddell, IWM HU6612; p. 799: Maureen Stuart-Clark, courtesy of Lady Allan; p. 819: Joseph Goebbels, © CORBIS; p. 839: Giovanni Guareschi, Ullstein.

Plate section, p. 1: above, USNA 242-HLB-2658-16; below, IWM HU5505; p. 2: right and below, IWM Department of Documents; bottom, IWM HU36121; p. 3: IWM HU5533; p. 4: above, HU2722; below, H2005; p. 5: above, USNA 306-NT-1205F-3; below, IWM E 18493; p. 6: IWM HU71891; p. 7: left, IWM CH7238; below, AWM 009304; p. 8: above, IWM E21848; below, IWM HU5605; p. 9: above, IWM RU1266; below, AWM 012347; p. 10: AWM MED 1555; p. 11: IWM Department of Documents; p. 12: above, USNA 238-NT-293;

below: IWM MH2111B; p. 13: above, USNA 111-SC-178198; below, AWM 128289; p. 14: right, USNA 111-SC-217401; below, USNA 080 G 218861; p. 15: left, USNA 111-SC-208-819-8; below, IWM HU3616; p. 16: left, USNA 111-SC-203874; below, IWM D21213.

INDEX

766, 778, 783–5; Malta
conference, 791; Yalta
conference, 800, 801, 806;
Rhine crossing, 825; at
Chartwell, 829–30; end of
coalition government,
848–9; VE-Day, 856; atomic
policy, 859; election defeat,
859
Churchill tanks, 708
Chuter Ede, James, 391–2,
510–11
Ciano, Count Galeazzo: on
Hitler, 43–4, 46–7; attitude
to war, 43–4, 110–11; on
Mussolini's relationship
with Hitler, 110–11, 129,
199; Lorraine on, 203; on
death of Mussolini's son,
335–7; on diary, 513;
execution, 513, 645
ciphers, *see* codes
Citizens' Advice Bureaux
(CABs), 317–18
Citrine, Sir Walter, 113, 118–19
Clan Fraser, SS, 275
Clark, Brigadier, 677–8
Clark, Bruce, 783
Clark, Mark W., 446, 449
Clarke, Dudley, 765–6
Clegg, Howard, 145–7, 194–5
Clive, Nigel, 181
Cobb, Ivo Geekie, *see*
Weymouth, Anthony

Cockhill, J. W., 20
codes and ciphers: German
codebreaking, 81, 331;
British codebreaking, 289,
442, 532, 569–71; Italian
intelligence, 331; Enigma,
387, 571; Triton, 387, 497;
British security, 564;
American codebreaking,
569–71; BRUSA treaty, 571
Cold War, 720, 737, 859
Colditz Castle, 22–3, 457–9,
826
Collins, General, 775
Collishaw, Raymond, 249
Colmar Pocket, 790
Cologne: bombing, 227, 414,
473; US forces, 801, 815,
816–8
Columbia Broadcasting
Service (CBS), 91
Columbus, 104–5
Colville, Sir John ('Jock'), 153,
829–30
Combined Operations
Pilotage Party (COPP), 530,
531
Comintern, 306–7, 543
Commandos: creation, 765;
raid on Rommel's HQ,
353–7; St Nazaire docks
raid, 395; Dieppe raid, 451,
460; Sark raid, 473;
Bordeaux harbour raid,

Germans and islanders,
730–2, 824; German
surrender, 848
Jesehonnek, Colonel General,
591
Jews: German attitudes to,
29–30; Hitler's policy, 39;
Warsaw Ghetto, 227–8,
229–31, 320, 393–4, 433–4;
518–20; Lodz Ghetto,
251–2, 320, 615–16, 667–8,
683–4; in Romania, 255–6,
321–2, 328–9; under
German occupation,
310–11, 381–2; Holocaust in
Poland, 326–8, 480–4, 564;
in hiding, 459; numbers
dead (1942), 466–7;
extermination policy, 498;
smuggled from Norway,
504–5; deportation, 533–4;
in Ukraine, 543; anti-
semitism in Britain, 565;
Soviet war crimes trial,
578–9; in Italy, 663–4; in
Holland, 700–1, 778–80; in
Corfu, 710; Holocaust
survivors, 808–9
Jodl, Alfred, 729, 848
Johnson, Ken ('Snakehips'),
264–5
Jones, R. V., 227
Jordan, Philip, 535–7
Jünger, Ernst, 615–17

Kahl, Pieter, 728–30, 751–3,
776
Kaplan, Chaim A., 229–31,
433–4
Kardelj, Edvard, 558
Kardorff, Jürgen von, 489,
490, 525–6
Kardorff, Klaus von, 489, 490,
526, 534
Kardorff, Ursula von, 489–90,
525–6, 533–4, 807–8
Karl Borromaeus Church, 425
Kasserine Pass, 523, 525
Katyn Wood massacre, 540,
619–20
Keitel, Wilhelm, 792
Kelsey, Marion, 411–13,
416–18
Kennedy, John Noble, 252–4,
286, 367–8, 473
Kennedy, Joseph P.:
appeasement policy, 38, 53,
212; Halifax meeting, 53–5;
Chamberlain friendship,
54, 64–5, 172–3; on fall of
France, 172–3; Lee
relationship, 212, 213;
Lend-Lease opposition,
255; Beaverbrook
conversation, 572–5
Kent, Tyler, 231–2
Kesselring, Albert, 524, 609,
654, 835, 848
Keyes, Geoffrey, 354–6

Saving Your Diaries from the Dustbin of History

Every day new and exciting materials concerning the Second World War come to light. Sometimes these are found by relatives and, happily, they become treasured family possessions. However, it is not unusual for them to be found in old chests of drawers by house-clearers and then thrown away. Even when their historical value is recognized by relatives or friends there is often puzzlement about what to do with the material. Giving or lending diaries to an established archive, or making a photocopy available, ensures the long-term professional preservation of the information. It also ensures the material is accessible to historians who are writing books about the war. This in turn means that the author of the diary is able to make a wider contribution to the history of the period that they so painstakingly recorded, or even perhaps to find their own 'place in history'.

Over the years I have given material I have come across to the Liddell Hart Centre for Military Archives at King's College London. The best locations to deposit war diaries are centres that specialize in the history of warfare, of which there are several. Some of the most important ones are:

- The Churchill Archives Centre, Churchill College, University of Cambridge, Cambridge CB3 0DS, tel.: 01223 336087, fax: 01223 336135.
http://www.chu.cam.ac.uk/archives/home.shtml
- The Imperial War Museum, Department of Documents, Lambeth Road, London SE1 6HZ, tel.: 020 7416 5000, fax: 020 7416 5374.
http://www.iwm.org.uk/corporate/contact.htm
- The Liddell Hart Centre for Military Archives, King's College, The Strand, London WC2R 2LS, tel.: 020 7848 2187 or 020 7848 2015, fax: 020 7848 2760.
http://www.kcl.ac.uk/lhcma/home.htm

There are also many specialist museums and archives dealing with particular branches of the services, corps or regiments. Wherever you live there will also be a specialist archive or a major library near you. In many cases this will be the local county archive or the 'special collections' section of the library of a nearby university. Many universities have units that deal with particular types of records. For example, the University of Sussex looks after the superb Mass-Observation Archive, and the University of Warwick hosts the Modern Records Centre.

Few war records are worthless, and our view of what is important is always changing. At one time the papers of generals and admirals were the main focus of interest; now the lives of ambulance drivers, munitions workers and children are considered no less fascinating. We cannot know which aspects of history future generations will wish to explore. However, we can take the trouble to preserve our family materials and offer our successors the richest opportunities for exploring every aspect of the past. Those who took the trouble to keep their diaries and served as 'witnesses to war' deserve nothing less.

THE FARAWAY WAR: PERSONAL DIARIES OF THE SECOND WORLD WAR IN ASIA AND THE PACIFIC
Richard J. Aldrich

The war that took place across Asia and the Pacific between 1941 and 1945 both united and divided nations across the globe. Yet beyond the bombing of Pearl Harbor and the dropping of the atomic bombs on Japan, the personal experience of war in this theatre has received relatively little attention – the primary focus having been on the action against Hitler in Europe. On the opposite side of the world the combatants were all fighting each other upon unfamiliar terrain far away from their homelands: as one Japanese soldier wrote in his diary, *'at this moment in the southern hemisphere, everybody's mind was just preoccupied with the memory of home.'*

Richard J. Aldrich brings to life the war through the diaries of people on all sides, with events recorded as they happened. A kamikaze pilot in the last days before his suicide mission; an injured Australian prisoner of war humbled by the heroic attempts of his fellow inmates to save his life by endangering their own; a young Japanese boy terrified by the rumours of impending atomic warfare; a British nurse in Malaya forced to abandon her patients following strict evacuation orders. Stories such as these are drawn into a chronological account of the war by Aldrich's expert month-by-month commentary.

The Faraway War offers a stunning and diverse range of diaries, focusing both on ordinary people, some of whose diaries are published here for the first time, as well as on more celebrated figures such as Evelyn Waugh, Charles Lindbergh, Harry Truman and Joyce Grenfell. With this second volume Richard Aldrich now completes the picture that he began with the European and Middle Eastern action in *Witness to War*, by creating an intimate and illuminating portrait of a whole world ravaged by war.

COMING SOON FROM DOUBLEDAY

0 385 60679 6

Doubleday

THE RIGHTEOUS
The unsung heroes of the Holocaust
Martin Gilbert

'A TIMELY BOOK FOR A NEW CENTURY . . . THE
QUESTIONS RAISED IN THIS BOOK LIE AT THE HEART
OF OUR HUMAITY' *Guardian*

'He who saves one life, it is as if he saved an entire world'

The Holocaust will be forever numbered amongst the darkest
of days in human civilisation. Yet even in that darkness, there
were sparks of light. Many will recognize the names of Oskar
Schindler, Raoul Wallenberg and Miep Gies. But there were
thousands of others throughout Europe who risked their own
lives to save Jews from the Nazis and their horrific campaign
of obliteration that was the Holocaust.

By the beginning of 2002, more than 19,000 non-Jews had
been recognized as Righteous (Among the Nations) by Yad
Vashem, the Holocaust museum in Jerusalem. Some were
officials, some were clergy; others were citizens of countries
who united in their efforts to protect Jews. Many were merely
individuals who had the courage to stand up against a
growing tide of collaboration and simply say: 'We did what
we had to do'.

Martin Gilbert, the foremost British historian of the Holocaust,
here presents the evidence collected over many years.
Cumulatively, these accounts, from every occupied country in
Europe, from the Baltic to the Mediterranean, from the Atlantic
to the Black Sea, and from inside the Third Reich itself, form
an inspiring tribute to those heroic individuals who, without
thought to the risk to their own lives, dared to challenge
barbarism, and hold out the hand of rescue to the Jews of Europe.

'MARTIN GILBERT BRINGS TOGETHER SOME
REMARKABLE STORIES OF COURAGE AND INGENUITY'
Matthew J. Reisz, *Independent*

0 552 99850 8

BLACK SWAN

THE PAST IS MYSELF
By Christabel Bielenberg

'IT WOULD BE DIFFICULT TO OVERPRAISE THIS BOOK.
MRS BIELENBERG'S EXPERIENCE WAS UNIQUE AND
HER HONESTY, INTELLIGENCE AND COMPASSION
MAKES HER ACCOUNT OF IT MOVING BEYOND WORDS'
The Economist

Christabel Bielenberg, a niece of Lord Northcliffe, married a
German lawyer in 1934. She lived through the war in
Germany, as a German citizen, under the horrors of Nazi rule
and Allied bombings. *The Past is Myself* is her story of that
experience, an unforgettable portrait of an evil time.

'THIS AUTOBIOGRAPHY IS OF EXCEPTIONAL
DISTINCTION AND IMPORTANCE. IT DESERVES
RECOGNITION AS A MAGNIFICENT CONTRIBUTION
TO INTERNATIONAL UNDERSTANDING AND AS A
DOCUMENT OF HOW THE HUMAN SPIRIT CAN
TRIUMPH IN THE MIDST OF EVIL AND PERSECUTION'
The Economist

'MARVELLOUSLY WRITTEN'
Observer

'NOTHING BUT SUPERLATIVES WILL DO FOR THIS
BOOK. IT TELLS ITS STORY MAGNIFICENTLY AND
EVERY PAGE OF ITS STORY IS WORTH TELLING'
Irish Press

'INTENSELY MOVING'
Yorkshire Evening News

0 552 99065 5

CORGI BOOKS

A SELECTED LIST OF FINE WRITING
AVAILABLE FROM TRANSWORLD PUBLISHERS

THE PRICES SHOWN BELOW WERE CORRECT AT THE TIME OF GOING TO PRESS. HOWEVER
TRANSWORLD PUBLISHERS RESERVE THE RIGHT TO SHOW NEW RETAIL PRICES ON COVERS WHICH
MAY DIFFER FROM THOSE PREVIOUSLY ADVERTISED IN THE TEXT OR ELSEWHERE.

All Transworld titles are available by post from:
Bookpost, PO Box 29, Douglas, Isle of Man, IM99 1BQ
Credit cards accepted. Please telephone 01624 677237,
fax 01624 670923, Internet http://www.bookpost.co.uk
or e-mail: bookshop@enterprise.net for details.
Free postage and packing in the UK. Overseas customers: allow
£2 per book (paperbacks) and £3 per book (hardbacks).